iPhone and iPad Apps for Absolute Beginners, iOS5 Edition

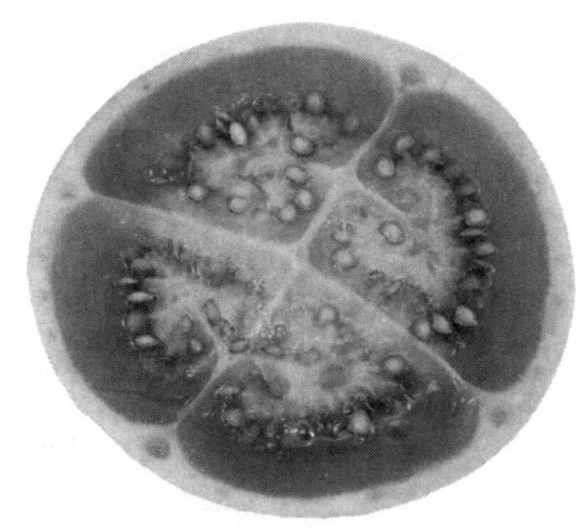

Dr. Rory Lewis

Apress®

iPhone and iPad Apps for Absolute Beginngers, iOS5 Edition

ISBN-13 (pbk): 978-1-4302-3602-1

ISBN-13 (electronic): 978-1-4302-3603-0

President and Publisher: Paul Manning
Lead Editor: Steve Anglin
Development Editor:Matthew Moodie
Technical Reviewer: Matthew Knott
Editorial Board: Steve Anglin, Mark Beckner, Ewan Buckingham, Gary Cornell, Morgan Engel, Jonathan Gennick, Jonathan Hassell, Robert Hutchinson, Michelle Lowman, James Markham, Matthew Moodie, Jeff Olson, Jeffrey Pepper, Douglas Pundick, Ben Renow-Clarke, Dominic Shakeshaft, Gwenan Spearing, Matt Wade, Tom Welsh
Coordinating Editor: Adam Heath
Copy Editor: Chandra Clarke
Compositor: MacPS, LLC
Indexer: BIM Indexing & Proofreading
Artist: SPi Global
Cover Designer: Anna Ishchenko

Distributed to the book trade worldwide by Springer Science+Business Media, LLC., 233 Spring Street, 6th Floor, New York, NY 10013. Phone 1-800-SPRINGER, fax (201) 348-4505, e-mail `orders-ny@springer-sbm.com`, or visit `www.springeronline.com`.

For information on translations, please e-mail `rights@apress.com`, or visit `www.apress.com`.

Apress and friends of ED books may be purchased in bulk for academic, corporate, or promotional use. eBook versions and licenses are also available for most titles. For more information, reference our Special Bulk Sales–eBook Licensing web page at `www.apress.com/bulk-sales`.

To my best friend, my wife, my life, my light, my Kera.

—Dr. Rory Lewis

Contents at a Glance

Contents

Foreword: About the Author

"Rory and I met in L.A. in 1983. He reminds me of one of my favorite film characters, Buckaroo Banzai—always going in six directions at once. If you stop him and ask what he's doing, he'll answer comprehensively and with amazing detail. Disciplined, colorful, and friendly, he has the uncanny ability to explain the highly abstract in simple, organic terms. He always accomplishes what he sets out to do, and he'll help you do the same."

Why you'll relate to Dr. Lewis

While attending Syracuse University as a computer-engineering student, Rory scrambled to pass his classes and make enough money to support his wife and two young daughters. In 1990, he landed a choice on-campus job as a proctor in the computer labs in the LC Smith College of Engineering. Even though he was struggling with subjects in the Electrical Engineering program, he was always there at the Help Desk. It was a daunting experience for Rory because his job was only to help his fellow students with computer lab *equipment* questions, but he invariably found his classmates asking deeper andharder questions: *"Dude, did you understand the calculus assignment? Can you help me?!"*

These students assumed that, because Rory was the proctor, he knew the answers. Afraid and full of self-doubt, he sought a way to help them without revealing his inadequacies. Rory learned to start with: *"Let's go back to the basics. Remember that last week the professor presented us with an equation...?"* By going back to the fundamentals, restating and rebranding them, Rory began to develop a technique that would, more often than not, lead to working solutions. By the time his senior year rolled around, there was often a line of students waiting at the Help Desk on the nights Rory worked.

Fast-Forward 17 Years

Picture a long-haired, wacky professor walking through the campus of the University of Colorado at Colorado Springs, dressed in a stunning contrast of old-schooland drop-out. As he walks into the Engineering Building, he is greeted by students and faculty who smile and say hearty hellos, all the while probably shaking their heads at his tweed jacket, Grateful Dead t-shirt, khaki pants, and flip flops. As he walks down the hall of the Computer Science Department, there's a line of students standing outside his office. Reminiscent of the line of students that waited for him at the Help Desk in those early years as a proctor in the computer lab, they turn and greet him, *"Good morning, Dr. Lewis!"* Many of these students at UC-Colorado Springs are not even in his class, but they know that Dr. Lewis will see them and help them anyway.

Past—Present—Future

Dr. Lewis holds three academic degrees. He earned a Bachelor of Science in Computer Engineering from Syracuse University. Syracuse's LC Smith College of Engineering is one of the country's top schools. It is there that Intel, AMD, and Microsoft send their top employees to study for their PhDs.

Upon completing his BS (with emphasis on the mathematics of electronic circuitry in microprocessors), he went across the quad to the Syracuse University School of Law. During his first summer at law school, Fulbright & Jaworski, the nation's most prolific law firm, recruited Rory to work in its Austin office, where some of the attorneys specialize in high-tech intellectual-property patent litigation. As part of his clerking experience, Lewis worked on the infamous *AMD v. Intel* case; he helped assess the algorithms of the mathematics of microprocessor electrical circuitry for the senior partners.

During his second summer in law school, Skjerven, Morrill, MacPherson, Franklin, & Friel—the other firm sharing the work on the *AMD v. Intel* case—recruited Rory to work with them at their Silicon Valley branches (San Jose and San Francisco). After immersing himself in law for several years and receiving his JD at Syracuse, Lewis realized his passion was for the *mathematics* of computers, not the legal ramifications of hardware and software. He preferred a learning and creative environment rather than the fighting and arguing intrinsic in law.

After three years away from academia, Rory Lewis moved south to pursue his PhD in Computer Science at the University of North Carolina at Charlotte. There, he studied under Dr. Zbigniew W. Ras, known worldwide for his innovations in data mining algorithms and methods, distributed data mining, ontologies, and multimedia databases. While studying for his PhD, Lewis taught computer science courses to computer engineering undergraduates, as well as e-commerce and programming courses to MBA students.

Upon receiving his PhD in Computer Science, Rory accepted a tenure-track position in Computer Science at the University of Colorado at Colorado Springs, where his research is in the computational mathematics of neurosciences. Most recently, he co-wrote a grant proposal on the mathematical analysis of the genesis of epilepsy with respect to the hypothalamus. However, with the advent of Apple's revolutionary iPhone and its uniquely flexible platform—*and market*—for mini-applications, games, and personal computing tools, he grew excited and began experimenting and programming for his own pleasure. Once his own fluency was established, Lewis figured he could teach a class on iPhone apps that would include *non*-engineers. With his insider knowledge as an iPhone beta tester, he began to integrate the parameters of the proposed iPad platform into his lesson plans—even before the official release in April 2010.

The class was a resounding success and the feedback was overwhelmingly positive, from students and colleagues alike. When approached about the prospect of converting his course into a book to be published by Apress, Dr. Lewis jumped at the opportunity. He happily accepted an offer to convert his course outlines, class notes, and videos into the book you are now holding in your hands.

Why Write This Book?

The reasons Dr. Lewis wrote this book are the same reasons he originally decided to create a class for both engineering and non-engineering majors: the challenge and the fun! According to Lewis, the iPhone and iPad are "*...some of the coolest, most powerful, and most technologically advanced tools ever made—period!*"

He is fascinated by the fact that, just under the appealing touch screen of high-resolution images and fun little icons, the iPhone and iPad are programmed in *Objective-C,* an incredibly difficult and advanced language. More and more, Lewis was approached by students and colleagues who wanted to program apps for the iPhone and would ask his opinion on their ideas. It seemed that, with every new update of the iPhone, not to mention the advent of the expanded interface of the iPad, the floodgates of interest in programming apps were thrown wider and wider. Wonderful and innovative ideas just needed the proper channel to flow into the appropriate format and then out to the world.

Generally speaking, however, the people who write books about Objective-C write for people who know Java, C#, or C++ at an advanced level. So, because there seemed to be no help for the average person who, nevertheless, has a great idea for an iPhone/iPad app, Dr. Lewis decided to launch such a class. He realized it would be wise to use his own notes for the first half of the course, and then to explore the best existing resources he could find.

As he forged ahead with this plan, Lewis was most impressed with *Beginning iPhone 3 Development: Exploring the iPhone SDK.* This best-selling instructional book from Apress was written by Dave Mark and Jeff Lamarche. Lewis concluded that their book would provide an excellent, high-level target for his lessons...a “stepping stones” approach to comprehensive and fluent programming for all Apple’s multi-touch devices.

After Dr. Lewis’s course had been successfully presented, and during a subsequent conversation with a representative from Apress, Lewis happened to mention that he’d only started using that book about half-way through the semester, as he had to bring his non-engineering students up to speed first. The editor suggested converting his notes and outlines into a primer—an introductory book tuned to the less-technical programming crowd. At that point, it was only a matter of time and details—like organizing and revising Dr. Lewis’s popular instructional videos to make them available to other non-engineers excited to program their own iPhone and/or iPad apps.

So, that’s the story of how a wacky professor came to write this book. We hope you are inspired to take this home and begin. *Arm yourself with this knowledge and begin now to change your life!*

Ben Easton
Author, Teacher, Editor

About the Contributing Authors

Ben Easton is a graduate of Washington & Lee University and has a B.A. in Philosophy. His eclectic background includes music, banking, sailing, hang gliding, and retail. Most of his work has involved education in one form or another. Ben taught school for 17 years, mostly middle-school mathematics. More recently, his experience as a software trainer and implementer reawakened his long-time affinity for technical subjects. As a freelance writer, he has written several science fiction stories and screenplays, as well as feature articles for magazines and newsletters. Ben resides in Austin, Texas, and is currently working on his first novel.

Brian Parks PhD Student, Computer Science and **Anthony Magee**, MS student at UCCS work with Dr. Lewis and assisted in studying the various versions of the beta Xcode.

Brian is in the Ph.D. program in Computer Science at the University of Colorado at Colorado Springs, where he regularly collaborates with Dr. Terrance Boult and Dr. Rory Lewis. He received his B.S. in Computer Science from Lehigh University, Pennsylvania.Brian specializes in software design and development techniques with an eye toward software engineering and architecture, especially with data-driven applications. Brian is also an educator and an academic; focusing on software engineering and design and, most recently, computer organization and assembly language programming while research focuses on computer vision and its relationship with psychological theories of vision.

Anthony is currently finishing work towards a Masters degree in Computer Science at the University of Colorado at Colorado Springs, where he also received his Bachelors degree.Anthony is experienced in the design and development of software and has spearheaded the implementation and release of several software applications over his career. He has specialized in several fields as part of his collegiate and personal interests. These include theoretical and applied mathematics, software design, user interface design, computer science education, computer vision, and the list continues to expand.

Brian and Anthony are the managing partners of Synapse Software.

About the Technical Reviewer

Matthew Knott is a Learning Platform developer and SharePoint expert. He has been programming since a young age and hasn't stopped learning since. An experienced C and C# developer, Matthew has recently started developing iOS apps to mobilize the Learning Platform. He lives in Wales, United Kingdom with his wife and two children and likes to write on his blog (`mattknott.com`) from time to time.

Acknowledgments

When I arrived in America in 1981 at the age of 20, I had no experience, money, or the knowledge to even use an American payphone. Since then, it's been a wonderful road leading to this book and my life as an Assistant Professor at two University of Colorado campuses. I am such a lucky man to have met so many wonderful people.

First, to my wife, Kera, who moved mountains to help with graphics, meals, dictations, keeping me working, and sustaining a nominal level of sanity in our house. Thank you, Kera.

To my mother, Adeline, who was always there to encourage me, even in the darkest of times when I almost dropped out of Electrical Engineering. To my sister, Vivi, who keeps me grounded, and my late brother Murray, a constant reminder of how precious life is. To Keith and Nettie Lewis, who helped me figure out those American payphones. To Ben Easton, Brian Bucci, and Dennis Donahue, all of whom invited me into their families when I had nobody.

A special thanks to Dr. Zbigniew Ras, my PhD advisor, who became like a father to me, and to Dr. Terry Boult, my mentor and partner in the Bachelor of Innovation program at UCCS.

Last, but not least, to Clay Andres at Apress—he walked me through this process and risked his reputation by suggesting to a bunch of really intelligent people that I could author such a book as this.

Many thanks to you all.

Preface

What *This* Book Will Do For *You*

Let me get this straight: you want to learn how to program for the iPhone or the iPad, and you consider yourself to be pretty intelligent—but whenever you read computer code or highly technical instructions, your brain seems to shut down. Do your eyes glaze over when reading gnarly instructions? Does a little voice in your head chide you, *"How about that! Your brain shut down six lines ago, but you're still scanning the page—pretending you're not as dense as you feel. Great!"*

See if you can relate to this...you're having an issue with something pretty technical and you decide to Google it and troubleshoot the problem. You open the top hitand somebody else has asked the exact same question! You become excited as the page loads, but, alas, it's only a bulletin board (a chat site for all those geeks who yap at one another in unintelligible code). You see your question followed by...but it's too late! Your brain has already shut down, and you feel the tension and frustration as knots form in your belly.

Sound familiar?

Yes? Then this book's for you! My guess is that you're probably standing in a bookstore or in the airport, checking out a magazine stand for something that might excite you. Because you're reading this in some such upscale place, you can probably afford an iPhone, a Mac, a car, and plane tickets. You're probably intrigued by the burgeoning industry of handhelds and the geometric rate at which memory and microprocessors are evolving...how quickly ideas can be turned into startlingly new computing platforms, into powerful software applications, into helpful tools and clever games...perhaps even into greenbacks! And now you are wondering if you can get in on the action—using your intellect and technical savvy to serve the masses.

How do I know this about you?

Easy! Through years of teaching students to program, I know that if you're still reading this, then you're both intelligent enough and sufficiently driven to step onto the playing field of programming, especially for a device as sweet as the iPhone or as sexy as the iPad. If you identify with and feel connected to the person I've described above, then I know you. We were introduced to one another long ago.

You are an intelligent person who may have mental spasms when reading complex code—even if you have some background in programming. And, even if you do have a pretty strong background in various programming languages, you are a person who simply wants an easy, on-point, no-frills strategy to learn how to program the iPhone and iPad. No problem! I can guide you through whatever psychological traffic jams you typically experience and help you navigate around any technical obstacles, real or imagined. I've done this a thousand times with my students, and my methodology will work for you too.

The Approach I Take

I don't try and explain everything in minute detail. Nor do I expect you to know every line of code in your iPhone/iPad application at this stage. What I will do is show you, step by step, how to accomplish key actions. My approach is simultaneously comprehensive and easy-going, and I take pride in my ability to instruct students and interested learners along a wide spectrum of knowledge and skill sets.

Essentially, I will lead you, at your own pace, to a point where you can code, upload, and perhaps sell your first iPhone/iPad app, simple or complex. *Good news*: the most downloaded apps are *not* complex. The most popular ones are simple, common-sense tools for life…finding your car in a parking lot, or making better grocery lists, or tracking your fitness progress. However, when you complete this book, you may want to graduate to other books in the Apress and Friends of ED series. You have quite a few options here, and down the road I'll advise you regarding the best ways to move forward. Right now, though, you may want to read a little about me so you will feel confident in taking me on as your immediate guide in this exciting app-venture.

May you experience great joy and prosperity as you enter this amazing and magical world.

Peace!

Rory A. Lewis, PhD, JD

Chapter 1

Before We Get Started

This introductory chapter will ensure that you have all of the required tools and accessories to proceed fully and confidently through this book. Some of you may already have Xcode, an up-to-date iOS simulator, and Interface Builder installed on your Mac and you may believe that because you are solid on these points, you are ready to jump right in. If so, you may want to jump ahead to Chapter 2 and start immediately on your first program.

It will behoove you, though, to understand why I teach certain things and skip over others. For those of you who have never programmed in Objective-C, it is quite a challenge—even for my engineering students who know Java, C, and C#. Nevertheless, with the appropriate preparation and mindset, you will accomplish programming in Objective-C.

So—I urge you to read on. The time you will invest in this chapter will be well worth it in peace of mind and confidence. Chapter 1 will help to structure the way that your brain will file away all of the rich content that is to come.

Necessities and Accessories

In order to program for the iPhone and/or iPad, and to follow along with the exercises, tutorials, and examples presented in this book, you'll need to have 5 minimal requirements. You may not completely understand them right now, but that's OK—just roll with me for a second. I'll explain everything as we go through these steps. Briefly, the 5 you need are:

- A Mac
- The correct operating system for your Mac called an "OS X"
- Registration as a developer (discussed in detail below)
- The correct operating system for your iPhone, called an iOS
- The correct Software Development Kit for your iPhone, called an SDK that runs a program called Xcode.

Let's go into some of these in a bit more detail.

First, you will need an Intel-based Macintosh running Lion (OS X 10.7.2 or later). If your system was bought after 2006, you're OK. I purposely program everything on a MacBook bought in 2006. All of the videos on the net are screencast from either my MacBook from 2006, or if I broadcast from my 2010 iMac, I first run it on my MacBook bought in 2006. You don't need the latest revved up Mac. If you haven't bought one yet, I suggest you get a basic, no-frills MacBook Air. If you do own an older Mac, then you may be able to add some RAM. Make an appointment at the Genius Bar at an Apple Store and ask them to increase the RAM as much as possible. Also, ask them explicitly: "Can this old computer run Lion *at least* 10.7.2, iOS5, and Xcode 4.2 or later?"

If you do not have a Mac, then keep in mind that, as mentioned, I have made a point to code and run every program in this book on Apple's smallest and cheapest model, the MacBook. Apple has discontinued the MacBook; they now sell the MacBook Air for $999, which is more advanced than the Author's MacBook. You can purchase a MacBook on eBay and other such sites. See Figure 1–1.

Figure 1–1. *I use the cheapest 2006 Mac on the market, the MacBook, to perform all the coding and compiling in this book. Essentially, there is no need at all to buy a more expensive or higher-end Mac to perform all the exercises.*

Second, you will need the correct OS X. As I write this, it is OS X 10.7.2. We need to make sure that you have the latest and greatest operating system (OS X) inside your Mac. I cannot tell you the number of emails and forum questions that show that many of you will think: *"Ahh my code probably did not compile correctly because Dr. Lewis has a different OS X or/and iOS on his machine ..."*

> **NOTE:** The operating system that runs your computer (OS X) is different from the iPhone/iPad Operating System, commonly known as "iOS." Even if you think that everything is up to date, I suggest that you follow along with me and make sure that your system has the latest OS X and the latest iOS inside it. As you follow along with me and tackle all the programs that I teach you in this book, there will be times when your code will not work the first time you run it. In fact, most of the time your code will not work the first time you run it (or "compile it" as us geeky guys say.) So! Let's take care of this now.

Close every program running on your Mac, so that the only program running is "Finder". Go up to the little apple located on the upper left-hand corner of your Mac and select "About This Mac," as illustrated in Figure 1–2.

Figure 1–2. *Go to your Desktop, click on the Apple, and select "About This Mac."*

Once you have selected this, you will see a window called "About This Mac," as illustrated in Figure 1–3.

Figure 1–3. *The "About This Mac" window, and Xcode version window. Here you can see that my MacBook is using OS X 10.7.2. We will discuss iOS later in this chapter. If you have already installed Xcode (or after you install Xcode), under "Xcode," click on "About Xcode" and you will see what version you are running (as shown here on the right).*

Note again that I have OS X 10.7.2 and this is the operating system I will use for this book. By the time you read this book, it will most likely have changed to a higher level. You need to bear two things in mind here. First, you need to update to that latest OS X, as shown below, and secondly, you need to go to the book's online forum to see if there is anything you need to know about changes in the new version of the OS X that may impact this book. So, let's look at how you need to update your system to the latest OS X.

With all of your programs closed except for "Finder," go back up to the apple in the upper left-hand corner of your Mac and select "Software Update …," as illustrated in Figure 1–4. Next, simply follow the instructions and the four screen prompts, as illustrated in Figure 1–5.

Figure 1–4. *Go to your Desktop, click on the Apple and select "Software Update..."*

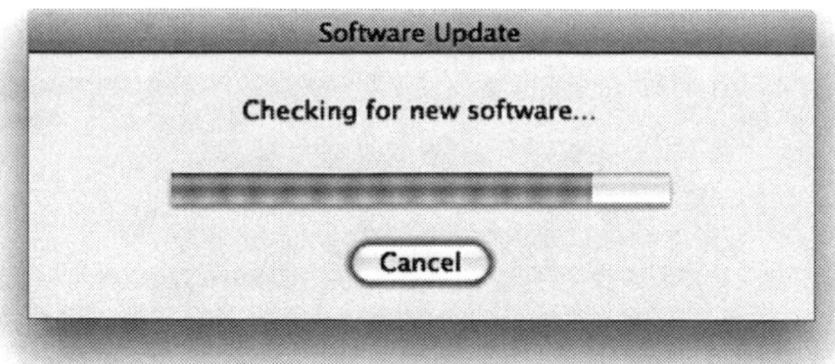

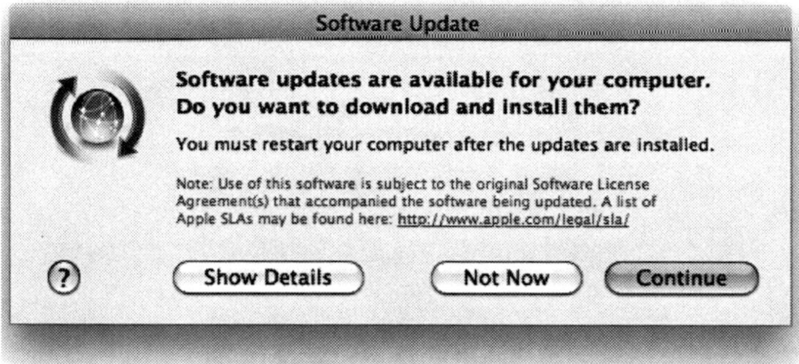

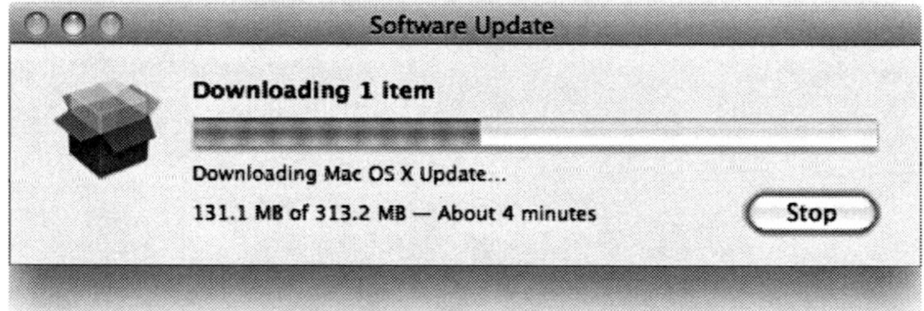

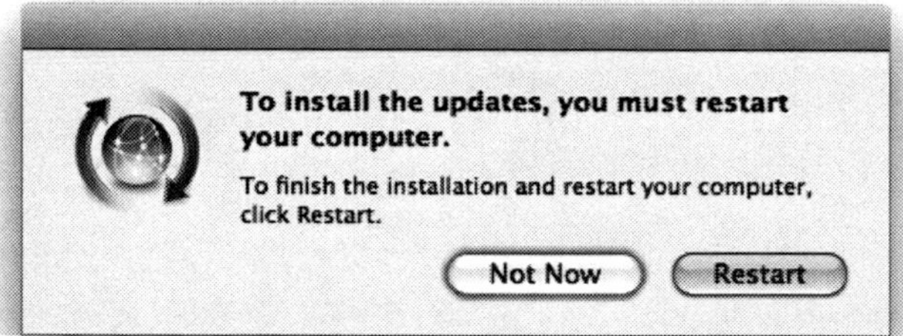

Figure 1–5. *Top - Checking for new software; 2nd from the top - Select the option to download the new software; 2nd from the bottom - Wait for your new software to download; Bottom – Select "Restart" to have your Mac properly install the new software.*

If, by the time you are reading this book, you realize that the OS X, and/or the iOS make my pictures appear dated, then do not freak out. I have a forum that is always online where I and many volunteers love to help others. We always update the forum with news regarding recent updates of the OS X and the iOS. Visit the forum here: `www.rorylewis.com/ipad_forum/` or `bit.ly/oLVwpY`. See Figure 1–20.

Thirdly, you will need to become a registered developer via the iPhone/iPad Software Development Kit (SDK) and download Xcode. If you are a student, it's likely that your professor has already taken care of this, and you may already be registered under your professor's name. If you are not a student, then you will need to follow these numbered steps to sign up.

> **NOTE:** Even if you absolutely do not want to be a developer, you can still download Xcode with your purchase of Lion or buy it at the Mac store. I have yet to have a student last for more than a week trying alternatives to this. The $100 allows you to have access to the Apple developer tool kits, tutorials, example code, and help forums, and to receive a provisioning license to run your apps on a physical iPhone or iPad. Lastly, you're reading this book so you can make an app and sell it on iTunes store and make $$—you need to pay the $100 for this alone. Buying a Mac, Xcode, and this book—but not buying the $100 registered license—is like paying to learn to drive a car, buying a car, but then never obtaining a driver's license. Many of the tools that I teach you to use in this book to debug assume you have a license. It's your choice.

1. Go to `developer.apple.com/programs/ios/` or `bit.ly/qu04ow`, which will bring you to a page similar to the one shown in Figure 1–6. Click the Enroll Now button.

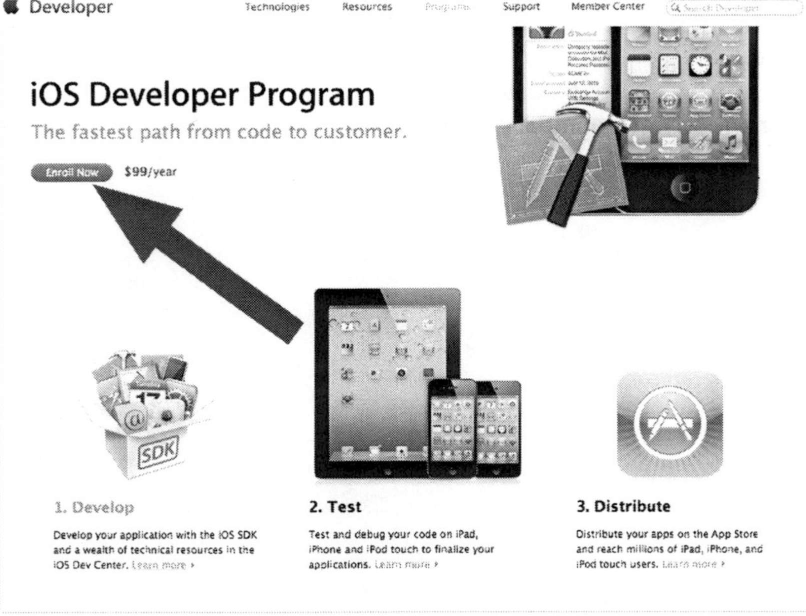

Figure 1–6. *Click the "Enroll Now button".*

2. Click the Continue button, as illustrated in Figure 1–7.

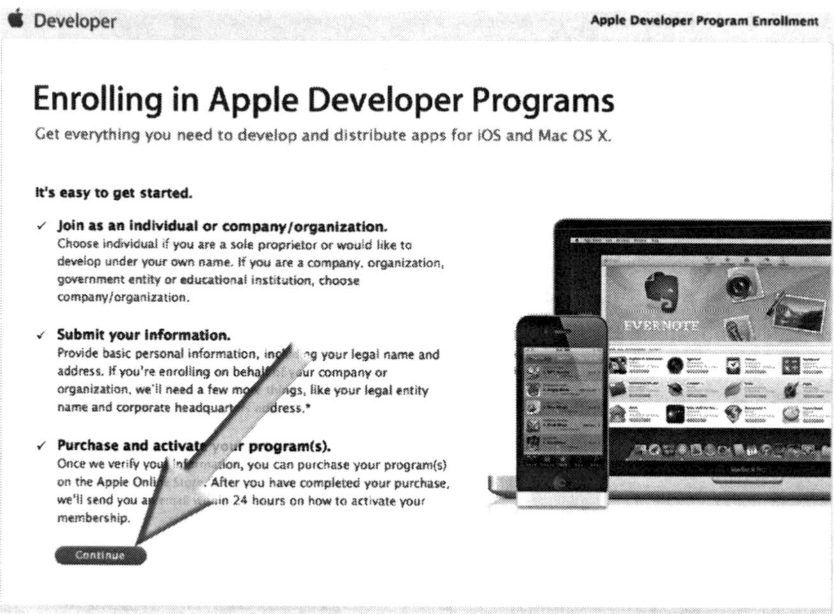

Figure 1–7. *Click the Continue button.*

3. Most people reading this book will select the "I need to create a new account for ..." option (arrow 1 in Figure 1–8). Next, click the Continue button as illustrated by arrow 2 in Figure 1–8. If you already have an existing account, then you have been through this process before. Go ahead with the process beginning with the "I currently have an Apple ID ..." option, and I'll meet you at step 6, where we will log onto the iPhone/iPad development page and download the SDK.

Figure 1–8. *Click the "I need to create an Apple ID…" option to proceed.*

4. You are probably going to be enrolling as an individual, so click the Individual link, as illustrated in Figure 1–9. If you are enrolling as a company, click the Company option to the right and follow the appropriate steps; I'll meet you at step 6.

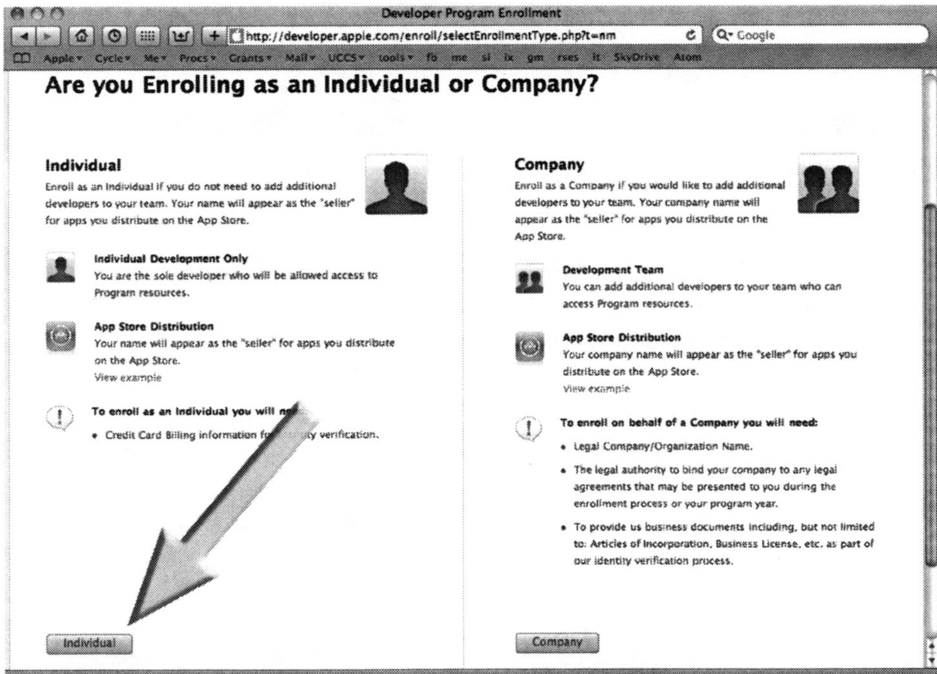

Figure 1–9. *Click the Individual option.*

5. From here, you will enter all of your information, as shown in Figure 1–10, and you will pay your fee of $99 for the Standard Program. This provides you with all of the tools, resources, and technical support that you will need. (If you're reading this book, you really do not want to buy the Enterprise program at $299, as it is for commercial in-house applications.) After paying, save your Apple ID and Username; then receive and interact with your confirmation email appropriately.

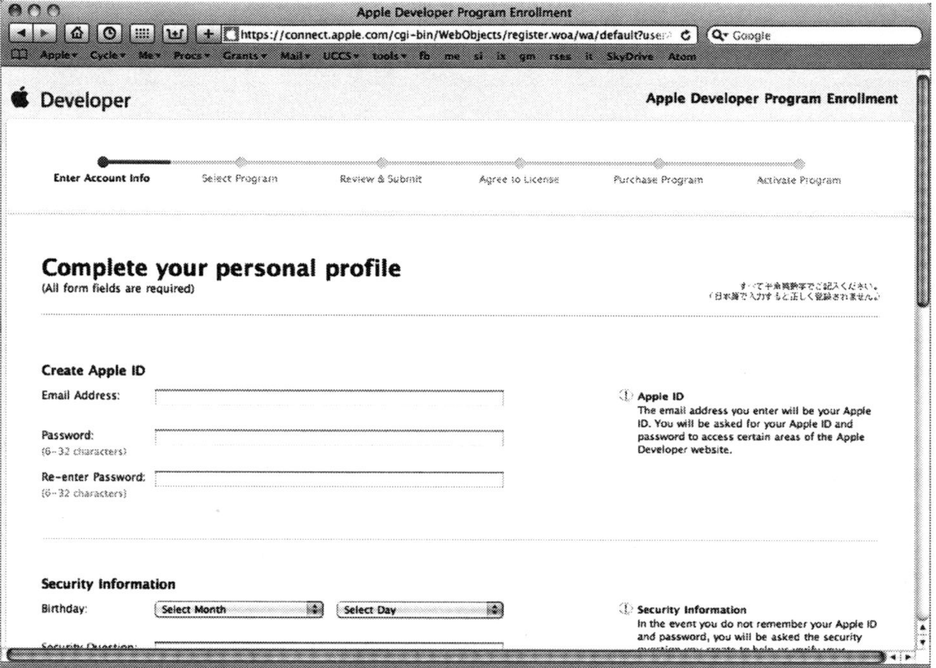

Figure 1–10. *Enter all of your information accordingly.*

NOTE: Before we move onto Step 6, you will want to make sure that you have received your confirmation email and have chosen a password to complete the last step of setting yourself up as a *bona fide* Registered Apple Developer. Congratulations!

6. Use your Apple ID to log into the main iPhone/iPad development page at `developer.apple.com`. This page has three icons for the three types of Apple programmers. As shown by the arrow in Figure 1–11, click on the top icon—iOS Dev Center—to get to the download page for iPhone/iPad Operating System software.

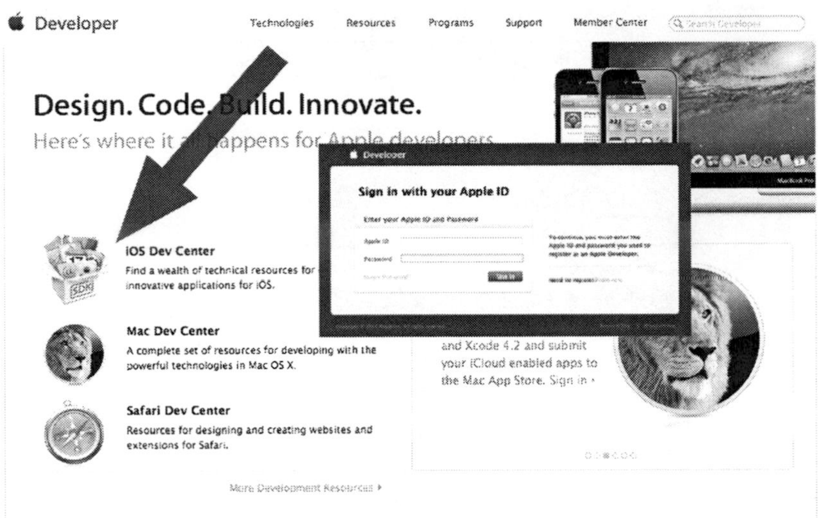

Figure 1–11. *For now, click on the "iOS Dev Center" icon indicated by the arrow. Later, you may also want to program apps for the Mac Computer or the Safari Web Browser.*

> **NOTE:** While we're here, let's go over the other 2 download options. The icon below the iOS is for people who want to download an environment to program wonderful things that run on a Mac. The third and last icon is for people who want an environment to program apps that operate inside Safari's web browser. Maybe one day you will want to connect your cool zany innovative idea that has made thousands of dollars to Safari. Well, this is the place you will want to do that.

7. After logging in to iOSDev with your username and password, as described in step 6, you will see a screen similar to that shown in Figure 1–12. The iOS Dev Center contains all the tools necessary to build iPhone and iPad apps. Later on you will spend time here, but for now we just want to go to the Developer Page of the latest build of the iOS SDK. Locate the 'Downloads' icon indicated by the arrow and click it. You may notice that this only takes you to the bottom of the page, as illustrated in Figure 1–13. Whether you scrolled down or clicked down here, just click on the "*Download Xcode 4*" button so that you can get to the Xcode 4 and iOS SDK 4.3 page.

> **NOTE:** Again, at the time I wrote this book, Xcode 4.2 and iOS SDK 5 were the latest versions. The chance is great that by the time you read this book, these may have larger numbers. This is not a problem; just go on to Step 8. If, by chance, something has really thrown us all a curve ball, it will be discussed and solved for you in easy-to-read English at our forum located at `www.rorylewis.com/ipad_forum/` or `bit.ly/oLVwpY`.

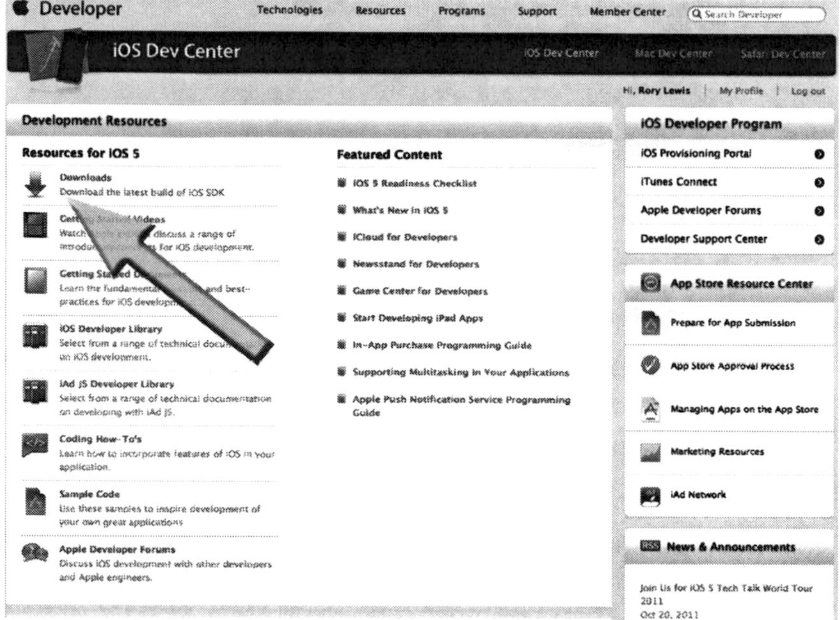

Figure 1–12. *This takes you to the bottom of the page, as shown in Figure 1–13.*

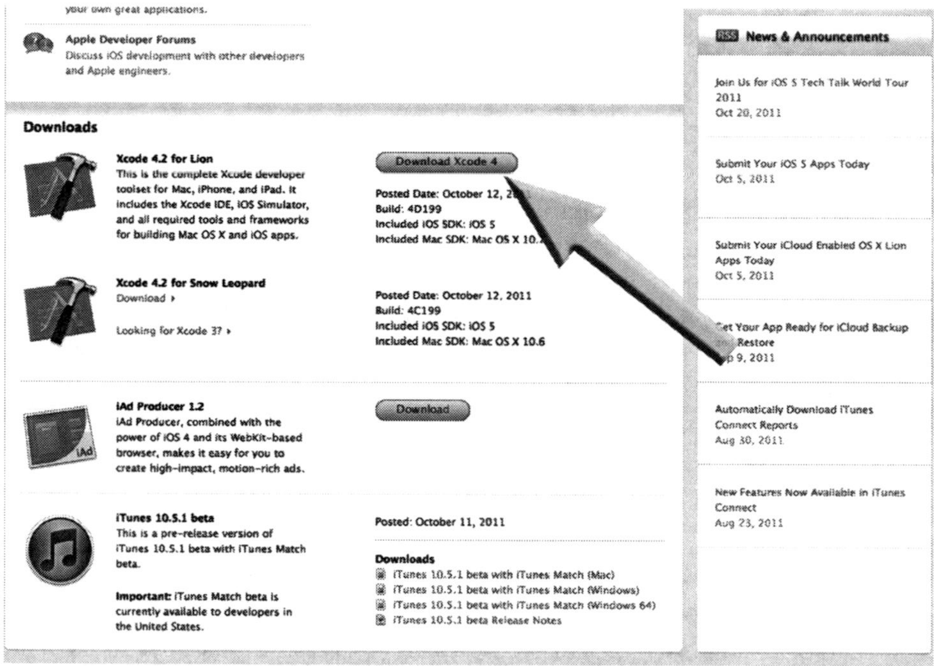

Figure 1–13. *Click on the "Download Xcode 4" button and that will take you to the Xcode 4 Developer Page.*

8. I know you're probably thinking: "*Gee, I just want to download it!*" Remember that there are thousands of downloads at Apple.com. This page, illustrated in Figure 1–14, is called the Xcode 4 Developer Page and it has all of the relevant downloads for you. For now, we want to click on the latest version. These figures show the latest version at the time of this printing. It WILL be different by the time you read this in print. Right now, the latest version available at this point is *"Xcode 4.2 for Lion,"* so this is the link that is indicated by the arrow. It will look similar at this point—click on it.

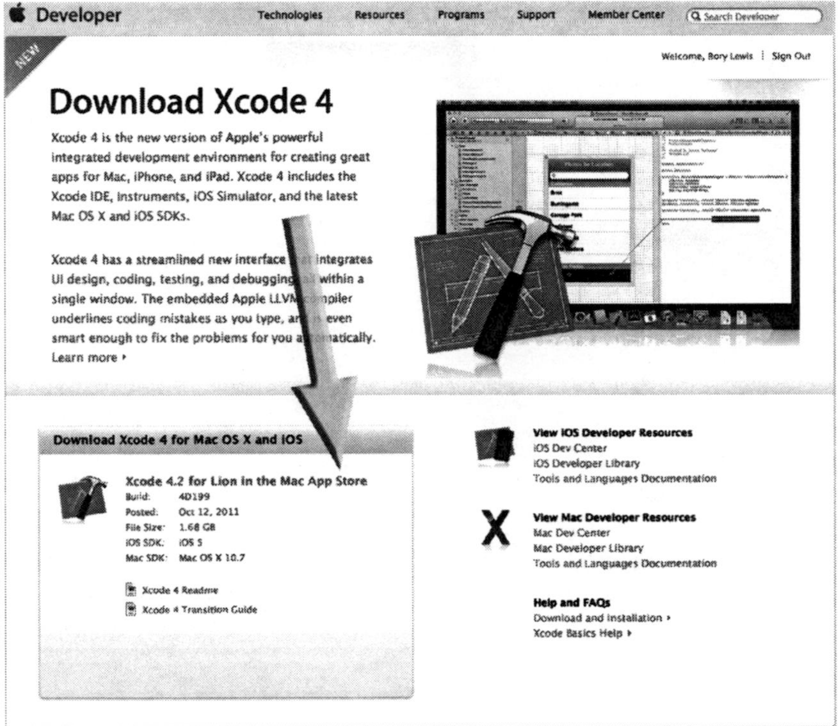

Figure 1–14. ***Click on the "Xcode 4.2 for Lion in the Mac App Store" link.***

9. Your download will start and, depending upon your connection speed, it may take somewhere between 2 to 15 minutes. Your screen should look something like the one shown in Figure 1–15.

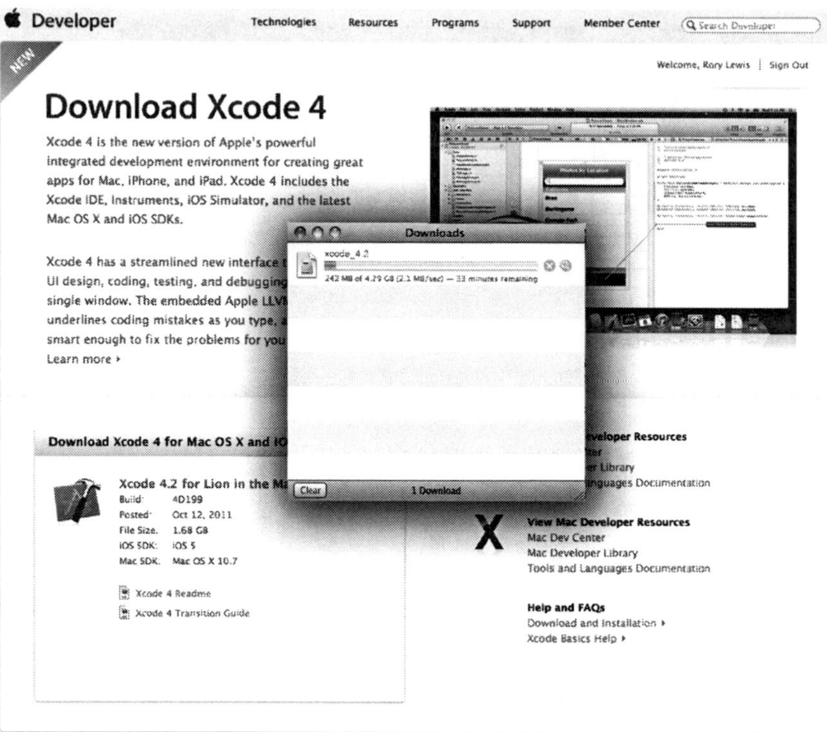

Figure 1–15. *Wait for the download to complete.*

10. Once the download has completed, the Xcode and iOS SDK drive icon will appear on your desktop and a window with your Xcode and iOS SDK.mpkg will appear, as shown in Figure 1–16. Click on the "*Xcode and iOS SDK.mpkg,*" as indicated by the arrow in Figure 1–16.

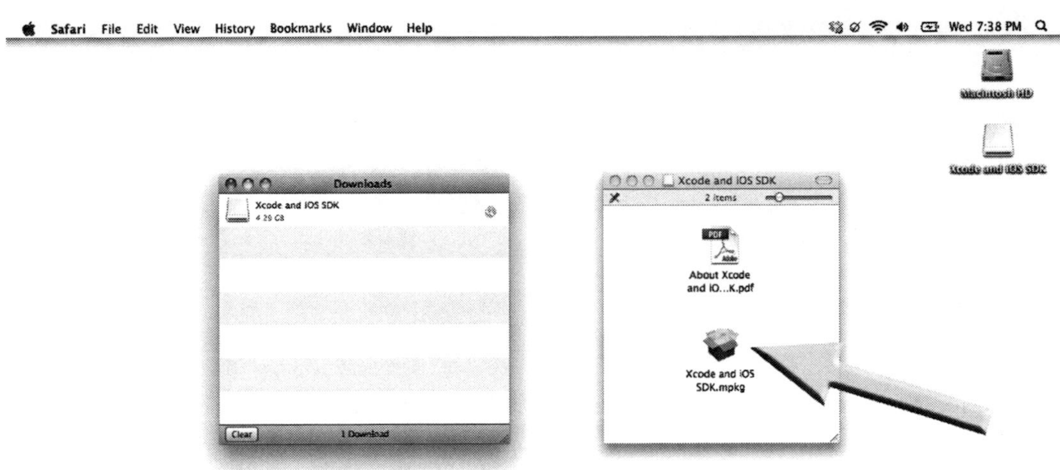

Figure 1–16. *Click on the "Xcode and iOS SDK.mpkg" icon.*

11. Once you have clicked on the Xcode and `iOS SDK.mpkg` icon, a security verification window will open up. Click on the "*Continue*" button as shown by the arrow in Figure 1–17. Next, you will see the "*Install Xcode and iOS SDK*" window, as shown in left-hand image in Figure 1–18. Now click on "*Continue,*" as indicated by the arrow. After several minutes, the installation will be complete and you will see a "*The Installation was Successful*" window appear. Click the "*Close*" button, as indicated by the arrow in the right-hand image in Figure 1–18.

Figure 1–17. *The security verification window. Click on the "Continue" button.*

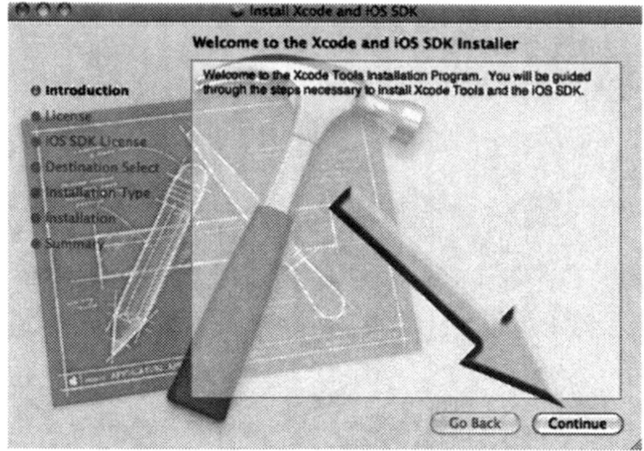

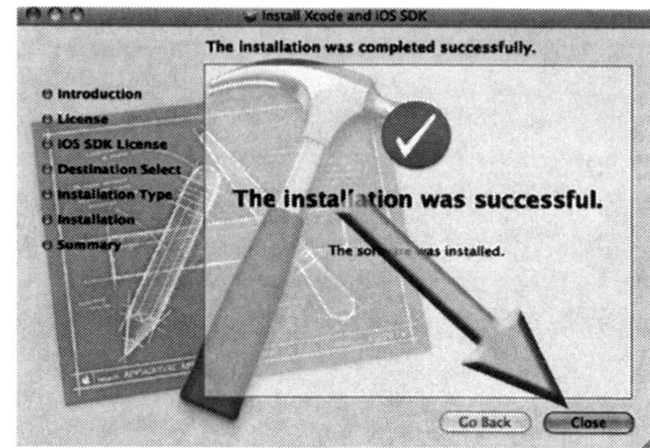

Figure 1–18. *The "Install Xcode and iOS SDK" window. Click on the "Continue" button.*

12. Included with the Apple SDK that you've now downloaded is Apple's integrated development environment (IDE). This programming platform contains a suite of tools, sub-applications, and boilerplate code that all enable us to do our jobs more easily. We will use Xcode, Interface Builder, and the iPhone/iPad Simulator extensively, so I advise you to bring these icons to your dock (see Figure 1–19) as described in Step 13 below. This will save you tons of time searching for them.

Figure 1–19. *Xcode, Interface Builder, and the iPhone/iPad Simulator—locked & loaded, ready to roll!*

13. Bring Xcode to your dock by choosing **Macintosh HD ➤Developer ➤ Applications ➤ Xcode.app** and dragging it onto your dock, as illustrated in Figure 1–19. In the same way, bring Interface Builder to your dock by choosing **Macintosh HD ➤ Developer ➤ Applications ➤ Interface Builder.app** and dragging it. Finally, bring the iPhone/iPad Simulator to your dock by choosing **Macintosh HD ➤ Developer ➤ Platforms ➤ iPhone/iPad Simulator Platform** and dragging it. I've placed them together at the center of my dock, as illustrated in Figure 1–19.

> **NOTE:** Whenever I say "iPhone" or "iPad," I am referring to any iPhone or iPad OS device. This includes the iPod touch. In addition, when I say Macintosh HD, yours may have been named something different.

What I Won't Teach You

With your Xcode, Interface Builder, and iPhone/iPad Simulator tools installed and ready to access easily, you're ready to roll. But wait! You need to know where we're going.

First, though, let me say something about where we won't be going—what I will *not* be covering. I will not attempt to teach you how every line of code works. Instead, I will take a subsystem approach, indicating which pieces or sections of code will serve you in which situations.

While this book is designed to impart to you, the reader and programmer, a comprehensive understanding and ability, we will be dealing in molecules rather than atoms or subatomic particles. The emphasis will be on how to recognize general attributes, behaviors, and relationships of code so that you need not get bogged down in the symbol-by-symbol minutiae. I will get you to a place where you can choose those areas where you may want to specialize.

Computer Science: A Broad and Diverse Landscape

Consider this analogy: suppose that the iPhone/iPad is a car. Most of us drive cars in the same way that we use computers. Just as I would not attempt to teach you how every part of the car works if I were giving you driving lessons, I would not—and will not—approach iPhone and iPad programming with fundamental computer engineering as the first step.

Even great mechanics who work on cars every day rarely know the fundamental physics and electronics behind the modern internal combustion engine, not to mention all the auxiliary systems. They can drive a car, diagnose what's wrong with it when it needs servicing, and use their tools and machines (including computers) to repair and tune it optimally. Similarly, clever programmers who create the apps for the iPhone and iPad rarely know the fundamental coding and circuit board designs at the root of the Apple platforms. Nevertheless, they can use these devices, they can envision a new niche in the broad spectrum of applications needs, and they can use their tools and applications—residing on their desktops and laptops—to design, code, and deliver their ideas to the market.

To continue with this analogy, programming the iPhone or iPad is like playing with the engine of your car—customizing it to do the things you want it to do. Apple has designed a computing engine every bit as fantastic as a V8 motor. Apple has also provided a pretty cool chassis in which we can modify and rebuild our computing engine. However, we have restrictions on how we can "pimp" our iPhone/iPad cars. For those of you who have never pimped a car, I will demonstrate how to maximize creative possibilities while honoring these restrictions.

I'm going to show you, without too much detail, how to swap oil filters, tires, seats, and windows to convert your vehicle into an off-road car, a hot rod, a racing car, or a car that can get us through the jungle. When you've mastered this book, you will know how to focus on and modify the engine, the transmission, the steering, the power train, the fuel efficiency, or the stereo system of the car.

Why Purgatory Exists In Objective-C

My Assumption: you've never worked on a car, and you've never gotten grease on your hands, and you want to pimp one of the world's most powerful automobiles—with a complex V8 engine. I'm going to show you exactly how to do this, and we're going to have fun doing it!

First, you need to know a little about how we even came to have the souped-up car with the V8—that is, the iPad. In 1971, Steve Jobs and Steve Wozniak met, and five years later they formed Apple, producing one of the first commercially successful personal computers. In 1979, Jobs visited Xerox PARC (Palo Alto Research Center), and secured the Xerox Alto's features into their new project, then called the *Lisa.* Although the Alto was not a commercial product, it was the first personal computer to use the desktop metaphor and graphical user interface (GUI). The Lisa was the first Apple product with a mouse and a GUI.

In early 1985, Jobs lost a power struggle with the Board of Directors at Apple, resigned from the company, and founded NeXT, which was eventually bought out by Apple in 1997. During his time at NeXT, Jobs changed some critical features of the code on the Macintosh (Mac) to talk in a new language—a very intense but beautiful language called Objective-C. The power of this language was in its ability to efficiently use objects. Rather than reprogramming code that was used in one portion of the application, Objective-C *reused* these objects. Jobs' brain was on overdrive at the time, and this incredible code took this new language of Objective-C to new heights. His inspiration was fused into the guts of the Mac by creating a metalanguage we call Cocoa. A metalanguage is a language used to analyze or define another language. As I've indicated, Objective-C is a very challenging beast, and you can think of Cocoa as the linguistic taming of the beast, or at least the caging of the beast.

As an “absolute beginner” to the world of programming, you cannot be expected to be concerned with the subtleties of coding language distinctions. I am simply giving you an overview here, so that you will have a rough historical context in which to place your own experience. The main point I’m making here is that Objective-C and Cocoa are very powerful tools, and both are relevant to the programming of the iPhone/iPad.

Houston, We Have a Problem

This is the essence of the challenge that intrigued me, and led to the design of my original course. How can one teach non-engineering students, perhaps like you, something that even the best engineering students struggle with? At the university level, we typically have students first take introductory programming classes, and then proceed to introductory object-oriented programming, such as C# or C++.

That being said, we are going to dive *head on* into Objective-C! At times, I’m going to put blindfolds onto you; at other times, I’m going to cushion the blows. There will be times when you may need to reread pages or rewind video examples a few times—so that you can wrap your head around a difficult concept.

How We’ll Visit Purgatory Every Now and Again

At specific places in my courses, I know that half the class will immediately get it, a quarter will have to sweat over it before they get it, and the remaining quarter will struggle and give up. This third group will typically transfer out of engineering and take an easier curriculum. I know where these places are, and I’m not going to tell you. I’ll repeat that. I will not tell you.

Don’t worry, I won’t allow you to disturb a hornet’s nest (of Objective-C issues) and get stung to death. Nor will I mark off those concepts that you may find difficult. I’m not going to explain this now. Just accept it! If you just relax and follow my lead, you’ll get through this book with flying colors.

When you do find yourself in one of those tough spots, persevere. You can always reread the section, rewind the video examples, or—most importantly—go visit the Forum where many people, including myself, are often online and ready to help you immediately. We may refer you to somebody else's solution or we may help you directly. So go to the forum, say "hello" to the crowd, and become immersed by first seeking help from others and then going back to help others. The forum is located at: `www.rorylewis.com/ipad_forum/` or `bit.ly/oLVwpY`. See Figure 1–20.

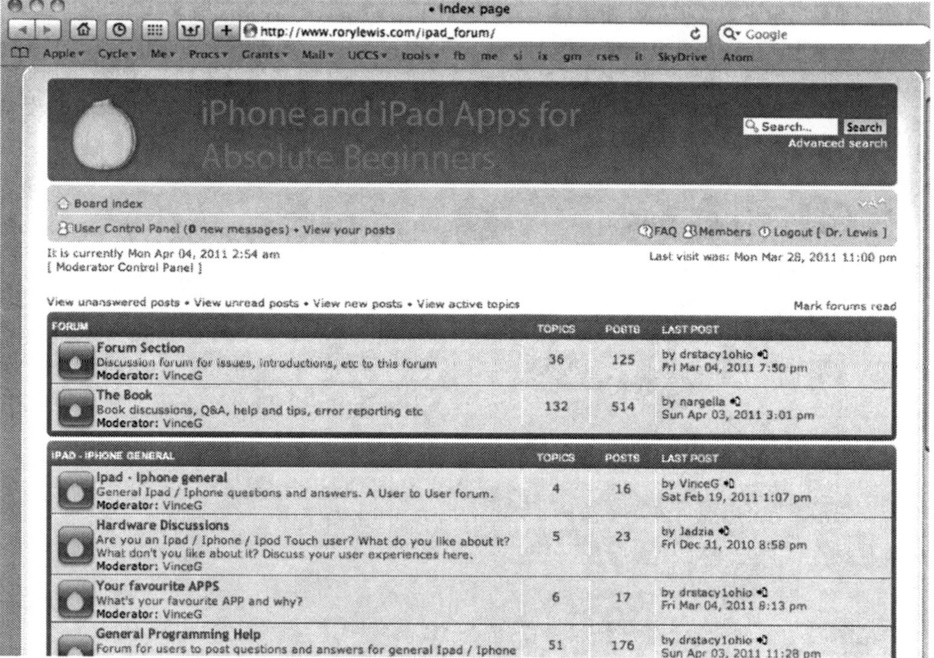

Figure 1–20. *Visiting the Forum can help if you find yourself in a tough spot.*

Looking Forward... *Beginning iPhone 4 Development: Exploring the iPhone SDK*

Down the line, some of you may want to continue your iPhone and iPad programming adventure by reading Dave Mark and Jeff Lamarche's book, *Beginning iPhone 4 Development: Exploring the iPhone SDK* (Apress, 2009). Remember the analogy of becoming a mechanic for an automobile with a V8 engine mounted on a basic chassis? Their book presumes that the readers know what a carburetor is, know what a piston is, and that they can mount racing tires and super fly rims on their friends' pimped-up wheels.

In other words, they assume that you understand the fundamentals of object-oriented programming: that you know what objects, loops, and variables are, and that you are familiar with the Objective-C programming language.

On the other hand, I assume that you don't know, for example, what a "class" is, or what a "member" or "void" is. I imagine that you have no idea how memory management works on an iPhone/iPad and, furthermore, that you never had an interest—*until now*—in understanding an array, or an SDK.

What You Will Learn

When students start a challenging class, I have found that it works wonders to have them create something really cool, and with relative ease. At each stage of this process, I will typically present an example that you can read, see, and digest right away. Later on, we will return to analyze some of the early steps and go into more detail. I will explain how we accomplished some task or action the first time *without even knowing it*. Then, by comparing the first time through with subsequent modifications, you will learn how to tweak the program a little here, a little there. This way, you'll stay on track—motivated and inspired to absorb the next new batch of tricks, lessons, and methods.

Creating Cool and Wacky Apps: Why I Teach This Way

You've heard the bit about how we best remember things: doing is better than seeing, which is better than hearing, and so on. Well, I know that students love humor—and guess what! We remember funny stories and lessons much better than we remember dull and boring ones. I have found that, without exception, when students work on code that is fun and wacky, they tend to spend much more time solving it.

The more we apply ourselves mentally toward the solution of a problem, the more neural connections are made in our brains. The more neurons we connect, the more we remember and—most importantly—the less apt we are to waste time on ineffective methods.

The more time we spend on a particular topic, the more chance there is that you will experience gut feelings about whether a particular methodology for solving a project is on track or not. So, as we proceed, be aware that I am employing humor to burn computer science and Objective-C concepts and methods into your brain without your exerting any conscious effort.

It is common for my students to contact me after receiving a difficult homework assignment. First, they'll send me a tweet asking if they can Skype me. One particular night, I was playing chess with a colleague when I received a tweet asking if I was available. "Of course," I responded. I warned my colleague, also a professor at the University of North Carolina, that students he knew were about to appear on Skype. When they buzzed in, sure enough, they were four of my electrical engineering students, wide-eyed and smiling. *"Hey, Dr. Lewis, we finally got it, but Dude! The last method you assigned..."*

When we finished our conversation, and I turned off my Mac, it was 12:30 a.m. My colleague asked, "Rory, I never called a professor this late in the evening—much less *after midnight*! Shouldn't they ask these questions during office hours?!" He was probably right, but after thinking about it for a minute I replied, "I'm just happy that they're working on my wacky assignment!" As we set up the next chess game, he murmured something about how I might be comfortable in the insanity ward.

The point is that I want you to read this entire book. I want you to work all the examples and to feel elation as you complete each assignment! I have done everything I can to make this book enjoyable. If you choose to engage with the ideas contained herein, this book will change your life!

By the way, successfully navigating these lessons will make you a certified geek. Everybody around you will sense your growing ability and will witness your transformation; as a result, they will seek you out to request that you write apps for them.

Evangelizing to Your Grandmother... What You Coded Is Crucial!

It's important that you not let complex code turn you inside-out. Just two minutes ago, a student walked into my office—so confused that he couldn't even tell me what it was he didn't know. He said something like, "My second order array worked fine in-line, but not as a class or a method." I said, "No, that's too complex! Here's an easier way of saying it..."

I described how he had a long line of "stuff" going in one end and being spat out the other—and it worked really well. But, when he put it in a *method*, he couldn't see the start of the long line of stuff; when he put it in a *class*, he couldn't see *any* of the stuff!"

"Wow! I know what I did wrong, Dr. Lewis. Thank you!" Now, as I type this, he's explaining it to his two buddies who came in yesterday and tried to ask the same question. Don't worry. The confusion that drove these questions—such as the distinctions between "classes" and "methods," and other coding entities—will be covered later in this book. All in good time!

If you can keep your feet on the ground and transform complex things into simpler ideas, then you can remember them—and master them. Grasp this concept, and you will be able to convert your far out ideas into code—and who knows where that will take you! This is why I am so determined to impart to you the ability to convert things your grandmother wants to be able to do into iPhone and iPad programming language.

How Does This All Work?

Before we start our first program in Chapter 2, it's critical that you are able to step back and know where we've been, where we are now, and where we will go next. In other words, you may ask yourself: How do I convert an innovative idea for an iPhone or iPad app into money in my back pocket? How does this work? Does it even work or are all those crazy stories of people making massive amounts of money from iPhone and iPad Apps untrue?

So, are these stories of Apps-to-Riches true? This is easy to answer. As of March 02, 2011, when Steve Jobs revealed the iPad 2, he announced that Apple had paid a cumulative $2 billion to developers for apps sold in the App Store (see Figure 1–23, #9). Note that only eight months earlier Apple announced that it had paid out $1 billion to iPhone and iPad app developers since the App Store launched in July 2008.

A sum of $2 billion has never been paid to programmers before. You are entering a booming, epic event in computers and technology. Reading this book and learning how to program apps is going to change your life. During this new post-PC era, Apple has single-handedly created a never-before-seen environment for developers to take advantage of these more personal and powerful machines. This vibrant community of programmers that you are about to enter has helped push Apple's count of apps up to more than 350,000. But still you may ask: How does this work?

I have created map of how the innovative process works and you need to understand this to know where you are going with this book. Looking at Figure 1–21, I want you to start by looking at ...err...YOU! Yes, that's you there, at #1, sitting next to a bag of money represented by #11, which is the 11th of 12 steps. Starting at #1, which is you with your brilliant innovative idea, you take your idea to #2, which represents the OSX on your Mac. Once you open your Mac, you are accessing the SDK (#3), which includes the iPhone/iPad Simulator (#4), Interface Builder (#5) and Xcode (#6), all lying on a gray strip that is part of your SDK iOS. These items (#4 to #6) will be explained in detail later; 90 percent of this book deals with the items in this strip. The only thing not covered here is where you convert your idea into code by programming in Objective-C.

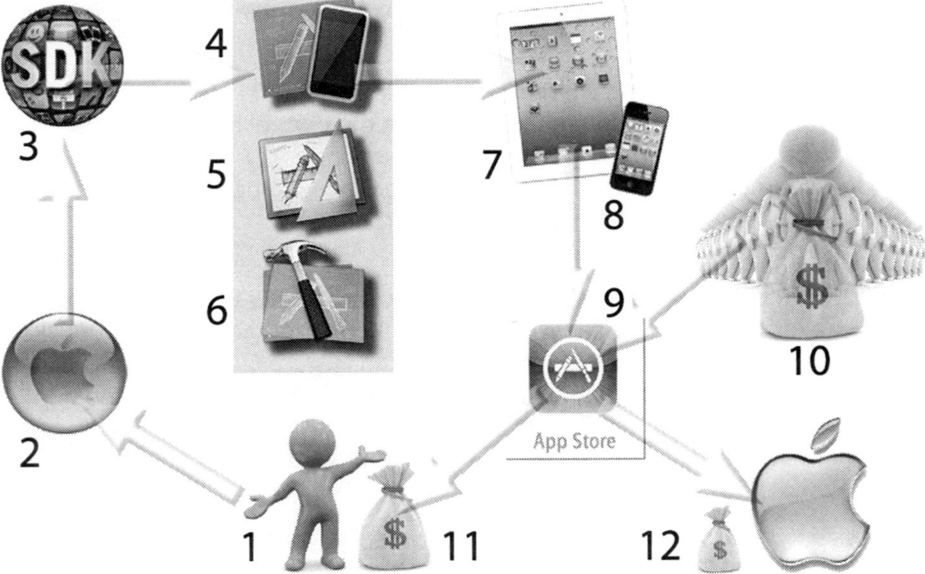

Figure 1–21. *The iPhone and iPad app programming landscape*

> **NOTE:** In Figure 1–21, the gray box contains the Interface Builder (#5) which technically is not supposed to exist in these latest versions of Xcode. The problem is that it's still there, just in the background and we still use it extensively in Storyboarding (Chapter 7) onwards. So, be aware that some will say Interface Builder is gone (they're wrong) and that we are not using it (wrong again. We do after Chapter 7). To the left of this area is where you've already been: Remember that you have a Mac with an OSX (#2) purchased after 2006 and running Mac OS X 10.7.2 or higher, and we've just walked through the process of downloading the iPhone and iPad SDK (#3) (Figures 1–6 through 1–20). We have also extracted the iPhone/iPad Simulator (#4), Interface Builder (#5) and Xcode (#6) and positioned them onto your dock (Figure 1–12).

In Chapter 2, we will start using Xcode (#6), Interface Builder (#5), and the iPhone/iPad Simulator to turn you into a bona-fide geek! In your geeky state you will test your Apps on real iPads (#7) and real iPhones (#8). Once you know that your code works fanatabulously (that's my geekdom word), you will upload your app to the App Store (#9) where people with money (#10) will download your app by paying the App Store money. The money that is received by the App Store is split up, with two-thirds of it going to you and one-third going to Apple.

We're going to run all of the programs we create by compiling them to one of several possible locations—the icons for these are to the right of the central gray area. The primary location will be the iPhone/iPad Simulator. The secondary locations will be your local iPhone and/or your local iPad. Lastly, we could use iTunes to upload your iPhone and/or iPad App to the App Store, where people can purchase it or download it for free. This is where we are going.

The two central objects in Figure 1–21, as you now know, are where we will spend the vast majority of our time within this book. We'll be using Xcode to type in code, just like the serious geeks do. I'll show you how to operate all of its features, such as file management, compilation, debugging, and error reporting. Interface Builder is the cool way Apple allows us to drag and drop objects onto our iPhone/iPad apps. If you want a button, for instance, you simply drag and drop it where you want it to be located on the virtual iPhone or iPad.

Essentially, we'll use Xcode to manage, write, run, and debug your app—to create the content and functionality. We'll use Interface Builder to drag and drop items onto your interface until it looks like the colorful and cool application you envisioned—to give it the style, look, and feel that suits your artistic tastes.

After we integrate all of the interface goodies with the code that we wrote in Xcode, we might get advanced and tweak the parameters that deal with memory management and efficiency. But that's jumping too far ahead in our story.

Our Road Map: Using Xcode and Interface Builder

Very often, authors of programming books do the same old thing. First, they present a very simple, ubiquitous "Hello World" application and then they throttle the user with intense code that loses a great many readers and students straight away. Utilizing Objective-C (being run in Cocoa) along with the iPhone and iPad SDK, I've had to really rethink this introductory process. I have identified four challenges here:

- Teaching you "Hello World" and then going into advanced technologies and APIs would be counter-productive.
- It makes no sense to randomly choose one of the many ways to say Hello to the world from your iPhone or iPad. They are all going to be necessary to have in your toolkit at a later date.
- Trying to write a simple "Hello World" application in Objective-C is more involved than the beginner is ready for, unless we break up the process into stages or layers.
- Deciding how to progress slowly, get comfortable, and become familiar with the nomenclature and the process, and then get to Storyboarding and other more advanced concepts.

My solution to overcoming these issues is simple. I'll show you how to say hello to the world from your iPhone/iPad in not one, not two, but quite a few different ways. Each time, we'll go a little bit deeper, and we'll have a blast as we do so.

Each time you travel down the road into the land of Xcode, you are immediately asked what type of vehicle you'd like to drive. A Jeep? A race car? A convertible? By focusing on basics, I am going to show you how to "drive" in Xcode. The objective here will be to gain competence and confidence in whatever style of vehicle we must access. So, let's take a look at exactly what these different vehicles have to offer. Here, I would like you to follow along with me.

Getting Ready For Your First iPhone/iPad Project

Assuming that you have already downloaded the SDK and installed Interface Builder, Xcode, and the iPhone/iPad Simulator, open up your Mac and click the Xcode icon on your dock. Your screen should look similar to Figure 1–22. Up pops the Welcome to Xcode window; it includes all of your iPhone and iPad resources.

Figure 1–22. *After clicking the Xcode icon, you will see the "Welcome to Xcode" screen.*

As indicated by arrow 1, make sure you keep the "*Show this window when Xcode launches*" option checked. You'll find many valuable resources here that will come in handy. I suggest that, after you have completed Chapter 4, you take a little time to explore these resources—give them a test drive, so to speak. This practice will open all kinds of creative doors for you.

Without actually starting a new project, let's walk up to the showroom floor and check out some of the models we might be driving. To open a new project in Xcode, click on the Xcode icon. When it opens, you can do one of two things: either click on the number 2 and then number 3 arrows as indicated on Figure 1–22, or enter Command + Shift + N (⌘⇧N), simultaneously. This will open a new window that showcases the different types of vehicles that you can drive in the land of Xcode.

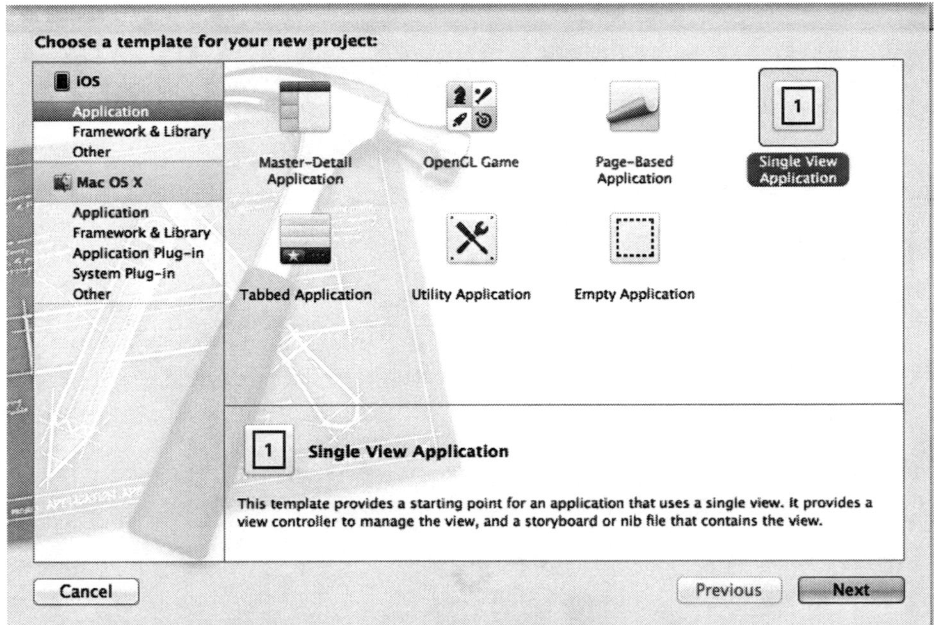

Figure 1–23. *The new window that showcases the different types of vehicles that you can drive in the land of Xcode.*

Figure 1–23 displays the seven vehicle models: Master-Detail Application, OpenGL Game, Page-Based Application, Single View Application, Tabbed Application, Utility Application and Empty Application.

Early on, most of our travel in Xcode will be by one of the latter two styles shown. Switching back to computer terms, View-based Application and Window-based Application are the structures that we will utilize in the basic development cycle for the iPhone/iPad. It is here that we will access cool gadgets and components.

Don't worry: I haven't forgotten our goal of creating a simple "Hello World" application. We will say hello to the world while using a number of the six options, and you will become familiar with each. Before we drive our car, let's make sure the key works in the ignition—or in computer land, let's check that the iOS compiles a blank document and brings up the iPhone/iPad Simulator. Click on Single View Application, as shown in Figure 1–23. Looking at your screen, you should see something very similar to that of Figure 1–24. First call it "test," as indicated by arrow 1, then make sure you select iPhone as depicted by arrow 2, and then click on the "Next" button as indicated by arrow 3.

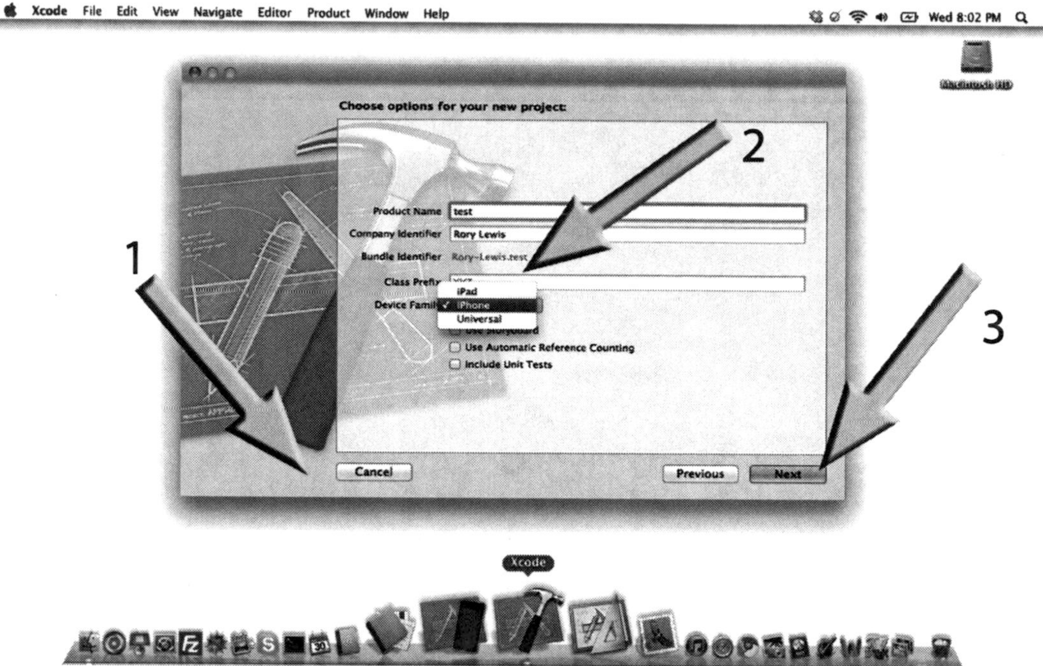

Figure 1–24. *Let's go for a test drive.*

If your program does not default to saving it onto your Desktop, then navigate your way to your Desktop and the click on the "Create" button, as illustrated in Figure 1–25.

Figure 1–25. *Navigate to your Desktop and create your test app.*

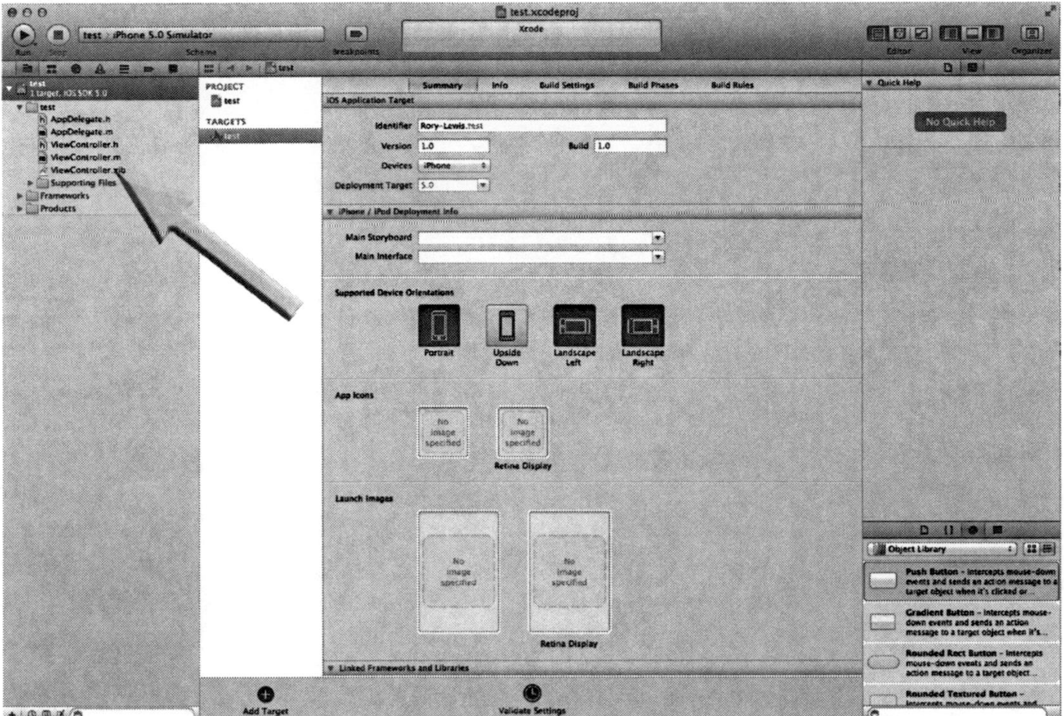

Figure 1–26. *The initial Integrated Development Environment (IDE) screen.*

Figure 1–26 shows the initial view of Xcode 4's integrated development environment (IDE). We will not get tangled up in explaining everything right now. All I want you to do is to click on any of the any of the files that end with an ".h" or an ".m". Now click on the `testViewController.h` file, as indicated by the arrow in Figure 1-26. This will bring up the screen shown in Figure 1–27, where I want you to run your blank app by clicking on the "go" button as indicated by the arrow. Oh Yeah! The iPhone in the iPhone/iPad Simulator pops up, as illustrated in Figure 1–28. Congratulations! You've loaded Xcode and you've taken it for a test drive. It's time to realize that you're just about to embark into a whole new world.

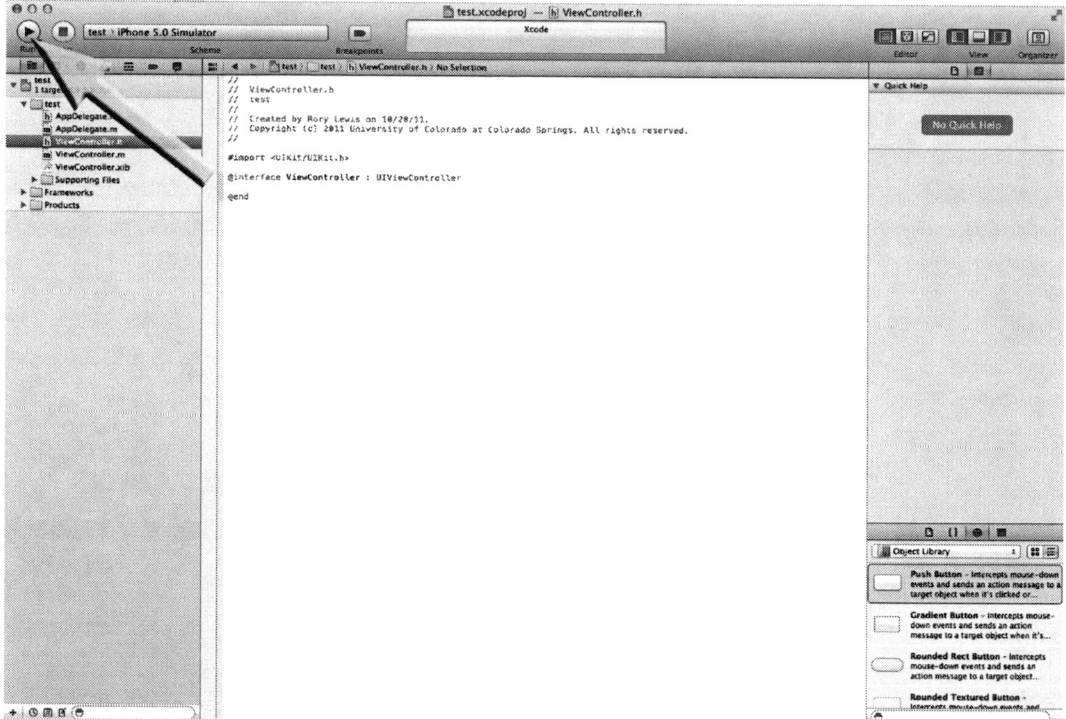

Figure 1–27. *Run it!*

Figure 1–28. *Your first test-drive.*

The Accompanying Screencasts

All figures shown in this book have been captured from my screen as I write the code—in a screencast. For example, the `helloWorld_001` example in Chapter 2 is located at `www.rorylewis.com/docs/02_iPad_iPhone/06_iphone_Movies/002_helloWorld_002.htm` or `bit.ly/quO4ow`.

It is not necessary to view the aforementioned screencast, since I have included all the instructions in Chapter 2. However, I've heard students say that it's fun to retrace what they heard in the lesson. These video examples tend to be rather condensed. If you would like to follow along with the screencasts, please note these recommendations:

- Stop the video when I get ahead of you. Rewind it and get back on track with me.
- After you can complete the project in full, save the screencast to another folder. Then, go through it again with fewer stops until you can master it… and compile it.
- For the competitive among you, perhaps a goal is to execute the code in time with me as I go. Generally, though, I want you to feel good and comfortable with programming at a high level. It would behoove you to practice this for all the examples in the book.

The Accompanying PDFs

I also provide a PDF version of the keynote slides that I give to my students at the University of Colorado. These PDFs—which are not required, but merely supplemental—show all the slides from this chapter. There are also links for those of you who want to probe deeper into subject matter that is not covered in this book.

> **NOTE:** You can access videos and supplementary materials at the `www.apress.com` web site.

Pretending Not to Know: The Art of De-Obfuscation

Before we begin in earnest, I want to reiterate that I am going to show you how to program while knowing only the essentials. As we move forward, I will explain concepts a little deeper. However, I will only do this once we've gotten your head wrapped around the easy concepts. This is a new way of teaching, and I have had great success with it.

You may think I've completely lost my mind, but I ask you to follow my instructions anyway. If you have a question that I don't appear to address, trust me that it's not important at the time. We will cover it down the road!

How We'll Travel Through Each Step

This book is completely inclusive. Even though I provide video tutorials for the exercises in this book, you don't need any of it. You can read this book alone, without any Internet connection, and everything that you need you can find within these pages.

So, now that you've finished checking your system parameters, signed up as an official Apple developer, downloaded the SDK, extracted the essential tools, and configured your dock, it is time to advance to Chapter 2 and create some code.

A LITTLE EXERCISE

Looking at Figure 1–28, you see that on the test drive we ended up with an iPhone popping up on the iPhone/iPad Simulator. Well, what about the iPad? Well, that's what I'd like you to do on your own. See if you can get the iPad in the iPhone/iPad Simulator, as illustrated in Figure 1–29. The clues are seen in Figure 1–24 and in Figure 1–29 where, under the test folder, is a brand new folder called test 2.

Figure 1–29. *iPad2 in the iPhone/iPad Simulator.*

Chapter 2

Blast-Off!

The first program we shall attempt, as mentioned in Chapter 1, will be a basic and generic "Hello World" application. This Blast-Off chapter emulates precisely what I have found, through experience, to work very well in the lecture halls when teaching this course. I use this simple, innocent, benign "Hello World App" as a basis to introduce students to the most critical skill sets that they will use over and over again. As happens with my own students, by the time you finish Chapter 2, you will know how to run your first app in 3 different ways, according to each of the following sections:

2.1. iPhone Simulator.

2.2. iPad Simulator reading your iPhone environment (pseudo iPad).

2.3. iPad Simulator.

In my lectures, I want to keep the flow of adrenaline by continuously creating app after app and getting that geeky feeling of conquering the world. Therefore, I leave §2.4 to 2.6 for a special Saturday class that is optional for students who want to create their own business selling apps and making money. Likewise for you, the reader, I suggest that you only do §2.1 to 2.3 and then go to Chapter 3, as this will keep the flow going. Our first adventure with this new set of tools will be saying "Hello" to the world from the View-based Application template in Xcode. Later, we will say "Hello" to the world from the Navigation-based Application template, first in a very basic way and then with some modifications.

Besides the information I present here in this book, including various screenshots, I also offer you screencasts of myself going through each of the examples in this book. Downloads for that will assist you in getting through this book, as will lecture notes, 3rd party resources, and pertinent YouTube videos—all of which can be accessed by clicking on the blue Xcode 4 icon located top center at: `www.rorylewis.com`.

Running Your App on the iPhone Simulator

In this first example, we are going to click on a button that will have text appear above it saying "Hello World."

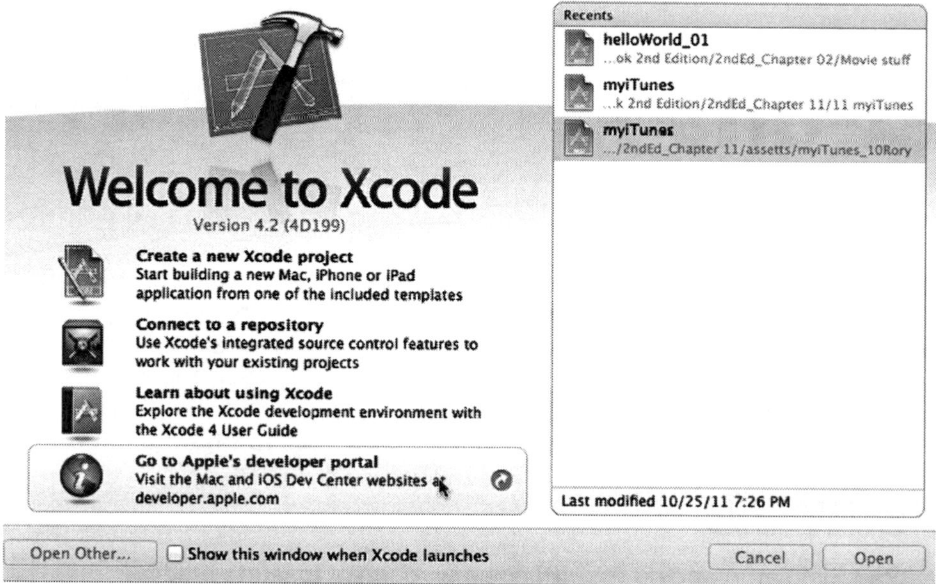

Figure 2–1. *Click the Xcode icon in your Dock to open it. You will be presented with the "Welcome to Xcode" frame, as discussed in Chapter 1.*

1. Before opening Xcode, first close all open programs so that you will be able to optimize your processing capabilities and focus your undivided attention on this new material. Press Command + Tab (⌘→|) and then Command + Q (⌘Q) to close everything, until only the Finder remains on your screen. Find and click the Xcode icon in your Dock to open it. You will be presented with the Xcode "Welcome" screen discussed in Chapter 1. See Figure 2–1.

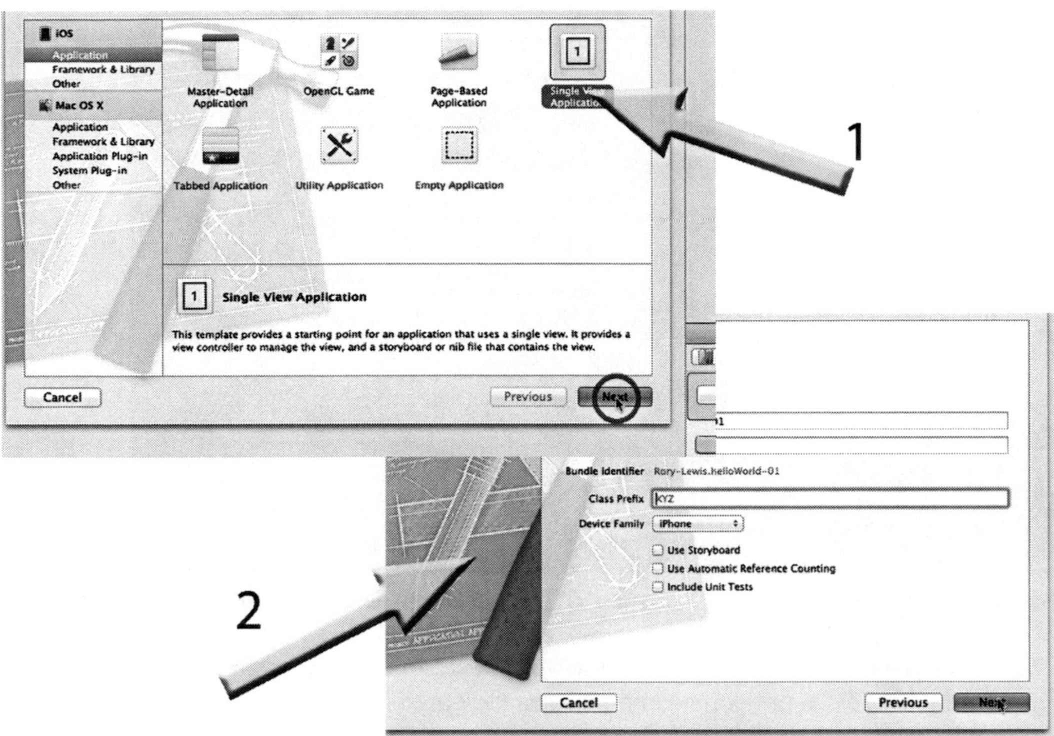

Figure 2–2. *Name it* `hello_World_01` *and use your name or company name for the Company Identifier. For the Device, select iPhone.*

2. Now open a new project in Xcode. The two ways to accomplish this are by using keyboard shortcuts or by clicking your mouse. I *strongly* suggest that you use keyboard shortcuts. These will save you time and make you feel like a pro. Be aware that the best way to *not* get work as an iPhone and iPad app developer is to use your mouse for functions that can be done via shortcuts. Using your keyboard, press Command + Shift + N at the same time. These three keystrokes appear in Figure 2–1 as ⌘⇧N. (If you were using your mouse to open a new project, you would choose *Create a new Xcode project*.) Select View-Based App and then press Return (↩). Name it `helloWorld_01`, enter your name, and select iPhone, as depicted in Figure 2–2.

NOTE: My View-based Application template icon was highlighted by default; yours may not be. Regardless, click on it, and save the new project to your desktop as `helloWorld_01`.

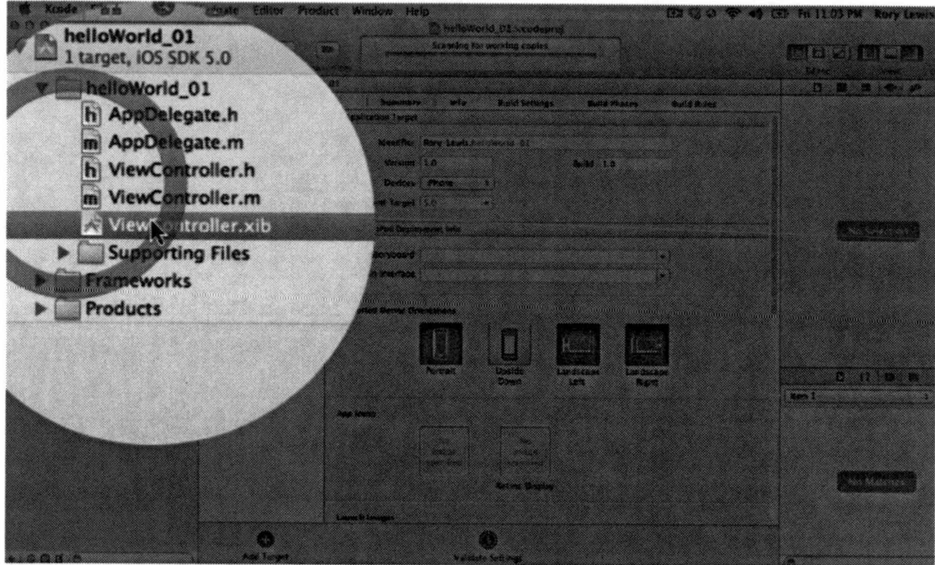

Figure 2–3. ***Click the*** `helloWorld_01 ViewController.xib` ***to open the Interface Builder.***

3. As soon as you save this project to your desktop, Xcode instantiates the `helloWorld_01` project environment, as indicated by the name on the top of the window (see Figure 2–3). If this looks a bit scary, stay cool... don't freak out! This is Apple's way of arranging all of the goodies that you will eventually use to write complex apps. For now, just follow along and try to set aside all the questions you may be asking. Xcode has created 6 files:

   a. 2 *classes* that contain two files (a *header* file (`.h`) and an *implementation* file (`.m`)). Two of them end in `Appdelegate` and two of them end in `ViewController`. We will get back to this later. Right now just know this: Each "class" is comprised of two files: a header file and an implementation file.

   b. 2 *nib* files (`.xib`).Don't ask yourself what "nib" means yet. Just open the file where you can see a visualization of your program. In due time, you'll get to know plenty about nibs.

As shown in Figure 2–3, double-click to open up the `helloWorld_01 ViewController.xib` (pronounced "nib") file that is located in the manila-colored `helloWorld_01` folder that is located inside of the blue Xcode folder located at the top left-hand side of the Navigator Area of your Xcode environment.

NOTE: There is a slight possibility that your Navigation Pane, which bears the folders seen in the highlighted circle in Figure 2–3, is closed. This is not a problem. To open your utility area, go to the upper left of the workspace window, which includes inspectors and libraries. Use the View Selector in the toolbar to open and close the navigator, debug, and utility areas. You may also need to again select the black folder icon called the Project Navigator located directly under the "Run" button— it looks like the "play" button in iTunes.

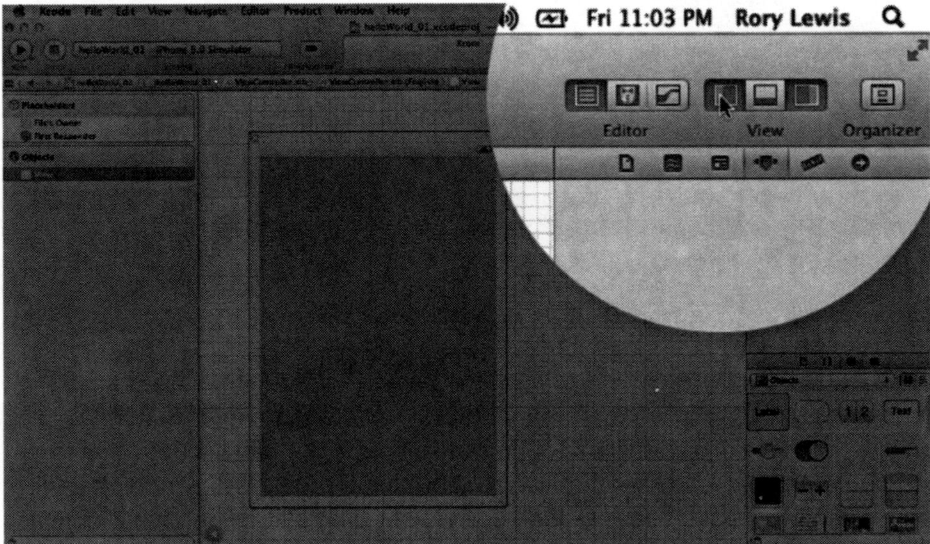

Figure 2–4. *Open the Utilities Pane by clicking on the Utilities Icon in the View Selector.*

4. We need to open the utility area located to the right of the workspace window (see Figure 2–4), which includes inspectors and libraries. Navigate to your View Selector, which contains 3 icons, and select the far right icon called the Utilities Icon.

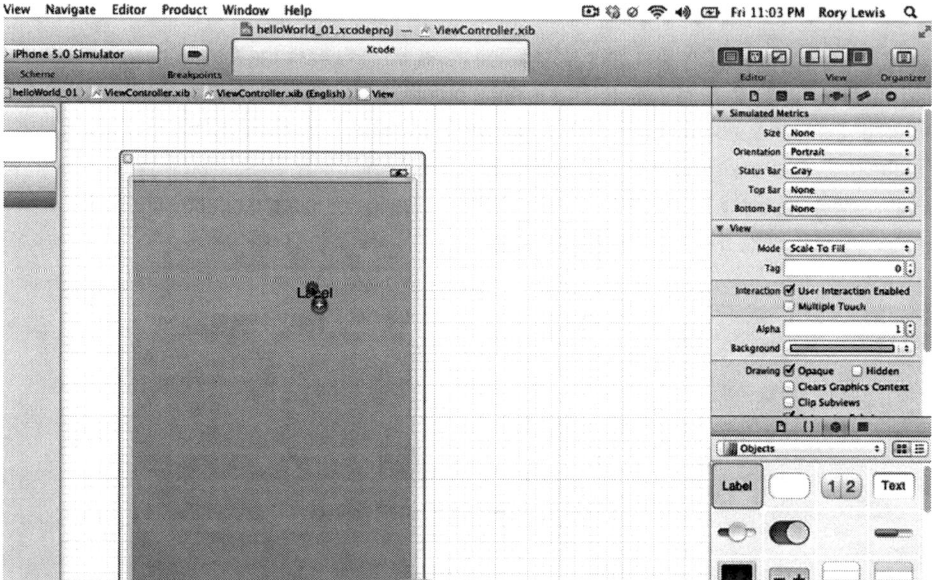

Figure 2–5. *Drag out a label onto your canvas. Delete its text and center its content.*

5. We now need to drag some goodies from the library onto our canvas. First, however, let's think about what we're going to do. We are going to click on a button that will have text that will appear above it saying "Hello World!" Therefore, we need something to click on; that will be a button and we need a label that will contain the text that says "Hello World!" Easy! First drag a label onto your canvas, as shown in Figure 2–5. Move it to a height that suits you and then move it horizontally until the blue center line appears. At this point, you will let it go, nicely centered in the middle of your canvas. Now, this label will eventually contain the text "Hello World!" so drag the label's side handlebars out to the right and left to make it a little larger, to about the same size shown in Figure 2–5. Now go to the Text box and delete the text label so that it is blank, as shown in Figure 2–5. Lastly, still looking at Figure 2–5, notice how my arrow is hovering over the "centered text" icon. Do the same and click it so that when your "Hello World!" text appears in the label, it will be nicely centered inside the centered label. Beautiful. Now let's move onto the button.

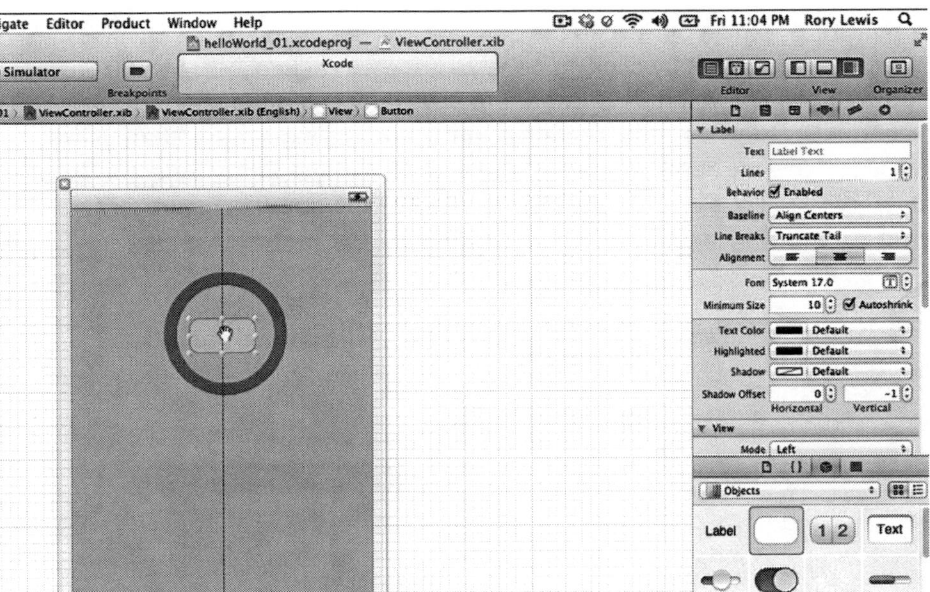

Figure 2–6. *Drag a button onto the canvas.*

6. Drag out a button and place it below your text, moving it left to right until the center lines tell you it's centered. At that point, you let it go, as shown in Figure 2–6. Immediately double click on it and type the text "Press Me" (see Figure 2–7).

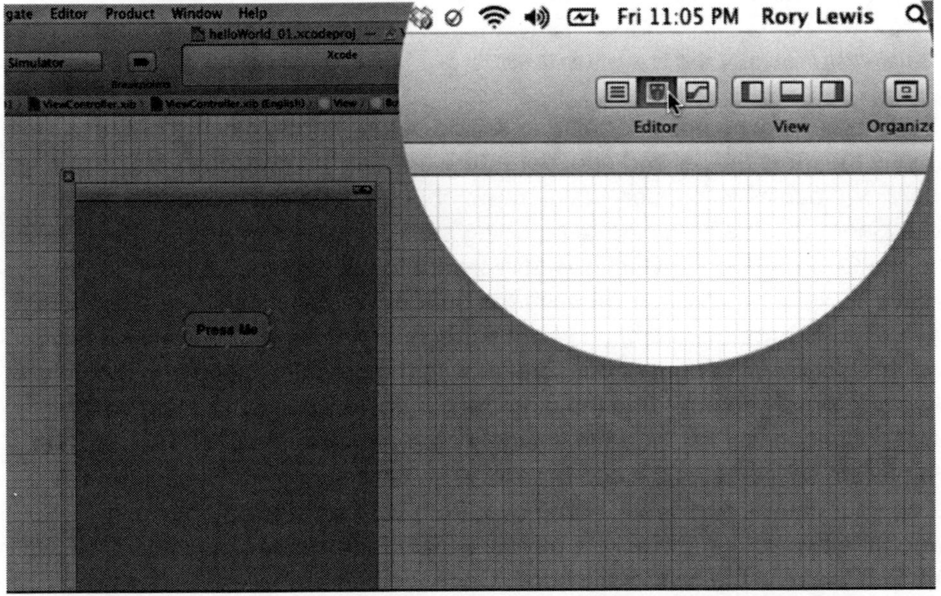

Figure 2–7. *Close the Utilities folder, save your work, and open the Assistant, as indicated by the arrow.*

7. We are finished loading our two items onto the canvas, so go to the Utilities Folder again and close it by clicking on it, as shown in Figure 2–7. As you are finished with this file, you may also want to save it by using the shortcut Command + S, (⌘S).This is the preferred method of saving—rather than using your mouse. Now we need to open up the Assistant in the Editor Selector, located to the left of the View Selector. This is indicated by the arrow in Figure 2–7.

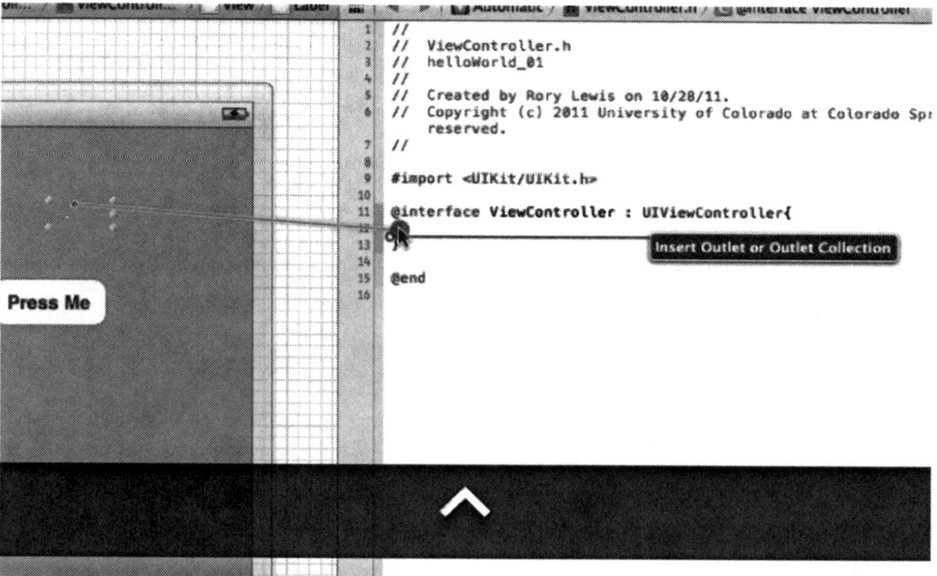
// ViewController.h
// helloWorld_01
// Created by Rory Lewis on 10/28/11.
// Copyright (c) 2011 University of Colorado at Colorado Sp
reserved.
#import <UIKit/UIKit.h>
@interface ViewController : UIViewController{
Insert Outlet or Outlet Collection
@end
Press Me

Figure 2–8. *Control-drag from your Label to create an Outlet.*

8. For those readers who once dabbled in Xcode before Xcode 4 came out, this next section is the most radical and cool departure from all the previous versions of Xcode. For those newbies, don't think twice about it; let's just move forward in blissful ignorance. We are going to be doing something here in Step 8 that is new, called the Open URL contextual menu. We want to tell the label to print out text that says "Hello World!" when we push the button. We call these things "outlets" and we used to have to code these from scratch. In Xcode 4, however, we have the source code on the right of our screen, with the graphical builder in the center, and we can simply control-drag (holding the control key while dragging your mouse) connections. First, add the squiggly brackets after the `UIViewController` and hit return so it creates the end bracket and some space. Now, click on the label on your canvas and control-drag over from your label to any place in-between the two squiggly brackets of your `@interface` method, as shown in Figure 2–8 (we're in the header file here). Once the black label appears saying Insert Outlet, release your mouse.

> **NOTE:** The Assistant uses a split-pane editor, which is where much of the Xcode 4's dazzle appears. Remember that you can open the Assistant automatically by Option-clicking a file in the project navigator or symbol navigator pane.

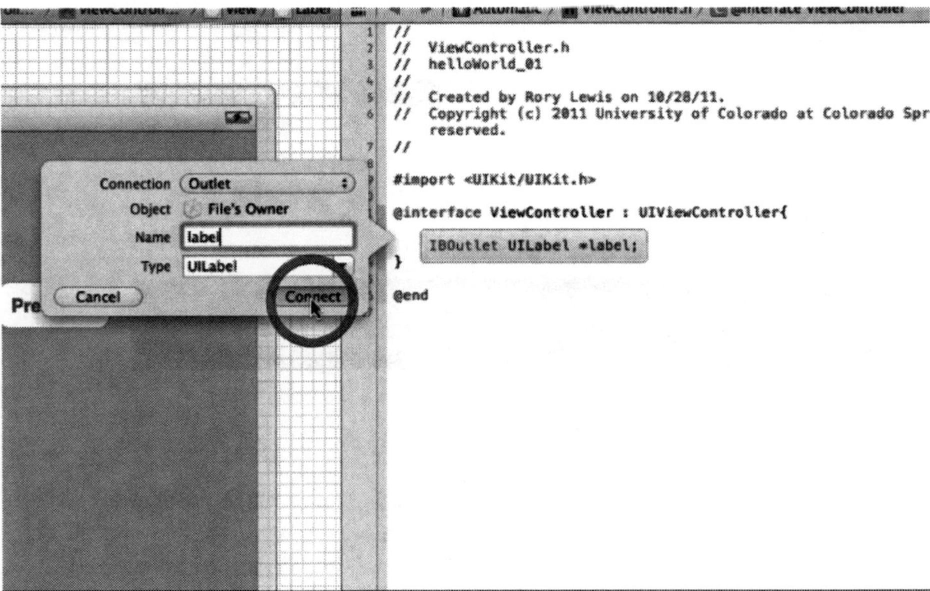

Figure 2–9. *Make the* `IBOutlet` *a label.*

9. As mentioned in Step 8, we want the connection type to be an Outlet—and the people at Apple figured this is what you probably need—so by default, it appears so we keep it selected. Don't worry about Object and File's Owner right now. You can name the label anything you like, but for now, name it label as I have (see Figure 2–9), so your code will look the same as mine when and if you compare yours to my video, the images in this book, or the code you download from my website. Don't worry about the `UILabel` for now either. Now hit return (↩) and you will see that the code `IBOutlet UILabel *label;` magically appears. You can see it highlighted in the text below. We will discuss this in detail in "Digging the Code" at the end of this chapter. For now, let's move on.

```
#import <UIKit/UIKit.h>

@interface helloWorld_01ViewController : UIViewController {

    IBOutlet UILabel *label;
}

@end
```

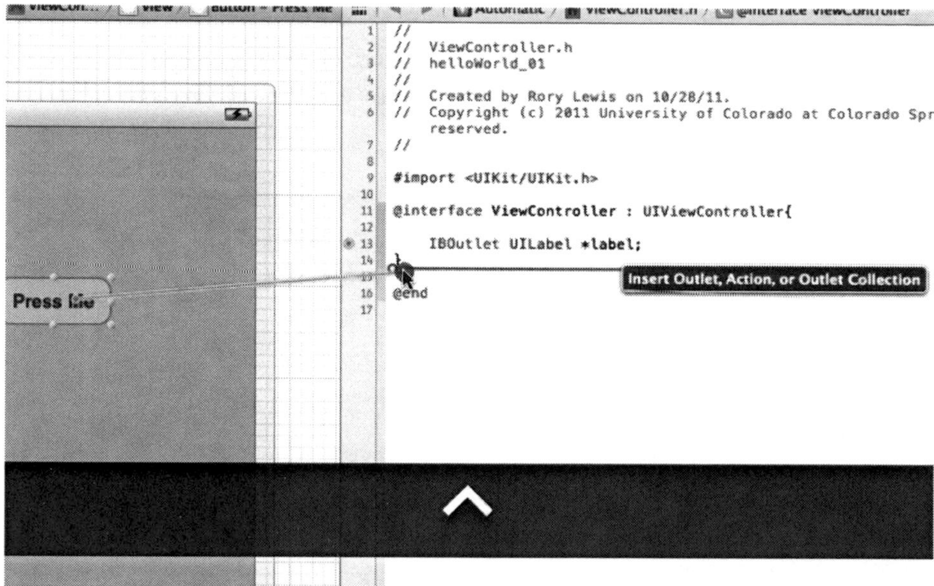
//
// ViewController.h
// helloWorld_01
//
// Created by Rory Lewis on 10/28/11.
// Copyright (c) 2011 University of Colorado at Colorado Spr
reserved.
//
#import <UIKit/UIKit.h>
@interface ViewController : UIViewController{
IBOutlet UILabel *label;
}
@end
Insert Outlet, Action, or Outlet Collection

Figure 2–10. *Control-drag from your button to create an Action.*

10. Now we need to place some code behind the button we dragged onto the canvas so it can do the "action" we want it to do. In our case, we want the button to tell the label we connected in Step 9 to say stuff. We call this "declaring an action." For now, we just need to associate the button with action code; we'll later define exactly what these actions will be. So just as we did before with the label, click on the button in your canvas and control-drag over from your button to just below the closed squiggly bracket, as shown in Figure 2-10. Once the black label appears saying Insert Outlet, Action… release your mouse.

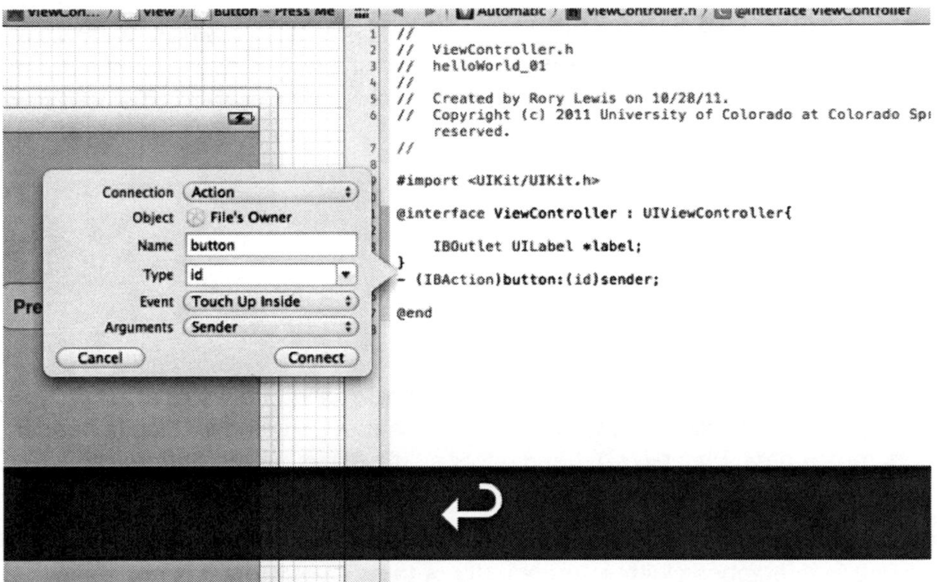
Connection Action
Object File's Owner
Name button
Type id
Event Touch Up Inside
Arguments Sender
Cancel
Connect
//
// ViewController.h
// helloWorld_01
//
// Created by Rory Lewis on 10/28/11.
// Copyright (c) 2011 University of Colorado at Colorado Sp
reserved.
//
#import <UIKit/UIKit.h>
@interface ViewController : UIViewController{
IBOutlet UILabel *label;
}
- (IBAction)button:(id)sender;
@end

Figure 2–11. *Creating your actions for your button.*

11. As mentioned in Step 10, we want the connection type to be an action, so you will need to change the connection type from an Outlet to an Action by selecting it from the drop-down menu. Again, don't worry about Object and File's Owner right now. Name it "button" and ignore everything else for now. This is illustrated in Figure 2–11.

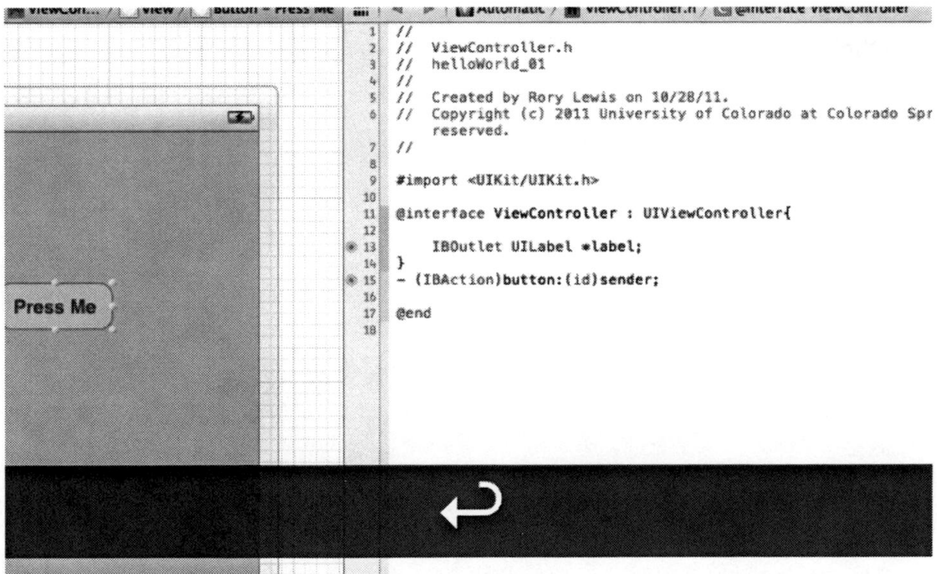
Press Me
//
// ViewController.h
// helloWorld_01
//
// Created by Rory Lewis on 10/28/11.
// Copyright (c) 2011 University of Colorado at Colorado Spr
reserved.
//
#import <UIKit/UIKit.h>
@interface ViewController : UIViewController{
IBOutlet UILabel *label;
}
- (IBAction)button:(id)sender;
@end

Figure 2–12. *Completing your* `ViewController`*'s header file.*

12. Hit return (↩) and you will see `-(IBAction)button:(id)sender;` which appears as shown below and in Figure 2–12. Yes, we will discuss this in detail in "Digging the Code" at the end of this chapter. Right now, let's keep moving.

```
#import <UIKit/UIKit.h>

@interface helloWorld_01ViewController : UIViewController {

    IBOutlet UILabel *label;
}
- (IBAction)button:(id)sender;

@end
```

Before moving on to Step 13, we need to look around and see where we're at. Remember, back in Step 3, I said that we have 2 *classes* that contain two files (a *header* file (`.h`)and an *implementation* file (`.m`)). Let me talk a little bit about the difference between these two files: one with the `.h` suffix, the other with the `.m` suffix.

The `ViewController` manages the interactions your code has with the display, and it manages the user's interactions with your code. It contains a view, but it is not a view itself. You only have a minimal understanding of the `ViewController` *class*, so far. What I want you to get, though, is that, as mentioned in Step 3, every class consists of two parts: the *header* (`.h`) file and the *implementation*(`.m`) file.

I want you to read this next part aloud, and I don't care if you're in the bookstore! OK? "*We tell the computer in a header file what types of commands we will execute in the implementation file.*" Now, let's say it again in context with our code: "*We tell the computer in the* `helloWorld_01 ViewController.h` *file what types of commands we will execute in the* `helloWorld_01 ViewController.m` *file.*"

Well, admit it—that wasn't so bad!

Let's get back to the example:

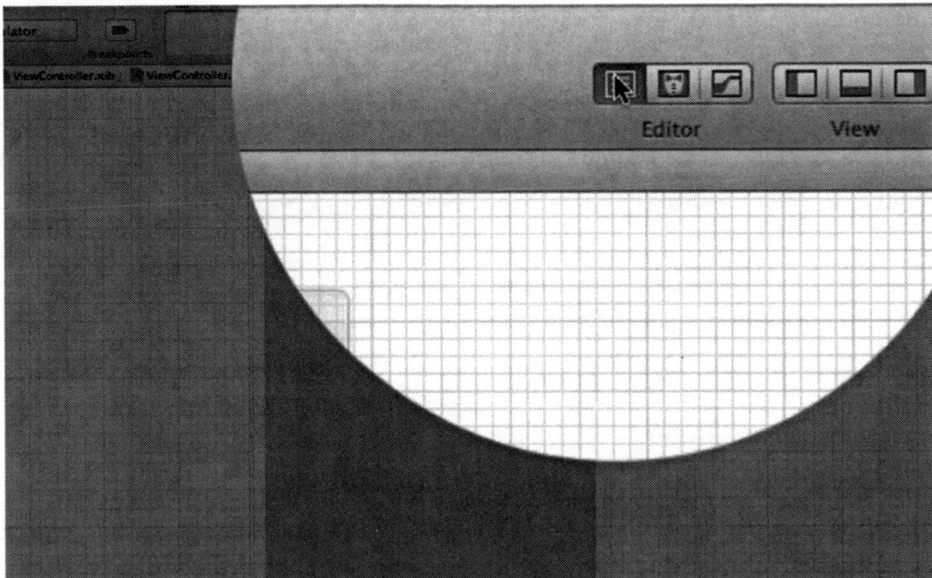

Figure 2–13. ***Switch to the Standard Editor.***

13. To move on to the implementation file from this point, get into the habit of first switching views and going from the Assistant Editor (remember we did this in Steps 2–7) to the Standard Editor. To do this, go to the Editor Selector located to the left of the View Selector and click on the Standard Editor, as shown in Figure 2–13.

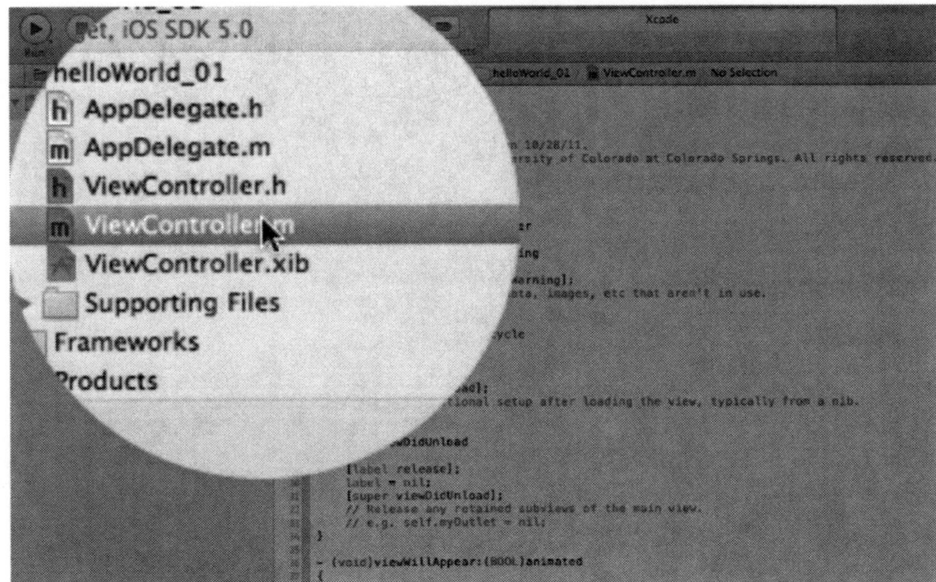

Figure 2–14. ***Open your*** `helloWorld_01 ViewController's` ***implementation file.***

14. Once in the Standard Editor, select your ViewController's implementation file, as shown in Figure 2–14.

Recall how, in Step 10, we "*declared an action*" when we control-dragged the button into our header file's code? Remember that in the header file we "declare" actions, while in the implementation file we "implement" actions. Here in your ViewController's implementation file, we are going to implement the actions that we want to happen when somebody presses on the button. Specifically, we want it to say, in the label, "Hello World!" "Mmm, how do we do this?" you may ask. Well, we need to type your very first code to start your journey towards geekdom. Yup, you're going to code text. Take a deep breath and follow along.

Looking at the text of your helloWorld_01 ViewController's implementation file, we see that the clever people at Apple programmed Xcode to already write a number of methods that need to happen in the background just to get your app with label and buttons running on your iPhone. For now we will ignore these methods, starting at the first one named dealloc, which deallocates memory and going down to the end until we get to one named - (IBAction)button:(id)sender. Mmm… wait a minute, that's the code that appeared in Step 12, right? Right? Well, almost. That code ended with a semicolon ";" because, in the header file, we declared this action. Xcode knows we now need to implement this action in the implementation file, so it rewrites it for us, not as a declaration but as a method. It does this by substituting the colon with squiggly brackets. You need to remember this rule. You will use it over and over again.

> **NOTE:** A declaration in .h becomes a method in the .m file by replacing the colon with squiggly brackets!

After reaching the implementation of your action that you declared in the header, I want you to place your cursor in between the two squiggly brackets, as indicated in the code below. Click there and read below.

```
#import "helloWorld_01ViewController.h"
@implementation helloWorld_01ViewController
- (void)dealloc


- (IBAction)button:(id)sender {
}
@end
```

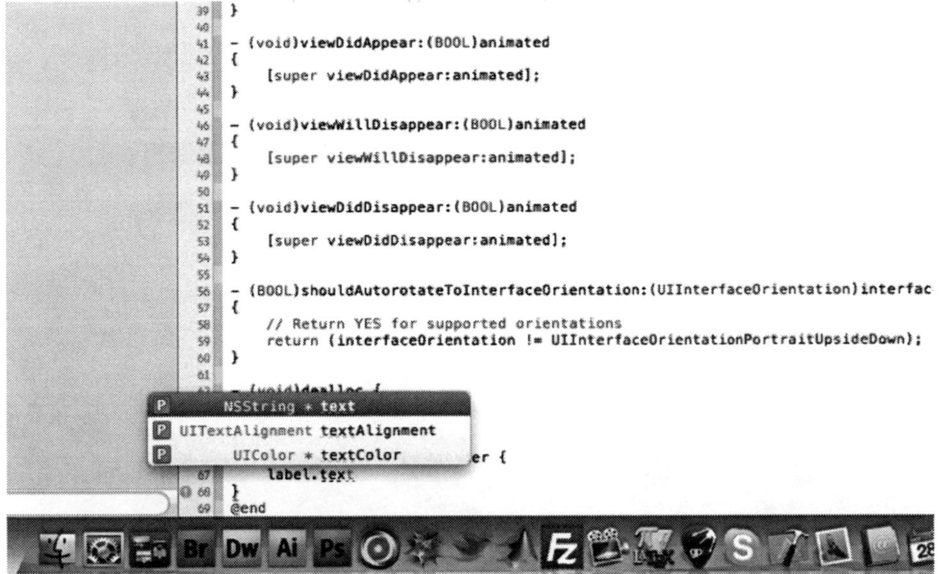

Figure 2–15. *As you enter the text "label.text" auto completion suggests code. If you agree with the selection, then press the Tab (⇥) key and Xcode places the command into your code.*

15. The code I want you to type is `label.text = @"Hello World!"` but it's not that straightforward because, as you type, something really cool happens. Xcode figures out what you're probably going to want to code in its auto completion window, as illustrated in Figure 2–15. If you agree with the selection, then press the Tab (⇥) key and Xcode places the completed, correctly typed and spelled command into your code. If the one it suggests is not the correct one, but you see the correct one a few commands down, just arrow down (↓) until you reach the correct selection and then press ⇥. Cool, huh? After you have written `label.text,` continue on to Step 16.

```
- (void)viewDidDisappear:(BOOL)animated
{
    [super viewDidDisappear:animated];
}

- (BOOL)shouldAutorotateToInterfaceOrientation:(UIInterfaceOrientat:
{
    // Return YES for supported orientations
    return (interfaceOrientation != UIInterfaceOrientationPortraitU|
}

- (void)dealloc {
    [label release];
    [super dealloc];
}
- (IBAction)button:(id)sender {
    label.text = @"Hello World!";|
}
@end
```

Figure 2–16. *Type in the text you want the label to say after the "@" directive.*

16. Now we need to type `@"Hello World!";` which is what we want to say. Your code should look like that depicted in Figure 2–16. If you wanted to say "*I can feel I'm becoming a geek!*" instead, then type `label.text = @"I can feel I'm becoming a geek!";`.

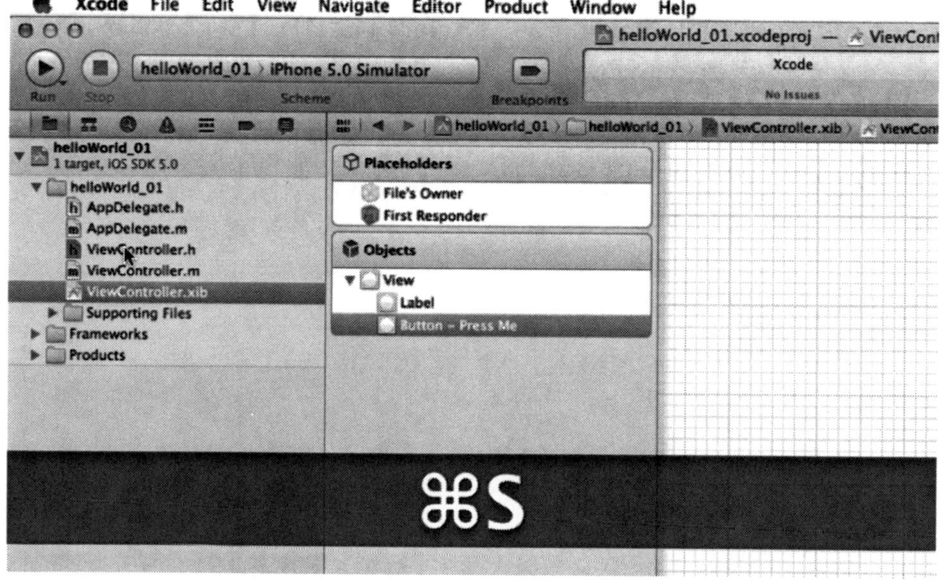

Figure 2–17. *Save your work: ⌘S.*

17. Save your work ⌘S, as shown in Figure 2–17. Please try not to use your mouse; try to make a new habit by always pressing the Control+S (⌘S) every time you want to save. This will make you feel and look really smart and geeky. You may also want to check that your header files and nib files are also saved because, during the course of reading these instructions, you may have had to go back and change files. Well, you need to go back and save them. So go ahead and save everything now. If the file is highlighted in gray, then it means you need to save them too.

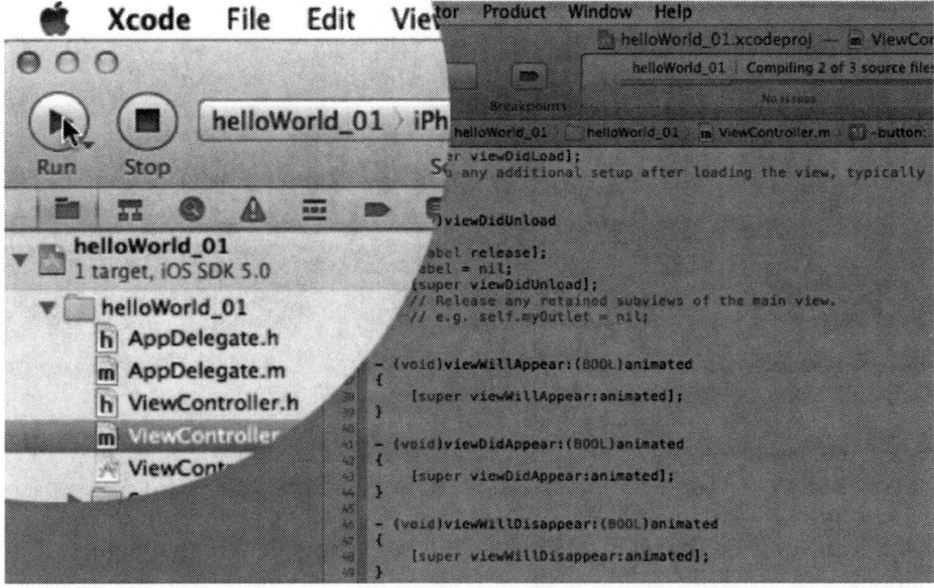

Figure 2–18. *Run it!⌘R.*

18. Press ⌘R and run it, as described in Figure 2–18.

As Figure 2–19 shows, the iPhone simulator loads your very first app, waits for you to press the button, and then says "Hello World!".

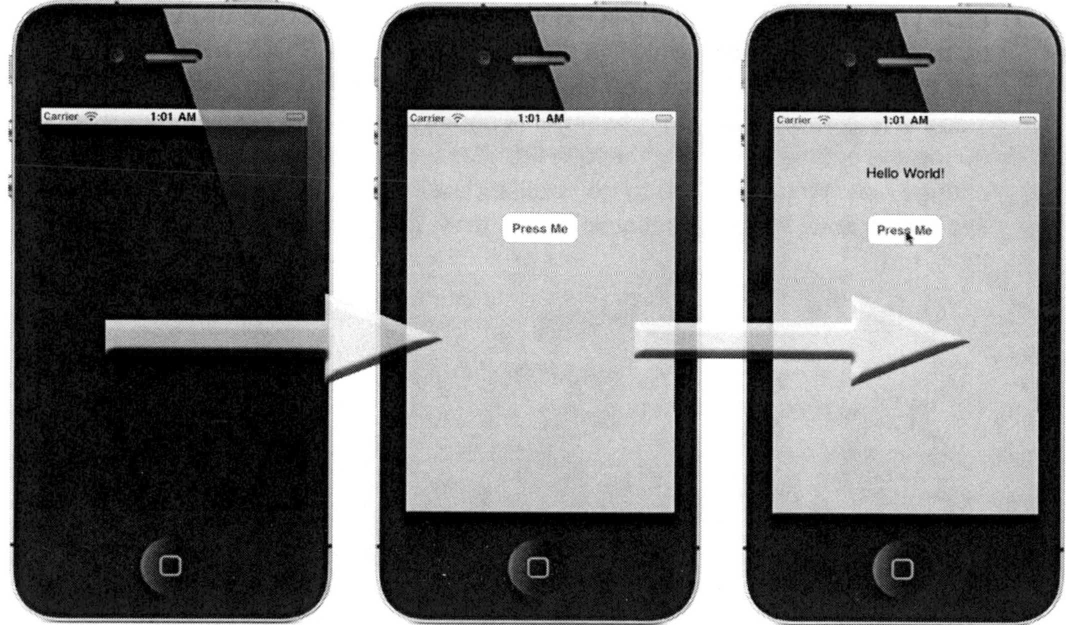

Figure 2–19. *The iPhone simulator, loading and waiting for the user to press the button, and then saying "Hello World!"*

Congratulations, my friend! You have really done something very special today. I know you may have cursed me a couple of times, or floundered here and there, but in getting here you've just done something very special with your life. You've gone from being a user to a coder. You've taken that very difficult leap from being a user of technology to a coder of technology. We still have a few things to do, so take a break. Walk the dog; do something that does not involve technology, even if it's walking out to the street. Take a minute to realize that you're beginning a long journey. It will be difficult at times, but it's one wherein you can hold your head high and say: "Yeah, I code iPhone and iPad apps!"

Running your app on the iPad Simulator that reads your iPhone environment

Two methods are available for running your iPhone app on the iPad simulator:

- First we'll change the environment from the iOS simulator, so, while still in the iPhone simulator, I want you to click on **Hardware ➤ Device ➤ iPad** so that we can see how your first app runs if it were being run on an iPad (see Figure 2–20).The result is the display presented in Figure 2–21.

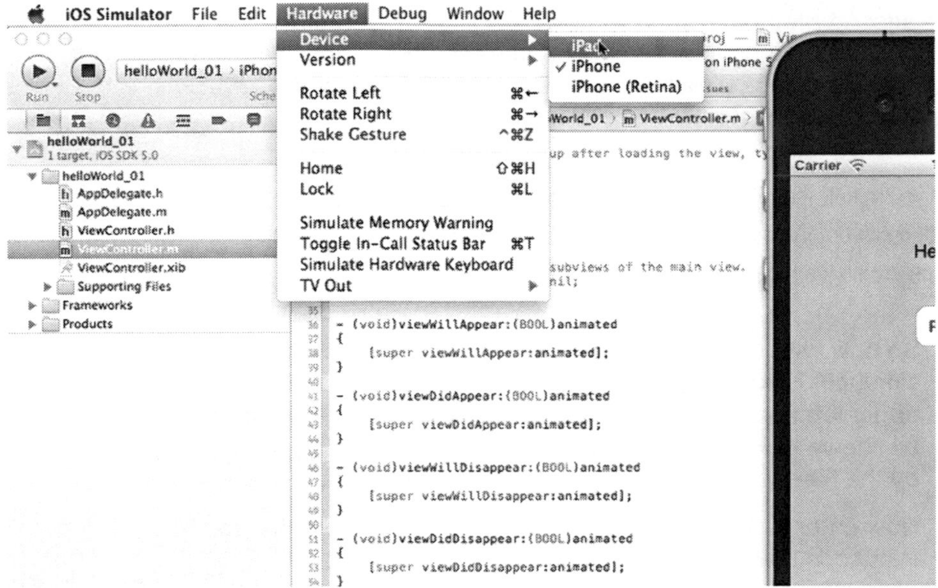

Figure 2–20. *Let's see how your iPhone app runs on the iPhone simulator.*

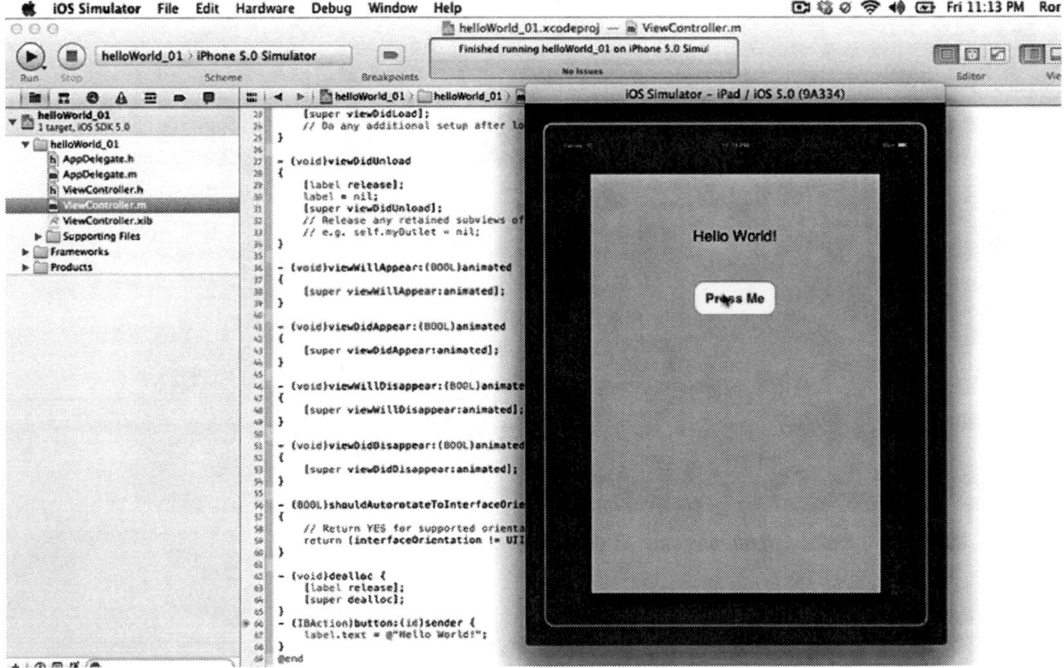

Figure 2–21. *Initially it appears in the iPhone mode. Click on the zoom and view it full screen as shown here.*

- The second method is achieved by changing the output device from within Xcode. To do this, I want you to close your iPhone simulator by first making sure you're in the simulator and then entering Command + Q (⌘Q). You should now be back in Xcode.

> **NOTE:** If you're not, then it means you've had other programs up, which is something I asked you to not do. In order for you to follow along exactly, you really need to keep your desktop and running programs identical to how I am teaching you.

  a. So now with Xcode open, change your scheme to the iPad simulator by clicking on the Scheme drop-down menu on the upper left hand portion of your ribbon and select iPad Simulator, as shown in Figure 2–22. Right now it says iPad 4.3 Simulator, but by the time you read this book it probably will be a higher number.

  b. Now enter ⌘R to run it. Again, you will come up with the same instances displayed in Figure 2–21.

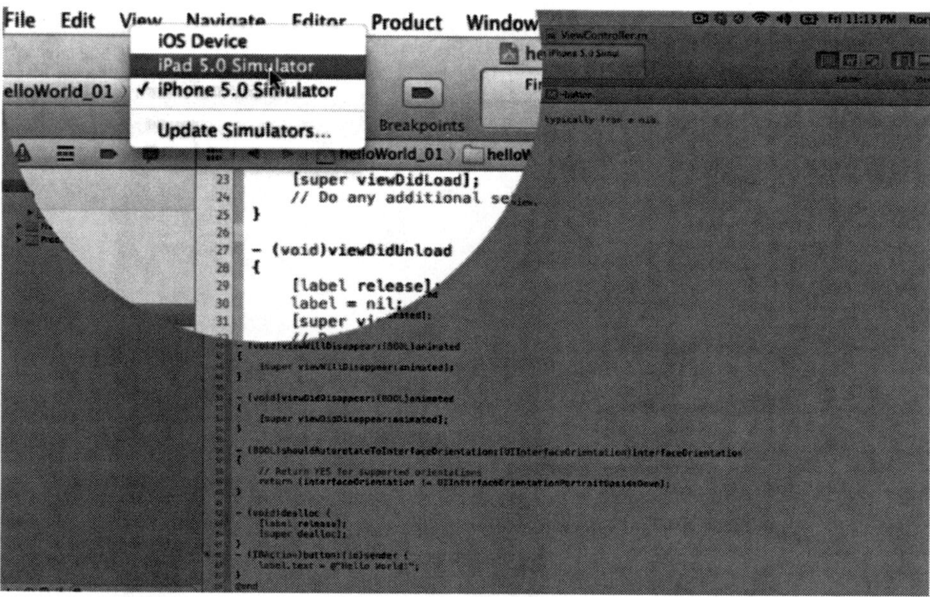

Figure 2–22. *Second method of running your iPhone app in the iPad simulator.*

Running your App on the iPad Simulator

`helloWorld_02` – iPad Simulator

At the beginning of this chapter, I made a deal with you. I said we were going to take a very simple app and run it in all the different forms possible. Specifically, I said we would run your first app on:

- §2.1. The iPhone Simulator: (✔ see Figure 2–19).
- §2.2. The iPad Simulator reading the iPhone environment (✔ see Figure 2–21).
- §2.3. The iPad Simulator.

At this point, you have already completed the first two goals of running it on the iPhone simulator, with the latter being the iPad reading an iPhone app. But this is not really an iPad app. A real iPad app is made specifically for the iPad and cannot be run on an iPhone because all the graphics and sizes of screens are specifically designed for the iPad and are too large to be viewed on the iPhone.

Looking at Figure 2–21, you can see that the first image on the left shows your iPhone app inside the iPad and scaled exactly to the size of an iPhone. When you clicked the zoom, it simply zoomed and expanded everything larger to fit inside the iPad. Well, this is what I refer to in class as being "pseudoiPad," as it's not the real deal. So let's go ahead and show you how to make an app specifically for the iPad.

1. We will need to close your `helloWorld_01` app in Xcode by entering ⌘S to save it and then ⌘Q to quit Xcode. You should now be looking at your empty desktop, except for the `helloWorld_01` folder right under your Mac hard-drive icon. Good. We are now going to run `helloWorld_02`, which will be exactly like `helloWorld_01` except for a couple of steps.

2. Open up Xcode and enter Command + Shift + N at the same time. Recall that these three keystrokes appear in Figure 2–1 as ⌘⇧N. Select View-Based App and then press Return (↩). Now stop and look at Figure 2–23: in Figure 2–2, we named it `helloWorld_01`. However in Figure 2–23, we name it `helloWorld_02`. Most importantly, in Figure 2–23, we select iPad, NOT iPhone as we did in Figure 2–2. With this done, I want you to try remember all of the steps we performed in `helloWorld_01` until you run it, whereupon you will come up to only the right hand image of Figure 2–21.

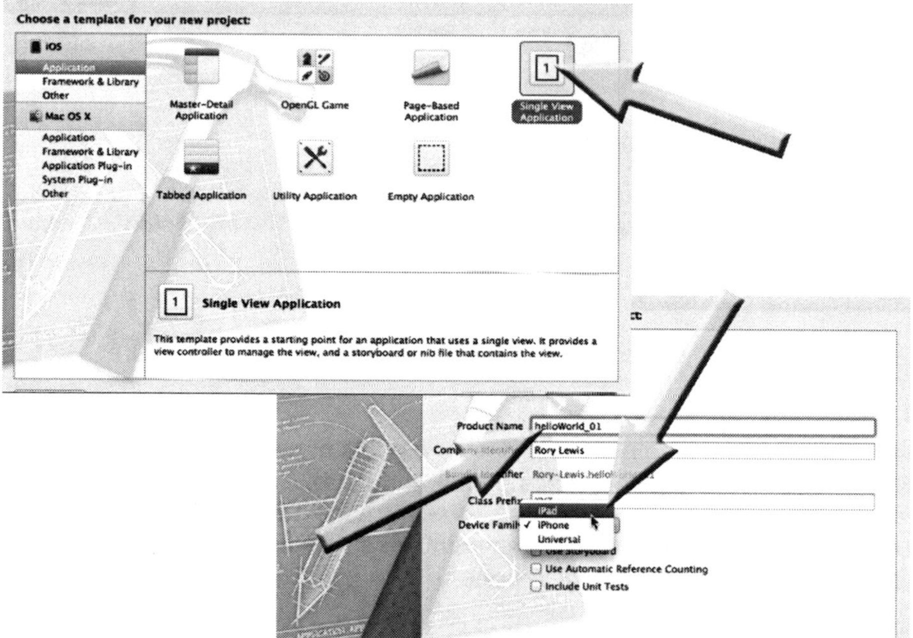

Figure 2–23. *Open Xcode, select the Navigation-based Application template, and then save a new project file to your desktop.*

Huh? Yes that's what I said: I make my students in the lecture hall redo `helloWorld` all over again, but now as a "real" iPad app and I encourage them to try and not peek at their lecture notes, to try doing it on their own. If you have to look at your notes, or this book, that's fine. But try to do it over and over again, until you can do this without looking at any notes at all.

Running your App on Physical Devices

> **TIP:** You may want to skip this section. Read the following carefully.

After you have set up your device and profiles, you can continue on with steps §2.4, running your app on your iPhone, §2.5, running your app on your iPad based off of an iPhone environment and §2.6, and running your app on your physical iPad.

Whatever your decision is, you will need to first do the following organizational chores. Right now, on your beautiful clean open desktop, you only have two folders containing your 2 `helloWorld` programs. We need to make a place to store all of your programs that will make sense to you as you continue to read this book. Create a folder in your Documents folder called *My Programs*, and then save the files named `helloWorld_01` and `helloWorld_02` there by dragging them to that folder. Now, with a fresh, clean empty desktop, close all programs. Press Command + Tab and then Command + Q to close everything until only the Finder is left on your screen

> **NOTE:** For students in my class or at other universities, I or your professor has already taken care of this. If you are not a student and did not pay your $99 in step 5 in Chapter 1, or/and you do not have an iPhone or iPad, then skip ahead to Chapter 3.

Digging the Code

At the ends of chapters, I include this section called "Digging the Code," wherein I start to feed you insights into the meaning of much of the code that miraculously appeared or that I just instructed you to type. What I have found, though, is that the human brain makes its own associations if it keeps on doing something over and over again and certain outcomes occur each time we repeat that action. I have found that if I first allow students to fly through huge amounts of code in sheer ignorant bliss, it does a great deal of good because it allows their brains to make connections that only they can make. So here in "Digging the Code" I start feeding you little snippets, just the right ones that connect the dots as to why we put this code here or that code there. Later, as we get towards the end of the book, you will feel totally comfortable really digging the code and getting into it. For Chapter 2, however, we have not repeated enough actions for you to make your own associations. So, for now, take a deep breath and I'll see you in Chapter 3.

Chapter 3

Keep on Truckin'

Now that you've gotten your feet wet from programming your first two iPhone and iPad apps, I want you to tell yourself that you have to *keep on truckin'* with more apps, more practice, and create a more natural connection of synapses in your brain. Initially, many traditional Computer Science colleagues of mine had disdain for my approach of blindly hauling newbie programmers through code without explaining it all. Over the years, I've learned exactly when to tell you what's going on and when to just jostle you through the code. Most importantly, you need to keep on truckin' and keep your brain dialed into Xcode.

This third "Hello World" application introduces you to some cool new concepts such as Strings, Delegates, and slightly more complex code. Remember that this is Objective-C; it's a pretty complex and difficult language, so I will explain only what I deem necessary. This brings up a difference between Chapter 3 and Chapter 2. Recall that in Chapter 2, when I mentioned digging the code, I said: "For Chapter 2, however, we have not repeated enough actions for you to make your own associations." Well, here in Chapter 3, we start really getting into digging the code. So let's get on with the next application. When it's done, take a break, and then be ready to go back and review lines of your input, as we focus on certain portions of the code, and look at how it all works together.

Besides the information I present here in this book, including various screenshots, I also offer you screencasts, which are available at my website. You can use the short URL, go to rorylewis.com, as indicated below when you click on the Xcode 4 icon, and then go to either *video tutorial* or *downloads*:

- Short URL: ow.ly/50ksH
- Manual URL: www.rorylewis.com

helloWorld_03 – An Interactive View-Based App

In your first two programs, `helloWorld_01` and `helloWorld_02`, you said "Hello" to the world using a view-based platform that housed a button. This third app will also be a view-based app, but a little complexity will be added to it. When a user interacts with this third app of yours, they will first be prompted to enter their name into a Text Field object. Once they have entered their name into the Text Field object, and they press the Press Me button, text will appear saying that the name entered is in fact the person saying "Hello World!"

Before you get started with the next method, you need to save `helloWorld_01` and `helloWorld_02` in a folder of your choice that is *not* on the desktop. Create a folder in your Documents folder called "My Programs," and then save the file named `helloWorld_01` there by dragging the entire folder inside your My Programs folder. Now, with a fresh, clean, empty desktop, close all other programs you may have running by selecting programs. Press Command + Tab (⌘⇥) and then Command + Q (⌘Q) to close everything until only the Finder is left on your screen.

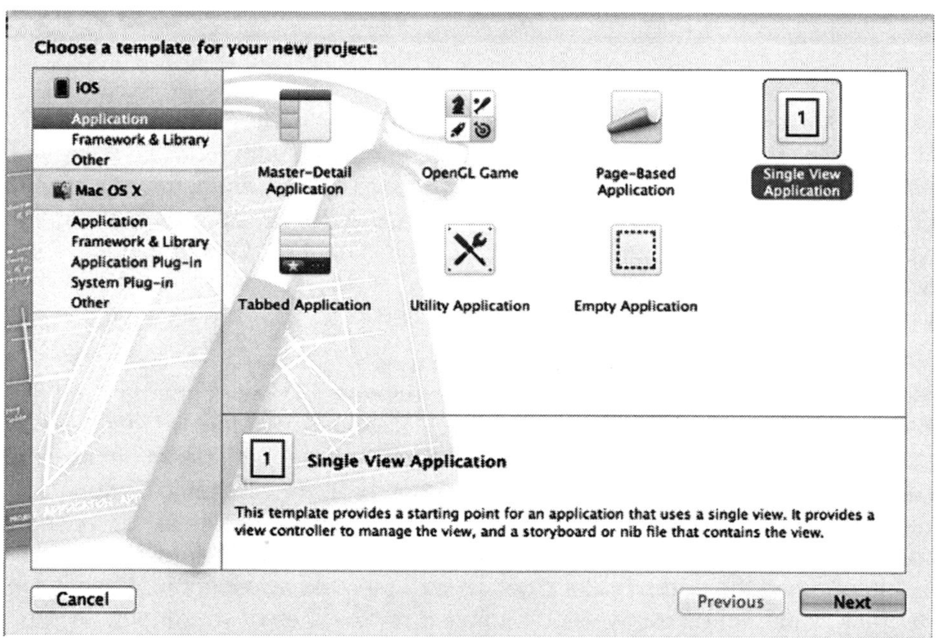

Figure 3–1. *Open Xcode, select the View-based Application template, and then click the Next button.*

1. Now, just as you did in the first example, launch Xcode and open a new project by using your keyboard shortcut: ⌘⇧N. Your screen should show the New Project wizard as depicted in Figure 3–1. You may find that your View-based Application template was highlighted by default because of the last example. If, however, your View-based Application template is not selected, then click on the View-based Application icon, and then click the Next button, as indicated in Figure 3–1.

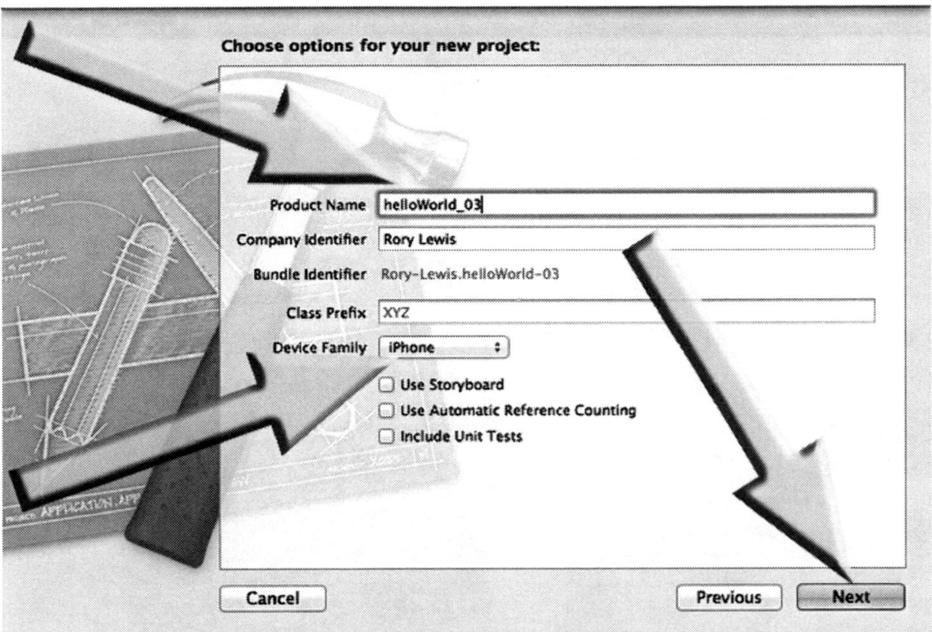

Figure 3–2. *Name your project, make sure it's for an iPhone, and then click on the Next button.*

2. You are going to call this third project `helloWorld_03`, so type that in the Product Name box, as shown in Figure 3–2. The Company Identifier should automatically be defaulted to your Xcode license name. Remember that `helloWorld_02` was created for an iPad, so the Device Family on your computer may still be set to iPad. Whatever the case, make sure that `helloWorld_03` is set for the iPhone family. In the event that your "Use Storyboard", "Use Automatic Referencing Counting" or "Include Unit Tests" are checked by default, uncheck them. Once this is done and your screen looks like that shown in Figure 3–2, click the Next button.

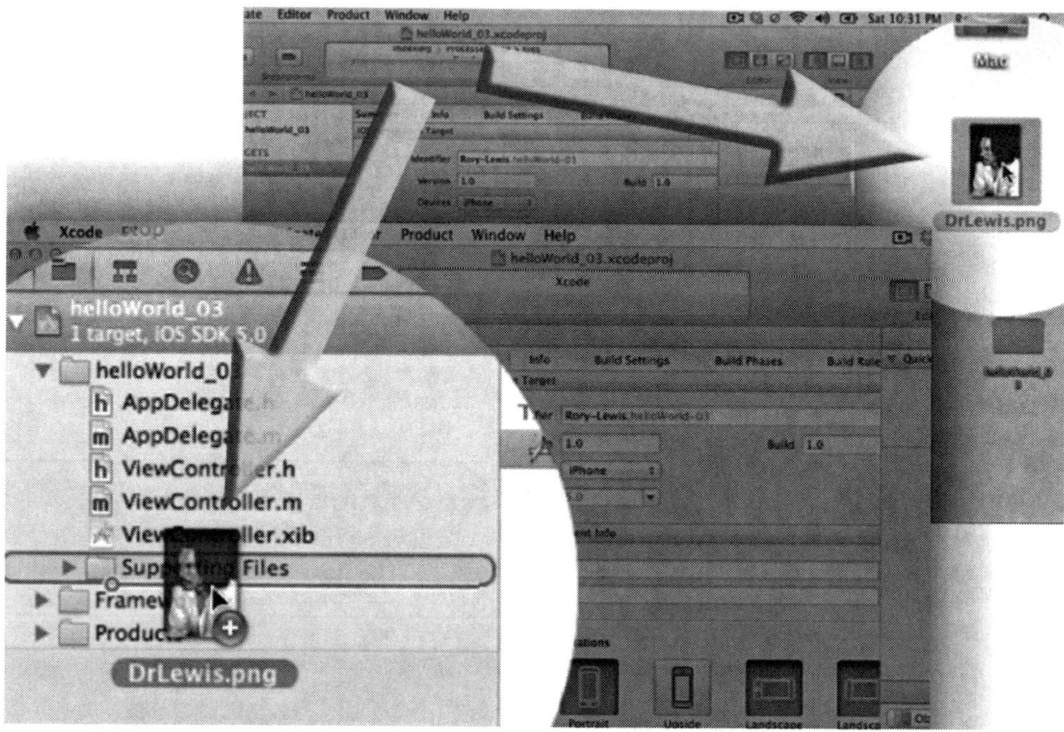

Figure 3–3. *Drag a picture of yourself from the desktop into your Supporting Files folder.*

3. For this homework assignment, my students are required to take a photo of themselves, crop it into a 320 × 480 image, and then save it as a `.png` file. This way, I can associate names with the correct faces in a faster manner. For those of you who are reading this book and are not my students, go ahead and get a picture of yourself, crop it to 320 × 480, and save it onto your desktop as a `.png` file. If you do not have access to a graphics editor, then feel free to use the picture I used for this project. You can download it at ow.ly/50ksH (scroll down to the third video tutorial from the top, `helloWorld_03`, and click on the box icon). A compressed file will be downloaded to your computer with the picture I used in this example, named `DrLewis.png`. Place it onto your desktop. Once it is on your desktop, press Command + Tab (⌘-⇥) until Xcode is highlighted. Release the ⌘-⇥ keys, at which point Xcode will now fill your screen again. Minimize Xcode slightly so you can see the desktop with your picture, or for some of you, the picture of me as illustrated in Figure 3–3. Grab it, drag it over to your Supporting Files folder, and drop it inside the folder.

NOTE: Just in case you noticed, along with the positive attributes associated with giving you the exact code and images of me programming precise code that is taken directly from my online tutorials, there comes a negative aspect: you seeing me make errors. In this case, I accidently missed the Supporting Files folder. I said "Oops" and quickly dragged it from the helloWorld_03 folder into the Supporting Files folder, which is exactly when the image from Figure 3–3 was snapped. In case you noticed this, ignore it. Just drop your file into the Supporting Files folder, and let's move on.

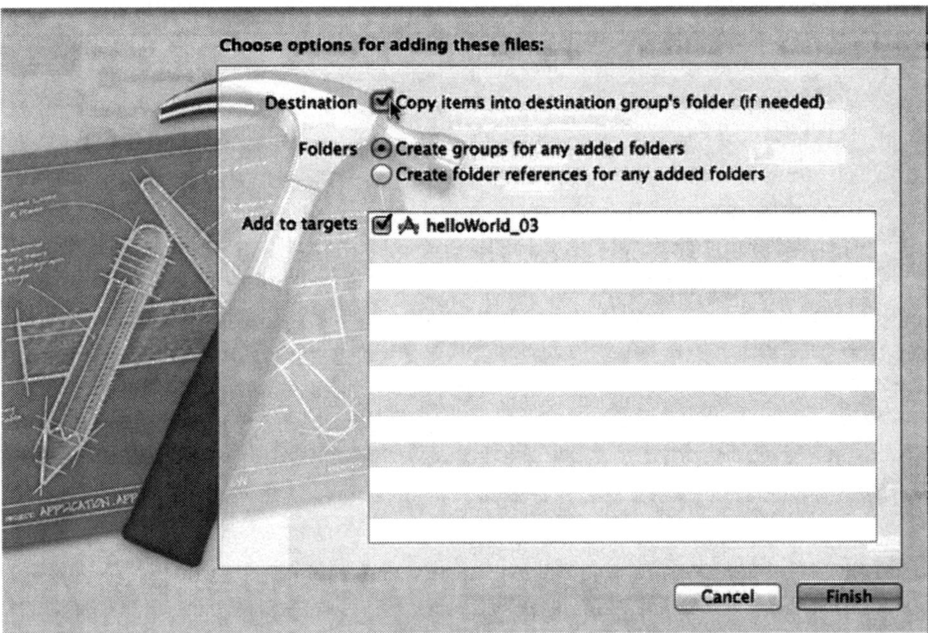

Figure 3–4. *Complete importing your image by selecting the "copy items into destination …" option and clicking on the Finish button.*

4. One of the most common mistakes that I see students make happens at this simple stage of Xcode management: they forget to check the "Copy items into destination group's folder if needed" checkbox. When you import a file into the Supporting Files folder on your computer, if you do not check "Copy items into destination group's folder" everything will work fine, giving you a false sense of security. In this case, even though Xcode is told that your supporting files, such as the image in this example, reside in your Supporting Files folder, what's really happening is that there's a little note saying: "Dude, I take no responsibility for this, the file is not here, it's still on the owner's desktop!" So you, the writer of your code, go on doing your homework. Every time you run your code, and Xcode calls to access a supporting file, this irresponsible "Pointer Reference" guy just keeps saying, "It's not here—it's still on your desktop!" So you finish your homework and everything works great. You smile as you zip up your work and send it to me. I give you a zero and then you cry. Why? Well, the irresponsible pointer reference is telling me that your reference files are on *my* desktop. Nope! It's not on my desktop, it's on yours, and you get zero out of 10 for being negligent and depending on a Pointer Reference dude rather than selecting the "Copy items" check box. This way, you fire the Pointer Reference and have the file in your program. This way, when you zip it up and send it to me, and I open up your work to grade, it opens with all your relevant files in the exact place you want. So after dragging your picture into the Supporting Files folder, check the "Copy items into destination group" check box, as shown in Figure 3–4, and then click Finish. Now you're in good standing, and will not be brought to tears by the Pointer Reference dude.

NOTE: I can hear you asking "Why even give us this option then?" Here's a simple answer that covers most but not all bases. Let's say that you were designing a game or program that has a database of millions and millions of files, movies, characters, or possible responses that a player may say, and this database was too large to fit on an iPhone or iPad. Here, you would not check the "Copy items into destination group" box, and allow the Pointer Reference dude to say, "Yo, I take no responsibility for any of this, it's not really here, it's at this URL located at http://www.wherever.com."

Creating the User Interface

OK, now we're ready to start dragging and dropping items onto your View Design area, the image that the user sees when they look at their iPhone.

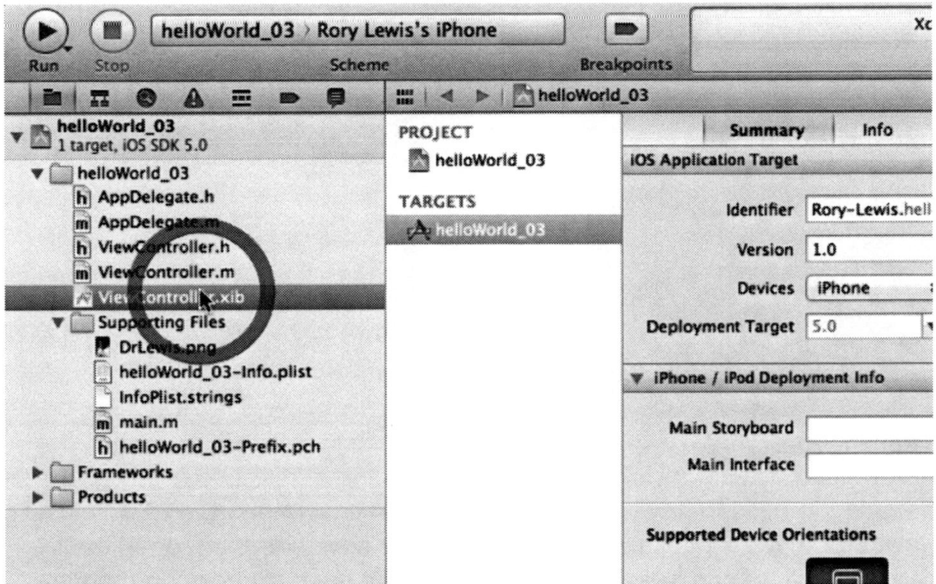

Figure 3–5. *Open your nib file.*

5. In order to do this, you open up your nib file, just as you did in the two previous apps. So, open up your `nib` file by going to your helloWorld_03 folder and selecting the `helloWorld_03ViewController.xib` file, as illustrated in Figure 3–5.

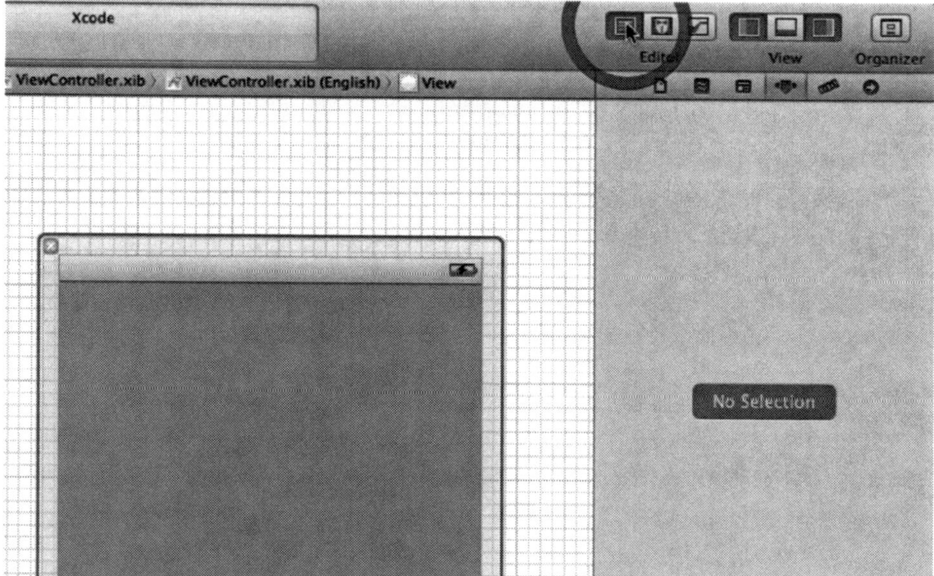

Figure 3–6. ***Close the Navigator View.***

6. You're going to need to have space in the Xcode 4 environment, so first, close the Navigator View, because we do not need it for now, and then, open the Utilities View, so we can see the tools and icons we need to dress up the View Design area. In Figure 3–6, you can see that I am closing the Navigator View. See Figure 3–34 for more details on Xcode 4 nomenclature.

Figure 3–7. *Drag a UIImageView onto your View Design area.*

7. With your Utilities pane open, as shown in Figure 3–7, go to the bottom section of the panel and, making sure that you have selected the icons view (depicted by four little squares on the icon above the right-hand arrow in Figure 3–7), drag a UIImageView onto your View Design area. The reason we need a UIImageView is because we need to have an image of you underneath the buttons and text labels. That picture that you just dragged in needs to have a place where it can live. A UIImageView is just the guy for this job. He is going to reside underneath all of your buttons and embrace whatever picture you tell him to embrace.

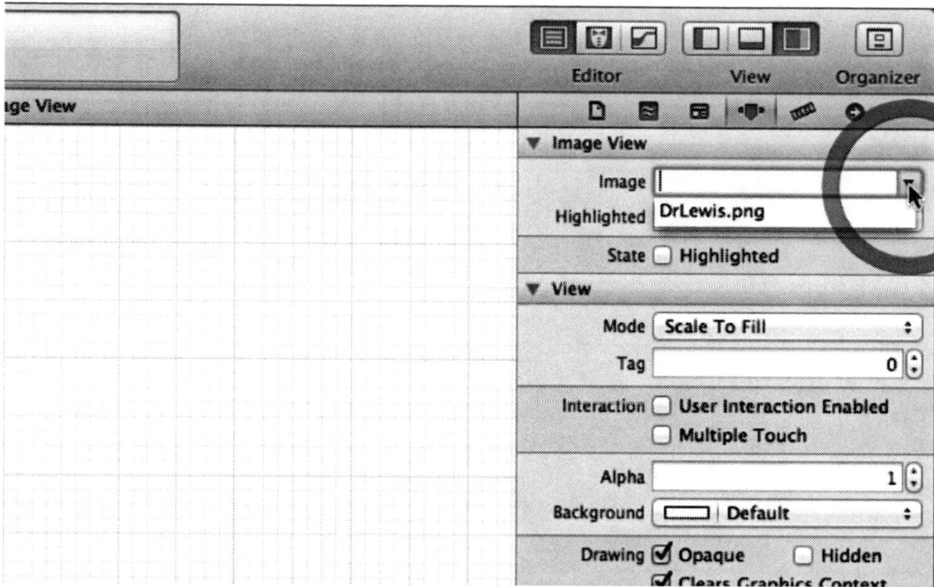

Figure 3–8. *Associate your selected image with your UIImageView.*

8. Remember the image that you dropped into the `Resources Folder` back in Figure 3–3? Well that's the image that you will want the `UIImageView` to be, so you just drag it onto your `View Design area` to encapsulate it. To do this, you need to tell it to do so, and this is done by making sure that you have selected the `Attributes Inspector` in the `Inspector Bar` (see the icon under "`View`" in Figure 3–8, or as explained in Figure 3–33 at the end of this chapter). With the `Attributes Inspector` open, click on the `Image` drop down menu, and guess what you'll see. You'll see the name of the file you dragged into the `Resources Folder`. Select it, and *Voila*! The image appears in your View Design area. Isn't that cool?

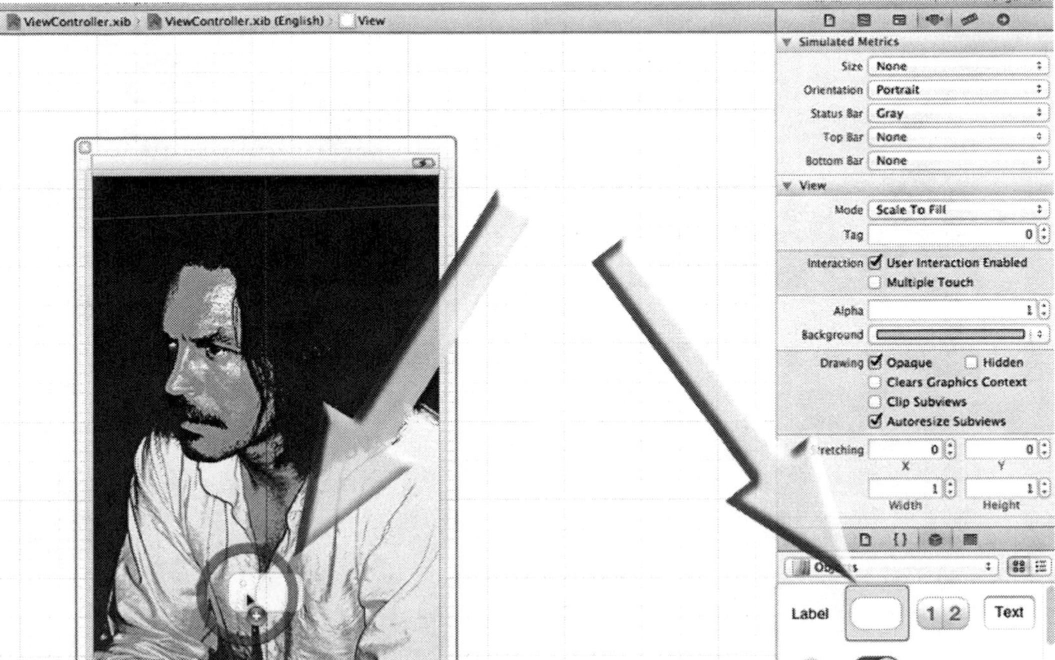

Figure 3–9. *Drag a button onto your View Design area.*

9. Drag a button from your Library onto your View Design area and place it at the bottom, as illustrated in Figure 3–9. Make sure it's nicely centered. Just to remind you: when you click on this button, your code will invoke an action that will grab the name of the person that the user entered into a Text Field object, and it will output that person's name in a label followed by the text, "Hello World!"

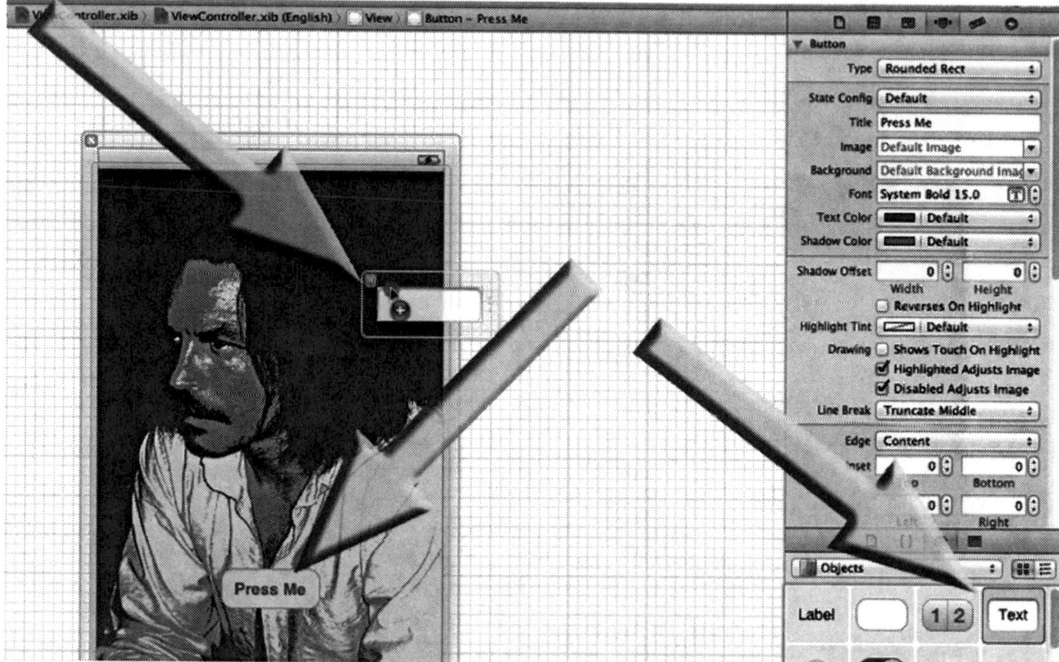

Figure 3–10. *Type "Press Me" on the button, and then drag a Text Field object onto your View Design area.*

10. Immediately after releasing your button, double click on it and type, "Press Me", just as you did in the two previous assignments. Now go back to your Library and drag out a Text Field object onto your View Design area, placing it towards the top (as illustrated in Figure 3–10) and nicely centered. Remember that the text that the user types into here will be sent out to the label when they press the button saying "Press Me."

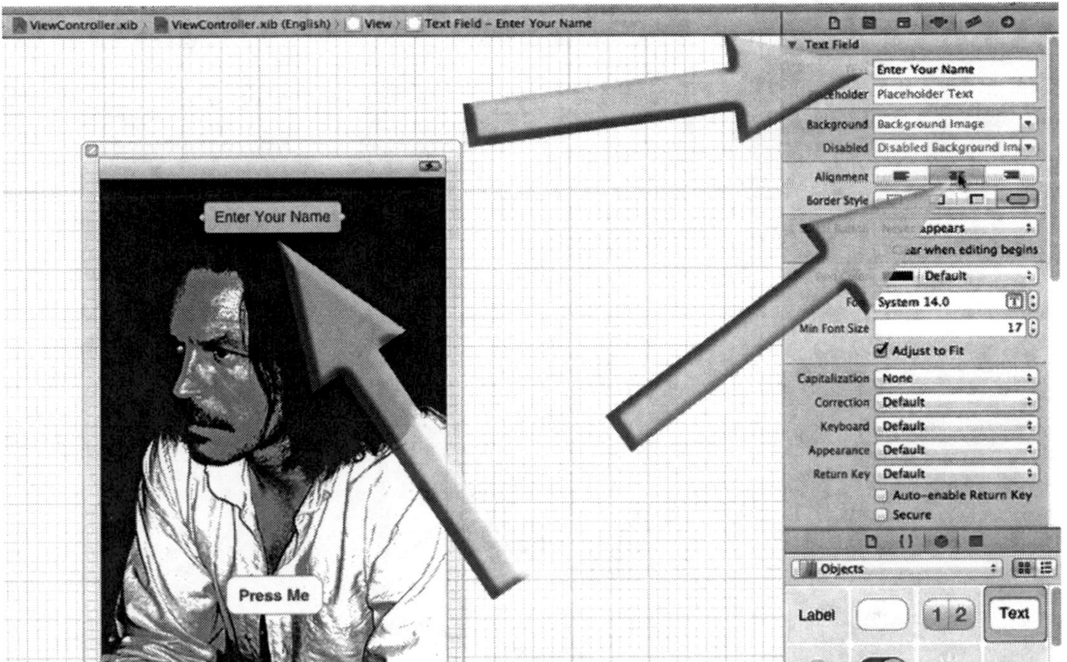

Figure 3–11. ***Center your Text Field object, enter the text "Enter Your Name" in the text field, and center the text.***

11. After centering your Text Field object and expanding it in your View Design area, as illustrated in Figure 3–11 (where it says "Enter Your Name"), click in the text field, go over to your Utilities Inspector pane, and enter the text that you want the user to see when they look inside the Text Field object. You want to tell the user to enter their name here, so type "Enter Your Name" inside the text field box. Also, center this text so that it is centered inside the text field box, and make sure that the text field box is also centered in the View Design area.

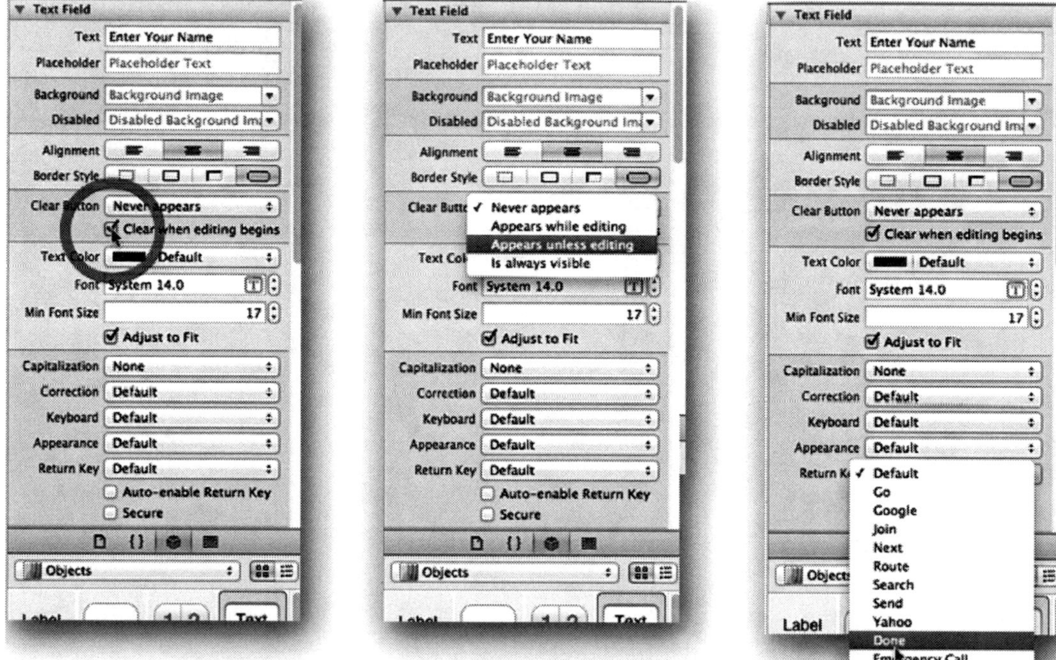

Figure 3–12. *The three steps that ensure that the text in the Text Field object clears the instant the user activates the field. Also, note that a clear button icon is in the field, and "Done" appears on the Return Key (see Figure 3–32)*

12. Once the user starts typing, you want your prompt text to disappear. To make doubly sure that your text disappears, keep the `clear button` (the grey crossed icon) active in the `Text Field object`, which allows the user to press it to clear your text—just in case your professor uses a mouse to grade your homework on the simulator and wants to make sure you know two ways to delete the text in the `Text Field object`. You should also delete the word "Return" on the keypad's return key, and replace it with the text "Done." I have illustrated the aforementioned three steps in Figure 3–12.

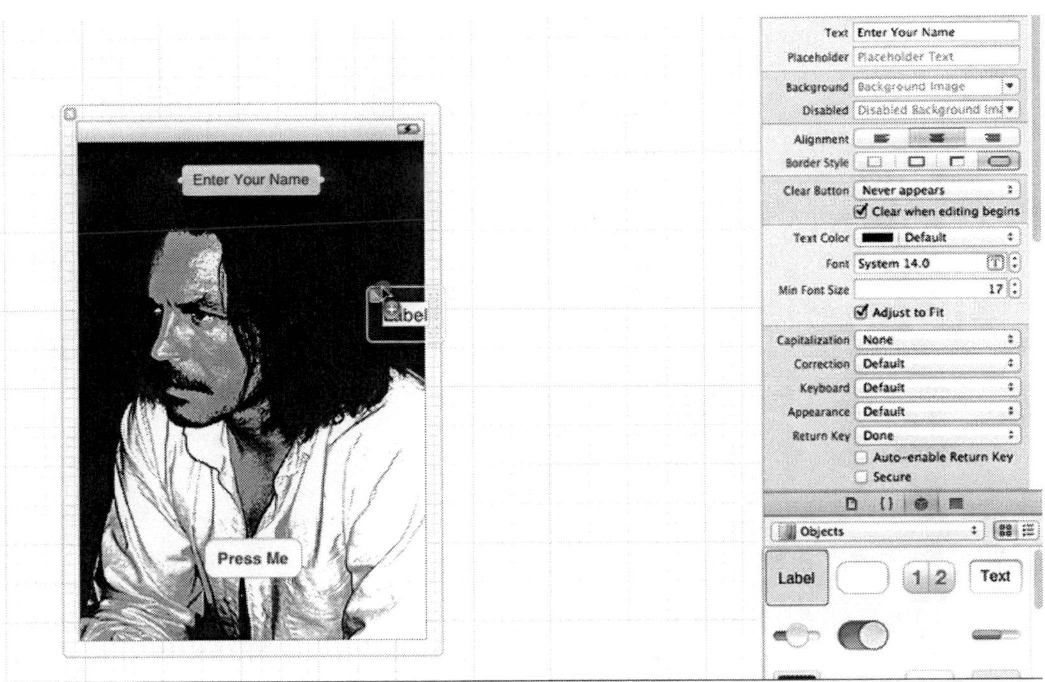

Figure 3–13. *Drag a Label object onto your View Design area.*

13. Once the user has entered their name into the `Text Field object`, and they press the button, you need to display the user's name and text in a label. You have yet to place a Label object onto the View Design area, so do it now, by dragging it from the Library onto the `View Design area`, as illustrated in Figure 3–13.

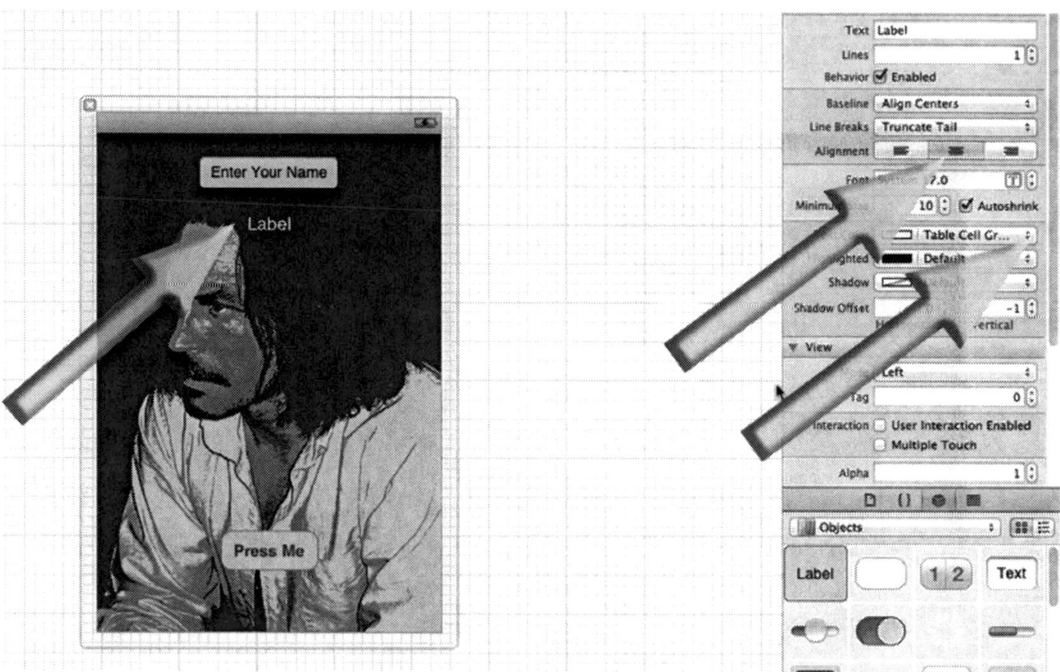

Figure 3–14. *Center and expand your Label object. Also, change the text color if necessary, and center the inside of the Label object.*

14. Place the Label object just below your Text Field object, and expand it, while still keeping it centered, with respect to the View Design area. Do this by quickly expanding one side and then expanding the other until the purple center line appears. This is the fastest method of expanding and centering at the same time. Next, center the text inside the Label object, and then, depending on the color of the picture, change the text color to make sure it stands out. In case of Figure 3–14, the color behind the text was black, so it was changed to white.

Connecting to the Code

OK, you are now through with dragging objects from the Library onto the View Design area. Let's connect these objects to your file's owner, so you can associate it with code.

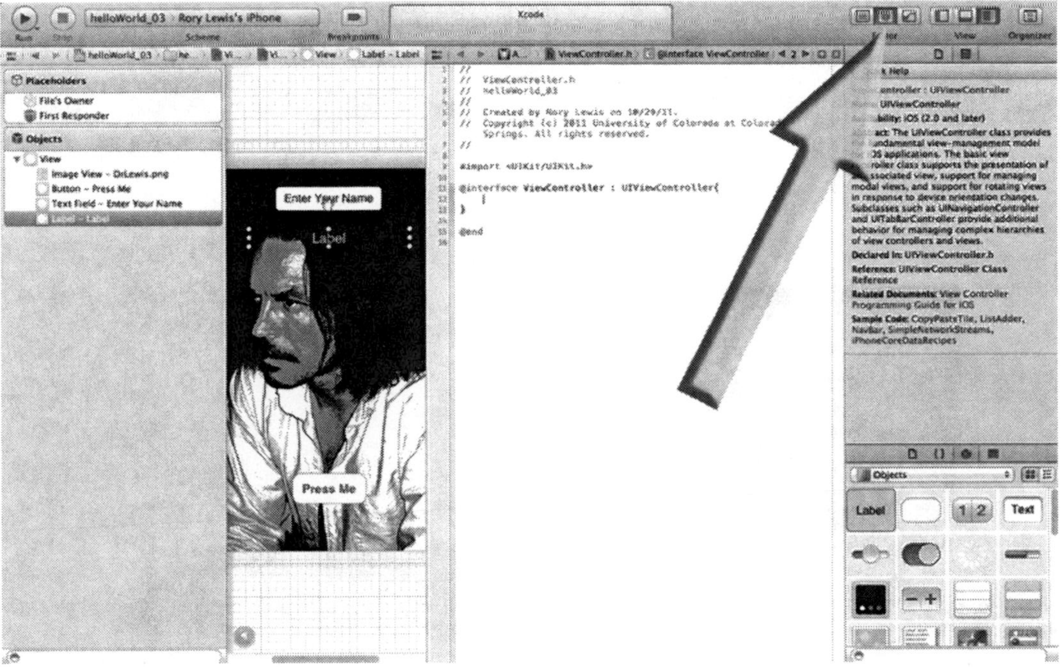

Figure 3–15. *Open the Assistant Editor.*

15. One of the really cool properties of Xcode 4 is that in the "olden" days, when Xcode first came out, you had to enter Control + Command + Up Arrow (^⌘↑) or Control + Command + Down Arrow (^⌘↓) to zip back and forth between files that the clever people at Apple knew we would want to switch between. These connected pages and files are called *counterparts,* but you don't have to know that because in Xcode 4, the Assistant Editor figures out cool ways to plop them all there on the screen for you. Right now, you should start connecting code with all of the goodies that you have brought onto the View. So, go to the Editor Selector with your mouse, as shown in Figure 3–15, and select the Assistant Editor, which looks like the chest of a person wearing a tuxedo. Here you'll see how the layout changes. Just for fun, you may want to select the button immediately to the left of the Assistant Editor, called the Standard Editor, and you'll see that now you have one screen—just like in the old days. Anyway, with the Assistant Editor selected, let's move on.

> **NOTE:** You can also use keyboard shortcuts to open up the Assistant Editor Option, Command + Return (⌥⌘↩) and Command + Return (⌘↩) to open up the Standard Editor. There are thousands of keyboard shortcuts; some make it into superstardom and some never make it out of books and blogs. These two shortcut keys are being mentioned because even though Xcode 4 is still young, I'm seeing myself and others starting to use these two commands naturally.

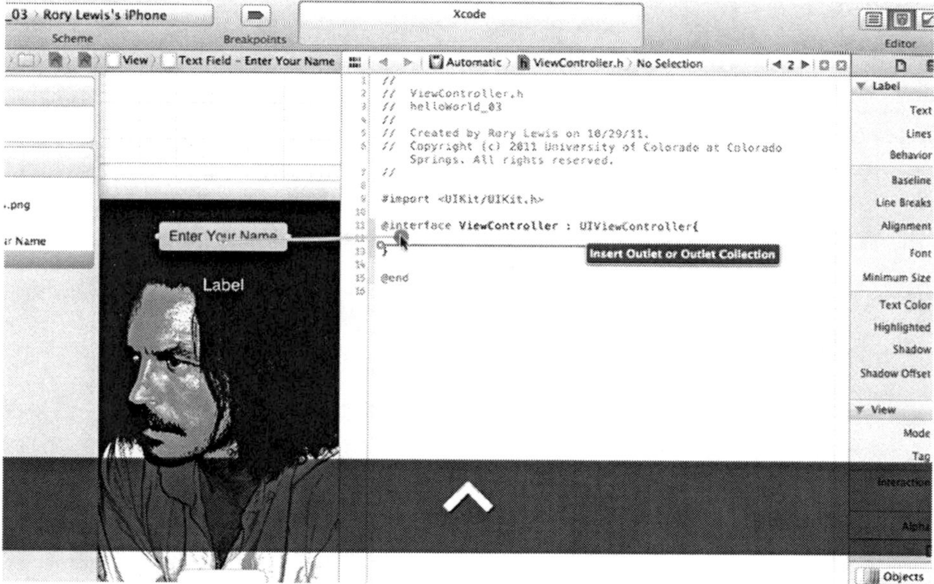

Figure 3–16. *Control-Drag a connection from your text box in Interface Builder directly into your header file.*

16. As you can see, you're back at a familiar screen that shows Interface Builder with your header file centered in the middle. Here you want to associate Outlets and Actions with the buttons and labels you dragged onto the View Design area. The last two times you did this, you were told to drag from this to that. Now, however, you are going to use a little bit more of the correct nomenclature, so that you can sound a little more geeky. Click once inside the text box, and then control-drag from the text box to your header file, placing it between the two curly braces. If you were to control-drag over to an invalid destination then Xcode would not display the insertion indicator, which is shown in Figure 3–16.

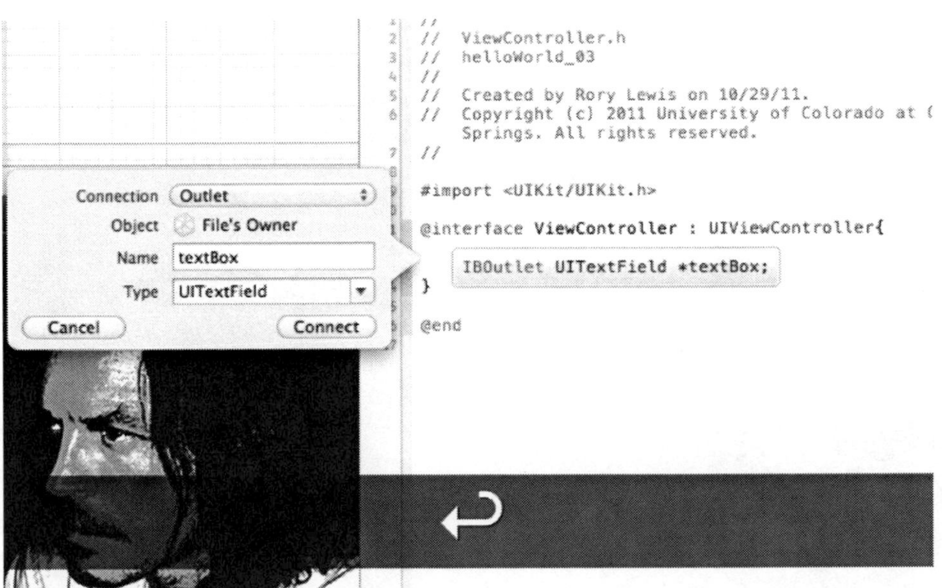
Connection
Outlet
Object
File's Owner
Name
textBox
Type
UITextField
Cancel
Connect
//
// ViewController.h
// helloWorld_03
//
// Created by Rory Lewis on 10/29/11.
// Copyright (c) 2011 University of Colorado at (
Springs. All rights reserved.
//
#import <UIKit/UIKit.h>
@interface ViewController : UIViewController{
IBOutlet UITextField *textBox;
}
@end

Figure 3–17. *When the text box's connection dialogue appears, specify what type of connection you plan to use in your code.*

17. When you see the insertion indicator appear as you control-drag over to the area between the two curly braces, release the mouse button. Xcode displays the dialog box, where you will want to tell it that this needs to be an outlet, so don't select anything as this is the default. This is illustrated in Figure 3–17. Later on, why this is done and what this Outlet stuff is all about will be explained. Right now, just make sure that you give it a name. In Figure 3–17, it was called `textBox`. Once this is done, click on the Connect button, and see how the Outlet code magically appears.

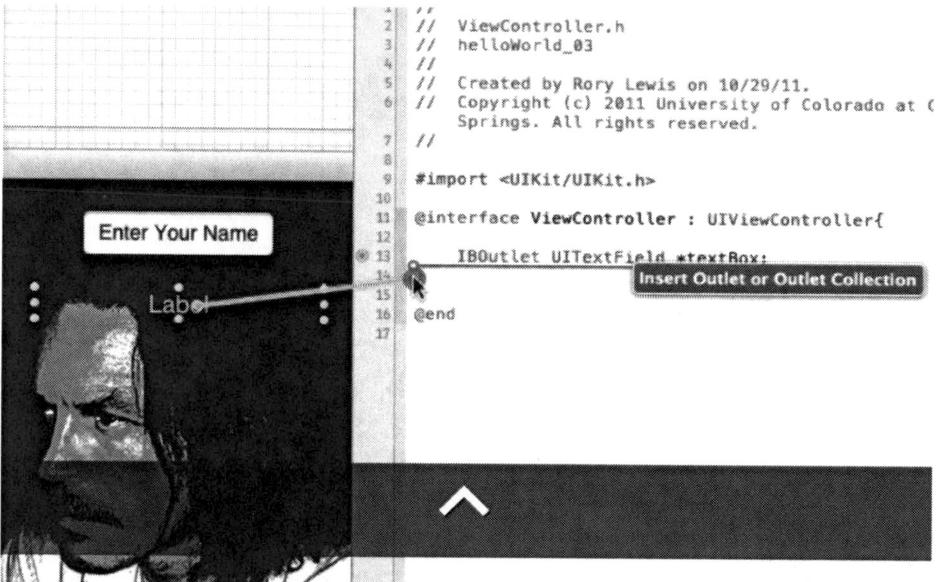
// ViewController.h
// helloWorld_03
//
// Created by Rory Lewis on 10/29/11.
// Copyright (c) 2011 University of Colorado at (
Springs. All rights reserved.
//
#import <UIKit/UIKit.h>
@interface ViewController : UIViewController{
IBOutlet UITextField *textBox;
Insert Outlet or Outlet Collection
@end
Enter Your Name
Label

Figure 3–18. *Control-drag a connection from your label in Interface Builder directly into your header file.*

18. Click once inside the label and control-drag it into your header file, placing it below your textBox outlet, inside the two curly braces. Drag until you see the Display the Insertion indicator, as shown in Figure 3–18.

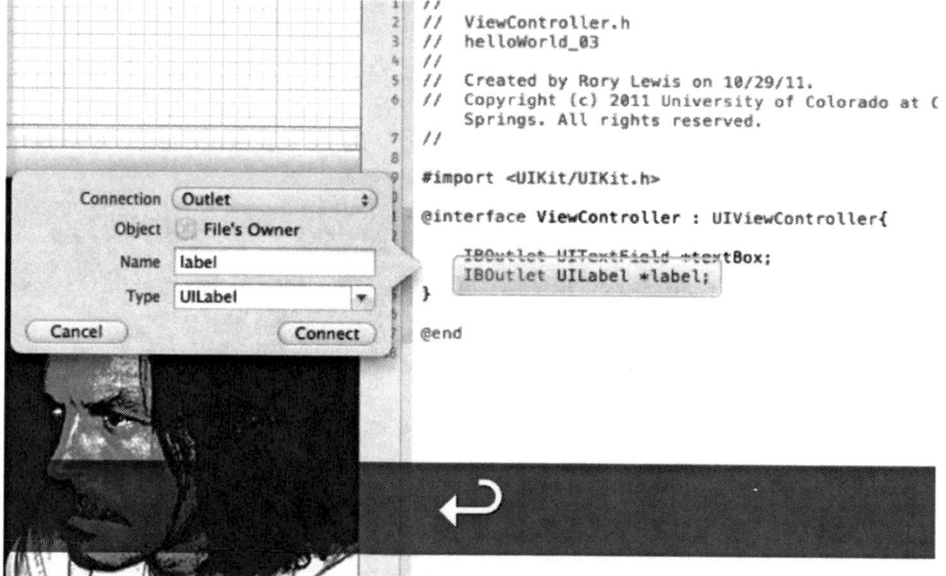
// ViewController.h
// helloWorld_03
//
// Created by Rory Lewis on 10/29/11.
// Copyright (c) 2011 University of Colorado at (
Springs. All rights reserved.
//
#import <UIKit/UIKit.h>
@interface ViewController : UIViewController{
IBOutlet UILabel *label;
}
@end
Connection Outlet
Object File's Owner
Name label
Type UILabel
Cancel
Connect

Figure 3–19. *When the label's connection dialogue appears, specify what type of connection you plan to use in your code.*

19. Just as you did with the `textBox` when you made it an outlet, you want to do the same here when the label's dialogue box opens. Leave it as an outlet on the top drop down and simply give it a name. In Figure 3–19, it was called "label." When you click Connect, it plants some very cool outlet code that you did not even have to program! So you have two lines of code that were automatically added: one when you dragged over the `textBox`, and the other when you dragged over the label. Both of these will be outlets. Are you thinking that the button, like the other ones, will be an action? This is correct. But getting back to these outlets—when you look at this code, without understanding everything, all you need to know about each of these lines of code, as seen in Figure 3–19, is the following:

```
IBOutlet UITextField *textBox;
```

This adds an outlet to a text box.

```
IBOutlet UILabel *label;
```

This adds an outlet to a label, just as you did in previous examples.

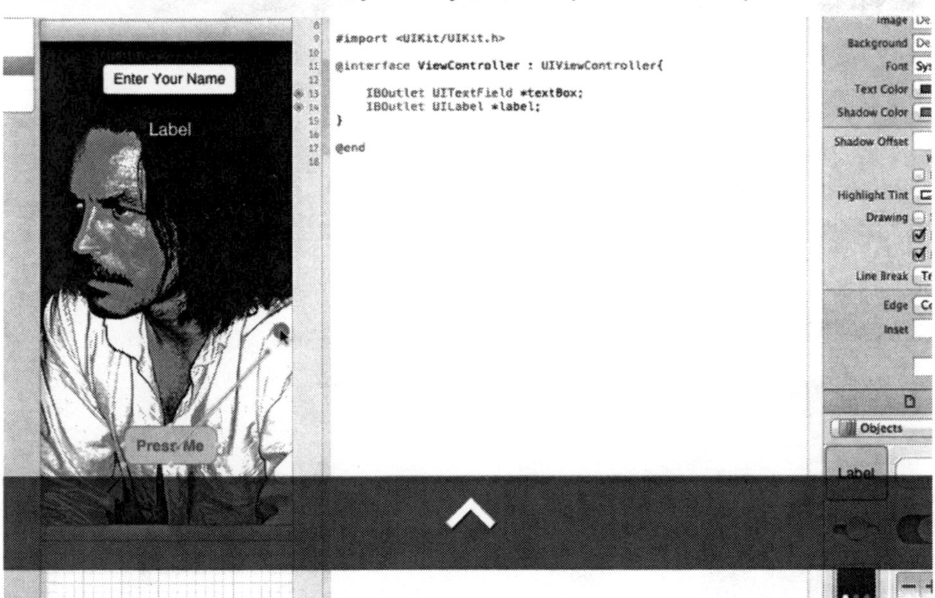

Figure 3–20. *Control-drag from the button into your header file.*

20. Click once on the button that says "Press Me" (as shown in Figure 3–20), and control-drag towards the area below the `@interface` directive and its curly braces.

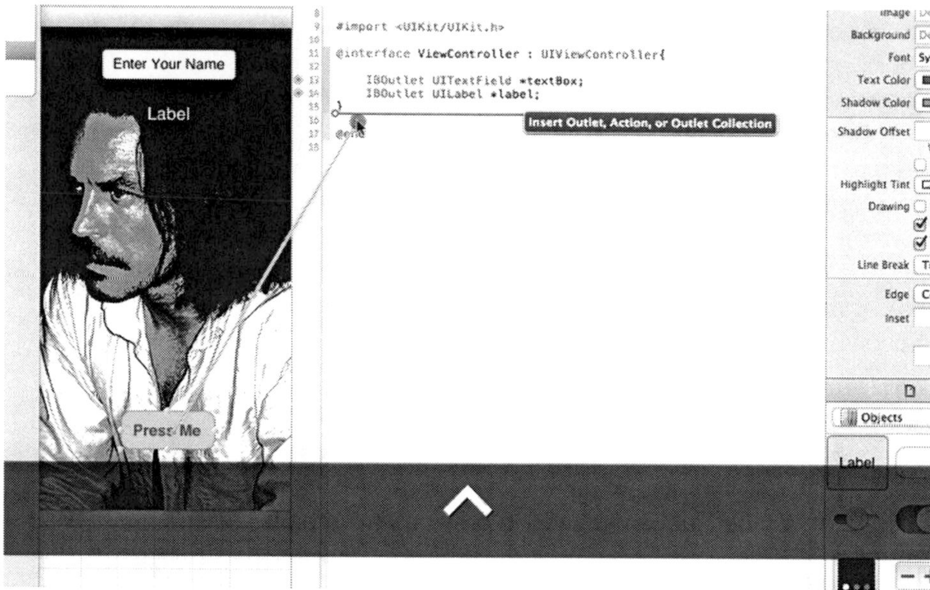

Figure 3–21. *The insertion indicator now has three options.*

21. Control-drag until you see the insertion indicator, as shown in Figure 3–21. Note that as you drag over to this area, Xcode already knows that this could be one of three options, not two, as shown in the insertion indicator for your label and text box outlets. See how this also includes a third option: "Action." Now, release the mouse button when properly located after the curly braces.

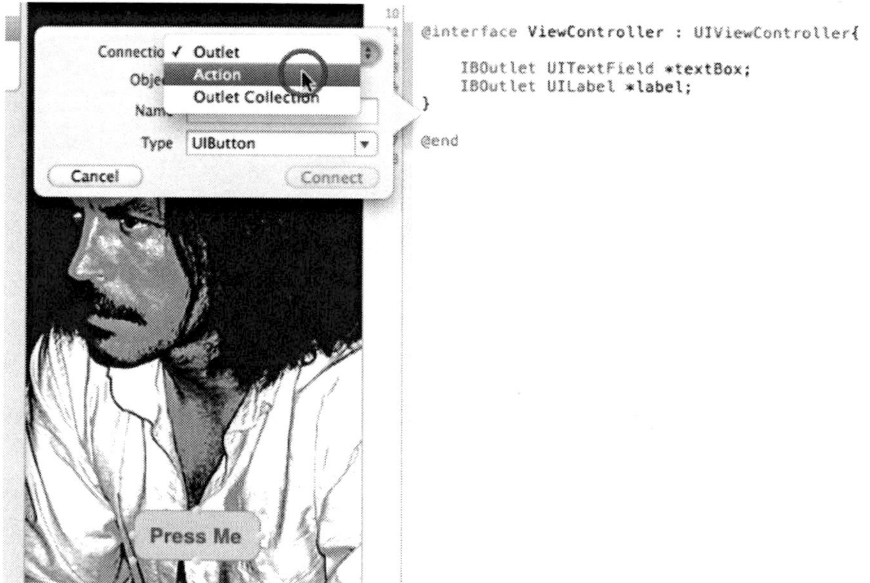

Figure 3–22. *Open the drop down menu and change the type of connection to an Action.*

22. The first thing you need to do here is change the connection type in the top drop down menu in the dialogue box from an *outlet* to an *action*. This is just like you did before with the outlet. See Figure 3–22.

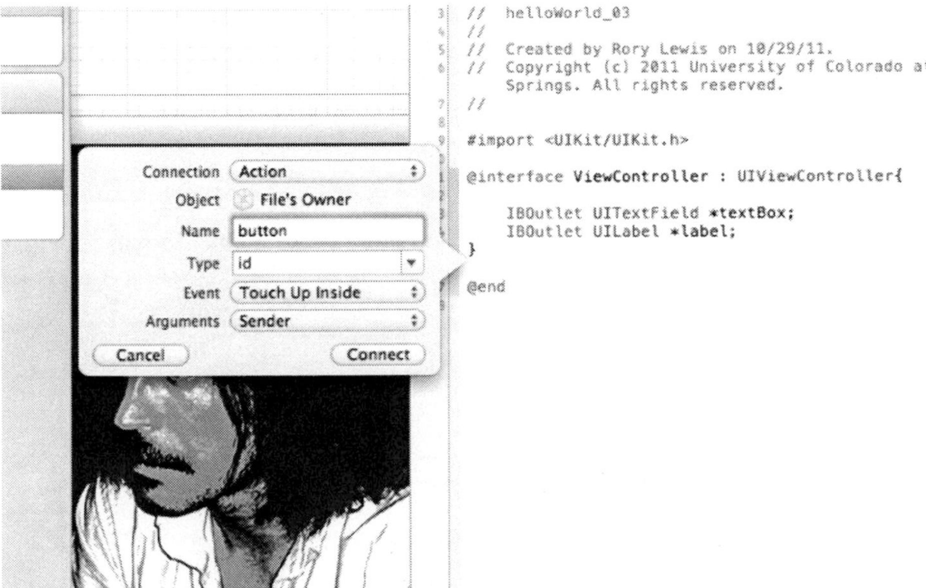
Connection Action
Object File's Owner
Name button
Type id
Event Touch Up Inside
Arguments Sender
Cancel
Connect
// helloWorld_03
//
// Created by Rory Lewis on 10/29/11.
// Copyright (c) 2011 University of Colorado a
Springs. All rights reserved.
//
#import <UIKit/UIKit.h>
@interface ViewController : UIViewController{
IBOutlet UITextField *textBox;
IBOutlet UILabel *label;
}
@end

Figure 3–23. *Name this action "button" and click on the Connect button.*

23. After changing this button from an outlet to an action, as shown in Figure 3–23, you still need to name it. In Figure 2-23, it is named `button`. Now, click on the Connect button. You will now see code appear as follows

```
- (IBAction)button:(id)sender;
```

READ IT ALOUD

Looking at this code, let's talk about it briefly. Don't worry if you space out. What I will ask you to do is what I make my students do in class, and that is to read the following out loud three times:

This is called a *method* and you could have named it "monkey" if you wanted to. If you did, it would look like this

```
- (IBAction)monkey:(id)sender;
```

I only want you to know two things about this method you called "monkey." First, that it has a *return type,* and second, that it has an *argument.*

- `monkey`'s return type: Our `monkey` method returns stuff to us, which is explained by saying: "Method `monkey`'s return type is an `IBAction`." Read the bold code louder.

```
- (IBAction)monkey:(id)sender;
```

- monkey's argument: monkey's argument is of type (id), which in your case, points through the sender to the button you dragged into the header file in Figure 3–23. Read the bold code louder.

```
- (IBAction)monkey:(id)sender;
```

OK, you can now take a nice deep breath. You are done with peaking under the hood for a while. You are also done with the header file, and now you can move onto the implementation file.

Avoiding an Annoying Error

But before you move onto the implementation file, you have to do a little housekeeping.

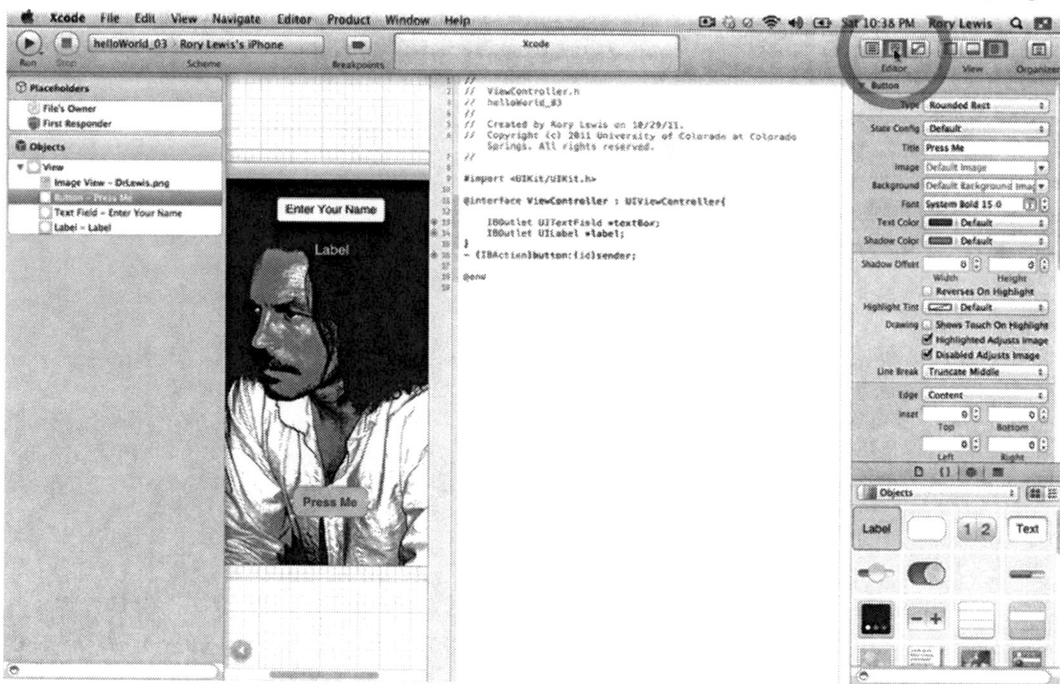

Figure 3–24. *Close the Assistant.*

24. You can see in this 3rd tutorial that Xcode 4 has done some remarkable things. However, as I write this book, a number of frustrated Xcode 4 programmers are encountering an irritating error. Before you move to the next step, I will show you how to avoid this error. (There is a chance that this quirky attribute of Xcode 4 will have been fixed by the time you read this.) Close the Inspector, as shown in Figure 3–24, and then open up the Utilities pane again.

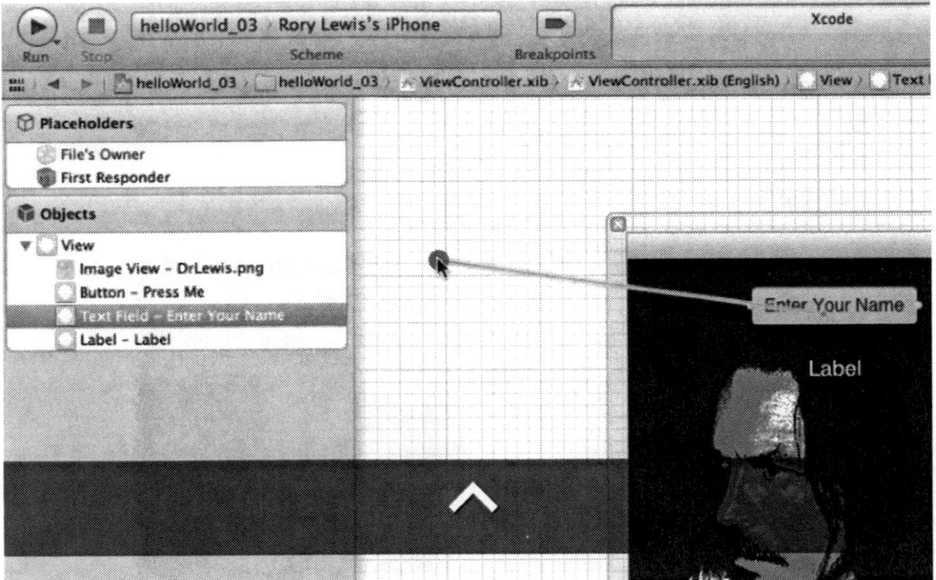

Figure 3–25. *Connect your text box to the delegate – Part 1: Activate* `textBox` *and start control-dragging.*

25. The way you have been connecting objects from Interface Builder directly into the code has been really cool, except that it seems that you cannot leave everything to the clever folks at Apple to make all the connections for you—yet. So, click once in the text box and control-drag to File's Owner. If you do not connect this to the delegate then you will get a very irritating error called a SIGABRT, which means Xcode is going to abort because it cannot connect. It's really bad news, but the good news is that you can avoid it. Here's how.

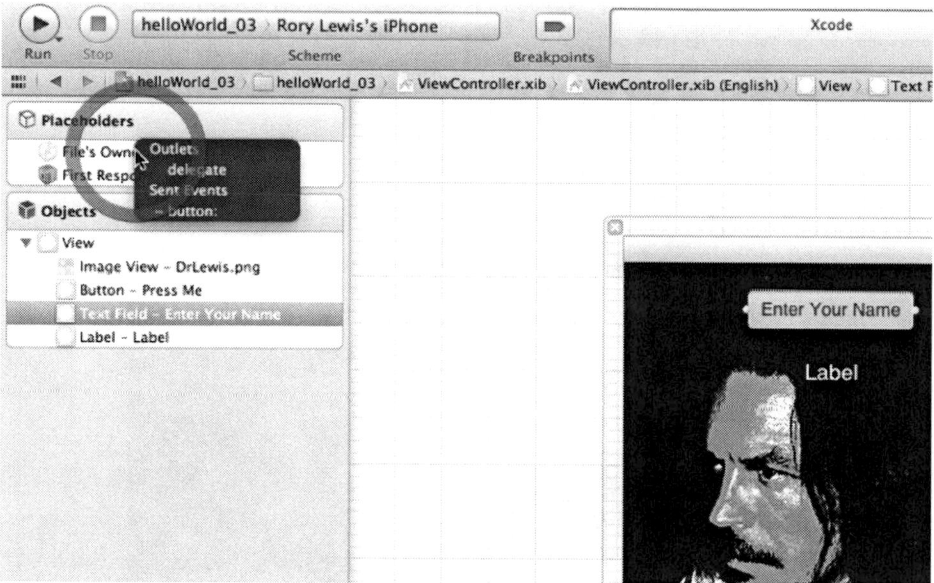

Figure 3–26. *As you near File's Owner, you will want to connect it to the delegate.*

26. As you near File's Owner, it presents you with a dark-gray contextual dialogue that tells you that you've already connected File's Owner to the button and the delegate, but you know better—it's still dangling there. You want to connect `textBox` to the delegate. Move your mouse right over it and when it activates, let go of the mouse. See Figure 3–26. With this done, you've connected all the goodies you dragged onto the View with the header file. The geeky way to say this would be to say: "Yo, dude, all my actions and outlets are now functionally connected!" Sounds pretty good, huh? What's more, you kind of understand what you've been doing! You brought buttons, text boxes, and labels onto your View. Then you wired them up to function as either outlets or actions. Now, all that's left is to dial in some code where necessary.

Setting up the Coding Environment

Before dialing in the code you need to do a little more housework.

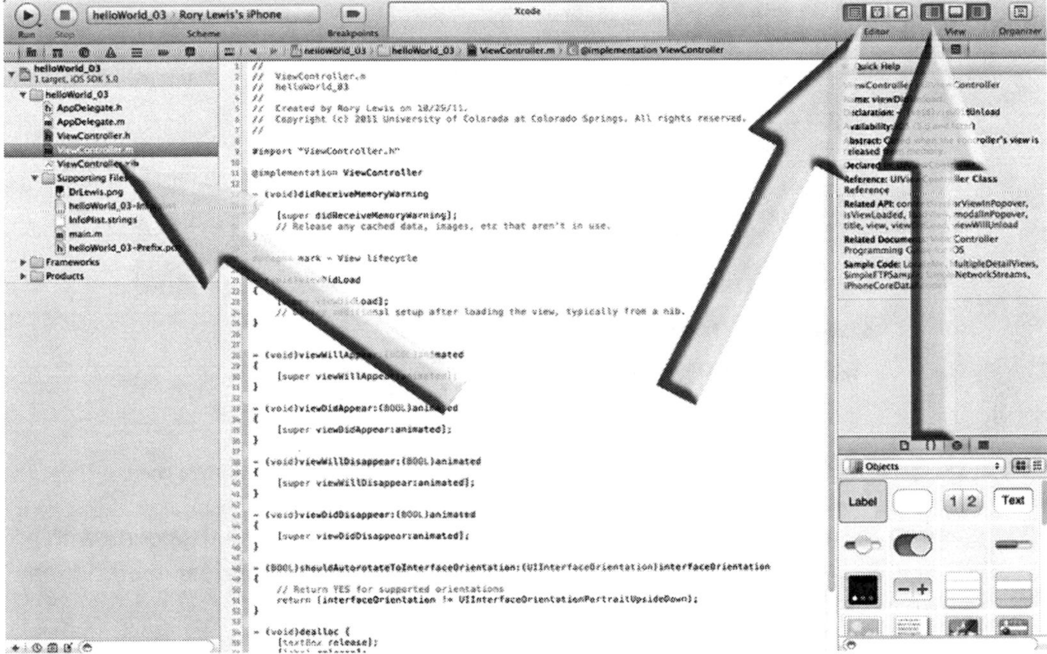

Figure 3–27. *Open the Navigator, and then go to Standard View and save everything.*

27. First, let's get your screen in a manner conducive for writing code, by clicking on the Navigator (see the right arrow in Figure 3–27), and then on Standard View (middle arrow, the left icon in the Editor section). With this done, please get in the habit of saving things. Go over to your nib, header, and implementation files that are now colored dark grey, click on each one, and save them by pressing command + S (⌘S). Or use Apple+Option+S to save all. Please do not use your mouse to save, as I will magically appear, take your book away, and declare that you have failed in your endeavor to become a geek. If you decide to work for a computer company after reading this book and they see you using your mouse to save, they will laugh at you because geeky people do that to those who save with a mouse. I'm serious!

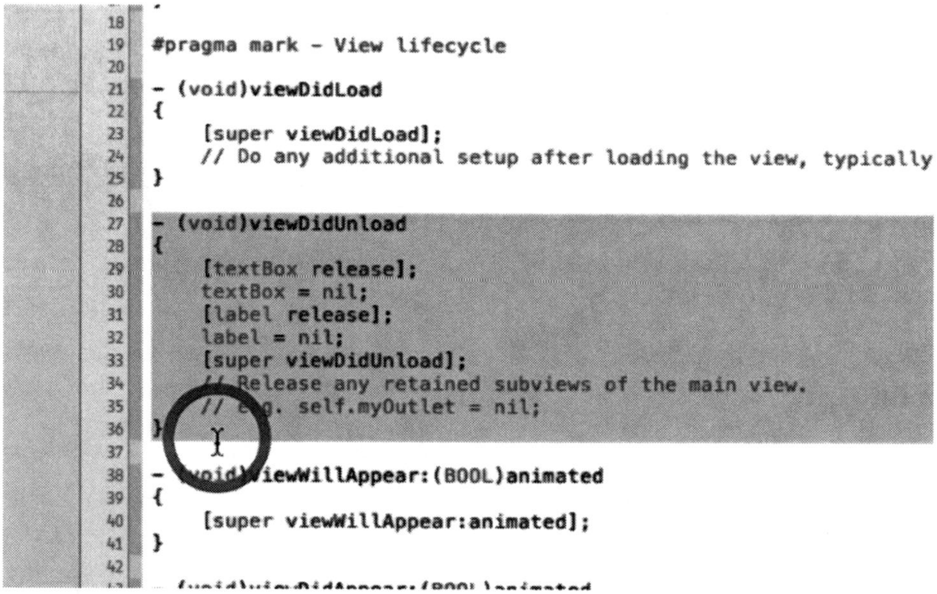

```
#pragma mark - View lifecycle

- (void)viewDidLoad
{
    [super viewDidLoad];
    // Do any additional setup after loading the view, typically
}

- (void)viewDidUnload
{
    [textBox release];
    textBox = nil;
    [label release];
    label = nil;
    [super viewDidUnload];
    // Release any retained subviews of the main view.
    // e.g. self.myOutlet = nil;
}

- (void)viewWillAppear:(BOOL)animated
{
    [super viewWillAppear:animated];
}
```

Figure 3–28. *Open the ViewController's implementation file and delete unnecessary boilerplate code.*

28. Click on the ViewController's implementation file. That's the one that ends with a `.m`, as in `helloWorld_03ViewController.m`. Delete the `viewDidUnload` method, as shown in Figure 3–28.

Creating a Programming Roadmap

You're now ready to get into some code that does something useful.

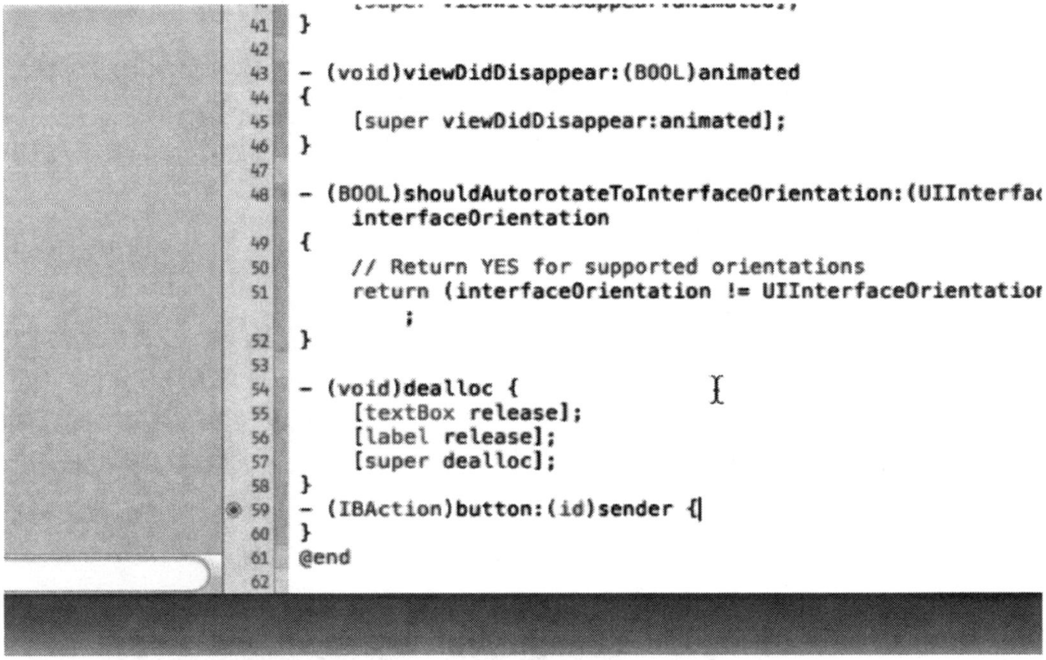

```
}

- (void)viewDidDisappear:(BOOL)animated
{
    [super viewDidDisappear:animated];
}

- (BOOL)shouldAutorotateToInterfaceOrientation:(UIInterfac
    interfaceOrientation
{
    // Return YES for supported orientations
    return (interfaceOrientation != UIInterfaceOrientatio
        ;
}

- (void)dealloc {
    [textBox release];
    [label release];
    [super dealloc];
}
- (IBAction)button:(id)sender {
}
@end
```

Figure 3–29. *The raw IBAction button method, before you start programming it.*

29. There are two items of interest for you here: first, what and where you are programming, and second, a roadmap that will guide you as you program your first chunk of code:

- **Looking at *what* you are programming:** You can see in Figures 3–22 through 24, that you have the method `(IBAction)button:(id)sender{…}`, which looks pretty similar to the action instantiated when you dragged over an action connected to your button from the interface builder to your header file. The only difference is that in the implementation file you need to implement what needs to happen when a person presses this button. To do this, you substitute the semi-colon with curly braces, and it's in these curly braces that you are going to instruct what exactly will happen when a person presses this button.

> **NOTE:** I'm going to explain this twice: first, as an overview and then again in a specific way that I have developed for newbie Objective-C programmers. I will be doing this quite often in the book. It really works well so bear with me and come along for the ride.

- **Your roadmap:** Looking at Figure 3–29, your road map states that you will have two text strings that you should call `Name` and `Output`. `Name`, `NSString`, receives text that the user enters into `textBox`. Clear `Output NSString`, and then let it receive the text from `NSString`. After placing it in front of ":says Hello World!", it sends this to Label so the viewer can see it. Lastly, clean out `Output NSString`.

The code is divided into 5 steps:

1. Create strings to manage your text input and output
2. Manipulate the text around
3. Display your hard work
4. Housekeeping
5. Get rid of the keyboard

Step One: Create strings to manage your text input and output

First, you should type the two `NSString` statements in between the curly braces. What you're doing is creating two strings of text called `NSStrings`, that you will call `Name` and `Output`. Make the contents of the `NSString *Name` contains the contents of the text that the user types into the `textBox`. Next, make the `NSString *Output` contain nothing, or in essence, clean it out by forcing "nil" into it. The "*" represent pointers that point to a memory address that will contain the contents of each `NSString`.

```
- (IBAction)button:(id)sender {
    NSString *Name = textBox.text;
    NSString *Output = Nil;
}
```

Step Two: Manipulate the text around

Underneath the two `NSString` statements, type out the `Output` line as shown below.

```
- (IBAction)button:(id)sender {
    NSString *Name = textBox.text;
    NSString *Output = Nil;
    Output = [[NSString alloc] initWithFormat:@"%@ says: 'Hello World!", Name];
}
```

With this typed out, look at the %@ in the following code

```
@"%@ says: Hello  World!", Name];
```

This is going to be written in progressively technical ways, such as:

- The %@ puts the stuff inside Name before the "says: Hello World!".
- The %@ puts the text located at a place in memory pointed to by Name, and then places that text from the memory before the "says: Hello World!".
- The %@ puts the text located in memory by pointer Name, and then places that text from the memory before the "says: Hello World!".
- The %@ places the string at *Name before the "says: Hello World!".

OK, that wasn't too bad. The descriptions went from totally non-geek text to gradually getting a little more geeky each time. In class, we play games where I challenge students to get in groups and try to do their own "road to geekdom" innovations. What I'm going to ask you to do, before you do the next one, is explain the above progression to a person close to you who knows nothing about computers. Read the four bullet points to them. When they cannot get it, explain it to them in YOUR WORDS. You will learn so much from this. Most of you will realize that they can already see that you've started the transformation from dude to geek.

OK. So moving on, I want you to focus on the [[NSString alloc] initWithFormat:@ in the line

```
[[NSString alloc] initWithFormat:@"%@ says: Hello  World!", Name];
```

Here it goes:

- The [[NSString alloc] initWithFormat:@ allocates the text saying "somebody says: Hello World!" in a way that makes sense to human beings.
- The [[NSString alloc] initWithFormat:@ allocates all those electrical signals in the iPhone's microprocessor using the code that the clever people at Apple programmed in their initWithFormat code, that converts the machine language representing "somebody says: Hello World!" into text that makes sense to human beings.
- Once it has converted everything to say "somebody says: Hello World!" into text, you store it in Output, as shown in the following code

```
Output = [[NSString alloc] initWithFormat:@"%@ says: Hello  World!", Name];
```

Step Three: Display your hard work

Next, you need to get the text that is being held in Output onto the screen of the user's iPad or iPhone. Students often tell me at this point that they think they're done. Nope. Your text is just lying there inside your microprocessor. You want it out on the screen so the viewer can read it. Recall that you created a perfect place for it in Figure 3–13? Go there, and meet me back here.

Cool huh! You need to put the text lying in Outlet into Label. So type in

```
label.text = Output;
```

What you've done here is accessed something that is called the "text property," set it to be whatever is in Outlet, and then dump it onto your screen inside Label.

```
- (IBAction)button:(id)sender {
    NSString *Name = textBox.text;
    NSString *Output = Nil;
    Output = [[NSString alloc] initWithFormat:@"%@ says: 'Hello World!", Name];
    label.text = Output;
}
```

Step Four: Housekeeping

You are not going into this now. But you need to stop memory leaks. One of the most common reasons for the iTunes store to reject your app is because it has memory leaks. This is too complex for now, and your brain is tired. Just know that the alloc you used means that you now need to release the memory. So write a comment for your own reminding, as you dig the code in later chapters.

```
//release the object"
```

Then, actually release it by typing

```
[Output release];
```

```
- (IBAction)button:(id)sender {
    NSString *Name = textBox.text;
    NSString *Output = Nil;
    Output = [[NSString alloc] initWithFormat:@"%@ says: 'Hello World!", Name];
    label.text = Output;
    [Output release];
}
```

Step Five: Get rid of the keyboard

Once the user enters their name and hits the Done button (see right hand image of Figure 3–12), you need to add a little code to make sure the keyboard is dismissed.

You do this by implementing a special kind of delegate method called textFieldShouldReturn. Right now, you do not have to worry about delegates, first responders, and so on. All I want you to know is that this code reassigns the first responder, your keyboard, and the text field that is active (typing in one's name), which saves it in your toolbag and reuses it every time you need to wipe out the keyboard.

```
- (BOOL) textFieldShouldReturn:(UITextField *)theTextField{
    [textBox resignFirstResponder];
    return YES;
}
@end
```

OK! You're done with code!

I want you to feel proud of yourself! You've allowed me to guide you through some treacherous waters of Objective-C code, and even if you're not feeling like you've absolutely wrapped your head around the code, no problem. Objective-C is an incredibly difficult language and the fact that you're still reading this means you're doing awesome. Remember that as you do more of this it all comes together and gets dialed in beautifully. For those of you who have understood what you've done so far in the way that I'm presenting it to you, congratulations!

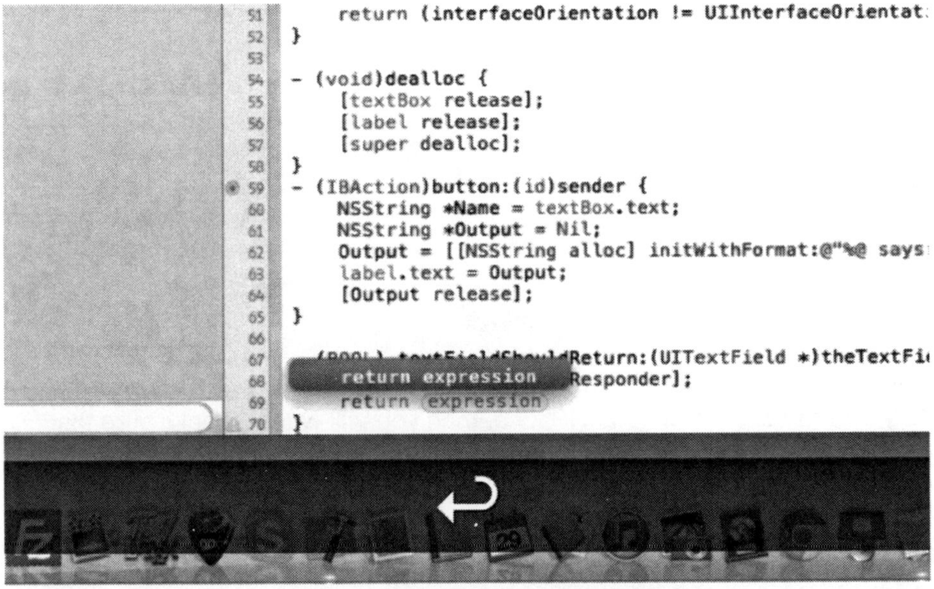

```
    return (interfaceOrientation != UIInterfaceOrientat
}

- (void)dealloc {
    [textBox release];
    [label release];
    [super dealloc];
}
- (IBAction)button:(id)sender {
    NSString *Name = textBox.text;
    NSString *Output = Nil;
    Output = [[NSString alloc] initWithFormat:@"%@ says
    label.text = Output;
    [Output release];
}

- (BOOL) textFieldShouldReturn:(UITextField *)theTextFi
    return expression    Responder];
    return expression
}
```

Figure 3–30. ***Coding the delegate method textFieldShouldReturn.***

30. Figure 3–30 shows the completed button method and the `textFieldShouldReturn` method being typed in with Xcode's code completion doing its work. Once this is done you are finished coding. Yeah!

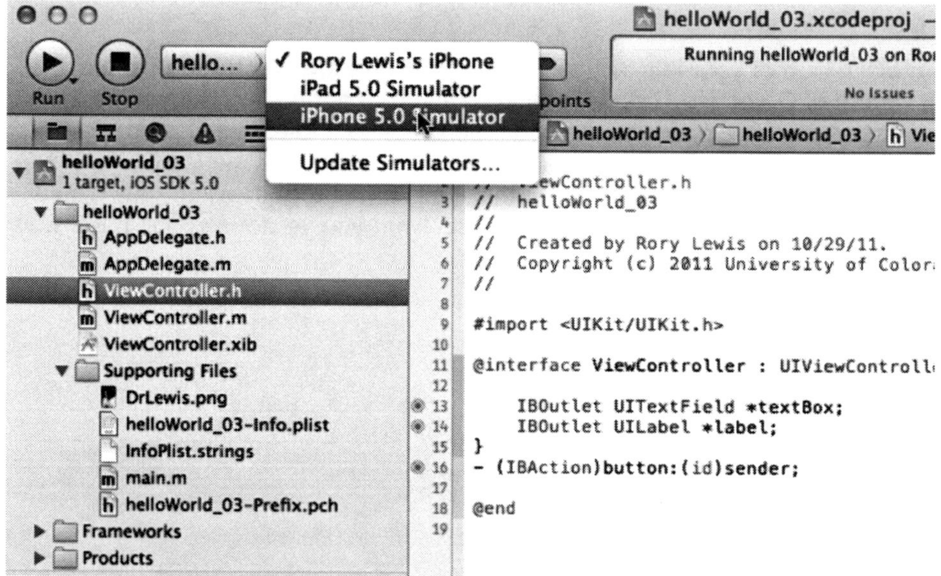

Figure 3–31. *Make sure you will be running to the correct target.*

31. First, let's make sure that you have saved everything. Now, if you ran your last app to your iPad or to your actual iPhone, then you will want to make sure that you change the "target" to be the iPhone simulator, as shown in Figure 3–31.

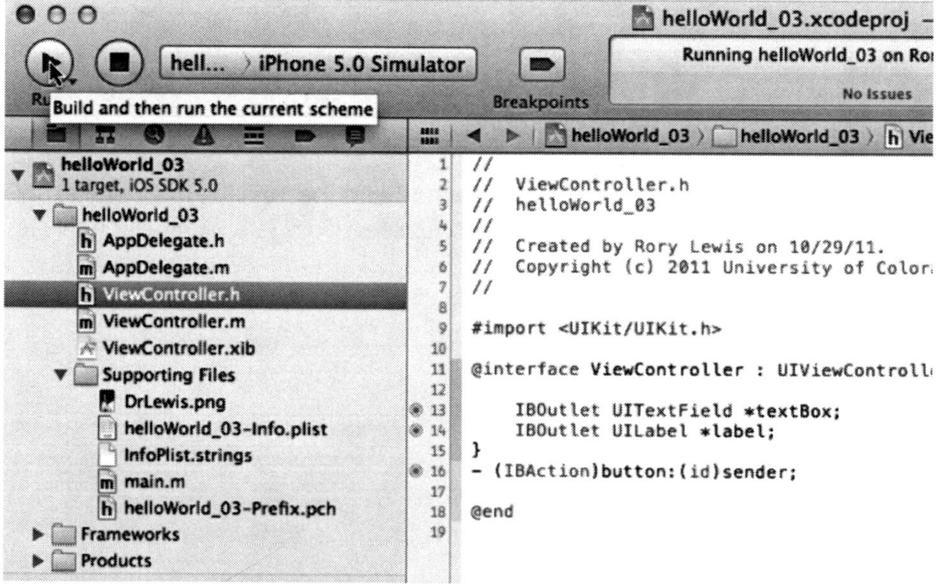

Figure 3–32. *Let's run it!*

32. You have worked really hard on this one, and now it's time to see the fruits of your work. Hit the Run button, as shown in Figure 3–32, and let's see your app come to life!

Figure 3–33. *The four states of your app.*

33. If you're using your own picture then yours will obviously be in the background. Starting on the left hand side of Figure 3–32 and moving to the right:

    a. The first image shows the text box asking the user to enter their name.

    b. The instant one clicks in the text box, the text disappears and the keypad appears.

    c. The third image shows the state of your app once the user hits the Done button.

    d. The last image shows the final state of all your hard work, which appears when the user hits the Press Me button. Congratulations!

Digging the Code

In these reviews, we will go over some of the code we have written, and I will reference familiar code and explain the processes in more detail. Here, I will introduce you to more technical terms that you will use in future chapters and in communicating with other programmers.

Consider this analogy: In `helloWorld_01` and `helloWorld_02` I taught you how to get into a car, turn the ignition, press the accelerator, and steer as you moved forward. In `helloWorld_03`, I guided you with similar directions, but as you drove toward your destination, I explained how the car is a hybrid engine and that it has some gasoline components and some electrical components. We talked about classes and methods, strings, outlets, and actions.

Now you've arrived at our destination; you've completed `helloWorld_03`, and I will open the hood and show you how, when you pressed the accelerator, it either pumped gasoline into the engine, or sometimes used the electric motor. When you look under the hood, I'll show you where these components are located. However, by the time you reach the end of the book, look under the hood, and dig the code, I will describe the amount of gasoline being squirted into the pistons by the carburetors, the exact torque and heat emission of the electric motor, and so on. Guess what—you'll be able to handle it!

One last comment about this section that is *really important*: Digging the Code is a section that I encourage you to read *without* definitive understanding. It's OK if you only partially "get it." Of course, if you happen to attain full comprehension of the subject in all its details, well that's great. What I suggest, however, is that you read these sections at the end of each chapter loosely because:

- I have received hundreds of emails from readers from the first edition of the book saying that knowing it was OK to blank out and not feel pressured to understand the code really worked out for them.
- Also, my students love it when at the end of each class, I make them turn off their Mac, put down their pens, Zen and zone out, and just casually listen to me. I've had students knocking on my office telling me in many colorful ways how the Zenning and zoning really worked for them.

Note that my research is in neurological acute brain injuries, where I study the brain and neural interconnectivity. This methodology of first connecting neurons and then infusing the deeper connective associations when the brain is relaxed is one that I've developed over the years. So, I want you to consider my former readers' and students' opinions about this matter and absorb my theorem.

> **NOTE:** Becoming an eloquent, knowledgeable, and financially thriving coder takes neurological leaps, during states wherein your brain is open to absorbing new data without the hypothalamus releasing anxiety hormones that pollute the ability of your neurons to create new connections, which allows linking logic and code to ontological reasoning.

So Zen out, zone out, and read in a meditative state with no fear. When that voice says, "You're not understanding it all," say: "That's OK, Dr. Lewis said so, now go away!" You will Zen and zone through:

- Nibs, Zibs, and Xibs
  - Instances and Instantiation
- Methods
  - Instance methods and class methods
- Header Files
- The Inspector Bar
- NSStrings
- Memory Management

Nibs, Zibs, and Xibs

Remember back in Figure 3–5, I instructed you to open your nib file. You could see that it was written "xib", and to make it more confusing, a minority of coders call them "zib" files. Just ignore them, refer to xib files by pronouncing them as "nib." At a recent conference in Denver, *360iDev for iPhone Developers,* it was clear most of the presenters referred to `.xib` files as "nibs" not "zibs." But no matter how we refer to them, it's important for us to understand what's going on with these files. What are they? Do we need them? Do you need to know how they work?

Do you recall, from Step 5, Figure 3–5, how you opened Interface Builder view when you clicked on that nib file? It was here that you saw your view and began dropping and dragging items onto your View Design area. What's going on here?

It turns out that when you examine nib files at the level of Cocoa or Objective-C, you see that they contain all the information necessary to activate the UI (User Interface) files, transforming your code into a graphical iPhone or iPad work of art. It's also possible to join separate nib files together to create more complex interactions, as you'll see later in this book. But in order to follow along, you need to add two words to your vocabulary: "Instances" and "Instantiation."

- **Instances:** All the information that resides in these files is put there so that it can *create an instance of* the buttons, the labels, the pictures, and so forth that you've entered. This collection of commands is plonked down and saved into your nib files to become the UI. The code and the commands taken together become real, and they are sensed by the user—seen or heard, or even felt.

- **Instantiation:** Remember in Step 29 and Figure 3–29, I explained that you can see that you have the method -(IBAction)button:(id)sender{…}, which looks pretty similar to the action *instantiated* when you dragged over an action connected to your button from the Interface Builder to your header file in Figures 3–22 through 24? Well the term *instantiate* is sometimes used in a similar fashion when you first save a new project. The computer *instantiates*—makes real and shows you the evidence for—a project entity created by assigning it a body of subfiles. In `helloWorld_03`, you saw how in Step 27 I asked you to go over to your nib, header, and implementation files that were colored dark grey? Well excuse me, how did these files get here? Did you program them or make them? Nope, Xcode instantiated these when you created your project. Xcode gave your project "arms and legs": two AppDelegate files and two ViewController files.

> **NOTE:** You are now manipulating these arm and legs to do cool stuff that we call apps, and sell them on the iTunes store.

We say that we've "created an instance" of something when we've told the computer how and when to grab some memory and set it aside for some particular process or collection of processes such that, when the parameters are all met, the user has an experience of this data (i.e., whatever was assigned in memory). Sometimes we refer to these collections or files of descriptions and commands as *classes*, *methods*, or *objects*. In this code-digging session, these terms might seem to run together and appear as synonyms, but this is not the case. As you read on, you will come to understand each term as a distinct coding tool or apparatus, each to be employed in a particular situation, relating to other entities in a grammatically correct way.

When we say that you created an instance of the buttons and labels in your nib file, what we're really saying is that, when you run your code, a specific portion of your computer's memory, known by its address, will take care of things in order to generate the user experience you have designed. Each time your application is launched on an iPhone or iPad, the interface is recreated by the orchestrated commands residing in your nib files. Consider the nib file associated with the action depicted in Figure 3–9. You dragged a button from the Library into the View window, and thus you *created an instance* of this button. If somebody were to ask you what that means, you might look them in the eye, with a piercing and enigmatic look, and say:

> *"By creating an instance of this button, I have instructed the computer to set aside memory in the appropriate* **.xib** *file, which, upon the launching of my app, will appear and interact with the user, precisely as I have intended."*

Wow!

Methods

The next concept I would like to explore a little more deeply is that of *methods*. As I did with nibs, I am only going to give you a high-level look this time. You've already used methods pretty extensively, so I'm simply going to tell you what you did.

Looking at Figure 3–23, after you dragged the button onto your header file, you changed it from an outlet to an action and clicked on the Connect button. Then you saw an instantiation of code appear

```
- (IBAction)button:(id)sender
```

I then suggested that to make things clearer, you could have named the method `monkey`, making it become

```
- (IBAction)monkey:(id)sender;
```

Here, you are instructing the computer to associate an action with a button.

- The first symbol in this piece of code is a minus sign (-). It means that `monkey` is something we call an *instance method.*
- On the other hand, if you had entered a plus sign (+) there, as in + `(IBAction)`, we would have called it a *class method*.

One symbol announces (to the processor) an instance, while another symbol announces a class. What these two statements have in common, though, is the method `monkey`. Furthermore, just by the name alone, you can see that this is an action that will be performed in Interface Builder. Yup, that's what that `IB` in front of the `Actions` means. See how Steve Jobs was really saying to himself when he designed Cocoa and Objective-C on his NEXT computers, that he wanted `Actions` and called them `IBActions`, so as to remind himself and other coders who used his code that when we typed in `IBAction` it was for `Actions` used in Interface Builder.

Consider this analogy: a programmer says, "Here comes an app that will assist you in drawing a nice, pretty house." That is a header type of announcement. Then, the programmer enters specific instructions for how the house will be constructed, how it will sit on/against the landscape, what kind of weather is in the background, and so on. "Draw a slightly curving horizon line one third from the bottom of the display, and midway on this, place a rectangle that is 4 × 7, on top of which is a trapezoid with a base length of…," and so on. These specific, how-to instructions belong in the implementation file, for they describe the actual actions—the *method*—of drawing the house.

So, to connect your button to a method named `hello`, you added this code as shown in Figure 3–24.

```
- (IBAction)hello:(id)sender;
```

This *created an instance of* your hello method. Then, you created a place in memory to execute the code inside your hello method.

Header Files

Look at this code, not in terms of methods but instead from the dimension of it being a header file and how it relates to its implementation file. I want you to go back to the point in time after you dragged and dropped your items that I called "goodies" onto the header file. Looking back at Figure 3–24, I want you to focus more on the bold text.

> **NOTE:** When naming things in code, you will represent "User Interface" with the initials UI. You will represent "Interface Builder" with the initials IB.

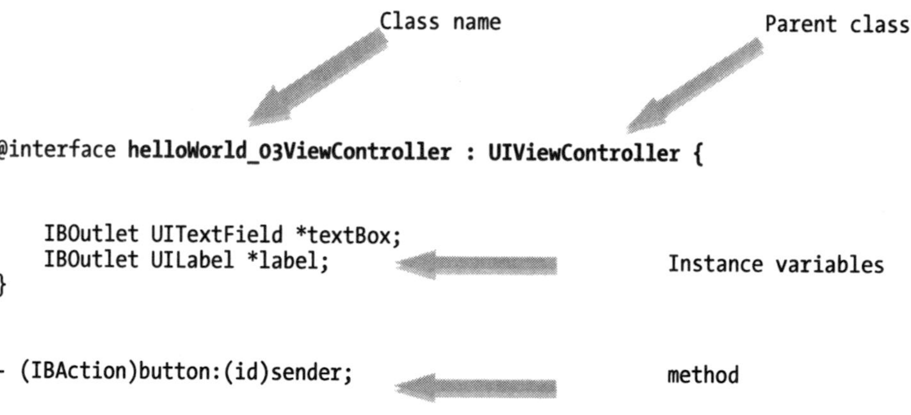
Class name
Parent class
@interface helloWorld_03ViewController : UIViewController {
IBOutlet UITextField *textBox;
IBOutlet UILabel *label;
}
Instance variables
- (IBAction)button:(id)sender;
method

```
@end
```

There are two things to note here. First, the @ symbol talks to the innermost part of Xcode, which transforms your code into actions, and second, that it's got something essential and important to announce. In fact, we call any statement beginning with @ a "directive." This @interface directive tells Xcode that you have interface stuff concerning helloWorld_03, and that the particulars will be enclosed within brackets {}.

Before you began dragging outlets into your code in Figure 3–16, notice how the opening bracket, "{" was empty! You had not said anything yet, right? You knew what you wanted to do, so you got the compiler's attention with the @interface directive, by creating your IBOutlets (Interface Builder Outlets) to write on your UILabels (User Interface Labels) and to have a separate Action associated with your button.

The Inspector Bar

Back in Step 8, Figure 3–8, while briefly explaining the Inspector Bar, I said that we'd get into it a little more. So as promised, here is some insight as to how the Inspector Bar is set up.

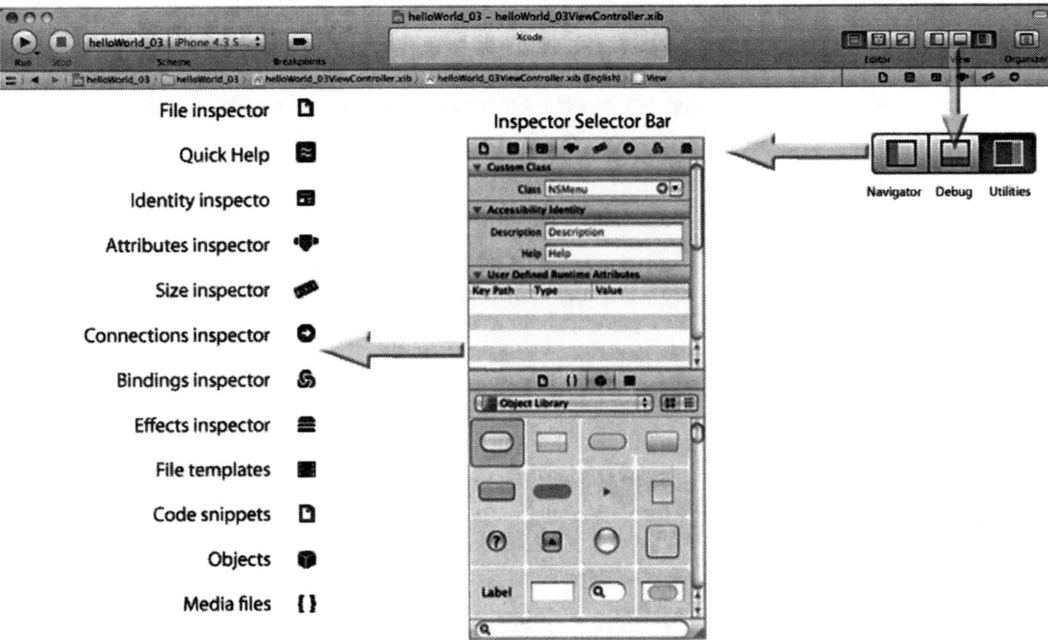

Figure 3–34. *Focusing in on the Inspector Bar.*

In Figure 3–33, I've recreated how I illustrate the Inspector Bar in class on the marker board. As you become familiar with the Xcode 4 environment, you will find yourself using the Inspector Selector Bar to choose a workspace that you will need at any phase of your coding. For now, let's zoom in on the most intense view: the Utilities View. Clicking on Utilities View, as shown in the top right-hand of Figure 3–33, you will see how I've created a zoomed up version of the Inspector Selector Bar, with its submenus located to the left of the panel. Starting at the top:

- ***File inspector:*** This is where one manages file attributes such as name, type, and path within your project.
- ***Quick Help:*** Just what it says.
- ***Identity inspector:*** Gives access to deep stuff such as class names, access, and labels.
- ***Attributes inspector:*** For adjusting attributes available to an object.
- ***Size inspector:*** Allows you to tinker with an interface object's initial size, position, and auto sizing.

- ***Connections inspector:*** Allows you to view the outlets and actions for your interface objects.
- ***Bindings inspector:*** For configuring bindings for view objects.
- ***Effects inspector:*** To adjust animation protocol such as transitions, fades, and other visual characteristics of selected objects.
- ***File templates:*** Common templates that you can drag from the library to the project navigator.
- ***Code snippets:*** Like clip art but for coders—snippets of source code that you can use by dragging into your files.
- ***Objects:*** You use these interface objects by directly dragging onto your nib file in the Interface Builder editor window.
- ***Media files:*** Just as it says, they are graphics, icons, and sound files that can be dragged directly to your nib file in the Interface Builder editor window.

NSStrings

Going back and digging a little deeper into the `NSString` statement in your implementation file, I went over this with sufficient detail while you wrote it. Here are five terms that I want you to associate about `NSStrings` `with`:

- `Output` is your returned value

```
Output = [[NSString alloc] initWithFormat:@"%@ says: Hello World!", Name];
```

- On the right-hand side of the equal sign is the message

```
Output = [[NSString alloc] initWithFormat:@"%@ says: Hello World!", Name];
```

- `NSString alloc` is the receiver

```
Output = [[NSString alloc] initWithFormat:@"%@ says: Hello World!", Name];
```

- `initWithFormat` is the method name

```
Output = [[NSString alloc] initWithFormat:@"%@ says: Hello World!", Name];
```

- `@"%@ says: Hello World!"` and `Name` are the parameters

```
Output = [[NSString alloc] initWithFormat:@"%@ says: Hello World!", Name];
```

More on Memory Management

At the end of Step 29, Figure 3–29, in "Step Four: Housekeeping," we spoke a little about `alloc` and how you allocated memory and released it at critical times in your app. I want you to have one last look at the implementation code you wrote for the button, but view it in terms of memory leaks and management.

```
- (IBAction)button:(id)sender {                    alloc+1
   NSString *Name = textBox.text;
   NSString *Output  = nil;
       Output = [[NSString alloc] initWithFormat:@"%@ says: Hello World!", Name];
   label.text = Output;
   //release the object
   [Output release];                        release-1
   }
```

Looking above, you can see how you first allocated some memory for your string. This is represented by the superscript $^{+1}$, to show that you have gone up one level and are allocating memory. Each time you go up one level, you need to also fall down one level by releasing that memory as shown by the $^{-1}$ at the release. It's really easy— when you `alloc` you need to release. In Objective-C, this is called reference counting. Where I see students suffer is those times that after they `alloc` they will also perform a retain. If you do find yourself having to retain some memory after you've allocated, then view it as [alloc+1] + [retain+1], which means that you have gone **two**, not one, levels up. This means that you need to release not once but twice. In summary:

- [alloc^{+1}] needs + [release^{-1}]
- [alloc^{+1}] + [retain^{+1}] needs [release^{-1}] + [release^{-1}]

Alright!

You're still here! Awesome! Take a break for at least 6 hours, and don't sweat over not getting all of the code you've been digging around in here. Hope you Zenned and zoned out beautifully. See you in Chapter 4.

Chapter 4

Buttons & Labels with Multiple Graphics

In this chapter, we'll tackle our fourth program together, and it's time to quicken the pace a bit. As in Chapter 3, you'll be able to simply view the screen shots and implement the code if you remember most of the details—steps that have been described repeatedly in the previous examples. You'll get fewer figures pertaining to each step, yet more procedures; we will be using the short bursts of information introduced in Chapter 3.

In addition, as in Chapter 3, once you have completed the program, we will do a code review in the "Digging the Code" section. Initially, we will cover some of the same aspects and concepts we discussed in that section in Chapter 3, and then we will zoom in on some of the new code. Not only will we go a little deeper, but we will also expand our horizons to consider other computing concepts that link up to this deeper level of analysis.

You will probably also notice a change of style in Chapter 4, for we will be moving away from the "elementary" language used in previous chapters. I will also be doing less hand-holding for you with the images. I will start weaning you off arrows—all the information is there, so if you cannot immediately find what I am referencing in the text, you will need to think a little and find it. Think of it as an exercise to force your neurons to make some associations by taking baby steps. So, let's pick up the pace—a little faster, a little more advanced, and using more of the technical nomenclature.

Most importantly, when we get to step 29, we will take twenty minutes of class time to open the hood and really get our hands dirty delving into some critical code concepts that you will need to wrap your head around in order to move on through the book. Don't worry; I make it easy.

Again, if you don't grasp every concept and technique fully, that is perfectly okay! Relax and enjoy this next example. However, before we start our fourth app, we will take a brief glance at our road map.

Roadmap Recap

Thus far, we've gone through three examples where we said "Hello world!" from inside the iPhone/iPad. You've had an opportunity to familiarize yourself with the creative process in the context of programming apps: go in with an idea and come out with a tangible, working product. Several times I asked you to ignore heavy-duty code that I judged would be distracting or daunting. You may have also noticed that when you did try to understand some of this thicker code, it made sense in a weird, wonderful, chaotic way. Well, as we progress forward, we are going to make the "chaos" of the unknown less unsettling.

Before dealing with this issue, let me also put you at ease by telling you that when it comes to Objective-C, our programming language, I have yet to meet a single advanced programmer who actually knows every symbol and command. Just as in other industries, people tend to get very knowledgeable in their specific domains and specializations (e.g., integrating Google Maps to a game or an app).

An analogy I like goes like this: Car mechanics used to be able to strip an engine down completely and then build it back up—presumably better than it was. Nowadays, car mechanics are very specialized, with only a handful knowing how to completely strip down and rebuild a specific modern-day car. We get an expert in Ford hybrid engines, or an expert in the Toyota Prius electrical circuitry, or a specialist in the drum brakes that stop big rigs, and so on. There is nothing wrong with this!

This is similar to how you are proceeding. You have just gotten your hands greasy and dirty by *successfully* programming three apps. Now, if all goes according to plan, you are going to delve even deeper when you get to step 29 and walk toward the future, brimming with confidence. I know from experience that the confidence of my students can be derailed if they are intimidated or blown away by too much complexity or technicality. I have found that students can handle bumps in the road if they know where they are going, and if they know that the rough stretches won't get too scary or dangerous.

helloWorld_04: A View-based Application

Right this second—feel good about yourself! You are already quite deep into the Forest of Objective-C. If you lose your way, remember that besides the information I present here in this book, including various screenshots, I also offer you screencasts, available at my website. You can use the short URL, go to *rorylewis.com* as indicated below where you click on the *Xcode 4* icon, and then go to either *video tutorial* or *downloads*:

Short URL: `http://ow.ly/50ksH`

Manual URL: `http://www.rorylewis.com` ⇨⇨ video tutorial / downloads

Figure 4–1. *Create or download three .png image files: a bottom layer, a top layer, and a desktop icon. Save them all to a beautiful, clean desktop.*

1. As usual, let's begin with a clean desktop and only four icons: your Macintosh HD and three image files (shown as icons in Figure 4–1). As I'm sure you have gathered by now, I think it's essential to have an uncluttered desktop, and I want to encourage you to continually hone your organizational mindset. Using our familiar shortcuts, close all programs. You are welcome to download these images (from either `ow.ly/5l1w8` for the downloads page or from the videos page at `ow.ly/5l1wS`), which will become key building blocks of this project, but we really want to encourage you to find and prepare images of your own. That way, you'll have more passion about this assignment. You have two basic choices at this point: download the images from the aforementioned links or prepare your own. Assuming that you are willing to go through the effort of creating three distinct photo files of your own choosing, pay attention to the following guidelines.

Figure 4–2. *STAIR.png; this is the background image—or bottom layer.*

2. The size of the first picture, STAIR.png, as shown in Figure 4-2, will be the iPhone standard of 320 pixels in width by 460 pixels in height. This will be the bottom layer of two images, so we'll call it the *background* layer. Our background, then, is a photograph of the stairs leading out the back of the Engineering building, here at the University of Colorado at Colorado Springs. We will use this picture as a backdrop for a picture of Immanuel Kant—the greatest philosopher of all time—a man whose philosophy formed the basis of that of many of our founding forefathers who framed the Constitution. More importantly to us, he was the man who began mapping parallels between mathematical logic and words in speech. When the program is run, the background will display and, once a button is clicked, up will pop the photo of Immanuel Kant at the top of the stairs. Take a quick peek at Figure 4-39. How nice—Immanuel Kant has decided to return to University! This is our scenario then: You will find many times in programming that you will want your user to see a familiar background, and then when a button is pressed, somebody (or something) unusual or unexpected suddenly appears. This helloWorld_04 will teach you this.

Figure 4–3. *This is the modified top-layer image, which will overlay the background.*

3. In order to create the second image, which we'll call the *top* layer, copy the background layer photo, which, in my case, was `STAIR.png`. Then crop this copy to create an image with these exact dimensions: 320 × 299 pixels. Yes, I know the height is a strange number—but trust me! Now you have a roughly square copy of the bottom two-thirds of your background photo. Next, paste onto this a partial image—probably a cut-out of some interesting or unusual object. This will yield something like the image in Figure 4–3: Immanuel Kant, in front of the background scene. This modified top layer will, of course, be saved as a `.png` file. Thus, you will end up with a prepared top layer that consists of the bottom section of the original background photo, with some interesting person or object pasted over it. You can probably guess that we're going to program the computer to start with the background image, and then, with some user input, insert the top layer—with bottom edges matching up flush, of course. This will give the illusion that our interesting guest, or object, suddenly materialized out of nowhere. Our top layer will not affect the space near the upper part of the background; we are reserving this region for the text that we will also direct the computer to insert. We go this route because the iPhone and iPad do not support `.png` transparency.

Figure 4–4. *This is the image for the screen icon!*

4. The third image file is an icon of your choice. As in the previous chapter, you may want to customize your icon. In my case, I took a portion of the photograph of Immanuel Kant's face and put it into my "icon" file, as shown in Figure 4–4. Once you have all three of these images—the bottom layer, the top layer, and the icon—save them onto your desktop, which will make it look similar to that of my desktop displayed in Figure 4-1.

NOTE: Remember that icons for the iPhone have a recommended size of 57 x 57 pixels as illustrated in Figure 4-4. However, note that if your app is an iPad-only specific app, then you will want to make a cool, slightly larger icon of 72 × 72 pixels. Be sure to stay mindful of these dimensions.

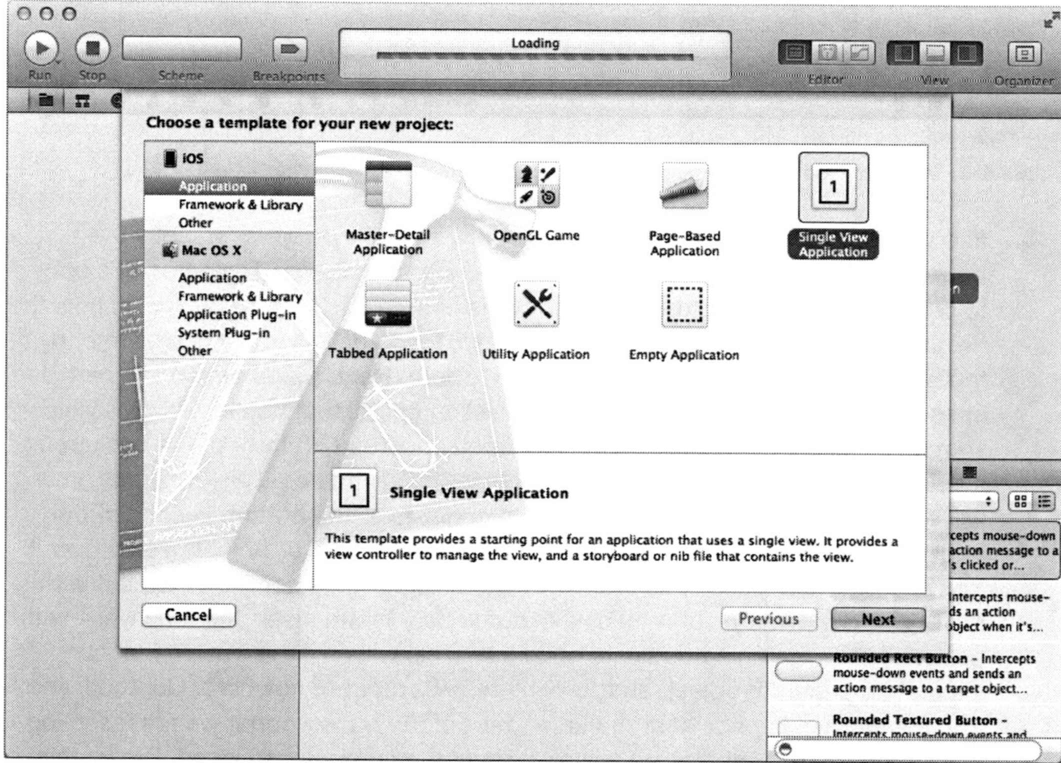

Figure 4–5. *Enter ⌘⇧N and select Single View Application from the New Project window.*

5. Now, just as you did in the first example, launch Xcode and open a new project by using your keyboard shortcut: ⌘⇧N. Your screen should show the New Project Wizard as depicted in Figure 4–5. You may find that your *Single View Application* template was highlighted by default, because of the last example. If, however, your *View-based Application* template is not selected, then click on the *View-based Application* icon, and then click on the *Next* button, as indicated in Figure 4–5.

   You may be thinking that a view-based application template is usually used to help us design an application with a single view, and that we should pick another option—because we've just made two views, the image of the stairs and the modified image of the stairs with Immanuel Kant in it. This reasoning would appear to be sound because navigation-based applications yield data hierarchically, using multiple screens. That choice would seem to be the right one for this project, except that this is actually not the case here.

We will be dealing with only one perspective onto which we will superimpose an image, not a view. If we were going to have portions of our code in one navigation pane, and other portions of our code in other navigation panes, then we probably would choose a navigation-based application. In this current project, though, we are going to manipulate one view in which we will superimpose images, rather than navigate from one pane to another. In essence, we'll be playing tricks with a single view.

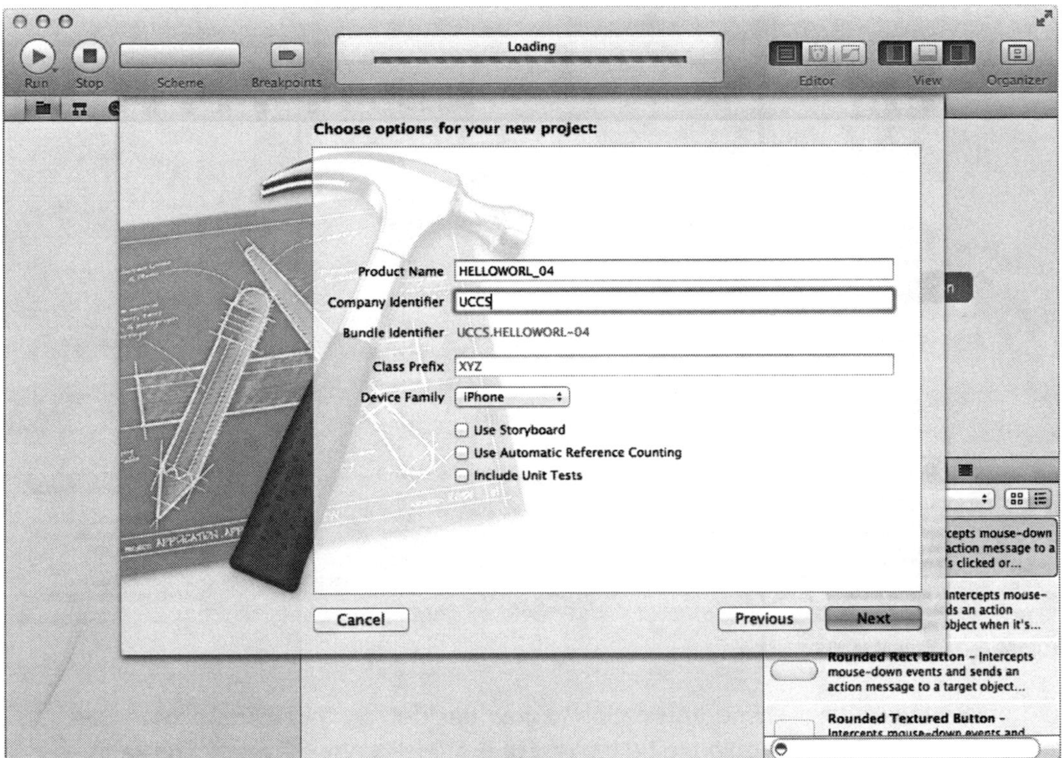

Figure 4–6. *Name your project and define whether it's an iPhone or iPad project. .*

6. Seeing as this is the fourth `helloWorld`, we will name it `helloWord_04`. When making the video example, I accidently hit the caps lock key with my big fat fingers, so mine is all caps, as you can see in Figure 4-6. I purposely kept all my errors on so that the code looks exactly as it does on the video here: `ow.ly/5l2rb`.

NOTE: For the rest of this chapter, I will continue to call this app `helloWorld_04`, even though I accidently left the caps lock key on. You have named yours `helloWorld_04`, so this is how we will move forward.

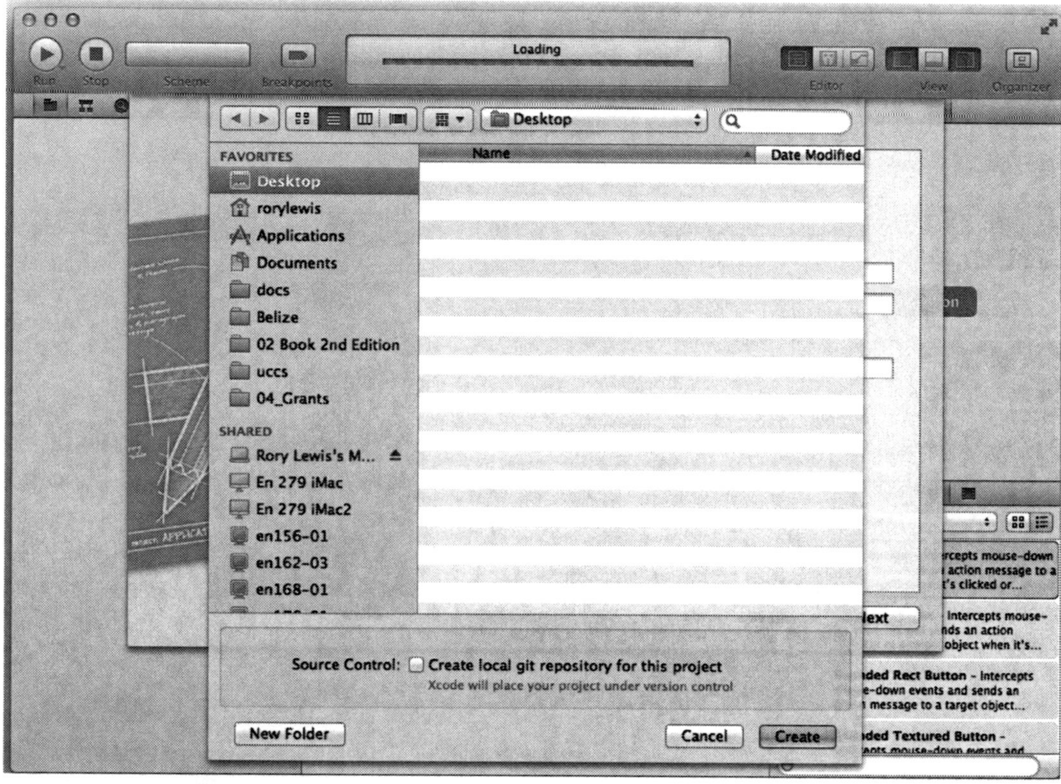

Figure 4–7. *Save it to the desktop.*

7. Save your View-based Application to your desktop as "`helloWorld_04`." See Figure 4–7. This is going to be the last of our "Hello World!" apps. I'd like to suggest that, once you've completed this program, you save all of these in a `Hello World` folder inside your `Code` folder. You will probably find yourself going back to these folders at some point to review the code.

   Later in the book, when we go into the details of Objective-C and Cocoa, there is a good chance that you'll scratch your head and say, "Damn—that sounds complicated, but I *know* I did this before. I want to go back and see how I connected these files in those 'Hello World!' exercises I did at the beginning of this book."

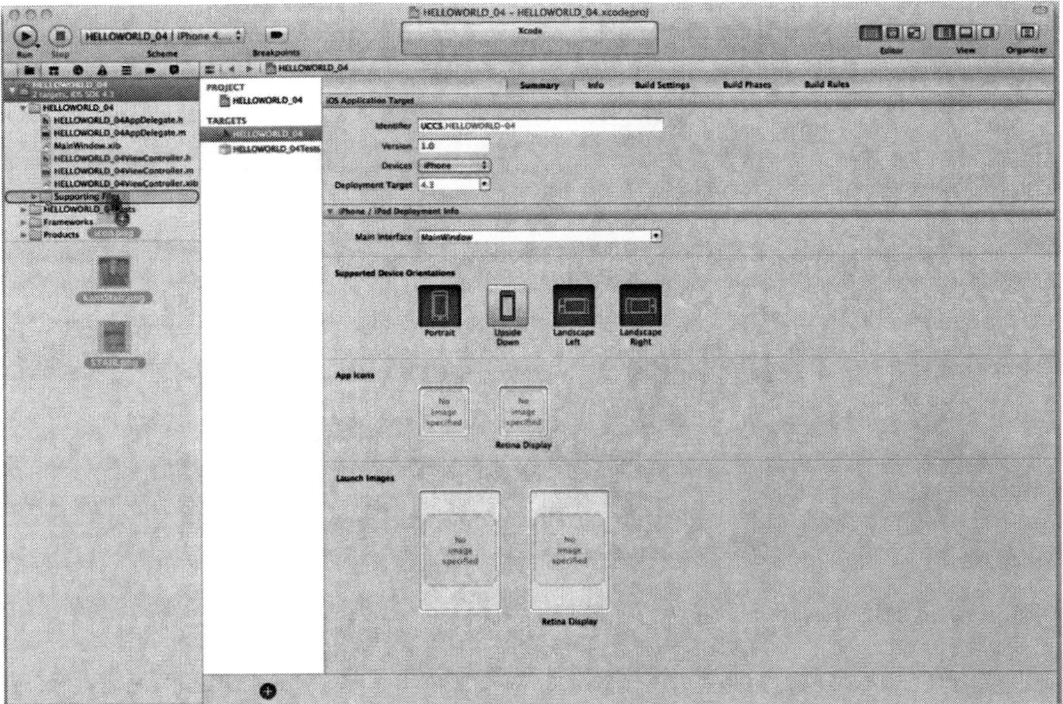

Figure 4–8. *Drag your three images into the Supporting Files Folder.*

8. Select all three of your images and drag them into your Supporting Files folder. I hope you are now beginning to see that Xcode has instantiated a project named `helloWorld_04`, as shown in Figure 4–8. As mentioned earlier, we're moving on from our elementary language and I will be throwing out some technical jargon that is more specific. Note that when the folder highlights, it means that the object is selected. Focus on where your cursor is—that is the point at which the folder will react. Once it highlights, drop the object in by releasing the mouse. Sometimes students get confused because it seems that the images should be able to drop into the folder but it will not highlight. This is because the folder opens, or highlights, only when you mouse carrying all of the pictures hovers over the folder. So remember that when you are dragging objects over to the folders, focus on where your mouse is and ignore everything else.

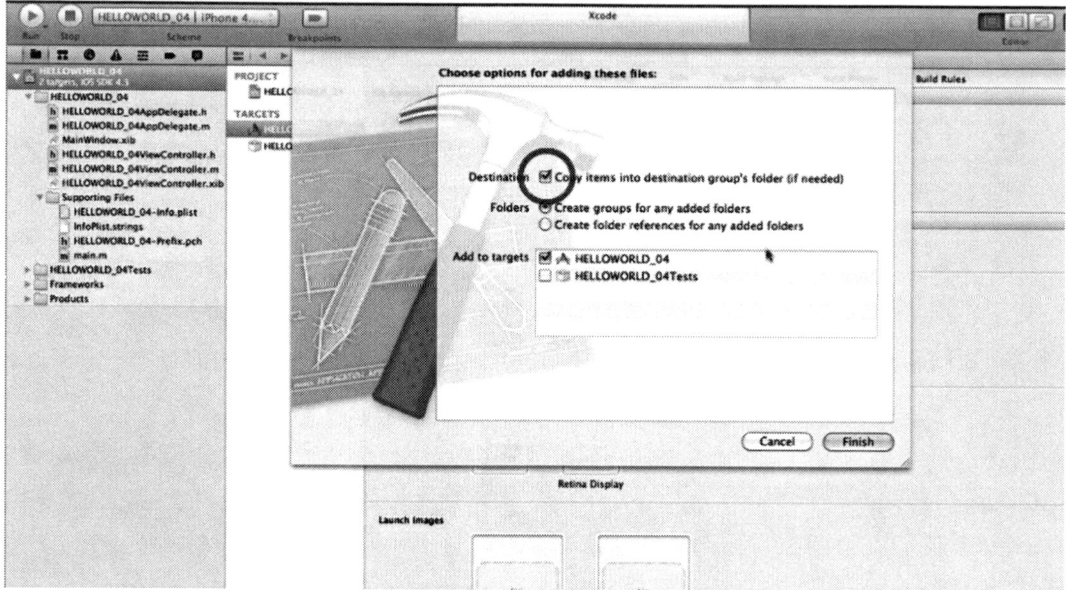

Figure 4–9. *Check the "Copy items into the destination group's folder…" box.*

9. After dropping the image into the `Resources` folder, you will be prompted to define whether the image will always be associated with its position on your desktop or whether it will be embedded with the code and carried along with the application file, as shown in Figure 4–9.

   We want it to be embedded, of course, so click the "Create groups for any added folders" box. Also, check the "Create groups for any added folders" box. Then click "Finish" (or press Enter).

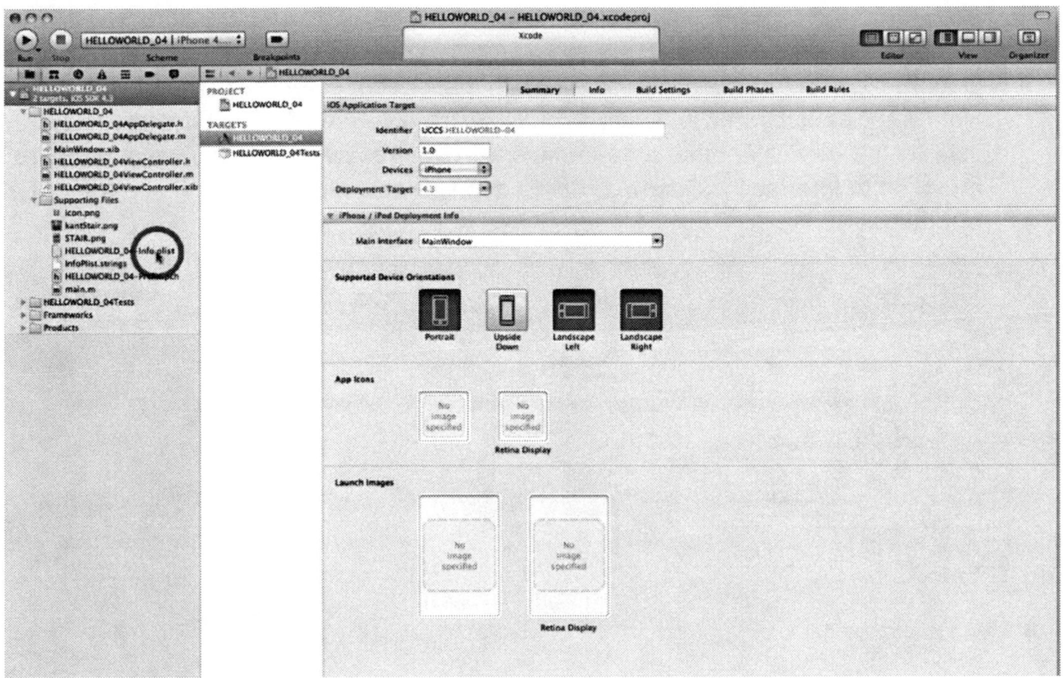

Figure 4–10. *Open the plist file so that we can associate our icon picture.*

10. We created an icon image file called `icon.png`. We want this one to show up on the iPhone/iPad, rather than the generic icon. To do this, double-click on the info.plist file in the `Resources` folder, as shown in Figure 4–10.

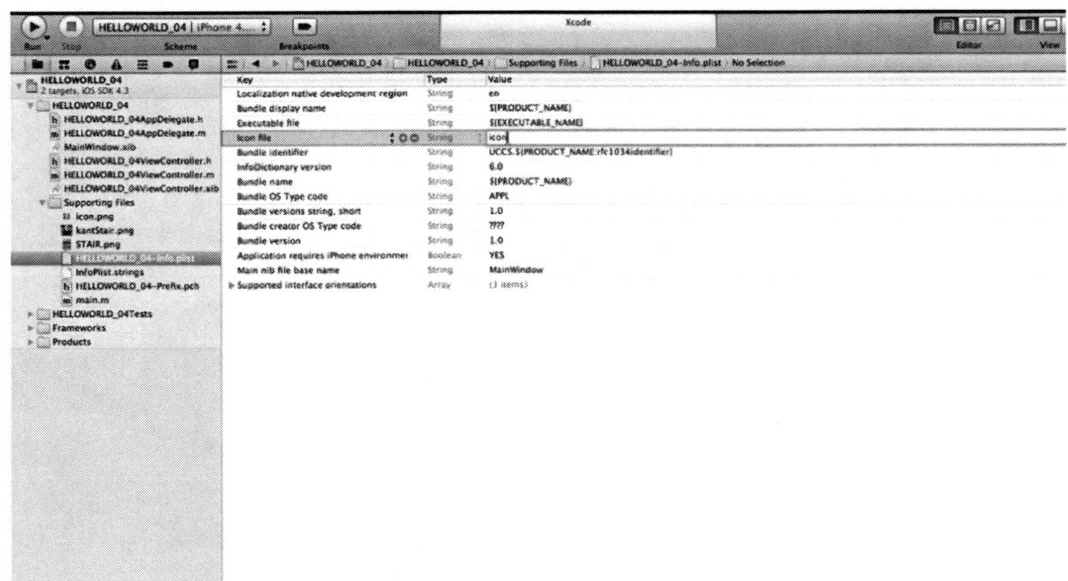

Figure 4–11. *Select the Icon file's value cell and enter the name of the picture you want to associate as the icon*

for your project.

11. Double-click on the Icon file's value cell. In that space, enter the name of your icon file: "`icon`" as illustrated in Figure 4-11. Now, save your work. The *plist* (property list), by the way, is another area that we will explore later. For now, we're ready to move on to Interface Builder in order to connect and associate various pieces of our puzzle.

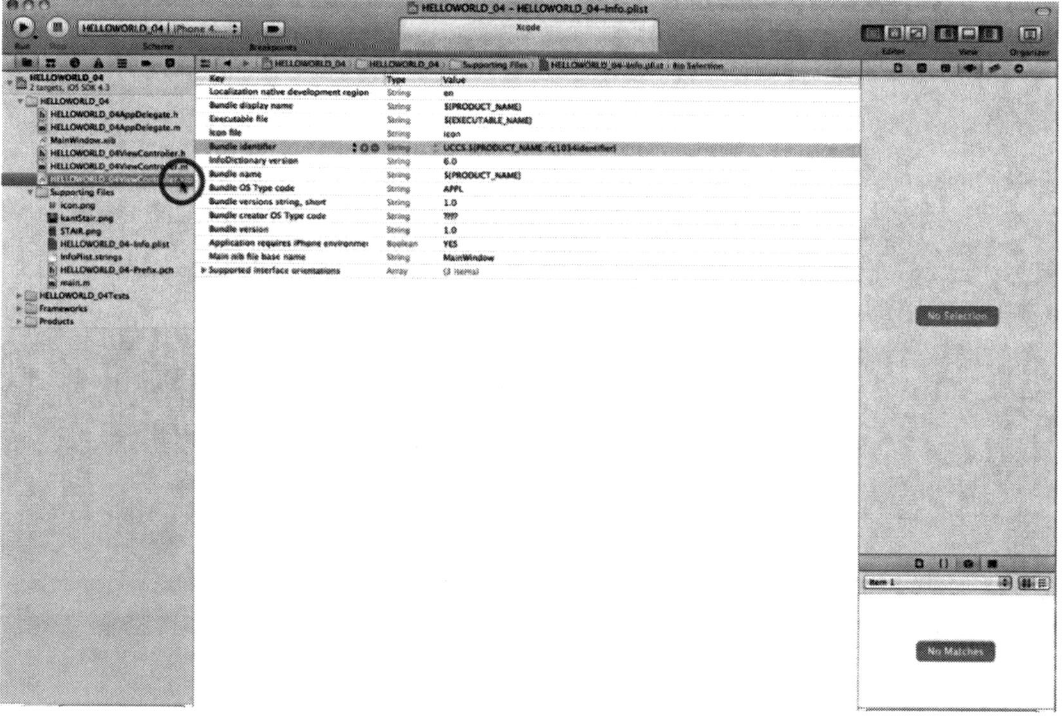

Figure 4–12. *Open your nib file.*

12. Click on your nib file, as illustrated in Figure 4-12, because it's time to start building the objects we'll need for our project. You should be seeing a pattern now—first we dump our images into the Resources folder, then we drag our objects onto the View, and finally we link the objects up with code.

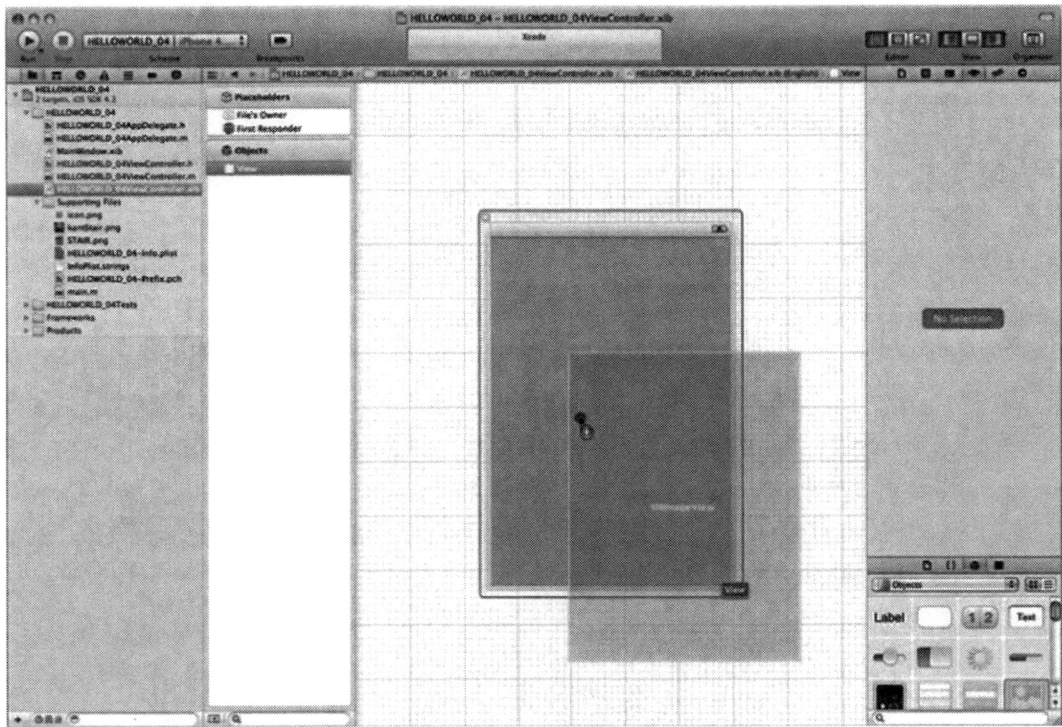

Figure 4–13. *Position the `UIImageView` onto the View screen, flush with the bottom.*

13. Your top layer image will be placed over the base layer when the user pushes the button. Therefore, we want to handle the base layer in the same manner as we have in the past. Scroll down in your library to the Cocoa Touch item folder and locate the Image View icons. Drag one onto your View frame, as illustrated in Figure 4–13.

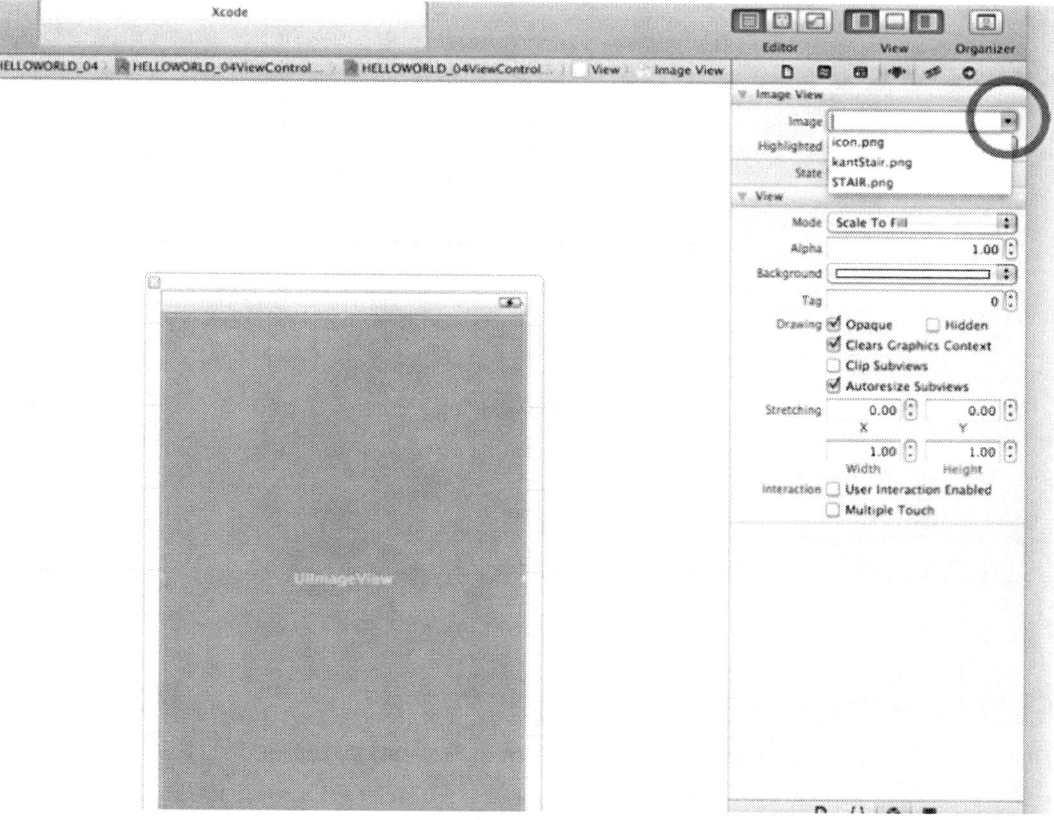

Figure 4–14. *Associate an image with `UIImageView`, which you've just dragged onto the View screen.*

14. We want to connect 320 x 460 `STAIR.png` to our Image View so that it will appear. Go to the Information tab of the Image View Attributes window, open the drop-down window, and select the image, as shown in Figure 4–14.

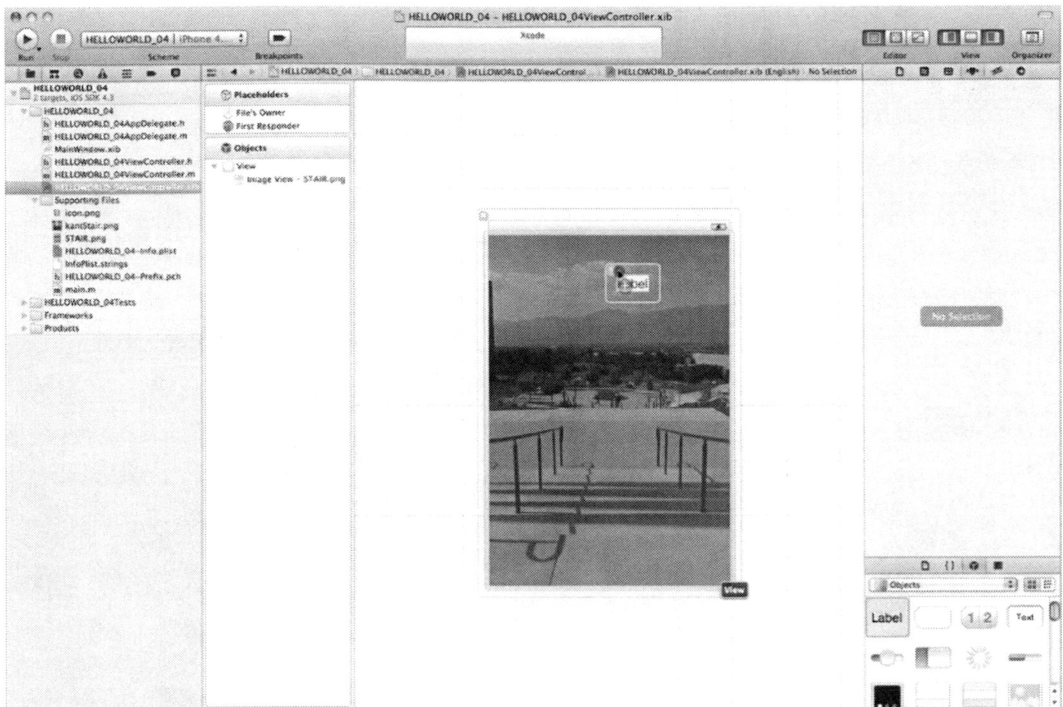

Figure 4–15. *Drag a label onto the View.*

15. Earlier, we decided that when the user presses the button, Immanuel Kant should appear and announce, "Hello World, I'm back!" We decided that the method we would employ would be a *label instance variable*—with a text property assigned with "Hello World, I'm back!" So, drag out a label that will be our instance variable, and we will assign the text "Hello World, I'm back!" onto the Base View later. When you put the label onto the View, repeat the way that you adjusted the size in the earlier assignments; i.e., widen it so it can fit this text. See Figure 4–15.

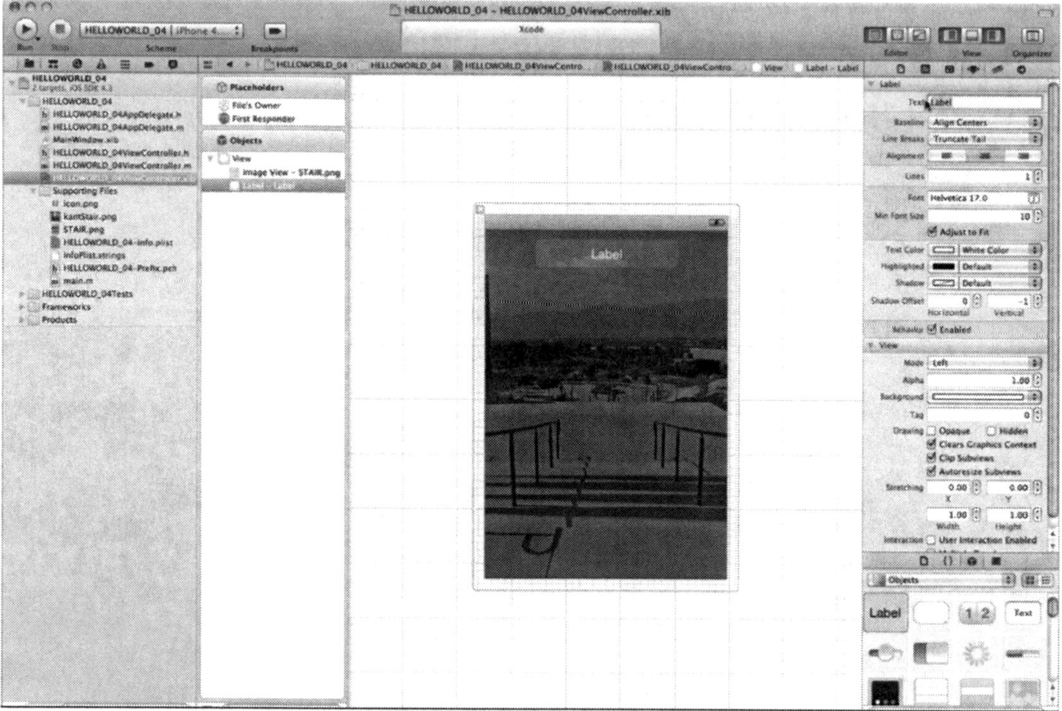

Figure 4–16. *Center the text and make it white.*

16. Just as you've done before, center the text and change its color to white in the Properties frame. Refer to Figure 4–16, and look over to the right-hand side to see that the center text and white text properties have been selected.

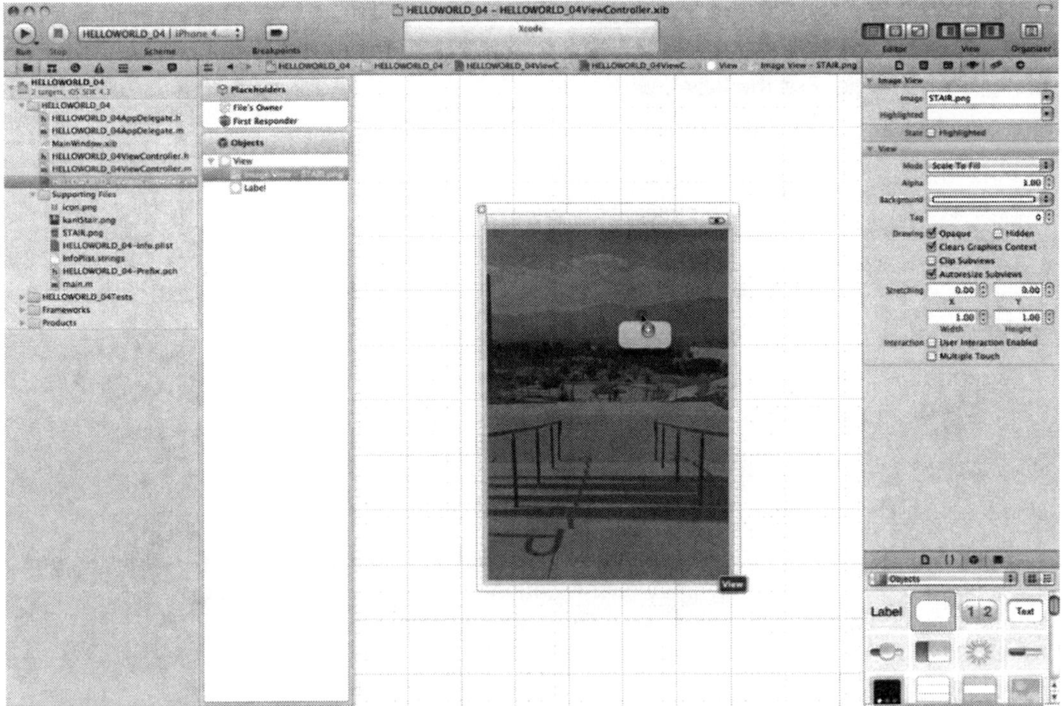

Figure 4–17. *Drag a button onto your base layer.*

17. We want the picture and the text to appear when a button is pressed, so we need a button. Go ahead and drag one onto your base layer and in its title field enter "Guess who's on campus?" as shown in Figure 4–17. When users see a button asking this question, they will be compelled to press it. When they do, we want Immanuel Kant to appear, saying, "Hello World, I'm back!" You may want to adjust the size of the button as we've done before. If you are inclined to make your button fancier than the one I created on the video, you may want it to look pretty cool and show some of the underlying image. While still in the Image View Attributes window, scroll down and shift the Alpha slider to about 0.30. Jumping ahead, you may want to start thinking about what we're doing in terms of the code we will soon write. We're looking at two `IBOutlets:` a label and the underlying base image. Each category "whispers" something to Interface Builder. One says that we want a `UILabel` class to use text that the pointer `*label` points to; the other says that the `UIImageView` class will put up an image located at a place the pointer `*uiImageView` points to.

Well, what have we done so far in Interface Builder? We've installed the background image and inserted a button that will trigger these two `IBOutlets`. Now, while still taking a minute to think ahead about what happens each time we drag outlets onto our header file, let's take a high altitude view of what we will be doing here:

```
- (IBAction)someNameWeWillGiveTheButton:(id) sender
```

This line, in fact, invokes our two friends, our two `IBOutlets` for the label and background image. For the label, with:

```
label.text = @"Hello World, I'm back!";
```

and the image, with:

```
UIImage *imageSource = [UIImage imageNamed: @"kantStair.png"];
```

To make the above all work in the implementation file, we will need to perform some action on the header file. We have to set the label and the image up—we say we need to declare them.

We will declare the label with:

```
IBOutlet UILabel *someNameWeWillGiveTheLabel
```

and we'll declare the image with:

```
IBOutlet UIImageView * someNameWeWillGiveTheImageView
```

Then, we will do something that we have not done yet and that I will explain at the end of the chapter in the "Digging the Code" section. We will perform something we call "Synthesis" on both of our `IBOutlets`. To do this we will run two "@property" statements:

```
@property (nonatomic, retain) IBOutlet UILabel *someNameWeWillGiveTheLabel
```

and for the image:

```
@property (nonatomic, retain)IBOutlet UIImageView *someNameWeWillGiveTheImageView
```

Also, we will synthesize the above in our implementation file, with:

```
@synthesize label, uiImageView
```

OK, that was a quick mental journey into the future. So, that means we're ready for action. We've created a button that will call our two friends; all we need to do now is to create the image and the label, and then associate them with the appropriate pieces of the code.

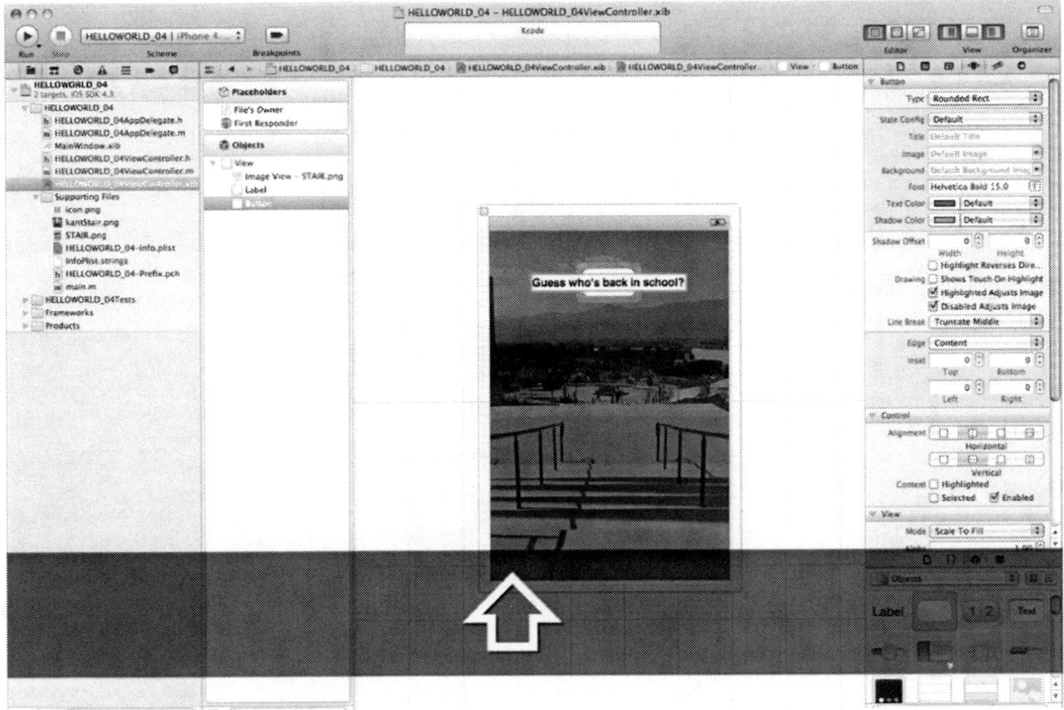

Figure 4–18. *Write the button text.*

18. We need the button to entice the user to press it. So we'll ask the user: "Guess who's back in school?" by double clicking on the button and writing the text in the button. You may notice that the button cleverly adjusts its size to accommodate the text width. See Figure 4–18.

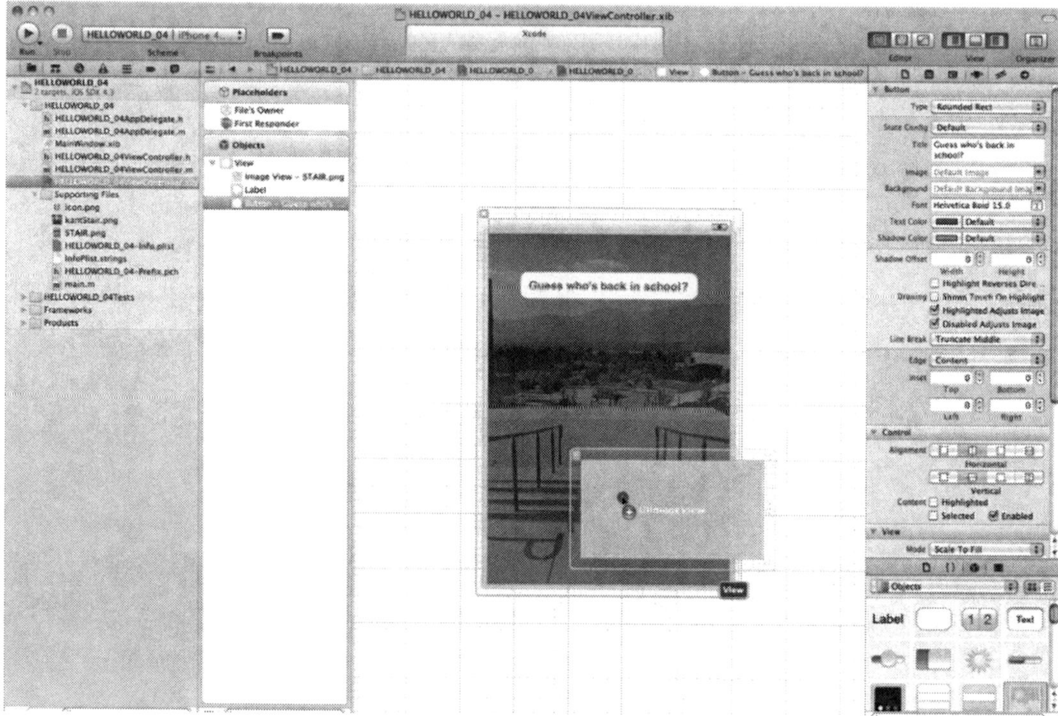

Figure 4–19. *Drag the second image view onto the View.*

19. Let's think about this for a second now. When the button is pressed, we want the `kantStair.png` image to appear on top of the background, `STAIR.png`. On what does it arrive? It's carried onto the screen by way of an Image View. Therefore, drag an Image View onto the screen, as shown in Figure 4–19. After you have dragged an Image View onto the screen, we want to place it flush to the bottom edge of the iPhone/iPad screen. We don't want the image floating in the middle of the screen, but instead to appear as if it's projecting from the bottom. Once you've dragged the image to the screen, just let it go. We have not yet configured the size or placement of the image. That's next!

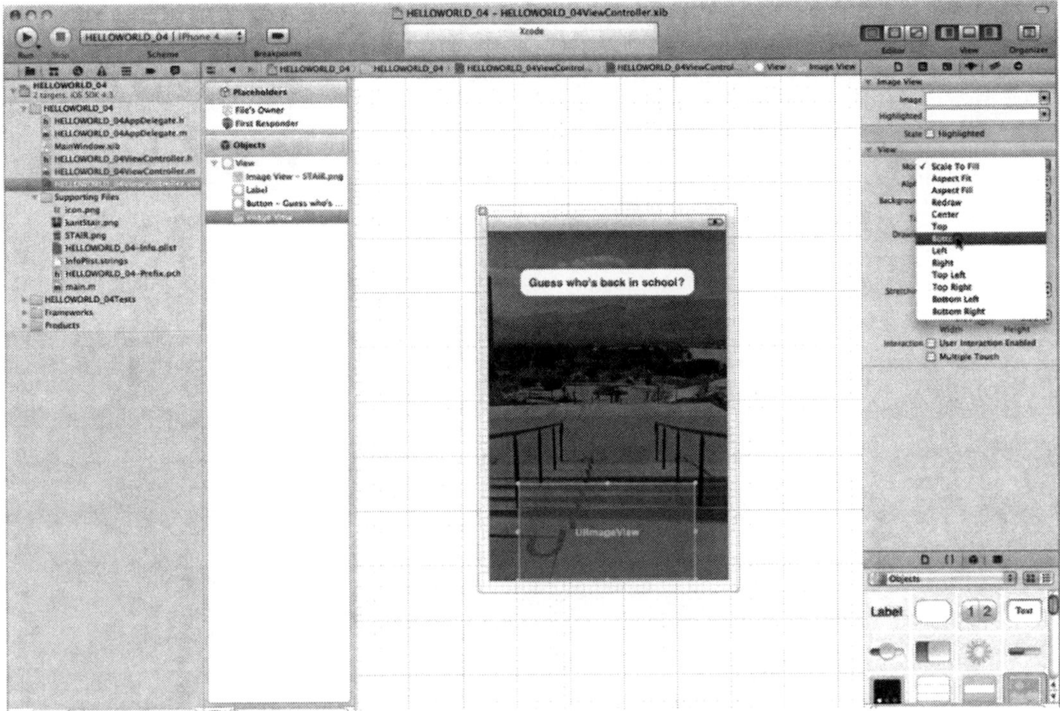

Figure 4–20. *Adjust the location of the second image view.*

20. Go to the Image View Application dialog frame and then click on the View tab. Here, you will see that the alignment option of Center is checked by default. We want to change that to Bottom, as illustrated in Figure 4–20. Before moving onto the next step, take a minute to align the label and button with each other, and in context with the center of the screen, as depicted in Figure 4–20.

You are now done with dragging items out onto the View. We have our label, a button, and two image views. Now let's save everything and start putting some code behind these items that we've dragged onto the view.

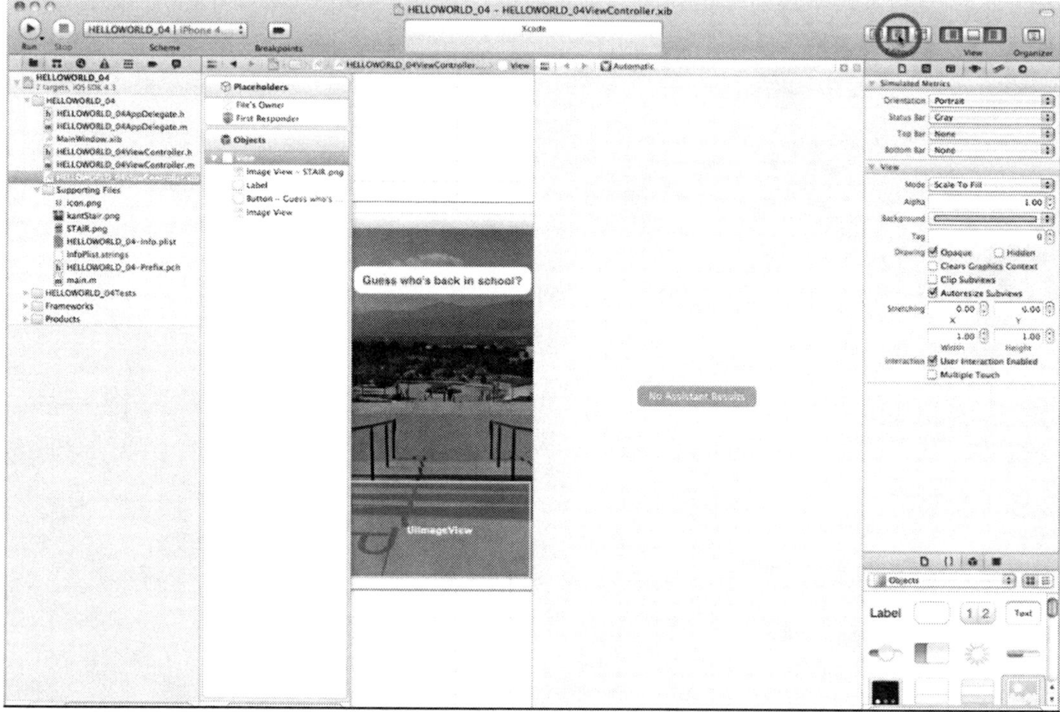

Figure 4–21. *Click on the Assistant.*

21. You now want to start tweaking your screen view to accommodate code. Just as we have done in the three earlier apps, we start moving from the Interface Builder view to our coding view by clicking on the Assistant, as depicted in Figure 4–21.

Figure 4–22. *Show the Navigator*

22. The second item we need to show after invoking the Assistant is the Navigator, as illustrated in Figure 4–22.

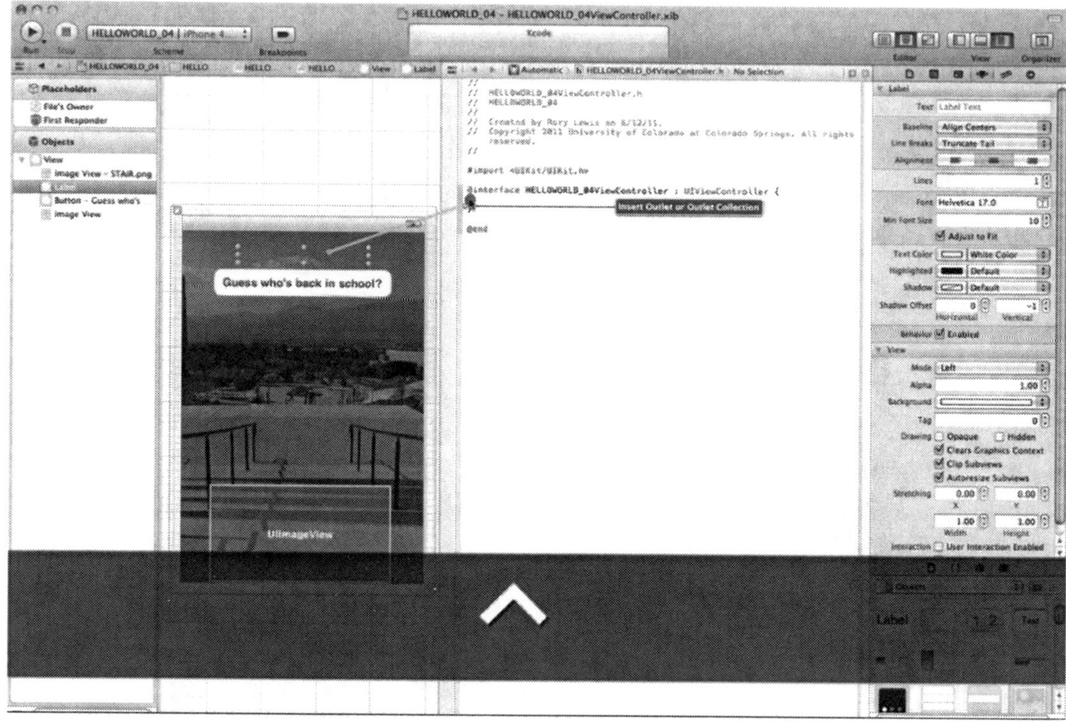

Figure 4–23. *Control-drag a connection from your label in Interface Builder into your header file.*

23. As shown in Figure 4–23, after clicking once on the label in your Interface Builder, Control-drag it into your header file, located inside the squiggly brackets of the `@interface` directive. Make sure that you keep on control-dragging out until you see the insertion indicator, as shown in Figure 4–23.

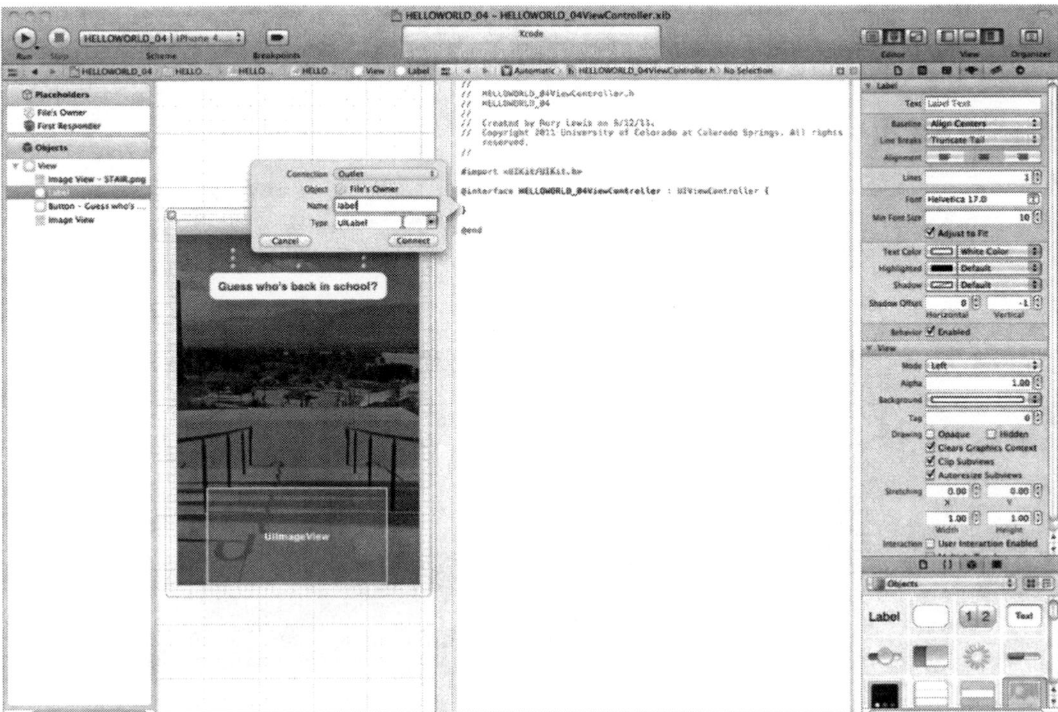

Figure 4–24. *Let's name the label outlet "label".*

24. As shown in Figure 4–24, when you've controlled-dragged your label out to the `@interface` directive, drop it in by letting go of your mouse and then call it "label" and leave it as an "outlet."

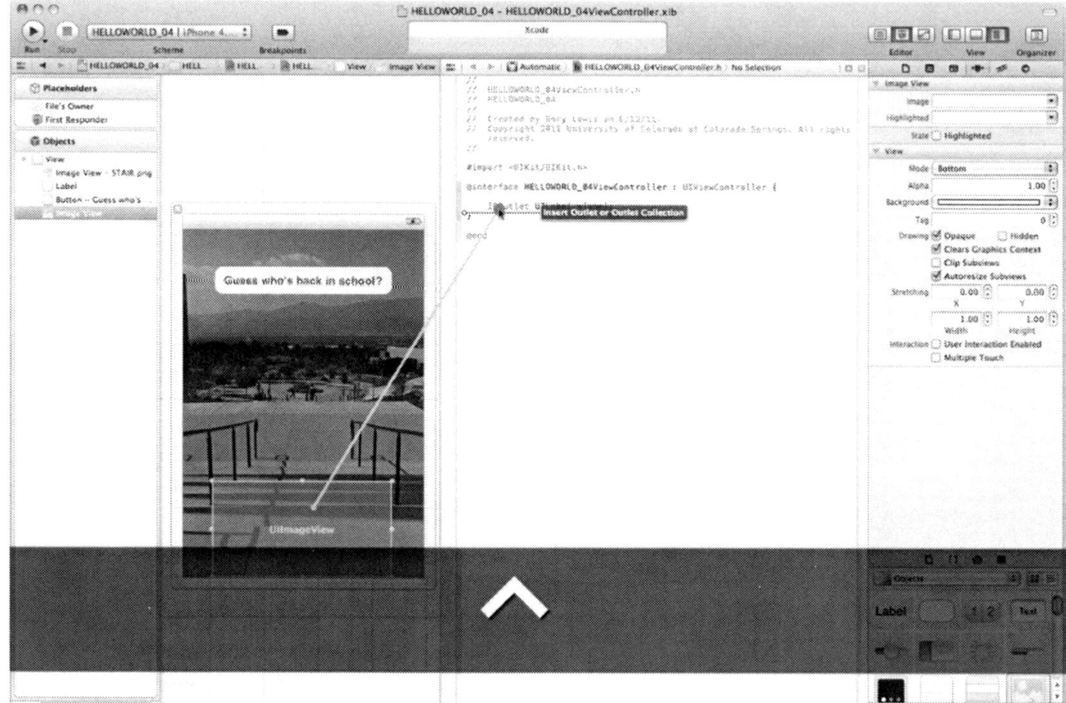

Figure 4–25. *Control-drag a connection from your second* `UIImageView` *in Interface Builder into your header file.*

25. After clicking once on the second `UIImageView` in your Interface Builder, control-drag it until you see the insertion indicator as shown in Figure 4–25. Make sure that when you control-drag into your header file, you go between the squiggly brackets of the `@interface` directive—directly under the label Outlet you've just created.

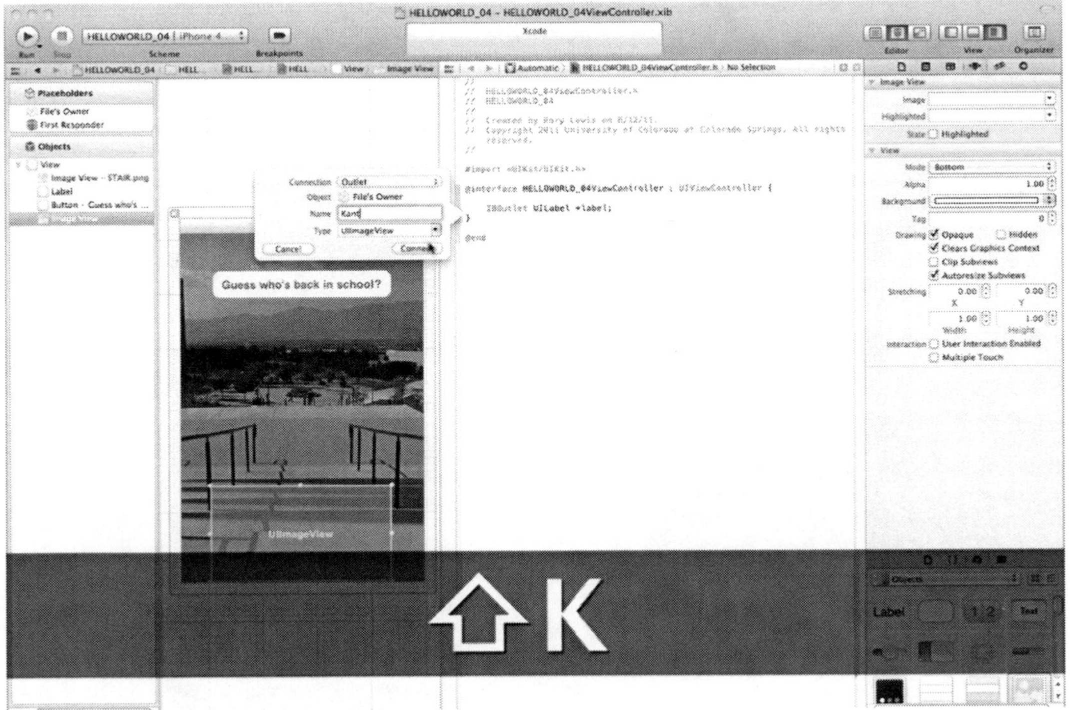

Figure 4–26. *Let's name the second* `UIImageView` *outlet "Kant".*

26. As shown in Figure 4–26, when you've control-dragged from the second `UIImageView` out to the `@interface` directive, drop it in by letting go of your mouse and then call it "Kant" and leave it as an "outlet" connection type.

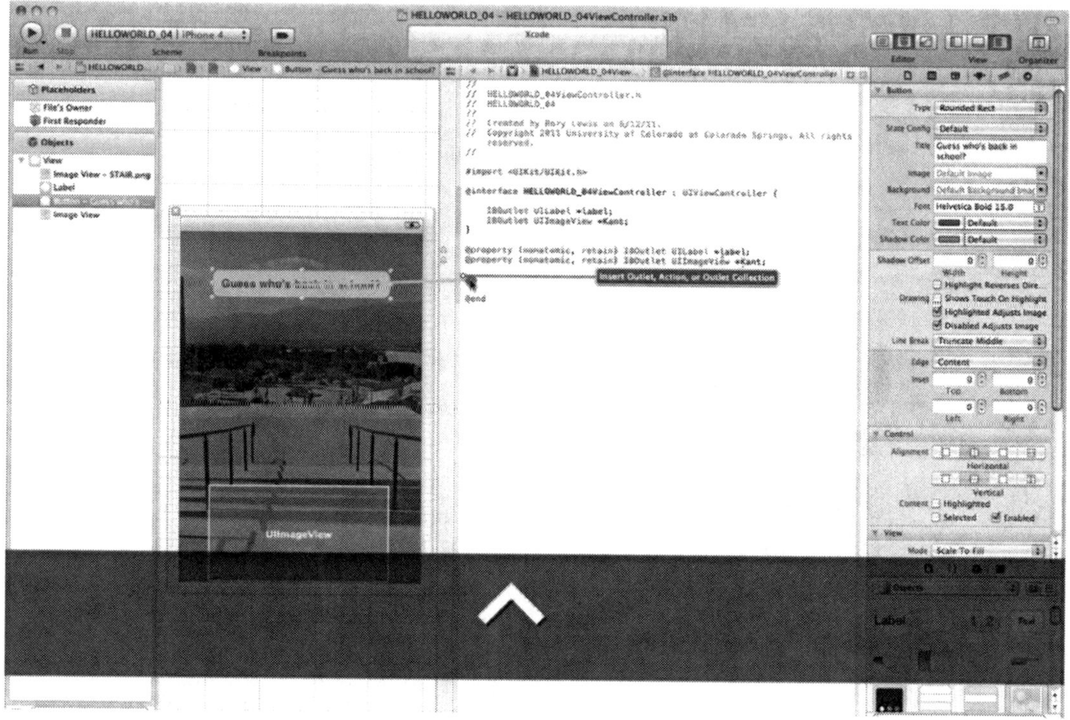

Figure 4–27. *Control-drag the button into your header file.*

27. Click once on your button and control-drag to the area below the `@interface` directive and its squiggly brackets. This is shown in Figure 4–27.

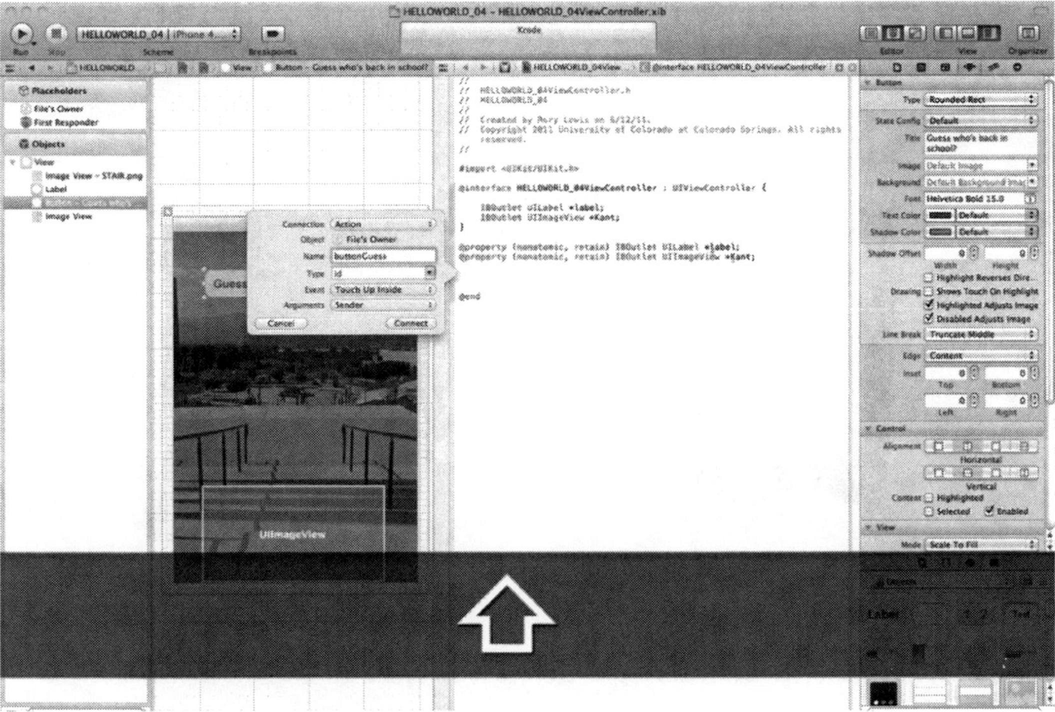

Figure 4–28. *Open the drop-down menu and change the type of connection to an Action.*

28. Change the connection type in the top drop-down menu in the dialog box from an Outlet to an Action. This is just like we did before. See Figure 4–28.

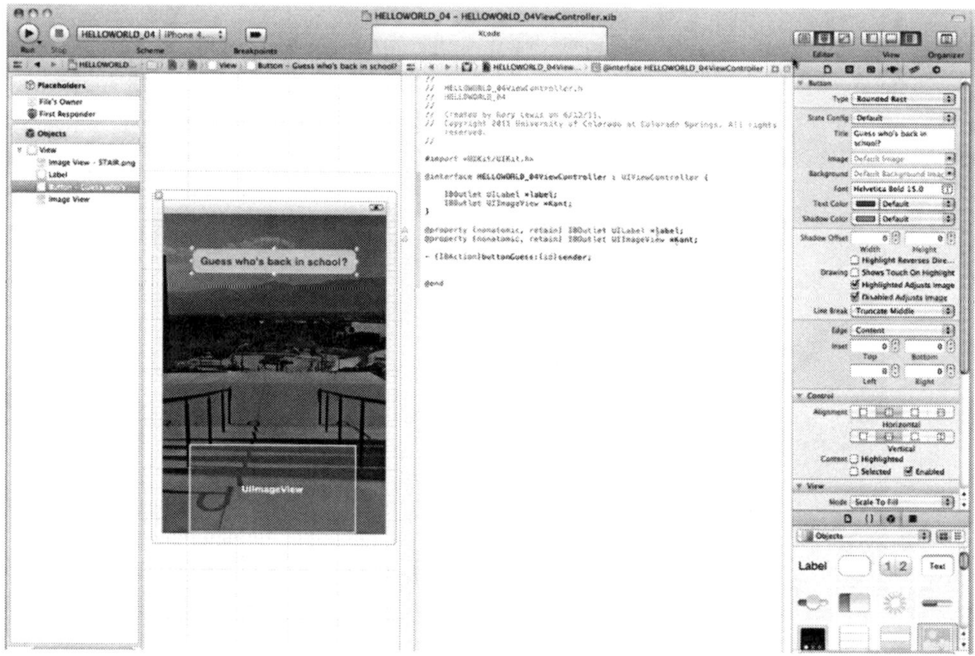

Figure 4–29. *This is how your code should appear, after you've completed the Synthesize and Button actions.*

29. At this point, we are going to focus and think about what we're doing. In class, I make sure that the students are 100% focused on this section. I force them to rewrite this section in their own words. I also include this section on quizzes, mid-term examinations, and the final examination. For readers at home, I will ask that you read this when you have a fresh mind and that you re-read it and convert the following into your own notes. Get up, get a pen and paper, and rewrite this section in your own words—just like I make my students do in the lecture hall.

> **NOTE:** Do not write this on your Mac because then you will start to cut and paste. Get up and grab a pen and a piece of paper. This is critical.

We are going to write statements that I've alluded to earlier that we called "synthesize" statements. However, to really grasp it, we need to dig a little deeper into outlets and actions as well, so in this section we will talk about `IBOutlets`, pointers, properties of management & control, and adding `IBActions`. However, before we get into this, let's look at what you have in your header file, what we will change, and then what we're going to focus on.

This is what your code looks like so far (Figure 4-29):

```
#import <UIKit/UIKit.h>

@interface helloWorld_04ViewController : UIViewController {
```

```
    IBOutlet UILabel *label;
    IBOutlet UIImageView *Kant;
}

- (IBAction)buttonGuess:(id)sender;

@end
```

You will type the bold text into your code right now, without thinking about what you're doing:

```
#import <UIKit/UIKit.h>

@interface helloWorld_04ViewController : UIViewController {

    IBOutlet UILabel *label;
    IBOutlet UIImageView *Kant;
}

@property (nonatomic, retain) IBOutlet UILabel *label;
@property (nonatomic, retain) IBOutlet UIImageView *Kant;

- (IBAction)buttonGuess:(id)sender;

@end
```

Understanding IBOutlets

In previous chapters, we have already discussed the `.m` and `.h` extensions in detail. We've been doing what most Cocoa and Objective-C programmers do—start off by programming the header files. In geekspeak, you'd say; "After dragging out objects onto the View, we opened the header and control-dragged our `IBOutlets` and `IBActions` into the header file." If anybody were to ask you on the forum to explain, you may tell them to, "Click on the disclosure triangle in your `Classes` file and open the file with extension `ViewController.h`!"

You've already programmed three previous header files, so you should be accustomed to just flying over this portion of your code. However, this time we're going to put on the brakes and think about what we're doing. For all our previous examples, we've only had to use one `IBOutlet`, a thing that allows us to interact with the user. Let's get more technical and specific, for that statement is too elementary. Let's dig deeper into what an `IBOutlet` is so that, when we get to the "Digging the Code" section, you'll be able to really understand it.

Looking at the code in bold, let's see if we can find our way to a deeper understanding of these elements:

```
#import <UIKit/UIKit.h>

@interface helloWorld_04ViewController : UIViewController {

    IBOutlet UILabel *label;
```

```
    IBOutlet UIImageView *Kant;
}

@property (nonatomic, retain) IBOutlet UILabel *label;
@property (nonatomic, retain) IBOutlet UIImageView *Kant;

- (IBAction)buttonGuess:(id)sender;

@end
```

Look at the first line:

```
#import <UIKit/UIKit.h>
```

This is what permits us to use the `IBOutlet` keyword. We use `#import` to import the `UIKit`, which is the user interface (UI) framework inside the huge body of core chunks of code called `IPhoneRuntime`, which is a stripped-down version of the OS X operating system found on a Mac. Of course, `IPhoneRuntime` is smaller, so it can fit onto an iPhone or an iPad.

When we import the `UIKit` framework, it delivers to our toolbox the ability to use tons of code Apple has already written for us—called *classes*—one of which is the very cool and popular class that you've already used: `IBOutlet`. The `IBOutlet` keyword is a special directive called an "instance variable" that tells Interface Builder to display items that you want to appear on your user's iPhone or iPad. In turn, Interface Builder uses these "hints" to tell the compiler that you'll be connecting objects to your `.xib` files. Interface Builder doesn't connect these outlets to anything, but it tells the compiler that you will be adding them.

Keeping inventory of what we'll be using: 1) the background image of the stairs; 2) the top-layer image of Kant; 3) the text of what he will be "saying" upon his return to the campus. In our exercise, we'll be using two `IBOutlets`—one dealing with the text in our label where Kant says "Hello World, I'm Back!" and the other with our second view where Kant magically appears.

Knowing that we need two `IBOutlets`, we can visualize how it will look. We start by focusing inside the brackets that follow `@interfacetestViewController : UIViewController`. Our code will need to appear as follows:

```
#import <UIKit/UIKit.h>

@interface helloWorld_04ViewController : UIViewController {

IBOutlet UILabel *label;
IBOutlet UIImageView *Kant;
}

@property (nonatomic, retain) IBOutlet UILabel *label;
@property (nonatomic, retain) IBOutletUIImageView *Kant;

- (IBAction)buttonGuess:(id)sender;

@end
```

As you can see, by only looking at the bold code and imagining that you have not programmed anything else but the bold code, these `IBOutlets` are just placeholders; one will produce text for what Kant says, and the other will produce a picture that is superimposed on top of the background.

We know that when we shoot text out onto the iPhone or iPad screen we use the `UILabel` class. This class draws multiple lines of static text. Therefore, go ahead and type in `UILabel` next to your first `IBOutlet`, as shown in the following code. Now, consider what we will need for the second `IBOutlet`. We know that we want to impose the top layer image as shown in Figure 4–03. A good idea here would be to use the `UIImageView` class because it provides us with code written by Apple that can display either single images or a series of animated images. With this said, enter the `UIImageView` class next to your second `IBOutlet`:

```
#import <UIKit/UIKit.h>

@interface helloWorld_04ViewController : UIViewController {

IBOutletUILabel *label;
 IBOutletUIImageView *Kant;
}

@property (nonatomic, retain) IBOutlet UILabel *label;
@property (nonatomic, retain) IBOutlet UIImageView *Kant;

- (IBAction)buttonGuess:(id)sender;

@end
```

As you can see it now makes sense when we say that we have two `IBOutlets`:

- We let one call the `UILabel` class to control the text.
- We let the other call the `UIImageView` class to control the second image.

Pointers

Now that we have the means to push text and an image onto the screen of the iPhone/iPad, we need to specify which text and which image. We sometimes use predefined code, created by the folks at Apple, which does what it does by virtue of referencing or pointing to our resources—that is, our text and images. As you are beginning to see, this is the context in which we will be using pointers.

In previous examples, we told you not to worry about that star thing (*). Well, now it's time to take a look at it. Let's focus for a moment on how these (*) things—*pointers*—do what they do. We need an indirect way to get our text and picture onto the screen. We say "indirect" because you will not be writing the code to accomplish this—you will use Apple's code to retrieve these. You will call up pre-existing classes, and then these classes will call up your text and your image. That is why we say this is an indirect means of obtaining your stuff.

Consider this little analogy. Suppose you make a citizen's arrest of a burglar who breaks into your house. You call the police and, when they arrive, you point to the criminal and say, "Here's the thief!" Then the policeman, not you, takes the criminal away to be charged.

Now, you want to display text on your iPhone/iPad. You call `UILabel`, and when it "arrives," you point to your words and say, "Here's the text." Then the `UILabel`, not you, deals with the text.

You will do likewise when you want to display an image on your iPhone/iPad. You call `UIImageView`, and when it "arrives," you point to your photograph or picture and say, "Here's the image." Then, the `UIImageView` code, not you, deals with the picture.

Perhaps you're asking yourself what the names of these pointers are, or need to be. The good news is that you can give them whatever names you want. Let's point the `UILabel` to `*label` and the `UIImageView` to a pointer with the name of `*Kant`. So again, looking at the code you've just written:

```
#import <UIKit/UIKit.h>

@interface helloWorld_04ViewController : UIViewController {

    IBOutlet UILabel *label;
    IBOutlet UIImageView *Kant;
}

@property (nonatomic, retain) IBOutlet UILabel *label;
@property (nonatomic, retain) IBOutlet UIImageView *Kant;

- (IBAction)buttonGuess:(id)sender;

@end
```

Some of the clever people at Apple describe their reasoning for creating and coding `IBOutlets` as giving a hint to Interface Builder as to what it should "expect" to do when you tell it to lay out your interface.

- One `IBOutlet` whispers into Interface Builder's ear that the `UILabel` class is to use text indicated by the `*label` pointer.
- The other `IBOutlet` whispers into Interface Builder's ear that the `UIImageView` class is to use the image referenced by the `*Kant` pointer.

We're not done yet. After we tell Interface Builder what to expect, we need to tell your Mac's microprocessor—through the compiler—that an important event is about to descend upon it. One of the most important things your compiler wants to know is when an object is coming its way. This is because objects are independent masses of numbers and symbols that weigh upon the microprocessor and put significant demands on it, and so the processor needs to be told by you, the programmer, when it needs to catch the object and put it into a special place in memory.

Objects can come in a wide variety of flavors—as conceptually different as *bird*, *guru*, *soccer*, and *house*. So, to allow the processor to handle its job when the time comes, we need to inform it that each object we will be using in our code has two specific and unique parameters or features: *property* and *type*.

Don't freak out! Providing this information is really easy, and it consists of two steps.

The first step is what we just covered: we give the compiler a head's up about objects we will be using by defining their two specific and unique features: property and type. The second step is this: When the microprocessor receives this data, it utilizes this information by synthesizing it.

- First, we declare that our object has a *property* with a specific *type.*
- Second, we instruct the computer to implement—or *synthesize*—this information.

In other words, we tell the compiler about our object by declaring it, including specific descriptive parameters of its *properties*. Then, we give the compiler the go-ahead to implement our object by telling it to *synthesize* the object.

But how do we do this declaring and implementing? We use tools in our code called *directives*. We signal directives by inserting `@` before stating our directive. This means that to declare what property our object has we put the `@` symbol in front of the word `property` to make it a property directive: `@property`.

When we see `@property` in our code, we know it's a property directive. Similarly, when we want to tell the compiler to process and synthesize; that is, to do its stuff on our object, we put the `@` symbol in front of our synthesis statement: `@synthesize`.

Saying the exact same thing we said before, but translated into geekspeak, we get:

- The `@property` directive *declares* that our object has a property with a specific *type.*
- The `@synthesize` directive *implements* the methods we declared in the `@property` directive

Easy, huh? OK, just two more points now, and then we'll get back to our code.

Properties: Management & Control

The first elaboration I want to make is that we also need to specify whether this property will be *read-only* or *read-write*. In other words, we need to specify whether it will always stay the same or whether it can mutate into something new. In geekspeak, we call this *mutability*. For the most part, we will use Apple code to handle the mutability of properties with respect to our objects.

In order to instruct the Apple code to handle the mutability property, we'll designate the property as "nonatomic." To apply this term meaningfully, try contrasting "nonatomic" with "atomic." Recall that "atomic" means powerful, and it implies the ability to go into the microscopic world and to effect change. Therefore, "nonatomic" must mean not-so-powerful, more superficial, and unmanipulable.

If we designate a property (such as mutability) as *nonatomic*, we are basically saying, "Apple, please handle our mutability and related stuff—I really don't care. I'll take your word for it!" At a later date, you may want to take direct control of this property, and then you *would* designate it as "atomic." At this time, though, we will use the more relaxed approach and let Apple handle the microscopic business. So, when it's time to choose one or the other designation, just use *nonatomic!*

The second elaboration I want to make at this point deals with *memory management*. We need to address the issue of how to let the iPhone/iPad know, when we store an object, whether it shall be *read-only* or *read-write*. In other words, we need to be able to communicate to the computer the nature of the memory associated with an object—in terms of who gets to change it, when, and how. Generally speaking, we will want to control this information, and keep it in our own hands—that is, to *retain* it. As you move through the remaining exercises in this book, we are going to keep the code in our own hands; we will retain the right to manage our memory.

We can summarize the addition of these details to the property directives, and how we would modify the code, as follows:

- The `@property (nonatomic, retain)` directive says the following:
  - Mutability should be nonatomic. Apple, please handle this!
  - Memory management is something we want to retain. We will maintain control.
- The `@synthesize` directive implements the methods we declared in the `@property` directive.

We have one more layer of complexity to add to this mix. We add those directives in two different files. We define the `@property` directive with a statement in the header file, and then we implement it by using the `@synthesize` directive in our implementation file.

- Header File: `helloWorld_04_ViewController.h`

```
@property (nonatomic, retain) //"our stuff"
```

- Implementation File: `helloWorld_04_ViewController.m`

```
@synthesize//"our stuff" we defined in @property in the header file.
```

We will need to write two of these for each of our two `IBOutlets`: one for the text, and the other for the picture. In addition, because we're still in the header file, we need to repeat this when we synthesize it in the implementation file. OK, time to go ahead and enter your code:

```
#import <UIKit/UIKit.h>

@interface helloWorld_04ViewController : UIViewController {

    IBOutlet UILabel *label;
    IBOutlet UIImageView *Kant;
}

@property (nonatomic, retain) IBOutlet UILabel *label;
```

```
@property (nonatomic, retain) IBOutlet UIImageView *Kant;

- (IBAction)buttonGuess:(id)sender;

@end
```

Yes, that seemed like a lot of explanation just to say: `@property (nonatomic, retain)`. Remember, though, that we're deep in the trenches… we're telling the computer that we want Apple to take care of mutability, but that we want to retain control of the memory. Later, we will synthesize these commands in the implementation file, for both `IBOutlets`.

`IBOutlets`? Remember them? Oh yeah—let's return to that part of your program. The `IBOutlet` for the text is `UILabel` with pointer `*label`, so we entered the code to control the text for the label as follows:

```
#import <UIKit/UIKit.h>

@interface helloWorld_04ViewController : UIViewController {

    IBOutlet UILabel *label;
    IBOutlet UIImageView *Kant;
}

@property (nonatomic, retain)IBOutlet UILabel *label;
@property (nonatomic, retain) IBOutlet UIImageView *Kant;

- (IBAction)buttonGuess:(id)sender;

@end
```

The `IBOutlet` for the picture is `UIImageView` with pointer `*uiImageView`, so enter the code for the picture:

```
#import <UIKit/UIKit.h>

@interface helloWorld_04ViewController : UIViewController {

    IBOutlet UILabel *label;
    IBOutlet UIImageView *Kant;
}

@property (nonatomic, retain)IBOutlet UILabel *label;
@property (nonatomic, retain)IBOutlet UIImageView *Kant;

- (IBAction)buttonGuess:(id)sender;

@end
```

```
        IBOutlet UIImageView *uiImageView;
```

Are we done with the header file yet? Not quite. We need to look at our IBActions. We've analyzed our IBOutlets, both of them, but now we're going to analyze the IBAction we used for our... can you guess?

Adding IBActions

Yes, we needed a button! So we made an IBAction for our button, as shown in Figure 4–28. We could "go deep" again, into the code for the IBAction, but this has been a challenging section. Let's save the technical part of this element for "Digging the Code." Meanwhile, just enter the new code that is highlighted here. See if you can anticipate the functions of the different pieces—or parameters—and we'll see how close you are later.

This is what we will be focusing on:

```
#import <UIKit/UIKit.h>

@interface helloWorld_04ViewController : UIViewController {

    IBOutlet UILabel *label;
    IBOutlet UIImageView *Kant;
}

@property (nonatomic, retain) IBOutlet UILabel *label;
@property (nonatomic, retain) IBOutlet UIImageView *Kant;

- (IBAction)buttonGuess:(id)sender;

@end
```

GO OUT NOW, AND TAKE A BREAK.

Figure 4–30. *Leave the Assistant and click on the Standard editor.*

30. We now need to redraw our user interface so that we can work on our implementation file. We need to leave the Assistant editor and click on the Standard editor, as shown in Figure 4–30.

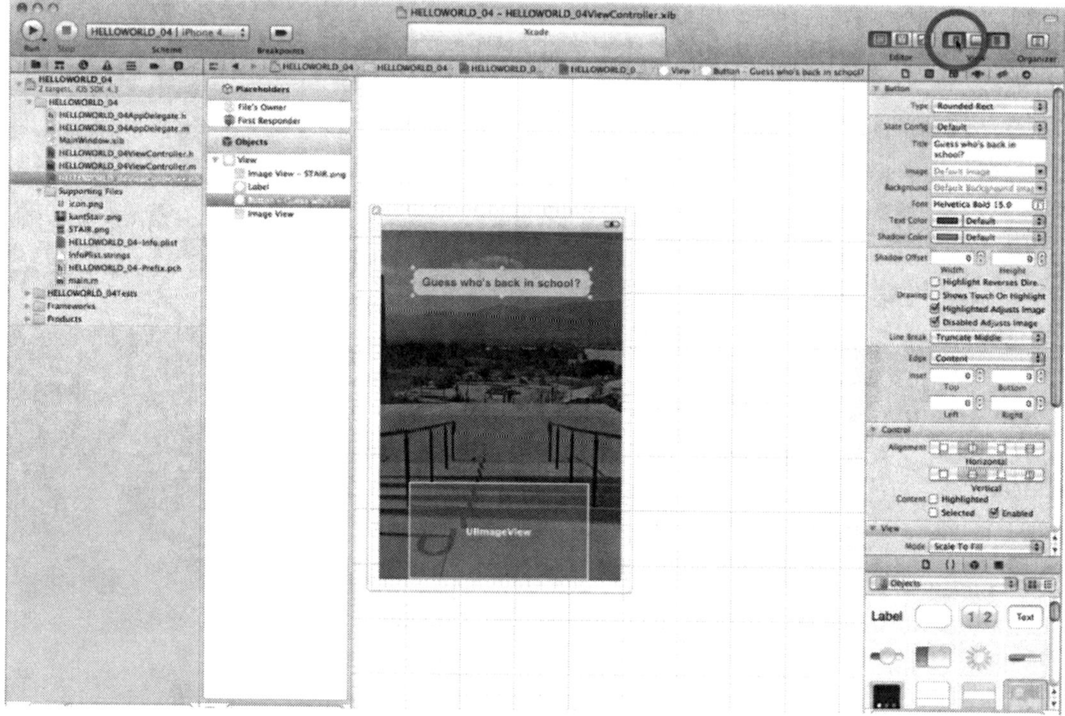

Figure 4–31. *Show the Navigator.*

31. We now need to show the Navigator, so we can jump from the header file into the implementation file. Of course, we have many different ways to do this, but for now just follow along, as this is the least complex means of doing this. See Figure 4–31.

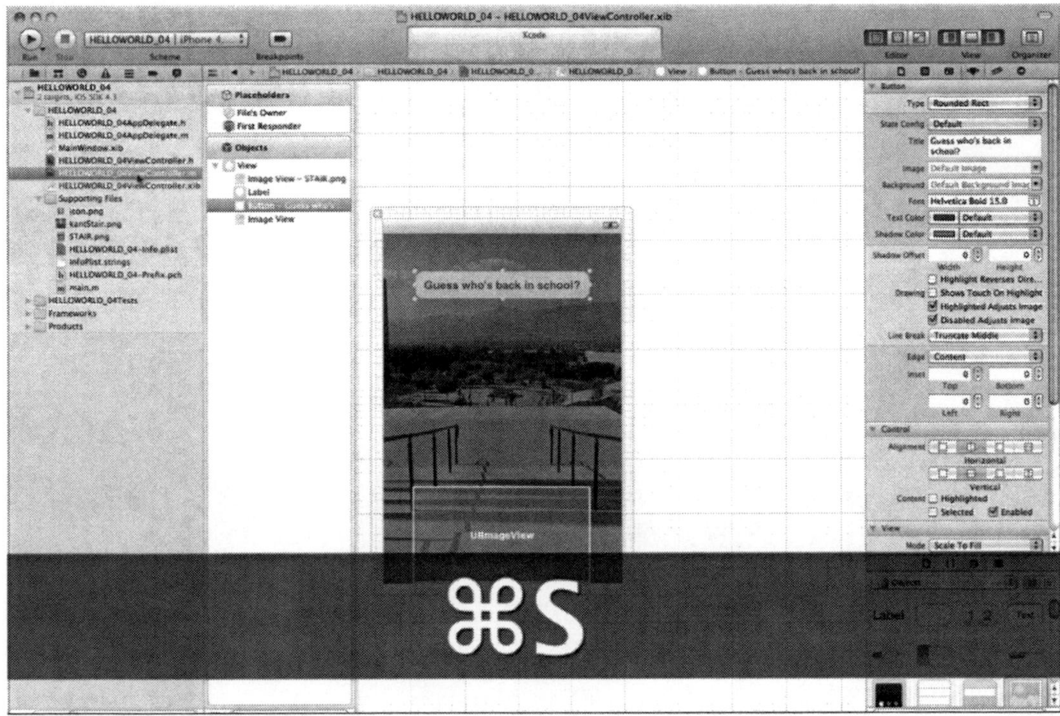

Figure 4–32. *Save your work and open the implementation file..*

32. Right now, the Interface Builder is showing our `.nib` file. Save everything and then go to your Navigator and click on the implementation file (`.m`), as shown in Figure 4–32.

Figure 4–33. *With the implementation file open we can now code.*

33. Now that you have your implementation file open, let's look at Figure 4–33 and first think of a means for providing synthesis. We've gone over making the `@property` directives for our label text and Kant image in the header file so that we would then have code the `@synthesis` statements for these two `IBOutlets` in our implementation file—so let's do it. Type in your synthesis code as shown below:

```
#import "helloWorld_04ViewController.h"

@implementation helloWorld_04ViewController
@synthesize label, Kant;

- (void)dealloc
{
    [label release];
    [Kant release];
    [super dealloc];
}
...

- (IBAction)buttonGuess:(id)sender {
}
@end
```

Figure 4–34. *Delete the* `viewDidLoad` *code.*

34. We do not need the `viewDidLoad` code, since we are manipulating it a little differently. Therefore, select it and then delete it, as shown in Figure 4–34.

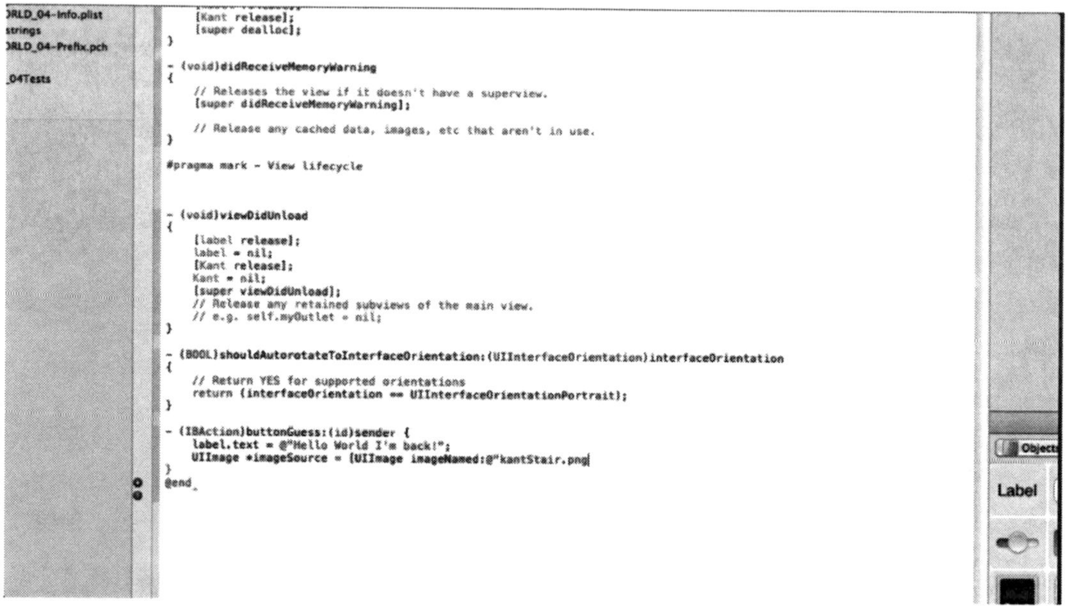

Figure 4–35. *Write the first two lines of the* `buttonGuess` *method.*

35. As indicated in Figure 4–35, we are now ready to program the code that will execute when the user presses the button. In other words, we are now ready to program the button's code. Scroll down until you get to the `buttonGuess` method that exists, but is currently empty.

```
#import "helloWorld_04ViewController.h"

@implementation helloWorld_04ViewController
@synthesize label, Kant;
...

- (IBAction)buttonGuess:(id)sender {

}

@end
```

When the user runs this app and presses the button, the image of Kant will appear instantly on top of the background staircase. He is going to "say" something via the embedded text. How about, "Hello World, I'm back!" To accomplish this, we need to associate the label instance variable with a text property assigned with our desired text as follows:

```
#import "helloWorld_04ViewController.h"

@implementation helloWorld_04ViewController
@synthesize label, Kant;
...

- (IBAction)buttonGuess:(id)sender {
```

```
label.text = @"Hello World I'm back!";
}

@end
```

Having completed the task of coding for the text, we now need to add the code that will cause the image of Kant to appear. For this, we will use a class method called imageNamed that will display the kantStair.png image, the top-layer photo we prepared at the beginning of this project. Enter the line bolded in the following code, immediately under the code you just entered for the text:

```
#import "helloWorld_04ViewController.h"

@implementation helloWorld_04ViewController
@synthesize label, Kant;
...

- (IBAction)buttonGuess:(id)sender {
label.text = @"Hello World I'm back!";
UIImage *imageSource = [UIImage imageNamed:@"kantStair.png"];

}

@end
```

Our pointer's name for the image is Kant, but right now the kant.png image file is in UIImage's assigned pointer called imageSource.

```
#import "helloWorld_04ViewController.h"

@implementation helloWorld_04ViewController
@synthesize label, Kant;
...

- (IBAction)buttonGuess:(id)sender {
label.text = @"Hello World I'm back!";
UIImage *imageSource = [UIImage imageNamed:@"kantStair.png"];
}

@end
```

We need to assign this automatically assigned pointer imageSource to the image of Kant as shown in the following code:

```
#import "helloWorld_04ViewController.h"

@implementation helloWorld_04ViewController
@synthesize label, Kant;
...

- (IBAction)buttonGuess:(id)sender {
label.text = @"Hello World I'm back!";
UIImage *imageSource = [UIImage imageNamed:@"kantStair.png"];
Kant.image = imageSource;
}

@end
```

If this doesn't quite make sense at the moment, that's OK. There sure are a lot of entities with "image" as part of their name, object, or association, and it is confusing. We'll be examining this topic more thoroughly as we move forward, so, right now, don't lose any sleep over it! Figure 4–36 illustrates how your code should appear at this point. Now save your work by entering ⌘S, and give yourself a pat on the back. You have worked through the header and implementation files at a much deeper level than in previous chapters. Even though you have walked through some of these technical functions before, you braved them again while remaining open to a deeper understanding. You also tackled a very difficult concept: synthesis.

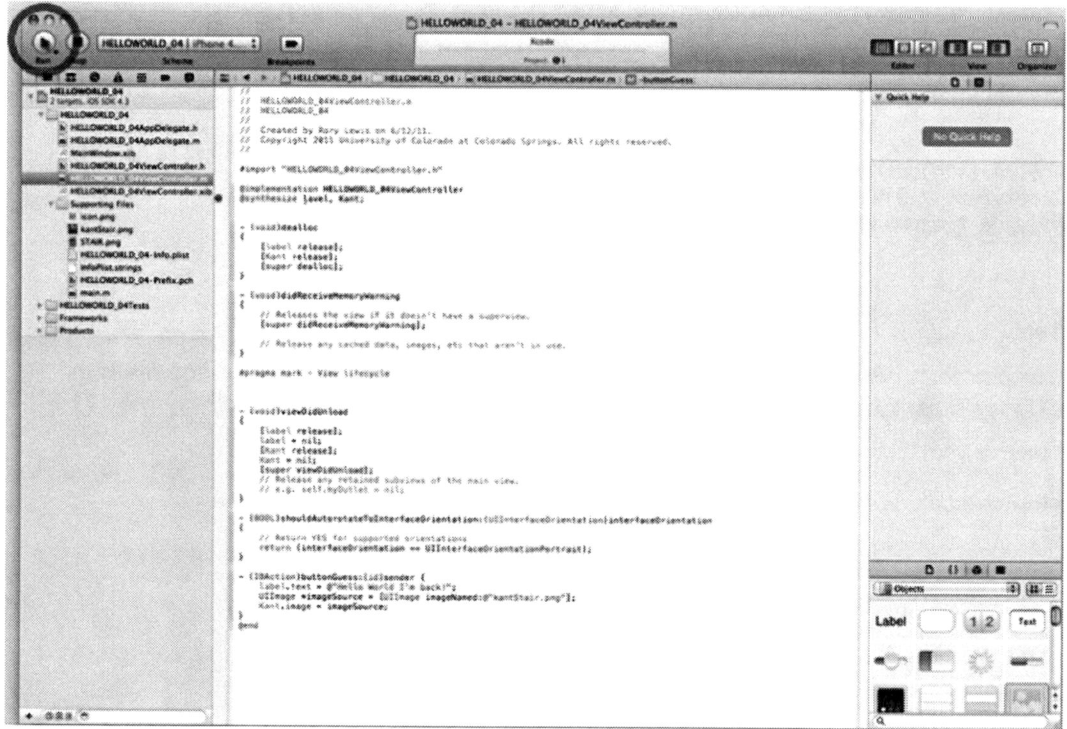

Figure 4–36. ***With the code all written, let's run it.***

36. Now that we are through writing our code, let's run it and see if we have any errors. See Figure 4–36.

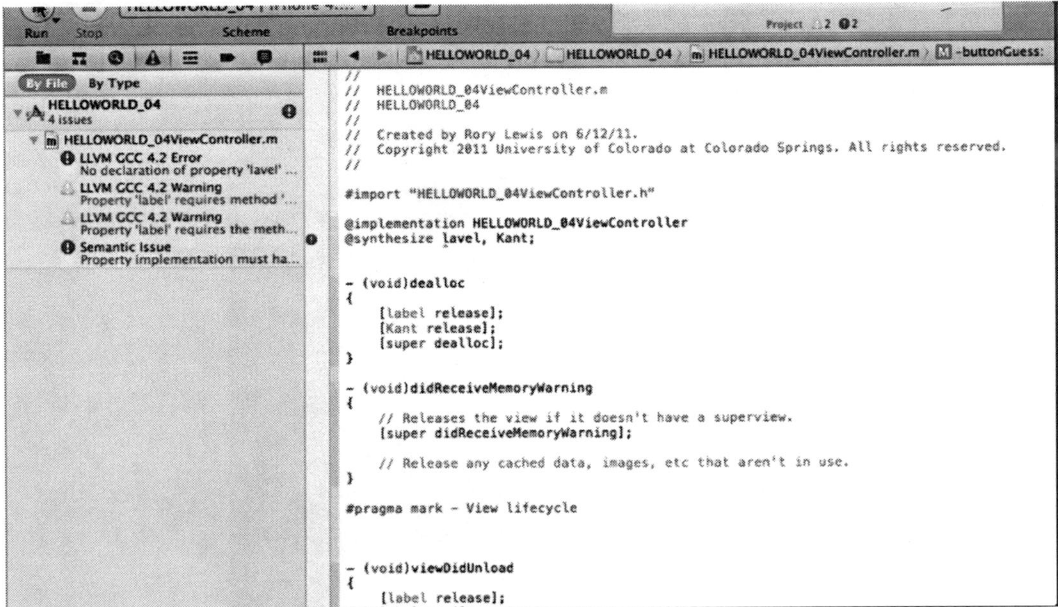

Figure 4–37. *Error! Misspelled label.*

37. As seen in Figure 4–37, we have errors. Clearly `lavel` should be `label`, so I changed it to `label`. You, of course, type very much better than I do so this means nothing to you—unless you have been diligently following each step in the video. Nonetheless, with the typo fixed, let's save it and run it again.

Figure 4–38. *Your screen as it runs.*

38. Figure 4–38 shows your screen with `helloWorld_04` running with the button clicked. Notice that the icons are still on the side, with the `helloWorld_04` folder below it.

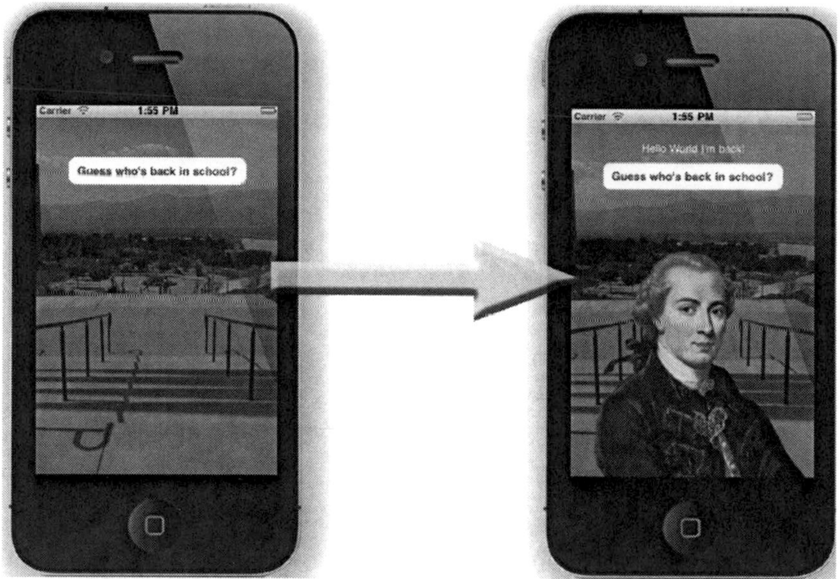

Figure 4–39. *The two* `helloWorld_04` *views.*

39. Figure 4–39 illustrates the two views of `helloWorld_04`. The first view is what we will see when the app first opens. Your images will be different of course, if you used your own, but apart from the background image your screen should look very similar. The second image is what appears when the button is clicked. The label text appears and the second image is superimposed on top of the underlying image.

Digging the Code

In this section, let's zoom into some of the key components that we encountered earlier in this chapter. I want to talk a little more about `IBOutlets` and `IBActions` – specifically how these include keywords… and even *quasi*-keywords. We'll also touch on pointers and their relationship to addresses in the code.

IBOutlets and IBActions

Earlier, we worked with `IBOutlet` and `IBAction` keywords, and now we're going to talk about a couple of related concepts. Strictly speaking, these are considered by many programmers to be "quasi-keywords."

The Appkit of Objective-C has converted original C language preprocessor directives, such as #define, into usable preprocessor directives. In geekspeak, we would pronounce this as "pound-define."

> **NOTE:** In the US, the "#" sign is often called the "pound" sign, especially in Objective-C and other programming contexts. In the United Kingdom, it is referred to as the "hash" character. Many iPhone/iPad developers have recently begun to refer to the #define preprocessor directive simply as the "define directive."

The #define preprocessor directive tells the computer to substitute one thing for another. That's an easy concept, right? For example, if I were to program the computer to substitute "100" every time it sees an instance of your name, our code in C would look like this:

```
#define yourName 100
```

This would tell the computer to substitute "100" each time it processes yourName—a variable that recognizes instances of your actual name.

Back to Xcode now, and our topic. In this context, the IBOutlet and IBAction quasi-keywords aren't really defined to be anything. In other words, they don't do anything substantial *for the compiler*, which is the core of the computer.

Quasi-keywords are flags, though, and they are important in the communication with the Interface Builder. When it sees the IBOutlet and IBAction quasi-keywords, it gets some of its internal code ready to perform specific tasks. It gets itself ready to deal with instance variables and all the hooks and connections that we make in that programming arena.

More About Pointers

It's difficult for many programming students to understand the concept of "pointers"—also sometimes known as the concept of *indirection*. It's not easy to explain this idea because it's one of the most sophisticated features of the C programming language.

Earlier in this chapter, I presented the analogy of seeing a criminal doing something, and then calling the police and pointing the police to where he is—so they, not you, can arrest the criminal. This analogy works for many students, but now let's go a little deeper.

If you were to ask a Computer Science professor what a "pointer" is, he would probably say something like "Pointers hold the address of a variable or a method."

"The *address*?" you ask. Well, consider this new analogy in the way of explanation.

Have you ever seen a movie in which a detective or some frantic couple is traveling all over the place, looking for clues to the treasure map, or the missing painting, or the kidnapped daughter? Sometimes they will spot a fingerprint, or a receipt, or even an envelope with a piece of paper containing a cryptic message—and these take the people one step closer to their goal—of finding the missing objects themselves.

We can call these pointers; they indicate the next place to go—for the solution of the given problem. They don't necessarily give the ultimate address, at which everything is handled and resolved, but they give us intermediate addresses or places to continue our work.

Thus, what the professor of Computer Science means is that pointers do not actually contain the items to which they direct us; they contain the locations within the code—the addresses—of the desired objects or actions or entities. This important feature makes the C-family of languages very powerful.

This simple idea makes it very efficient to turn complex tasks into easy ones. Pointers can pass values to types and arguments to functions, represent huge masses of numbers, and manipulate how we manage memory in a computer. Many of you are perhaps thinking that pointers are similar to variables in the world of algebra. *Exactly!*

In our first analogy, a pointer enabled an unarmed citizen to arrest a dangerous criminal by using indirection—that is, by calling the police to come and solve the problem. (Yes, the term "indirection" is an odd choice given that we are actually being *directed* toward the goal.)

Consider the following example where we use a pointer to direct us to the amount you have in your bank balance. To do this, let's define a variable called `bankBalance` as follows:

```
int  bankBalance = $1,000;
```

Now, let's throw another variable into the mix and call it `int_pointer`. Let us also assume that, for argument's sake, we have declared it. This will allow us to use indirection to indirectly connect to the value of `bankBalance` by the declaration:

```
int  *int_pointer;
```

The star, or asterisk, tells the family of C-languages that our variable `int_pointer` is allowed to indirectly access the integer value of the amount of money in our variable (placeholder): `bankBalance`.

To close, I want to remind you, and to acknowledge, that our digging around here is not an exhaustive or rigorous exploration into these topics... just a fun tangent into some related ideas. At this point, there is no reason for you to be bothered if you don't fully understand pointers. Seeds have been planted and that's what counts for now!

You've Said "Hello!"... but now, INDIO!

We can divide most iPhone and iPad apps into four different functions: **I**nteraction, **N**avigation, **D**ata, and **I/O** (Input/Output). We have seen enough apps to know that we can interact with them; we can navigate from one screen to another; we can manipulate and utilize data; and, we can provide input (type, paste, speak) and receive output (images, sounds, text, fun!).

Before we zoom in again to approach a program from any one of these specific areas, we need to first have a better grasp of how these different aspects of iPhone/iPad programming work, look, and behave. We also need to learn about their limitations and the pros and cons in terms of the projected or desired user experience and, because of the differences discussed above, whether the app is for the iPhone or the iPad. In `helloWorld_04`, unbeknownst to you, we continued to delve deeper into INDIO—Interaction, Navigation, Data, and I/O (input/output). Our code retrieved two images, by different means, which will interact with the user. This exercise took us closer to the I/O aspect of INDIO, which we have not quite wrapped our heads around because, simply put, we're not there yet.

Like a digital warrior, you are striding along a path into the forest of Objective-C, to a place where you will need to be accustomed to vaulting over rivers, hunting tigers, building fires in the rain, and so forth. So far, you've learned to start a fire with flint and steel—in dry weather—and you've gotten pretty good at hopping over streams. This lesson will teach you to vault over wider streams and, once there, to hunt tigers. Soon, you'll be equipped to fight the legendary demons of I/O in the daunting realm of INDIO.

As you gain a working knowledge of where any limitations and barriers exist, your journey through these four domains—all parts of a vast "forest"—will be more powerful and productive. A very important part of my job is to show you how to conduct yourself safely through the Forest of INDIO. Some sections of the forest are more daunting than others, but the good news is that you will be getting a nice, high-level view, as if from a helicopter! After our aerial tour, we will parachute down to the forest floor, open Xcode, and continue to explore the paths, the watering holes, and the shortcuts—to mark off the unnecessary sections and to be on the lookout for wild animals.

Model-View-Controller

As mentioned previously, the programmers who developed Cocoa Touch used a concept known as the Model-View-Controller (MVC) as the foundation for iPhone and iPad app code. Here is the basic idea.

Model: This holds the data and classes that make your application run. It is the part of the program where you might find sections of code I told you to ignore. This code can also hold objects that represent items you may have in your app (e.g., pinballs, cartoon figures, names in databases, appointments in your calendar).

View: This is the combination of all the goodies users see when they use your app. This is where your users interact with buttons, sliders, controls, and other experiences they can sense and appreciate. Here you may have a main view that is made up of a number of other views.

Controller: The controller links the *model* and the *view* together while always keeping track of what the user is doing. Think of this as the structural plan—the backbone—of the app. This is how we coordinate what buttons the user presses and, if necessary, how to change one view for another, all in response to the user's input, reactions, data, etc.

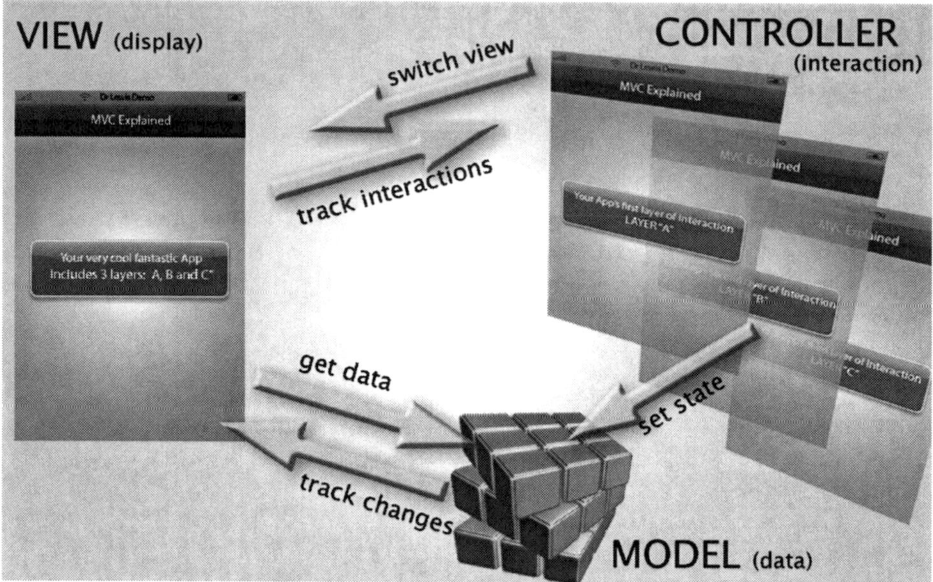

Figure 4–40. *The model, the view, and the controller (MVC).*

Consider the following example that illustrates how you can use the MVC concept to divide the functionality of your iPhone/iPad app into three distinct categories. Figure 4–40 shows a representation of your app; I've called it "MVC Explained." You can see that the VIEW displays a representation—a label—of "Your very cool fantastic App Includes 3 layers: A, B and C."

In the CONTROLLER section of the app, we see the three individual layers separated out, Layer "A," Layer "B," and Layer "C." Depending on which control mechanism the user clicks in the VIEW domain, the display the user sees, the CONTROLLER returns the appropriate response—the next view from the three prepared layers.

Your app will probably utilize data of some type, and this information will be stored in the MODEL section of your program. The data could be phone numbers, players' scores, GPS locations on a map, and so on.

As the user interacts with the VIEW section of the app, it may have to retrieve data from your database. Let's say your data contains the place your user parked her car. When the user hits a particular button in your program, it may retrieve the GPS data from the MODEL. If it's a moving target, it may also track changes in the user's position in relation to a car in the parking lot. Lastly, the CONTROLLER may change the state (or mode) of your data. Maybe one state shows telephone numbers, while another shows GPS positions or the top ten scores in a game. The CONTROLLER is also where animation takes place. What happens in the animation can affect and perhaps change the state in your Model. This could be done by using various tools, such as `UIKit` objects, to control and animate each layer, state, etc.

If this sounds complicated, bear in mind that you've already done much of this without even knowing it! In Example 1, you had the user press a button and up popped a label saying "Hello World!" This shows how you have already built an interaction with a `ViewController`. We will be delving further into these possibilities, of course. In Chapter 4, we will venture deeper into the **I**nteraction quadrant of the Forest of INDIO, and allow the user to add and delete table view items.

When we do this, I will do my best to keep you focused on the big picture when it comes to interactions… via **N**avigation. Our goal will be to have the user move from less specific information to more specific information with each new view.

In the Chapter Ahead

In Chapter 5, we will move into the next level of complexity: switch view applications. We will examine how a team of characters or roles within your code will work together to direct an outcome, or series of outcomes, that will give the user the sense of seamless flow.

You will learn about delegators and switch view controllers, classes and subclasses, and "lazy loads." We will get into the nitty-gritty of the `.xib` files, examine the concept of memory deallocation, and learn about imbedded code comments. It's getting curiouser and curiouser…

Onward to the next chapter!

Chapter 5

Touches

Here in our fifth app, we take a giant leap forward and really program some code. I want to say this right now: even though this is a big leap forward, there is always an easy ways out. Yes, I want you to do your very best to type in the all the code as you diligently follow the steps. Yes, I even want you to carry on when you feel like giving up; however, at this point, I want to clarify something with you, as I do with my students.

Redefining "Giving Up"

We need to talk about this for one page and I want you to read through this—you will probably need to in order to prepare yourself for this chapter. In the past, you may have associated "giving up" with totally relinquishing a dream you had. So let me share with you my outlook on three terms: "giving up," "dreams," and "goals". I want to talk about these terms in the context of the following four points:

- A person can have a dream until the day he or she dies. For example, one could dream of being a supernova geek who programs phenomenal multi-million dollar apps. A person could have that dream until the day he or she dies, even if he or she had never even touched an iPhone or knew what the word "Xcode" meant. This is because the equation that makes up a dream has no element of time.
- A goal, however, is simply a dream with an added element of time. Think about it. When the element of time in your goal's equation runs out, you FAIL! It's really simple. If you plan to become a supernova geek and sell a million apps within 12 months and you cannot compile "*hello world*" after 12 months, then you've FAILED!

- The more we accomplish goals within our time constraints, the more confident we become. That's why a good professor sets baby steps along the way to ensure that his or her students accomplish goals and feel really good about themselves. That's why good professors make little programs that move students a little closer to their ultimate goals. Each week, my students need to finish a set goal by programming an app. If they do not send me that completed app within the time limit, I fail them for that assignment! However, this is rare because rather than give up when it gets really hard, I have some back up angels that help my students succeed and meet their goals in time.
- Rather than give up when the going gets tough, you can
  - First, watch me program this code in the video at `http://bit.ly/qp6aCS` and simply follow along. I go a little fast to keep the video short, but you can always pause it. In June 2011, the average person paused the video 28.5 times (all viewers).The average student of mine paused the video 11.3 times.
  - Secondly, if watching the video does not result in total success, you can download my code for this program at `http://bit.ly/r1isYn`. Here, you can visually compare your code with mine. I tell students to try visually comparing first; if that doesn't work, I have them paste my code into either Pages or Word, and then paste their code into another similar document. After this, they should GO AWAY from their computers and check my code line by line against theirs.
  - Thirdly, if the preceding steps don't work, I don't want you to give up! I want you to paste my code into your code after you have dragged your icons from the nib file into your header file. This means that you still do steps 1 through to 30, which involve mostly dragging and dropping. Then, paste the implementation code into your implementation. When it compiles, I want you to then try it again on your own before moving on to the next chapter.

The preceding steps eliminate the possibility of you giving up on being a supernova geek. I LOVE receiving emails from students and readers telling me how proud they are of being geeks, and how they cannot believe that so many people are downloading and buying their apps. I especially love it when they tell me that they never programmed before in their lives, and how this book showed them they could program apps and not give up. A wife and mother of four in Helena, Montana brought me to tears when she told me that when her husband lost his job as a boiler maker, she bought my book and never gave up—she supported her family for over a year until her husband found another job. She still programs and sells apps.

Essentially, first and foremost, try your hardest to do it by just reading the chapter. If it's too much for you, then check out the video. If the video does not help, then download the code, move away from your computer, and check your code visually, line by line. As a last resort, you can paste my code into yours after you drag-and-drop the other elements into your code.

OK—let's do it.

Roadmap Recap

Going back to the car mechanic analogy, we understand that nowadays, as mentioned in the previous chapter, car mechanics are very specialized: only a handful know how to completely strip down and rebuild a specific car. So far, we have been peering over the shoulder of one such car mechanic, as he has changed and swapped specific components inside the engine. Today, you will build a very basic lawnmower engine. It will involve more steps than you've had to take thus far, but at the end of this chapter, you will have taken a huge leap forward.

As you build your lawnmower engine, there will be times that you look down and see a bigger mess of tools, nuts, and bolts than you have ever seen before. But hang in there. Follow me as I ask you to stand up from time to time and look at that "mess" from my point of view, not yours, and it will all make sense to you.

Touches: A View-Based Application

The *touches* app initially looks like the cover of this book. The lulu fruit however, can be moved around with your fingertips after you touch it. There are also three buttons on the top called Shrink, Move, and Change. The Shrink button is a special button; after you press it, the lulu fruit icon shrinks and the text inside the button automatically changes to Grow. Upon pressing the Grow button that used to be the Shrink button, the lulu fruit grows back to its original size. If you like, you can quickly have a look at Figures 5–45, 5–46, and 5–47. You can also see the app working right at the beginning of the video here: `http://bit.ly/qp6aCS`. Only look at the app working though—don't follow the video through the code, as I want to explain the code to you in a specific way.

CGAffineTransform Structs

We will also be working on animation code that the clever people at Apple wrote into a bundle called a *data structure*. This is a critical tool coders use to perform animations of their objects. The data structure can shrink an object, change its angle, move it, tilt it, and make it do all sorts of other cool animations. All the code that Apple uses to perform these animations is kept in vaults located in core animation data structures called *structs*. Apple explains this by saying that the "`CGAffineTransform` data structure represents a matrix used for **affine** transformations." Huh? What does that mean? It means that the `CGAffine` transforms all the critical points of an object you want to animate into a property called a *transform*. This property is simply a matrix. Once the object you want to animate is in this matrix, `CGAffine` is able to obey us when we instruct it to change our object's position, angle, shape, scale, and so on. This is what we'll do to the lulu fruit icon.

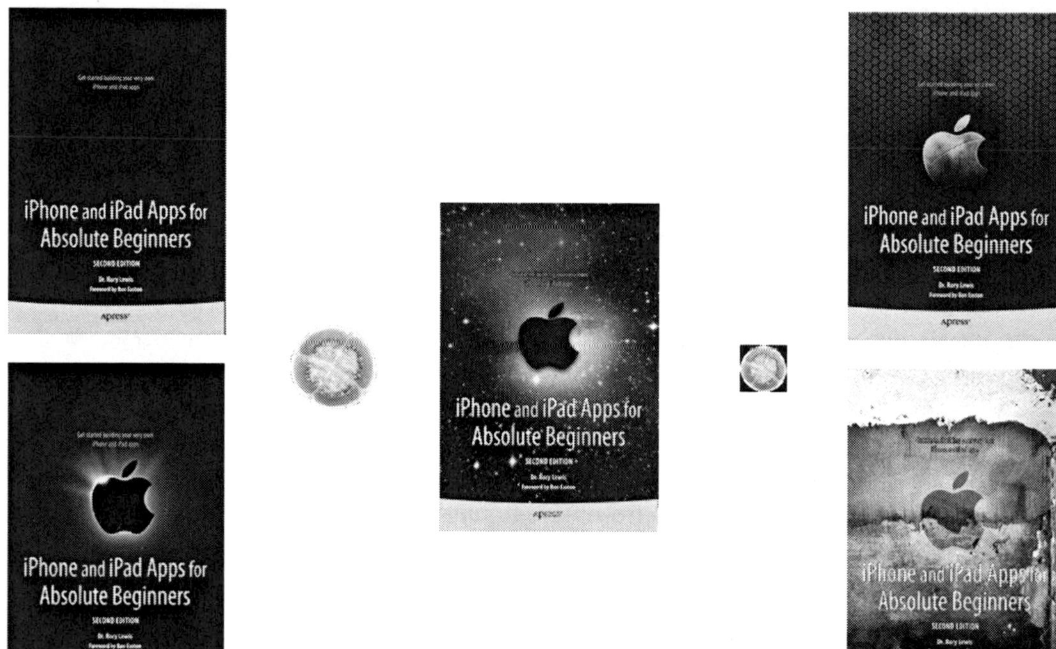

Figure 5–1. *The five background images and two lulu fruit icons downloaded from the repository*

1. Do I even need to say this ? Close all programs, delete all trash, and drag all your important files and folders to a proper destination so that you have a perfectly clean desktop. Download the images from `http://bit.ly/prqKsL` and upon unzipping the downloaded file, you will see seven images on your desktop. The five background images are various versions of the cover of this book. The first image will be the upper left-hand one in Figure 5–1, which is a picture of the front of the book without the lulu fruit icon. One can see that the lulu fruit icon is separate from the background pictures. The larger lulu fruit icon is the one that will be on the user screen and will be animated via the `CGAffineTransforms` we impose upon it. The smaller lulu fruit icon is the `icon.png` version. Our *Change* button will scroll through all five background images. The Shrink button and Move buttons will use `CGAffine` structs to animate the lulu fruit icon.

> **NOTE:** You can of course use your own images and icons. However, this is a long chapter even without spending resources on creating your own images. In class I tell students to hand in this homework assignment using my icons first. Later, they can use their own and if done on time (within three days), they can hand in their homework again with their own icons for extra credit. No students have done this yet.

Figure 5–2. *The seven images opened on your desktop, ready to launch into Xcode*

2. Your desktop should look similar to mine, as shown in Figure 5–2, with nothing but the seven icons and your Mac hard drive on your desktop. Once everything is clean and your images are stacked up and ready to go, YOU are ready to blast off!

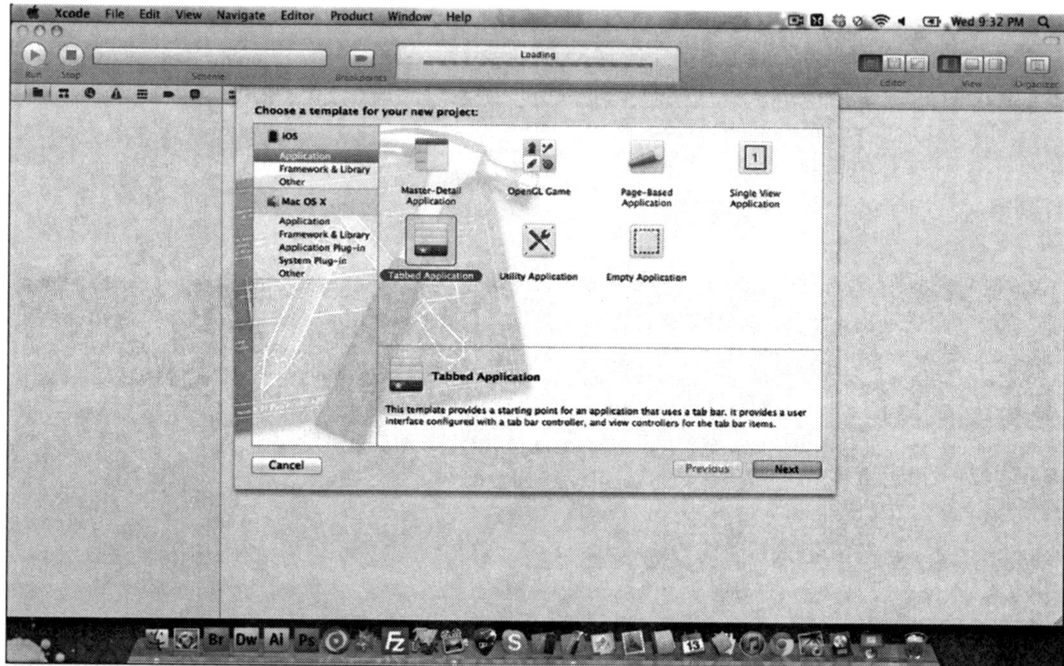

Figure 5–3. *Enter ⌘⇧N. Xcode 4.2 provides the option for a Single-View Application, which is the same as the older versions of View-Based Application.*

3. Like we have done before, launch Xcode and open a new project by using your keyboard shortcut ⌘⇧N. When you see the New Project wizard as depicted in Figure 5–5, you will want to click the *Single View Application* template.

   Once your New Project Window has opened and you have selected the Single View Application, I want you to press return ("Enter"), or click the Next button.

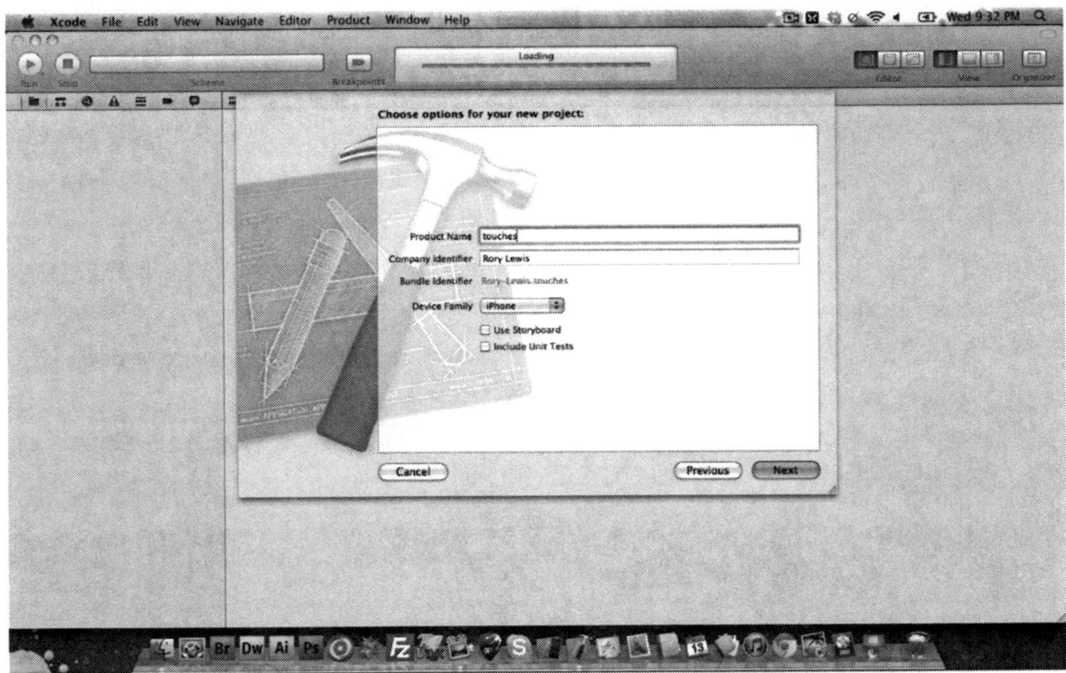

Figure 5–4. *Call your project "touches."*

4. Call your project "touches," and most importantly, remember to deselect the "Use Storyboard" option. Once the project is correctly named and the storyboard option is deselected, as shown in Figure 5–4, press Return or click Next.

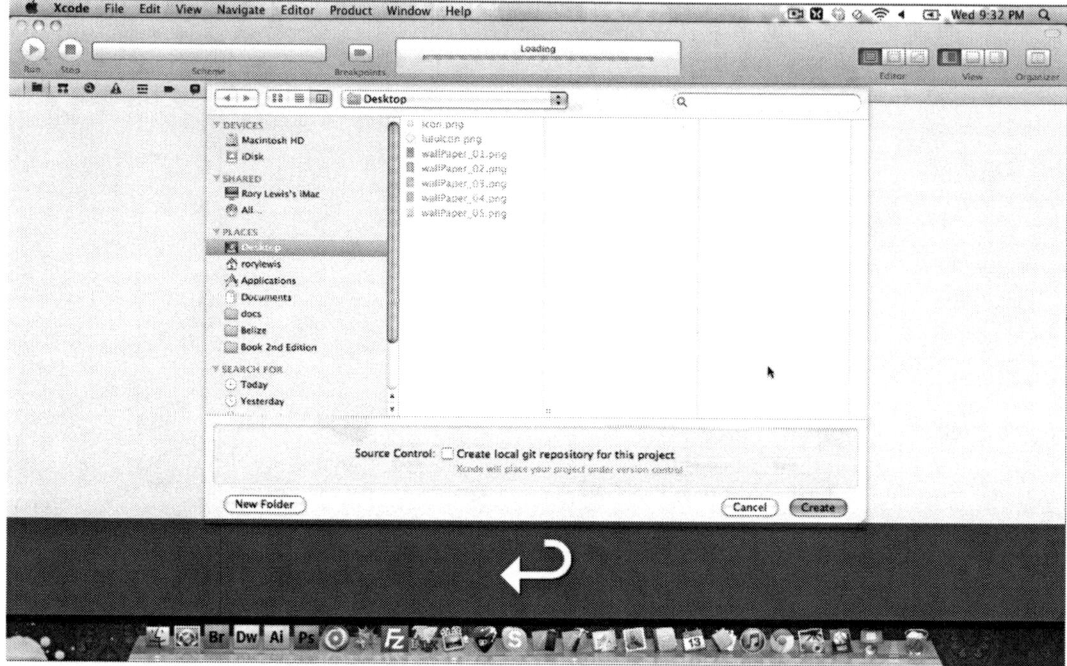

Figure 5–5. ***Select the option to save your project to your desktop.***

5. Save your project to your desktop. You can probably guess by now that we make sure that our current project is located on the desktop. After we're done with it, we place it an appropriate folder.

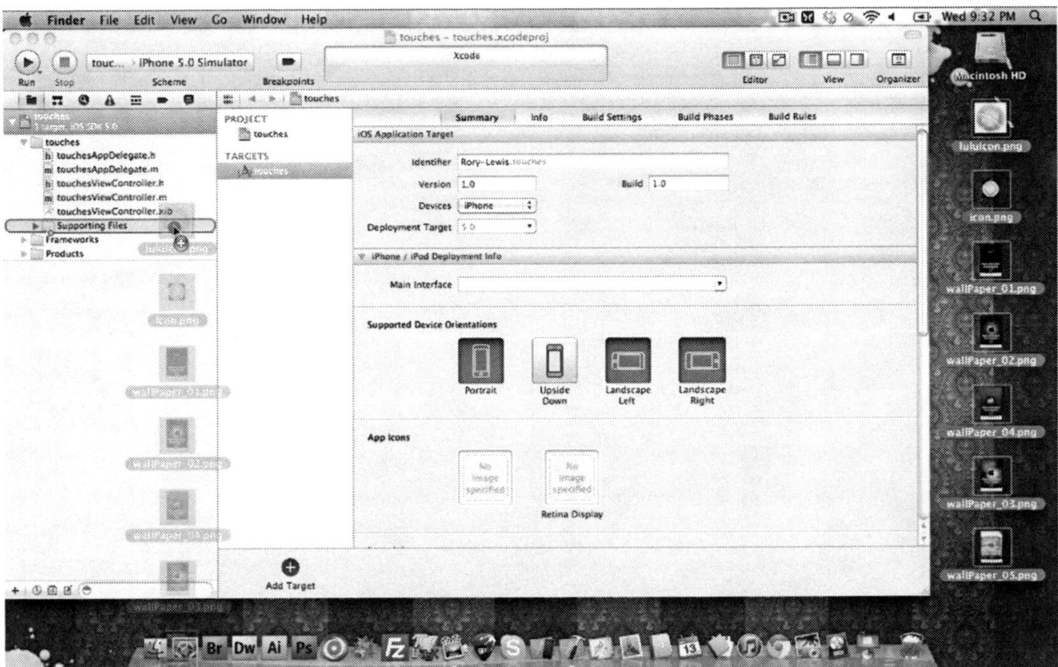

Figure 5–6. *Drag your images over to your Supporting Files folder.*

6. Initially, when Xcode instantiates itself, it will create a large window that nearly covers your entire desktop. Grab the bottom right-hand corner and shrink the window just enough to see the seven images you downloaded from the repository at `http://www.rorylewis.com`. As illustrated in Figure 5–6, drag all your images over into your Supporting Files folder in Xcode.

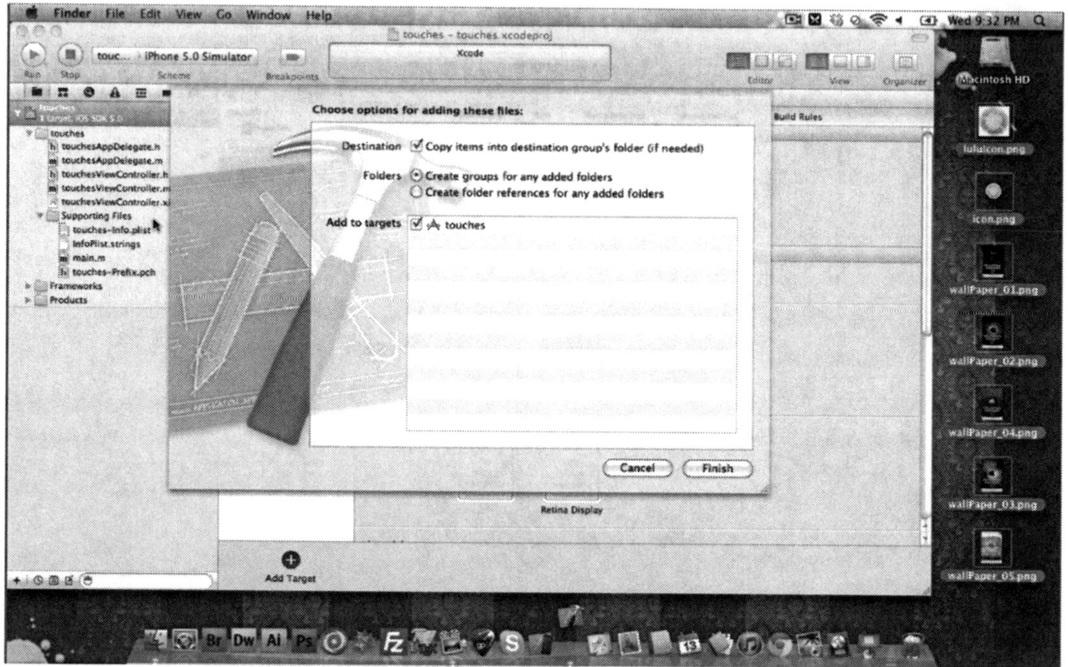

Figure 5–7. ***Check the "Copy items into the destination group's folder ..." box.***

7. After dropping the image into the `Resources` folder, you will be prompted to define whether the image will always be associated with its position on your desktop or embedded with the code and carried along with the application file, as shown in Figure 5–7. We want it to be embedded, of course, so click the "Copy items into destination group's folder ..." box. Also, check the "Create groups for any added folders" box. Then, click "Finish" (or press Enter).

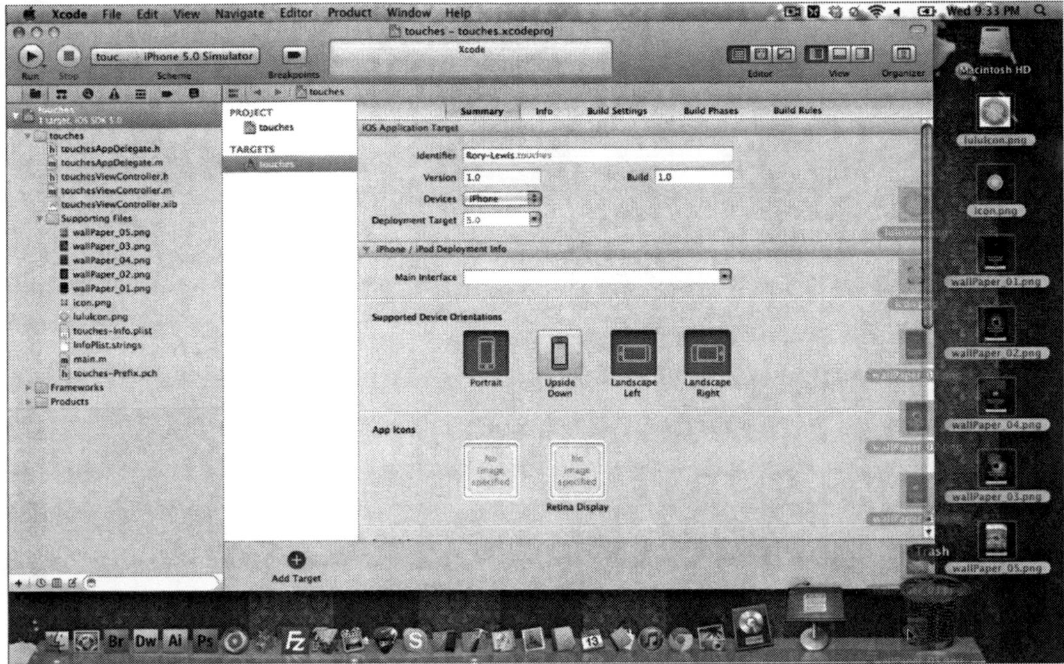

Figure 5–8. ***Drag your images into the trash.***

8. After you have dumped all your images into Xcode appropriately, there is really no need to keep them on your desktop or save them anywhere else. If you want to use them again in another version or if this run through does not work, simply open up the `touches` folder and they will all be there. There is no need to duplicate the images. So go ahead and trash the images that remain on your desktop, as shown in Figure 5–8.

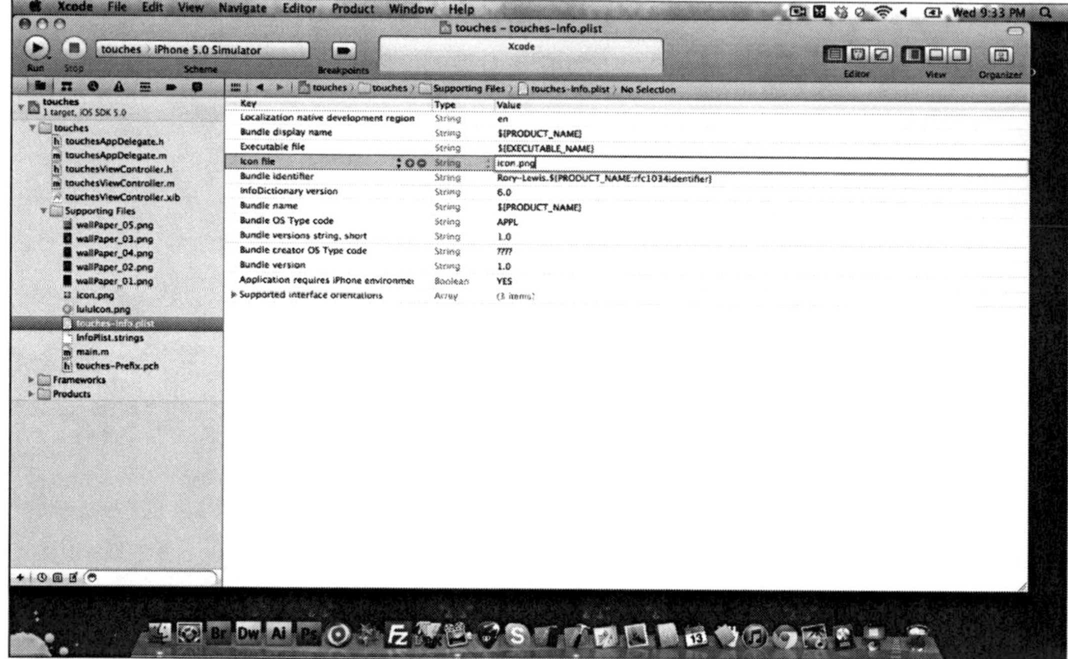

Figure 5–9. *Let's make your icon first.*

9. First, let's make the icon. Open up your plist while you are in the Supporting Files folder and enter "`icon.png`" into the icon name, as shown in Figure 5–9. It's not a bad habit to immediately connect your icon into the plist right after dropping in all your images. Once you leave this folder, you might forget to do it later.

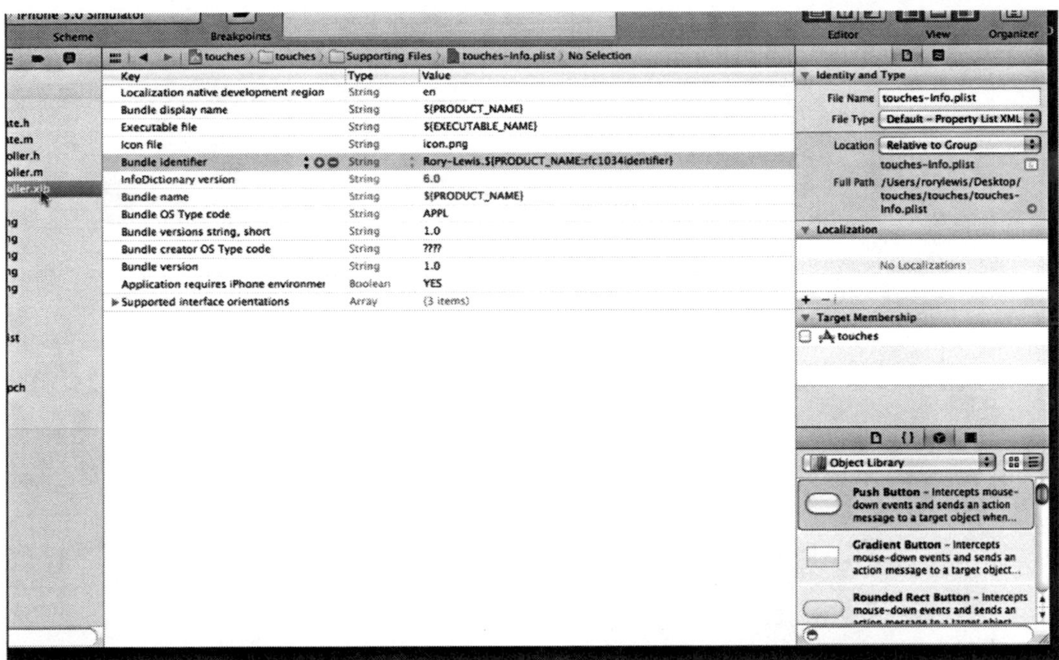

Figure 5–10. *Click on your nib file, open up the Utilities View, and close the Navigator View.*

10. Once you have associated your icon with `icon.png` or the name of your personal icon (if you named it differently), I want you to open your `touchesViewControllernib` file, as shown in Figure 5–10. As we have done before, we need more space, so let's also open the Utilities View, so we can see the tools and icons we need to dress up the View design area. Secondly, close the Navigator View, because for now, we do not need it.

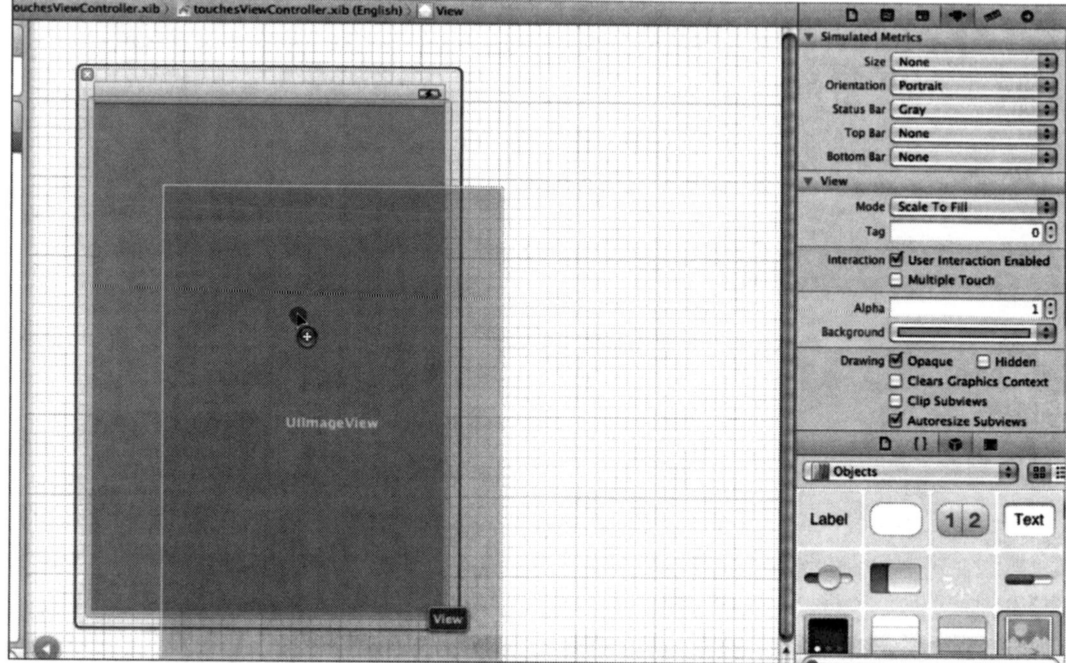

Figure 5–11. *Drag a `UIImageView` onto your View design area.*

11. With your Utilities pane open, drag a `UIImageView` onto your View design area, as shown in Figure 5–11. The `UIImageView` will hold the current backgrounds you downloaded named `WallPaper_01` to `wallPaper_05`. Later, I will explain how you will write code that will determine which of the five background images will be housed on this `UIImageView` at any particular point in time. But we do know that the Change button will fire up the code that will switch the background. So, you can guess that the next thing we need to do is drag some buttons onto the view design area.

> **NOTE:** Xcoders also call the View design area the View screen and View frame. So, whether a person says "*View design area,*""*View screen,*" or "*View frame,*" all these terms mean the same thing. I purposefully use the three terms interchangeably throughout this book.

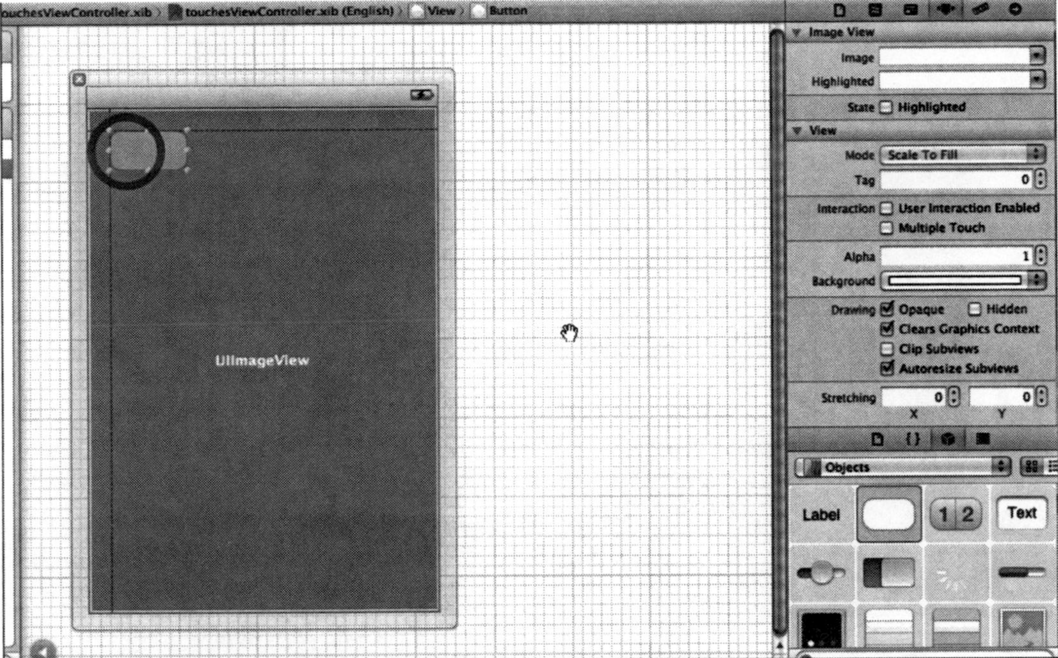

Figure 5–12. *Drag three buttons onto your View design area.*

12. As shown in Figure 5–12, start dragging three buttons onto the top of your View frame. Keep them in line with one another. Keep the outer two buttons lined up with the outer margins and keep the center button centered on the screen. The blue indicator lines will tell you when you move your button close to the range of each of the respective boundaries.

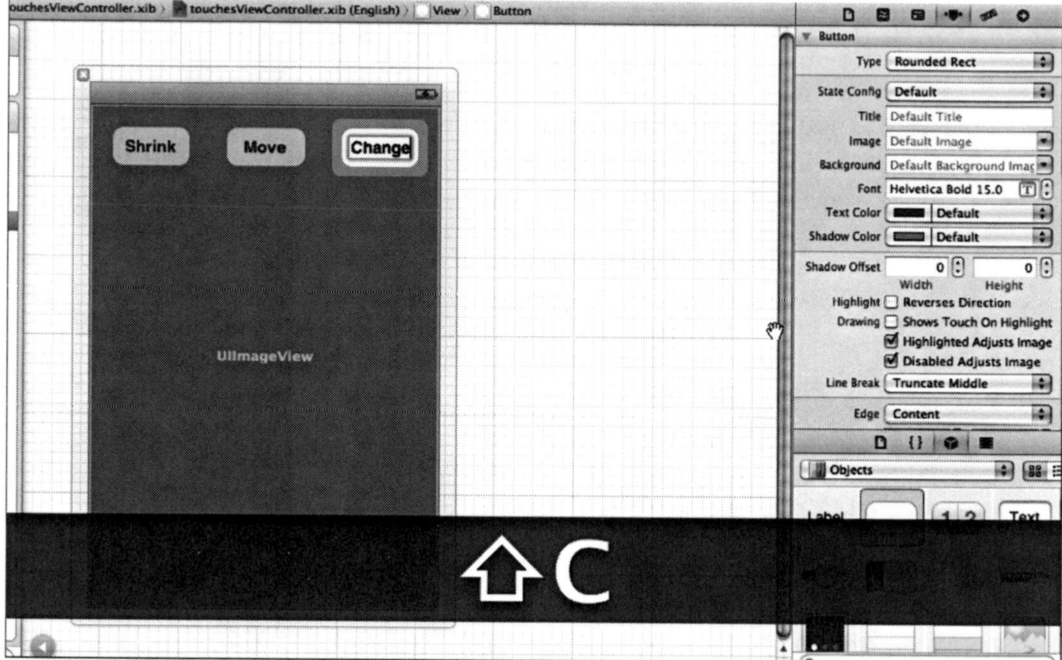

Figure 5–13. *Name your three buttons Shrink, Move, and Change.*

13. Once you have positioned your three buttons onto your View frame, click the buttons and name them. Name them Shrink, Move, and Change, as illustrated in Figure 5–13.

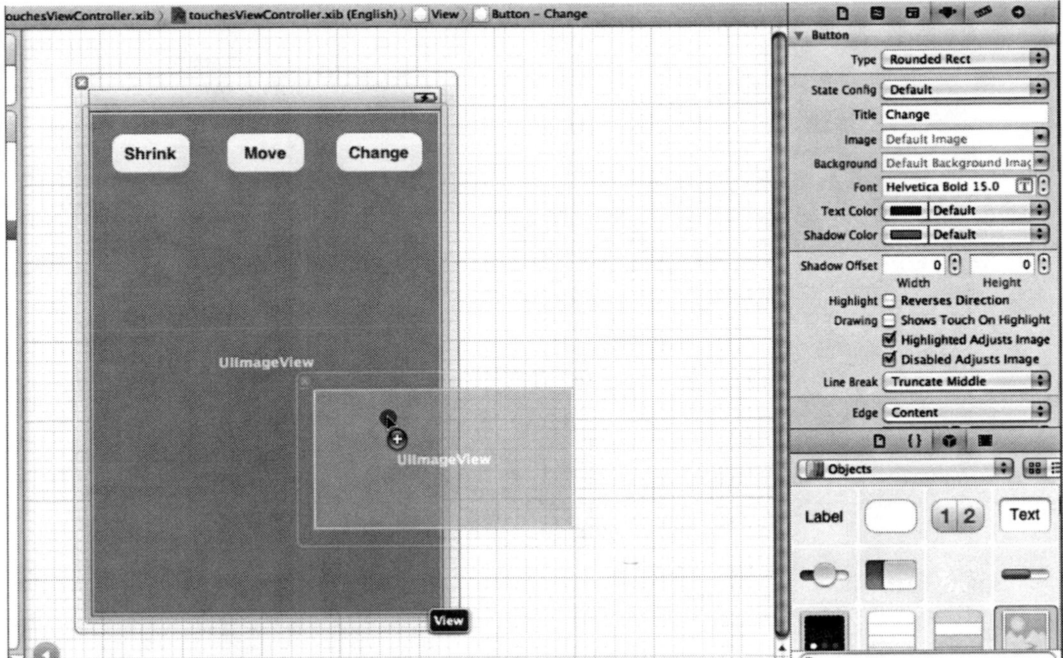

Figure 5–14. *Drag a second UIImageView onto your View design area.*

14. We now need another `UIImageView` to hold the lulu fruit icon that we can move around with our finger, scale with a button, and move with a button, so add another `UIImageView` onto your View frame, as shown in Figure 5–14.

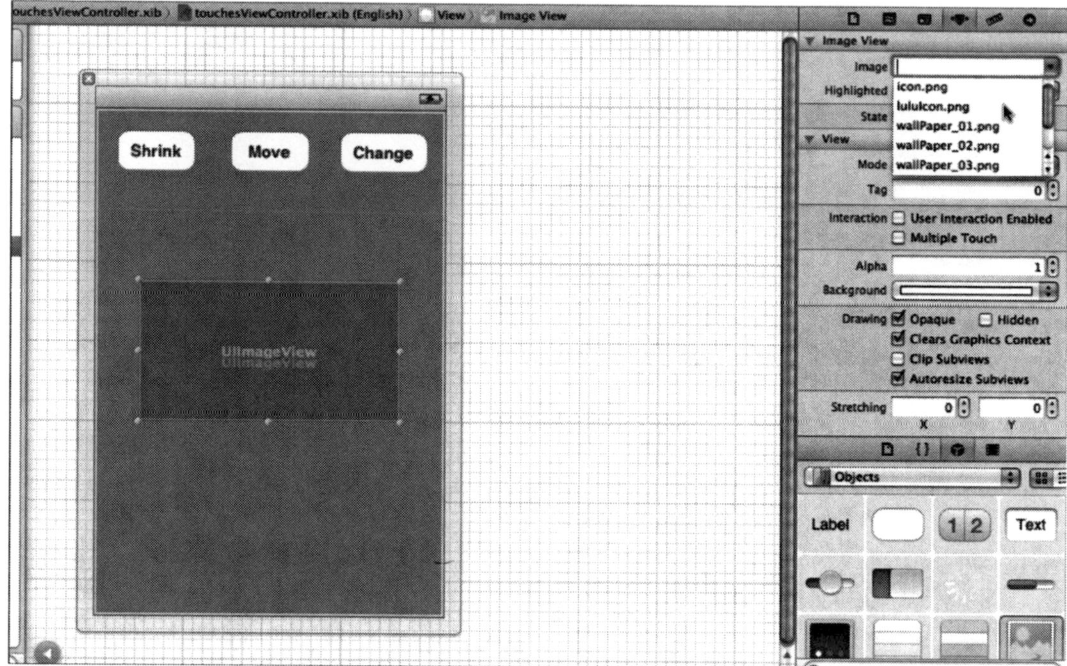

Figure 5–15. ***Associate the lulu fruit icon with the second UIImageView.***

15. With the second `UIImageView` selected, go to the image drop- down menu in the Attributes dialogue in your Utilities pane, as shown in Figure 5–15. Select the `luluIcon.png` to associate it with your second `UIImageView`.

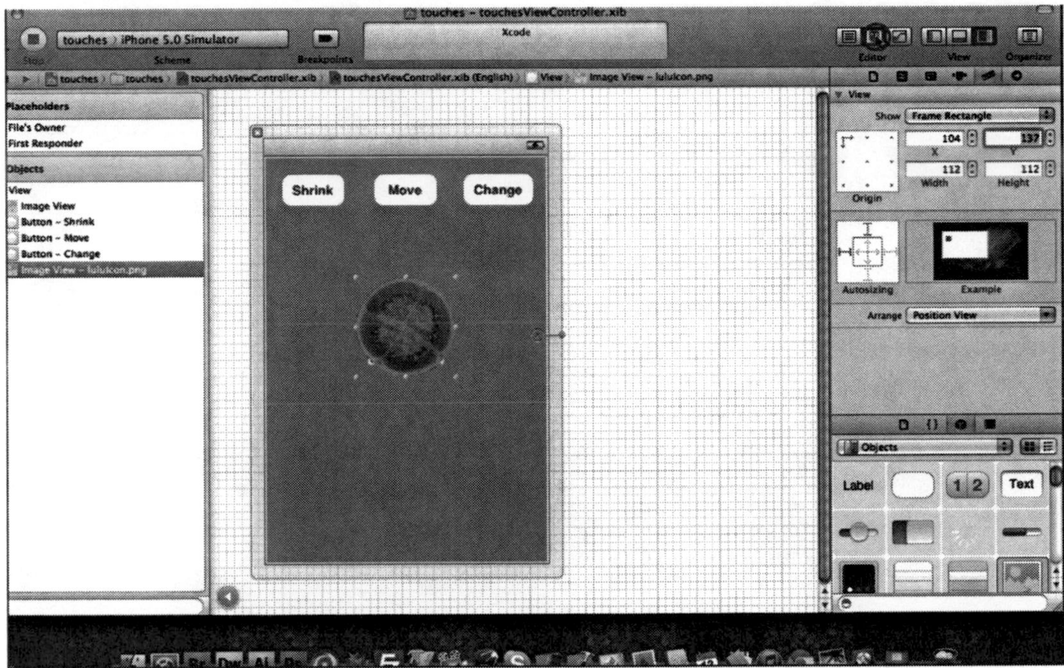

Figure 5–16. *Size and locate the luluIcon.png.*

16. Once the `luluIcon.png` appears inside the second `UIImageView`, I want you to leave the Attributes dialogue in your Utilities pane and click the Size inspector (⌘⌥5); make the width of the lulu icon a square consisting of 112 x 112 pixels. Also, set the y-axis height to be 137 pixels down from the top of the View pane. You can either center the icon manually (as I do) or do it in the x-axis box. This is illustrated in Figure 5–16.

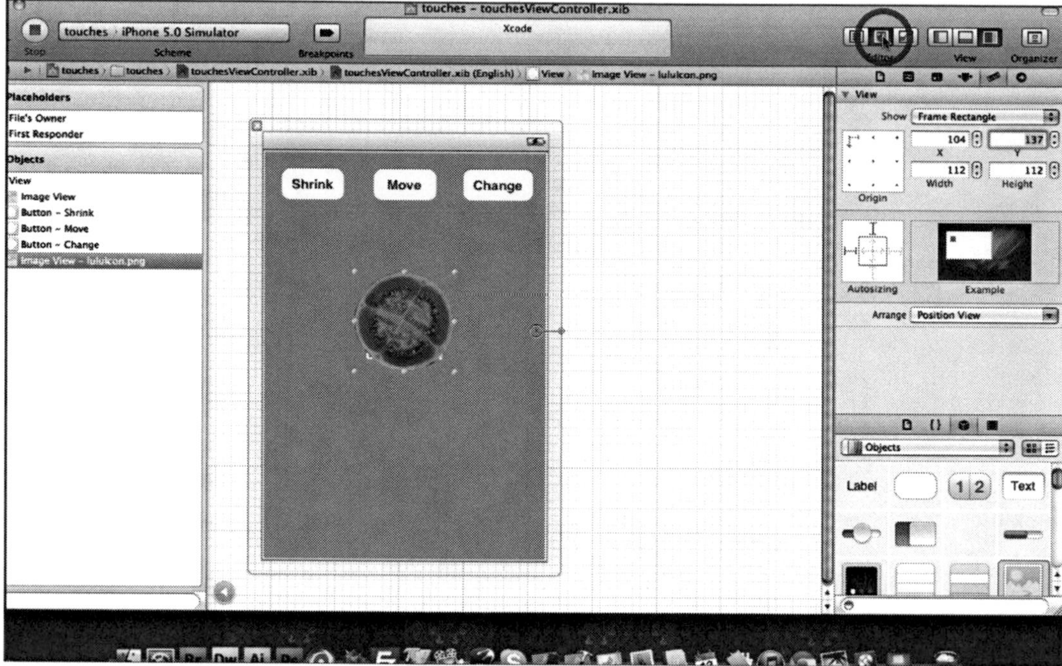

Figure 5–17. *Click the Assistant to bring up your* `touchesViewController` *header file.*

17. We have completed dragging and positioning all the items necessary onto your nib. Now we need to connect these items to your code, as we have done before. We need to work on the `touchesViewController` header file. Click the Assistant button and your screen will look similar to what is shown in Figure 5–17.

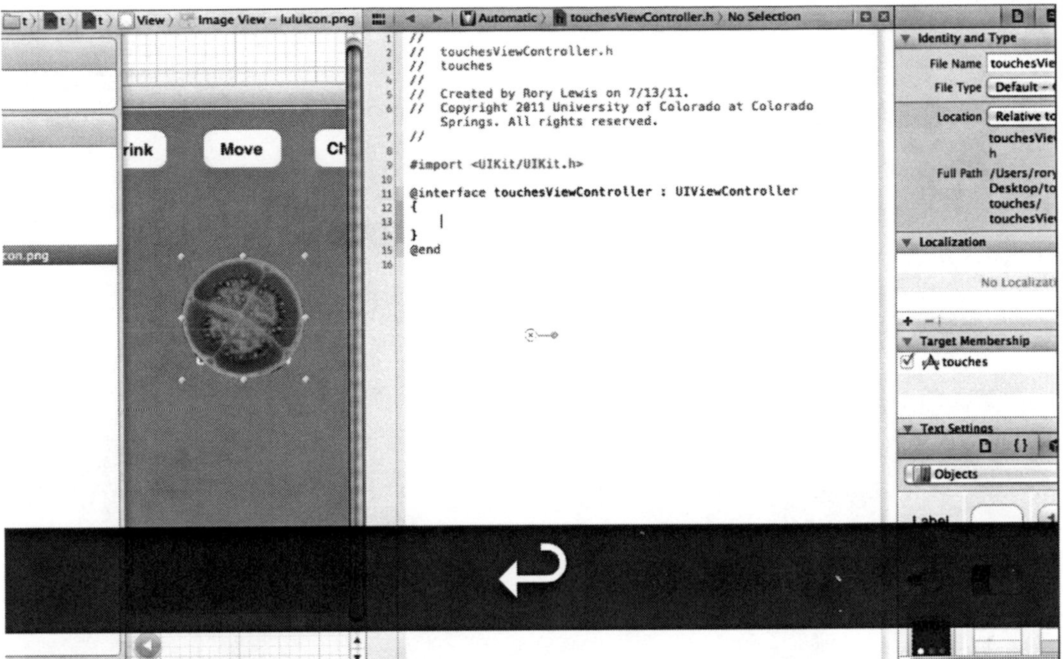

Figure 5–18. *Reposition your screen so you can work on the header file.*

18. There are potentially two things here. First, depending on how large your screen is, you may have to resize or position your View pane inside the nib so that you can see all three of your buttons. Secondly, add curly brackets to the `@property` directive, as illustrated in Figure 5–18.

> **NOTE:** If you are in Version 4.0 or earlier, you will not need to add squiggly brackets to your `@interface` directive, as they are automatically instantiated However, if you are using a higher, more recent version of Xcode, then you will probably have to add the squiggly brackets, as shown in Figure 5–18.

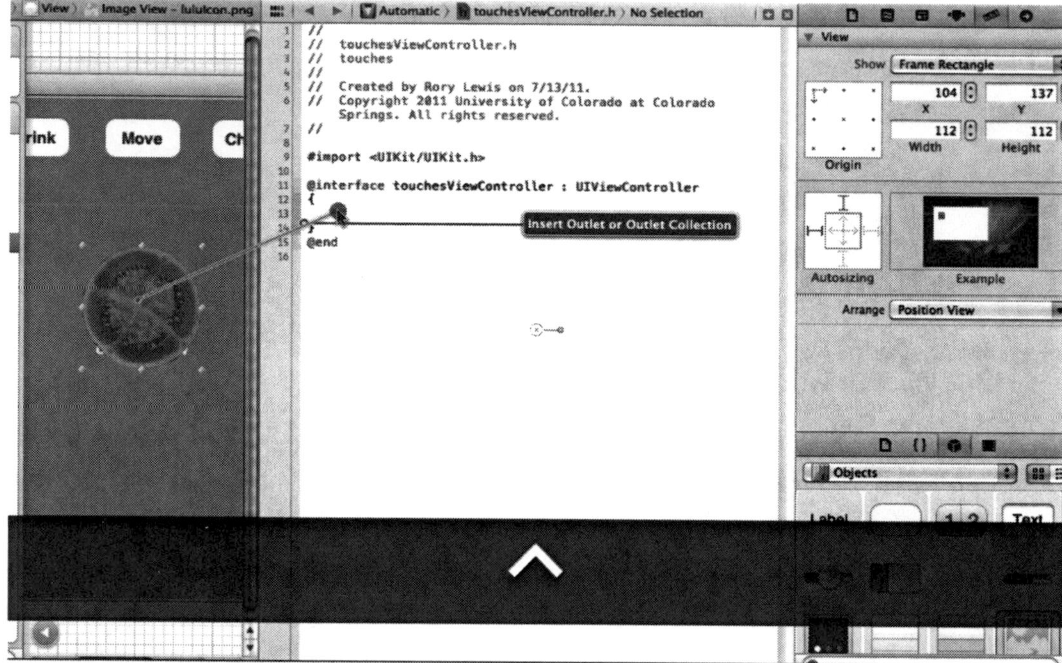

Figure 5–19. ***Control-drag a connection from your icon in Interface Builder into your header file.***

19. Typically, in the past, when we reached this juncture, I instructed you to just blindly start control-dragging outlets and action into your `@directive`. Today, however, we will first think about what we're going to do, so we can fuse synapses in your brain to understand how to create a robust header file. To recap what you have done in the past, I fed you a ration of Outlets and actions using the following very broad criteria:

- Outlets to connect nib file members with your `UIImageViews` code, which the clever people at Apple wrote for us
- Actions to connect your buttons with code we wrote in the implementation file

Now, we are going to grow up and move on. Remember how I mentioned that when we click the Shrink button, it shrinks the lulu fruit icon and the text inside it changes to Grow; then when we press the button again, it makes it grow? Well, we need to use the code the folks at Apple wrote that allows us to do cool things like change the colors, text, and other appearances inside a button.

> **NOTE:** This code provided by Apple is located in a class called `UIButton`. When we use this code, we say we are using an *instance of* `UIButton`. In short, we need an outlet for our Change button, so we can change the text in it to go from Shrink to Grow.

We will, of course, also need an outlet for the lulu fruit icon and the background that will hold whatever WallPaper_0x.png is being used. So, we will need three outlets. After we have correctly control-dragged our three outlets into the @properties directive, it will look something like this:

```
IBOutlet UIImageView *some variable name;
IBOutlet UIImageView *some variable name;
IBOutlet UIButton *some variable name;
```

Yup! We need to give each of these outlets variable names. Let's use myIcon for the icon, myBackground for the background, and shrinkButton for the button that shrinks the lulu fruit icon. You could use different names, but do that later. Follow along with me now and it will look like this:

```
IBOutlet UIImageView *myIcon;
IBOutlet UIImageView *myBackground;
IBOutlet UIButton *shrinkButton;
```

Insofar as the actions for the three buttons are concerned, they stay the same. We will still have three actions for our three buttons sitting right after and outside of the @properties directive, and the code will look something like this:

```
- (IBAction)some variable name:(id)sender;
- (IBAction)some variable name:(id)sender;
- (IBAction)some variable name:(id)sender;
```

Yup! We need to give each of these actions variable names. Let's use shrink for the Shrink button, move for the Move button, and change for the Change button. Again, you could use different variable names here, but for now just follow along with me. It will look like this:

```
- (IBAction)shrink:(id)sender;
- (IBAction)move:(id)sender;
- (IBAction)change:(id)sender;
```

OK! So let's get to it! Start off by control-dragging from your icon to the @properties directive, as illustrated in Figure 5–19.

NOTE: You may have noticed that sometimes I say "*Control-drag a connection from ____ in Interface Builder into your header file,*" and other times I say "*Control-drag a connection from _____ in Interface Builder into your @property directive.*" This is not to confuse you; it's to let you know that they mean the same thing and you may work for, hire, or meet people who use one or the other in their nomenclature.

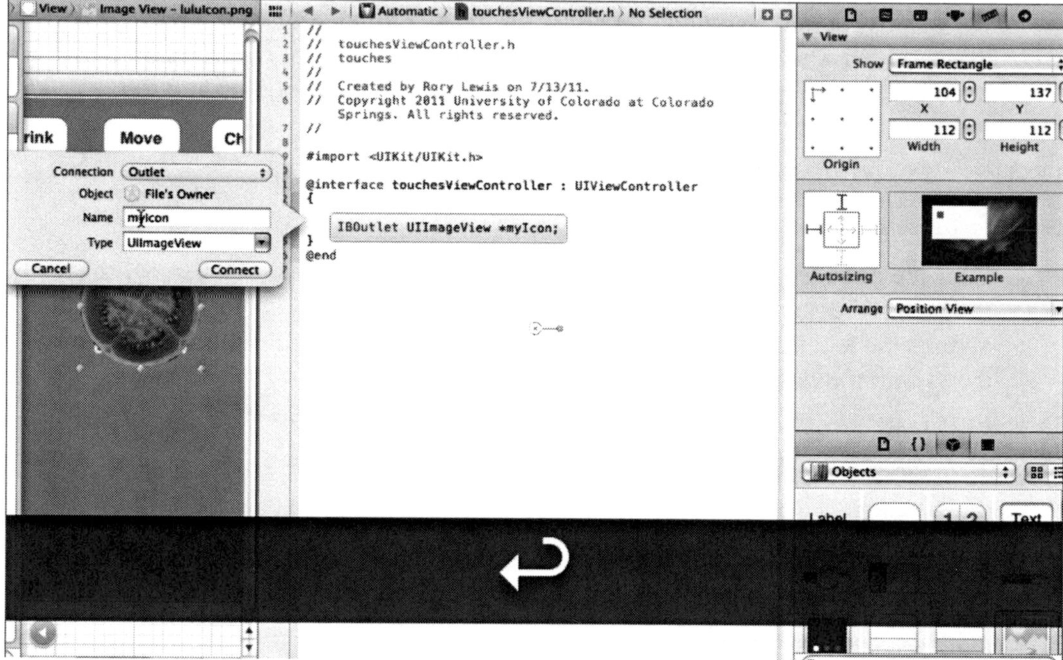

Figure 5–20. *Keep the icon as an outlet and name it "`myIcon`."*

20. As depicted in Figure 5–20, when you reel the fishing line into your `@property`, keep it as an outlet and name it `myIcon`.

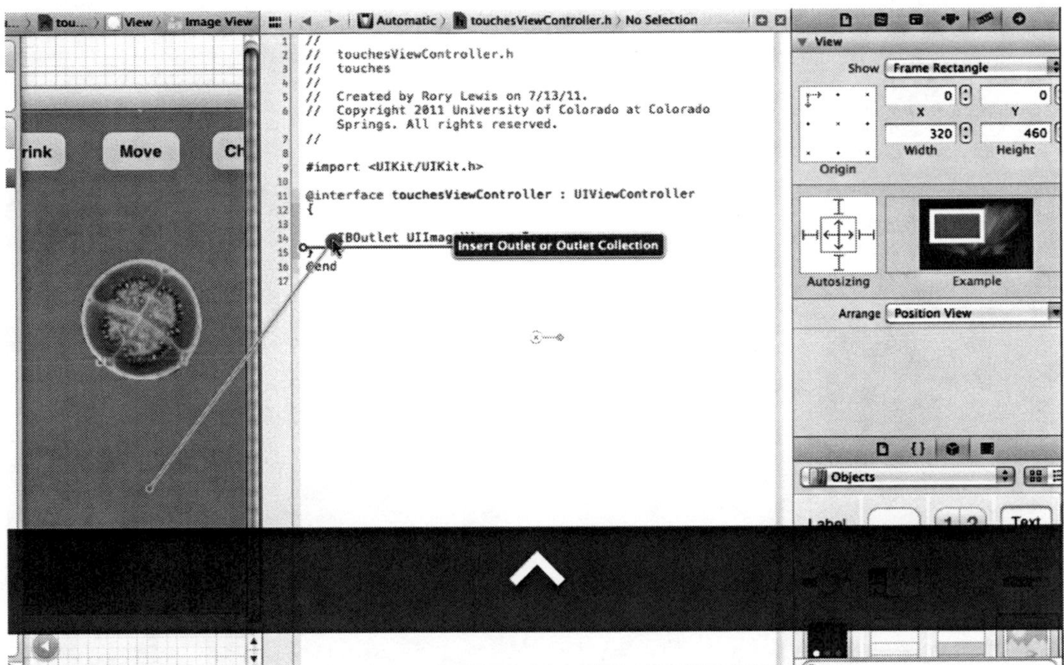

Figure 5–21. *Control-drag a connection from anywhere on the Background into the @property directive.*

21. Now, we need to connect the `UIImageView` we dragged into View Design Area with the header file's `@property` directive, as depicted in Figure 5–21.

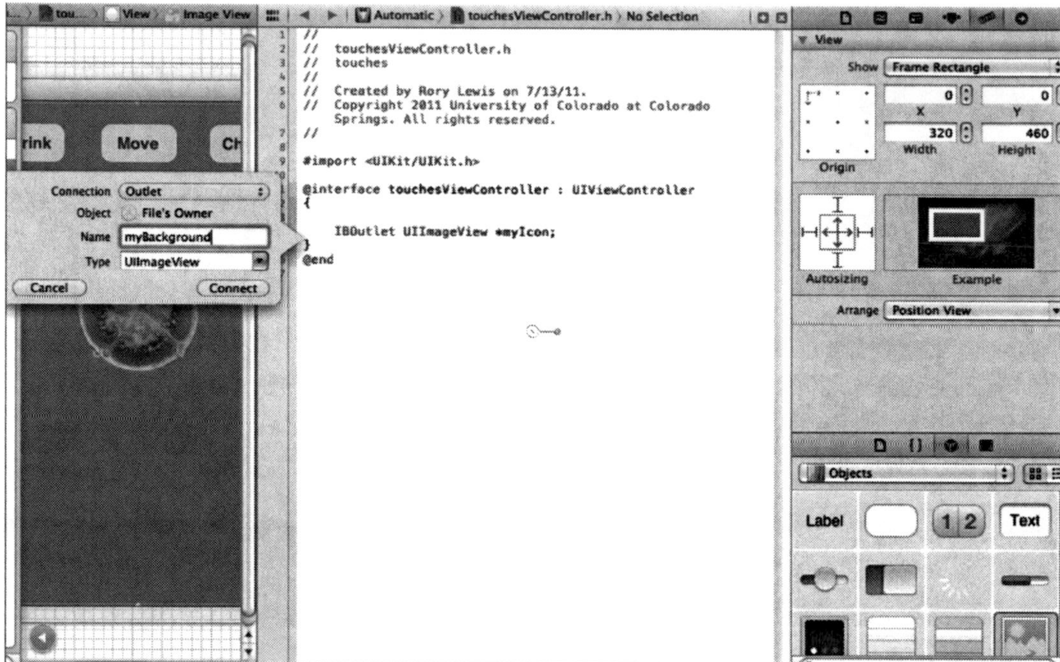

Figure 5–22. *Keep the icon as an outlet and name it "`myBackground`."*

22. As depicted in Figure 5–22, when you reel the fishing line into your `@property`, keep it as an outlet and name it `myBackground`.

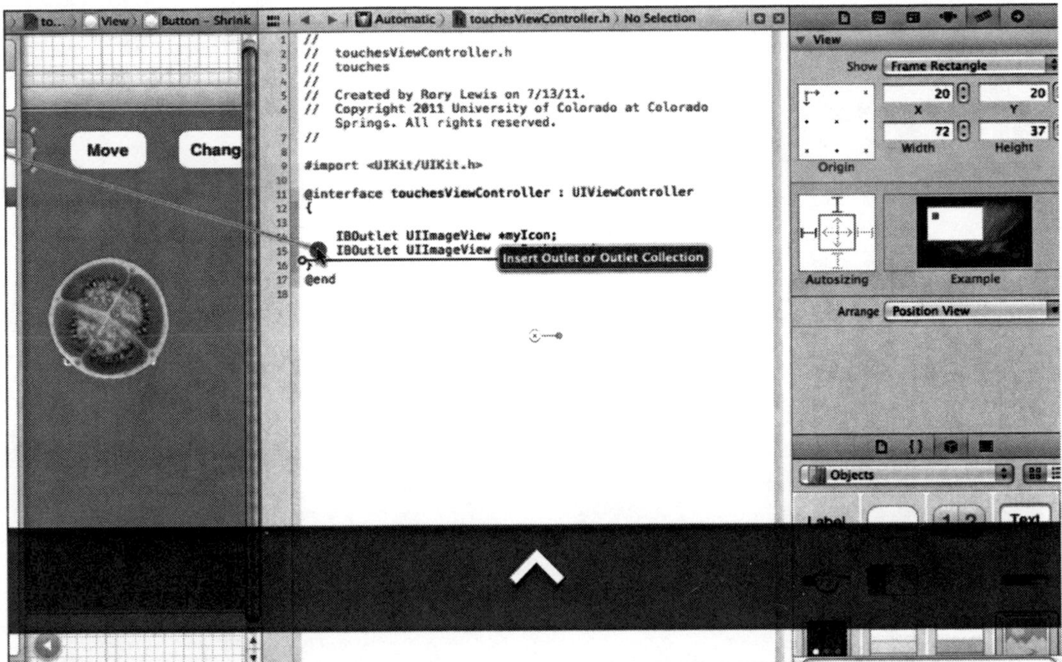

Figure 5–23. *Control-drag a connection from your Shrink button in Interface Builder into your header file.*

23. As shown in Figure 5–23, after clicking the Shrink button in your Interface Builder once, control-drag into your header file, in-between the squiggly brackets of the `@interface` directive. We have discussed in §19 why we are, for the first time, connecting a button to the `@property` directive. If you skipped that section, I strongly suggest you fully understand why we are connecting a button as an outlet.

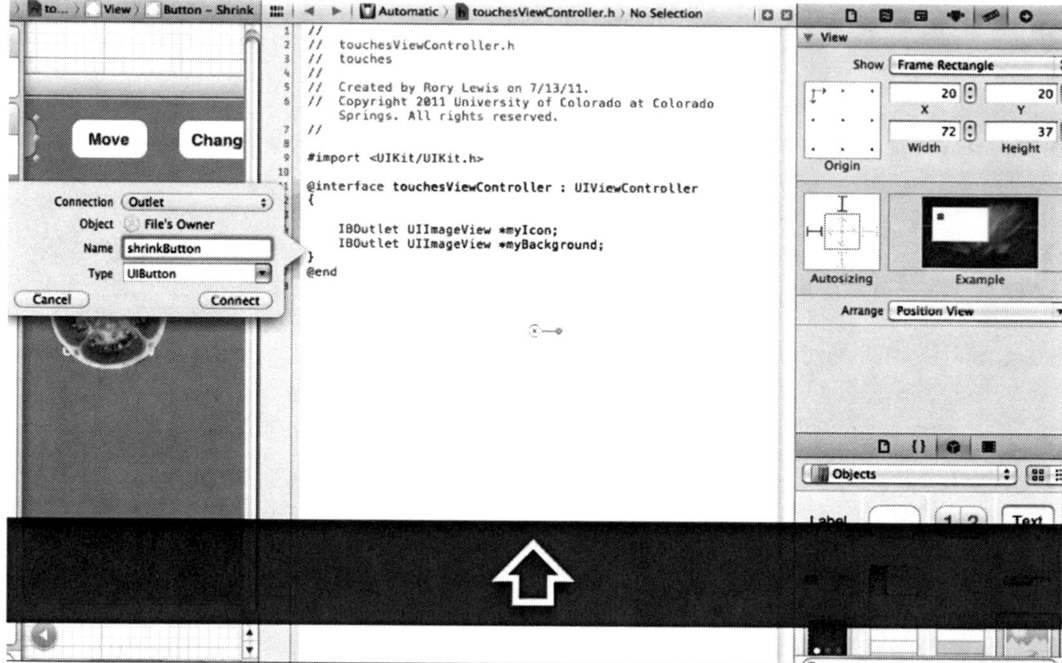

Figure 5–24. ***Keep the button as an outlet and name it*** `shrinkButton`.

24. As shown in Figure 5–24, when you've control-dragged out to the `@interface` directive, drop it in by letting go of your mouse and naming it `shrinkButton`—leave it as an outlet.

Coding the Header File

After we understand that we've connected our outlets we would typically leave the `@interface` directive, go outside of it, and connect our buttons as actions. In this case, we need to do something we've never done before: set up a few more variables and pointers. We will not go too deep into them, but I will emphasize ***why*** we need to do this.

We need to keep track of our images. Specifically we need to

- Keep track of the current image being displayed in the background. Remember we have five of them, so we'll call the current background `currentBackground`.
- We have to store these 5 background images somewhere. The typical way we do this is store all five images in a list we call an *array*. This means we will need to create an array. Let's call our array `bgArray`.

- We also need to know if the Shrink and Move buttons have been pressed because that will change the state. This is explained in detail later, but for now, the location and size of the icon changes and this affects what can be done to it next. So, we'll need to track two button states: the state of the Shrink button and the state of the Move button. Let's call them `hasShrunk` and `hasMoved`.
- Remember when I spoke about how we will use the `CGAffineTransform` class to help us manipulate our icon (see the "CGAffineTransform structs" section)? Well, we need to use the `CGAffineTransform` class to first move the lulu fruit icon when we press the move button, and then change the size of the lulu fruit icon when we press the shrink button. So, we need two `CGAffineTransforms`. Let's call one `translate` and the other `size`.

So we now have six items.

- An array we will call `bgImages`
- A way to keep track of the `currentBackground`
- The state of `hasMoved`
- The state of `Shrunk`
- A way to transform `translate` (the position of our lulu fruit icon)
- A way to transform `size` (the size of our lulu fruit icon)

Now that we have determined what we need and what we call them, we have one more thing to do: associate them with an internal means of doing what we want them to do. We have to associate them with a type. This is all very easy. Apple does it all for us. We just need to know what tools to reach for in our Apple tool bag and attach to each of these variables we have created.

- For the array, Apple has an `NSArray` that does the job beautifully.
- To keep track of the current background, let's just give each of the backgrounds a number of type integer (`int`).
- To keep track of the buttons, we just need to know whether they have been pressed. A simple "yes" or "no" will be cool. Hmm, that's Boolean isn't it? So we'll associate Booleans with our `hasMoved` and `hasShrunk` buttons.
- Lastly, we need to simply assign the `CGAffineTransform` class to our `translate` and `size` variables.

To emphasize how we will associate these named types to our six items, I want you to look at the following very carefully:

```
NSArray *bgImages;
int currentBackground;
bool hasMoved;
```

```
bool hasShrunk;

CGAffineTransform translate;
CGAffineTransform size;
```

This means that we need to type the preceding code underneath your three `IBOutlets` as follows:

```
@interface touchesViewController : UIViewController
{
    IBOutlet UIImageView *myIcon;
    IBOutlet UIImageView *myBackground;
    IBOutlet UIButton *shrinkButton;

    NSArray *bgImages;
    int currentBackground;
    bool hasMoved;
    bool hasShrunk;

    CGAffineTransform translate;
    CGAffineTransform size;

}
```

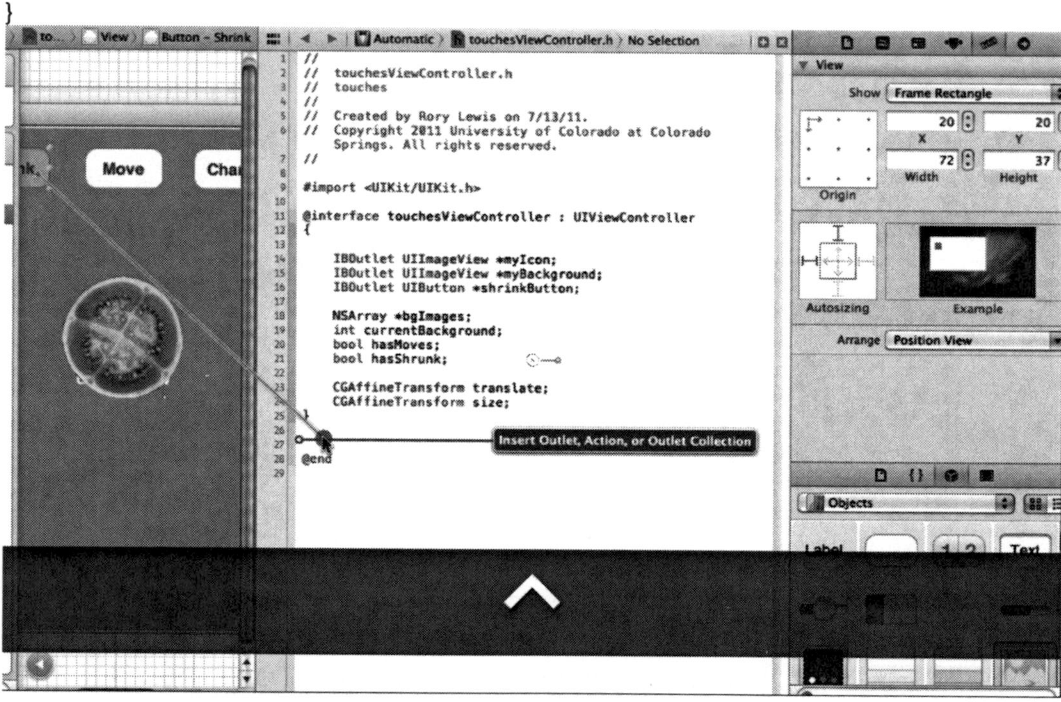

Figure 5–25. *Create a few more items and then drag your first button.*

25. Now and only now that we have correctly created and defined our variables do we start to connect our buttons, as actions, to the space below the `@directive`. Grab your Shrink button by clicking it and control-drag to the header file, right under the `@directive`, as illustrated in Figure 5–25.

Figure 5–26. *Change the default type of your Shrink button to Action.*

26. As shown in Figure 5–26, when you've control-dragged from the Shrink button to the header file, drop it in and make sure to change the type from outlet to action.

Figure 5–27. *Name it shrink.*

27. Once you have created the action for the shrink button, call it `shrink`. This is shown In Figure 5–27.

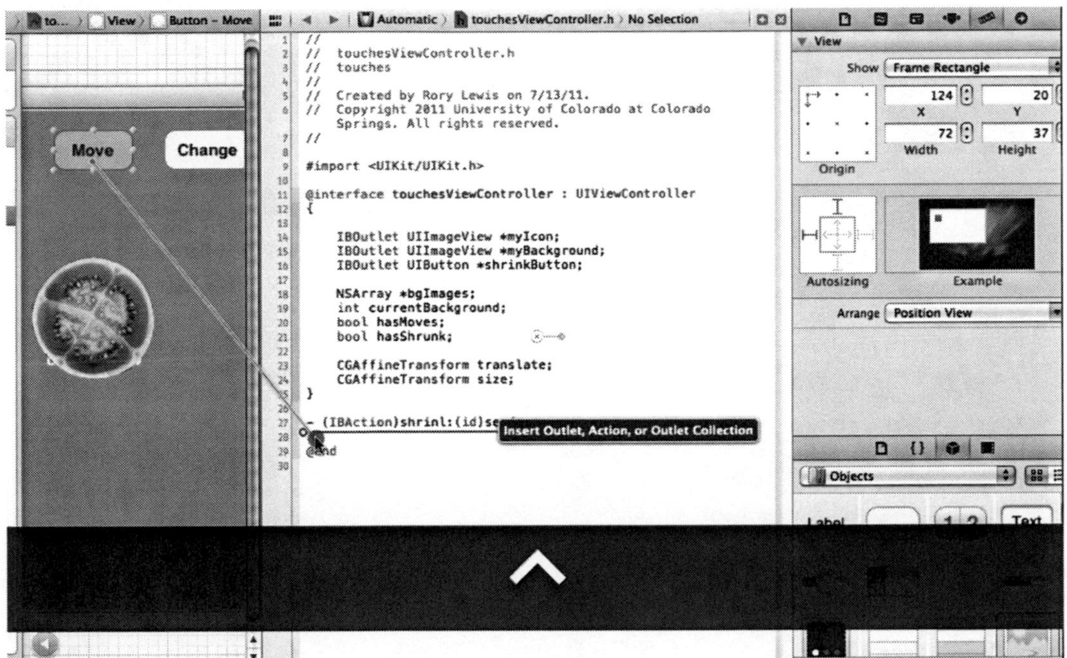

Figure 5–28. *Control-drag and create actions for the remaining Move and Change buttons.*

28. Now, on your own, control-drag first from the Move button and then from the Change button to the header file. Make sure you change them into actions and name them `move` and `change`. In Figure 5–28, you can see how it looks as we start control- dragging from the move button to the header file.

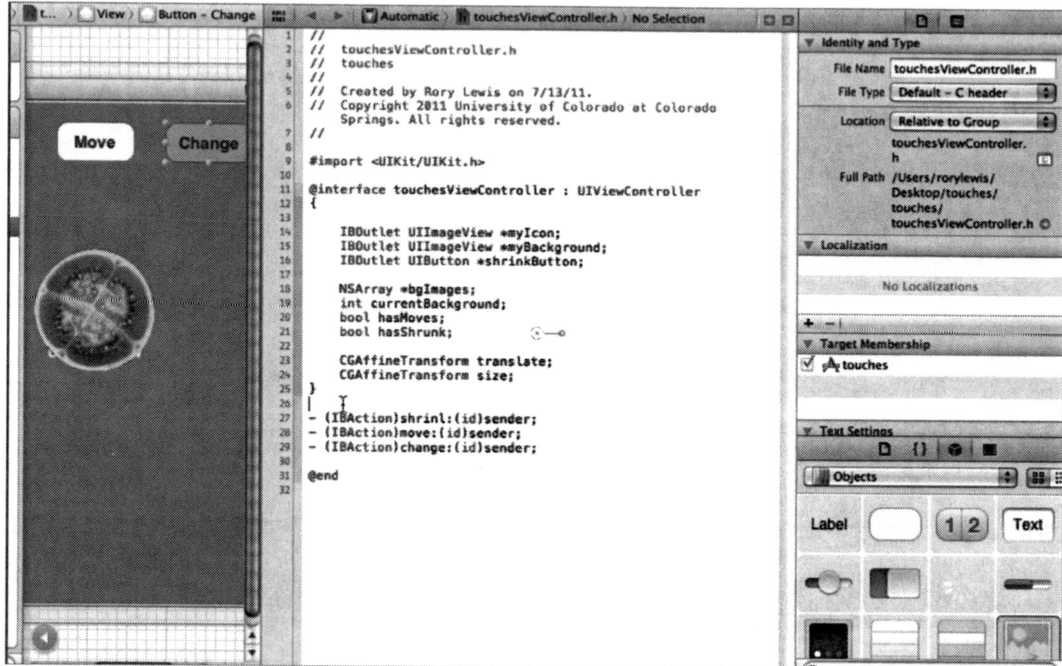

Figure 5–29. *Make space for the getters and setters after checking that this is how your code appears.*

29. Before moving on to creating the `@properties` for synthesis (getters and setters), I would like you to make sure that your code looks like mine in Figure 5–29.

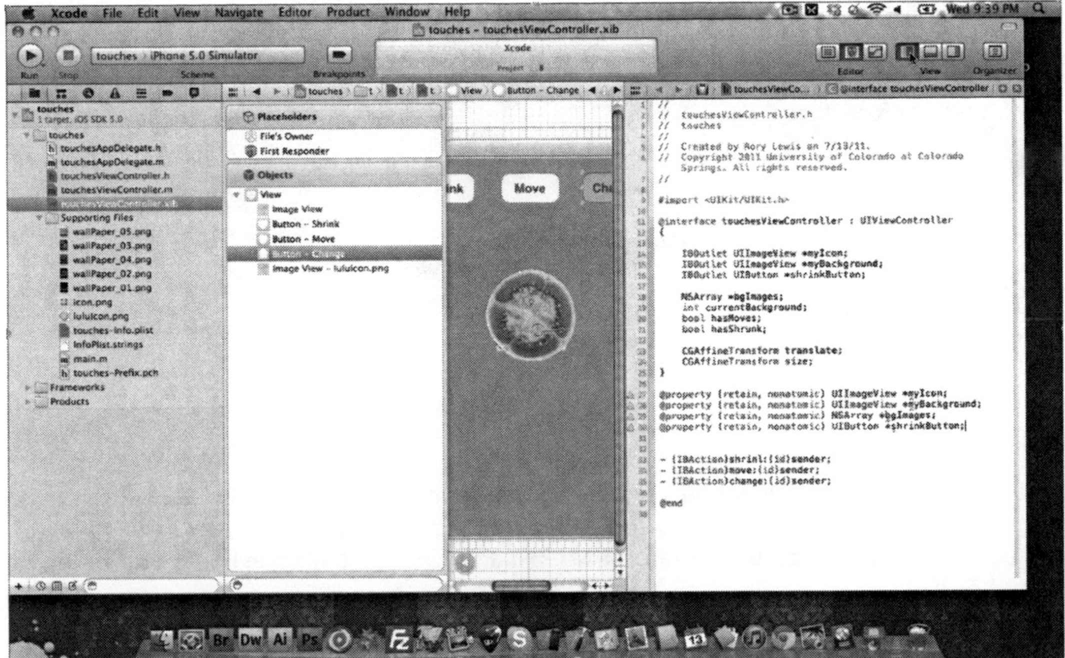

Figure 5–30. *After writing in your @properties, open the Navigator.*

30. We now need to enter your `@properties` for synthesis, as explained in Chapter 4. You need to synthesize your three `IBOutlets` and the array with an `@property` with `(nonatomic, retain)` directives. Recall from Chapter 4 that when we make the mutability nonatomic, we're asking Apple to handle this! Also, the retain means that with respect to memory management, we will maintain control. OK, now write in the following code right above the three `IBActions` you entered for your buttons, as shown in Figure 5–30.

```
@property (retain, nonatomic) UIImageView *myIcon;
@property (retain, nonatomic) UIImageView *myBackground;
@property (retain, nonatomic) NSArray *bgImages;
@property (retain, nonatomic) UIButton *shrinkButton;
```

With this done, we are now finished coding your header file. Before moving onto the implementation file, I strongly encourage you to check every letter, space, semicolon, empty line, and comma of your header code against mine. When you are done, let's move towards the implementation file. OK, so this is how your header file should look:

```
#import <UIKit/UIKit.h>
@interface touchesViewController : UIViewController
{

 IBOutlet UIImageView *myIcon;
 IBOutlet UIImageView *myBackground;
 IBOutlet UIButton *shrinkButton;

NSArray *bgImages;
```

```
 int currentBackground;
 bool hasMoved;
 bool hasShrunk;

 CGAffineTransform translate;
 CGAffineTransform size;
 UIButton *move;
}

@property (retain, nonatomic) UIImageView *myIcon;
@property (retain, nonatomic) UIImageView *myBackground;
@property (retain, nonatomic) NSArray *bgImages;
@property (retain, nonatomic) UIButton *shrinkButton;
- (IBAction)shrink:(id)sender;
- (IBAction)move:(id)sender;
- (IBAction)change:(id)sender;

@end
```

Once you are confident that every line of your code matches mine, you need to start getting your view area ready to do some huge coding. Start by opening the Navigator panel, which pops up on the panel on the left-hand side of your screen, as illustrated in Figure 5–30.

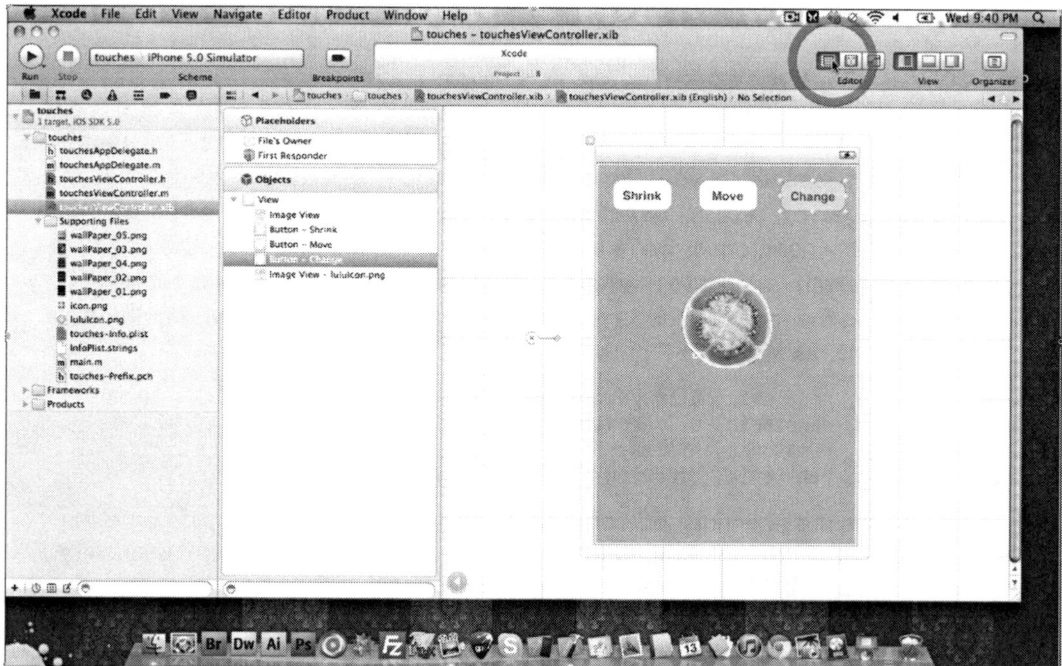

Figure 5–31. *After opening the Navigator, close the Assistant and click the Standard editor.*

31. We no longer need to see either the nib or the Assistant. We just need wide open spaces to code your implementation file. Now that you've opened the Navigator, close the Assistant and open the Standard editor, as illustrated in Figure 5–31. Now go into the navigation pane and click your implementation file: `touchesViewController.m`.

Working in the Implementation File

In this section, I will teach you how to go about the first two tasks; one needs to be performed immediately upon opening the implementation file. The first task is synthesis, which is typically only one line that you will code. Second is the `viewDidLoad` method that typically instantiates by itself; however, in more complex code, we need to add code into the `viewDidLoad` method, as we will today.

Synthesis

I have made a point to encourage students and readers to grow into the habit of always synthesizing in the implementation immediately after coding the `@property` directives in the header files. You may have noticed that both in Chapter 4 and in this chapter, the last code I wrote in the header file was the `@property` directives for synthesis. This is because if you get into the habit of immediately performing synthesis on the items you just coded in the header file, you will not forget to do it at all—you won't have to waste time going back and refreshing your memory as to what you were going to synthesize.

We just performed `@synthesis` on `myIcon`, `myBackground`, `bgImages` and `shrinkButton`. This is what we need to synthesize first when we open up the header. What follows is how I think about it; this makes it very easy.

```
@implementation touchesViewController
@synthesize   items you just performed @properties on
- (void)didReceiveMemoryWarning
...
...
...
```

Now, by plugging that idea into this application, we get

```
@implementation touchesViewController
@synthesize  myIcon, myBackground, bgImages, shrinkButton;
- (void)didReceiveMemoryWarning
...
...
...
```

viewDidLoad

The code inside the `viewDidLoad` method runs after machine language code reserves some space in memory for your View. You will notice that the first thing called inside `viewDidLoad` is its superclass, `superviewDidLoad`. **Now before you freak out**, just as rats are a subclass of rodents, viewDidLoad is a subclass of superviewDidLoad, so the first thing Apple gets viewDidLoad to do is call all the code from its superclass. It's here, at this exact moment of time, that we need to perform some tasks.

```
- (void)viewDidLoad
{
    [super viewDidLoad];
Set all our button and backgrounds to the start state
Create an array with all our wallpapers inside of it
Set how much the shrink button will shrink the lulu fruit icon
Set how much the move button will move the lulu fruit icon
Set the background image to the current background image

}
```

Set Buttons and Backgrounds to the Start State

Let's look at how to set all our buttons and backgrounds to their start state. This is to create a clean slate before the program starts to run. In order to create a clean slate in code, we need to set our state-changing variables to zero (or to nil). We have three such variables that tell us whether a state has changes: hasMoved, hasShrunk, and currentBackground. Remember that both hasMoved and hasShrunk are Booleans, so they can either be "YES" or "NO." The obvious start state for these is that they have not been moved yet. So, we need to set both hasMoved and hasShrunk to "NO." This leaves us with currentBackground, which keeps track of which one of our five wallpapers is currently In the background and viewed by the user. Recall that we assigned currentBackground to be of type integer. This is easy: we simply set it to zero. See the following bold print:

```
- (void)viewDidLoad
{
    [super viewDidLoad];
hasMoved = NO;
    hasShrunk = NO;
    currentBackground = 0;

Create an array with all our wallpapers inside of it
Set how much the shrink button will shrink the lulu fruit icon
Set how much the move button will move the lulu fruit icon
Set the background image to the current background image
}
```

Create Our Array with All Our Wallpapers Inside of It

Now, we need to create an array, which is just a list of things, and fill it up with our wallpapers. The supernova geeky way to say this is as follows: "We need to create an NSArray object and initialize it with some objects of type png." That's not too obtuse, is it? Recall that we did declare the array in our header file. Often, students are so fearful of arrays that they forget to declare them when they write their exam code. Recall in the header file we wrote "NSArray *bgImages," so we have declared an array and called it bgImages. Right away, we know we need to write "bgImages = (the stuff that will make our array come to life)." There are many complex ways to use arrays, but we will use the plain cheeseburger . . .or should I say . . . Apple methods using the NSArray initializers. They are pretty much the same as the factory methods, only you do the allocation yourself, which is in the form of NSArray.

```
name of your array = [[NSArray alloc] initWithObjects: @"your 1st object", @" your 2nd
object ", @" your 3rd object ", nil];
```

This looks all cluttered, so looking at the end of it, you'll see that all your objects are separated by commas; then, we tell the array it has ended by putting that""nil"" at the end. Let's do two things here. First, let's plug the real name of our array—bgImages—into the template, and then we'll take the contents between these commas and place them onto their own separate lines and see if this makes more sense.

```
bgImages array  = [[NSArray alloc] initWithObjects:
@"your 1st object",
@" your 2nd object ",
@" your 3rd object ",
nil];
```

Pretty cool, huh?! This really spooky code is actually making sense to you! Yeah! OK, we're not quite there yet though. We need to do one more thing before we bring this array to life. We need to wrap our heads around the UIImage class reference, which is an object the folks at Apple wrote to display images. Our objects are images, but really, they are filenames that contain images. We need to use the UIImage together with a method called imageNamed that returns image objects connected to filenames. So, for each file name, we need to use UIImage imageNamed. I have illustrated this as follows:

```
name of your array  = [[NSArray alloc] initWithObjects:
[UIImage imageNamed:@ »WallPaper_01.png »],
[UIImage imageNamed:@ »WallPaper_02.png »],
[UIImage imageNamed:@ »WallPaper_03.png »],
[UIImage imageNamed:@ »WallPaper_04.png »],
[UIImage imageNamed:@ »WallPaper_05.png »],
nil];
```

With that code, we have created an array that contains our five images. All we need to do now is insert it into our code. See the following bold print:

```
- (void)viewDidLoad
{
    [super viewDidLoad];
hasMoved = NO;
    hasShrunk = NO;
    currentBackground = 0;

bgImages = [[NSArray alloc] initWithObjects:
                [UIImage imageNamed:@ »WallPaper_01.png »],
                [UIImage imageNamed:@ »WallPaper_02.png »],
                [UIImage imageNamed:@ »WallPaper_03.png »],
                [UIImage imageNamed:@ »WallPaper_04.png »],
                [UIImage imageNamed:@ »WallPaper_05.png »],
                nil];
```

```
Set how much the shrink button will shrink the lulu fruit icon
Set how much the move button will move the lulu fruit icon
Set the background image to the current background image
}
```

Set How Much We Will Shrink the Lulu Fruit Icon

It's really easy to set how much we will shrink the lulu fruit icon when we press the Shrink button. Remember when we discussed at the beginning of this chapter how CGAffine is able to obey us when we instruct it change our object's position, angle, shape, scale, and so on? Well now we are going to use it. I have randomly decided to shrink the lulu fruit icon by 25%. This means that we need to tell CGAffine two things: first that we want to scale the image, and second, how much we want to scale it on the x- and y-axes. We want to use CGAffine to scale the stuff we use . . . hmmm . . . let's guess . . . Ah! how about CGAffineTransformMakeScale? Yes! We're correct. Ok, now for the next assignment. To scale the image by 25%, we need to scale both the x- and y-axes equally at 0.25; but before we enter this into the code, remember in our header file we created a variable called size of type CGAffineTransform? Well we need to set the size variable equal to the 25% shrinkage we tell the CGAffineTransformMakeScale code to perform. This is illustrated by the following:

```
- (void)viewDidLoad
{
    [super viewDidLoad];
hasMoved = NO;
    hasShrunk = NO;
    currentBackground = 0;

bgImages = [[NSArray alloc] initWithObjects:
                [UIImage imageNamed:@"WallPaper_01.png"],
                [UIImage imageNamed:@ »WallPaper_02.png »],
                [UIImage imageNamed:@ »WallPaper_03.png »],
                [UIImage imageNamed:@ »WallPaper_04.png »],
                [UIImage imageNamed:@ »WallPaper_05.png »],
                nil];
size = CGAffineTransformMakeScale(.25, .25);
Set how much the move button will move the lulu fruit icon
Set the background image to the current background image
}
```

Set How Much We Will Move the Lulu Fruit Icon

In the same way that we made CGAffineTransformMakeScale tell our size variable to hold the amount we will shrink the icon, we will now use Translation. This is a geeky way of saying how much we will make it travel across the screen in CGAffineTransformMakeTranslation to tell the move variable we created in our header file of type CGAffineTransform to hold the amount we want to move it. I have randomly chosen to only move our lulu fruit icon up 100 pixels on the y-axis. "Up" means we need to subtract pixels from the y-axis. We only want to subtract 100 pixels on the y-axis and leave the x-axis alone (0,-100). This is illustrated as follows:

```
- (void)viewDidLoad
{
    [super viewDidLoad];
hasMoved = NO;
    hasShrunk = NO;
    currentBackground = 0;

bgImages = [[NSArray alloc] initWithObjects:
                [UIImage imageNamed:@ »WallPaper_01.png »],
                [UIImage imageNamed:@ »WallPaper_02.png »],
                [UIImage imageNamed:@ »WallPaper_03.png »],
                [UIImage imageNamed:@ »WallPaper_04.png »],
                [UIImage imageNamed:@ »WallPaper_05.png »],
                nil];
size = CGAffineTransformMakeScale(.25, .25);
    translate = CGAffineTransformMakeTranslation(0,-100);
Set the background image to the current background image
}
```

Set the Background Image to the Current Background Image

The last job we need to do in the `viewDidLoad` is to set the background image to the current background image. What does this mean!? I can just hear you saying this out loud and scratching your head. Let's think about this. We have created an array that holds our five images. We will set each of those images with a number. When we press the Change button, whatever number image is on our background, we will replace it with the next one. We have set `currentBackground` to zero. So, the first time somebody presses the Change button, it will use the code we have yet to code to change the `currentBackground` from 0 to 0+1, which means that the current background will now be the next background in the array.

> **NOTE:** I am not going to explain the code at this point because most of us just paste it in when we need to get the object at an index and place inside a variable we created.

This is how I want you to use it now and later on your own: your variable that contains your image will be equal to [`bgImagesobjectAtIndex: your variable that in our case holds the back ground image`]. Don't think about this too much. Just use it as I have illustrated in the following code.

```
- (void)viewDidLoad
{
    [super viewDidLoad];
hasMoved = NO;
    hasShrunk = NO;
    currentBackground = 0;

bgImages = [[NSArray alloc] initWithObjects:
```

```
                [UIImage imageNamed:@ »WallPaper_01.png »],
                [UIImage imageNamed:@ »WallPaper_02.png »],
                [UIImage imageNamed:@ »WallPaper_03.png »],
                [UIImage imageNamed:@ »WallPaper_04.png »],
                [UIImage imageNamed:@ »WallPaper_05.png »],
                nil];
size = CGAffineTransformMakeScale(.25, .25);
    translate = CGAffineTransformMakeTranslation(0,-100);
 myBackground.image = [bgImages objectAtIndex:currentBackground];
}
```

```
- (void)viewDidLoad
{
    [super viewDidLoad];

    hasMoved = NO;
    hasShrunk = NO;
    currentBackground = 0;

    bgImages = [[NSArray alloc] initWithObjects:
                [UIImage imageNamed:@"WallPaper_01.png"],
                [UIImage imageNamed:@"WallPaper_02.png"],
                [UIImage imageNamed:@"WallPaper_03.png"],
                [UIImage imageNamed:@"WallPaper_04.png"],
                [UIImage imageNamed:@"WallPaper_05.png"],
                nil];

    size = CGAffineTransformMakeScale(.25, .25);
    translate = CGAffineTransformMakeTranslation(0,-100);

    myBackground.image = [bgImages objectAtIndex:currentBackground];
}

- (void)viewDidUnload
{
    [super viewDidUnload];
}

- (void)viewWillAppear:(BOOL)animated
{
    [super viewWillAppear:animated];
}

- (void)viewDidAppear:(BOOL)animated
{
    [super viewDidAppear:animated];
}

- (void)viewWillDisappear:(BOOL)animated
{
    [super viewWillDisappear:animated];
}
```

Figure 5–32. *Check that your code is complete in the implementation file.*

32. With all of this completed, your `viewDidLoad` should look like mine, as illustrated in Figure 5–32.

New Heading

We will be personally handling much of how we unload memory associated with our views. We will handle this with our own handwritten code as we switch from one background to the next, so we can delete some of the boilerplate code Apple instantiated for us.

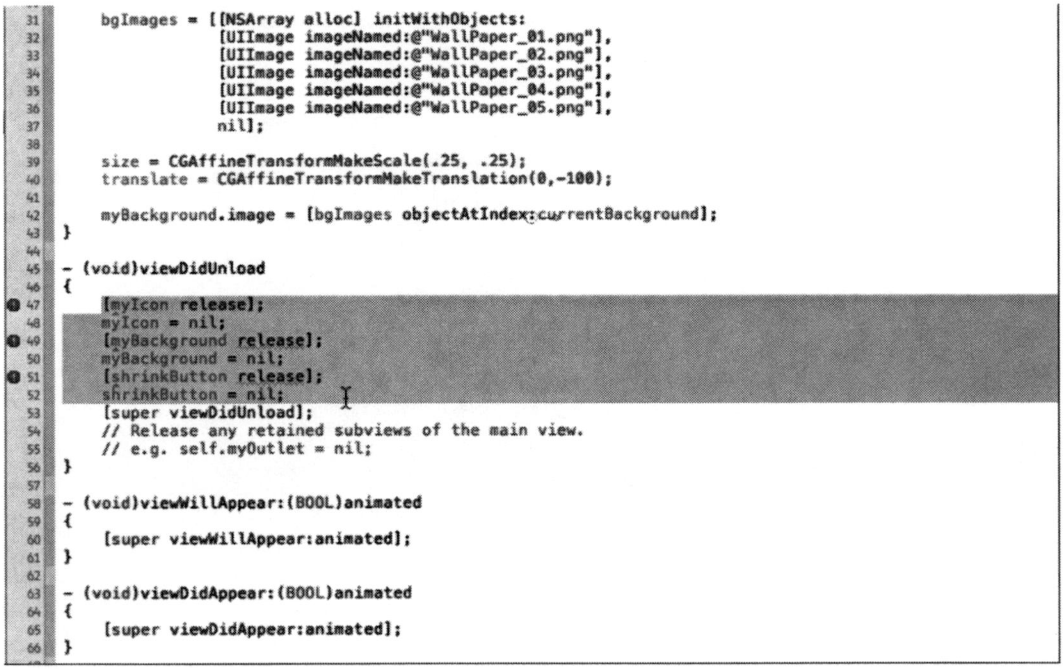

```
    bgImages = [[NSArray alloc] initWithObjects:
                [UIImage imageNamed:@"WallPaper_01.png"],
                [UIImage imageNamed:@"WallPaper_02.png"],
                [UIImage imageNamed:@"WallPaper_03.png"],
                [UIImage imageNamed:@"WallPaper_04.png"],
                [UIImage imageNamed:@"WallPaper_05.png"],
                nil];

    size = CGAffineTransformMakeScale(.25, .25);
    translate = CGAffineTransformMakeTranslation(0,-100);

    myBackground.image = [bgImages objectAtIndex:currentBackground];
}

- (void)viewDidUnload
{
    [myIcon release];
    myIcon = nil;
    [myBackground release];
    myBackground = nil;
    [shrinkButton release];
    shrinkButton = nil;
    [super viewDidUnload];
    // Release any retained subviews of the main view.
    // e.g. self.myOutlet = nil;
}

- (void)viewWillAppear:(BOOL)animated
{
    [super viewWillAppear:animated];
}

- (void)viewDidAppear:(BOOL)animated
{
    [super viewDidAppear:animated];
}
```

Figure 5–33. *Trim down your viewDidUnload.*

33. As illustrated in Figure 5–33, go to your `viewDidUnload` and select all the code from the beginning of `[myIcon release]` to the end of your `shrinkButton = nil` and delete it all.

```
- (BOOL)shouldAutorotateToInterfaceOrientation:(UIInterfaceOrientation)interfaceOrientation
{
    // Return YES for supported orientations
    return (interfaceOrientation != UIInterfaceOrientationPortraitUpsideDown);
}

-(void) touchesMoved:(NSSet *)touches withEvent:(UIEvent *)event{
    UITouch *touch = [[event allTouches] anyObject];

    if (CGRectContainsPoint([myIcon frame], [touch locationInView:nil]))
    {
        if (hasMoved == YES && hasShrunk == YES) {
            myIcon.transform = CGAffineTransformTranslate(size, 0, 0);
            hasMoved = NO;
        }

        if (hasMoved == YES && hasShrunk == NO) {
            //myIcon.transform = translate;
            myIcon.transform = CGAffineTransformMakeTranslation(0,0);
            hasMoved = NO;
        }

        myIcon.center = [touch locationInView:nil];
    }

}


- (IBAction)shrink:(id)sender {
    if (hasShrunk) {
        [shrinkButton setTitle:@"Shrink" forState:UIControlStateNormal];
    } else{
        [shrinkButton setTitle:@"Grow" forState:UIControlStateNormal];
    }

    if (hasShrunk == NO && hasMoved == NO) {
        [UIView beginAnimations:nil context:NULL];
        [UIView setAnimationDuration:1.0];
        myIcon.transform = size;
        [UIView commitAnimations];
        hasShrunk = YES;
    }
```

Figure 5–34. *Code your touchesMoved method.*

34. Now we are going to code the touchesMoved method. Yes, I know you don't even see it yet! What I want you to do after deleting the appropriate code in your viewDidUnload is scroll down through all the methods Apple instantiated for you. Scroll through your viewWillAppear, viewDidAppear, viewWillDisappear, viewDidDisappear, and shouldAutorotateToInterfaceOrientation. Now you will see three methods for our three actions we created in the header file for our three buttons.

```
- (IBAction)shrink:(id)sender {
}
- (IBAction)move:(id)sender {
}
- (IBAction)change:(id)sender {
}

@end
```

This is really great because we will place all our code inside these methods, but hold on . . .we're missing the method that will handle our touching and moving the lulu fruit icon with our fingertips! Yup, we need to create that from scratch. Right above the shrink method, which is at the top, I want you to create about four blank lines and then simply enter touches and code completion will bring up touchesMoved; press Enter, and then enter touches again, and the code completion will bring up touches withEvent:(UIEvent *)event{. Now you will have all four methods you need to code, as illustrated by the following, where I have highlighted the four variables we created in the header file.

```
-(void) touchesMoved:(NSSet *)touches withEvent:(UIEvent *)event{
}
- (IBAction)shrink:(id)sender {
}
- (IBAction)move:(id)sender {
}
- (IBAction)change:(id)sender {
}
@end
```

Now we can enter the code inside our touchesMoved class. But let's look at it from a high altitude to start off with. What do we want the touchesMoved method to do? Well, this may not seem obvious, but we simply want the touchesMoved method to do the following:

```
-(void) touchesMoved:(NSSet *)touches withEvent:(UIEvent *)event{
Grab code that can sense all touches on the screen
Check if a touch on the screen is on the lulu fruit icon. If yes then
Check if icon was moved and shrunk using buttons if yes then
Keep shrunk size and move icon to its position before move button
Check if icon was moved and not shrunk using buttons if yes then
Move icon to its position before move button
Set icon to be at the current touch location
}
```

Part of my teaching method is that I do not always teach you everything. You've seen this already when we blindly coded the first couple of hello worlds. At this point I'm going to teach you how to use certain tools to perform tasks. I will not teach you how all of these tools work right now, but I am going to teach you what tool to grab. At this point, we need to get code that can sense all touches on the screen. I want you to just remember that when you want the User Interface to do cool stuff with touches, we need to first call code Apple wrote that senses and records all touches. So, type in UITouches and one of the options the code completion will present is `UITouch *touch = [[event allTouches] anyObject]`, and this is the tool I want you to invoke before you do anything with touches. Don't think about how it works right now. Just know to call it at this point. Refer to the bold print in the following example.

```
-(void) touchesMoved:(NSSet *)touches withEvent:(UIEvent *)event{
UITouch *touch = [[event allTouches] anyObject];
Check if a touch on the screen is on the lulu fruit icon.  If yes then
Check if icon was moved and shrunk using buttons if yes then
Keep shrunk size and move icon to its position before move button
Check if icon was moved and not shrunk using buttons if yes then
Move icon to its position before move button
Set icon to be at the current touch location
}
```

Now we need an if statement to check if a touch on the screen is on the lulu fruit icon. We need to know that the iPhone looks at the rectangle that our object fits into, and see if the person's finger is within that rectangle. To do this, we use `if (CGRectContainsPoint([myIcon frame], [touch locationInView:nil]))`. You will only need to type in if and CGRect, and then touch and code completion will fill in the rest. We will nest two more if statements inside of this if statement. Notice how I have taken our road map tasks and nested them inside this `if` statement as illustrated in the following:

```
-(void) touchesMoved:(NSSet *)touches withEvent:(UIEvent *)event{
UITouch *touch = [[event allTouches] anyObject];
    if (CGRectContainsPoint([myIcon frame], [touch locationInView:nil]))
    {
Check if icon was moved and shrunk using buttons if yes then {
Keep shrunk size and move icon to its position before move button
}

Check if icon was moved and not shrunk using buttons if yes then {
Move icon to its position before move button
     }
Set icon to be at the current touch location
}
}
```

At this point, two nested conditions need to be inserted inside the `if` statement we just created. But let's think about this. All we want to do is test to see whether the lulu fruit icon has been moved by the buttons, and if it has, regardless of whether it's been shrunk, we need to reset whether it was moved back to a state in which it hadn't moved. The two conditions that would have moved the lulu fruit icon are: when we moved it and shrank it, or when we moved it and didn't shrink it; either way, we want to change the state to not being moved so that when the user's finger touches the lulu fruit icon, we can say, "*You were not moved, but now you are being moved*." We cannot say, "*You were moved and now you're being moved again*."

```
-(void) touchesMoved:(NSSet *)touches withEvent:(UIEvent *)event{
UITouch *touch = [[event allTouches] anyObject];
    if (CGRectContainsPoint([myIcon frame], [touch locationInView:nil]))
    {
        if (hasMoved == YES && hasShrunk == YES) {
            myIcon.transform = CGAffineTransformTranslate(size, 0, 0);
            hasMoved = NO;
}

if (hasMoved == YES && hasShrunk == NO) {
            myIcon.transform = CGAffineTransformMakeTranslation(0,0);
            hasMoved = NO;
}

Set icon to be at the current touch location
}
}
```

> **NOTE:** If you were watching the video, in the second if statement, I wrote `myIcon.transform = translate`, not `CGAffineTransformMakeTranslation(0,0);` It does not make too much difference, but it is better to use the latter. I did change it so in the code that you download, it will also be the latter.

The last thing we need to do is set the location of the icon to the exact position that the finger is moving it at any moment. This is stock boilerplate code that you will use over and over again to keep track of an object as one's finger moves it around the screen. We use the *variable name*.center = [touch locationInView:nil], as indicated in the following code:

```
-(void) touchesMoved:(NSSet *)touches withEvent:(UIEvent *)event{
UITouch *touch = [[event allTouches] anyObject];
    if (CGRectContainsPoint([myIcon frame], [touch locationInView:nil]))
    {
        if (hasMoved == YES && hasShrunk == YES) {
            myIcon.transform = CGAffineTransformTranslate(size, 0, 0);
            hasMoved = NO;
}

 if (hasMoved == YES && hasShrunk == NO) {
            myIcon.transform = CGAffineTransformMakeTranslation(0,0);
            hasMoved = NO;
     }

myIcon.center = [touch locationInView:nil];
    }
}
```

We have now completed writing the touchesMoved method. Compare your code to how mine looks in Figure 5–34.

Coding the Shrink Button

We now want to write the code we will invoke once the user presses the shrink button.

```
- (IBAction)shrink:(id)sender {
    if (hasShrunk) {
        [shrinkButton setTitle:@"Shrink" forState:UIControlStateNormal];
    } else{
        [shrinkButton setTitle:@"Grow" forState:UIControlStateNormal];
    }

    if (hasShrunk == NO && hasMoved == NO) {
        [UIView beginAnimations:nil context:NULL];
        [UIView setAnimationDuration:1.0];
        myIcon.transform = size;
        [UIView commitAnimations];
        hasShrunk = YES;
    }
    else if (hasShrunk == NO && hasMoved == YES) {
        [UIView beginAnimations:nil context:NULL];
        [UIView setAnimationDuration:1.0];
        myIcon.transform = CGAffineTransformScale(translate, .25, .25);
        [UIView commitAnimations];
        hasShrunk = YES;
    }
    else if (hasShrunk == YES && hasMoved == YES) {
        [UIView beginAnimations:nil context:NULL];
        [UIView setAnimationDuration:1.0];
        myIcon.transform = CGAffineTransformScale(translate, 1, 1);
        [UIView commitAnimations];
        hasShrunk = NO;
    }
    else {
        [UIView beginAnimations:nil context:NULL];
        [UIView setAnimationDuration:1.0];
        myIcon.transform = CGAffineTransformIdentity;
        [UIView commitAnimations];
        hasShrunk = NO;
    }
}

- (IBAction)move:(id)sender {

    if (hasMoved == NO && hasShrunk == NO) {
        [UIView beginAnimations:nil context:NULL];
        [UIView setAnimationDuration:1.0];
        myIcon.transform = translate;
        [UIView commitAnimations];
```

Figure 5–35. *Coding the shrink method*

35. Remember, in the header file, we created an outlet that allowed us to change the font from "Shrink" to "Grow" once somebody pressed the button? This is because we cannot allow the lulu fruit to be shrunk twice in a row, or it would virtually disappear! So, the first thing we need to do is change the text. The second thing we need to do is keep track of the possible state of the Shrink and Move buttons, so that we can tell the `CGAffine` to properly transform the lulu fruit icon for us. The code looks something like this:

```
-(IBAction)shrink:(id)sender
{
if it has not been shrunk, keep the text saying Shrink, else change it to Grow
if it has not been shrunk or moved - do stuff
else if it has not been shrunk and has been moved - do stuff
else if it has been shrunk and moved - do stuff
else - do stuff
}
```

To change the text, we will use the `setTitle` and `forState:UIControlStateNormal` using the following format: `your variable namesetTitle:@"your text" forState:UIControlStateNormal`. We have called the outlet for our Shrink button, `shrinkButton`, when we declared it many years ago in the header file. The text we will use will be "`Grow`"" once it has been changed, and then "`Shrink`"" once it has been changed again; this loop continues forever as illustrated by the following.

```
-(IBAction)shrink:(id)sender
{
```

```
    if (hasShrunk) {
        [shrinkButton setTitle:@"Shrink" forState:UIControlStateNormal];
    } else {
        [shrinkButton setTitle:@"Grow" forState:UIControlStateNormal];
    }
if it has not been shrunk or moved - do stuff
else if it has not been shrunk and has been moved - do stuff
else if it has been shrunk and moved - do stuff
else - do stuff
}
```

We write nested if statements by starting with an if and ending with and else; between the beginning if and the ending else if, we stick in all the else ifs we need. In our case, I have randomly chosen to arrange the if statements as follows: if 'both NO'; else if 'NO and YES'; else if 'both YES'; and finally else whatever remains, which is 'YES and NO'. Converting the aforementioned into code is illustrated as follows:

```
-(IBAction)shrink:(id)sender
{
    if (hasShrunk) {
        [shrinkButton setTitle:@"Shrink" forState:UIControlStateNormal];
    } else {
        [shrinkButton setTitle:@"Grow" forState:UIControlStateNormal];
    }

if(hasShrunk == NO && hasMoved == NO)
{
- do stuff
}
else if(hasShrunk == NO && hasMoved == YES)
{
- do stuff
}
else if(hasShrunk == YES && hasMoved == YES)
{
- do stuff
}
else
{
- do stuff
}
}
```

Before we "do stuff" to the state of the lulu fruit icon within each nested if, we need to perform, within each nested if, certain preliminary chores. We need to tell the microprocessor how many seconds we want the 'stuff' to last, and then, after doing whatever stuff we want to our lulu fruit icon (using CGAffineTransform), we need to update its state. This is illustrated in the following non-code, in plain English:

```
-(IBAction)shrink:(id)sender
{
    if (hasShrunk) {
        [shrinkButton setTitle:@"Shrink" forState:UIControlStateNormal];
    } else {
        [shrinkButton setTitle:@"Grow" forState:UIControlStateNormal];
```

```
    }

if(hasShrunk == NO && hasMoved == NO)
{
Start animation with duration of 1 second
- do stuff
Commit animations and update shrunk state
}
else if(hasShrunk == NO && hasMoved == YES)
{
Start animation with duration of 1 second
- do stuff
Commit animations and update shrunk state
}
else if(hasShrunk == YES && hasMoved == YES)
{
Start animation with duration of 1 second
- do stuff
Commit animations and update shrunk state
}
else
{
Start animation with duration of 1 second
- do stuff
Commit animations and update shrunk state
}
}
```

I will keep this non-code, plain English roadmap of these trivial chores in this state for a while, so it does not clutter up the coding landscape as we focus on more important elements. We now need to take a fairly high level approach to what we will do in each of the four cases.

1. **If:** *Both of the buttons have not been pressed* and we press the Shrink button, we will
    - Shrink the lulu fruit icon.
2. **Else if:** The Shrink button has not been pressed, but we do press the Move button, we will
    - Keep the icon where we moved it, but go ahead and shrink the lulu fruit icon.
3. **Else If:** Both the Shrink and Move buttons have been pressed, and we press the Shrink button again, we will
    - Grow the lulu fruit icon back up to its original state and move it to its moved location.
    - Recall that we have already coded the text inside the Shrink button to change from Shrink to Grow.

4. **Else if:** The Shrink button has been pressed, but the Move button has not been pressed, we will
   - Grow the lulu fruit icon back up to its original state and keep it in its current location.

Keeping the preceding scenario in non-code, plain English, this is how it will be placed inside the code:

```
-(IBAction)shrink:(id)sender

{
    if (hasShrunk) {
        [shrinkButton setTitle:@"Shrink" forState:UIControlStateNormal];
    } else {
        [shrinkButton setTitle:@"Grow" forState:UIControlStateNormal];
    }

if(hasShrunk == NO && hasMoved == NO)
{
Start animation with duration of 1 second
Shrink icon
Commit animations and update shrunk state
}
else if(hasShrunk == NO && hasMoved == YES)
{
Start animation with duration of 1 second
Keep icon moved and shrink icon
Commit animations and update shrunk state
}
else if(hasShrunk == YES && hasMoved == YES)
{
Start animation with duration of 1 second
Keep icon moved and change icon back to normal size
Commit animations and update shrunk state
}
else
{
Start animation with duration of 1 second
Move icon back to normal size and location
Commit animations and update shrunk state
}
}
```

Now, we will change it to real code.

- In the first case, to shrink the lulu fruit icon, do the following:
  - Set the transform of the lulu fruit icon to be the size that is contained in our variable `size`.
- In the second case, to keep the icon moved where we moved it, but still shrink it, we will do the following:
  - Set the transform of the lulu fruit icon to be located at the place where the transform method has moved it.

- But now we've lost "size," so we need to re- shrink it to .25 of its state.
- In the third case, to grow the lulu fruit icon back up to its original state and move it to its moved location, the following should be done:
  - Set the transform of the lulu fruit icon to be located at the place where the transform method has moved it.
  - Now, bring it back up to its original size.
- In the last case, to grow the lulu fruit icon back up to its original state and keep it in its current location, do the following:
  - Bring it all back to its original state.

Placing the preceding examples into the code gives us the following:

```
-(IBAction)shrink:(id)sender
{
    if (hasShrunk) {
        [shrinkButton setTitle:@"Shrink" forState:UIControlStateNormal];
    } else {
        [shrinkButton setTitle:@"Grow" forState:UIControlStateNormal];
    }

if(hasShrunk == NO && hasMoved == NO)
{
Start animation with duration of 1 second
myIcon.transform = size;
Commit animations and update shrunk state
}
else if(hasShrunk == NO && hasMoved == YES)
{
Start animation with duration of 1 second
myIcon.transform = CGAffineTransformScale(translate,.25, .25);
Commit animations and update shrunk state
}
else if(hasShrunk == YES && hasMoved == YES)
{
Start animation with duration of 1 second
myIcon.transform = CGAffineTransformScale(translate,1, 1);
Commit animations and update shrunk state
}
else
{
Start animation with duration of 1 second
myIcon.transform = CGAffineTransformIdentity;
Commit animations and update shrunk state
}
}
```

We now need to think about how we will update the shrunk state of the lulu fruit icon. In the first two cases, we did shrink the lulu icon, so we need to update the shrunk state to YES. In the last two cases, it was not shrunk, so we should update the shrunk state as being NO. See the following code:

NOTE: If this does not make sense, then think about it by looking at the explanation of the preceding code. Or just go along with it for now if your brain is tired—it's OK— just follow along.

```
-(IBAction)shrink:(id)sender
{
    if (hasShrunk) {
        [shrinkButton setTitle:@"Shrink" forState:UIControlStateNormal];
    } else {
        [shrinkButton setTitle:@"Grow" forState:UIControlStateNormal];
    }

if(hasShrunk == NO && hasMoved == NO)
{
Start animation with duration of 1 second
myIcon.transform = size;
Commit animations
hasShrunk = YES;
}
else if(hasShrunk == NO && hasMoved == YES)
{
Start animation with duration of 1 second
myIcon.transform = CGAffineTransformScale(translate,.25, .25);
Commit animations
hasShrunk = YES;
}
else if(hasShrunk == YES && hasMoved == YES)
{
Start animation with duration of 1 second
myIcon.transform = CGAffineTransformScale(translate,1, 1);
Commit animations
hasShrunk = NO;
}
else
{
Start animation with duration of 1 second
myIcon.transform = CGAffineTransformIdentity;
Commit animations
hasShrunk = NO;
}
}
```

Next, we will change the plain English chores within each nested `if` to actual code. We clear the state of the animation and set the animation to 1 second (I randomly chose 1 second, you can choose something else). After we perform our actions on the lulu fruit, we commit the actions. This is illustrated by the following code:

```
-(IBAction)shrink:(id)sender
{
    if (hasShrunk) {
        [shrinkButton setTitle:@"Shrink" forState:UIControlStateNormal];
    } else {
        [shrinkButton setTitle:@"Grow" forState:UIControlStateNormal];
    }
```

```
if(hasShrunk == NO && hasMoved == NO)
{
[UIView beginAnimations:nil context:NULL];
[UIView setAnimationDuration:1.0];
myIcon.transform = size;
[UIView commitAnimations];
hasShrunk = YES;
}
else if(hasShrunk == NO && hasMoved == YES)
{
[UIView beginAnimations:nil context:NULL];
[UIView setAnimationDuration:1.0];
myIcon.transform = CGAffineTransformScale(translate,.25, .25);
[UIView commitAnimations];
hasShrunk = YES;
}
else if(hasShrunk == YES && hasMoved == YES)
{
[UIView beginAnimations:nil context:NULL];
[UIView setAnimationDuration:1.0];
myIcon.transform = CGAffineTransformScale(translate,1, 1);
[UIView commitAnimations];
hasShrunk = NO;
}
else
{
[UIView beginAnimations:nil context:NULL];
[UIView setAnimationDuration:1.0];
myIcon.transform = CGAffineTransformIdentity;
[UIView commitAnimations];
hasShrunk = NO;
}
}
```

Lastly, we add some spacing between the sections within each conditional statement, and it should look very similar to my code in Figure 5–35.

Coding the Move Button

Programming the code that makes the Move button operate is exactly the same as the code we used for the Shrink button, except that we do not change the text inside the button, so leave that out.

```
- (IBAction)move:(id)sender {

    if (hasMoved == NO && hasShrunk == NO) {
        [UIView beginAnimations:nil context:NULL];
        [UIView setAnimationDuration:1.0];
        myIcon.transform = translate;
        [UIView commitAnimations];
        hasMoved = YES;
    }
    else if (hasMoved == NO && hasShrunk == YES) {
        [UIView beginAnimations:nil context:NULL];
        [UIView setAnimationDuration:1.0];
        myIcon.transform = CGAffineTransformTranslate(size, 0, -100);
        [UIView commitAnimations];
        hasMoved = YES;
    }
    else if (hasMoved == YES && hasShrunk == YES) {
        [UIView beginAnimations:nil context:NULL];
        [UIView setAnimationDuration:1.0];
        myIcon.transform = CGAffineTransformTranslate(size, 0, 0);
        [UIView commitAnimations];
        hasMoved = YES;
    }
    else {
        [UIView beginAnimations:nil context:NULL];
        [UIView setAnimationDuration:1.0];
        myIcon.transform = CGAffineTransformMakeTranslation(0, 0);
        [UIView commitAnimations];
        hasMoved = YES;
    }

}

- (IBAction)change:(id)sender {
    currentBackground++;
    if (currentBackground >=[bgImages count])
        currentBackground = 0;

    [UIView beginAnimations:@"changeview" context:nil];
    [UIView setAnimationDuration:1];
    [UIView setAnimationCurve:UIViewAnimationCurveEaseInOut];

    if (currentBackground == 1)
        [UIView setAnimationTransition:UIViewAnimationTransitionFlipFromLeft forView:self.view cache:YES];
```

Figure 5–36. *Coding the move method*

36. We are then left with the same four states. Simply change all the cases of "shrunk" to "moved" and it's identical. Check your code against mine in Figure 5–36.

> **NOTE:** I suggest that you first cut and paste the first "if" statements from the shrink method then swap out the shrinks and moves. After this, paste it three times; change the relevant cases of "if" to "else if" and "else." Lastly, change the scaling to moving in the `CGAffineTransformTranslates`.

Coding the Change Button

The only thing left to do now is to write the code that will change the backgrounds when we press the Change button.

```
            [UIView beginAnimations:nil context:NULL];
            [UIView setAnimationDuration:1.0];
            myIcon.transform = CGAffineTransformTranslate(size, 0, 0);
            [UIView commitAnimations];
            hasMoved = YES;
        }
        else {
            [UIView beginAnimations:nil context:NULL];
            [UIView setAnimationDuration:1.0];
            myIcon.transform = CGAffineTransformMakeTranslation(0, 0);
            [UIView commitAnimations];
            hasMoved = YES;
        }

}

- (IBAction)change:(id)sender {
    currentBackground++;
    if (currentBackground >=[bgImages count])
        currentBackground = 0;

    [UIView beginAnimations:@"changeview" context:nil];
    [UIView setAnimationDuration:1];
    [UIView setAnimationCurve:UIViewAnimationCurveEaseInOut];

    if (currentBackground == 1)
        [UIView setAnimationTransition:UIViewAnimationTransitionFlipFromLeft forView:self.view cache:YES];

    if (currentBackground == 2)
        [UIView setAnimationTransition:UIViewAnimationTransitionCurlDown forView:self.view cache:YES];

    if (currentBackground == 3)
        [UIView setAnimationTransition:UIViewAnimationTransitionCurlUp forView:self.view cache:YES];

    if (currentBackground == 4)
        [UIView setAnimationTransition:UIViewAnimationTransitionFlipFromRight forView:self.view cache:YES];

    [UIView commitAnimations];
    myBackground.image = [bgImages objectAtIndex:currentBackground];

}


@end
```

Figure 5–37. *Code the change method.*

37. We will essentially perform five jobs: increment the current background; make sure the incrementation keeps the images contained in our array; initialize the `UIView`; create animations for our backgrounds as they get loaded; and lastly, commit and change the background. Our starting roadmap for our change method is as follows:

```
-(IBAction)change:(id)sender
{
Increment background to the next background image
Check to see currentBackground doesn't go off the array
Initialize the UIView
Create animations
Commit and change
}
```

I have said before that each time we press the Change button, it will change the image by changing the number of the background image. If wallPaper_01 is presently housed in the background and we press Change, then we will increment it; meaning, we will add one and bring on wallPaper_02 as the next background. All this means is that each time the Change button is pressed, before we do anything else, we need to increment the currentBackground as follows:

```
-(IBAction)change:(id)sender
{
currentBackground++;
Check to see currentBackground doesn't go off the array
Initialize the UIView
Create animations
Commit and change
}
```

If we keep incrementing, then we will go beyond the number of images lined up in our array. Therefore, we need to reset the count back to zero once we reach the number of images in our array. This is illustrated by the following:

```
-(IBAction)change:(id)sender
{
currentBackground++;
if(currentBackground >= [bgImages count])
                currentBackground = 0;
Initialize the UIView
Create animations
Commit and change
}
```

To initialize the UIView, we need to do two things, but I've added a third task just to be cool. We have to reset (reboot, set to zero—however you want to say it), the beginAnimations method that those incredibly supercalifragilistic dudes at Apple wrote! Then, we need to set how long each animation is going to be. As I mentioned when we did the initializing before, I set the initializing in-between changes to 1 second. To be cool, I incorporated a third task: determining how smoothly each animation will start and end using the UIViewAnimationCurveEaseInOut method. This is illustrated by the following:

```
-(IBAction)change:(id)sender
{
currentBackground++;
if(currentBackground >= [bgImages count])
currentBackground = 0;
[UIView beginAnimations:@"changeview" context:nil];
[UIView setAnimationDuration:1];
[UIView setAnimationCurve:UIViewAnimationCurveEaseInOut];
Create animations
Commit and change
}
```

NOTE: To actually change the backgrounds, we need be careful how we wrap our heads around this concept. Read this carefully and do your best to follow along.

We divide the changing of each background into two steps.

1. First, we ask whether the current background's numerical value, or tag, is the one we're dealing with. If it's true, then we perform the code within the squiggly brackets (shown in the next bullet).
2. We will then use the setAnimationTransition method to perform whatever other method we have chosen. There are methods to curl up, curl down, move in from the left or right, flip this way, do that, or do this. Or you can create your own method . . . when you become an uber geek. Right now, I'm just using curls and page flips, so I will call these *transitions* appropriately.

Looking at it a little more closely, for each animation, we use the form as follows:

```
if(currentBackground ==the # we want)
[UIView setAnimationTransition:
➥UIViewAnimationTransition the animation we choose
➥ forView:self.view
➥ cache:YES];
```

Now repeating this method and using randomly chosen animations for each animation, the code takes on the following form:

```
-(IBAction)change:(id)sender
{
currentBackground++;
if(currentBackground >= [bgImages count])
currentBackground = 0;
[UIView beginAnimations:@"changeview" context:nil];
[UIView setAnimationDuration:1];
[UIView setAnimationCurve:UIViewAnimationCurveEaseInOut];
if(currentBackground == 1)
[UIView setAnimationTransition:
➥UIViewAnimationTransitionFlipFromLeft
➥orView:self.
➥view cache:YES];

if(currentBackground == 2)
[UIView setAnimationTransition:
➥ UIViewAnimationTransitionCurlDown
➥orView:self.
➥view cache:YES];

if(currentBackground == 3)
[UIView setAnimationTransition:
➥ UIViewAnimationTransitionCurlUp
➥orView:self.
➥view cache:YES];

if(currentBackground == 4)
[UIView setAnimationTransition:
➥ UIViewAnimationTransitionFlipFromRight
➥orView:self.
```

```
↳view cache:YES];
```

Commit and change

}

The last step, again as we did before we simply need to commit the change and execute the code:

```
-(IBAction)change:(id)sender
{
currentBackground++;
if(currentBackground >= [bgImages count])
currentBackground = 0;
[UIView beginAnimations:@"changeview" context:nil];
[UIView setAnimationDuration:1];
[UIView setAnimationCurve:UIViewAnimationCurveEaseInOut];
if(currentBackground == 1)
[UIView setAnimationTransition:
↳UIViewAnimationTransitionFlipFromLeft
↳orView:self.
↳view cache:YES];

if(currentBackground == 2)
[UIView setAnimationTransition:
↳ UIViewAnimationTransitionCurlDown
↳orView:self.
↳view cache:YES];

if(currentBackground == 3)
[UIView setAnimationTransition:
↳ UIViewAnimationTransitionCurlUp
↳orView:self.
↳view cache:YES];

if(currentBackground == 4)
[UIView setAnimationTransition:
↳ UIViewAnimationTransitionFlipFromRight
↳orView:self.
↳view cache:YES];

[UIView commitAnimations];
myBackground.image = [bgImages ↳objectAtIndex:currentBackground];
}
```

Check your code against mine, as illustrated in Figure 5–37. We're done! Can you believe that? All you need to do is run it and your code will work beautifully . . . Ahh ... NOT! Not unless you're a super geek!

Running the Code

Let me explain something. The odds that it will work are small and that's OK! It's OK that your code does not work at first. Expecting your code to run beautifully the first time is similar to what my mother told me a couple of years ago. She called from across town at 5:00 o'clock in the afternoon and said, "Darling I'm just leaving now; I know it's 5:00 o'clock, but I should be there soon because I hope there will not be too much traffic today!" I could not believe what she had just said. I replied, "Mom, rather than expecting to be here in 20 minutes hoping there will not be traffic only to be horribly let down, why don't you expect it to take one hour and enjoy that new Deva Premal meditation CD I bought you? Relax and enjoy yourself!"

Likewise, expect there to be errors. Debugging our code is a HUGE part of being a computer scientist and expecting not to see any is only going to let you down. If there were no errors then you'd be lucky!

Figure 5–38. *The opening screen*

38. Once you run it, you can do four things: press one of the three buttons or move the icon around on your screen. This initial view is seen in Figure 5–38.

Figure 5–39. *Some more views*

39. Figure 5–39 shows three images. The first background displays where the Shrink button is pressed and then it changes to Grow. On the third image, we see the beginning of the flipping of the background to the next background.

Figure 5–40. *Views of the change backgrounds*

40. Figure 5–40 illustrates the page curling to the fourth background and the lulu fruit icon being moved by the touches function.

Digging the Code

Typically, I spend time digging the code that we flew over. However, this chapter was a huge leap, and I could not justify leaving you to flip back to this section to understand what was going on while you typed the code. As far as going deeper into the code is concerned, there's not much left to dig into—we did a pretty thorough job on it. In the next Chapter, we will look at switch views; we will "quickly" run the code and then come back to what we really did in the "Digging the Code" section. Let's close this chapter and give your brain a break.

In the Chapter Ahead

In Chapter 6, we will move into the next level of complexity: switch view applications. We will examine how a team of characters or roles within your code will work together to direct an outcome, or a series of outcomes, that will give the user the sense of seamless flow.

You will learn about delegators and switch view controllers, classes and subclasses, and "lazy loads." We will get into the nitty-gritty of the `.xib` files, examine the concept of memory deallocation, and learn about imbedded code comments. It's getting curiouser and curiouser. . .

Onward to the next chapter!

Chapter 6

Switches

After finishing the touches app in Chapter 5, you can say that you've coded Objective-C apps without flinching! You are not alone if, while coding Chapter 5, you felt as though you were struggling to make your way across a tough and rocky road. I say this because all programmers have had to journey over this road. It's absolutely OK to look back on that chapter and think to yourself that you don't remember what you did. Yes, that's normal, and I'm about to prove to you that it's normal. First, I need to explain why you are going to take time out at this point.

In my experience, when teaching students languages such as C, C++, C#, Assembly, Machine Languages, Java, and the list goes on, many students drop out even when they seem to be doing fine. In recent years, I began to catch students as they neared this junction, and I would ask them why they were contemplating dropping out. They would all tell me something similar to this: "I can see I did the homework but I'm scared I will fail because it's just not sinking in. I don't grasp it." About four years ago I tried an experiment. When the students walked into the lecture hall they were in shock when I told them to close their text books, close their laptops, and put away their books because we were going to take a journey inside their brain and have a class on neurology. In fact, we were going to scientifically illustrate why many felt they were stupid, not getting it, and essentially feeling like a dork! The entire lecture hall collapsed in laughter. At the end of the lecture that I now call "Don't Freak Out! Let's Have a Look at Your Brain!" some students were crying and came up to me after class and thanked me. Not a single student dropped out.

Right now I bet that you feel you have not retained anything from Chapter 5 and that you feel a little overwhelmed and insecure in your geek abilities. Well, that's OK—just read on and you'll see why you feel a little uneasy. Even if you do feel confident at this point, you probably will falter at some point down the road as it gets harder, but I still want you to read on. This is important, so I want you to really understand this.

Don't Freak Out: Let's Look at Your Brain!

One of the best ways to explain this is to ask you something that has nothing to do with Objective-C and computer science. It's about childhood memories.

Do you ever smell something you've not smelt before and without any warning your brain immediately takes you back to a place in your early childhood? Yes, this happens to all of us. After smelling this smell, you will suddenly see everything clearly in your head: the walls, the people—it's all crystal clear and sometimes it may overwhelm you emotionally. You may feel blown away that you've not thought about those walls or images for many years, and now suddenly they're overwhelming your senses. Let me explain why this happens. I will use my smell of old-fashioned soap to illustrate this, and then show how this is related to the neural connectors you've just created.

Look at Figure 6–a. Under the first title, "ILLUSTRATION," you will see a very simplified illustration of how, once your brain receives a new input that it's never experienced before, it creates a nucleus housed inside a cell body that retains that event. This is connected to the rest of your brain by threads and axons. As you experience new events that relate to this new event, a tree of synapses and neurons connect to this nucleus. Some of these connections become quite full of what we call dendrites.

When I was a little boy in Durban, South Africa, I went down to where the servants were washing laundry. Back in 1963, most families used old-fashioned ammonia-filled soap that had a very distinct smell. This smell created a new nucleus in my baby brain. It connected with the joyful songs the Zulu servants were singing as they hand-washed the laundry. My brain also connected the imagery of the walls, the paint, and my dog Samson. These connectors of the singing, the walls, the paint and the dog formed four groups of connections to that new smell, as illustrated under "SYNTHESIZED" in Figure 6–a. Some groups immediately had more connections, such as songs, because I used to sing many Zulu songs as a small boy. The next biggest group was probably that of my dog. I've labeled the groups from 1 to 4 in order of size.

Many years later, in New York City, probably around 1993, I was rushing to keep an appointment with a law professor who had said he would meet me for lunch at a little restaurant. As I was running across 8th Avenue, I noticed some people cleaning the sidewalk in front of another restaurant. They were using soap and water and scrubbing it with these large straw brushes. Suddenly I smelt it. The smell I hadn't smelt since the time I was a three-year-old boy in that laundry room. I suddenly saw those servants, I could hear their songs and laughter, and I could see my old dog Samson. I became overwhelmed with that day, the people, the energy from so long ago, and I was so overwhelmed with emotion I stopped running and started crying. When I reached the restaurant, the law professor stood resplendent in his tweed suit and said: "Rory, it's OK that you're a couple of minutes late. Oh my gosh, are you crying?"

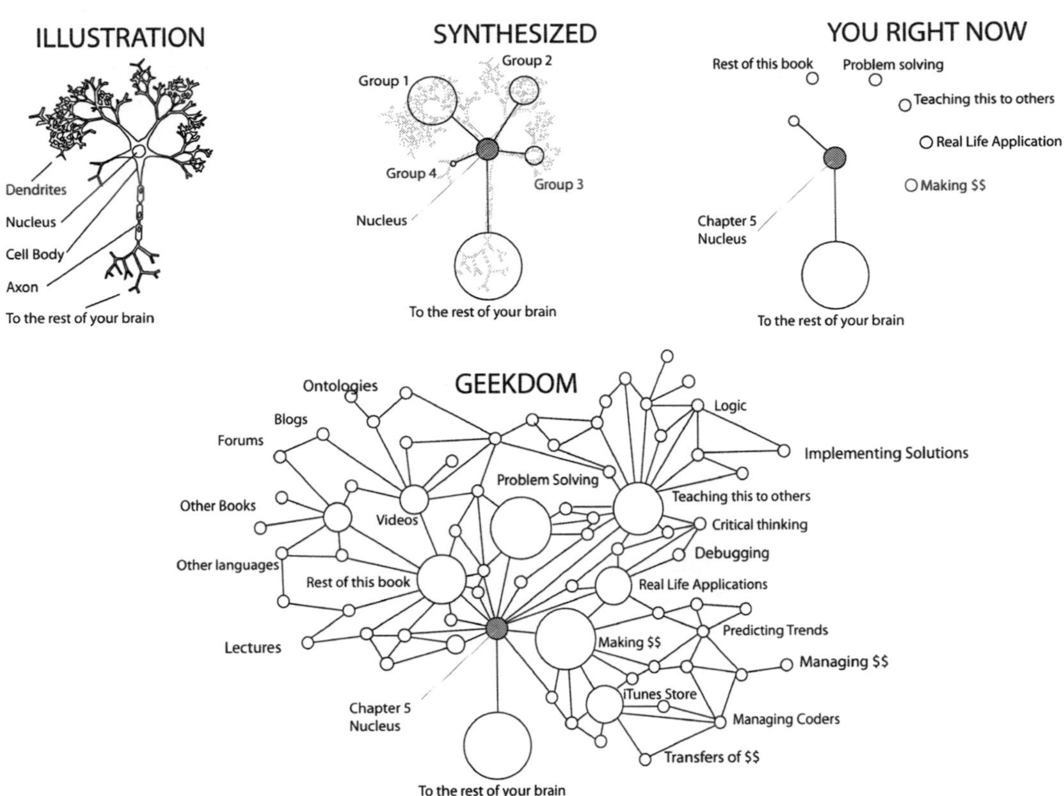

Figure 6–a. ***Don't freak out: Let's have a look at your brain.***

So what happened? What happens when you experience similar events? Why does this often happen with smell? Let's first look at events in life, such as the first time you realized that 1 + 1 = 2. Do you remember the first time you realized 1 + 1 = 2? Probably not. This is because after you created a nucleus associating 1 + 1 = 2 there were trillions of connectors going to 1 + 1 = 2. Every time you perform any function that related to 1 + 1 = 2 your brain makes a connection to the nucleus housing 1 + 1 = 2. Even as you flip through this book and it goes from page $_n$ to page $_{n+1}$, you make synaptic connectors to dendrites and groups of associations connected to 1 + 1. Somewhere in those trillions of 1 + 1 = 2 connectors are the visuals and sound effects of the room where you realized this, but it is lost in the maze of trillions of other connectors.

That rare smell though, that's different. Think about it. I have illustrated four groups associated with that smell from when I was three. Over the next 30 years, following the creation of that nucleus and the four groups linking it, there was never a connection made. It just lay there. However, as I crossed 8th Avenue and smelt that smell, it immediately invoked that same nucleus AND the contents of the four groups connected to that event. These connectors were STRONG because they were not interconnected with other complex relationships. This made the singing, the feeling I had towards my dog, the laughter, and the other events come hurtling into me.

Now go back to when you read Chapter 5 for a moment. Look at the "YOU RIGHT NOW" illustration in Figure 6–a. You created a set of nuclei when you made your way through Chapter 5. Let's imagine, for purposes of illustration, that it was only one event or one thing you learned while reading Chapter 5. The nucleus containing that knowledge is housed in the light grey circle. You may, at the most, have created one semblance of connectivity to some related thought or concept. That is why I connected one small group to the Chapter 5 knowledge nucleus. More importantly, notice that I have created five other groups of potential connectors to the Chapter 5: they are "rest of the book," "problem solving," "teaching to others," "real life application," and "making $$." Right now it's absolutely natural that these groups have *no connectivity* to the nucleus of Chapter 5's knowledge because you have not had time to create these connections. For example, right now, as you read this chapter, you probably "feel" like you have no connection to the knowledge you gained in Chapter 5. This is because there is no connection to it as you read this. There is also zero connectivity to making $$ from what you learned in Chapter 5, nor to the other groups.

I carefully choose topics, innuendo, and semantics to optimize, as best I can, connectivity between what I teach at the moment to what was taught in the past. By the time you reach the end of this book, create your first app, and sell it in the store, your brain will have begun to create many connectors to Chapter 5. I have illustrated this in Figure 6–a under GEEKDOM. Something that connects a huge amount of synapses to nuclei containing a difficult-to-understand concept is teaching others. It's great to go onto forums, such as mine at `www.rorylewis.com/ipad_forum/` or `bit.ly/oLVwpY`, and help out newbies with their questions (even if you are a newbie yourself) because it creates many connections to that difficult concept, making you smarter. In essence, helping others forces one to answer the same question in thousands of different ways. So I strongly encourage you to go to the forum, ask questions, and then, as you become wiser, help others.

So the first good news is that it's OK to feel disconnected to what you coded in Chapter 5. It's OK; you'll make those connections as you move forward. The second piece of good news is that Chapter 6 will not be as huge a leap as Chapter 5 was. Instead, you are going to take a break from serious code and connect new ideas to the synapses that you connected with code in Chapter 5. In fact, in both Chapter 6 and Chapter 7 there will be very little code! Instead, I will connect cool new thoughts to the portion of your brain that is associating code with ideas explored in Chapter 5. Once you have established these connections in your brain, you will associate more code. In Chapter 6, you will explore a popular method for navigating through iPhone apps using the platform of a "tabbed application." But for now, just relax and enjoy Chapter 6: Switches.

`switch`: A Tabbed Application

So far you have written code that allowed the user to poke or prod an iPhone or iPad in certain ways to make it do interesting things. This is now going to change. In this chapter, you will demonstrate how to create an iPhone app that allows you to do all of these cool functions without overwhelming your user, by dividing the functionality into several easy to locate tabs. This model, called the "tabbed model," is so popular amongst app developers that Apple has included a basic tabbed application project in the New Project options in Xcode. In other words, the people at Apple recognize how much programmers like to use this model, so they created most of the code you need. When you're all done writing this app, you'll have a display with two tabs at the bottom. The content of the first tab will be an image that you set using Interface Builder with a button overlaid on top of it. This button will cause Mobile Safari to open the Apress Publishing Web Site. The content of the second tab will be a different image, but you can set the image name and other attributes in the implementation file and only set up enough of a framework in Interface Builder to make that possible.

Obtaining the Resources

You can watch a video of the wild and crazy, beaming-with-life, groovy PhD student Brian Parks coding this switches app at `bit.ly/mX4pkk` and simply follow along with him. You can also download the code to this project at `bit.ly/vBSKMa` where you can visually compare your code with mine. Most importantly, you will either need to download the three images at `bit.ly/tIYl9Y` or create your own two images and icon using the same dimensions as mine: 320 × 480 pixels for the two large images, and, of course, 57 × 57 pixels for your icon.

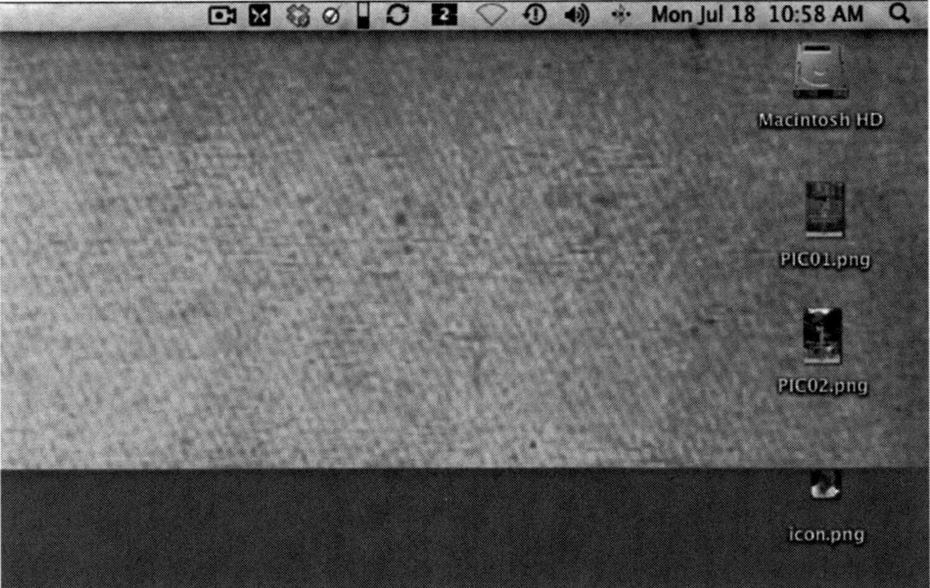

Figure 6–1. *Download the three images onto your squeaky clean desktop.*

1. Start off by cleaning out your desktop so there is nothing on it. Then either create your two 320 × 480 pixel images, one for each view, and then one icon, at 57 × 57 pixels, or download the three images used in the video, as illustrated in this book, at `bit.ly/vBSKMa`. This is shown in Figure 6–1.

Creating the App

Now let's create the app.

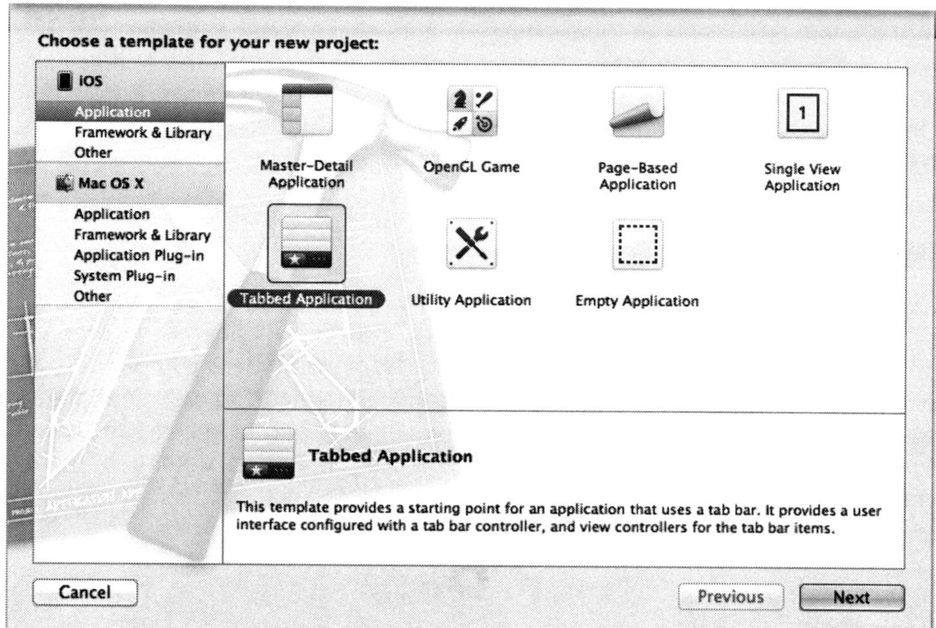

Figure 6–2. *Start a Tabbed Application.*

2. Start this app just like you've started all the apps so far: use ⌘⇧N to start a new project. Select "Tabbed Application" from the sheet that appears. This template sets up a significant portion of the tab framework for you, so you can focus on filling in the content and not worrying about the gory details of the interaction model. Click "Next." This is illustrated in Figure 6–2.

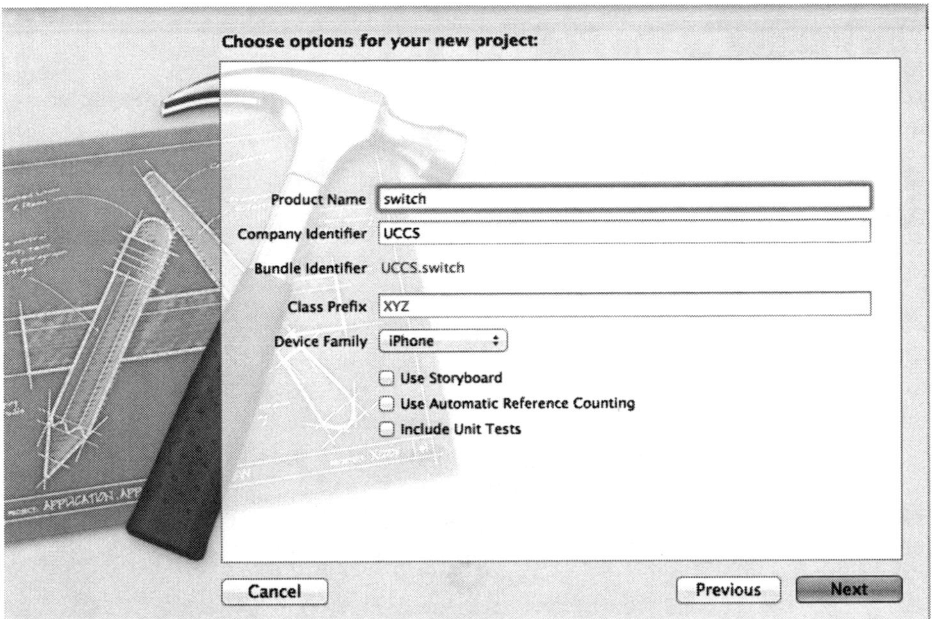

Figure 6–3. *Name the app "switch."*

3. As illustrated in Figure 6–3, name your app "switch" and ensure that both of the checkboxes are unchecked. "Use Storyboard" drastically changes how a tabbed application is set up and is explored in detail in Chapter 7. In this app, you'll specifically target the iPhone because tabs become cumbersome on the iPad.

Adding the Images to the Project

At this stage, it's probably a good idea to drag your imagery to use on the tabs, so you won't have to worry about it later.

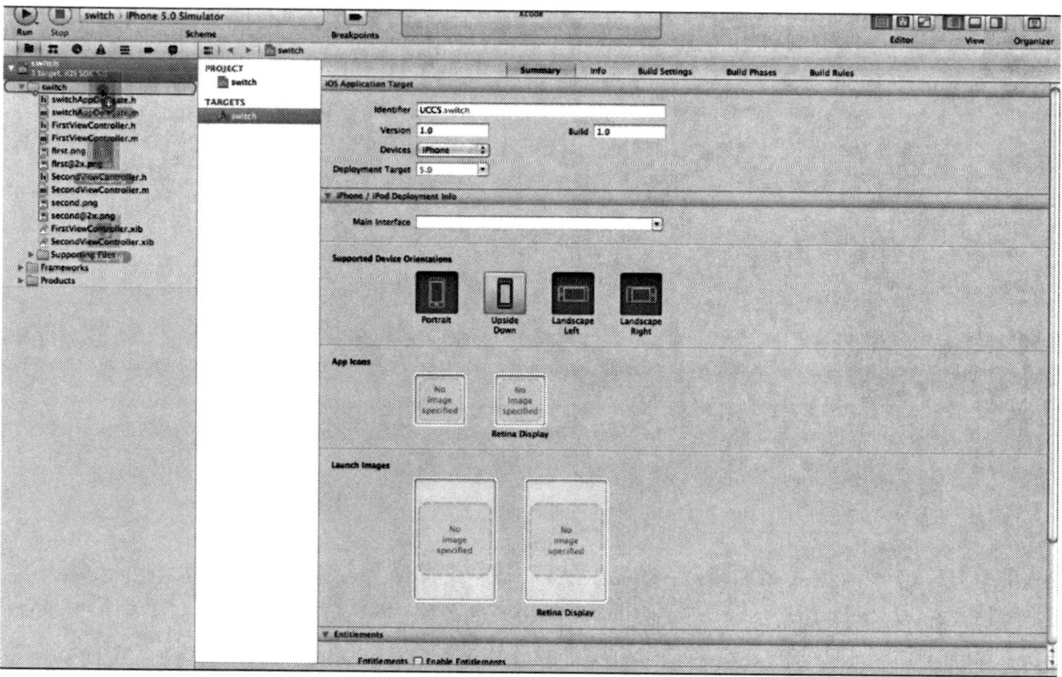

Figure 6–4. *Drag in your 3 images from the desktop.*

4. Drag your images from the desktop into supporting files, and in the process develop a very good habit for yourself. After dropping your images into the folder, you will be presented with a dialog, as shown in Figure 6–5.

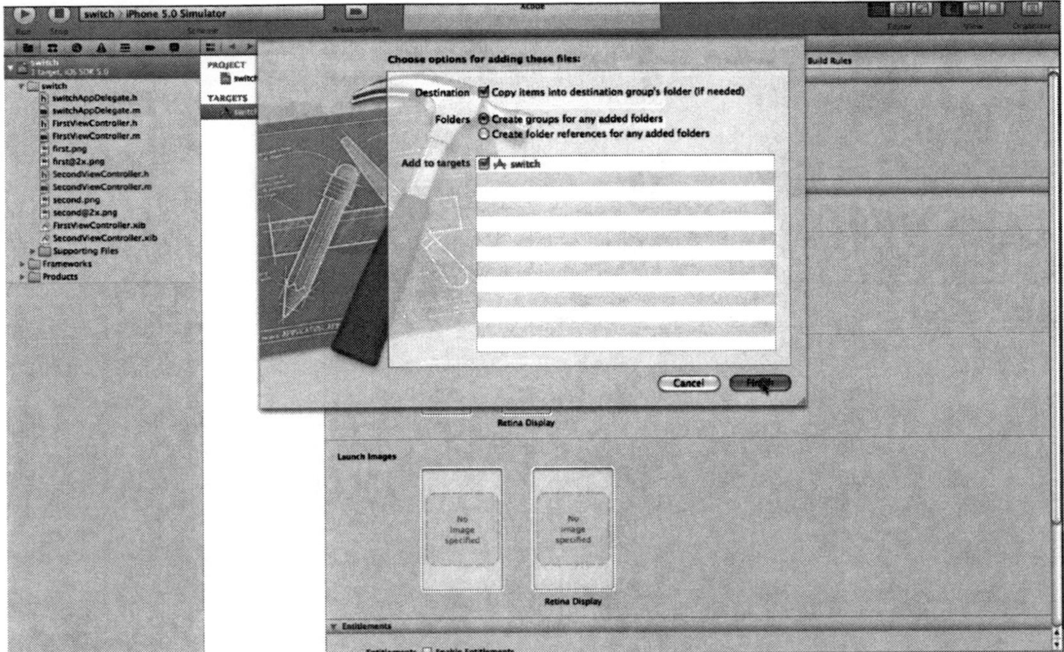

Figure 6–5. *Copy the items into the destination page's folder.*

5. Xcode recognizes that the images are not already part of this project, so it strongly recommends that you let it add them for you. As mentioned before, it's also making sure that it has encapsulated your images inside itself, so if you go elsewhere to run it then it will be able to find your images and display them. This dialog also gives you the opportunity to change the actions it is about to perform, but, in general, the assumptions it makes are correct, so accept Xcode's recommendations, as illustrated in Figure 6–5.

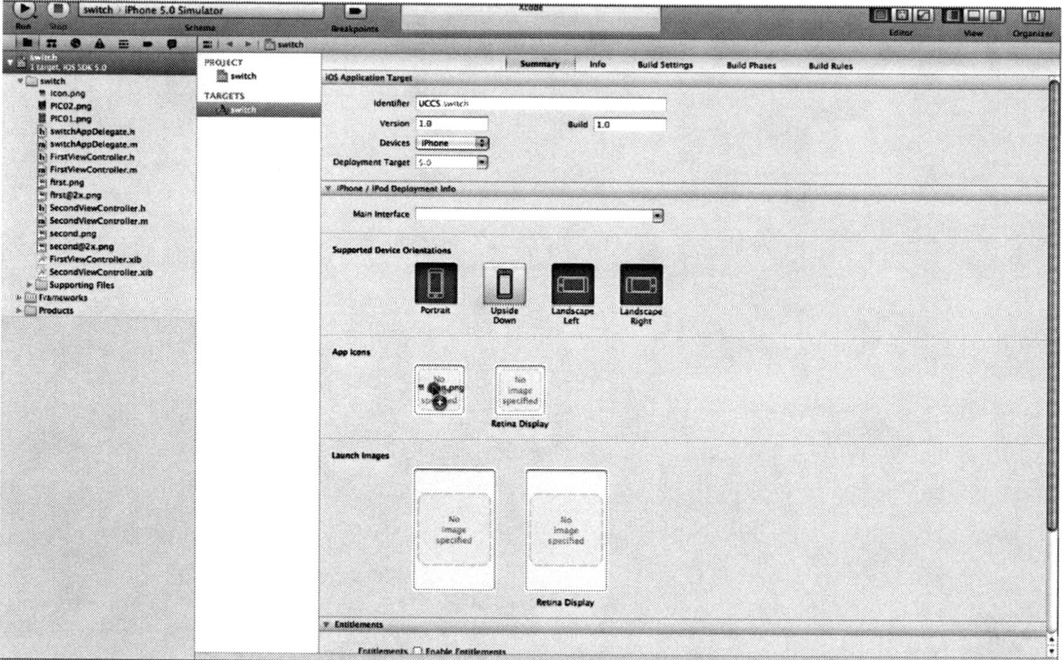

Figure 6–6. *Drag your icon to the app's icon property.*

6. Typically, you open the `plist` to include the icon. In this app, you see a new way to associate an icon with your app. So, drag your icon file to the app's properties. Notice how Xcode takes care of putting it in the right place in your project and setting up all the necessary linkages. This step is not critical if you don't have an appropriately sized `.png` readily available. You can always change the icon later. Note that it only allows you to drop the correct sized icon into each specific box. In Figure 6–6 you see the icon being dragged into the app's icon property.

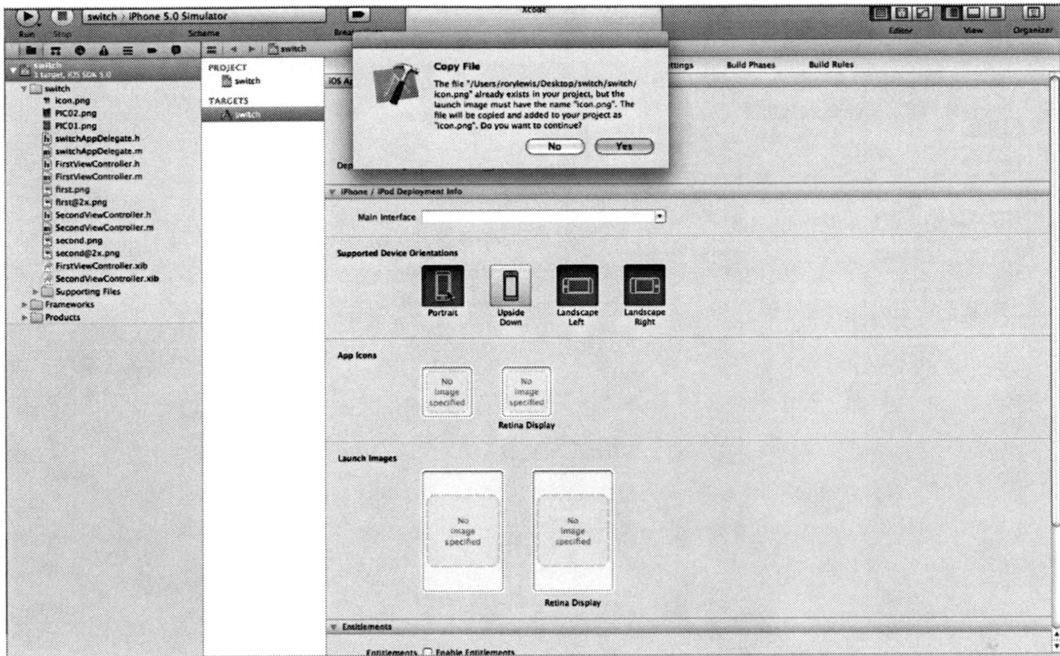

Figure 6–7. ***Warning that you dropped the images into the wrong place.***

7. Xcode displays a warning indicating that it will copy the icon from its current location to the "correct" place, which is fine. As with the previous warning, simply accept Xcode's recommendations. You, of course, will not see this if you dropped your images into the correct folder. This is illustrated in Figure 6–7.

Running the App

You do know that some of the readers of this book, and students from my former classes, actually work at Apple developing iOS code and doing the very special things you are about to see in this step. That's why I love to say, "The clever people at Apple have coded…" because these clever people at Apple include people just like you, who began right here, reading the first version of this book. Right now, you probably just want to see what the clever people have coded for the Tabbed Application.

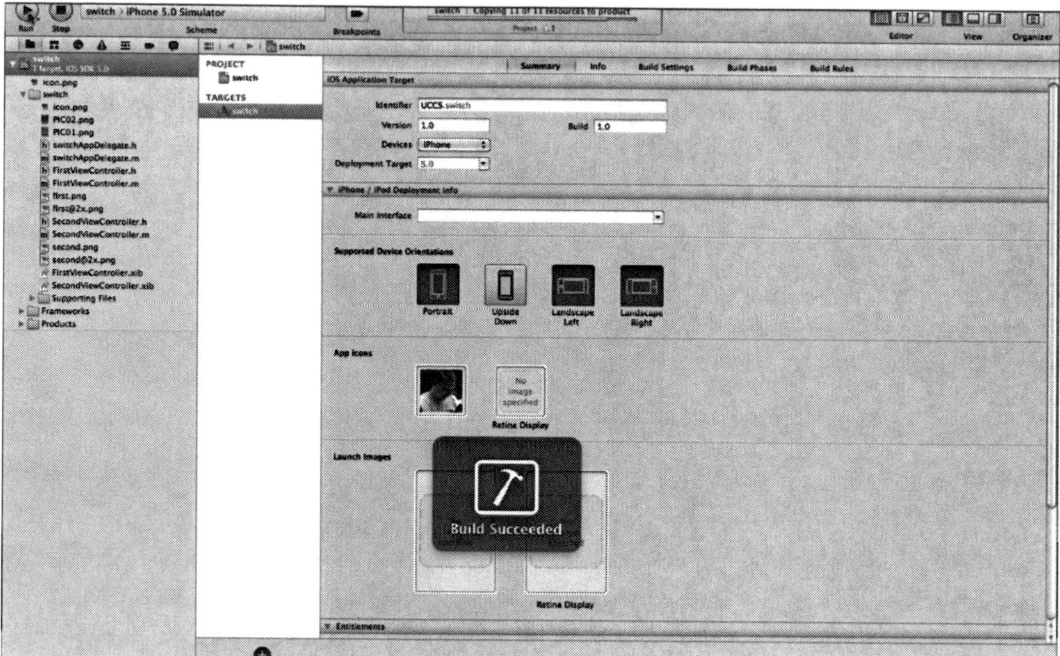

Figure 6–8. *Run it so we can see what Apple has already coded for us.*

8. Run the app by clicking the Run button or pressing ⌘R, as illustrated in Figure 6–8. If you've followed the instructions faithfully, you will see a "Build Succeeded" message and the iOS Simulator will start.

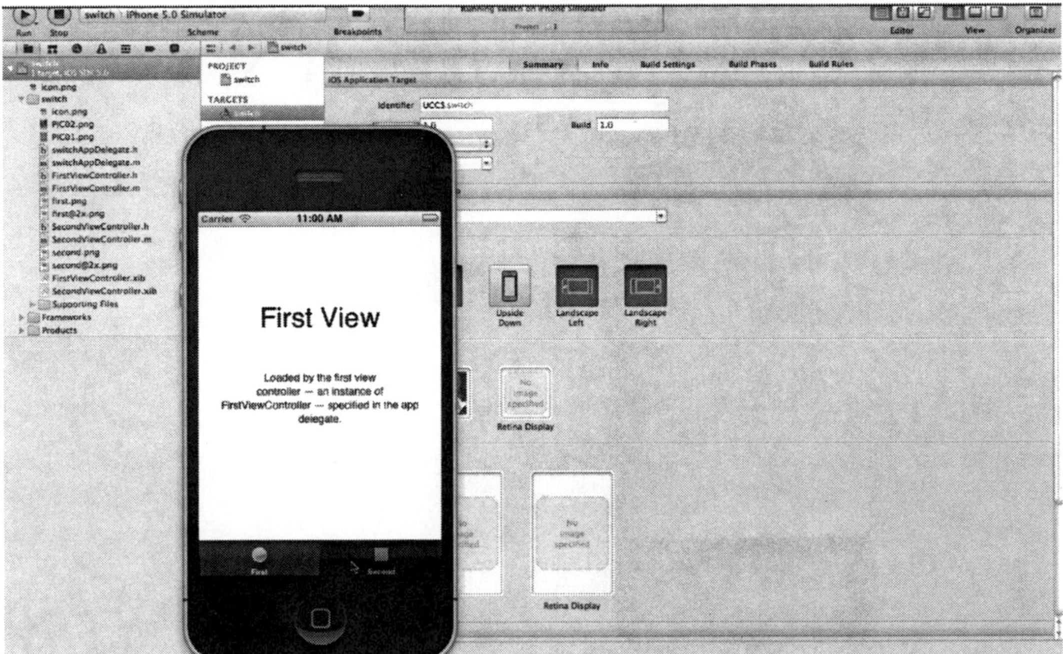

Figure 6–9. ***The first view to pop up will be the... First View.***

9. As illustrated in Figure 6–9, after you run the app you will see how the iOS Simulator pops up a First View. This is quite amazing. Those clever people at Apple have coded so much hardcore stuff and cool things that it leaves very little for you to do. Go ahead and play around with the app; click on the tabs to see that there really are, in fact, two different sets of content being shown. Remember that you haven't even touched the `.xib` files or any of the code! However, this is exactly the point where the magic of the Tabbed Application template ends and your creative input begins.

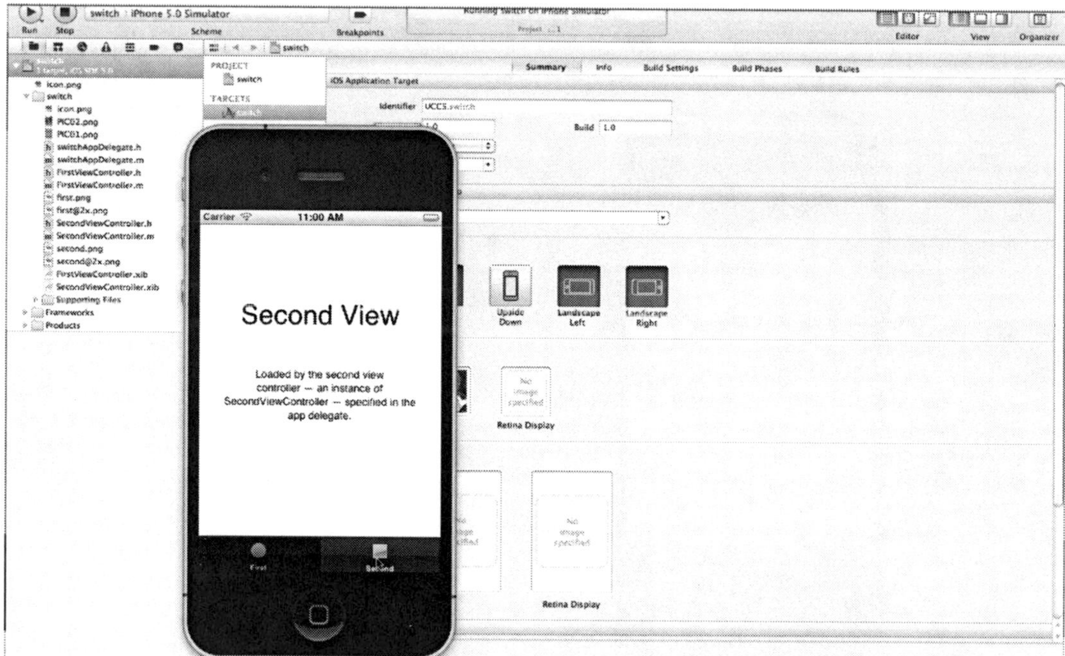

Figure 6–10. *The Second View appears when you select the "Second" tab.*

10. When you press the "Second" tab, located at the bottom of the screen, you will see that "Second View" pops up. So the tabs are actually working perfectly. I'm sure you will notice that while the Tabbed Application template sets up quite a bit and has prefilled some content, it's rather drab and uninteresting. Most importantly, it doesn't reflect anything that you might want it to do. Let's fix that.

Customizing the Tabs

That Second View that you see in Figure 6–10 can be replaced, along with the first introductory view, with code, or the next level of a game, or the details of an address tab or recipe. For your purposes, simply insert a first image into the First View and a second image into the Second View.

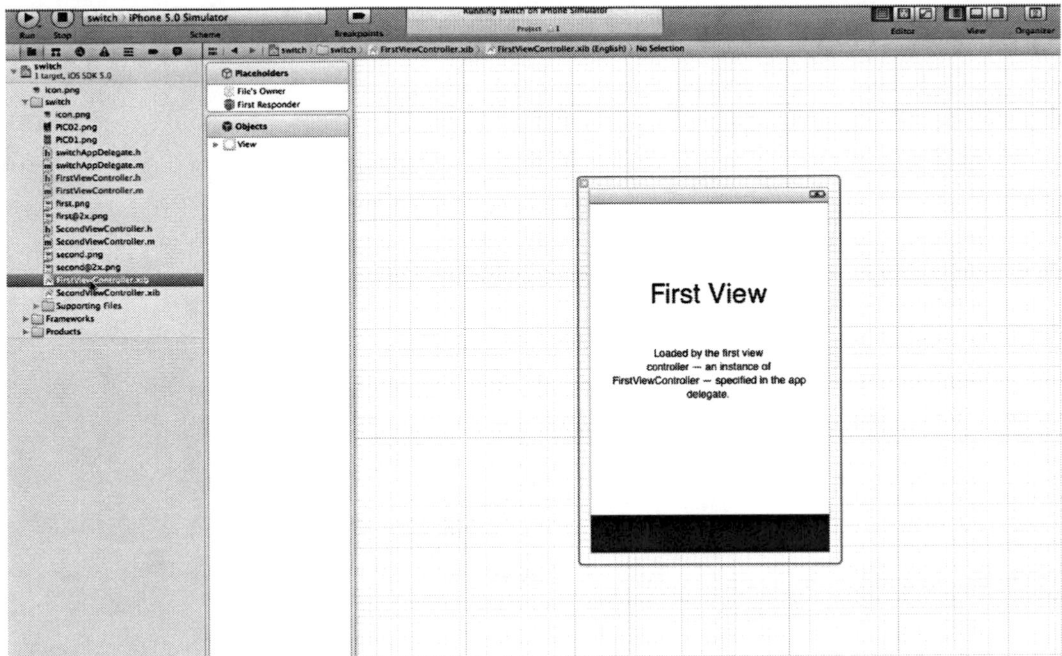

Figure 6–11. *Open up the First View nib file.*

11. Switch back to Xcode and click the "Stop" button. Select the `.xib` file called `FirstViewController.xib`, as shown in Figure 6–11. This shows what you saw in the iOS Simulator, minus the actual tabs on the Tab Bar. Let's set up your environment to make it easier for you to edit the nib (`.xib`). If you don't already have the Utilities View visible, click the appropriate view button to make it visible at the right side of the screen. You don't need the Debug View right now, so you can hide that. You don't really need the Navigator at the moment, either, but some developers (like Brian, the PhD student running this video) like to have it visible at all times. That is your choice.

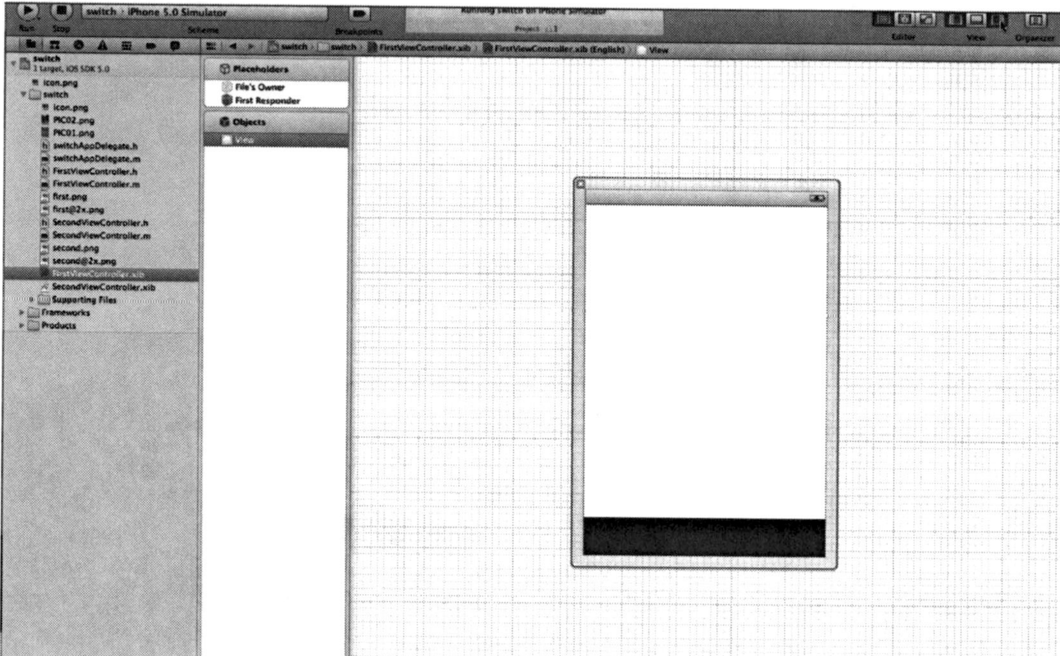

Figure 6–12. *Delete the UILabels.*

12. To use your own images, you need to get rid of the ones Apple has provided. Click each of the UILabels and delete them by pressing the Delete key while each is selected. Your screen should resemble Figure 6–12. Many tabs do have text content, but yours will not, so these UI elements are not necessary. This leaves you with a blank view, as can be seen explicitly in the left side of the Standard Editor.

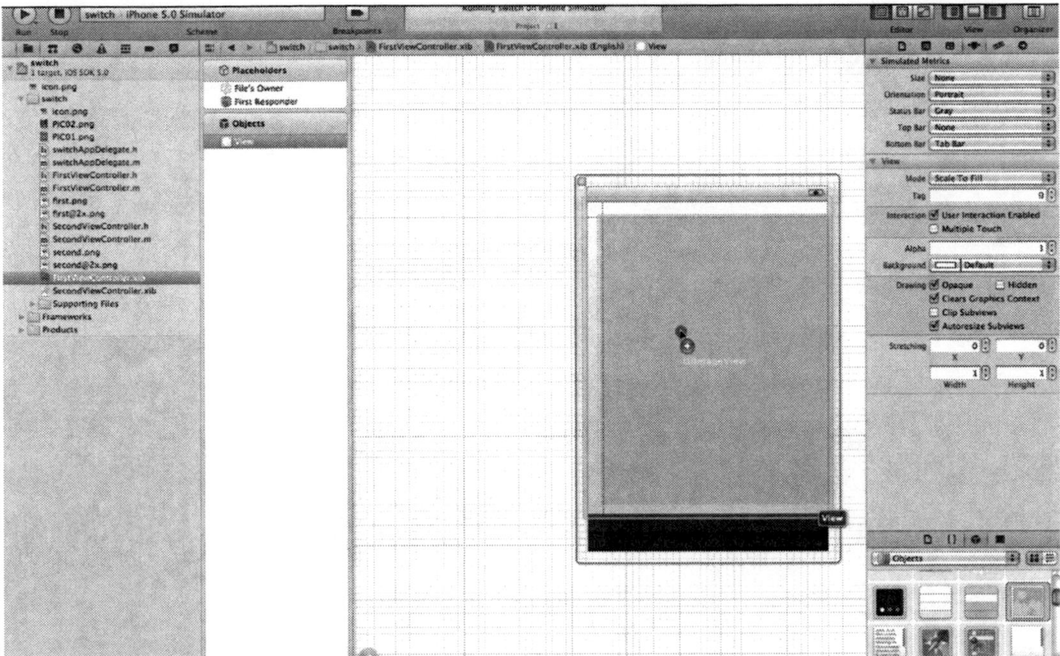

Figure 6–13. *Drag a UIImage onto your view.*

13. From the toolbox at the bottom of the Utilities View, find the image view (UIImageView) icon and drag it into the main area. As you do so, it expands to the same size as the area you can fill (in this case, the whole view). Use the guides to line up the UIImageView with the borders of the simulated iPhone window. This is illustrated in Figure 6–13.

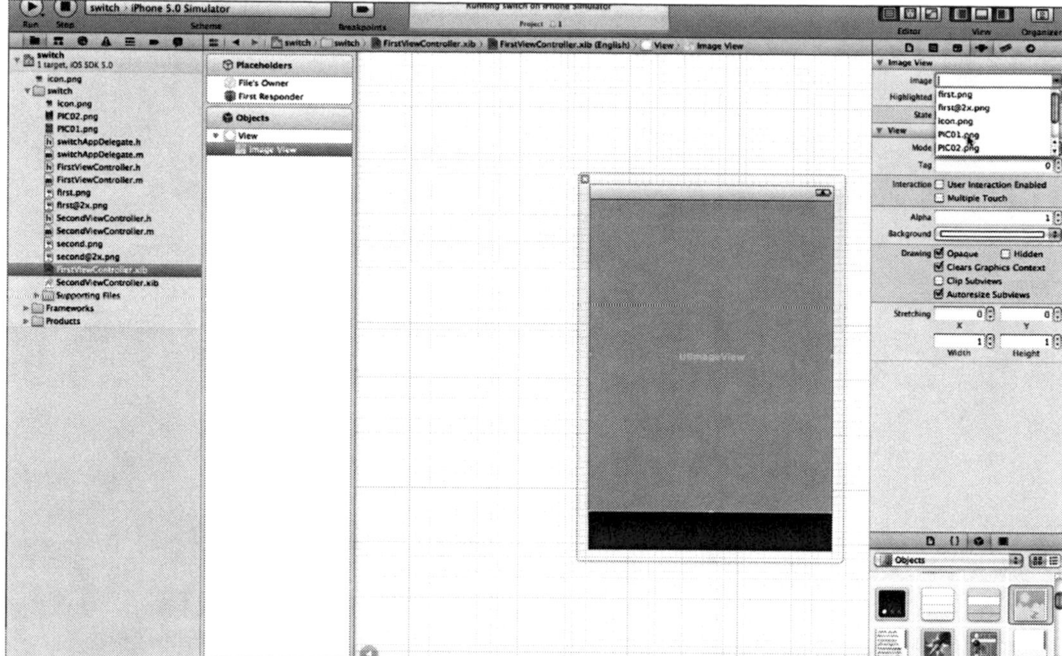

Figure 6–14. *Associate your first images with the first UIImageView.*

14. In the Utilities View, go to the Attributes Inspector (⌥⌘4) and click the Image drop-down, as shown in Figure 6–14. This list is populated with a list of images that Xcode has found in our project: `first.png` and `second.png` are the circle and square that Xcode has used as icons for each of the respective tabs, while `icon.png` is our app icon, leaving two entries that correspond to the images you dragged into the project in Figure 6–6. Select `PIC01` and Xcode will show it in the UIImageView.

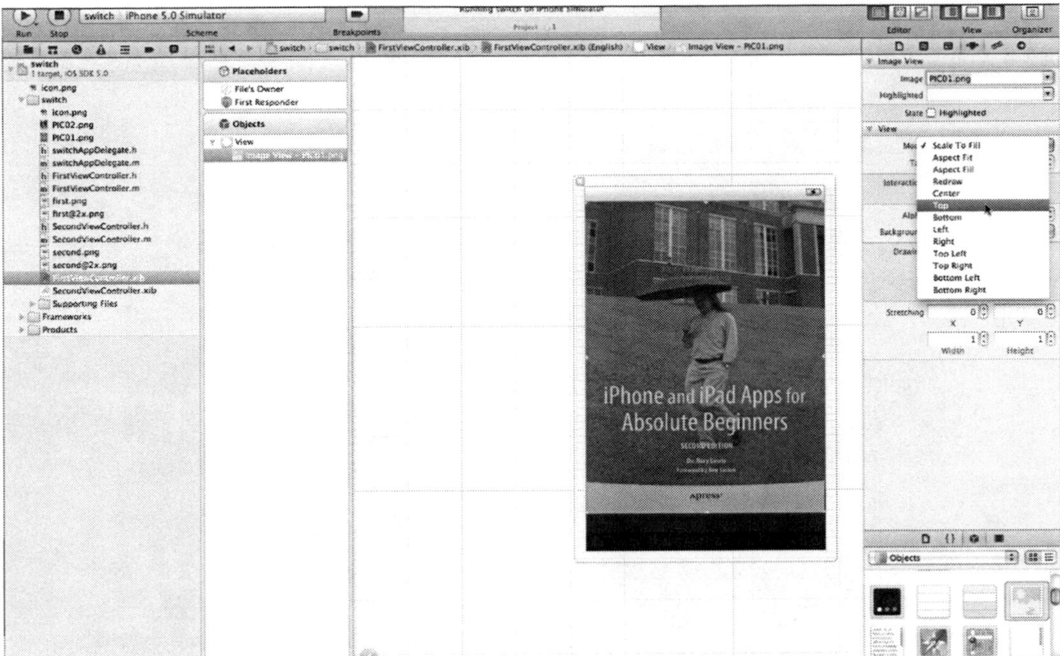

Figure 6–15. *Select a View Mode.*

15. As shown in Figure 6–15, you can now see `PIC01` being displayed on the view, and you should now see either `PIC01`, if you downloaded it from my site, or your own first image. You know the image is the correct dimension for a tabbed view, but it's still a good habit to line it up to the top or bottom, so that it fits exactly. In Figure 6–15, one can see Brian selecting a View Mode, placing `PIC01` at the top of the screen. I typically place it at the bottom. It makes no difference if your images are perfectly sized. This is your choice, though, so get into the habit of selecting a view mode that pleases you. I usually choose the bottom alignment because I don't want to cut off the bottom of the image. The other content view modes, and what they mean, are described in more detail later in the chapter.

Figure 6–16. *Run it and see what happens.*

16. Let's see what you have now. As expected, you can see in Figure 6–16 that the first tab looks exactly like the way you've set it up in Interface Builder.

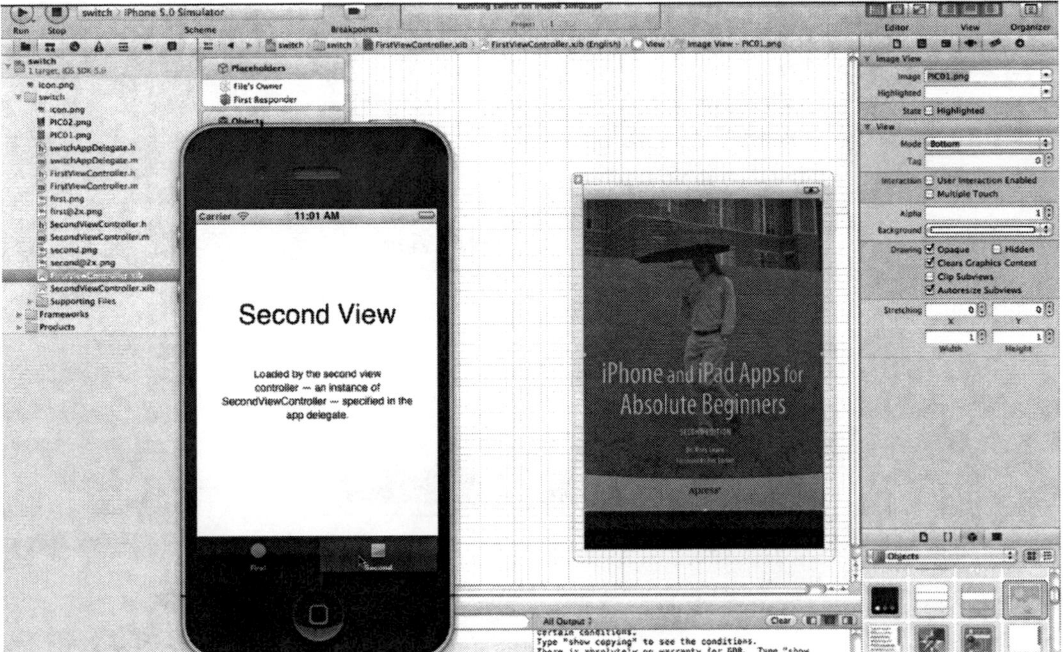

Figure 6–17. ***Second View still looks the same.***

17. Of course, you haven't changed anything on the second tab. Select Second View and see that, as expected, it still looks exactly the same as shown in Figure 6–17. Let's add an image to this tab, but instead of telling Xcode which image to load directly in Interface Builder, you can write a couple of lines of code that load the image when the tab is shown.

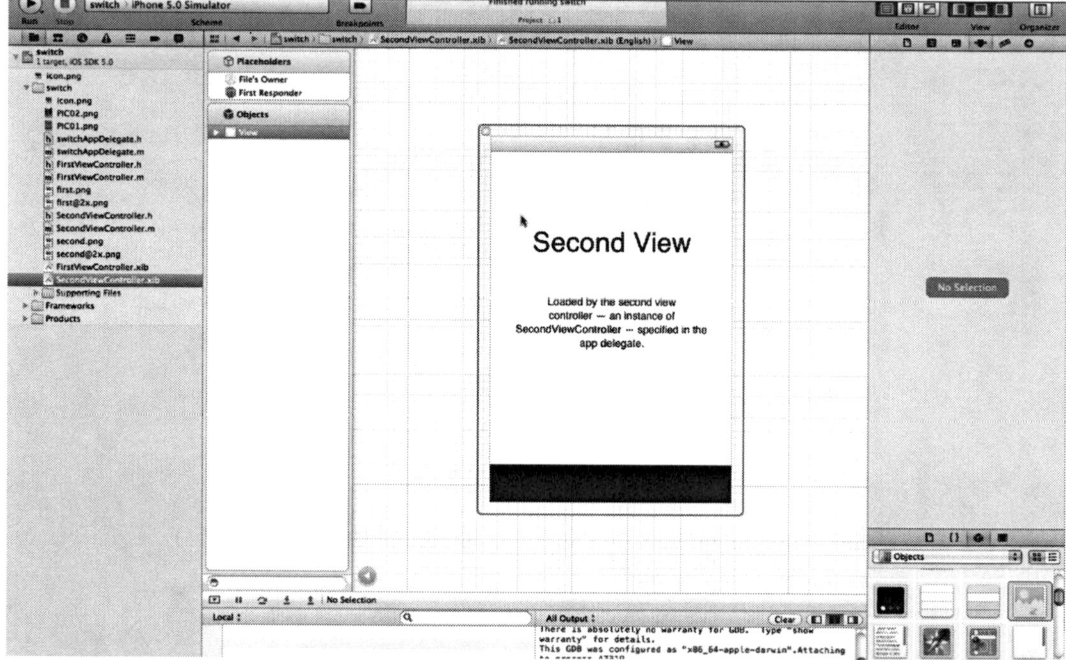

Figure 6–18. *Control-drag a connection from your icon in Interface Builder into your header file.*

18. Let's start by fixing up the Second View in exactly the same way you dealt with the first view. Select Second View in the Navigator and get your workspace set up. Again, select each label and delete it from the interface so that you have a clean UIView. This is illustrated in Figure 6–18.

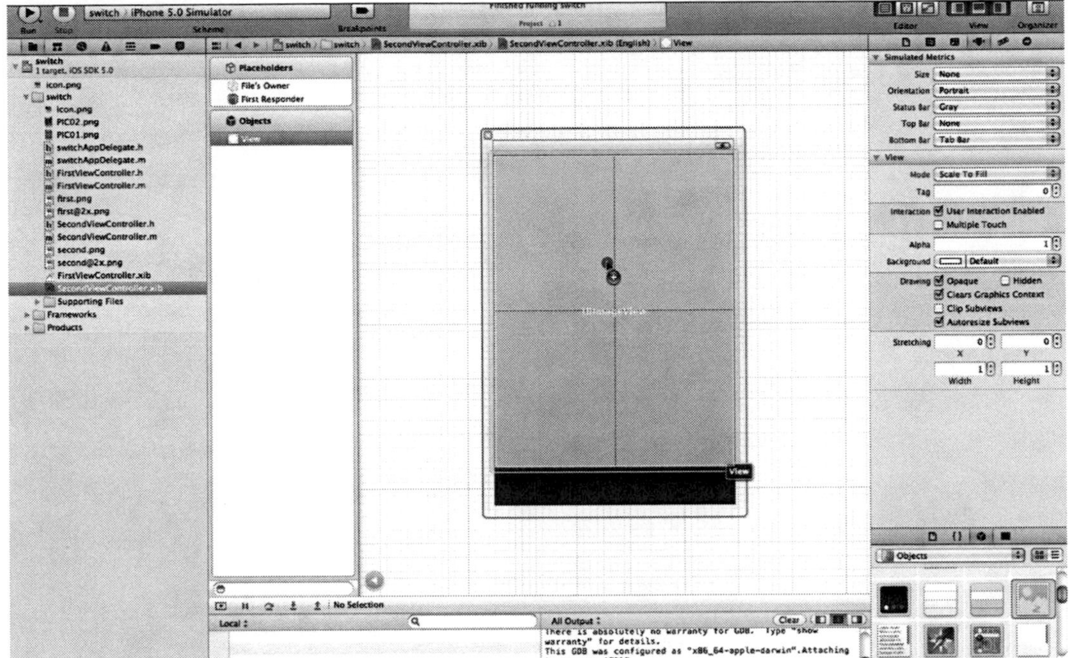

Figure 6–19. *Open the* `SecondViewController.xib` *and drag a UIImageView into the interface.*

19. You now need to work on the Second View. So open up the `SecondViewController.xib` and drag a new image view (UIImageView) into the interface just as you did for the first view in Figure 6–13, except now you are resizing the boundaries, as illustrated in Figure 6–19. Note that up to this point you haven't done anything differently. However, instead of using the Attributes Inspector to set the image and Content View Mode, you'll now do something a little different.

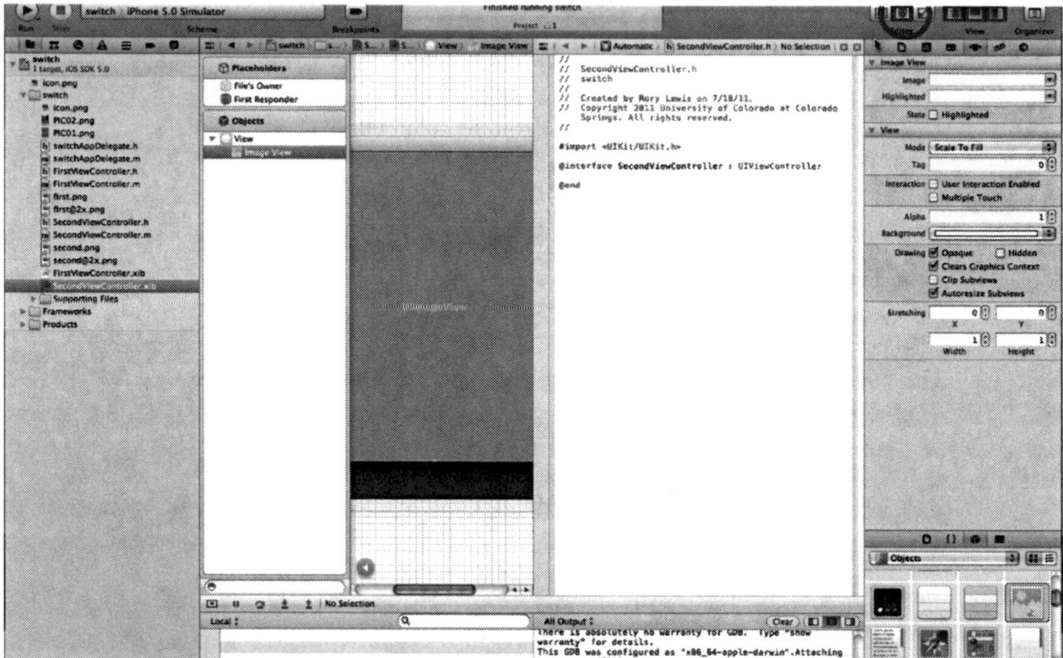

Figure 6–20. *Open the Assistant Editor.*

20. Pull up the Assistant Editor to show the header (`.h`) file that corresponds to your `SecondViewController.xib` file. This will allow you to indicate to Xcode how you wish to communicate between your code (which you'll write in a minute) and the interface that you've just finished designing. This is illustrated in Figure 6–20.

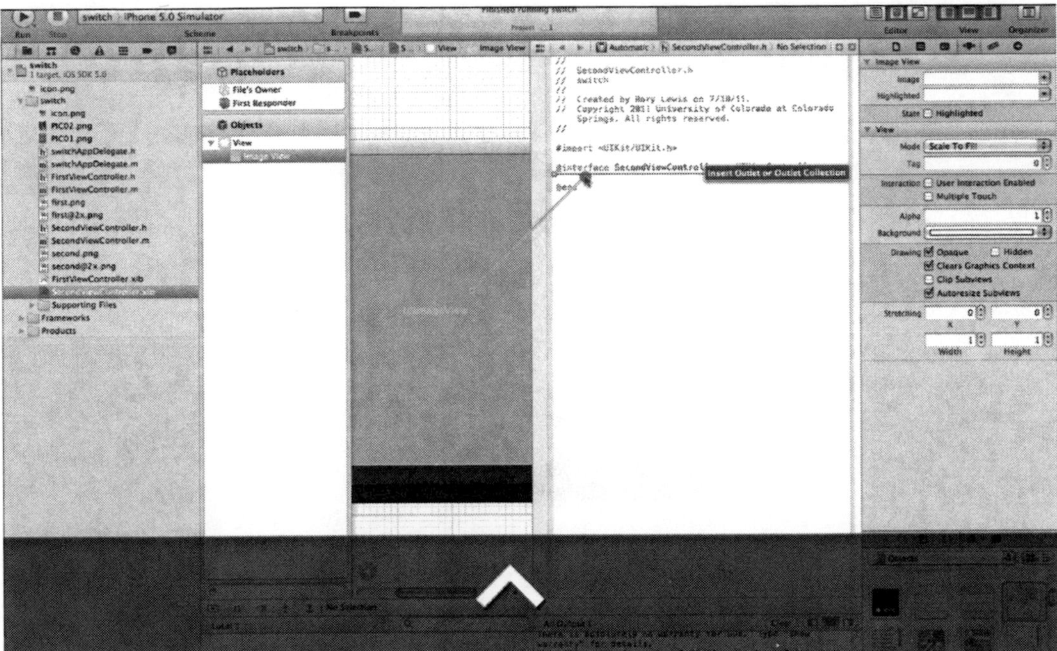

Figure 6–21. ***Control-drag an outlet into your header file.***

21. Control-drag from the UIImageView in the main drawing area to anywhere between the `@interface` and `@end` directives. As shown in Figure 6–21, Xcode will display a translucent message reading "Insert Outlet or Outlet Collection." Outlet Collections are a more advanced topic, but you've seen Outlets before and that's exactly what you're looking for.

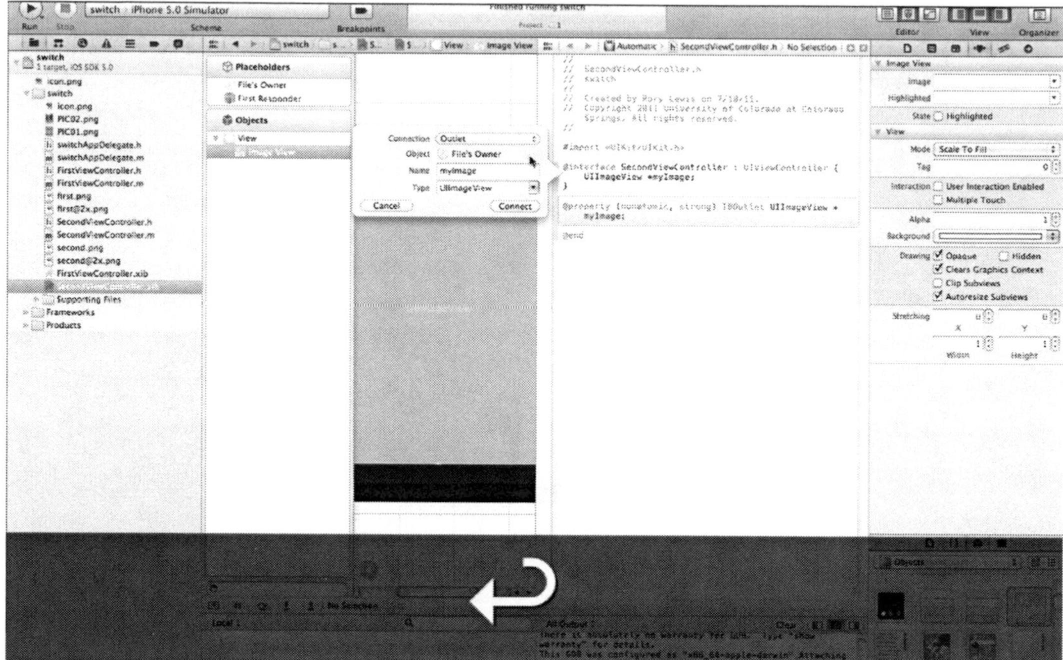

Figure 6–22. *Name the outlet "myImage."*

22. Upon letting go of the mouse button and completing the control-drag, Xcode presents you with a popover to get some additional information. You've already determined you want an Outlet, so all that remains is to give it a name, say "myImage," as illustrated in Figure 6–22.

Coding the Second View

Now let's write some code to make use of this new Outlet. To do so, select the file `SecondViewController.m` in the Navigator and find the method definition for `viewDidLoad`. It should look something like this:

```
- (void)viewDidLoad
{
[superviewDidLoad];
// Do any additional setup after loading the view, typically from a nib.
}
```

Add the lines in bold below, so that the method reads as follows (be sure to change `myImage` appropriately if you named your Outlet something different). Unless you named your image `PIC02`, you will have to change the text in quotes to the name of your image (without the "`.png`"):

```
- (void)viewDidLoad
{
    [superviewDidLoad];
// Do any additional setup after loading the view, typically from a nib.
```

```
    [myImagesetImage:[UIImageimageNamed:@"PIC02"]];
    [myImagesetContentMode:UIViewContentModeBottom];
}
```

These two lines of code are more or less equivalent to the changes you made in the Utilities View in Steps 14 and 15. The primary difference is that Steps 14 and 15 set these attributes directly in the nib file at development time, while the code you've just written sets these attributes at runtime, after the project has already been compiled onto our device. You'll look at the distinction between compile-time and runtime a little bit more in this chapter's "Digging the Code" section.

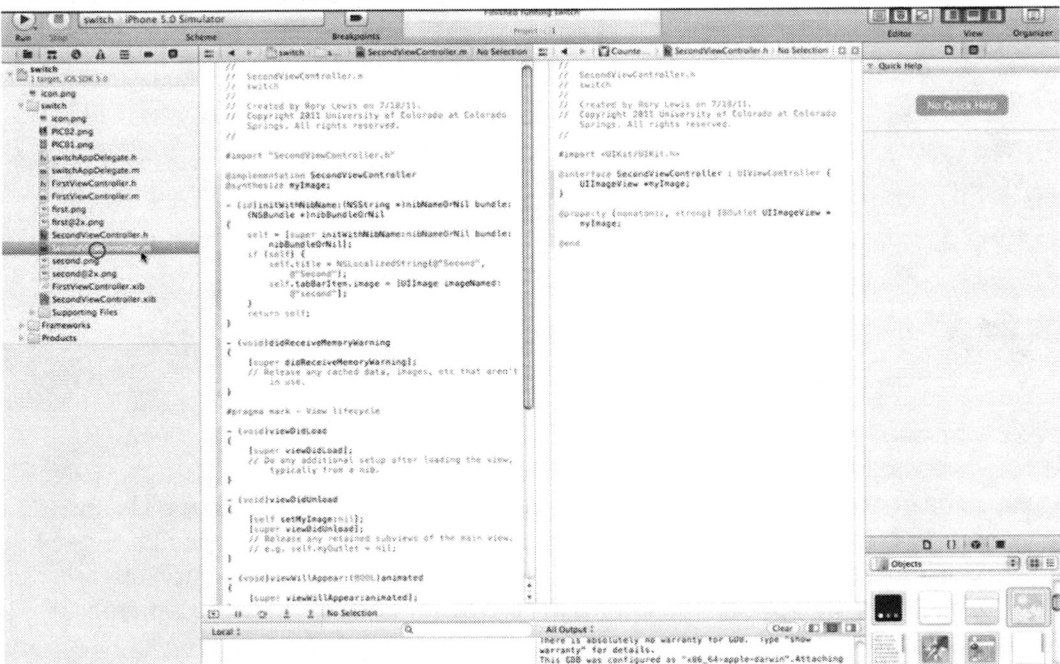

Figure 6–23. ***Time to write some code for the Second View.***

23. When this is done, check Figure 6–23 against your code; they should look similar. You can now close the Second View.

Adding a Button

You want to make a button that links up to the apress.com site—just for illustrative purposes of how to can include code in your view.

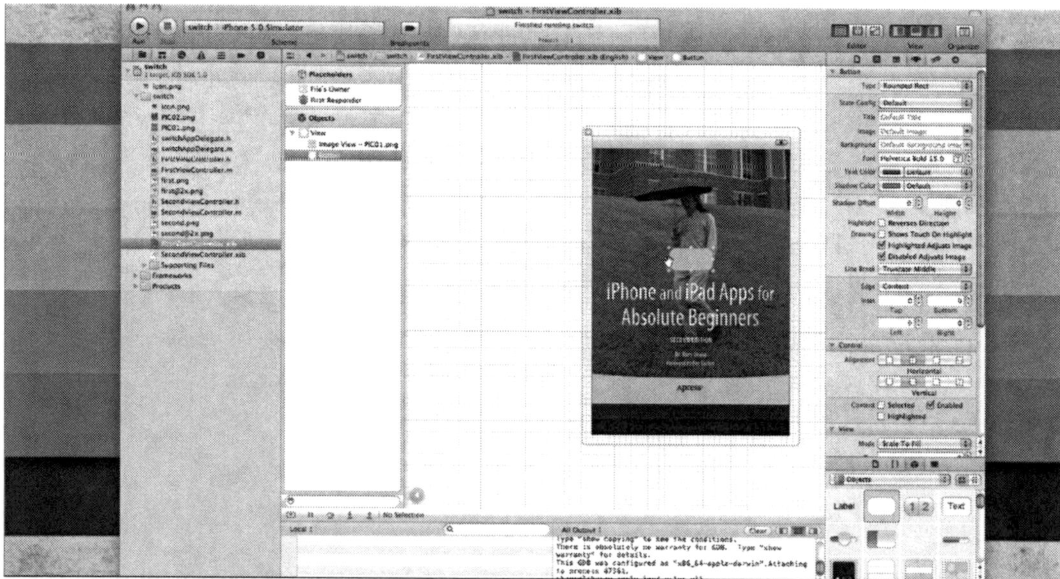

Figure 6–24. *Drag a button onto the First View.*

24. Let's do this on the First View: open up the `FirstViewController.xib` file and drag a button onto the image of me walking in the rain, as shown in Figure 6–24. Don't forget to type some text into the button. You can call the button that will take you to the Apress web site "Apress Web Site." You can name a button whatever you like.

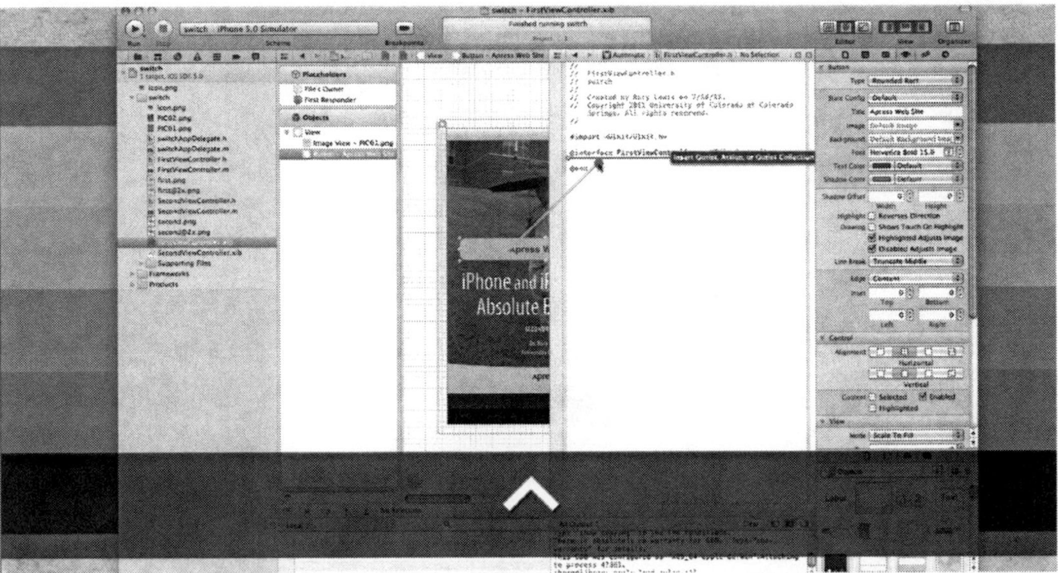

Figure 6–25. *Control-drag from the button into your header file.*

25. You've dragged so many buttons from nib files onto header files that all I need to say at this point is open the Assistant and control-drag an outlet onto your header, as illustrated in Figure 6–25. See how smart you are!

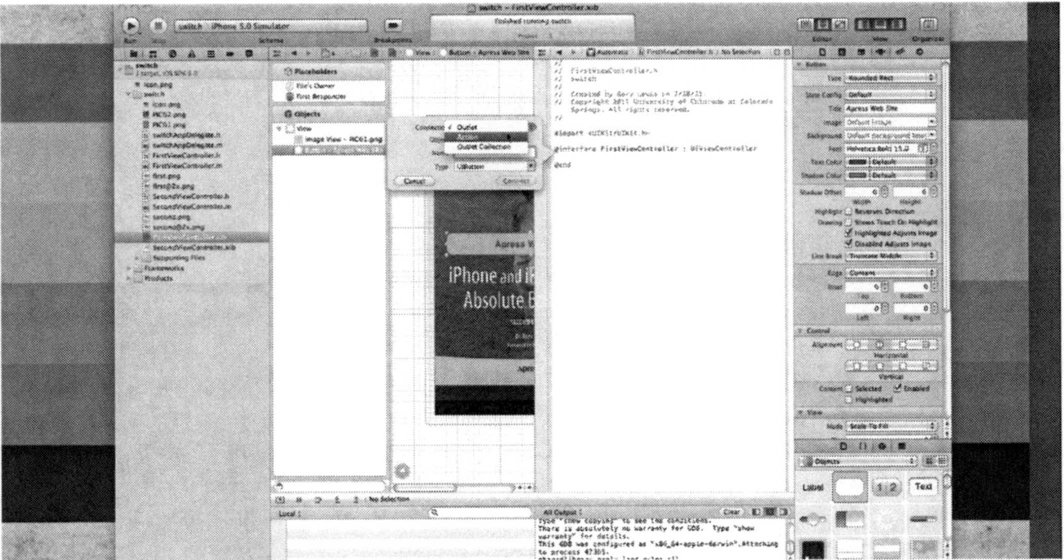

Figure 6–26. *Change the default Outlet to an Action.*

26. You know that if the button is going to perform an action then it cannot be an Outlet. Therefore, as illustrated in Figure 6–26, change the default Outlet to an Action.

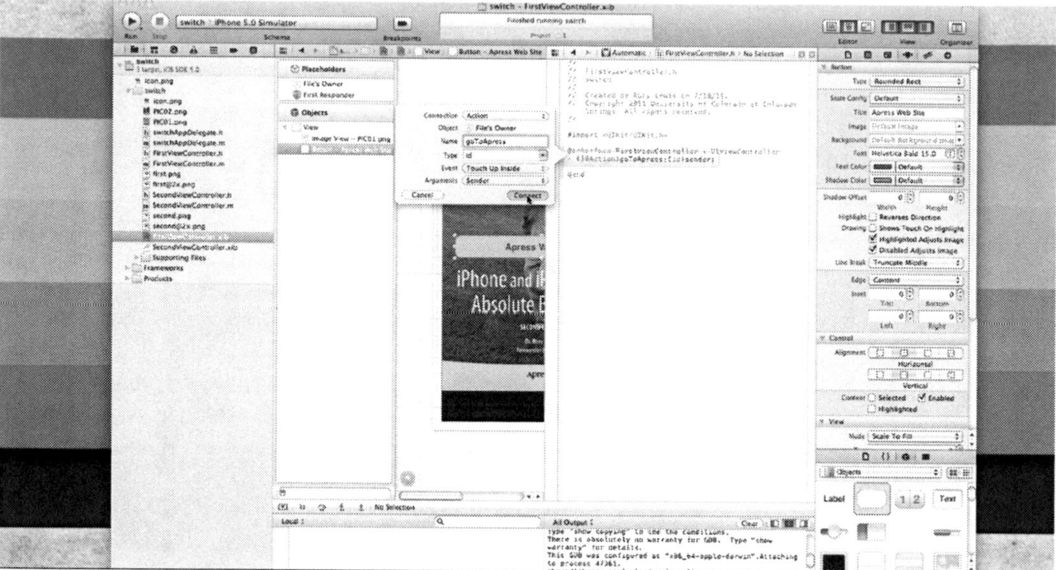

Figure 6–27. *Name the Action "goToApress."*

27. You want this Action to take a user to apress.com when they hit the button. You need to give the Action button a name, so let's call it `goToApress`, as illustrated in Figure 6–27. Once done, click Connect or press Return.

Coding the Button

You now need to code the button.

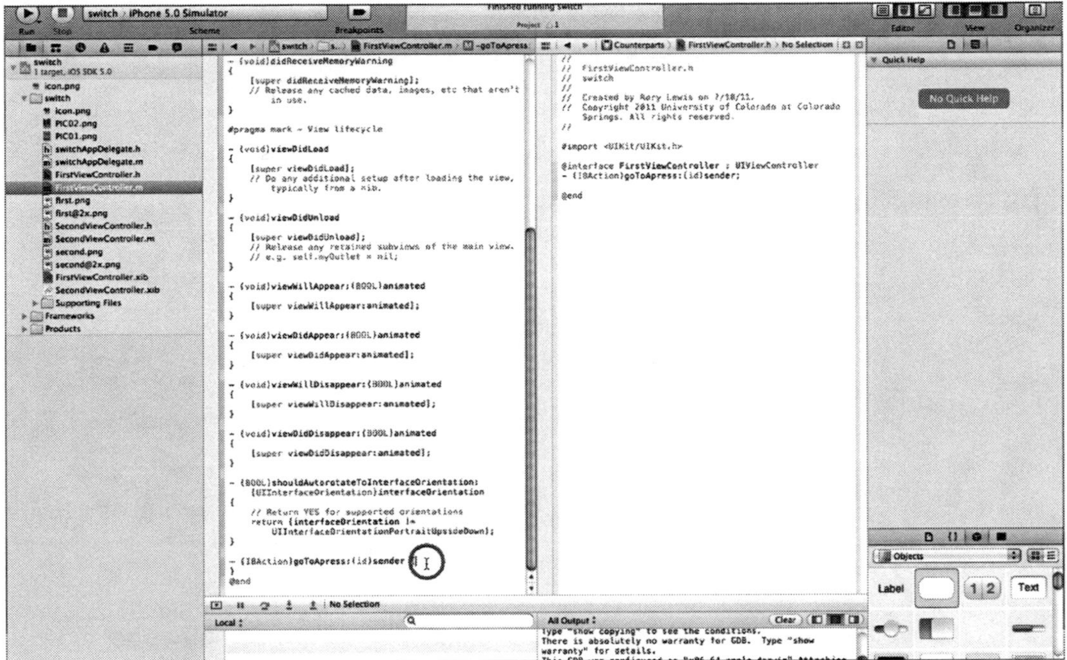

Figure 6–28. *Let's code the goToApress method.*

28. Open up your implementation file, as shown in Figure 6–28. You will see that that Xcode has also created a method stub for you (the framework for the method, but with no actual code that does anything useful). Click in this method and enter the following single line of code:

```
[[UIApplicationsharedApplication] openURL:[NSURL
↳URLWithString:@"http://apress.com"]];
```

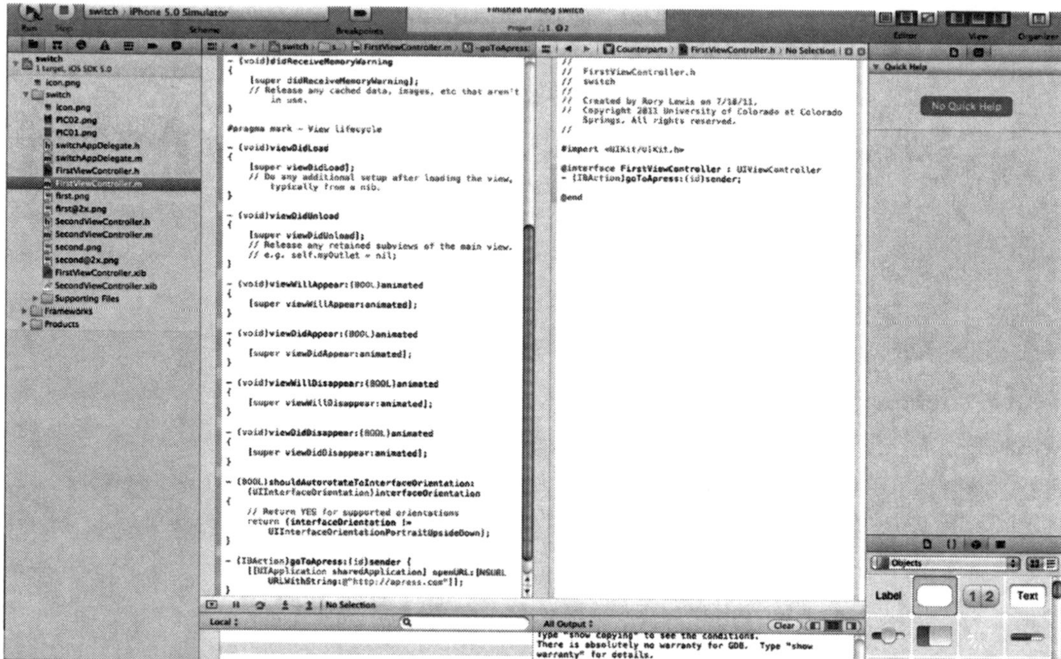

Figure 6–29. *Re-inspecting the code.*

29. When you think about it, it's really amazing that a seemingly complex operation like opening Mobile Safari from within your own app could have been condensed into a single statement by the people at Apple. So let's dissect the code you've just written, as shown in Figure 6–29.

In iOS, all apps are sandboxed into their own little piece of the system's resources. The topic of sandboxing is so complex that books can and have been written about the subject, so I won't go into detail here. Instead, it's sufficient to understand that iOS isn't going to let your app just do whatever it wants, so you have to use certain APIs that Apple has provided to tell the underlying system to do these things on your behalf.

In this case, send a message to the `UIApplication` class to obtain a reference to `sharedApplication`—that is, an object representing your application's gateway to the rest of the system. This object has a method called `openURL`, which does exactly that when passed an instance of `NSURL`.

In order to pass `openURL` an instance of `NSURL`, send the `NSURL` class the `URLWithString` message, which transparently converts the string you provide into an instance of `NSURL`.

Using the Button

It's time to test out the button.

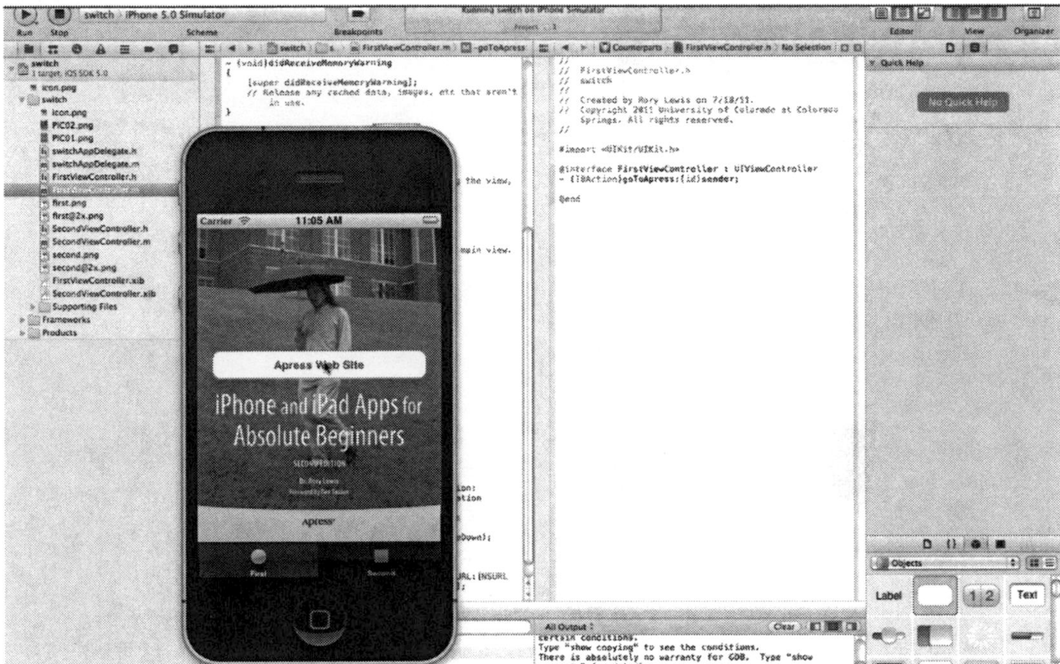

Figure 6–30. *Run it!*

30. As shown in Figure 6–30, when you run the app and click the button saying "Apress Web Site," your app will call off to iOS and launch Mobile Safari, as shown in Figure 6–31.

Figure 6–31. *The apress.com website on your iPhone!*

31. Congratulations! You've successfully completed your sixth iPhone app! See Figures 6–31 and 6–32.

Figure 6–32. *Your sixth iPhone app.*

Digging the Code

In this chapter, you quickly flew by a few advanced topics in order to get through the app. Let's take a step back from the code you've written and have a more in-depth look at some of these topics.

- In Step 15, you set a Content View Mode to alter how your image would be scaled and cropped to fit in the UIImageView. Take a look at what this means, and how each of the options differ from one another.
- In Step 24, I mentioned the difference between compile-time and runtime. For the purposes of writing the app, it was sufficient to know that the distinction led to two different ways of evoking the same resulting behavior. Here, I'll diverge into the philosophy of code and talk about why you might want to use one strategy over another in a given situation.

Content View Modes

In Step 15, you loaded an image into a UIImageView. If you used the images from the companion web site, the image was *mostly* the right size (it was exactly the same size as the full iPhone screen). Since the tab bar took up some of the available screen space, the space available for the UIImageView was a little shorter than your image. Xcode initially squished the image to make it fit. This view mode (the default) is called "Scale To

Fill" (`UIViewContentModeScaleToFill`) because it scales the image in both X and Y directions to fill the content frame.

Unless your images are exactly the same size as your UIImageView, this will result in distortion. This might be tolerable if you are loading images that you have created directly into your interfaces (either in Interface Builder or via the `viewDidLoad` method), but that limits what your app can do. On the other hand, if you will be loading an image of unknown or unrestricted dimensions, some of the other view modes will be more appropriate. Have a look at Figure 6–33 for a list of the available view modes.

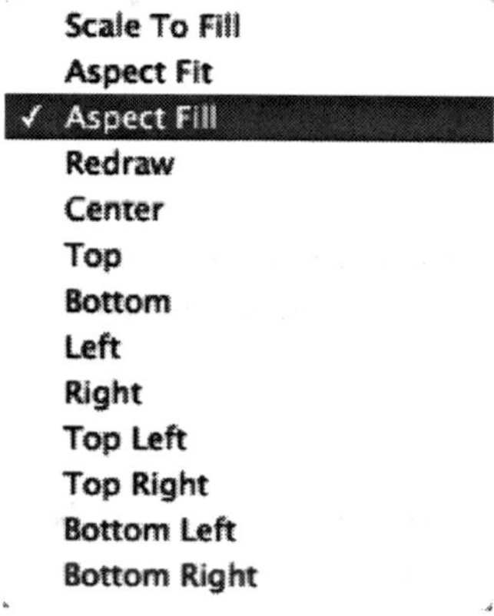

Figure 6–33. *Xcode's UIImageView Content View Modes.*

Starting at the top of the list in Figure 6–33, following Scale To Fill, *Aspect Fit* and *Aspect Fill* (`UIViewContentModeScaleAspectFit` and `UIViewContentModeScaleAspectFill`, respectively) will probably be the most useful to you.

- Aspect Fit. This scales the content, maintaining aspect ratio, until the largest dimension is equal to the corresponding dimension of the image view. Thus, if you have a UIImageView similar to the one in this chapter's app and a photo that was taken in landscape orientation, the image will be scaled so that the entire image is visible and empty space will appear above and below the photo in the interface.
- Aspect Fill. This scales the image until the other dimension fills the available space. This results in the entire view being filled with your image, at the expense of trimming off some of the image. Using the same example, this would cause the left and right edges of your photo to be trimmed.

The nine view modes at the bottom of the list (Center through Bottom Right) do no scaling at all on your image, and simply anchor the specified point in your image to the corresponding point in the content frame. For instance, choosing "Top Left" will cause the top left section of your image to be displayed so that the top edge is aligned with the top of the UIImageView, and the left edge is likewise aligned. Any extra image beyond the size of the content frame is cropped. In this app, you chose "Bottom" so that the bottom edges were aligned, and the extra portion of the image at the top was cut off.

The "Redraw" view mode provides a way to customize how your content scales and is a far more advanced topic than this discussion.

Compile-time and Runtime

In Step 24, I mentioned the terms *compile-time* and *runtime* in passing, noting that the distinction in that context was that the former meant you configured things in the Interface Builder part of Xcode and the latter meant you did this configuration by writing some code in your implementation file. That was a suitable definition of the terms at that time, but they can be defined a little more formally now.

Compile-time indicates that something happens when your project is compiled, or built, prior to being run on the simulator or on a real iOS device. These are things like the definition of classes in `.h` and `.m` files, the organization and layout of UIViews in your nib files, and the configuration you do in Xcode's various inspectors. Everything that is set at compile-time defines exactly the state your app will be in when it is started.

Runtime, on the other hand, describes the segment of time after your app has started running. This is when all the code you've written is actually executed, effecting changes in the state of the app from the way it was set up at compile time. In this chapter, you specified the image for the second tab through a message in your implementation file. Thus, the image to show was unspecified at compile time, but at runtime a series of instructions was executed to display the desired image in the UIImageView you provided.

Why is this difference significant? You proved, during the course of writing this app, that you can do the exact same thing at runtime as you could at compile-time. However, executing instructions to do what you wanted required several extra clicks and drags, and a few more lines of code. If you already know how you're going to configure something at compile-time, the advantages of writing code to do the same thing will diminish. However, if you want to dynamically change the properties of an object during the execution of the app (last chapter's app is a great example of this), it is obviously impossible to set all aspects of the state at compile-time.

In short, compile-time defines the starting state of your app, while runtime describes the actions that occur once your app begins running.

In the Chapter Ahead

In Chapter 7, you will move into the next level of complexity: *Storyboarding*.

Storyboarding is the new way Apple allows one to lay out how a user moves through an app, in much the same way that a movie producer sets up a storyboard to show how a movie will go from one scene to the next. Storyboarding has segues (pronounced "segways") that connect each view in your app with another. It is tempting to just go straight to storyboarding, but it's best to first learn a little about the code behind these buttons and images, as you have done. So take a break, and then let's move on to the land of storyboarding.

Chapter 7

Storyboards

This seventh chapter will introduce a new way to create an app quickly and visually. First, some views will be laid out and you will see how they can be connected without writing code, and you will get some neat transition animations for free. This new technique was first brought to the public's attention when Apple announced that they would be introducing a new and never-before-seen feature called Storyboards, which would be built into Xcode. It would allow the easy layout of workflow apps that use navigation and tab bars to transition between views.

Apple went on to say that the new storyboards would manage the view controllers for you, while visually creating an easy to manage geospatial view of your project. It would specify the transitions and segues that are used when switching between views, without having to code them by hand! Everyone waited with anticipation for the Beta to come out and, when it did, everyone was blown away. It changed the entire coding landscape.

Storytelling

When you tell a story, you communicate with others. Whether young or old, everyone loves a story. Storytelling is an integral part of daily communication with others. When you communicate with a user, you are telling them how to travel a path you've created that will bring them to a place where they will get what they want, be it a map, a song, a recipe, the weather, where they parked their car, a phone number, a movie, or something else. So why wasn't this thought of before? Why was the creation of apps seen as geeks programming code, while storytellers were seen as being something different? I'm not sure of the answer, but as I began to think about it, I realized that this was an incredible concept. Think of it. When Walt Disney began to think of the most efficient means to organize and structure cartoons, back in the early 1920s, he came up with the concept of storyboards. He would gather his artists together and they would mount a series of boards with key scenes from a story, and then they would organize these boards into a beautiful story. This technique became a huge success; it took over the movie industry, and it is the blueprint for planning every modern film. You can see a great movie that illustrates how Disney's storyboarding took over the industry here: `bit.ly/oWg5mc`.

The new iOS5 Storyboard feature is much the same, except you are not necessarily looking at pictures; you are looking at a geospatial representation of your app that allows you to organize it beautifully. Before iOS5 came out, nib files were used to define the user interface. There was no choice but to do this one view controller at a time. If you had 16 view controllers, you would have to define the user interface 16 times. Not only was this boring, but it became complex and confusing. Conversely, as you will soon see, a storyboard file captures all your user interfaces in one geospatial view, and gives you the ability to easily create and edit all your individual view controllers, and the transitions between your view controllers. You can move them around like a deck of cards, just like the guys at the Disney studios. It becomes easy to realize and edit the flow of the overall user interface and experience in your app.

Roadmap Recap

You now know enough of what happens behind the scenes to install a new way of doing things. It's as if you've spent enough time tinkering around with lawnmower engines and basic car engines that you can appreciate installing a brand new engine in your old car. As you install this new engine, you know that inside this engine are pistons, spark plugs, carburetors, and so on. You do not have to yank the engine open to know these items exist; you can just install it and connect it to the chassis, the drive train, and the electronics. In storyboarding, you are going to use a whole new method for designing your app; you will simply have to connect it to your outlets, view controllers, and the other elements of your app. You don't have to open up storyboard and look inside, as you know it works; you simply have to know how to connect things. So let's do it!

Roadmap: Four Phases

This app has been divided into four phases. The most important phase is the first one because it will be common for most of the potential uses for storyboarding. Because Phase I is the lowest common denominator for so many of the future storyboards you will find yourself doing, I focus on this quite a bit, and encourage you to perform exercises that will enable you to quickly become efficient at storyboarding. Phase I sets up the root of what will be done over and over again, and the three phases that follow are specific to this particular app.

- **Phase I** sets up the core of most potential storyboarding configurations.
- **Phase II** starts at Figure 7–22, and is comprised of setting up the view controllers for Male, Female, and Geek.
- **Phase III** starts at Figure 7–34, and is comprised of establishing the content of the view controllers.
- **Phase IV** starts at Figure 7–54, and is comprised of closure and coding.

Evolve: A View-based Storyboard Application

Once again, you will work with images that let you know where in the story you are. In more technical terms, you will use images rather than code to represent a state in your app. I encourage my students to use images because, if it does not work, then you know it's a bug in the high-level code that directs the user from state to state—not a bug in the code for a particular state.

In this app, you will see a funny set of states that show the state of a male, a female, and the other kind of human being—geeks. It will also show that when a man or a woman evolves into a higher state of consciousness they become geeks! Then, to add another state, for fun and to illustrate the purpose, it will be shown that when a geek evolves they become an Über Geek! As funny as this is, it simply gives us a nice set of diverse states that, in storyboarding, will be easy, but that in the old one-at-a-time nib manipulation would have been substantially more complex.

First, download the images from here: `bit.ly/p1L5cv` where you can also download the code or view the video. Once you have downloaded the `.zip` file containing the images, unzip the folder, and store the images on your desktop.

I will not be holding your hand as tightly as I have thus far. Instead, I will assume that you know how to perform some of the functions you have done repeatedly in this book. Yes, I will be talking to you in a more technical manner.

Phase I: Creating Core Storyboarding Configurations

Let's get going with Phase I, where you will build a core configuration.

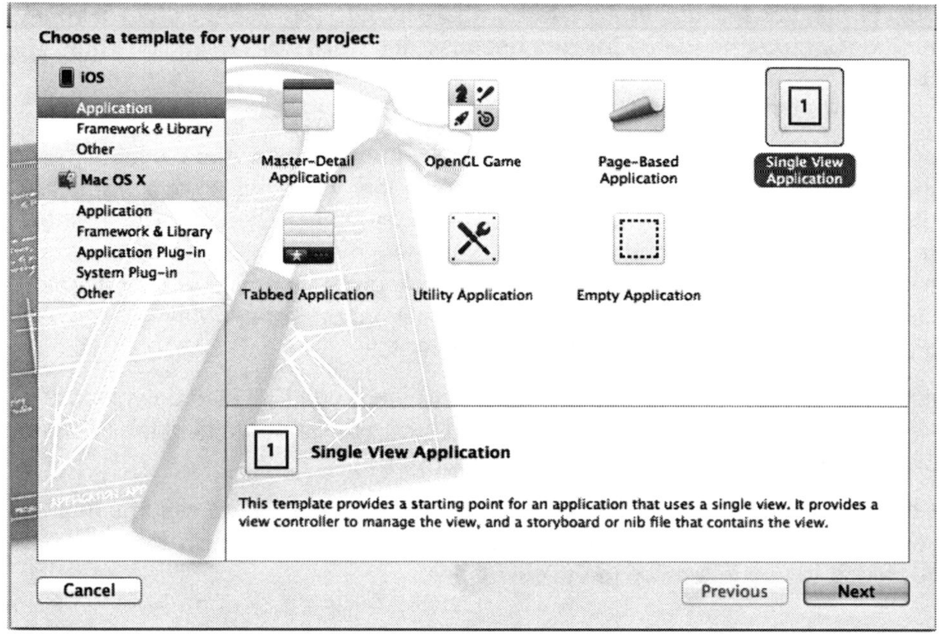

Figure 7–1. *Start by choosing a Single View Application skeleton. More views will be added later.*

1. OK, let's start a new project in Xcode by using your keyboard shortcut, ⌘⇧N, and selecting the Single View Application project type. The Single View Application will be the starting place for this application, and likely many more of this book's applications, as well as your own.

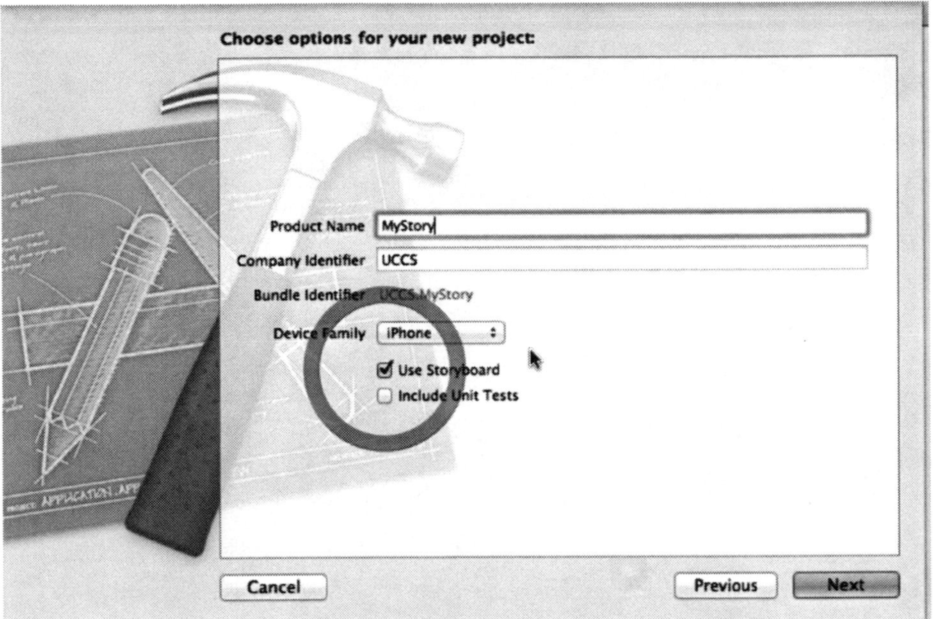

Figure 7–2. *Start with just an iPhone version of the app and the new storyboard feature selected to allow us to jump directly into design and layout. I named it "`MyStory`."*

2. Let's name this application "`MyStory`." The Company Identifier is not relevant to us at this time, so feel free to put something creative there. For simplicity, just target the iPhone device family at this time. The brand new "Use Storyboard" option will need to be checked. This will present you with a slightly different project layout once you've saved the project. Go ahead and click the Next button.

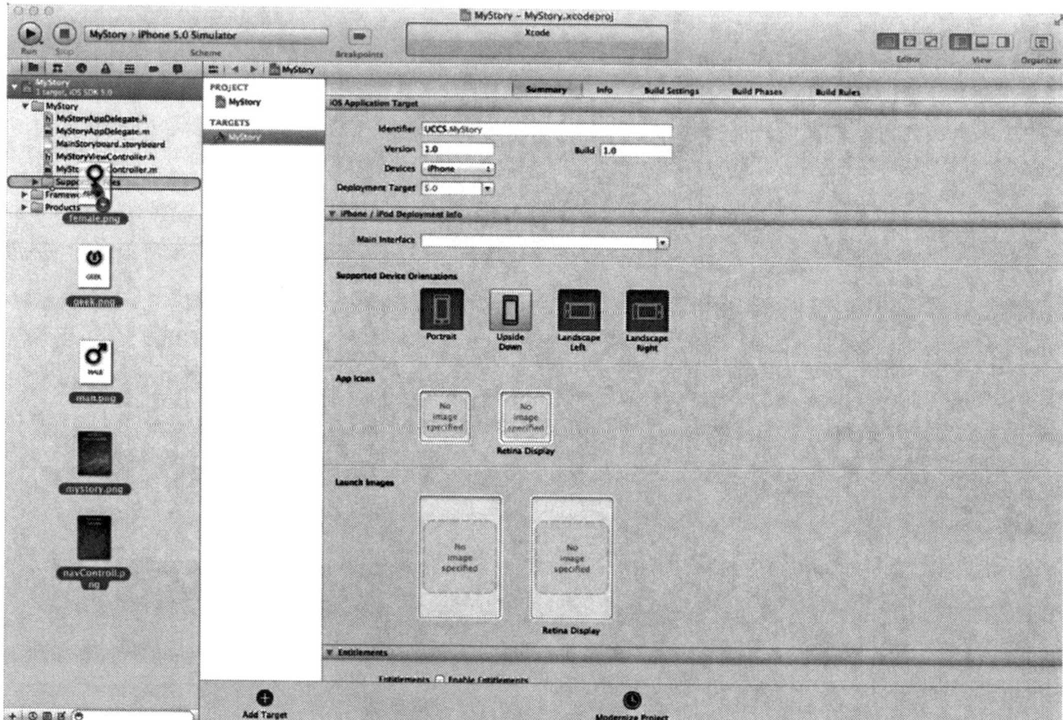

Figure 7–3. *Drag the images that you downloaded earlier to the project's "Supporting Files" directory in Xcode.*

3. The first thing to do is add some image files to the project by dragging them from the desktop to the project Supporting Files directory. This is just a logical directory, and the files can actually go almost anywhere in the `MyStory` directory. Be sure that these files are copied in the proceeding dialog box.

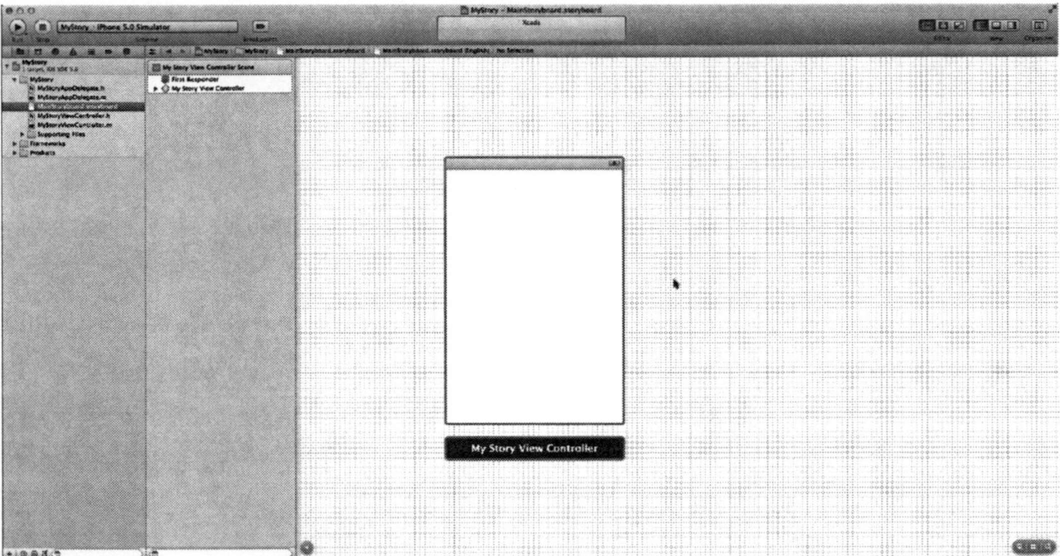

Figure 7–4. ***Select the "`MainStoryboard.storyboard`" file and you will be presented with your only default view.***

4. Now, select the "`MainStoryboard.storyboard`" file in Xcode's project file browser on the left. This shows you something a little familiar, a `UIView`. But this is not just a `UIView`, it also has an associated controller that is automatically created and linked to the view. You can add more views shortly, but one important thing to note here is that double clicking the grid pattern allows you to zoom in and out. You *must* be in normal viewing mode to add visual elements to the views.

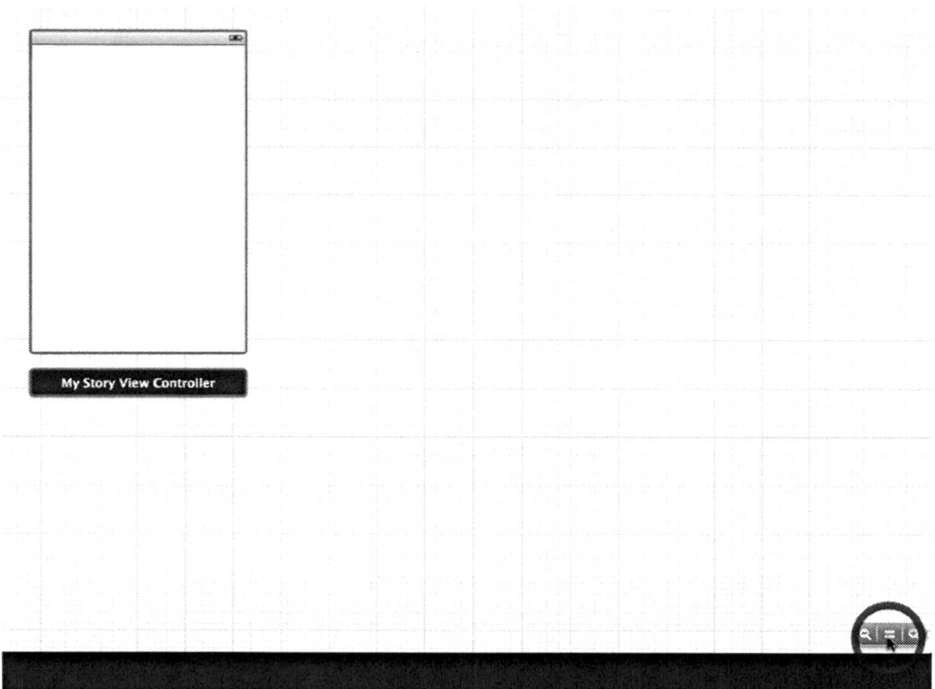

Figure 7–5. *Clicking this button returns you to normal viewing mode. The two buttons on either side allow you to zoom in and out.*

5. It's important to become familiar with the viewing and zoom modes, as you will constantly want to zoom in to edit a detailed view and then immediately zoom out again to view the entire storyboard. Clicking the center equal sign button returns you to the normal viewing mode. The two buttons on either side allow you to zoom in and out.

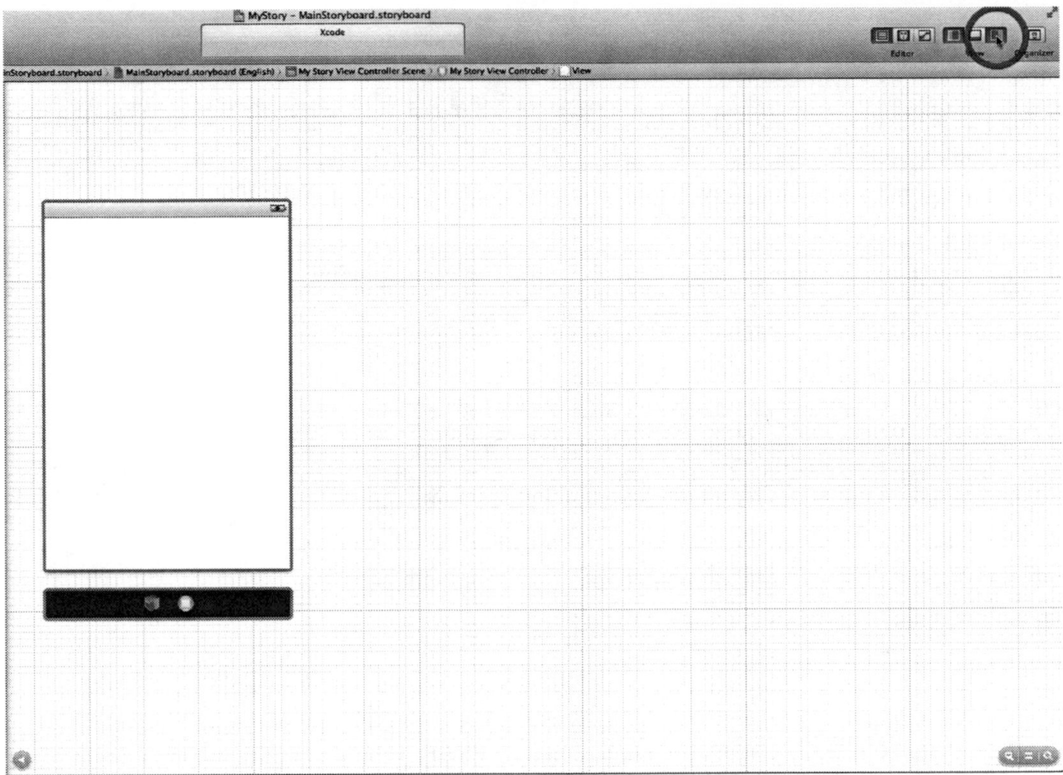

Figure 7–6. *You need to bring up the Utilities Panel to add some new views to the project.*

6. Bring up the Utilities Panel by clicking the button circled in red in Figure 7–6. Having a larger screen makes working with Xcode easier, as more and more panels and views take up valuable screen space.

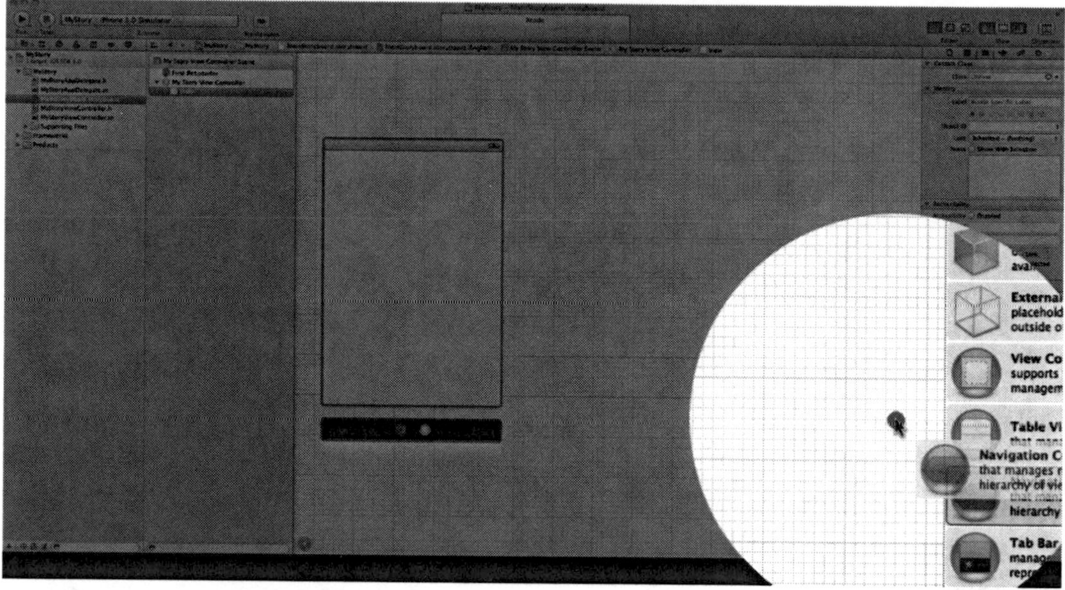

Figure 7–7. *Select a Navigation Controller.*

7. Once you have opened up the Utilities Panel, locate the "Navigation Controller" (`UINavigationController`). Select it and start dragging the Navigation Controller onto your Storyboard, as shown in Figure 7–7.

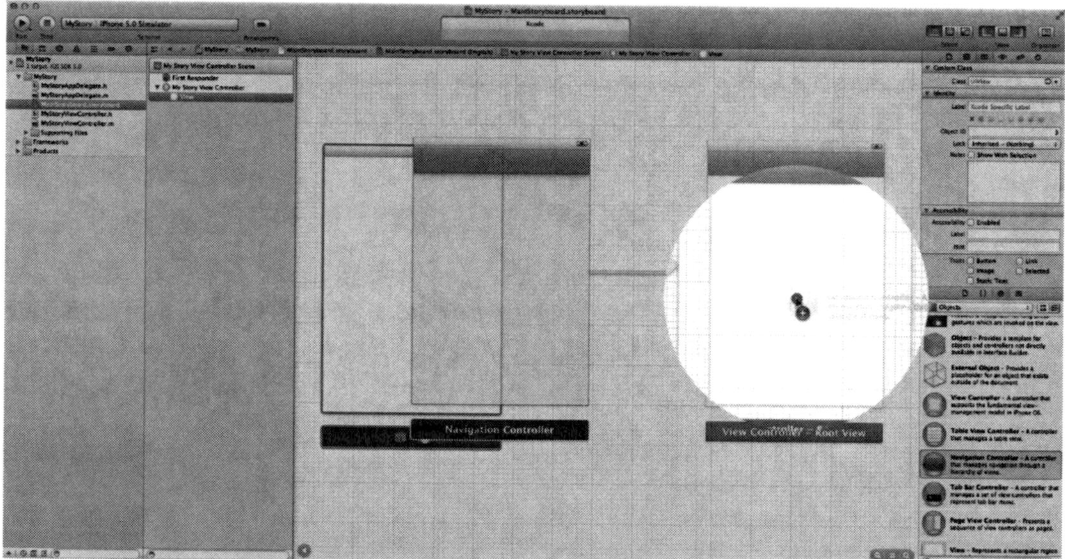

Figure 7–8. *Drag a new Navigation Controller to the storyboard area; placement is not important at this point. Two new views appear, with a link between them.*

8. As you drag the Navigation Controller onto the storyboard, you will see that instead of just a single view, you get a connected pair of controllers that are depicted as views. Drop it any place, as you are free to move it around as much as you need. This is, in fact, the case for almost everything that you will do in storyboards. You are not dealing just with views, you are actually seeing Apple instantiate each `UI` element into a set of views and controllers that allow you to build transitions. These transitions in Xcode are called segues (pronounced seg-ways), as shown in Figure 7–8.

> **NOTE:** A Segue (segway) is often articulated in music and performing arts realms when the musicians move without interruption from one song, melody, or scene to another. *We want a smooth transition from one scene to another.*

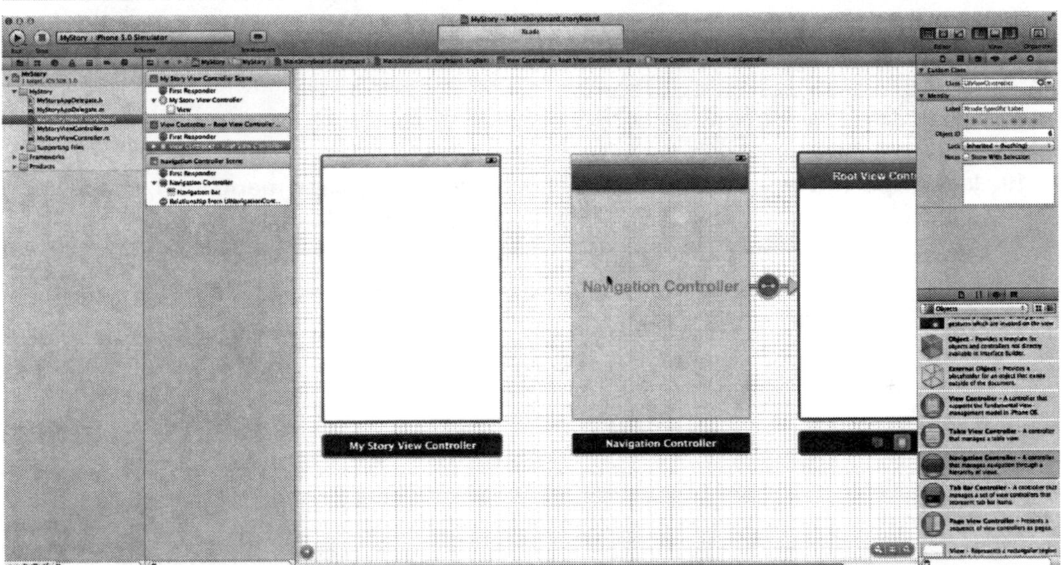

Figure 7–9. *Keep this first Navigation Controller as a simple view controller.*

9. You're going to leave this first Navigation Controller alone for a now. The reason is that this is the first view that the user will see, and all you want to happen here is to have access to the code Apple has provided for the logic associated to the blue navigation bar at the top of the view. Strictly speaking, the Root View Controller on the right is actually the first view that your user will see, as the Navigation Controller is pushed to the view stack. But for now, just arrange the controllers in an orderly fashion.

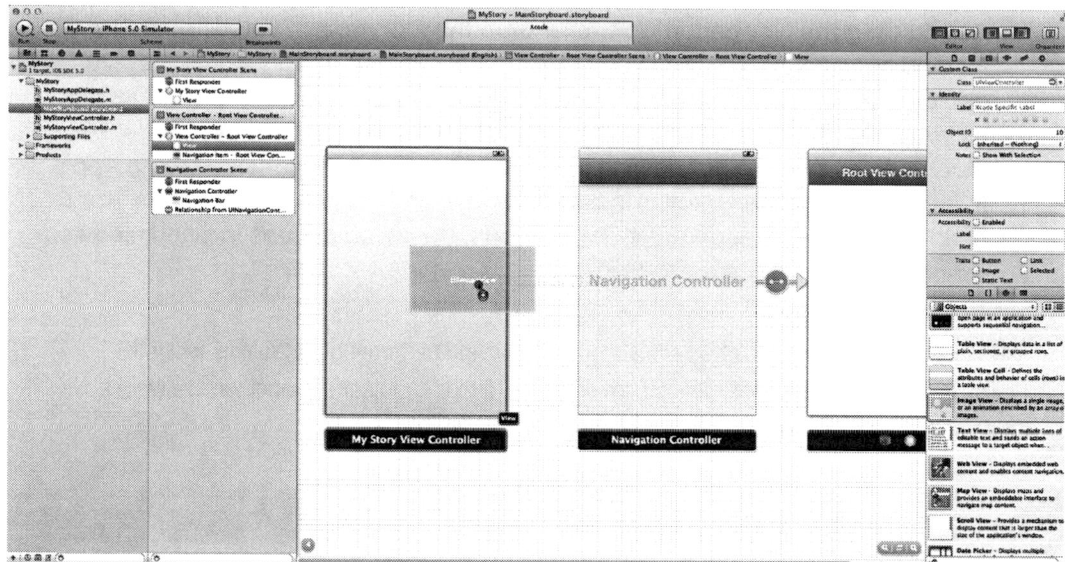

Figure 7–10. *Drag a `UIImageView` to your first view controller.*

10. In the app you will not have code in each state, as already mentioned; instead, you will have images, either made or, preferably, downloaded from my site. By now you know that images need to be parked in `UIImageViews`. So drag a `UIImageView` to your first view controller, so that you can place the `mystory.png` onto it. This is illustrated in Figure 7–10.

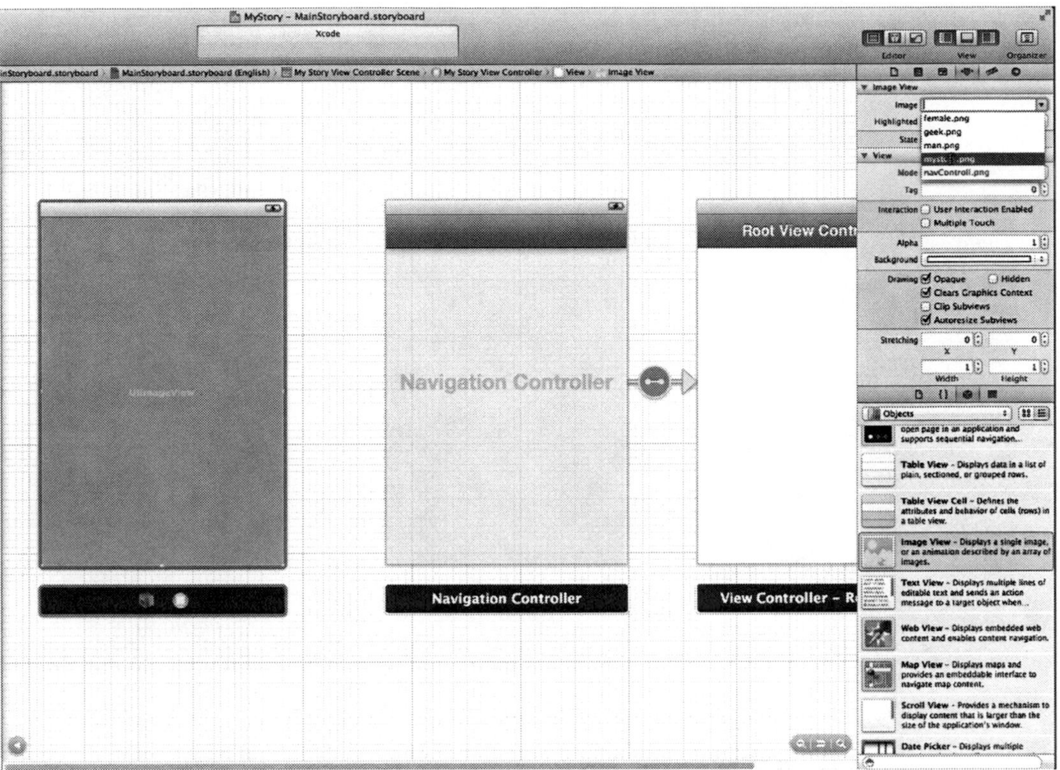

Figure 7–11. *Open the Utilities Panel and select the* `mystory.png`*.*

11. From the `UIImageView`'s settings in the Attributes Inspector found in the Utilities Panel, set the image to `mystory.png`, as illustrated in Figure 7–11.

Figure 7–12. *Drag a `UIButtonView` out to the main view controller so that you can have an actionable item in order to push the next view controller to the stack.*

12. As shown in Figure 7–12, you need to have a button on your main view controller, so drag a Round Rect Button (`UIButtonView`) onto it, so that you can have an actionable item to press, which will push the next view controller to the stack.

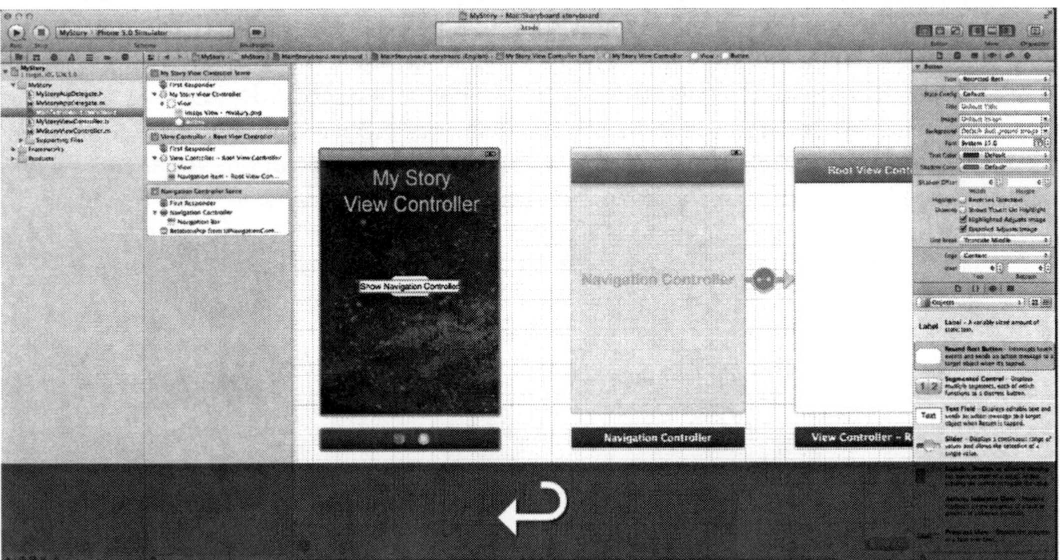

Figure 7–13. *Insert text into your button; I used "Show Navigation Controller."*

13. When the user presses this first button, you want it to take the user to the navigation controller. Let's tell the user this will happen if they press this button. This is illustrated in Figure 7–13.

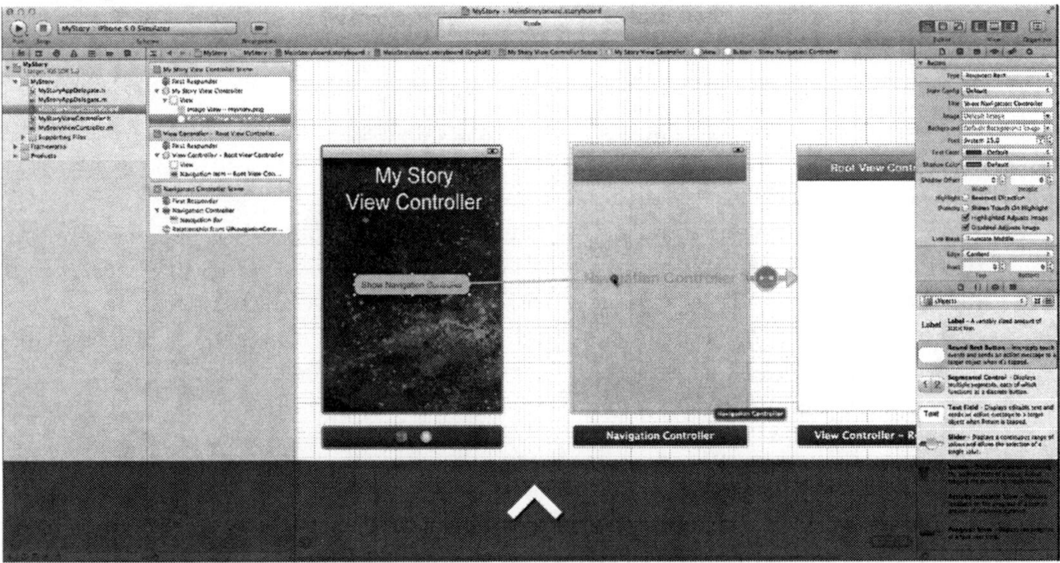

Figure 7–14. *Start the actual linking.*

14. This step is really the heart of storyboarding. Let's think about this. You want your user to be directed to the navigation controller when he or she presses the button saying "Show Navigation Controller." Rather than writing code, just link the button to the navigation controller. To do so, place your mouse over the button, and then control-drag and release over the Navigation Controller to create a transitional link. This is the magic—no code is written to make this transition with animation, as shown in Figure 7–14. It's just free! A gift that was written by the remarkably clever people at Apple that—if you don't mind me reminding you again—includes students and readers of the first edition of this book! So hang in there!

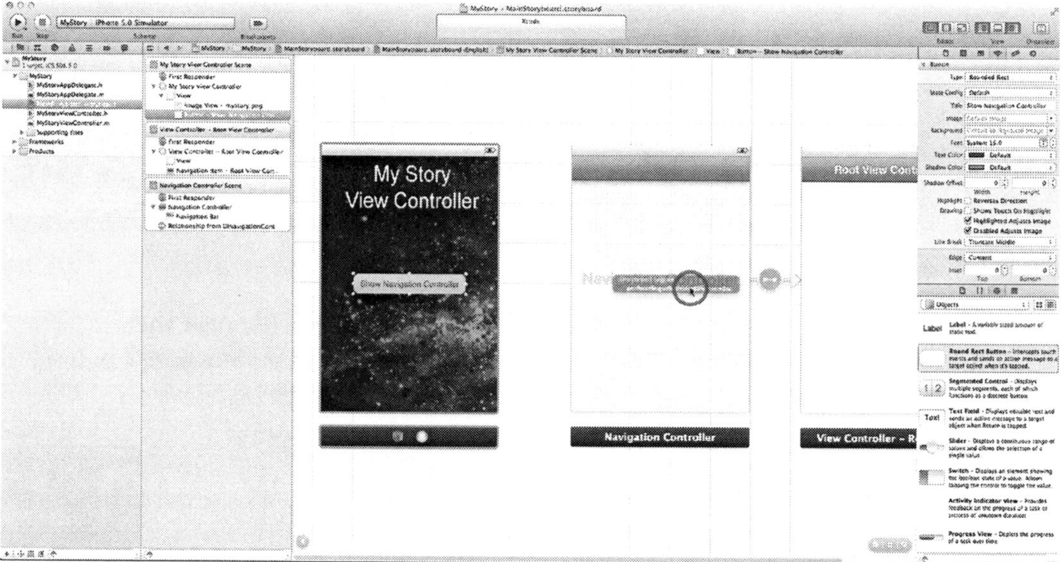

Figure 7–15. *Select the "`performSegueWithIdentifier:`" option.*

15. Upon dropping the connector onto the navigation controller, it comes up with the option `performSegueWithIdentifier:sender:`, which is the name of the method that holds all the code you need for connecting these two items appropriately using storyboarding. You may note that I have also added a section in Digging the Code that describes how to add the `performSegueWithIdentifier:sender` method programmatically. On the other hand, if you do not see this option, go to step 16.

> **NOTE:** You cannot create a segue by control-dragging from a `UIView` or the basic View Controller. You need an actionable item to create a segue, and the `UIButtonView` is an easy one to use.

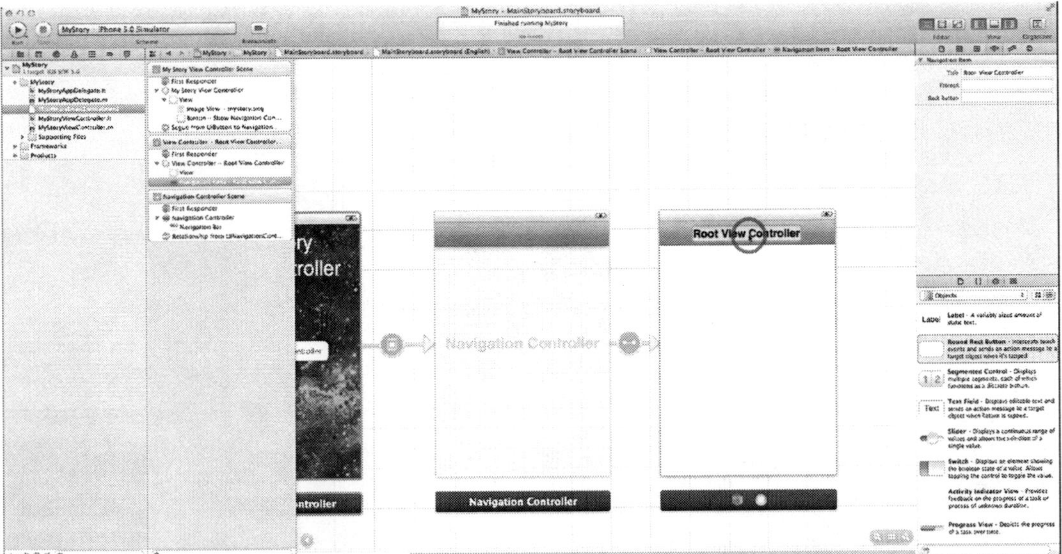

Figure 7–16. *Rename the Root View Controller's title bar to something a little better, such as "Root".*

16. You are now going to change the title of the Root View Controller to something useful. I suggest "Root" because you don't need to care about the aspect of the Model View Controller (MVC) when using the app. This label is also an integral part of the free naming of navigation buttons that you'll see when you run the app. This is illustrated in Figure 7–16. Naming these title bars is important for the user to understand where they are in your program, and how they got there. Double clicking the title bar, or typing in the Title section of the Attributes Panel, allows you to edit this value. When the user travels back and forth through a Navigation Controller, these labels appear in the title and the "back" button. You'll see this shortly when you test the app for functionality.

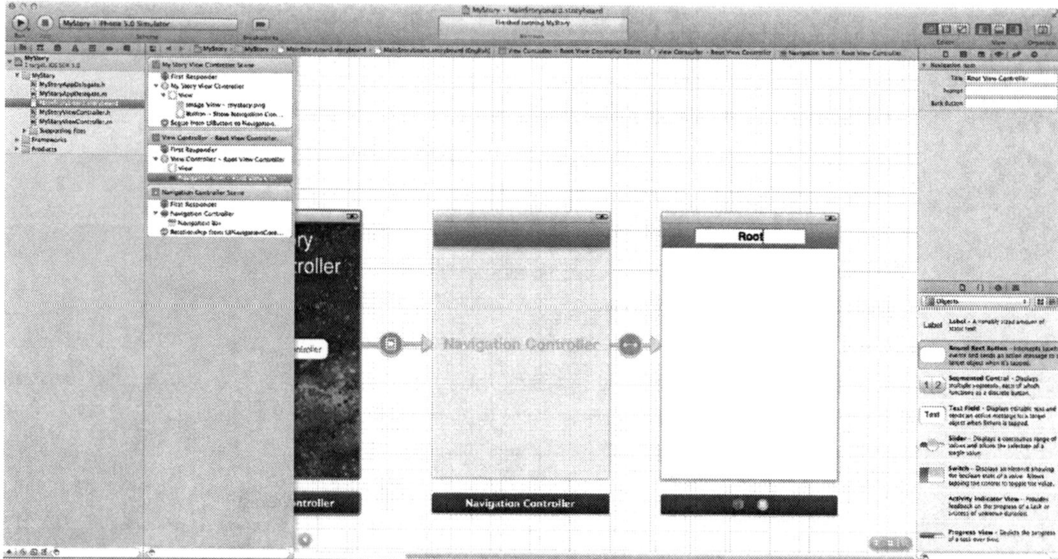

Figure 7–17. *Phase 1 is almost completed—you just need styles for segues and transitions, and then a test run.*

17. Before moving too far ahead, stop for a minute and catch your breath. You have successfully created the foundation not only for this storyboard app, but also for the methodology that you will use as the basis for many other apps, which is a view controller connected to your Root Navigation Controller. Essentially, you have created a view controller with a button that takes you to a navigation controller you have named "Root," as shown in Figure 7–17. The rest of your storyboard will blossom out from this root. Now, however, you will see segue styles, transition styles, and you will do a test run over the next three steps. Once you reach step 20, you will be asked to go back and run these first twenty steps.

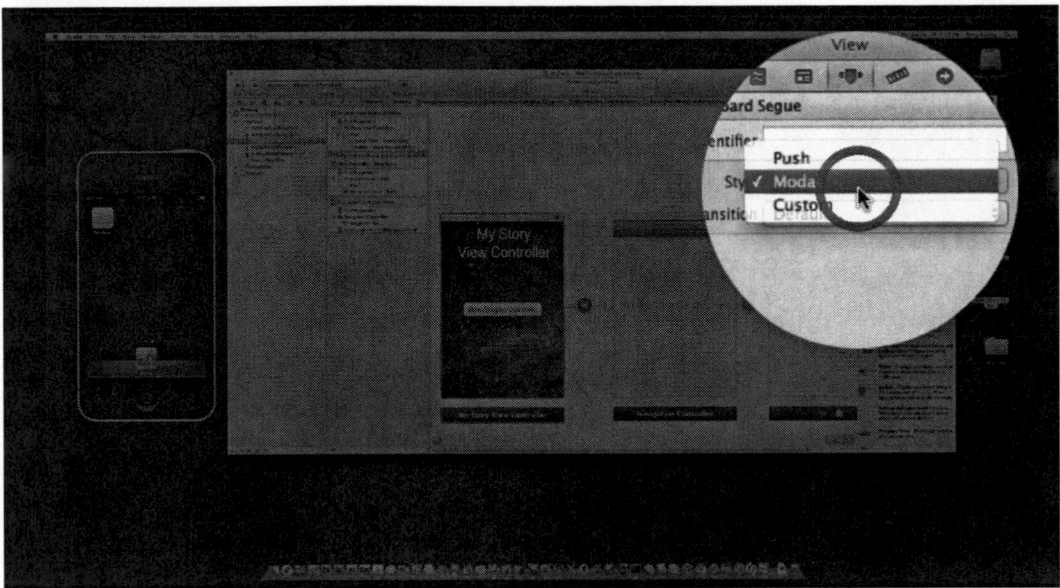

Figure 7–18. *Select the segue you have just created and select a segue style.*

18. Select the storyboard segue you created. Now let's choose a style of segue to use. In the Attributes Panel, you can select one of three style types of segue. "Push" is the standard slide in from the right animation. "Modal" is a type you can use for a segue that goes back and forth between two views. "Custom" requires that you write your own type of segue. Mmm, let's do that later, huh? Anyway, I want you to play around with these different styles, so that you become familiar with them. Different students have different tastes. For now, just leave the defaults because they work well, as illustrated in Figure 7–18.

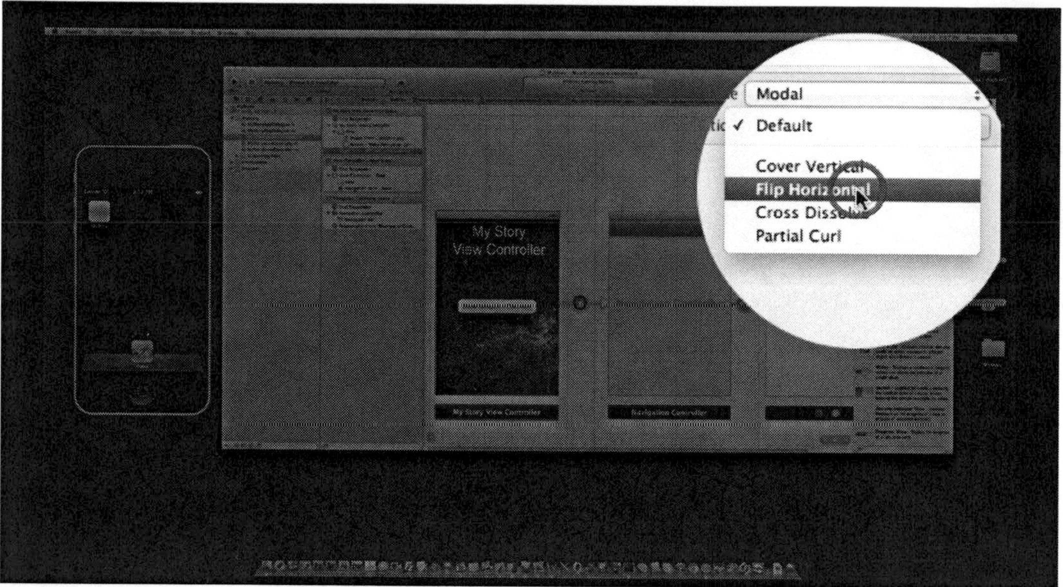

Figure 7–19. *Select the transition of your choice.*

19. Transitions are the animation types available for each style of segue. Again, just stick with the default. I chose the Flip Horizontal style for no particular reason other than it suits me. You can choose another style, if you want. Feel free to experiment here, but keep usability in mind. It is very easy to get too flashy with the animations. I often find that the popular apps, and smarter students, tend to have less flash and more utility and efficiency.

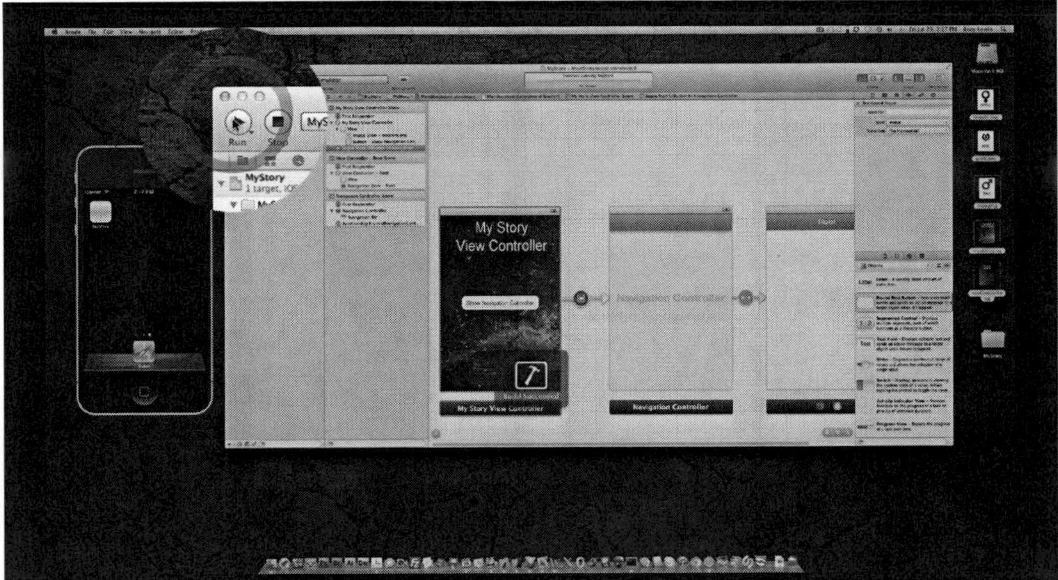

Figure 7–20. *Run it to see what you achieved in Phase 1.*

20. At this point, running the app will show you how little you actually had to do to get a working app with some direction. So, as depicted in Figure 7–20, hit that "Run" button and see what you have.

NOTE: You may want to emulate what I make my students do at this point. I make them erase everything they have done so far, except for the five icons on their desktop. Then I make them repeat these steps over and over again until they can 1) get up to this point, excluding steps 18 and 19; 2) run it; and 3) have it appear in the simulator within 50 seconds, without using the book.

I STRONGLY encourage you to do this!

Just as a golfer needs to practice his swing to create muscle memory, you need to be able to get to this point without even thinking. First, do it at your own pace with the book, and then go faster and faster until you get below 50 seconds! Yeah!

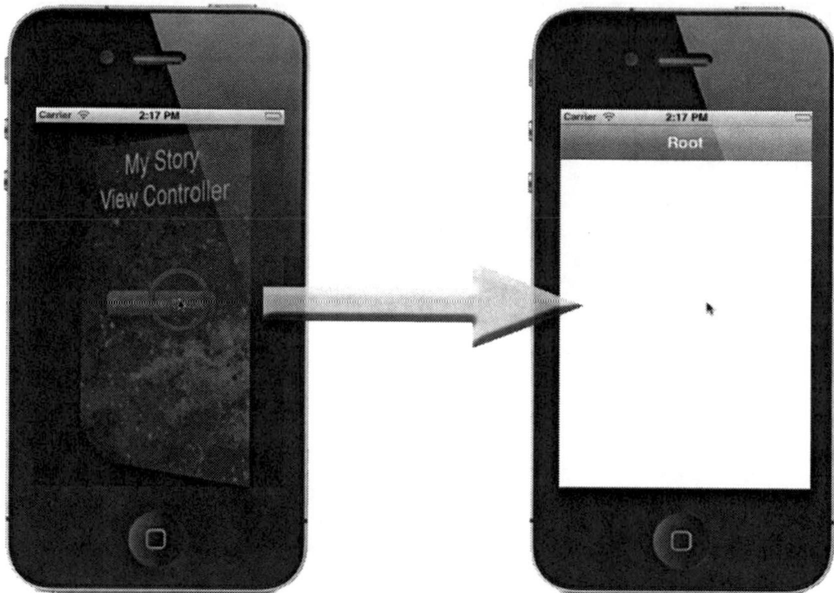

Figure 7–21. *And, sure enough, clicking the button flips the view and shows us a blank view, with a navigation bar at the top named "Root".*

21. After hitting the "Run" button, the simulator opens and voila! It works! You've hardly done anything, and used no code, simply having shifted, dragged, and connected a few items, and you now have a running app! Clicking the button flips the view and shows a blank view, with a navigation bar at the top named "Root," as depicted in Figure 7–21. Beautiful!

Phase II: Setting Up the View Controllers

Of course, you want to make this app do something more interesting than what you now have. Remember, in this evolving app you have three types of human—Men, Women and Geeks—and they can all potentially evolve into Über Geeks. This means that you need to have three views connected directly to your Navigation Controller. So, before you begin to drag three view controllers onto the storyboard, let's make sure:

- That you can see everything—enough for three horizontally placed `UIViewControllers`.
- That your alignment on the grid can be kept so that your connection lines don't get silly looking later on, and therefore harder to follow.

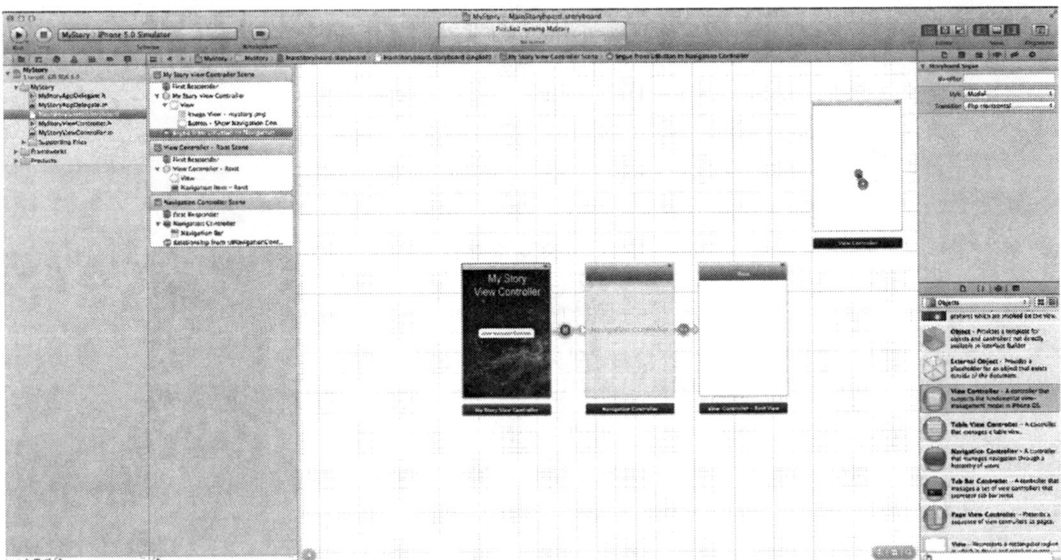

Figure 7–22. *Zoom out and drag a new view controller onto the storyboard.*

22. So, let's drop three more view controllers into the storyboard, to the right of the Root View Controller. Another way to do this is to drop one and then, while holding the option key, drag the first one to another position, which makes a copy. This is a personal preference, but it sure makes you look like a supercalifragilistic geek if you can do it. Anthony does a great job of this in the video seen here: `bit.ly/oMp984`. Try to get your screen looking like the one in Figure 7–22, which shows the first of the three `UIViewControllers` being dragged onto the storyboard. Remember, if you're having trouble with the zoom, just click the equal button in the zoom control area so that you can add other stuff to the individual controllers.

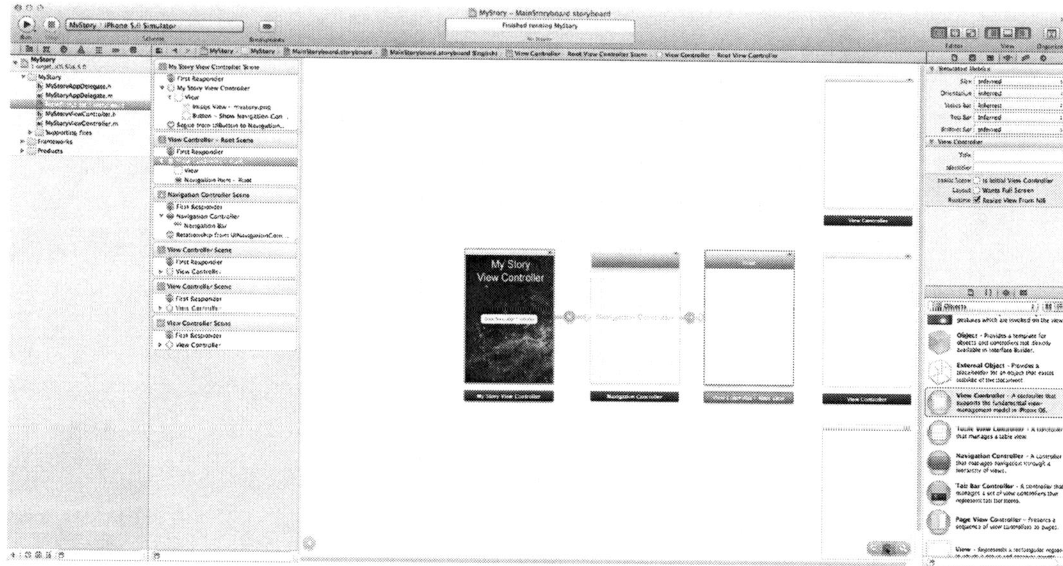

Figure 7–23. *Your storyboard after all three view controllers are placed onto the storyboard.*

23. As shown in Figure 7–23, this is how your screen should look after you have dragged all three view controllers onto your storyboard. Note that they are aligned, spaced equally apart, and locked into the grid.

> **NOTE:** Objects not sticking? It will get frustrating if you continually try to drag objects to a view and they never stick. So, be sure you return to the normal zoom level.

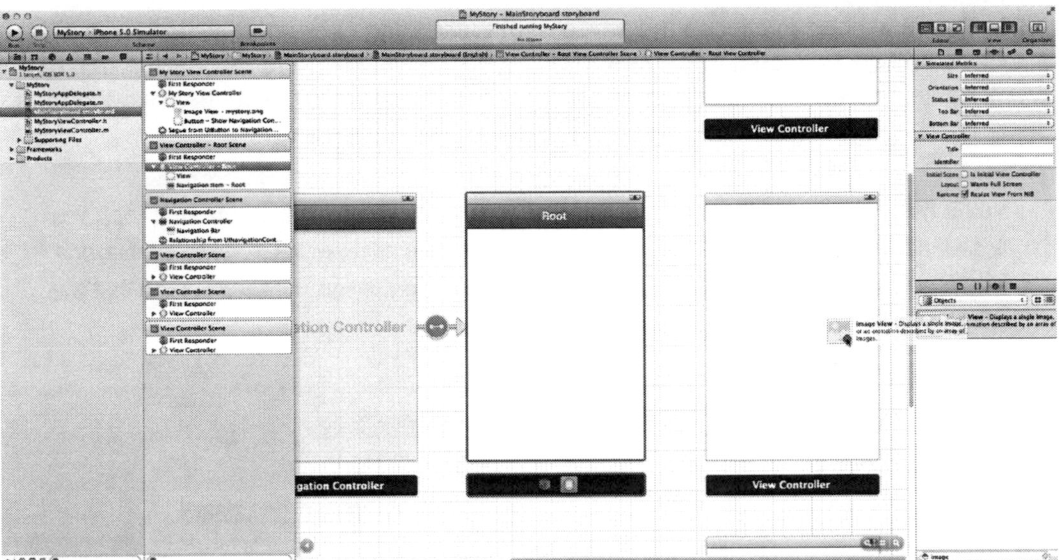

Figure 7–24. *Add a* `UIImageView`.

24. Looking into the immediate future, you still need to place four images: one image goes into your Root, and three images (representing Man, Woman, and Geek) are placed onto the three `UIViewControllers` you just created. I should not have to remind you that if you want to have an image appear on your app's view, you need to park those pictures on `UIImageViews`. For now, though, let's focus on the Root, where you need an image and buttons for going to the three images. Drag an Image View onto your Root, as shown in in Figure 7–24.

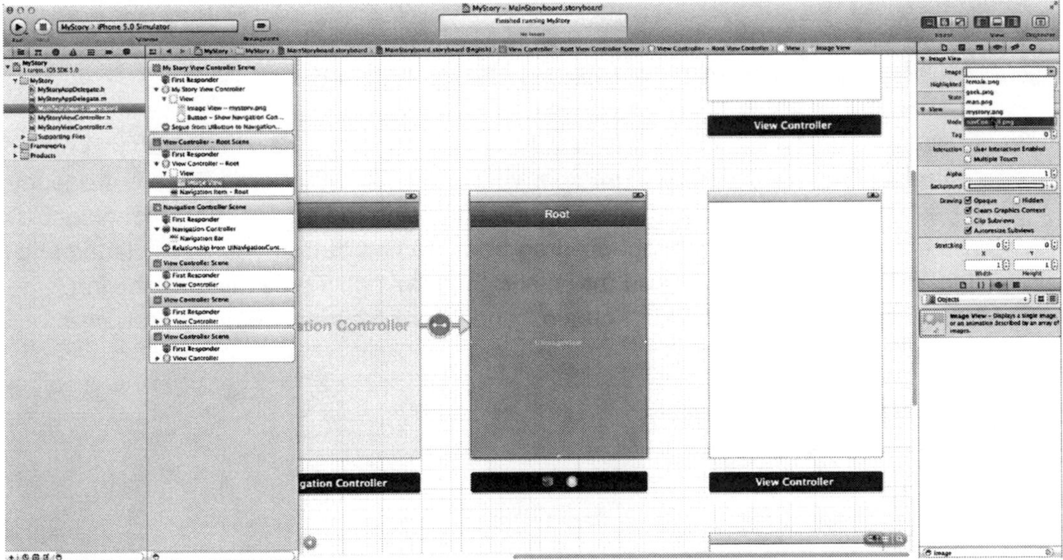

Figure 7–25. *Set the image in the Attributes Panel.*

25. You now need to choose the `NavControll.png` image I created, which is now located and selected from the Attributes Panel, as illustrated in Figure 7–25. Again, you can select any image you want. But, before you spend too much time creating your own image, keep the following note in mind.

> **NOTE:** Remember that in the months to come, as you use storyboarding to create your apps, you will not have an image here at all. Instead, you will have code representing a picker, a table, or a level of a game, to name a few examples. For now, just use my image, but keep in mind that you will later use greater things at this juncture of storyboarding.

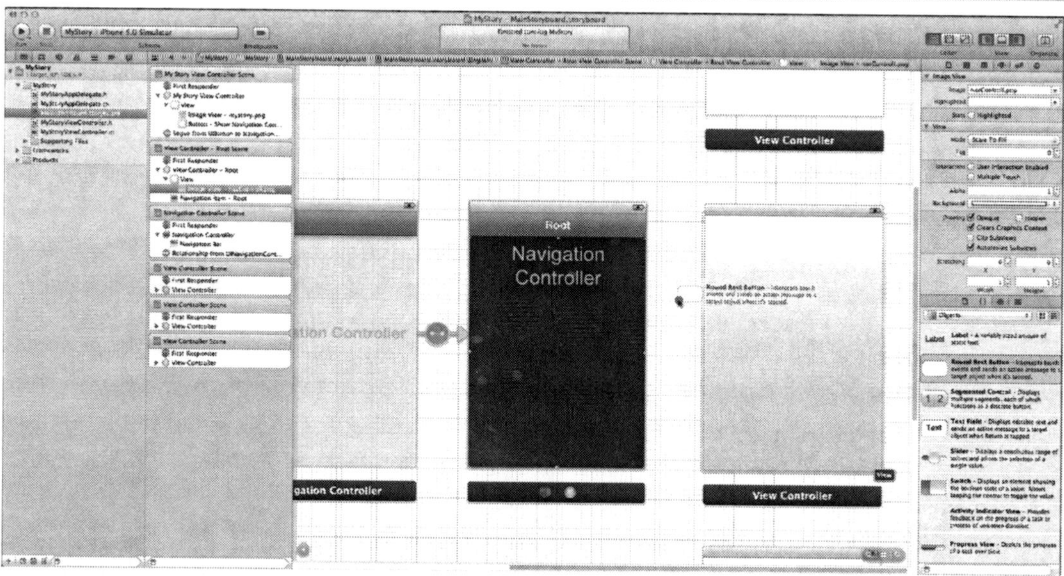

Figure 7–26. *Drag a `UIButtonView` to the navigation controller and duplicate it.*

26. As shown in Figure 7–26, add a new `UIButtonView` to the view. You can use each button's activation to move to another view. You can either drag three buttons, by repeating the process three times, or practice using the option-drag technique you tried once already. So, option-drag from the first button you have placed and duplicate it twice, as you need three, and these will now only need relabeling. Name these buttons "Male," "Female," and "Geek," in descending order, and resize them as you see fit.

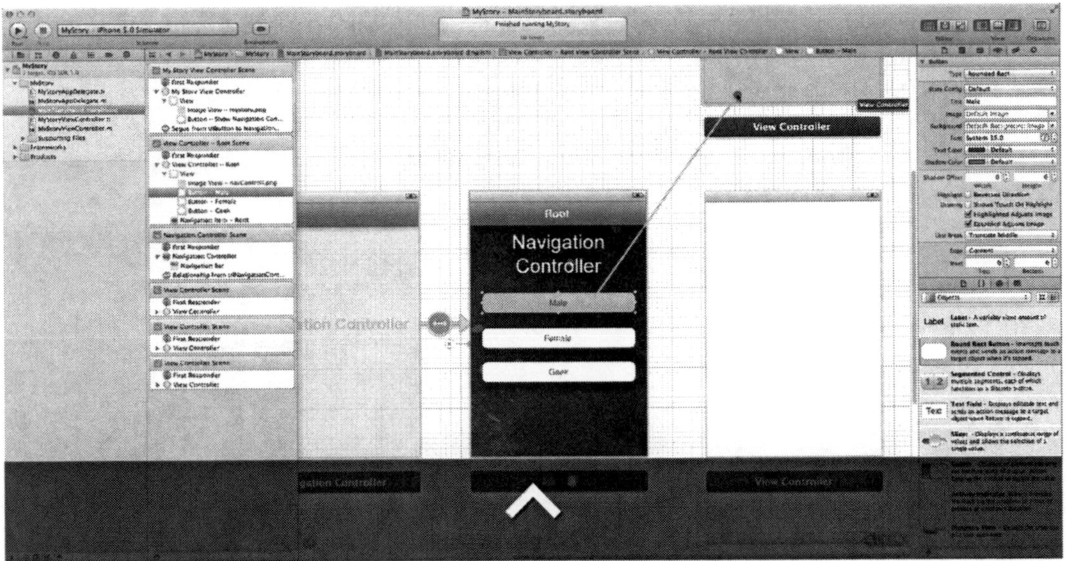

Figure 7–27. *Create more segues from each button to the three view controllers.*

27. You need to create segues from each of your three buttons to their associated view controllers. So, just as before, control-drag from each button to another view controller in order to create a segue link for each button. I connected "Male" to the top, "Female" to the bottom, and "Geek" to the center, as it will make the link lines look nice and organized. This is illustrated in Figure 7–27.

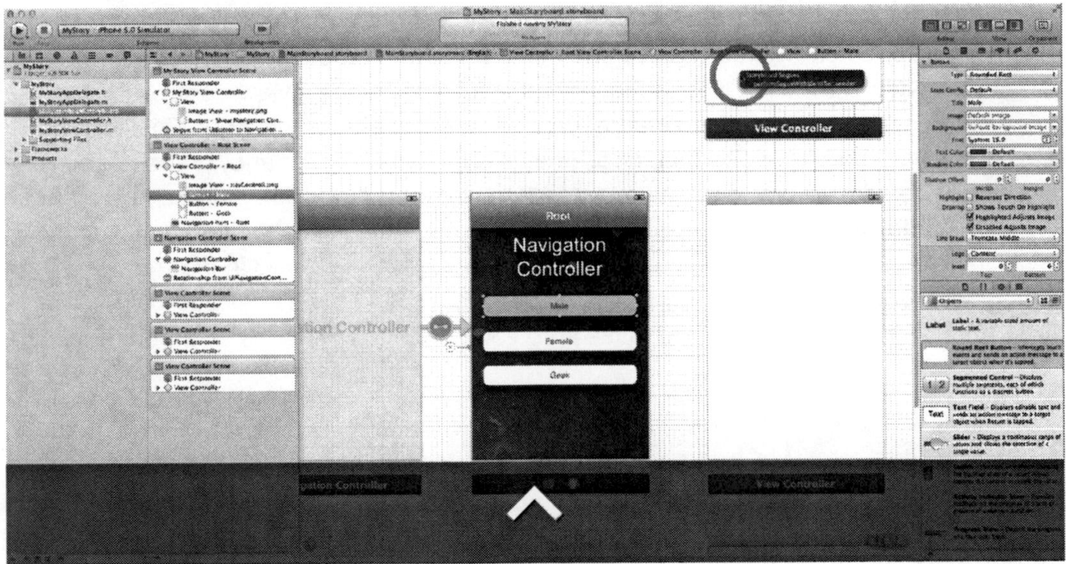

Figure 7–28. *Connect to* `performSegueWithIdentifier:sender:`.

28. Just as you did in 7–15, when you drop the control drag from the Male button to the Male view controller, you will get an option to select either modal, push, or custom, where you will leave it as the default, or you will see an option for `performSegueWithIdentifier:sender:` that holds all the code needed to connect these two items appropriately using storyboarding. This is illustrated in Figure 7–28.

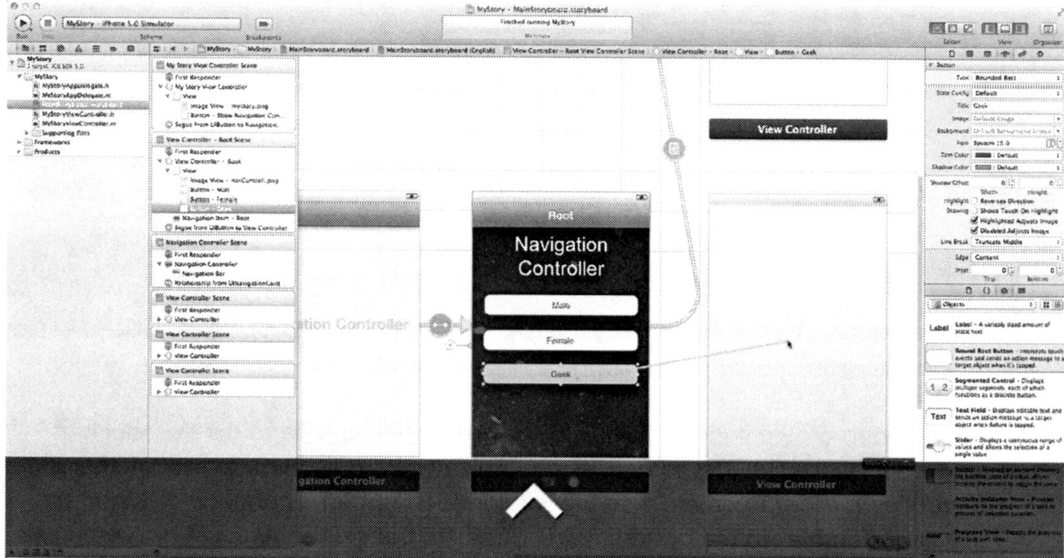

Figure 7–29. *Completed segue going to Male and segue to Geek in progress.*

29. Figure 7-29 shows the completed segue that connects the Male button to the Male view controller. Notice that I have placed the Geek's view controller in the middle, so that you can extend beyond in a later stage of this app. This illustrates how you may have one pattern or order for the user of your app, and another order of view controllers on your storyboard. You will also find, I have no doubt, that until you get a feel for how the segues show their visual connectivity, it will take a while to make them look as elegant as those illustrated in Figure 7–29. Don't get frustrated, it just takes a little practice to learn how far out to place the view controllers and how to make sure your grid alignment has symmetry between all the objects.

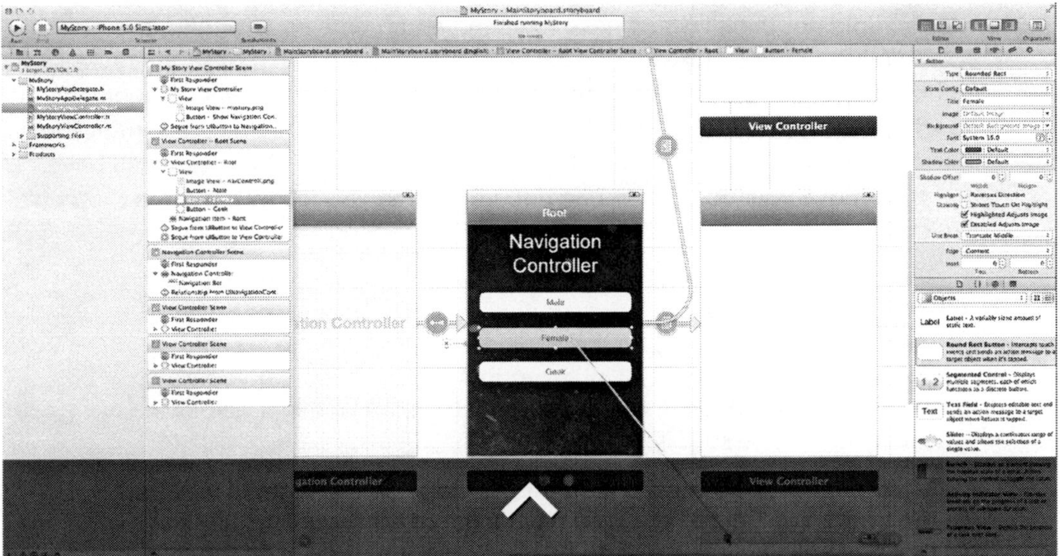

Figure 7–30. *Last segue, from the Female's button to its view controller.*

30. OK, for this last connection, all I will say is that you should create a segue from your Female button to its view controller. Figure 7–30 shows the first portion of this step, but there are steps I am not repeating.

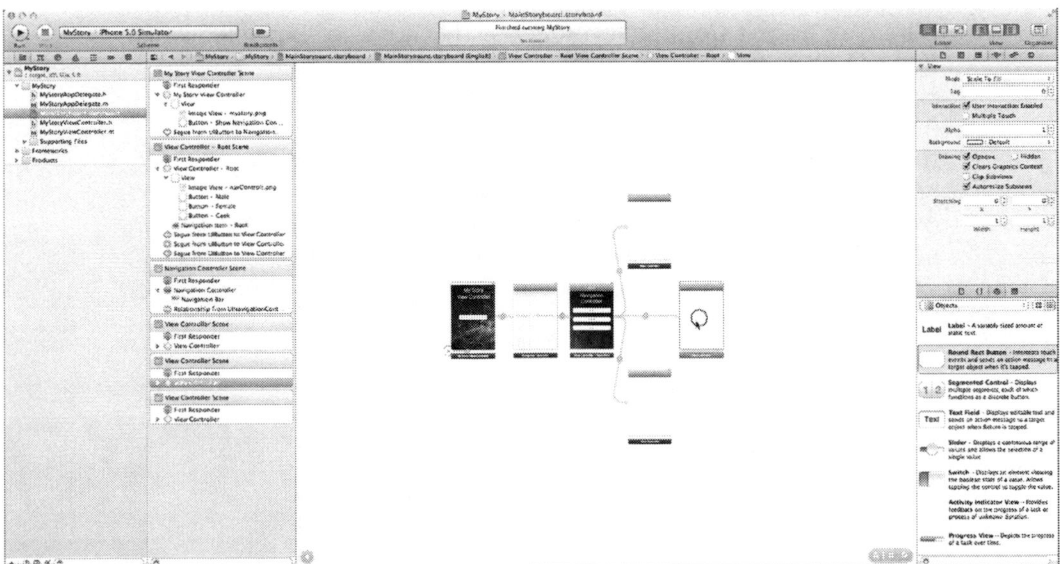

Figure 7–31. *Zoom out and arrange the views.*

31. Initially, I did not think I would have to spend much time on arranging the objects/views on the storyboard. However, after having some difficulty myself, and then seeing the wonderful spaghetti messes that some of my students came up with, I've decided to spend a little time coming up with some basic principles, that if adhered to will prevent a chaotic and tangled mess. Zoom out, as I have, and then move your objects around accordingly as you follow the three protocols I've developed:

    - **Mutual Exclusivity:** I've already mentioned the first tip, which is to keep the order of your buttons mutually exclusive from the order of your views. The buttons on the Navigation Controller go Male, Female, and then Geek. Maintaining that order on the storyboard would create problems, as it would violate some of the principles I will mention below.
    - **Maintain Initial Momentum:** If, for example, on the Woman view, at the bottom of Figure 7–31, you have a fan of 10 segues to 10 views that were all void of segues to the Geek branch, then keep those Woman-based segues going downward.
        - Looking at Figure 7–32, one can see a perfect example of how NOT to maintain initial momentum. Not only are the segue connections hidden, but they also overlap and disrupt the ability to follow where the segues start and end.
    - **Minimize Segue Connection Angles:** This is easier explained when first seeing it visually: look at the Male and Female segue connections from the Navigation Controller in Figure 7–31. Notice how they first slope back and then slope forward, as compared to the less angular connections from the Navigation Controller to the same two Male and Female views depicted in Figure 7–32 and onward. An easy way to adhere to this protocol is, once segue is connected, to move the object it is connected to horizontally and vertically, until the segue connection is almost perfectly horizontal or vertical.

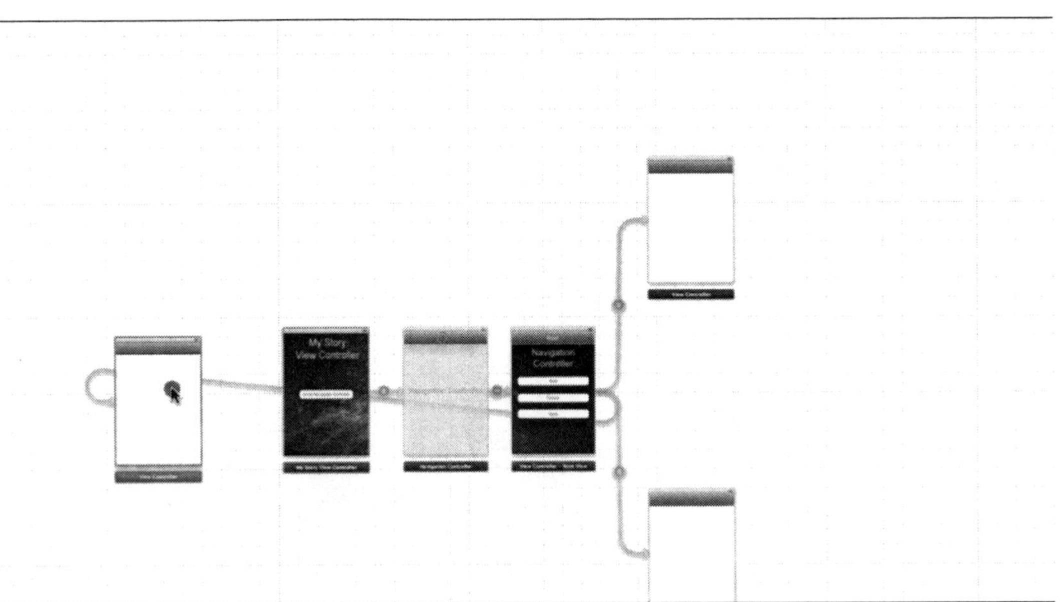

Figure 7–32. ***Oops! Violation of the second principle of "maintaining initial momentum" protocol.***

32. You really need to be careful how you place your objects because the GUI can make things look very odd, as illustrated in Figure 7–32, which demonstrates a violation of the protocol of "maintaining initial momentum." However, note that because you moved the Male and Female to the top and bottom, respectively, you can see that you have adhered to the protocol of minimizing segue connection angles.

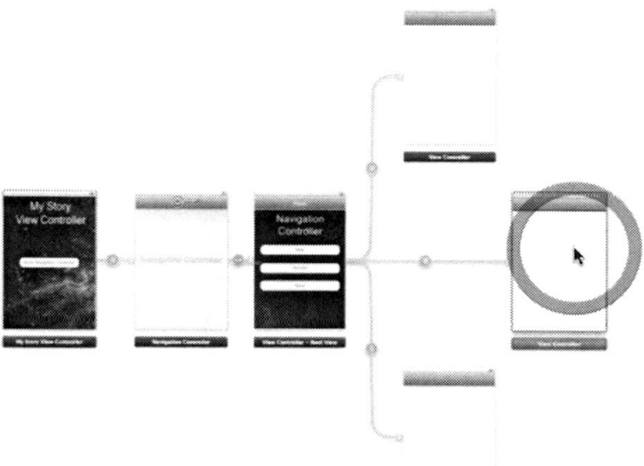

Figure 7–33. *Move Geeks forward.*

33. In order to comply with both the "maintain initial momentum" and the "minimize segue connection angles" protocols, move the Geeks object forward, as shown in Figure 7–33. Once the Geeks object is moved forward, you will be in adherence to all three protocols.

Phase III: Establishing View Controller Content

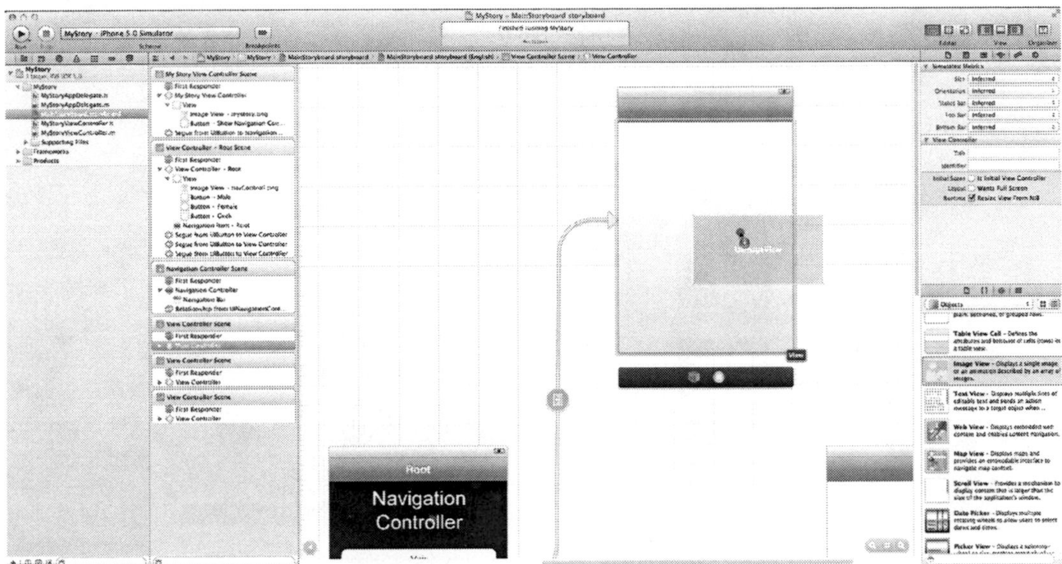

Figure 7–34. *Add a* `UIImageView` *to the Male view.*

34. Your next step will be to add images to your Male, Female, and Geek view controllers. Let's start at the top and drag an Image View onto the Male view, as shown in Figure 7–34.

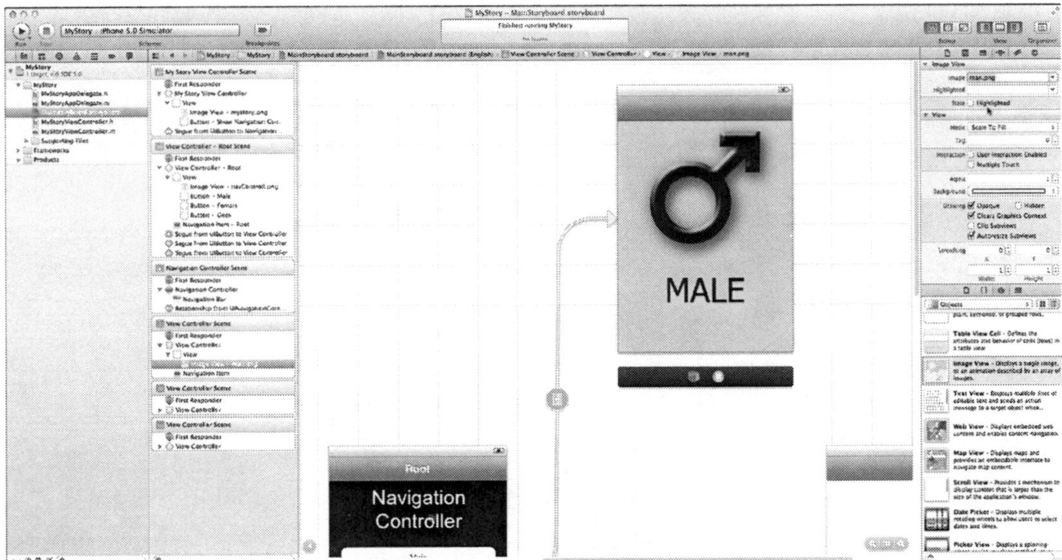

Figure 7–35. *Select the image to use for Male from the Attribute panel.*

35. Associate the man.png image with the Male controller by selecting it from the Attributes Panel, as shown in Figure 7–35.

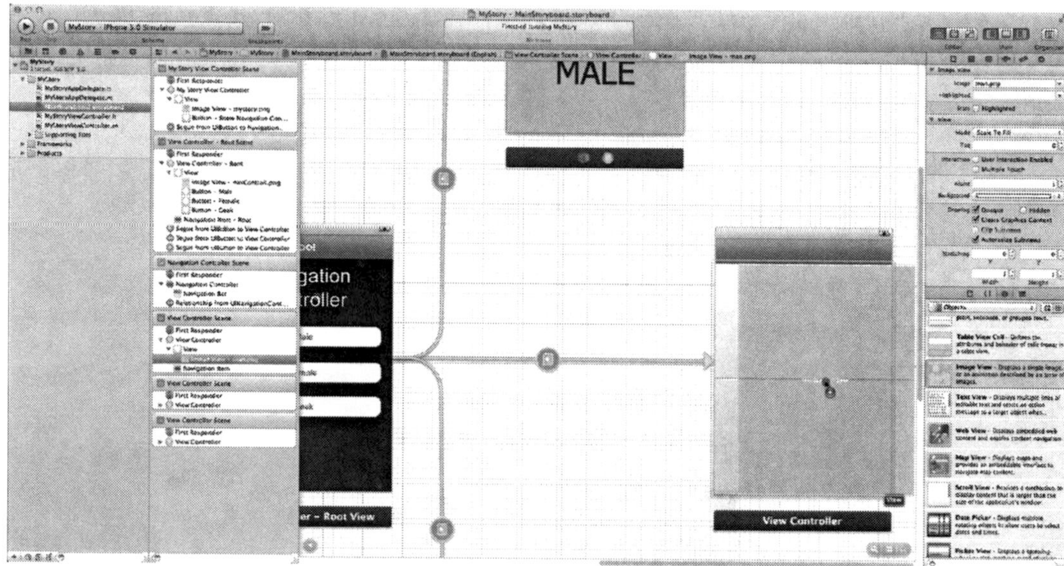

Figure 7–36. *Add a `UIImageView` to the Geek view.*

36. You now need to drag the `UIImageView` and associate an image with it—just as you did with Male—two more times. So let's do it: drag a `UIImageView` onto the Geek view, as shown in Figure 7–34.

> **NOTE:** Notice how the little icons in the segue lines depict the type of segue that will be performed.

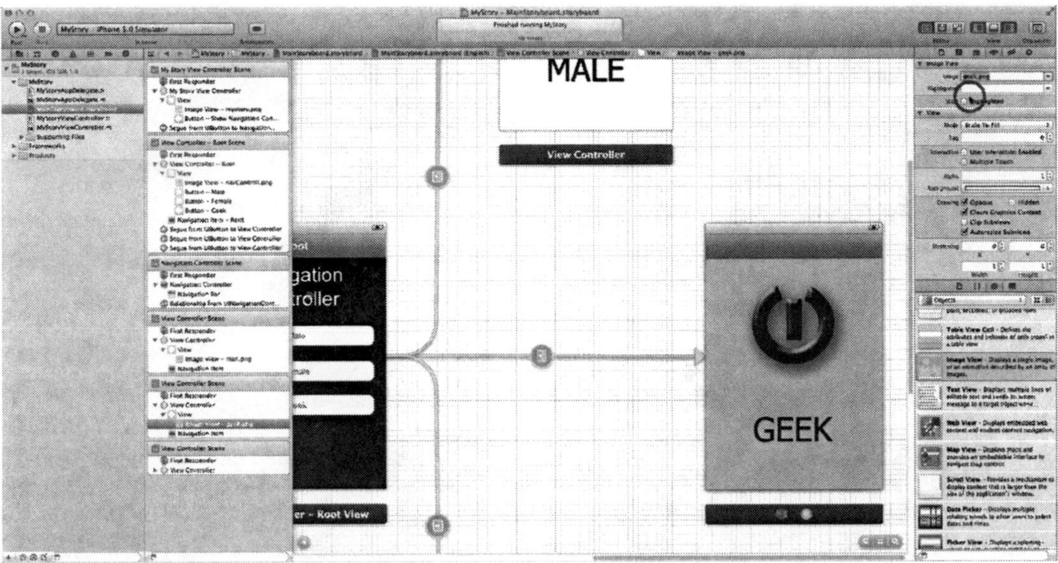

Figure 7–37. ***Select the image to use for Geek from the Attribute panel.***

37. Associate the `Geek.png` image with the Geek controller by selecting it from the Attributes Panel, as shown in Figure 7–35.

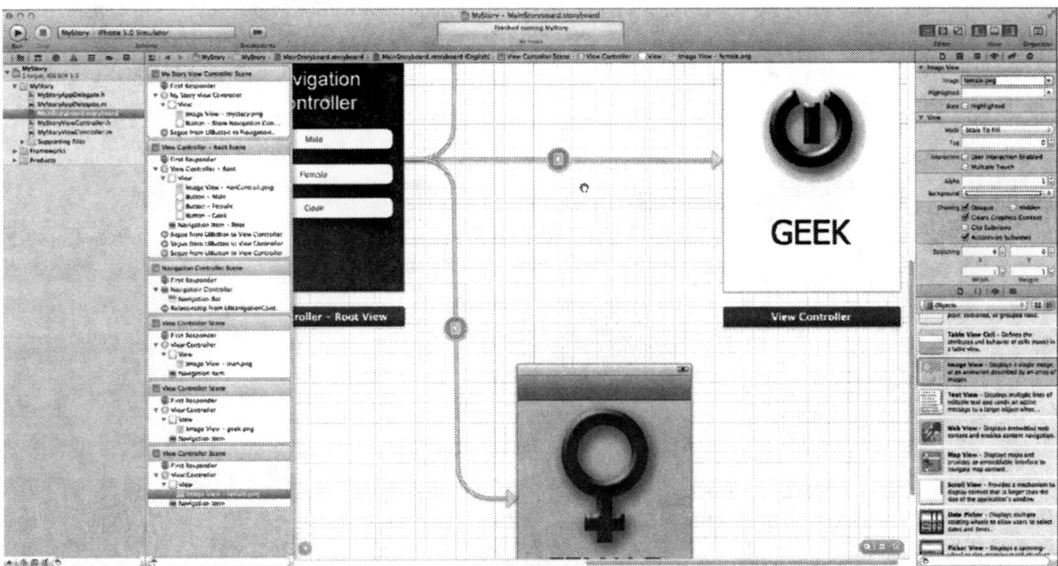

Figure 7–38. ***Add a `UIImageView` and select the image for Female.***

38. Yup! You can do this one on your own now. Add an `UIImageView` and associate the `female.png` with it. This is shown in Figure 7–38.

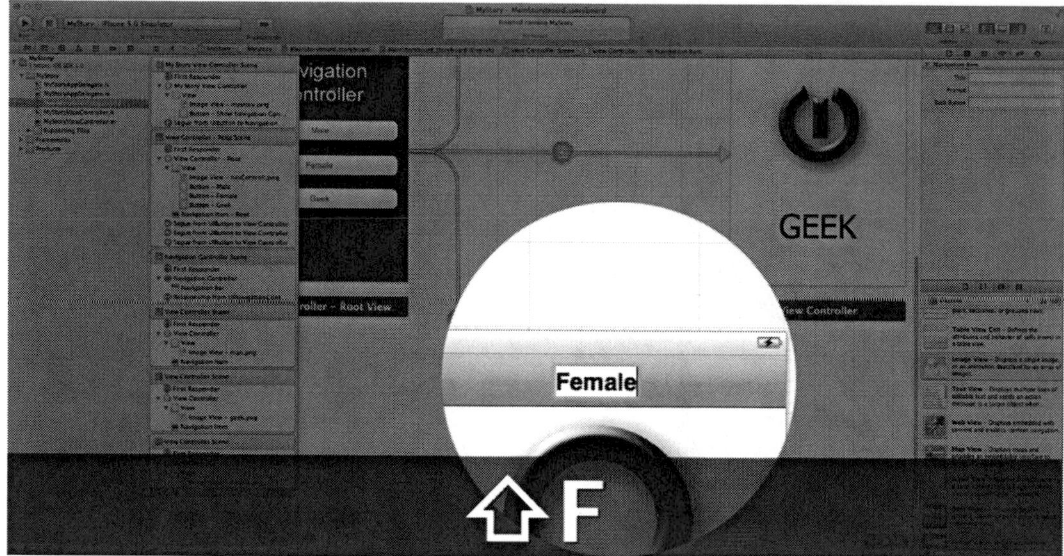

Figure 7–39. *Name the Female controller bar title.*

39. Naming the controller bar titles in storyboarding actually instantiates connectivity under the hood, and this eliminates the need for you to code some of these segues. This is explained in more detail in Digging the Code but, for now, just accept that applying names in a storyboard controller bar title is in essence a "freebie" with code. Do this with your Male, Female, and Geek controller bar titles. In Figure 7–39 you can see the default value of the Female controller changing to "Female."

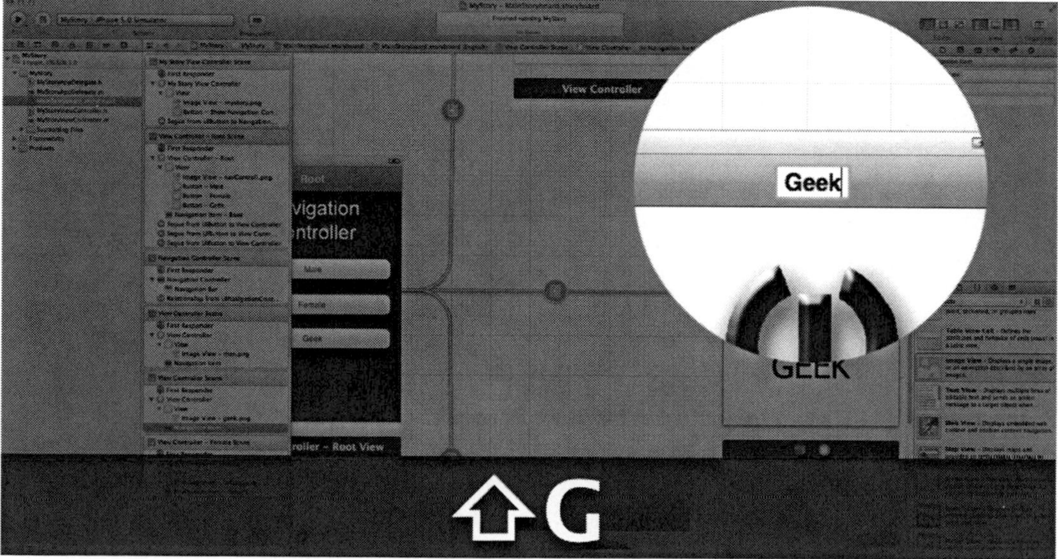

Figure 7–40. *Name the Geek controller bar title.*

40. Figure 7–40 shows the Geek controller bar title being renamed.

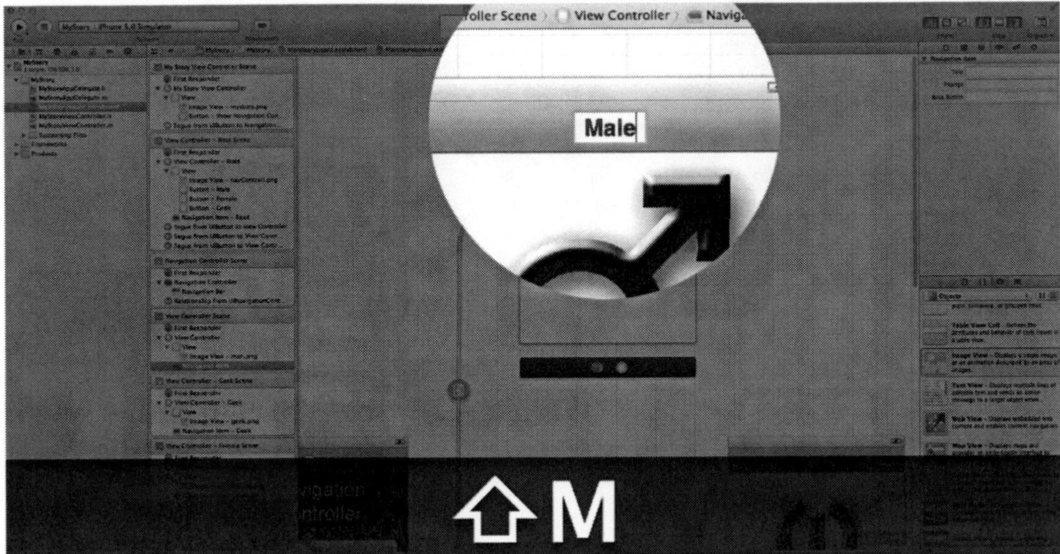

Figure 7–41. *Name the Male controller bar title.*

41. Figure 7–41 shows the Male controller bar title being renamed.

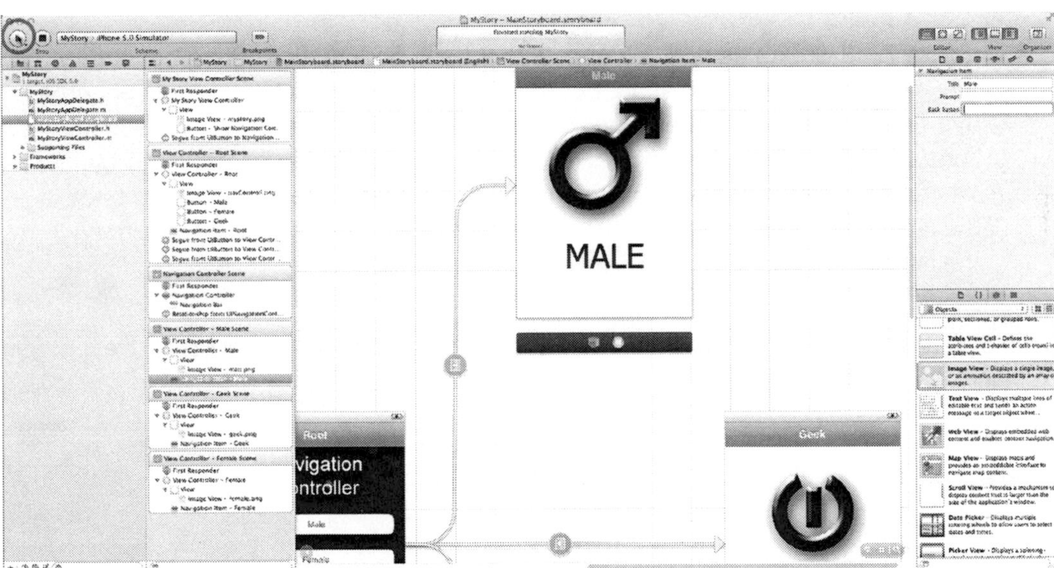

Figure 7–42. *Run it! Let's see if it all works correctly.*

42. Figure 7–42 shows how you perform a quick run to see if the segue connections and the images are all working correctly.

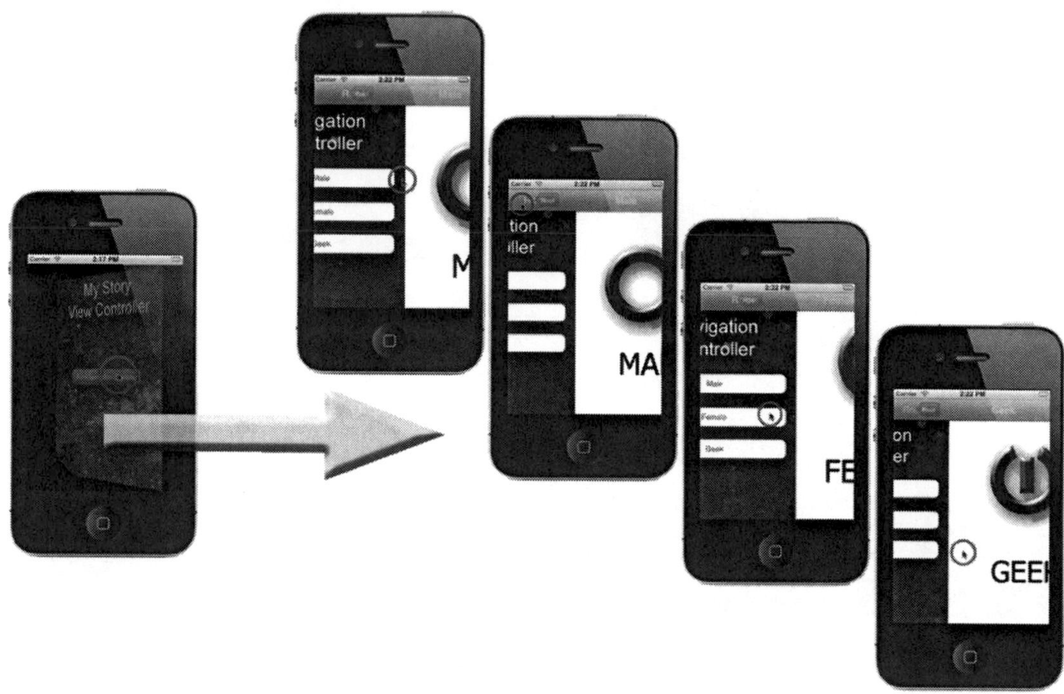

Figure 7–43. *Yes, it works!*

43. Figure 7–43 illustrates how the app, without any coding, is working beautifully. All the images show not one state, but the transition between two states connected by the segue. From the view controller on the very left-hand side, you see four images. The top image shows the click from the Navigation controller to Male. The next image, to the right, shows the click on the bar controller going *back* to the Navigation Controller. The remaining two images show segue transitions from the Navigation Controller to Female and Geek, respectively.

> **NOTE:** Because you did not change the segue type, you have the push effect for each of the three segue transitions created.

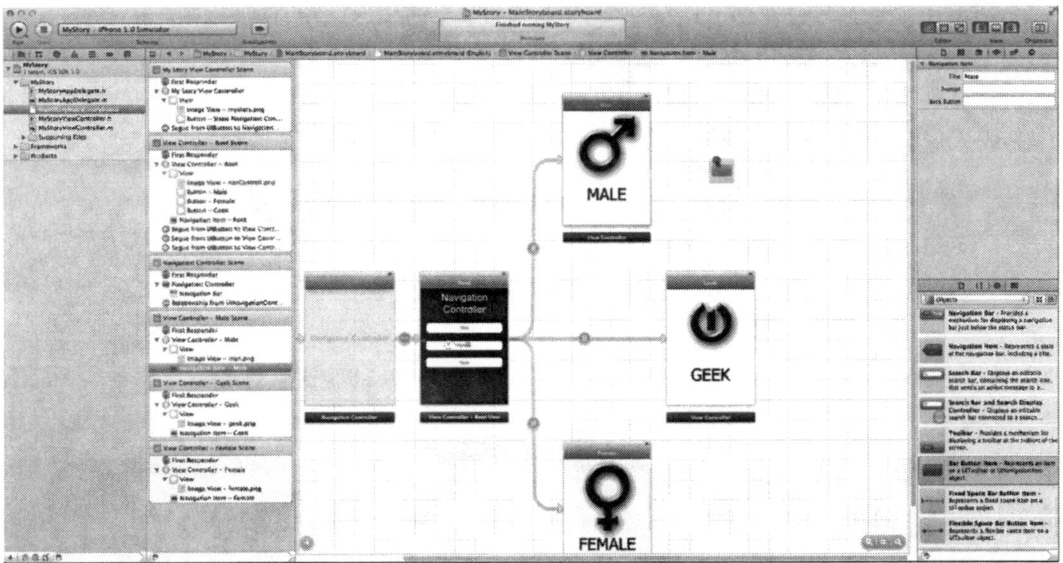

Figure 7–44. *Now let's "Evolve."*

44. You are now getting to the fun portion of this app that makes students laugh out loud in class. You understand that in this world there are Males and Females (for the most part!). In your app, you are going to show the world that evolution is still happening. You are going to show the world that both Males and Females can still evolve to a higher level of consciousness, and that, of course, is the state of being known as … yes, you got it … Geek! So you need to add a segue going from your Male and Female state to Geek. Mmm, do you know how you should do this? How about adding a "Button Bar Item" to both the Male and Female views' navigation bars and giving them the title "Evolve"? Then, after this, you can segue from these "Evolve" buttons to Geek. OK! Start off by dragging a "Bar Button Item" onto the Male, as shown in Figure 7–44. Once you have dropped your second Bar Button Item onto the Female, there is an important thing I want you to remember about Bar Button Icons. These buttons act just like regular `UIButtonViews`, but they look different, and they are designed to go in only one place, a navigation bar.

> **NOTE:** Bar Button Items act just like regular `UIButtonViews`, but they look different and are designed to go in only one place, a navigation bar.

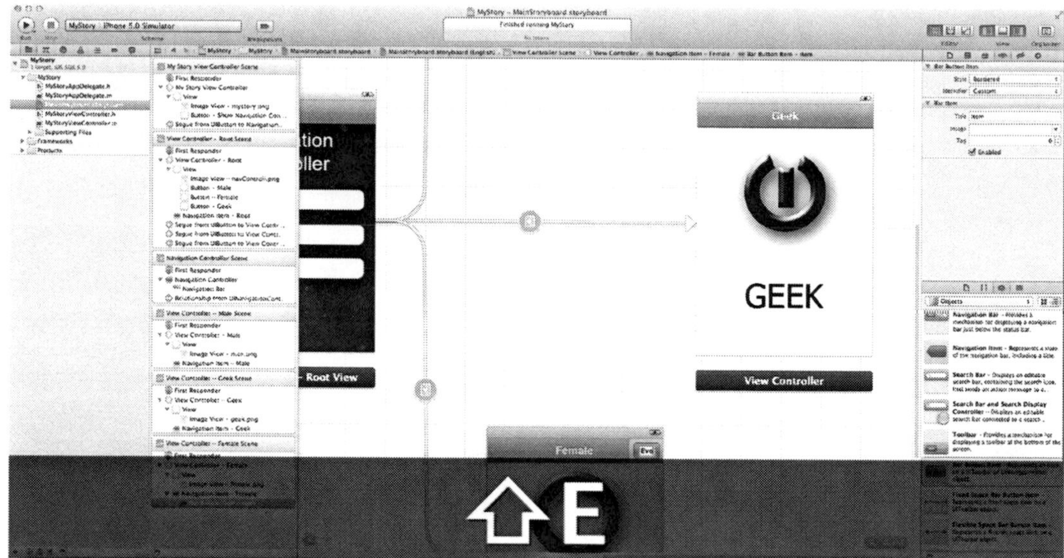

Figure 7–45. *Rename the Female Bar Button Item.*

45. As illustrated in Figure 7–45, rename the Bar Button Item you dragged onto the Female as "Evolve."

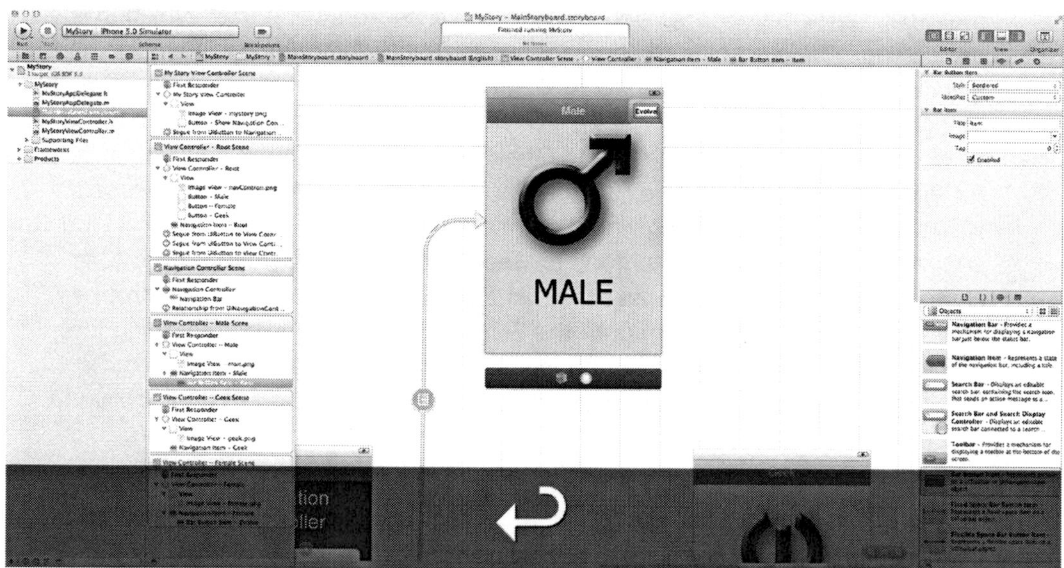

Figure 7–46. *Rename the Female Bar Button Item.*

46. As illustrated in Figure 7–46, click on the Bar Button Item you dragged onto the Male. Now name it "Evolve."

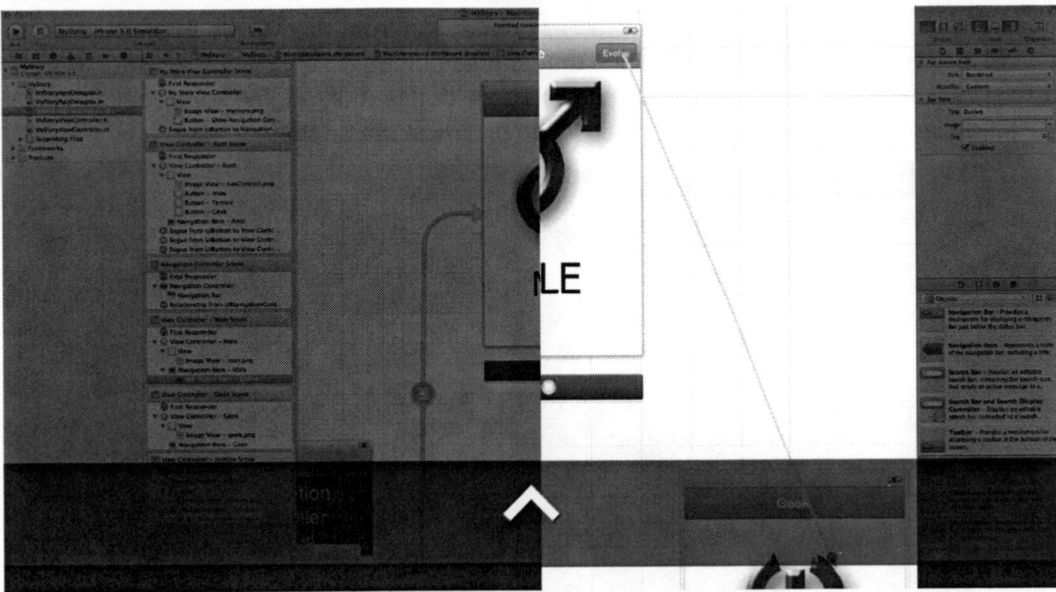

Figure 7–47. *Control-drag from the Male's Evolve button to the Geek view controller.*

47. You want to segue from the Evolve button to Geek. Click on the Male's Evolve button and control-drag to the Geek's view controller. What you have here is a new way to get a segue to another view. Note that I kept the transitions linear for simplicity. They can have loops or be entirely circular. This is illustrated, exactly as shown on the video, in Figure 7–47.

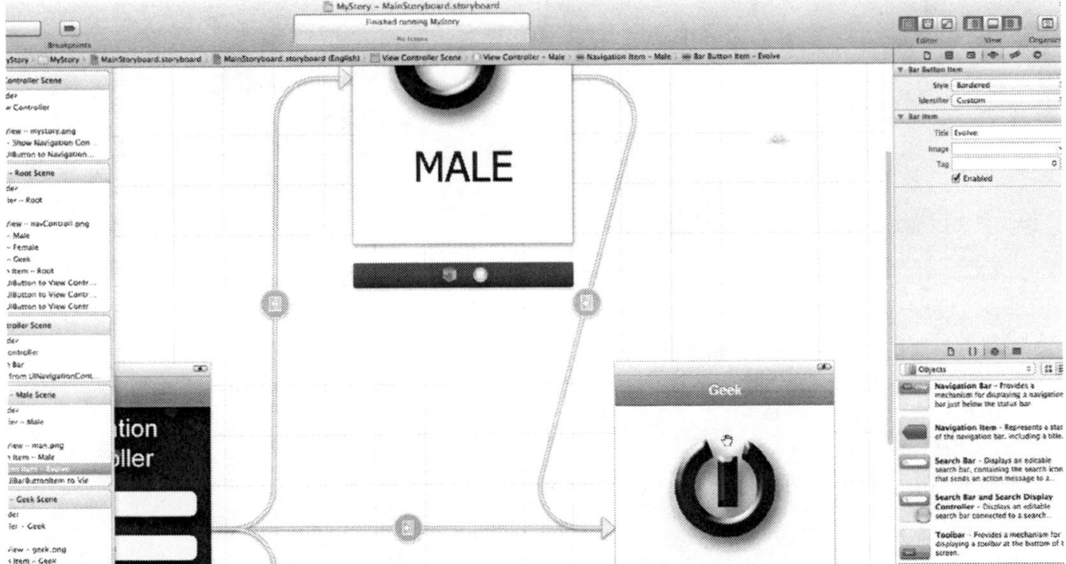

Figure 7–48. *Completed connection from the Male's Evolve button to the Geek object.*

48. Figure 7–48 illustrates the completed connection from the Male's Evolve button to the Geek object. You may notice that, at this point, you improve a violation of the third protocol, which is the "minimize segue connection angles" protocol. So go ahead and move it to the right until you minimize the angles.

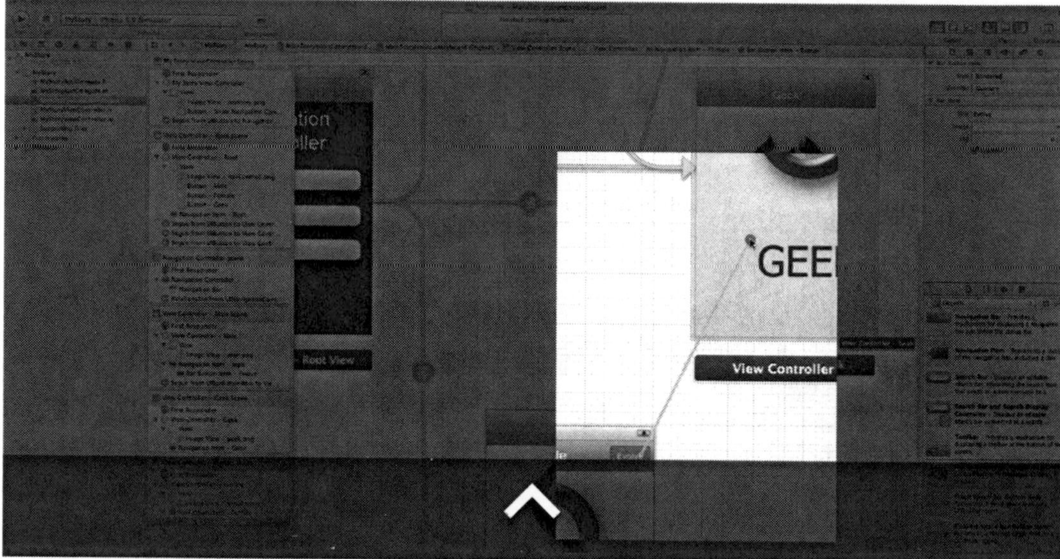

Figure 7–49. ***Segue from the Female's Evolve button to the Geek Object.***

49. Now that you have connected the Male's Evolve button to the Geek object, do the same for the Female. This is illustrated in Figure 7–49.

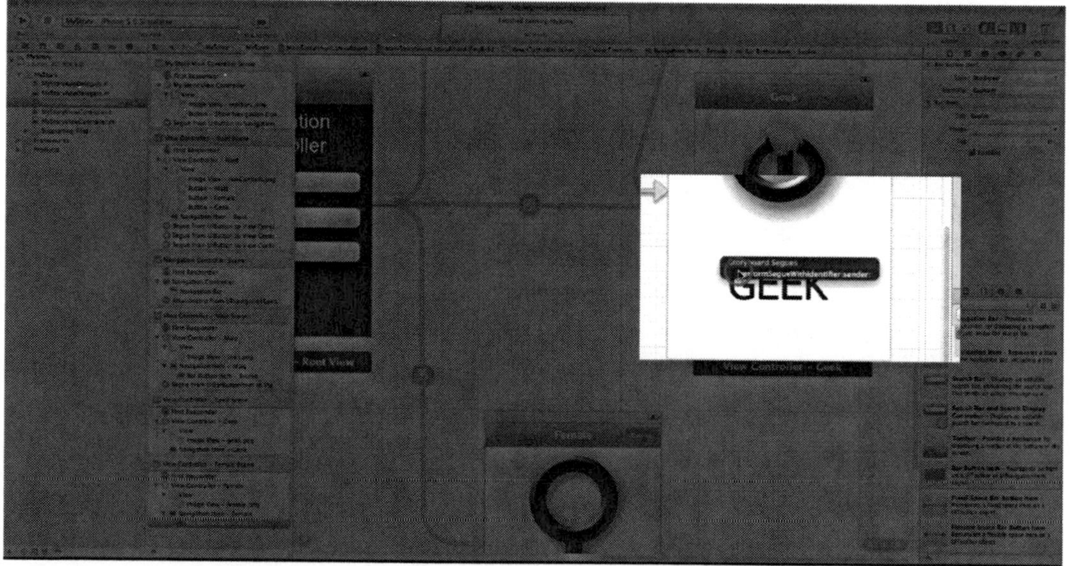

Figure 7–50. ***Just in case you forgot, or thought I forgot… Mmm!***

50. Figure 7–50 reminds you that I am no longer telling you every single step. For the last three segues, if you come up with the option of modal, push, or custom, leave it as the default, or, as you did before, use the `performSegueWithIdentifier:sender:` that holds all the code needed to connect these two items appropriately using storyboarding. If you have been doing it on your own and forgot that I was not telling you to do each of these steps, then you're doing great. If you struggled a bit during the last three `performSegueWithIdentifier:sender:` let me remind you that I am letting the leash go a little and allowing you to think of things on your own. I have designed the book so that, as you become more confident, you can simply look at the figure comments and fly. OK, let's move on!

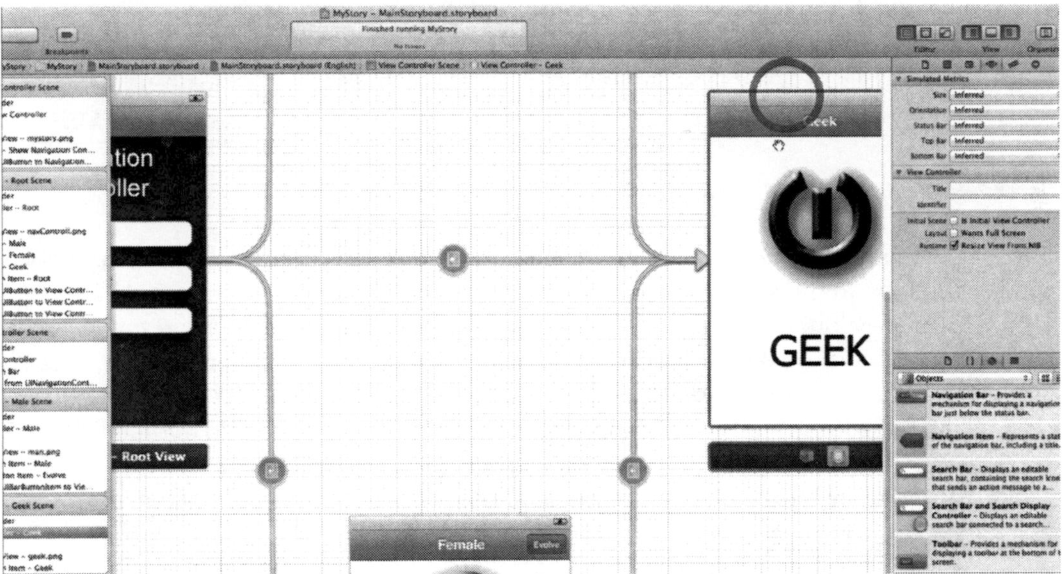

Figure 7–51. *Complying with the third storyboard protocol.*

51. Getting back to what was said in step 48, move the Geek object out and make it comply with the third protocol. This is illustrated in Figure 7–51. After a while, you will not think of protocols one, two, or three, and you'll simply find yourself doing a little rearranging here and there until you have a mouth-watering symmetrical layout!

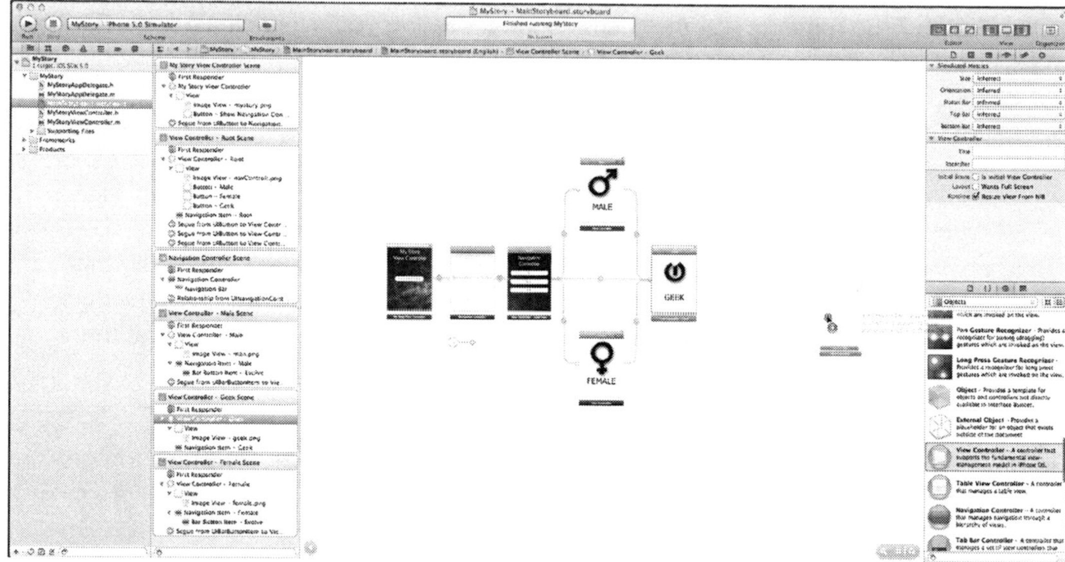

Figure 7–52. *One last* `UIViewController`*!*

52. Now that you've been living in the geek world for a few chapters, you've probably caught on to the fact that geeks know something of which normal people are completely ignorant. Yup! There is an even higher state of humankind than a geek! These special geeks, who evolve into a higher state of consciousness, are called Über Geeks. Über Geeks are very rare and can only be recognized by geeks. But this will be illustrated in your app. So, you essentially need to add *another* state of human evolution beyond that of Geek! You need to add one last `UIViewController`, which will demonstrate how to gain programmatic access to the controller and its data. This is illustrated in Figure 7–52.

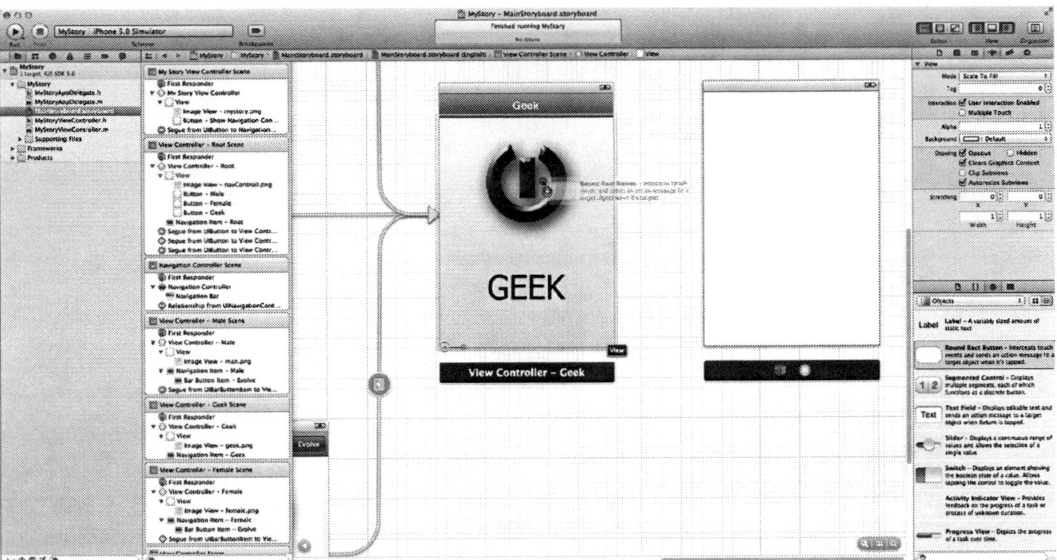

Figure 7–53. *You can use a simple invisible button over your background imagery as a simple hack to avoid spending time working on a fancy button.*

53. As you know, only geeks know that there is a state of human consciousness that is higher than a Geek. The next state up, Über Geek, is invisible. So you need to make an invisible button that only geeks will know segues to the higher Über Geek state of consciousness. Mmm, I can just hear you thinking, "How do we make an invisible button?!" Well, it's all part of being a geek. Normal humans even think that the geek symbol is the "Power" symbol! Geeks know it's really the geek symbol. There are also secret ways of doing things, like running the universe and all computers and gaining access to all kinds of cool things via invisible secret doors and gateways. Today you are evolved enough to learn how to make an invisible button. Read this carefully, and make sure you do not let non-geeks read this, please! As shown in Figure 7–53, drag a seemingly innocent, benign round rectangular button onto your Geek object.

Phase IV: Working on Closure and Coding

You're into the final phase now, so let's finish the app.

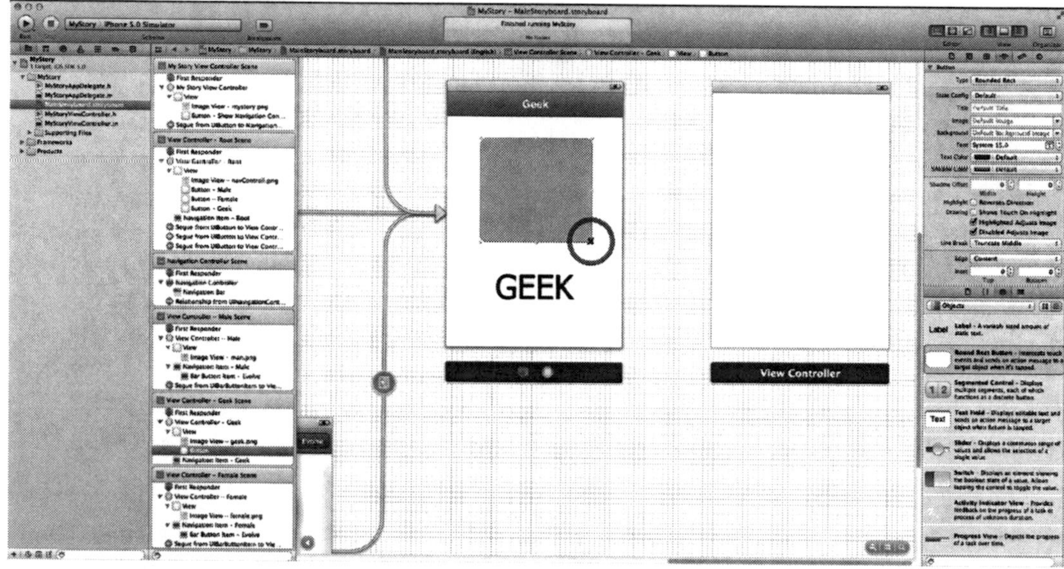

Figure 7–54. *Cover the entire Geek symbol, for starters.*

54. As illustrated in Figure 7–54, once your button is placed on the Geek object, expand the button so it covers the entire Geek symbol.

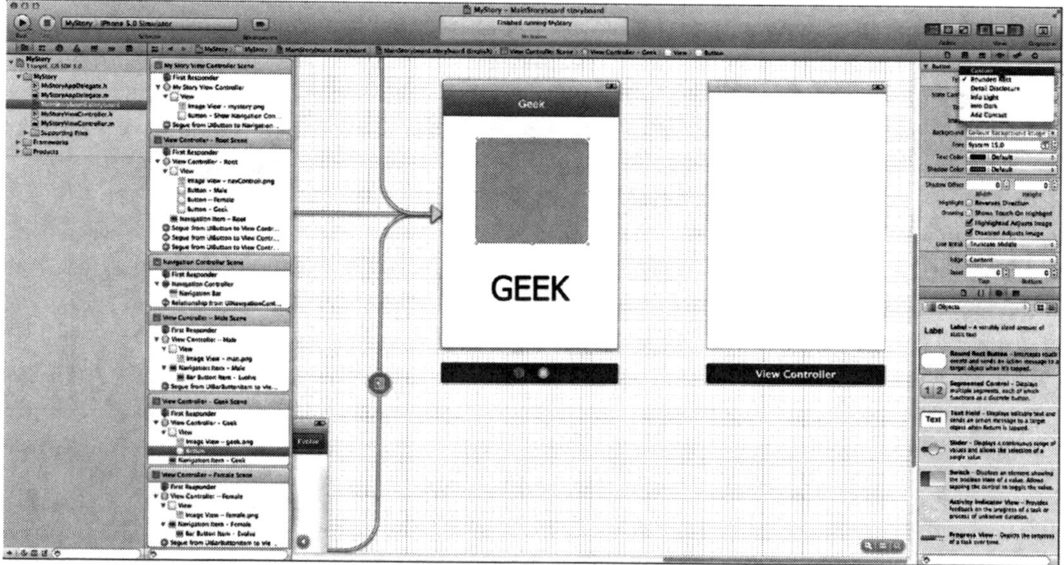

Figure 7–55. *Make that button vanish into thin air!*

55. You want to make it invisible, so, as illustrated in Figure 7–55, set the button type to Custom and the GUI will immediately default to making the button invisible, though still clickable for geeks!

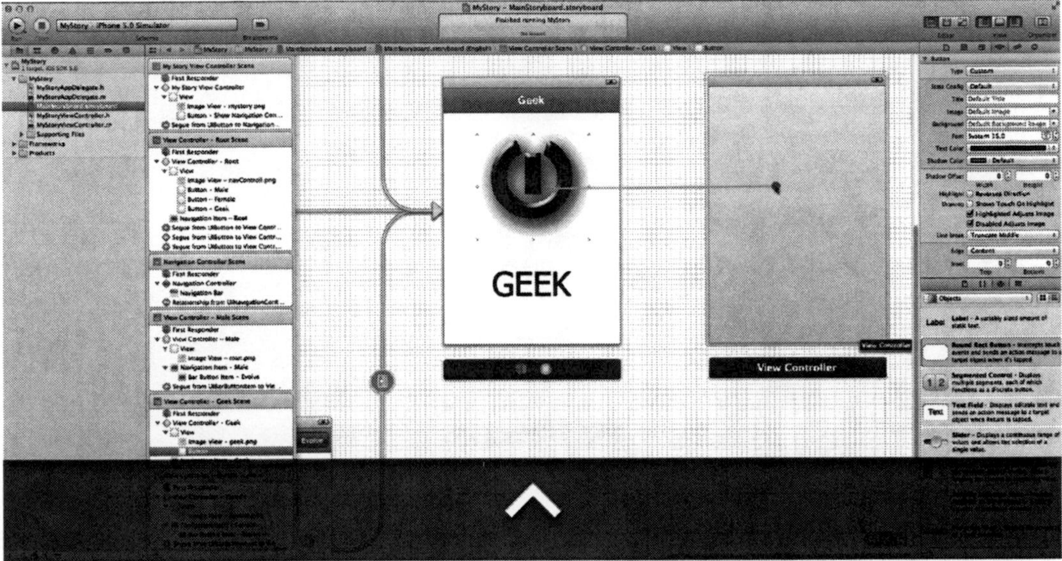

Figure 7–56. *Control-drag from the invisible button to the next View Controller.*

56. Now that you've made your invisible button, you need to make a segue to the next transition. Click where you know your invisible button is, and then control-drag over to the new view controller, as illustrated in Figure 7–56.

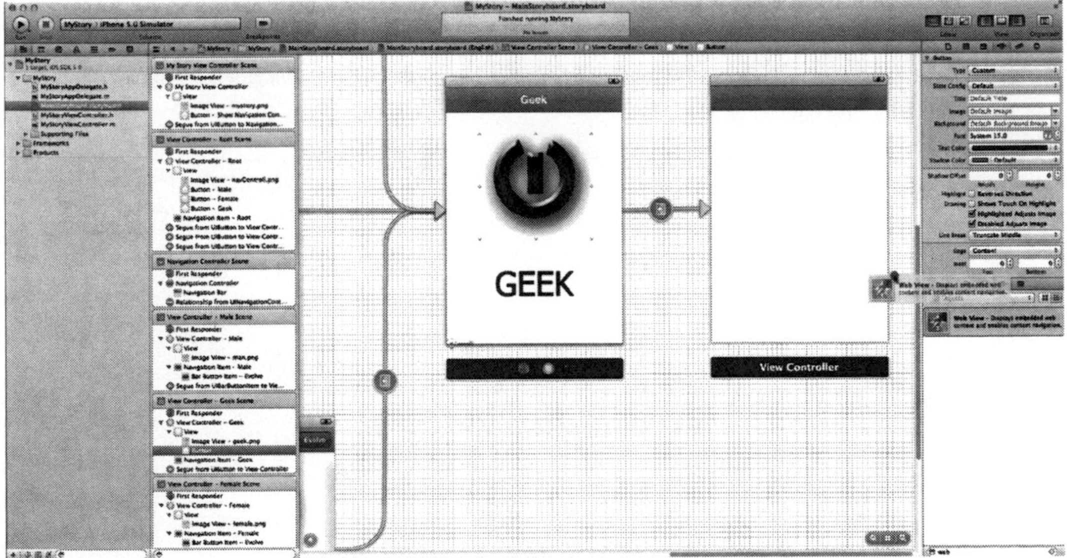

Figure 7–57. *This time, let's add a Web View to the view.*

57. For this last state, you will, for learning purposes, have a little more than an image. Let's insert a URL. To insert a URL, drag a Web View into the view. I go deeper into the additional bells and whistles associated with `UIWebView` in the Digging the Code section, but for now, drag a default `UIWebView` into the Über Geek's View Controller. This is illustrated in figures 7–57 and 7–58.

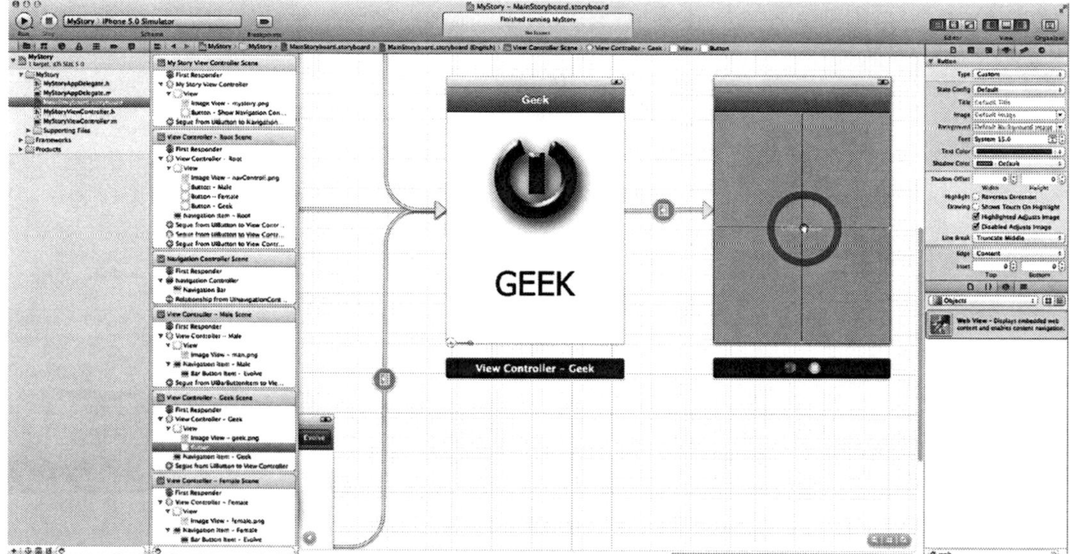

Figure 7–58. *Placement of the Web View.*

58. Figure 7–58 illustrates how you place the Web View into the Über Geek's View Controller.

> **NOTE:** I always make the links first to avoid resizing things inside my views when the navigation bar is added to the new view.

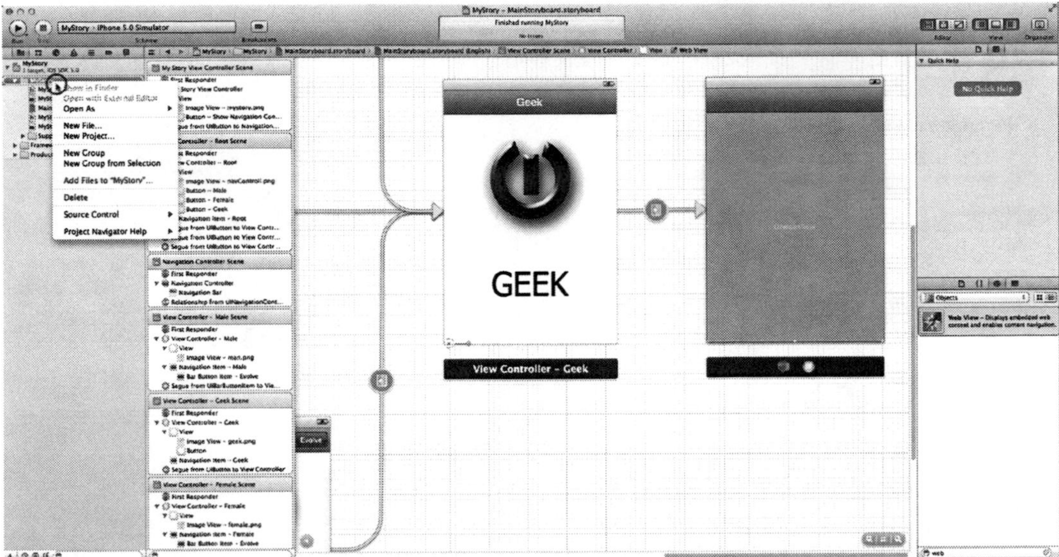

Figure 7–59. *Create a new class.*

59. Recall how I said that in this example you will use images rather than code. Well, that was true for everything you've done so far, but you need to see, at least once, how to insert code behind one of these states. This is the reason I've chosen a very simple URL with a couple of lines of code, which will at least connect a few synapses in your brain about how to add code. So, for this new Web View, you are going to create a new class, which you'll connect to this last view, and access some data in the view controller programmatically. Right-click (or control click) the main directory in the project and select New File, as shown in Figure 7–59. If you can do this on your own, then skip to step 61 and Figure 7–61. If you need a little guidance, then continue to the next step.

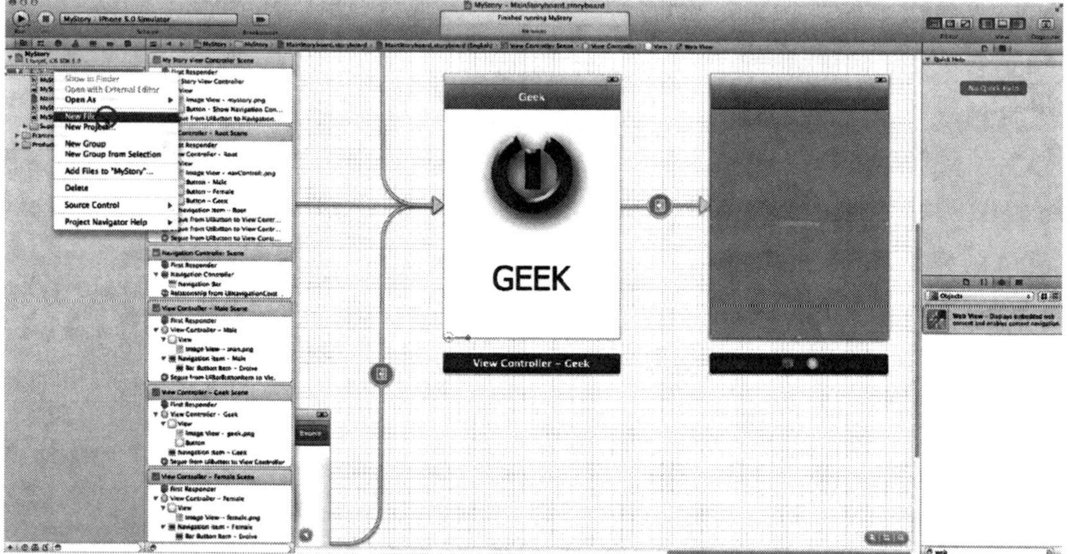

Figure 7–60. *Select "New File"*

60. Use your keyboard shortcut ⌘N, or select New File, as illustrated in Figure 7–60.

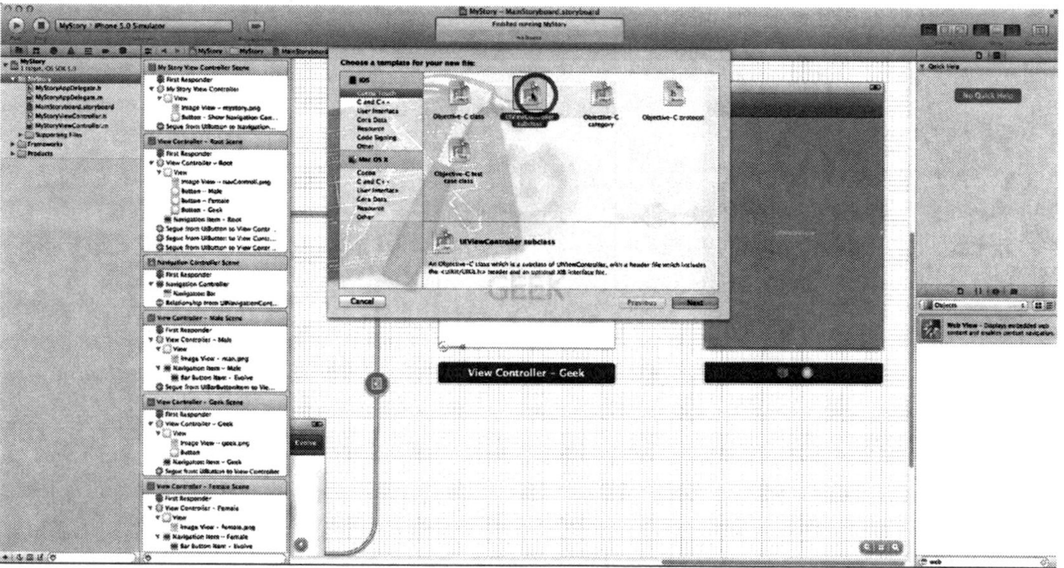

Figure 7–61. *Select a `UIViewController` subclass.*

61. Select a `UIViewController` subclass, as shown in Figure 7–61. From a technical standpoint, one can say that this corresponds to the same type as the object in the GUI builder.

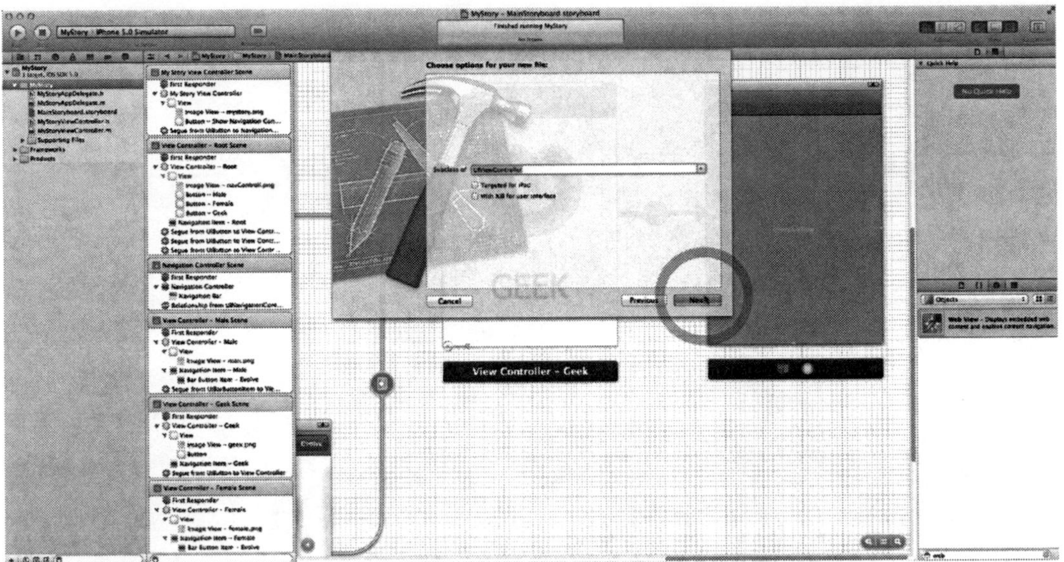

Figure 7–62. *Click Next.*

62. As shown in Figure 7–62, click Next.

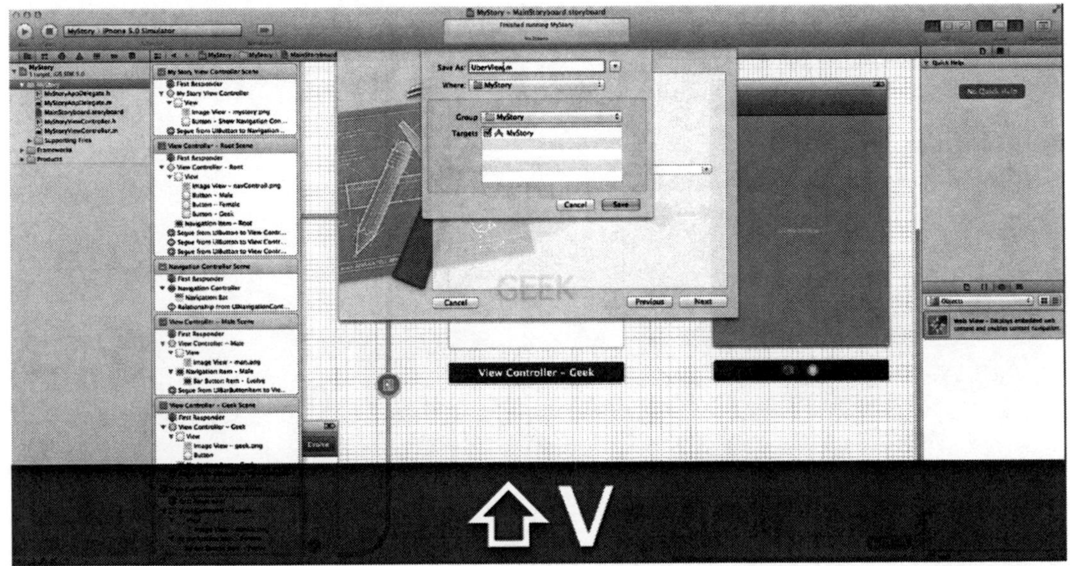

Figure 7–63. *Name the new class* `ÜberView`*.*

63. As shown in Figure 7–63, let's name the new class `ÜberView`, and click Save.

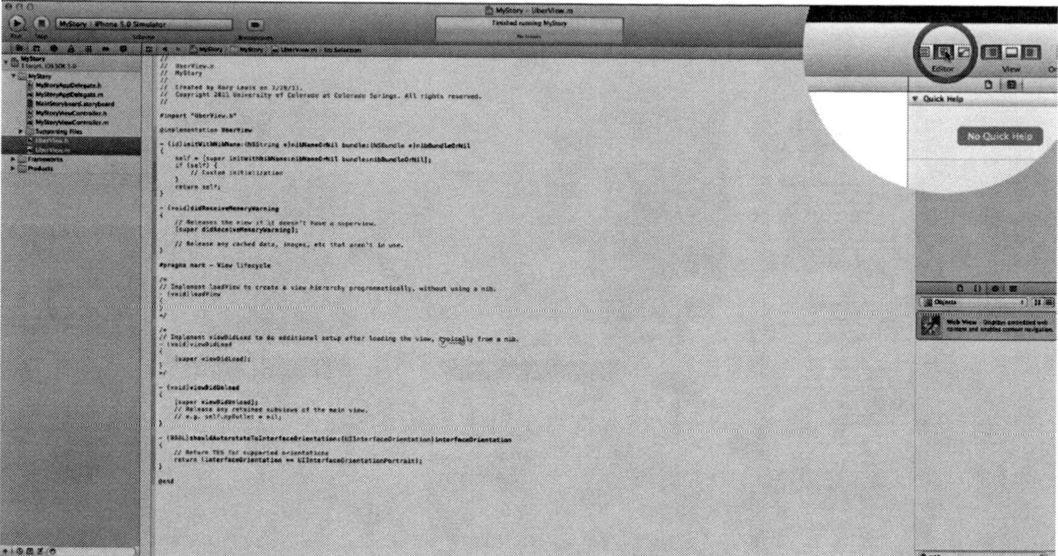

Figure 7–64. *Bring up the Assistant.*

64. Bring up the Assistant so that you can see the storyboard and the header files at the same time, as shown in Figure 7–64.

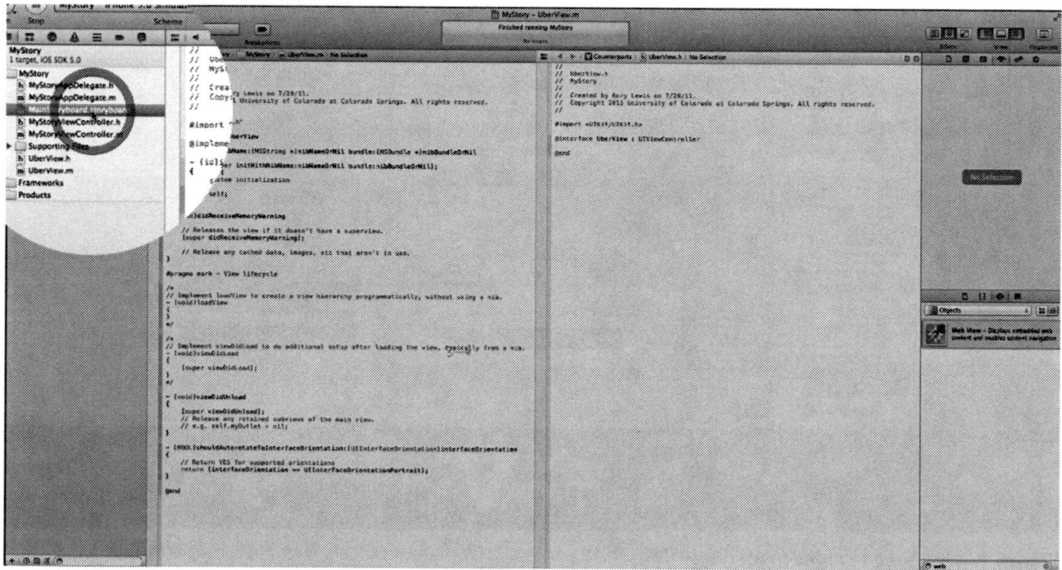

Figure 7–65. *Bring up the storyboard file in the main editor.*

65. Click the storyboard file again to bring it up in the main editor, as this will make the associated headers appear in the right editor, as shown in Figure 7–65.

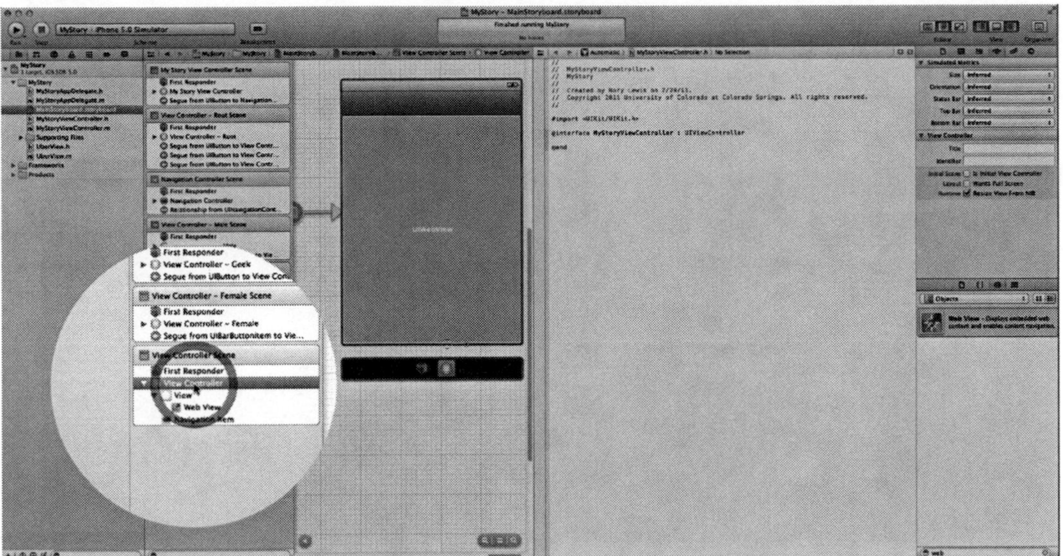

Figure 7–66. *Select the appropriate View Controller.*

66. Unlike in previous apps, things are a little more complex now, so you need to help the Assistant bring up the correct view. In order to tell the Assistant Editor what to bring up, simply select the view controller that holds your Web View. This is illustrated in Figure 7–66. Notice, in the column of View Controllers, they are ordered according to the order of creation. You can see your Male, Female, and Geek view controllers amongst the others you made, and then down at the bottom is the one you just made, called "View Controller Scene" because you have yet to name it. This is the view controller you want.

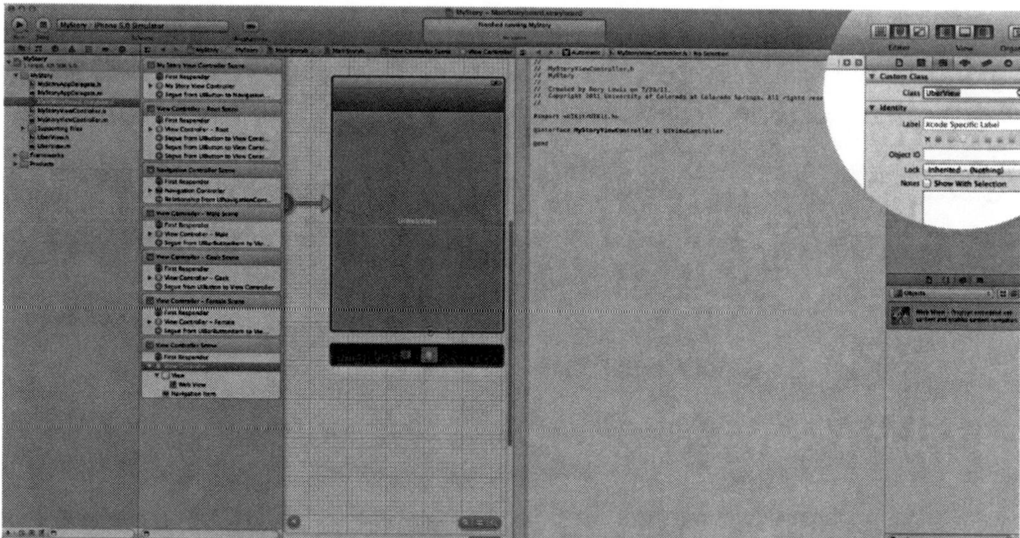

Figure 7–67. *Set the class of your view controller.*

67. You now need to set the class of this new view controller to `ÜberView` in the Attributes Panel, as shown in Figure 7–67.

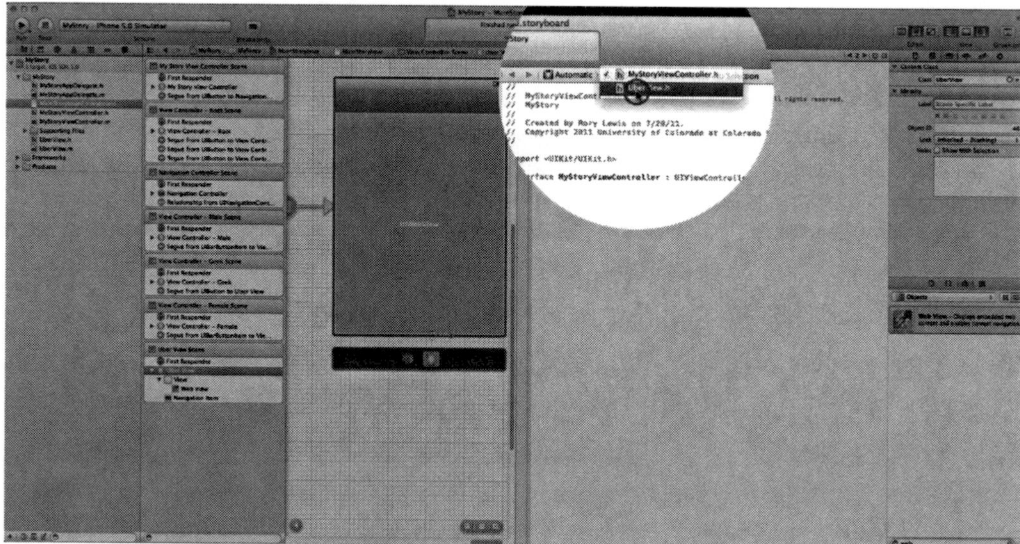

Figure 7–68. *Select the `ÜberView.h` file.*

68. You need to create `UIOutlets` for your URL, so you need to have the Assistant open the `ÜberView.h` file. You need to explain to the Assistant that this is what you need because the Assistant Editor has more than one choice for what you might want to edit. Furthermore, when things get a little complex, as they are here, it usually gets it wrong, so you need to select the header file, as shown in Figure 7–68.

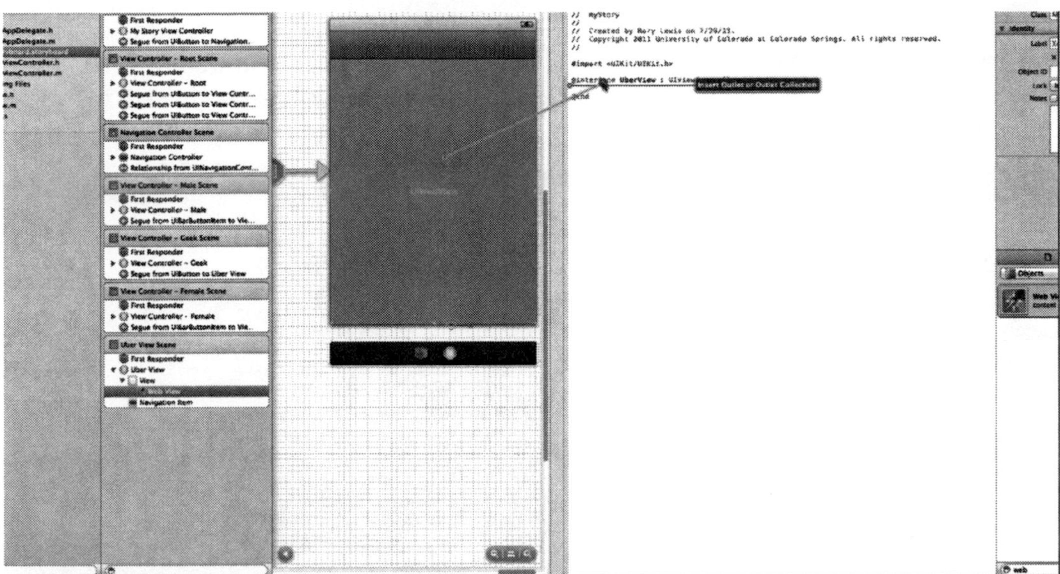

Figure 7–69. *Control-drag to your header file.*

69. Now that you've set up your Assistant correctly, simply control-drag from your `UIWebView` over the header file and drop it under `Überview's` `@interface` to let Xcode do its work, as shown in Figure 7–69.

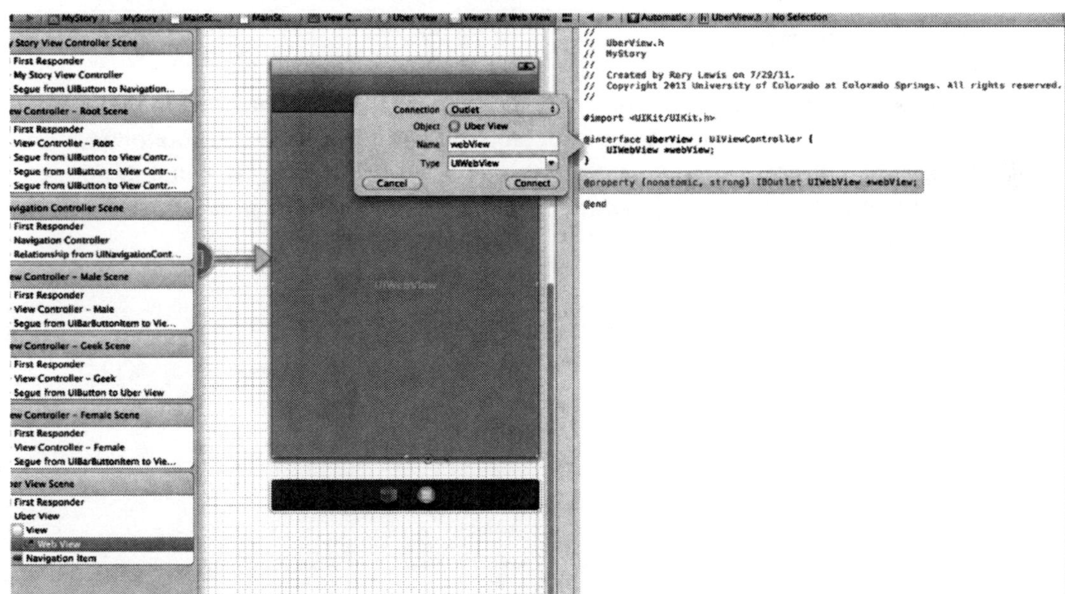

Figure 7–70. *Name your Outlet.*

70. Of course, you need to keep it as an Outlet, meaning that all you need to do is give it a name. You can name it anything you please, but if you want to check your code against mine, then I suggest you name it what I named it, `webView`, as shown in Figure 7–70.

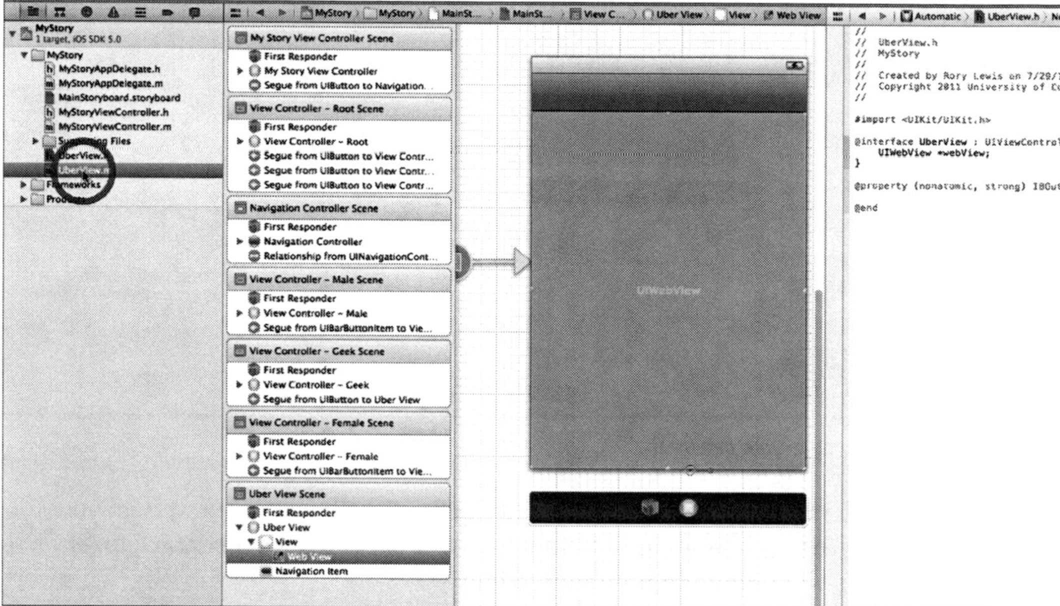

Figure 7–71. *Open the implementation file.*

71. When you insert code into a state such as this, you will probably do a little more than use a URL. You will need to bounce back and forth between your header and implementation file, to say the least. So let's do it here, as we will want to add a few bells. Back in the implementation file for the new controller class, you can make your Web View do stuff. This is shown in Figure 7-71.

Figure 7–72. *Let's code!*

72. Uncomment the `viewDidLoad` method, as that is where you want to initiate your web content loading code. See Figure 7–72.

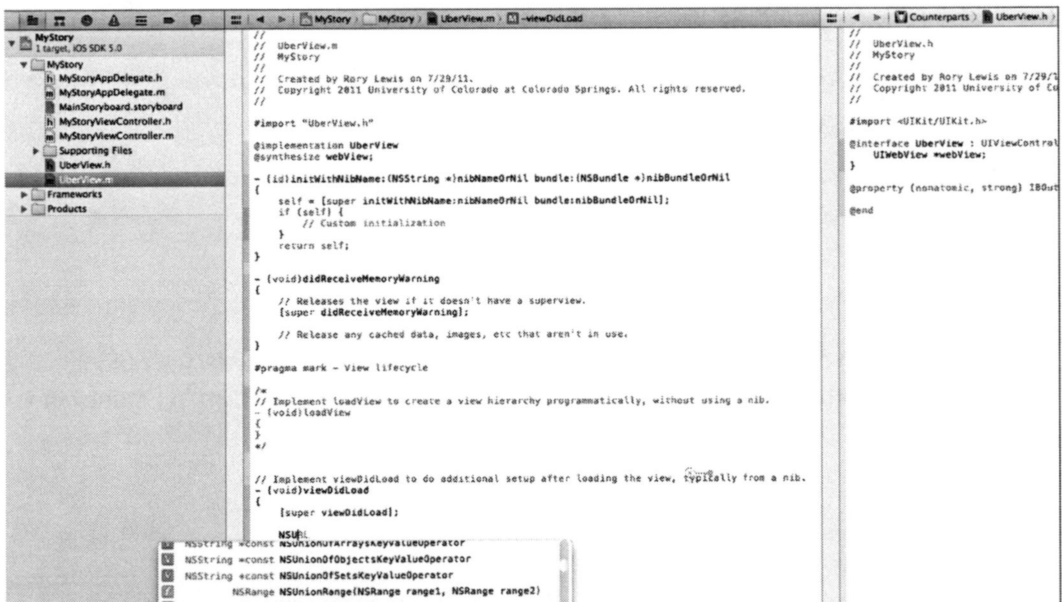

Figure 7–73. *Start with a* `NSURLRequest`.

73. You need to delegate data flow for your URL request, so start with a

NSURLRequest, which will automatically do this. See Digging the Code for information on NSURLRequests. See Figure 7–73.

```
    if (self) {
        // Custom initialization
    }
    return self;
}

- (void)didReceiveMemoryWarning
{
    // Releases the view if it doesn't have a superview.
    [super didReceiveMemoryWarning];

    // Release any cached data, images, etc that aren't in use.
}

#pragma mark - View lifecycle

/*
// Implement loadView to create a view hierarchy programmatically, without using a nib.
- (void)loadView
{
}
*/


// Implement viewDidLoad to do additional setup after loading the view, typically from a nib.
- (void)viewDidLoad
{
    [super viewDidLoad];

    NSURLRequest* request = [NSURLRequest requestWithURL:[NSURL URLWithString:@"http://www.
        synapsesoftware.net/about/two.html"]];
    [self.webView loadRequest:request];
}


- (void)viewDidUnload
{
    [self setWebView:nil];
    [super viewDidUnload];
    // Release any retained subviews of the main view.
    // e.g. self.myOutlet = nil;
}

- (BOOL)shouldAutorotateToInterfaceOrientation:(UIInterfaceOrientation)interfaceOrientation
{
    // Return YES for supported orientations
    return (interfaceOrientation == UIInterfaceOrientationPortrait);
}

@end
```

Figure 7–74. *Add the URL to the request.*

74. You need to add the URL address to the request and ask the webView object, which you linked to with an Outlet, to load your request, as shown in Figure 7–74.

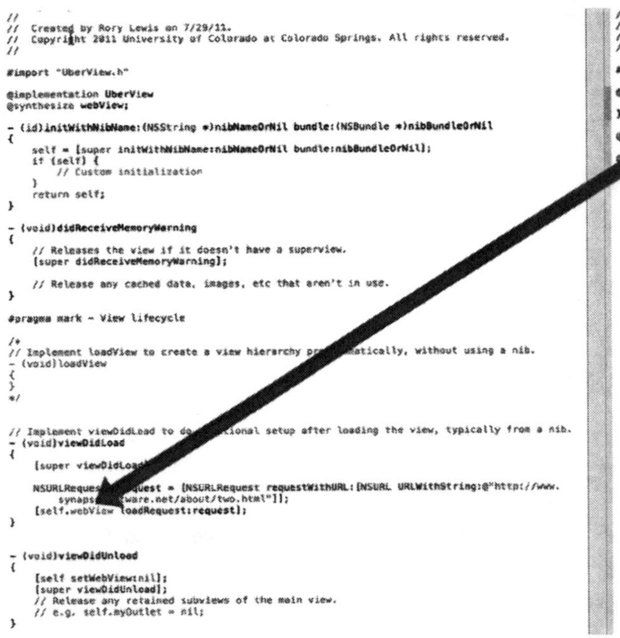

Figure 7–75. IMPORTANT: *The* `webView` *outlet linkage.*

75. This is important. Somehow, students have a hard time getting this, so I've illustrated this in both the video and the book. You need to associate the `webView` outlet linkage in your header file with the conditions set forth in your implementation file. I have illustrated this in Figure 7–75. Essentially, you want to add the URL to the request and ask the `UIWebView` object, which you made an `IBOutlet` for, to load your request. Below is the code for both the implementation and header files. Study it, and make sure you understand the `webView` correlation between the two files.

```
// Header:

#import <UIKit/UIKit.h>

@interface UberView : UIViewController {
    UIWebView *webView;
}

@property (nonatomic, strong) IBOutlet UIWebView *webView;

@end


//Implementation Files:
#import "UberView.h"

@implementation UberView
@synthesize webView;
```

```
- (id)initWithNibName:(NSString *)nibNameOrNil bundle:(NSBundle *)nibBundleOrNil
{
    self = [super initWithNibName:nibNameOrNil bundle:nibBundleOrNil];
    if (self) {
        // Custom initialization
    }
    return self;
}

- (void)didReceiveMemoryWarning
{
    // Releases the view if it doesn't have a superview.
    [super didReceiveMemoryWarning];

    // Release any cached data, images, etc that aren't in use.
}

#pragma mark - View lifecycle

/*
// Implement loadView to create a view hierarchy programmatically, without using a nib.
- (void)loadView
{
}
*/

// Implement viewDidLoad to do additional setup after loading the view, typically from a
nib.
- (void)viewDidLoad
{
    [super viewDidLoad];

    NSURLRequest* request = [NSURLRequest requestWithURL:[NSURL
URLWithString:@"http://www.synapsesoftware.net/about/two.html"]];
    [self.webView loadRequest:request];
}

- (void)viewDidUnload
{
    [self setWebView:nil];
    [super viewDidUnload];
    // Release any retained subviews of the main view.
    // e.g. self.myOutlet = nil;
}

-
(BOOL)shouldAutorotateToInterfaceOrientation:(UIInterfaceOrientation)interfaceOrientatio
n
{
    // Return YES for supported orientations
    return (interfaceOrientation == UIInterfaceOrientationPortrait);
}

@end
```

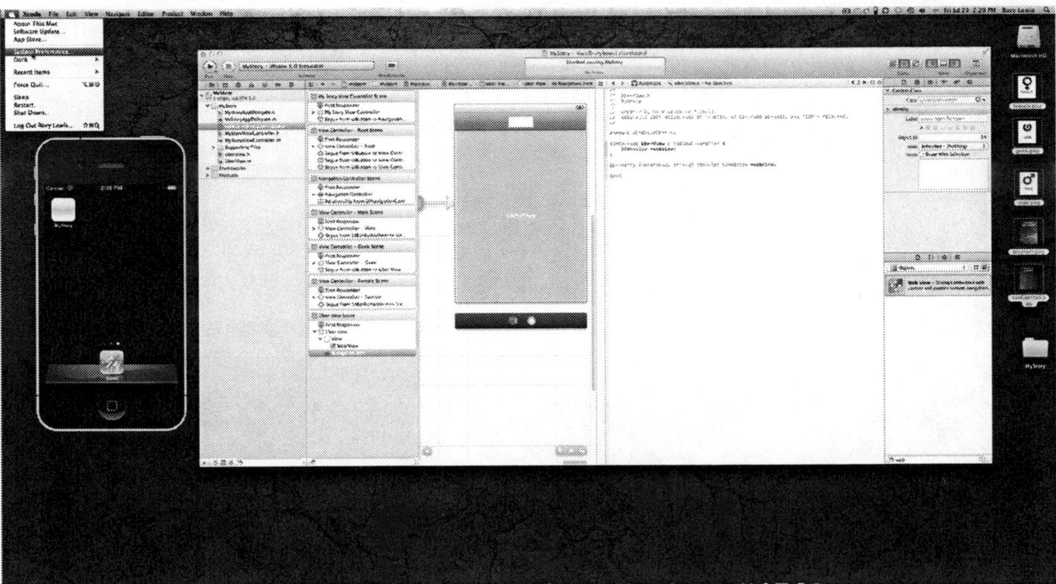

Figure 7–76. *You want a proper Ü character ... but a Lion crossed your path!*

76. As a geek, you likely want to have the proper "Ü" character in your last view controller's navigation bar. Initially, in the video and in figures 7–76 through 7–85, I explained exactly how to do this. It was a beautiful thing. But then something happened along the way. Mac OS X Lion removed the need for this entirely; an unexpected surprise. Now, you simply hold the u key until a little window appears, and you make the selection you need. Similar variations are available for other characters. You can explore these at your leisure. So, all these steps, between figures 7–76 and 7–89, were going to be taken out, but then something else funny happened. Many universities and community colleges had recently updated to Mac Leopard and would not have a Lion license for another year, at least. So this meant that there would be thousands of students left clueless as to how to create the proper "Ü". So, if you have Lion, hold the u key down until the correct letter appears, and then go to Figure 7–86. If you do not have Lion, then follow along. Start by opening the System Preferences app from the Apple menu, as shown in Figure 7–76.

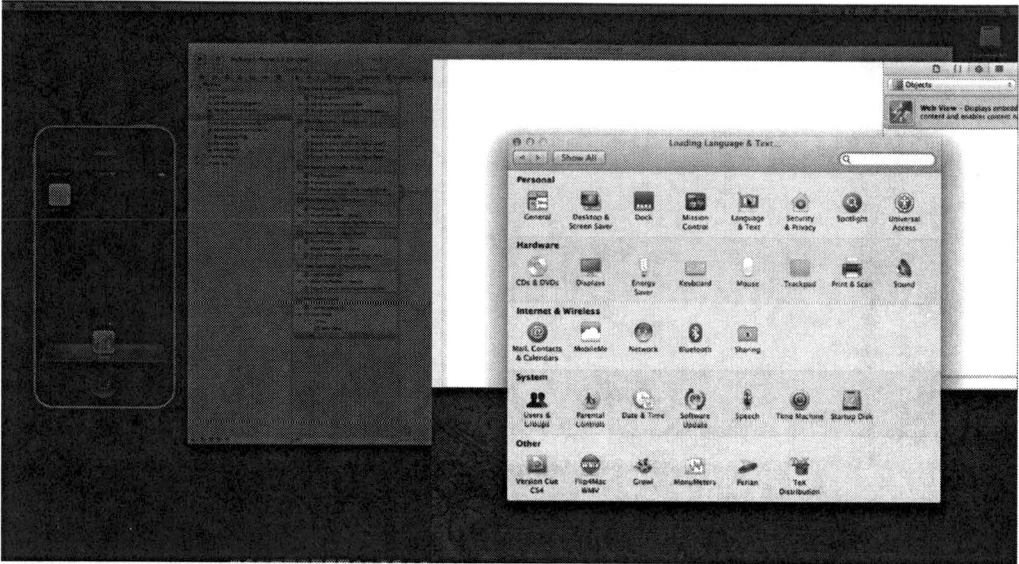

Figure 7–77. *Open the Language & Text preferences panel.*

77. Open the Language & Text preferences panel in the top row, as shown in Figure 7–77.

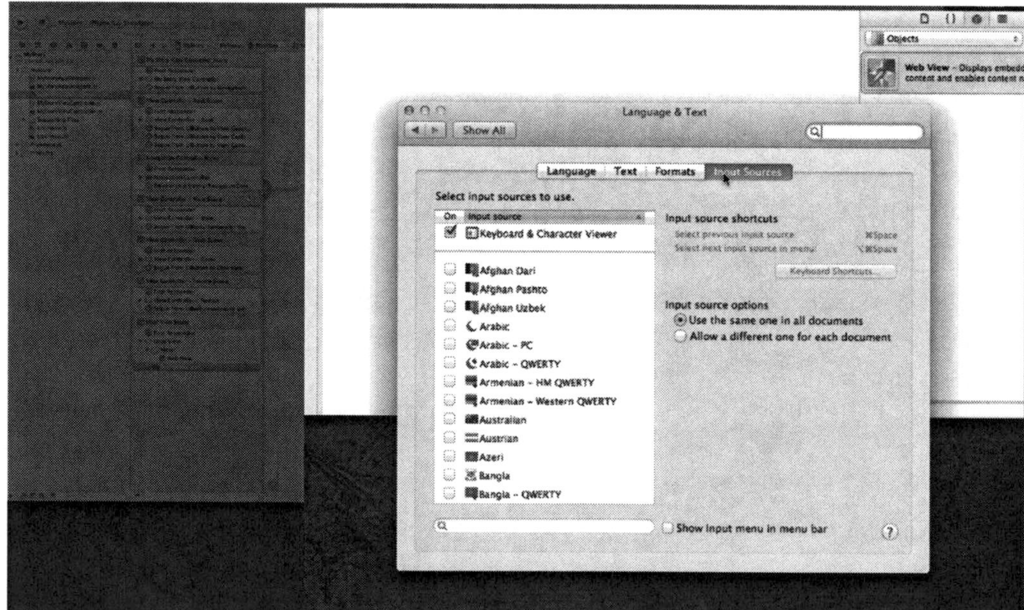

Figure 7–78. *Select the Keyboard & Character Viewer.*

78. In the Input Sources tab, select the Keyboard & Character Viewer from the source list. Also, turn on the menu item, as shown near the bottom in Figure 7–78.

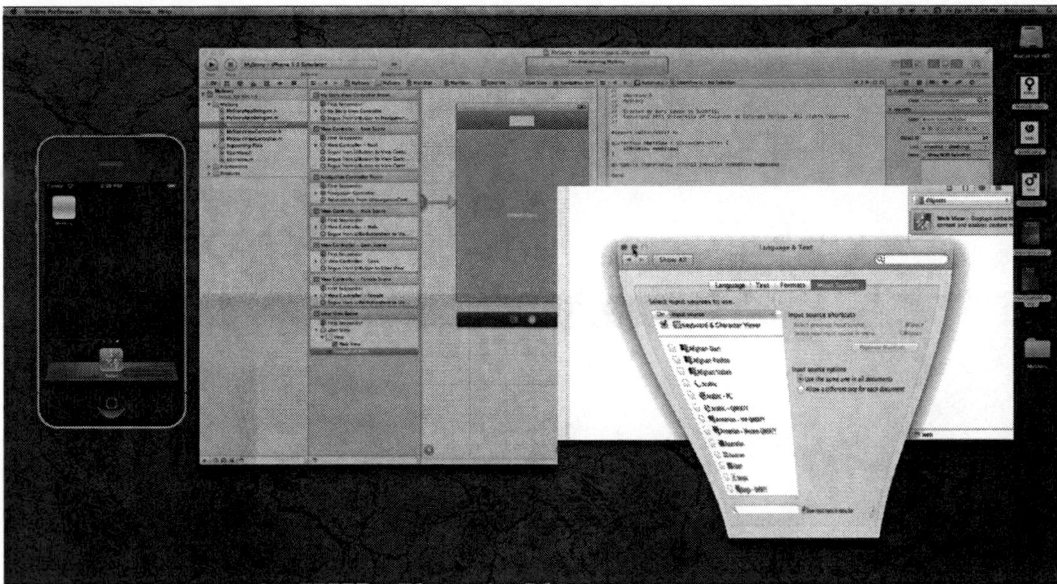

Figure 7–79. *Minimize this window to free up screen space.*

79. Now, minimize this window to free up screen space. You'll turn the menu item back off later. See Figure 7–79.

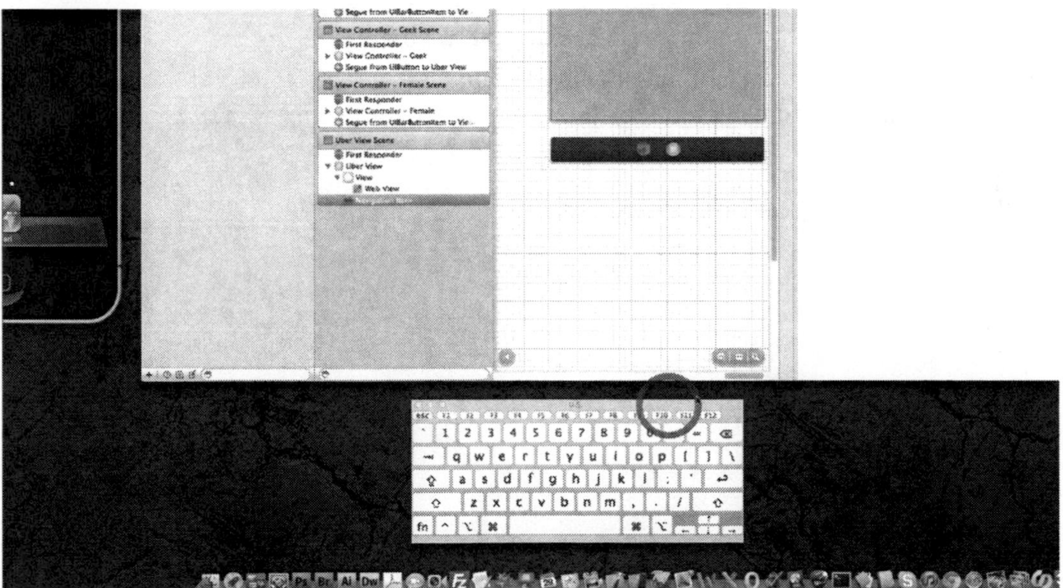

Figure 7–80. *Bring up the Character Viewer.*

80. Now, from the new icon that popped up in the menu bar, select Show Character Viewer. A tiny keyboard shows up. As you type on your keyboard, the keys will be highlighted, as shown in Figure 7–80.

Figure 7–81. *You want the orange keys.*

81. Holding the option key shows a plethora of symbols that you can type. The orange keys are for special keys with marks above the characters in other languages, such as “ö” or “ê”. Mmm, this is exactly what you want. See Figure 7–81.

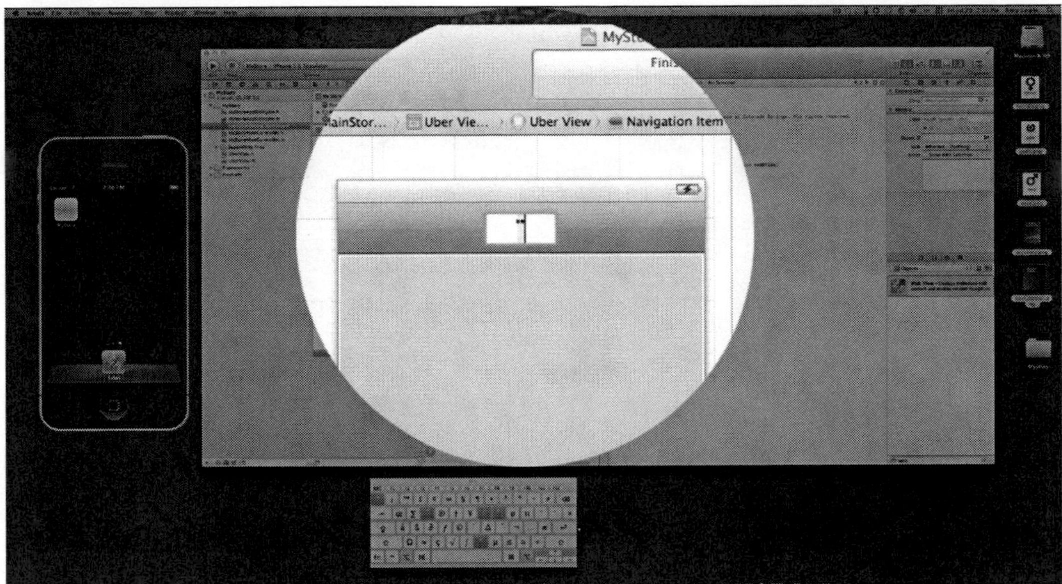

Figure 7–82. *Enter your Über Geek!*

82. Back in Xcode, double-click the `ÜberView`'s title bar to edit it. Start by typing option-u and watch the little keyboard below. Now you have two dots in a yellow box. The next letter you type will have these marks above it. Type shift-u. Ta-da—Ü. Finish it with "ber Geek," as shown in Figure 7–83.

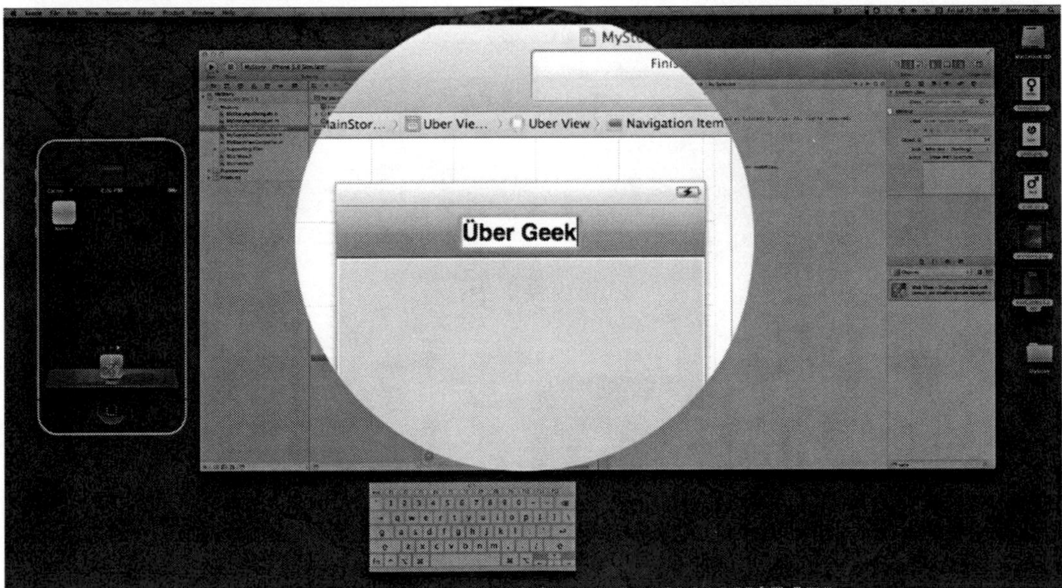

Figure 7–83. *Voila! You now have a proper spelling for Über.*

83. Figure 7–83 shows the proper spelling of Über Geek.

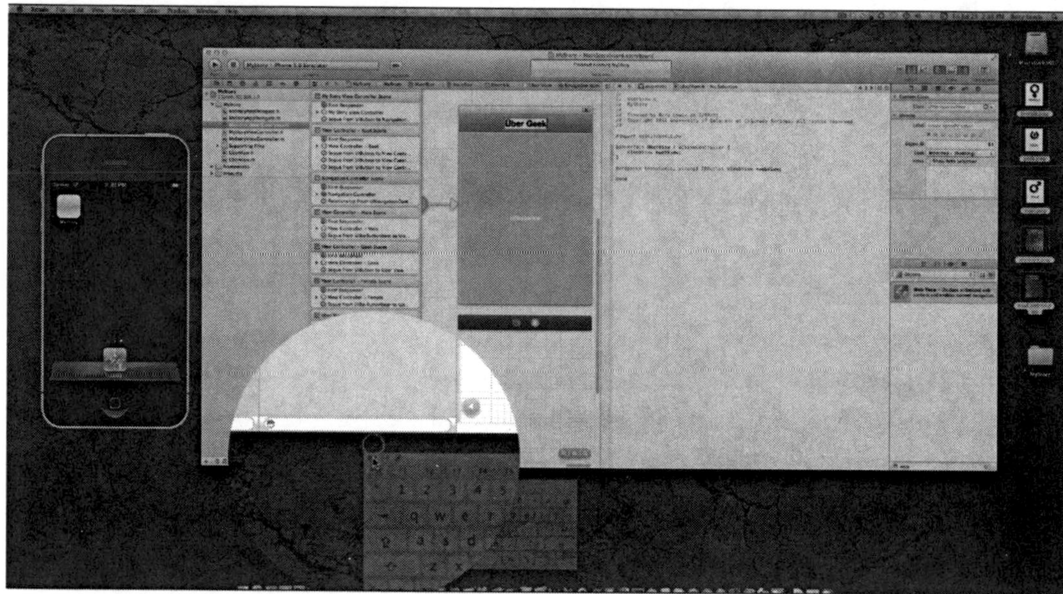

Figure 7–84. *Close the keyboard.*

84. Figure 7–84 illustrates how you can close the keyboard just like any other window.

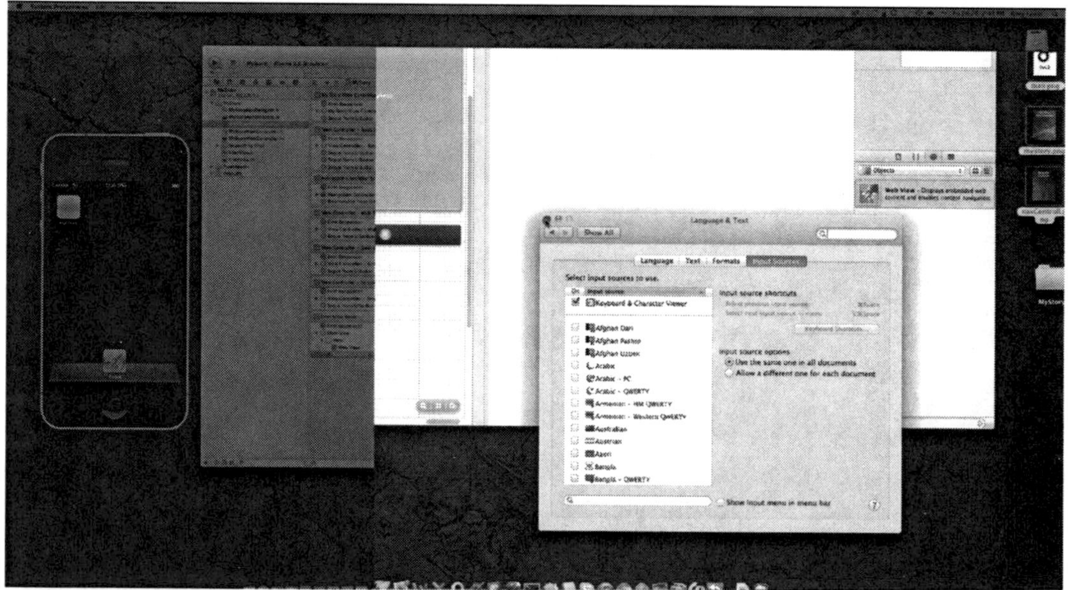

Figure 7–85. *Hide the menu item.*

85. As mentioned earlier, you may want to hide the menu item from the preference panel that you minimized earlier, as shown in Figure 7–85.

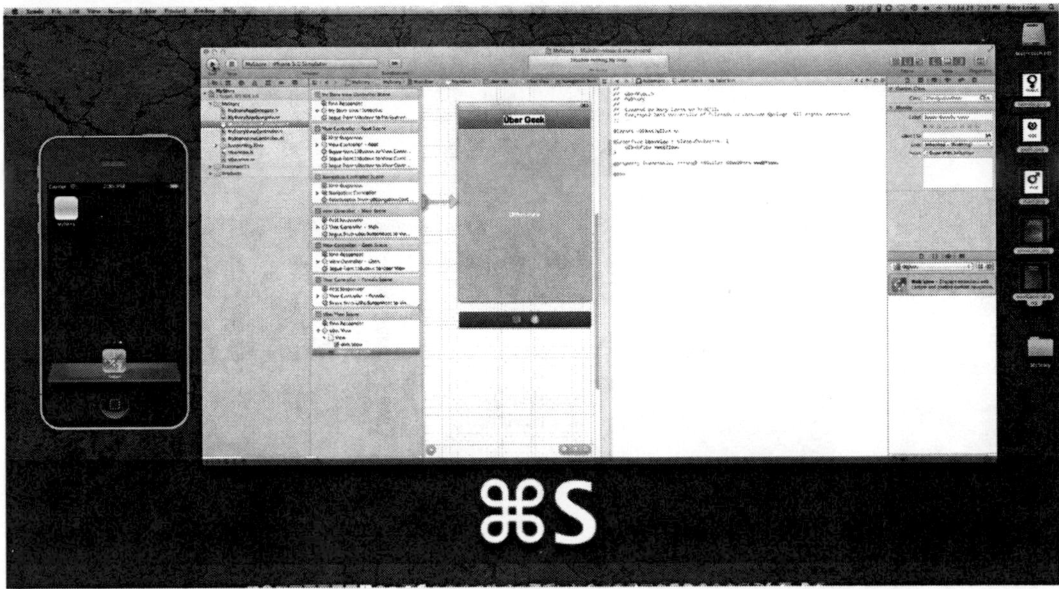

Figure 7–86. *Save it!*

86. Let's save everything and test it out, as shown in Figure 7–86.

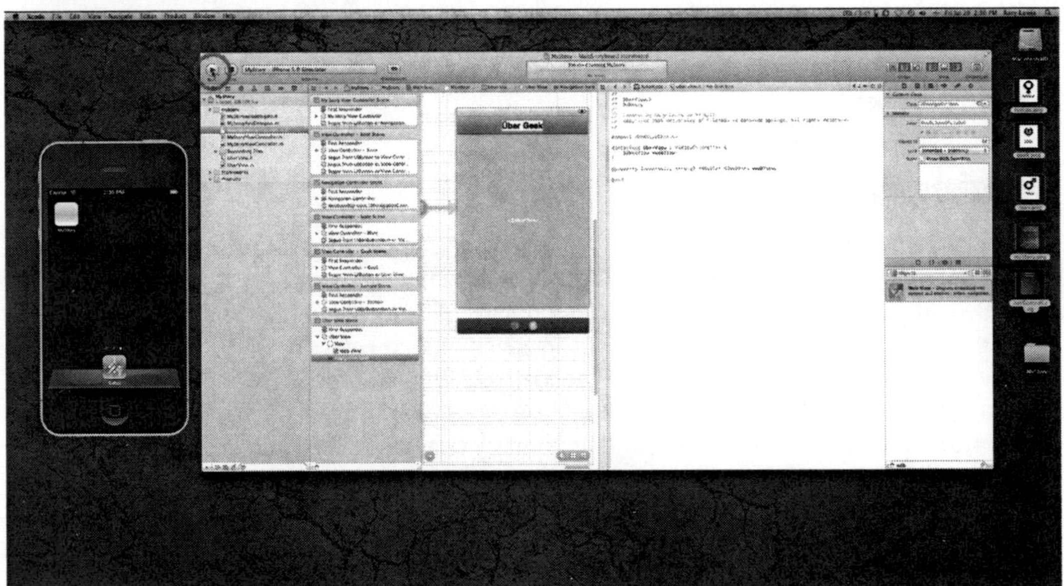

Figure 7–87. *Run it!*

87. Figure 7–87 illustrates the final step—running it.

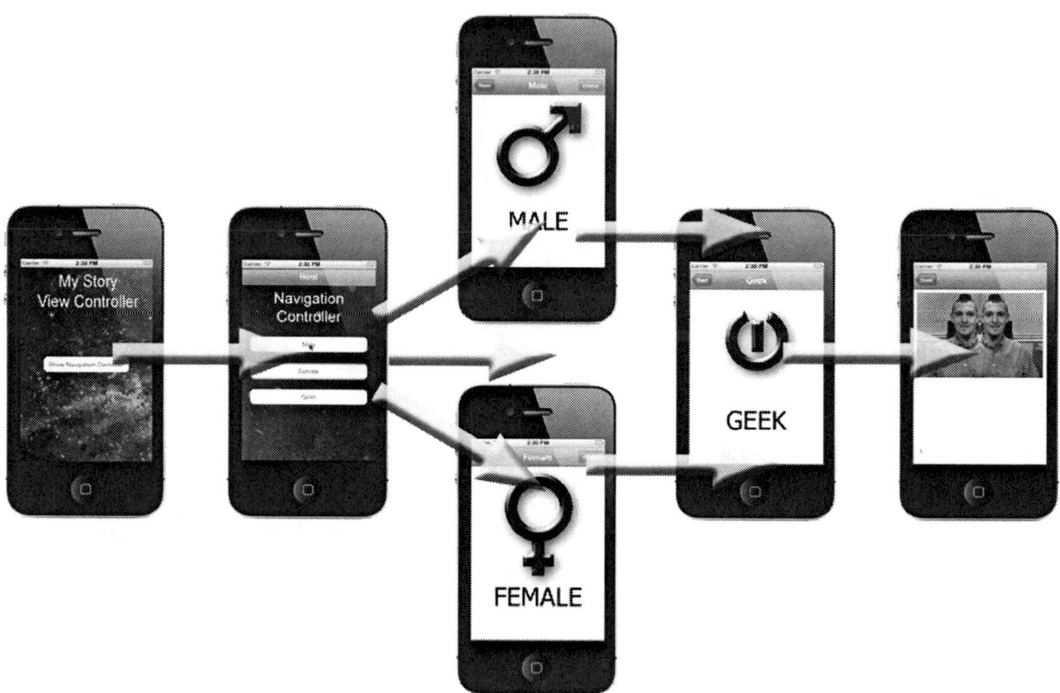

Figure 7–88. *Try to keep track in your head—as you can see, Anthony lost his head, and then found another, and then realized he had not lost his first head to begin with, and now he has two!*

88. Well done!

Digging the Code

Yes, I know this has been quite exhausting. Students are completely worn out after this class. I've tried to understand why this is so. When I tell them this is much easier than programming, they look at me as if I've lost my head. With this in mind, I have decided to do the next chapter as a recap, but using a business model so that two birds can be killed with one stone, allowing you to practice what you learned in this chapter while adding just enough of a twist that it allows business owners, and other innovative minds, to see how to apply storyboarding to a financial model.

With this in mind, the Digging the Code section of this chapter will be kept as an advanced reference, which you can come back to later when you try an advanced version of storyboarding. So, either move straight on to Chapter 8 or just glance through Digging the Code, without freaking out if you don't absorb anything. Just let your brain see what's here, zone out, take a break, and move on to the next chapter.

Storyboard View Controllers, iOS4 and Programmatically Creating Them.

The question I get asked the most by students, and folks on the web, is whether storyboards will be compatible with iOS4. I am not sure why so many people want to know this. Move forward, embrace new technology, and keep moving forward into new territory. But the answer is NO! Storyboards never have been, and never will be, compatible with iOS4 because they are based upon new runtime classes only available in iOS5 and Lion. The next most popular question is whether one can program the storyboard. Mmm, let's see, that is almost like saying, “OK, I have a car I can drive, but can I get out and push it?”

I cannot understand why so many people want to change it, or try to get under the hood. I could understand this if you had first mastered storyboarding and found huge gaps that you want to get around. However, in this case, as I write this, storyboarding has hardly been out very long, and people who have not done a single storyboarding app want to know if they can change it. I am going to answer this question, though, because by the time this book is released there is a chance that the latter will apply.

To answer this, you need to view storyboarding from the runtime point of view. The transitions and segues between view controllers ought to be viewed in runtime. Here, one will note that there is indeed a mechanism to instantiate segues programmatically.

- First, looking at how to program and tweak an existing segue programmatically, you need to look at the code that exists between the current view controller and the destination view controller. This is where you will be able to trigger your segue programmatically, using the `performSegueWithIdentifier:sender:` method of `UIViewController`.
- Second, if you do not have a segue between your view controllers, but you have defined your destination in your storyboard file, then you are in luck. You can load the view controller programmatically with the `instantiateViewControllerWithIdentifier:` method of `UIStoryboard`. After you have done this, you can connect your view controller by simply pushing it on a navigation stack. Warning—do not attempt to access it through Interface Builder. I've seen some of my students' Macs completely crash.
- Finally, if your storyboard is not connected to your destination view controller, you can create it programmatically, however the author has not explored this in depth in the Apple Dev site. It is there—I have no idea why you would want to do this, but it is in the View Controller Programming Guide for iOS.

If you do want to understand storyboarding, it is important to remember two things:

- First, it inherits from, and conforms to, `NSObject`
- Second, its framework is from `/System/Library/Frameworks/UIKit.framework`.

The important issue I want you to understand is that, right now, you can program endlessly using what you already know about storyboarding. Keep in mind the basics, and really understand these basics. Forget about programming storyboards programmatically. Use it as it is, and understand the basics.

The first basic function of storyboards that you must know is that they all need to begin with an initial view controller that represents the starting point of your app and connects to your user interface. This will be the first screen your user sees. In your case, it was the My Story View Controller. If you have a bug, you may want to check your transitions to the initial view controller in a different storyboard file, which is the storyboard file specified in the application's `Info.plist` file, using the `UIMainStoryboardFile` key, which is the initial view controller that is loaded and presented automatically when your program begins.

In the Chapter Ahead

In Chapter 8, we will introduce you to the world of debugging. We will first take a broad look at the debugging landscape. We will talk about some of the intimidating debugging tools, what they mean, when you may use debugging in the future, and most importantly how you can debug now using a very simple tool.

You will learn how to find a bug in code you wrote in a previous chapter. But more importantly you will embrace the art of debugging rather than view it as an endless, hopeless, bottomless pit.

Onward to the bugs that await us in the next chapter!

Chapter 8

Debugging

As you begin the eighth chapter, you'll start operating at a higher level. You may notice that in this chapter I use a different approach to teach you about debugging. In order for you to understand why this is an important chapter, I want you to consider the road that led me to presenting this chapter and its exercises.

So, what's the beef with debugging?

In 1988, at the University of Montana in Bozeman, I found myself in my first computer science class. It was fun getting out of the Electrical Engineering building every now and again to dabble around in software. We'd rush over—sometimes in bitter, minus 20-degree weather and blinding snow—to get to the Computer Science building across the quad. During my class in Pascal, an old language we used to learn with FORTRAN in order to get to the C Programming Language (which was a categorical imperative for all the geeks at Bozeman), something amazing happened.

I was trying to compile an in-class exercise. But every time I tried to compile my code that day, errors would appear in those glowing green numbers on the black screen. Back in those days, there was no indication of how many errors had occurred, or what or where they could be. It only said, "ERROR: FAILED TO COMPILE." I could not fix it, and suddenly my love for computer science began to plummet at a precipitous rate. Upon seeing how upset I was, the TA immediately went to the front of the class, and in a loud, piercing voice that got everyone's attention, announced:

> *Listen, class. I don't want to see y'all getting weird and upset like Rory over there. Your code will NEVER COMPILE THE FIRST TIME!! Do you hearhhhh me? Your code will NEVER compile the first time, so just get over it!*

I'll never forget that—especially now, as I see so many young computer science and engineering students drop out of computer science in their freshman year, right at the point that debugging and arrays hit them.

I also remember something my uncle told me when I was just a kid in Durban, South Africa, my place of birth. He was teaching me to surf in the huge, treacherous waves, and he said that if I wanted to handle the ten- to twenty-foot surf, first I had to learn how to “wipe out.”

> *Rory... you WILL wipe out. You WILL be held under the water for 15 to 20 seconds, so it is imperative that you learn how to survive a huge wipe. That way, you'll be fearless out there!*

Wow! I could not believe it took me years to associate these two analogous situations and their lessons. After that, I started making my students go back to code that they knew they could handle and having them program mistakes into it. Then, I’d have them give it to a partner, and guide one another as each debugged the other’s code. Over the years, debugging tools have evolved. In fact, debugging tools themselves have become very complex and intimidating to students. With this in mind, I have created a segue for you into learning to love debugging and feeling inspired to learn more complex debugging tools. You are at a stage where you are going to write more code than you ever have before. You WILL get errors, and I want you to be able to handle these tough times. This is why I am going to teach you the first lesson of crashing and burning.

> **NOTE:** You WILL crash. Let’s learn how to crash quickly, survive, and get back to flying!

Xcode’s Debugging Landscape

When you look at the debugging landscape, you will see a simple tool standing alone among a bunch of complex-looking debugging programs. In this chapter, I am going to use the simple debugging tool to teach you how to find a bug in the code you have written. In the section entitled “Digging the Code,” I will elaborate on the more difficult but very much stronger debugging tools—I’ll essentially bring them to your attention and introduce you to how they work, when to use them, and how to learn more about them when you reach a point in coding that is outside the domain of this book.

Xcode's Tools

Before you get started, I want to talk about some of the more advanced, sometimes intimidating debugging tools that we will dismiss for now and check back on later. Xcode has steadily been building up its debugging tools, and provides a very powerful set of debugging environments you can use to find bugs and kill them in a way that will not harm your code with careless extraction. In "Digging the Code," we'll take these tools on a test drive with some images for reference. For now, I’ll just briefly introduce them to you.

NOTE: For Xcode debugging tools to work, you must make sure that you install the iOS SDK corresponding to the iOS release that you have running on your Mac. If they do not match, debugging will not work. For example, if you have a device running iOS 4.2, but you do not have the corresponding SDK installed on your computer—you will not be able to debug.

Xcode's Tools: Text Editor

The first tool is the text editor that gives you the ability to debug code directly within the lines, as you may have noticed when your code does not compile and all those little red exclamation signs pop up all over it! Text editor allows you to add and set breakpoints; keep tabs on your "call stack"; access the value of variables by hovering the mouse pointer over them; execute just a single line of code; and step into, out of, or over function or method calls.

Xcode's Tools: Debugger Window

The second tool that comes along with Xcode is called the "debugger window." When you start to work with code that is really intense, or just lots of it, you will become friends with the debugger window, because not only does it provide all the same debugging features as the text editor using a traditional interface, but it allows you to see your "call stack" and the variables associated with it. Suppose you had a stack called "dog," and your variables associated with that stack were breed, sex, age, and name. If upon looking at your stack, you only saw sex, age, and name, then you'd immediately know that breed was missing. This is a simple example analogous to saying that what NASA does is shoot big pieces of metal into space, sometimes with people in them. The debugger window is a cool, powerful instrument you may come to really appreciate one day.

Xcode's Tools: GDB Console

The third tool, called the GDB console, comes wrapped in the Xcode IDE. It is a text-based GNU debugger with more functionality than the debugger window and a decent GUI that makes it easier to step through your code. In my experience, when you see coders on the GDB console flying through iterations at lightning speed, it usually means that they have been on GDB for a while. That, in turn, means that the coder is either at the Über-Geek or Superkalifragilistic-Geek level!

Xcode's Tools: Console Output and Device Logs

The fourth debugging environment provided in Xcode simply interacts with stuff that you already know goes on. I'm sure you've seen, when apps and programs sometimes crash, that the iOS on your Mac produces log entries to your console that indicate drill-down code when it crashes. You can produce console messages in your iOS applications, too. Coders will often go to the NSLog function, because these console logs helps coders debug at a lower level. The key phrase here is "lower level." If you wind up at an interview, they may ask you what you use to debug when you need to look for a bug that apparently exists at a lower level. You're answer for this should be: "Of course, we all use the console output and device logs to see the lower level code via the NSLog functionality." Oh, yeah—they will love you!

Xcode's Tools: NSZombie

The fifth debugging tool provided by Xcode works specifically for memory leaks. Before Xcode 4.2 we had to personally monitor what portions of our code were using our set amount of memory. When we were finished with one piece of code, we had to release the memory from that method or class so it could be used by the next section of code being executed. With this said, though, it's important to know when to enable NSZombie on a section of code.

Turning on `NSZombieEnabled` allows us to view logs that tell us the status of our memory—particularly our deallocated memory, as indicated below.

```
2011-09-10 20:01:12.8813 storyboard[2019:f2c] *** -[GSFont ascender]: message sent to
deallocated instance 0x127910
```

Xcode's Tools: Shark

The sixth debugging tool is quite popular and, like NSZombie, is specifically aimed at debugging memory leaks. The difference is that it's relatively fun to play with the user-friendly shark GUI. Shark gives us access to system-level events like interrupts and virtual memory. You can see how each thread talks to other threads in your code, and if memory is dropped, leaked, or causes a "bottleneck" during that interaction. Shark is a tool you will likely see in your work with Xcode, so remember that name for now.

Xcode's Tools: Unit Testing

The seventh and last tool provided by Xcode is what we call "unit testing." Unit tests comprise the platform or foundation of how an efficient project manager sets everything up on a huge coding project so that a suite of tests will run on each line of code *as it is written* to make sure everything works as expected.

If a project manager does not use unit testing and finds that his or her 30-person, 40,000-line Xcode project is not working... it's almost too late to start debugging. Unit testing is typically used by larger, well run Xcode companies. Just know that if you get an interview with such a company, you should spend some time practicing unit testing examples: at the interview they WILL ask you if you have unit testing experience, and it will be awesome to say "Yes, dude! I'm all over unit testing." Hmm, that may not be the best response, but you get the idea. Unit testing is way out of the scope of this book, but I will introduce it to you later, just so you can say you've all met each other!

Our Tool: FileMerge.app

Remember "learning to wipe out"? Well, `FileMerge.app` is what we will use to do this. I used to think that giving my students and readers of my books access to the code of the apps presented in this book would be all they needed to figure out what was wrong with their code. However, I was wrong: simply downloading the code from my website to their desktops was not enough to solve all of their problems. Being the geek that I am, I love to keep track of things, and I can tell you that over the last year I have sent more than 6,070 email responses containing a link to my source code to newbie geeks. Out of the 6,070 people that received this email and downloaded my code, 4,208 of them STILL could not debug their code! Clearly, I was doing something wrong, and I needed to revise my pedagogy. SO, I did.

I present my answer in this chapter, which shows you how to download my source code, use `FileMerge.app` to debug your code against my code, and find your mistake—in other words, it teaches you how to wipe out (or in computer terms, "crash").

In Chapter 7, I introduced storyboarding. It was fun dragging objects around the canvas and connecting them with segues. Now, you will start putting a lot of code behind those objects to make them shinier and more intelligent. And I do mean a LOT of code. You need to know how to debug using `FileMerge.app`, comparing my code against yours. This is a lesson I insist you take, even though you may think you're too cool for it.

switch-mistake: A Lesson in the Art of Crashing

You are going to revisit Chapter 6's switch code, but this time you will not code the entire app, and most importantly you will force an error. Then, you will download my code from the website, open up `FileMerge.app`, and debug your code. Now, you may ask, why don't we just do switches in Chapter 6 and then pop back here and do the debugging? The answer is threefold:

- First, as I said, you won't be using all the code you wrote in Chapter 6's switches, and you need to do it in a different order. So, you need to do it again from scratch, following step by step in this chapter.
- Second, the naming of the code will be different. I want you to have a different name on the code you write in this chapter so your bug does not pop up. I'll explain this later.
- Third, I just want you to practice redoing an app with which you already feel comfortable. This way, your error and the debugging becomes your primary focus.

Starting the Project

So, the first thing we need to do is clear off your desktop and download the source code and the images from my website.

- Download the images here: `bit.ly/raKxPe`.

NOTE: I provide only minimal instructions on each step leading up to the point where you create your bug. This is because you've already done this exercise, and now I'm taking the kid gloves off.

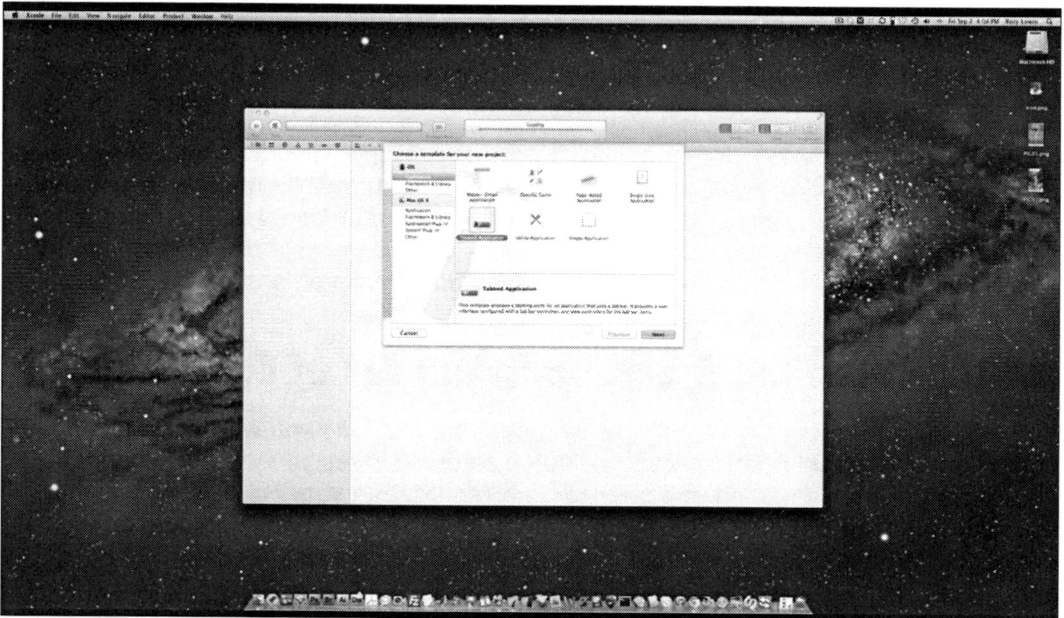

Figure 8–1. *A clean desktop with the three images downloaded, ready to open a new project*

1. With a clean desktop containing only the three images downloaded, open a new project by using the keyboard shortcut ⌘⇧N. When you see the New Project wizard as depicted in Figure 8–1, you will want to click the *Tabbed Application* template.

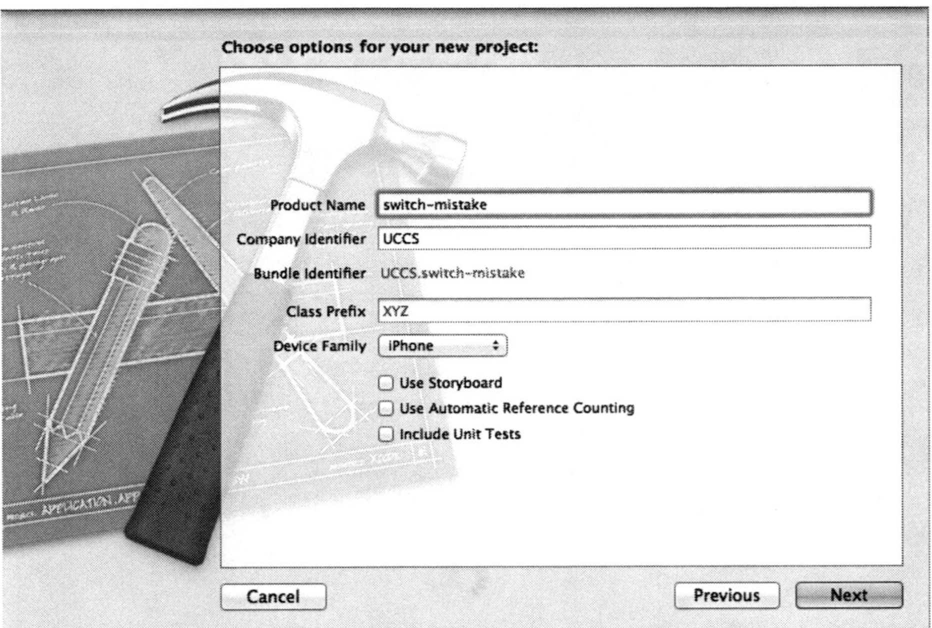

Figure 8–2. *Name it "switch-mistake" and click "Next".*

2. As shown in Figure 8–2, name it "switch-mistake," target it for the iPhone, deselect the *Use Storyboard* option, and click *Next* or hit ↩ on your keyboard.

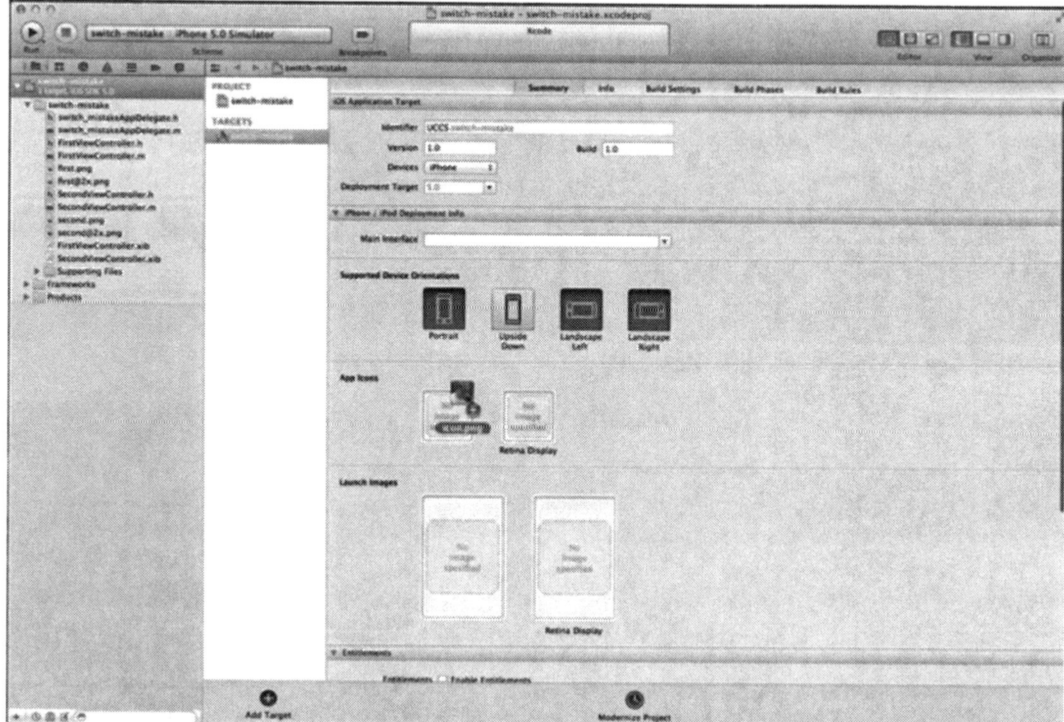

Figure 8–3. ***Drag the icon to the App Icon box.***

3. Drag the application icon, `icon.png`, from your desktop to the *App Icon* box, as shown in Figure 8–3.

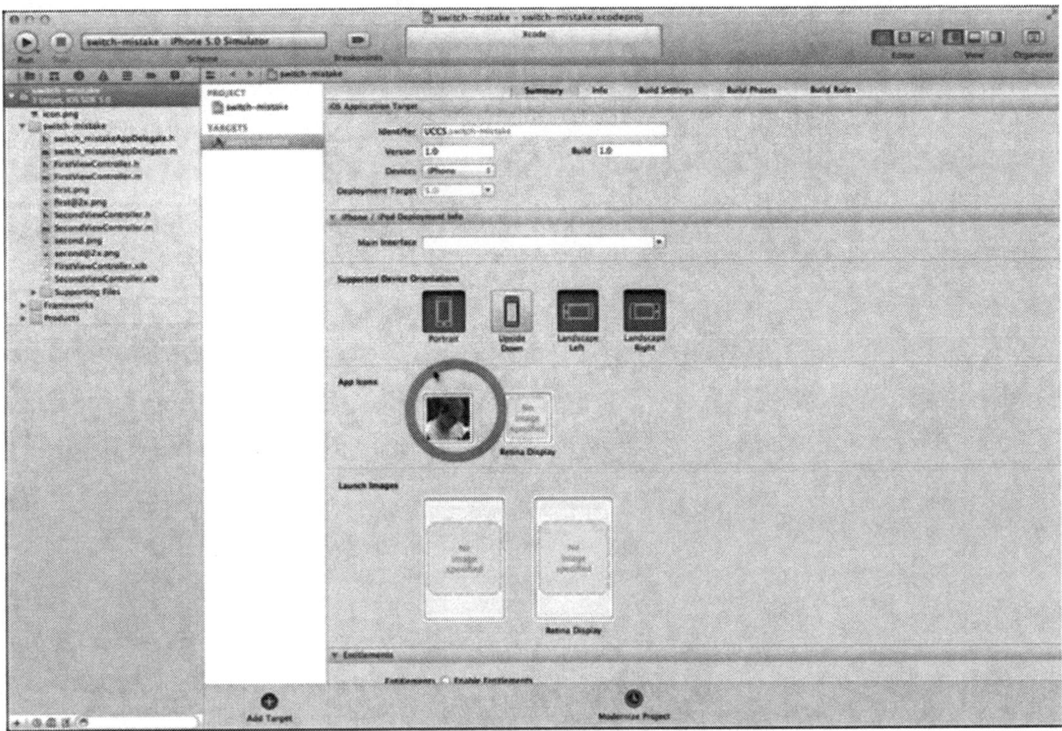

Figure 8–4. *App Icon properly dropped into the box*

4. Figure 8–4 shows the icon correctly dropped into the App Icon box. Note that you usually determine which image will be your icon by using the `plist`. Here, you are using the drag and drop method for the second time.

Creating the Views

Now that you have an icon, you can begin building the app.

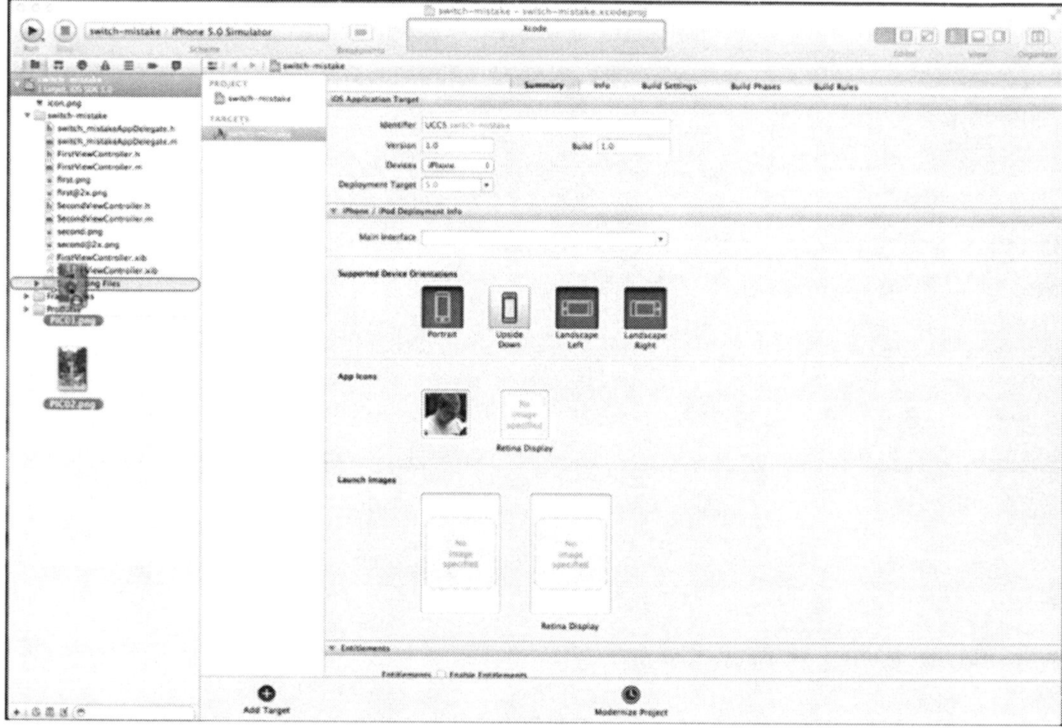

Figure 8–5. ***Drag and drop the remaining two images into the project.***

5. Drag and drop the two remaining images from your desktop into the *Supporting Files* folder, as illustrated in Figure 8–5.

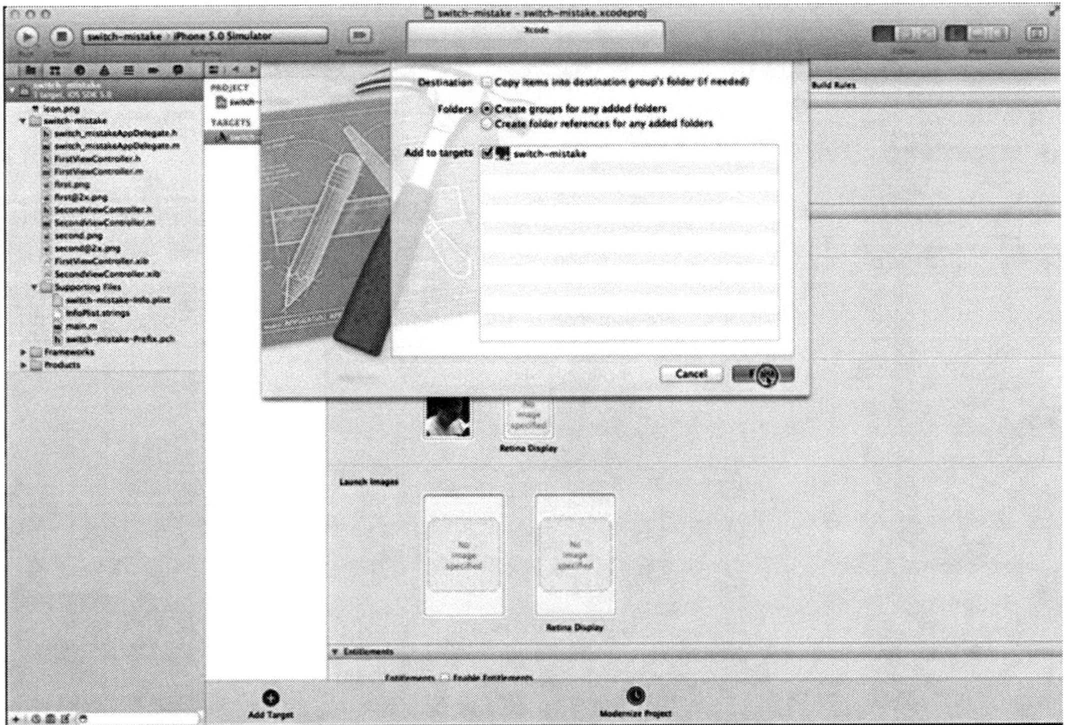

Figure 8–6. ***Create groups for added folders and add the icon image to your targets.***

6. After you have dropped all your images into the project resources folder, make sure to check your dialog box prompt. Make sure that *Create groups for any added folders* is checked and that the project is selected under *Add to targets*. This is shown in Figure 8–6.

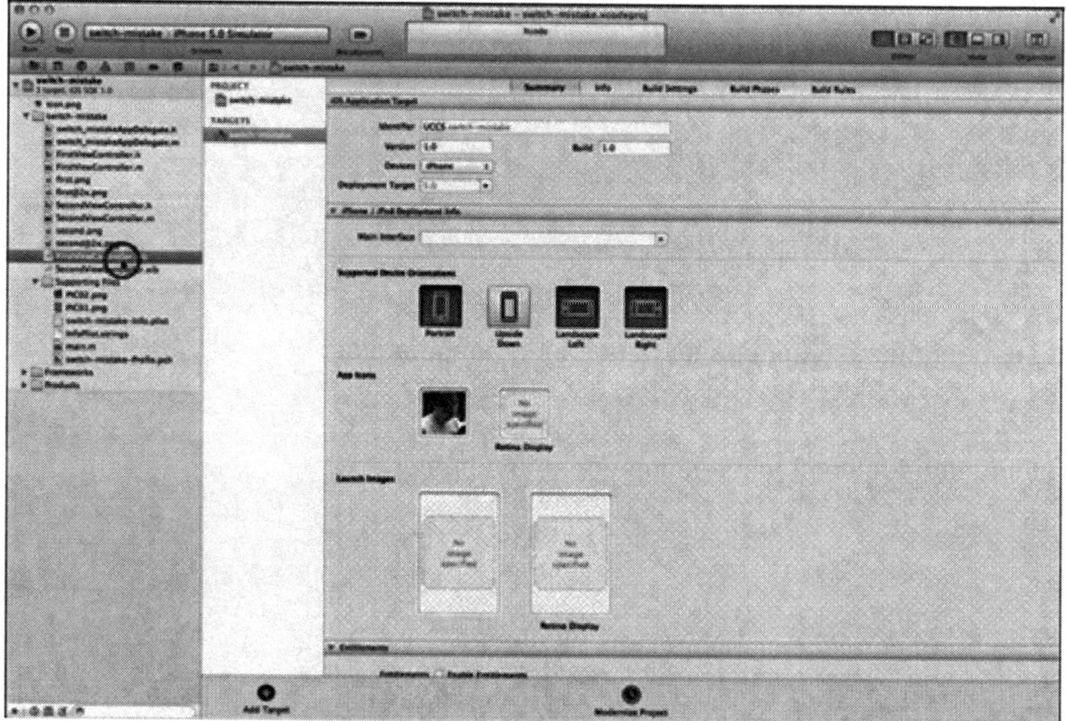

Figure 8–7. *Open* `FirstViewController.xib`*.*

7. Open `FirstViewController.xib`, as shown in Figure 8–7.

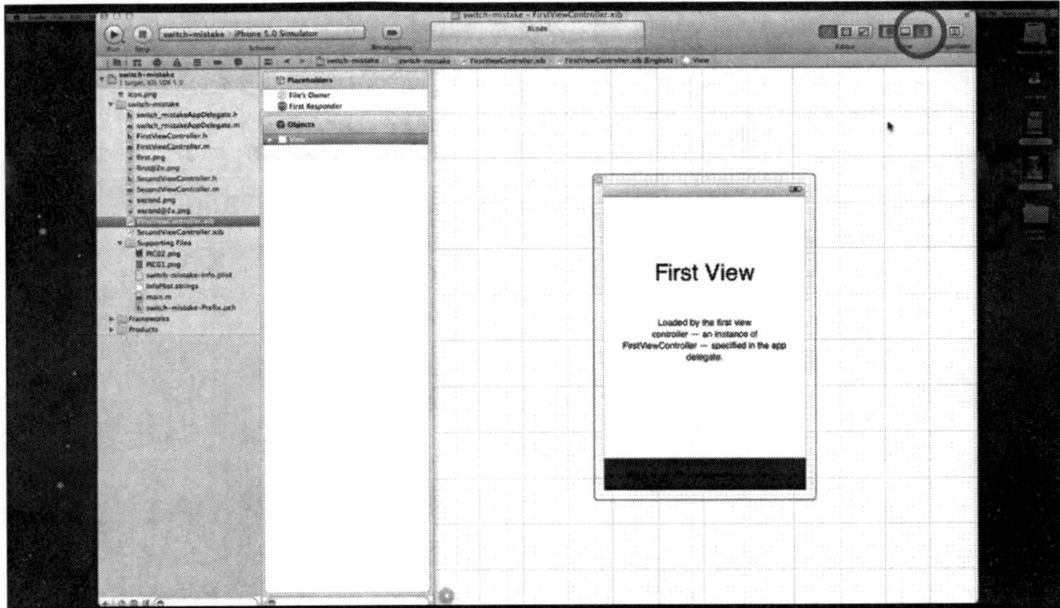

Figure 8–8. *Open the Utilities Inspector.*

8. You need to grab stuff from the library, so open up the *Utilities Inspector*, as shown in Figure 8–8.

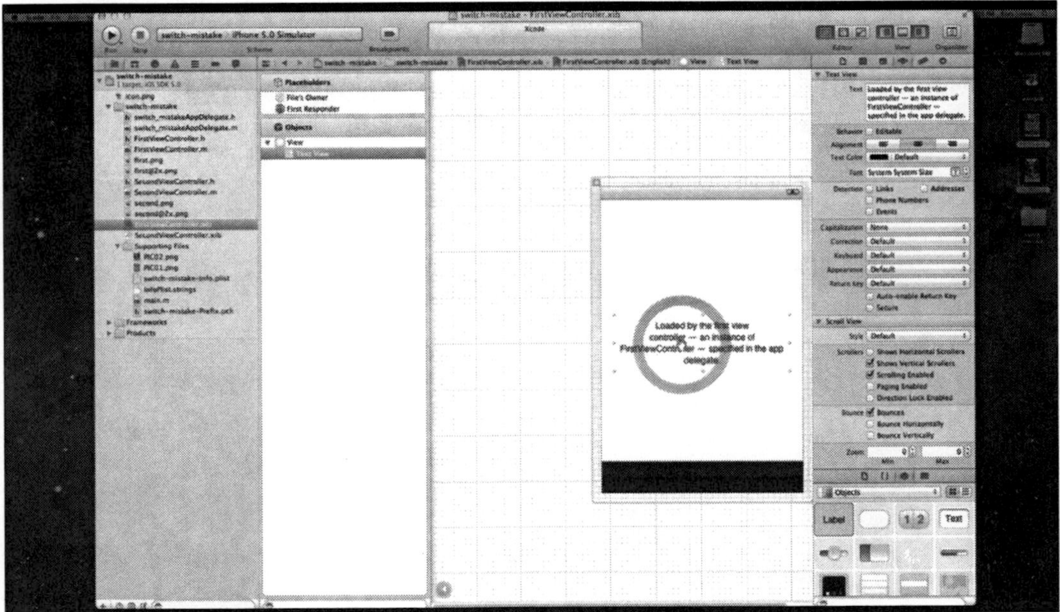

Figure 8–9. *Delete the default labels.*

9. You need to clear out the First View to add your content, so delete the First View label and the label with the text that starts: *Loaded by the first view....* Figure 8–8 shows the latter label being deleted. The First View label has already been deleted in Figure 8–9.

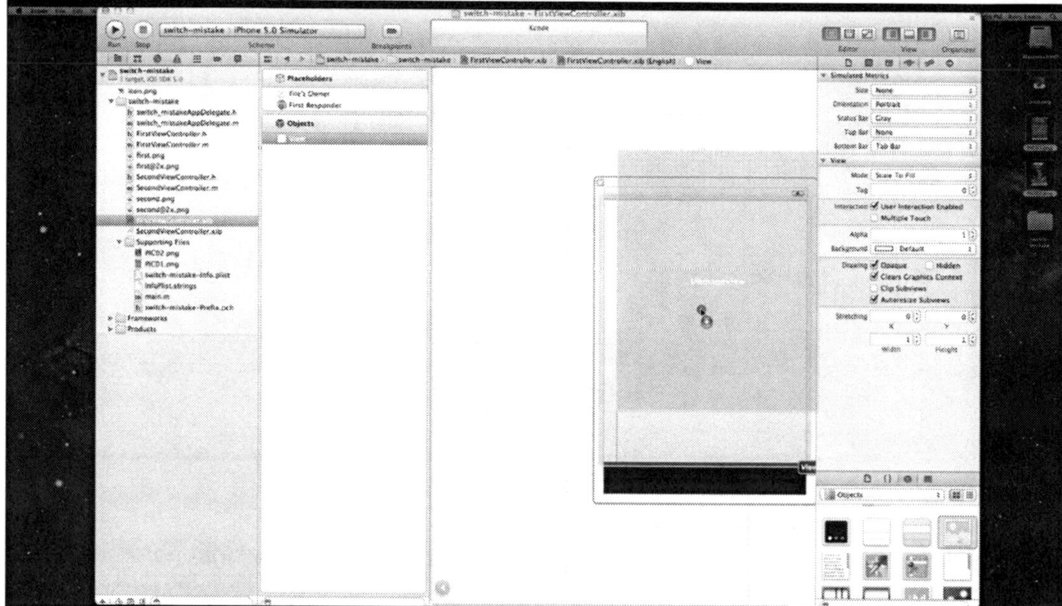

Figure 8–10. *Drag a `UIImageView` onto your view design area.*

10. With your Utilities panel open, drag a `UIImageView` onto your view design area, as shown in Figure 8–10.

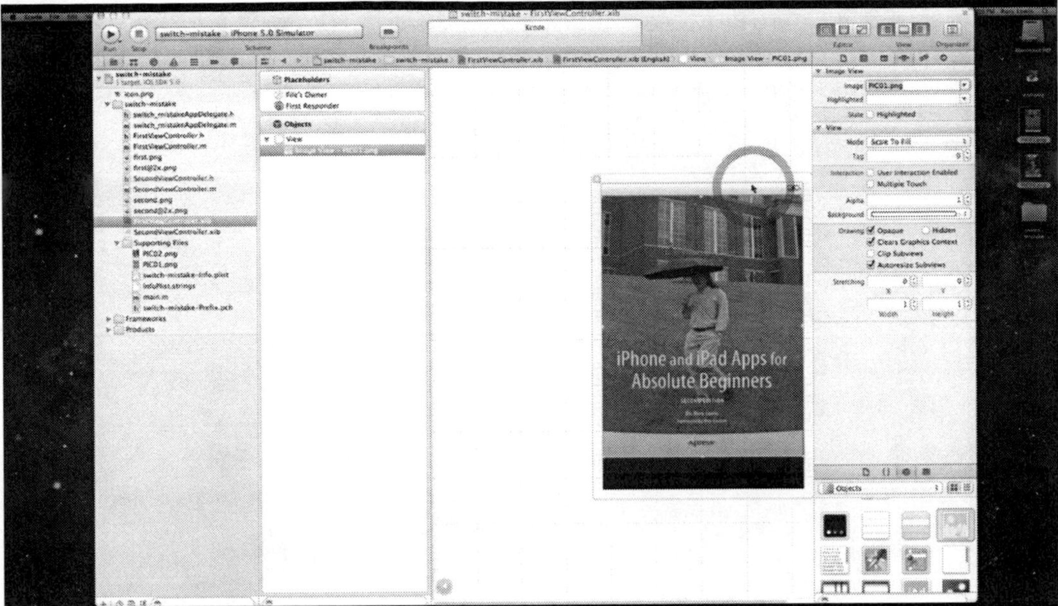

Figure 8–11. *Associate* `PIC01.png` *with the First View.*

11. With the first `UIImageView` selected, go to the image drop-down menu in the *Attributes* dialog in your Utilities panel, as indicated in Figure 8–11. Select `PIC01.png` and associate it with your first `UIImageView`.

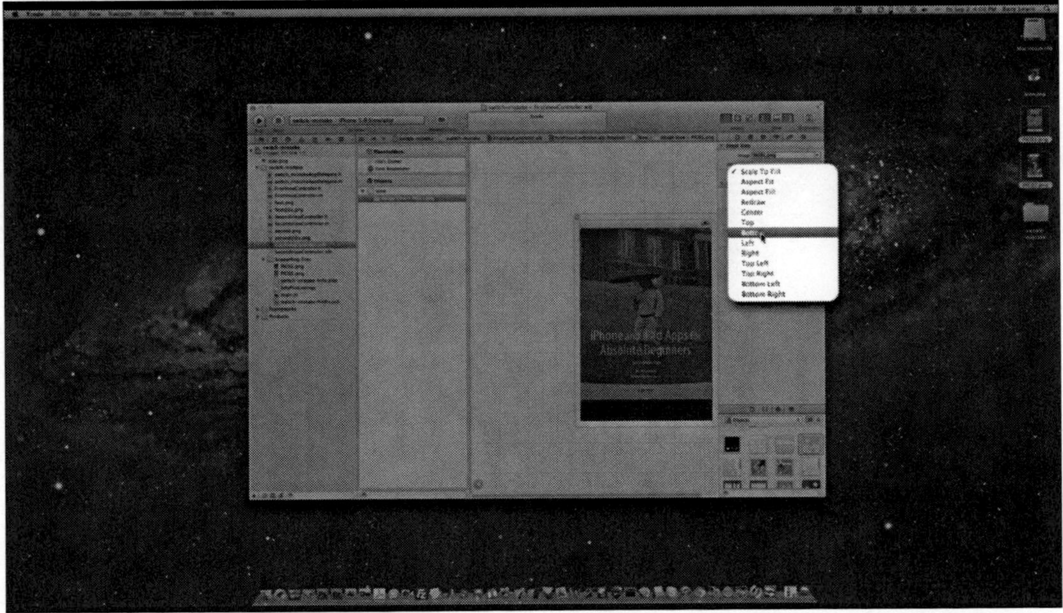

Figure 8–12. *Select "Bottom" for the View Mode.*

12. As shown in Figure 8–12, now click *Mode* and select “Bottom” from the drop-down menu.

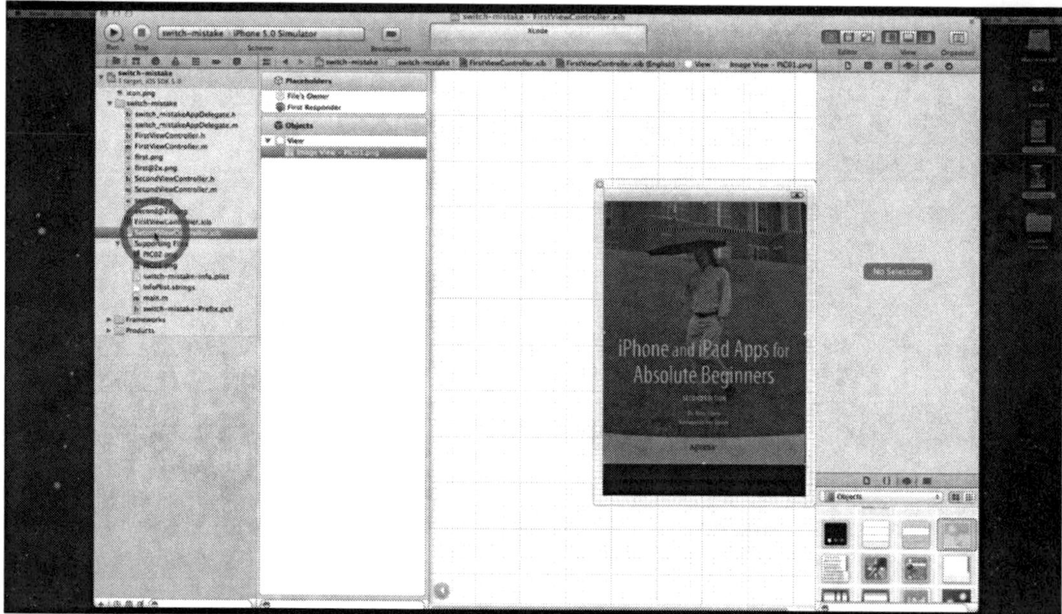

Figure 8–13. *Open the Second View Controller.*

13. Open the *Second View Controller*, as illustrated in Figure 8–13.

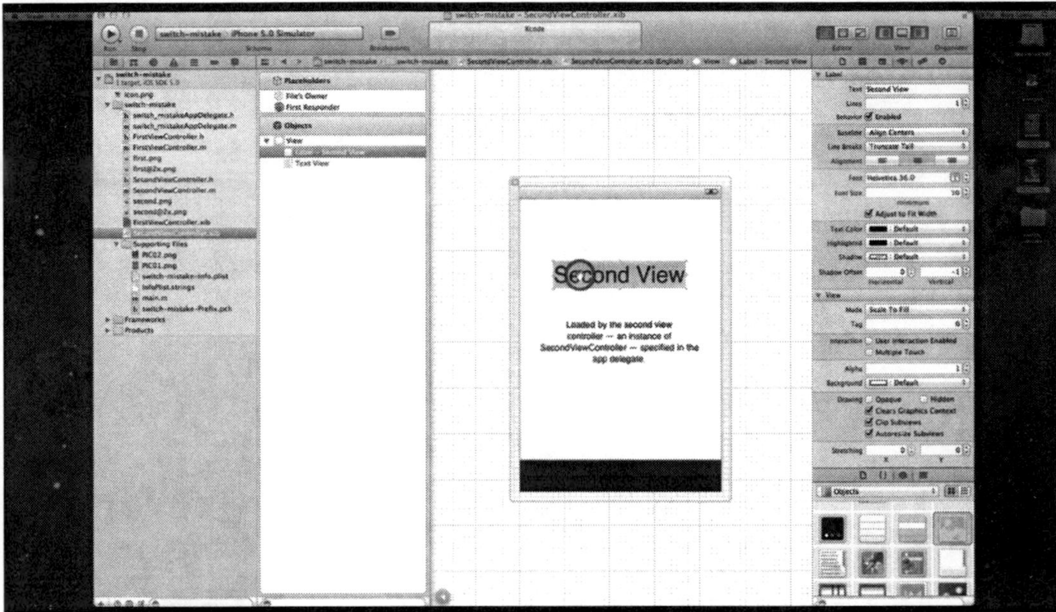

Figure 8–14. *Delete the Second View's labels.*

14. Figure 8–14 shows deleting the labels in the Second View, just as you did in the First View.

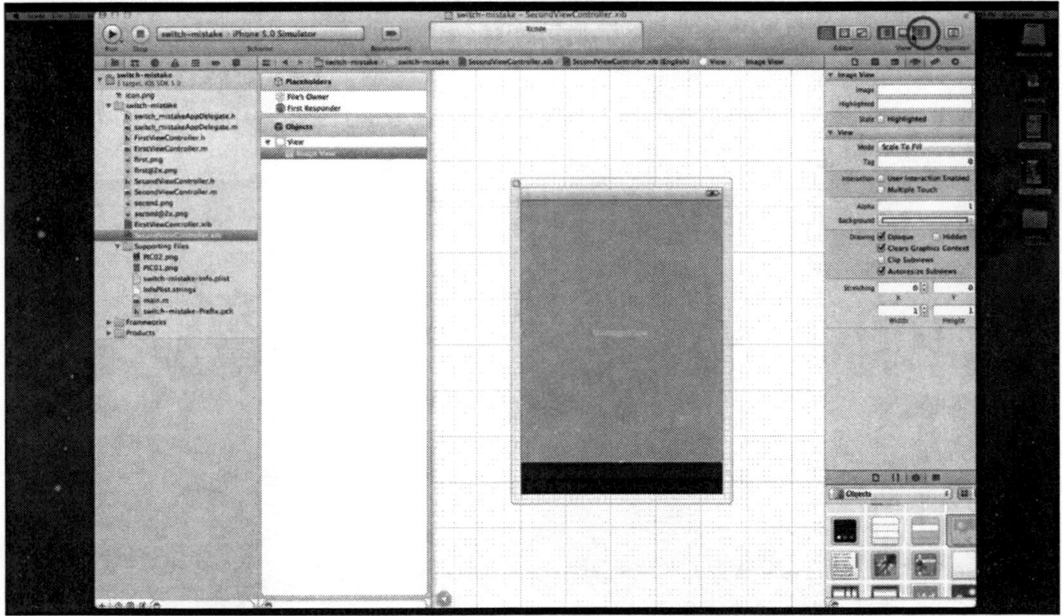

Figure 8–15. *Close the Utilities panel.*

15. Close the Utilities panel, as shown in Figure 8–15.

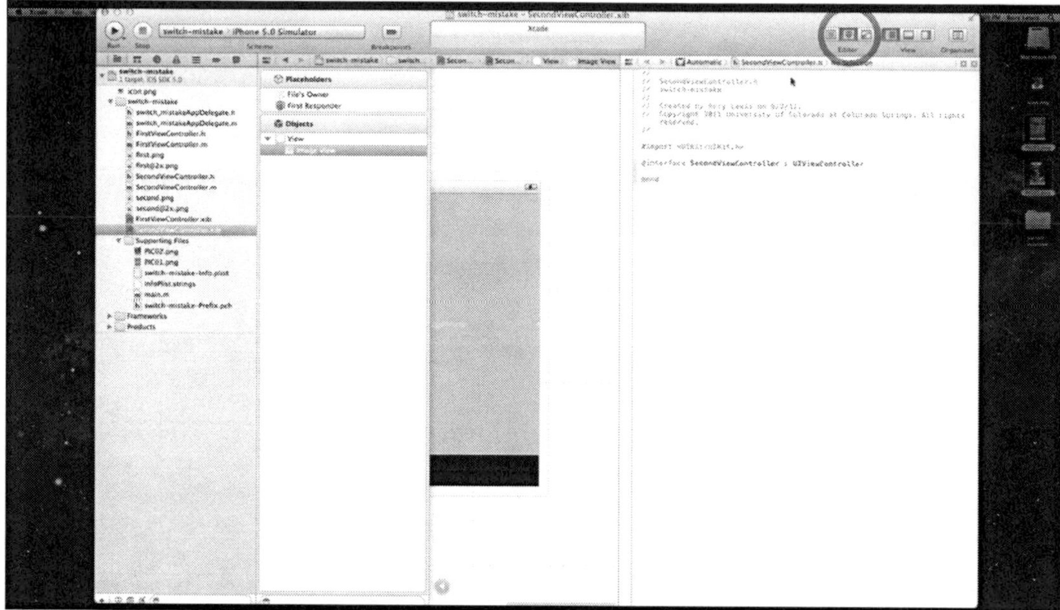

Figure 8–16. *Open the Assistant.*

16. Open the *Assistant*, as illustrated in Figure 8–16.

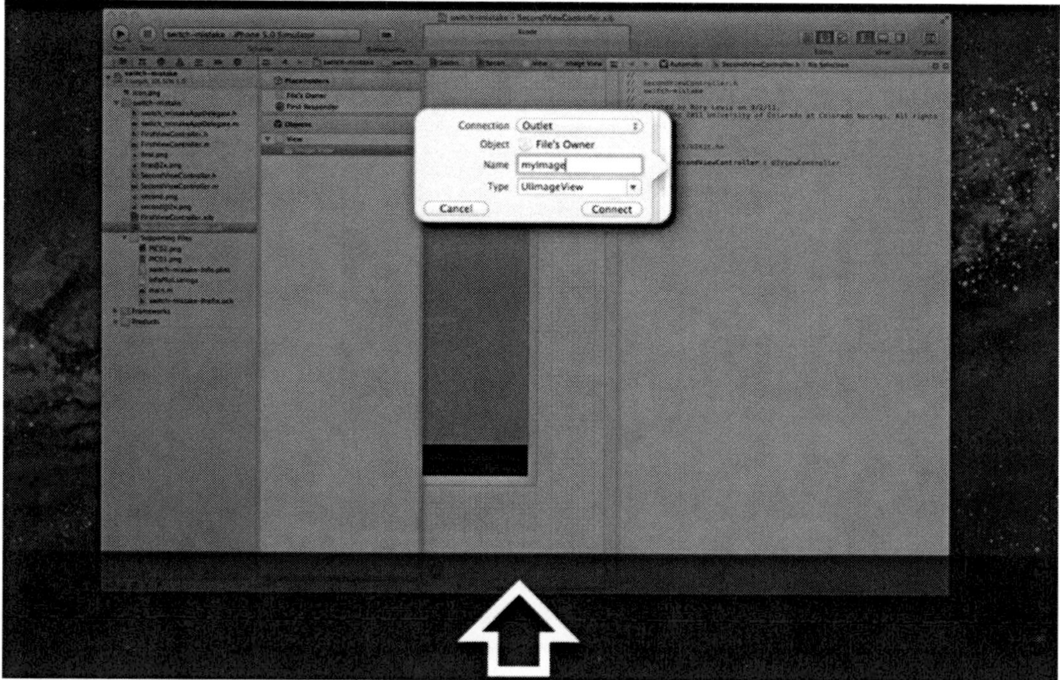

Figure 8–17. *Set up an outlet and call it "myImage."*

17. Control-drag onto the `SecondViewController` header file and set up an outlet called "myImage," as shown in Figure 8–17.

Creating the Bug

You need to enter code for the outlet you created and introduce the bug. Then you can debug your app.

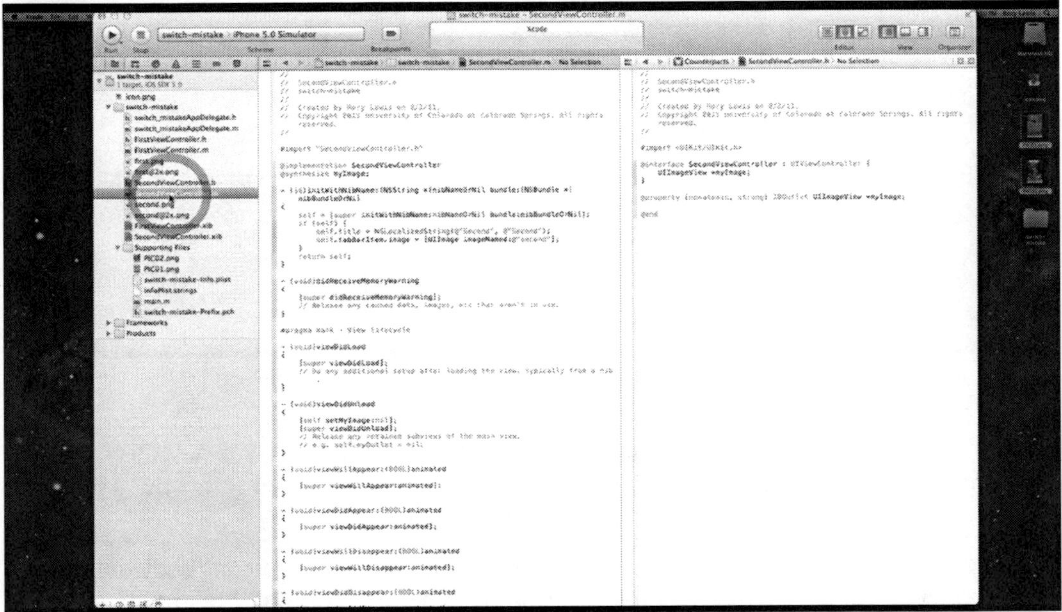

Figure 8–18. *Open* `SecondViewController`*'s implementation file.*

18. Open the *Implementation* file, as shown in Figure 8–18.

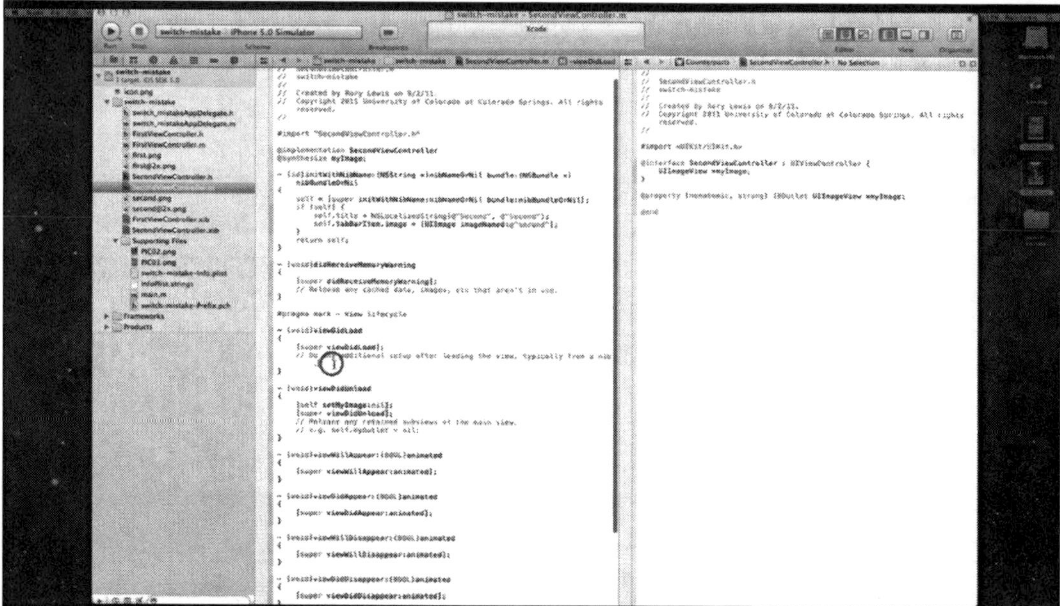

Figure 8–19. *Click in your `viewDidLoad` method.*

19. You're going to make the First View load the image incorrectly. So, let's code this now. Go to the **`viewDidLoad`** `method and click between the curly brackets to start codin`g, as illustrated in Figure 8–19.

Once you open `viewDidLoad`, set the `UIImage` to *PIC02* (recall that you already set the First View to *PIC01* in Interface Builder), you want to set the content, the image, to be placed in scale to the bottom of the view. This is a mistake, of course, and functions as the bug that you will track down later in the example. This error doesn't exist in my app's source code (and you didn't insert it in Chapter 6), so we can use my app to track down the problem by comparing the files.

This bug will not generate an error, but it will look "off" when you run it, just odd enough to serve as a situation where you can efficiently find the bug you inserted and change it to the correct code. The code inside `viewDidLoad` is as follows:

```
- (void)viewDidLoad
{
    [super viewDidLoad];

    [myImage setImage:[UIImage imageNamed:@"PIC02"]];
    [myImage setContentMode: UIViewContentModeScaleAspectFit;];
}
```

So, we will now pretend that "unbeknownst to you," `UIViewContentModeScaleAspectFit` is just going to make your life miserable. There will be shouting in the streets, children will be separated from their mothers, people will stop calling you a geek, and you will go to the forum at `bit.ly/oLVwpY` crying, "What happened to my code!?"

Just pretend, OK?

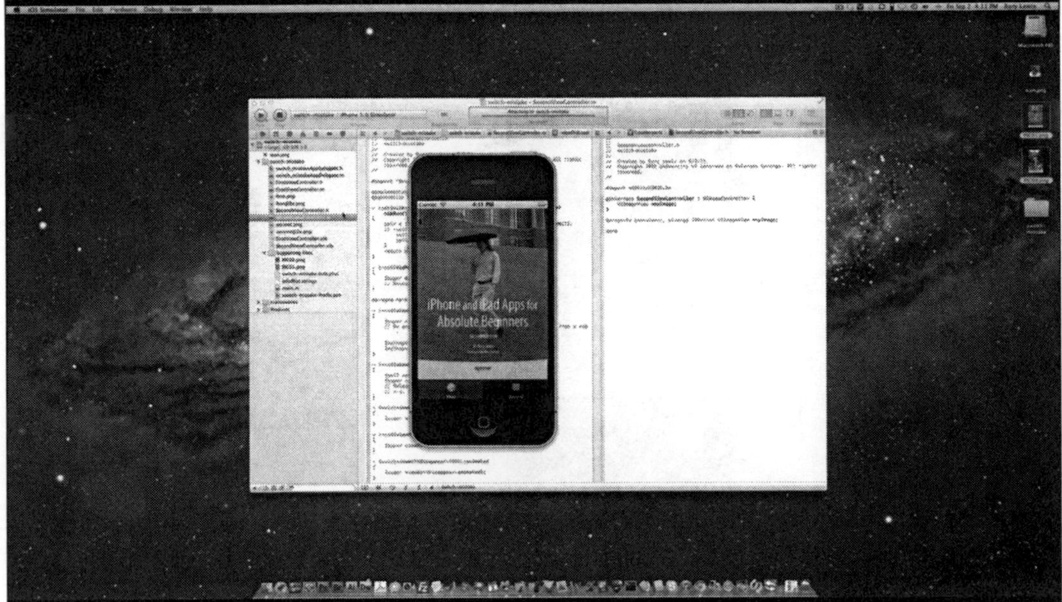

Figure 8–20. *Let's run it!*

20. As depicted in Figure 8–20, when we run the app and view the First View, all is well. But, then...

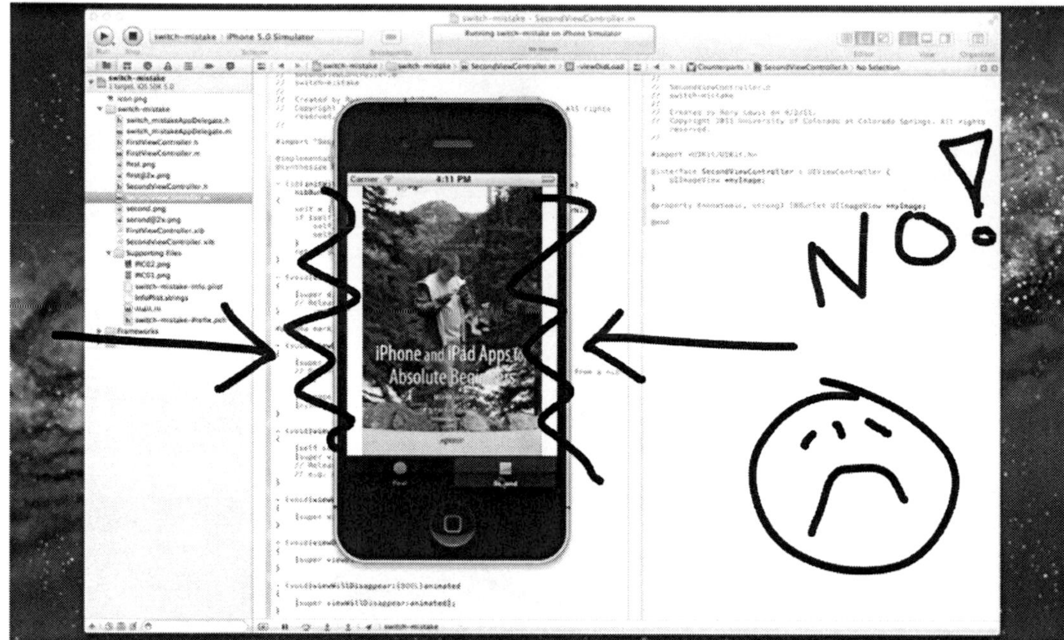

Figure 8–21. *Uh-oh! We have a problem, Houston!*

21. You have only ten minutes left to hand this assignment to Dr. Lewis. With the Second View looking like this, you know your app will get a D. What will you do? (See Figure 8–21.)

Comparing the Source Files

Now, you are going to look at the online code to see where you went wrong by comparing your code with that of the online project.

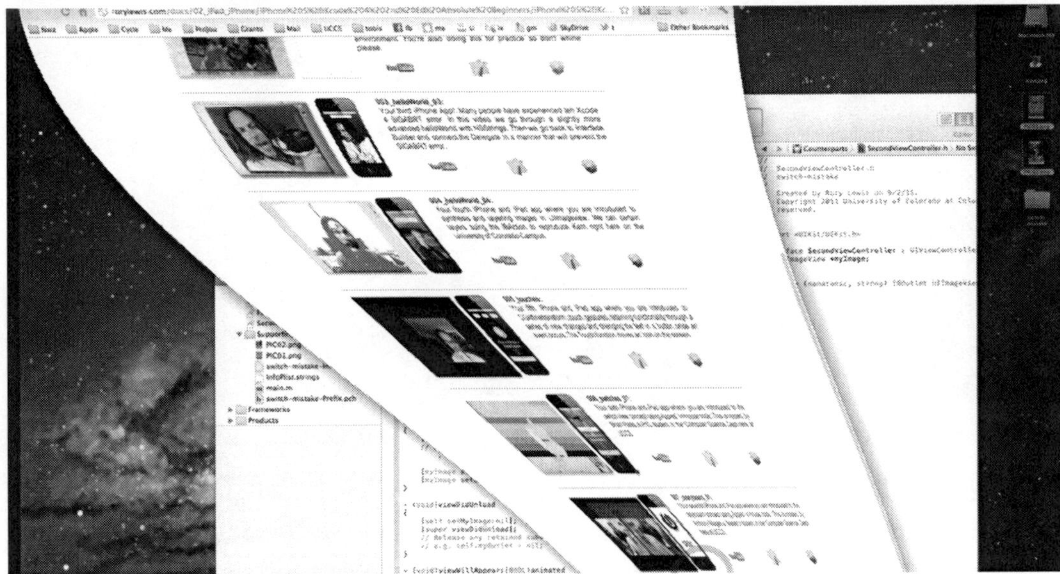

Figure 8–22. *Go to Dr. Lewis's website with all the downloads.*

22. To download the source code, go to `bit.ly/oEQcu6`. In the video, I kept my browser minimized, so Figure 8–22 shows me maximizing my browser.

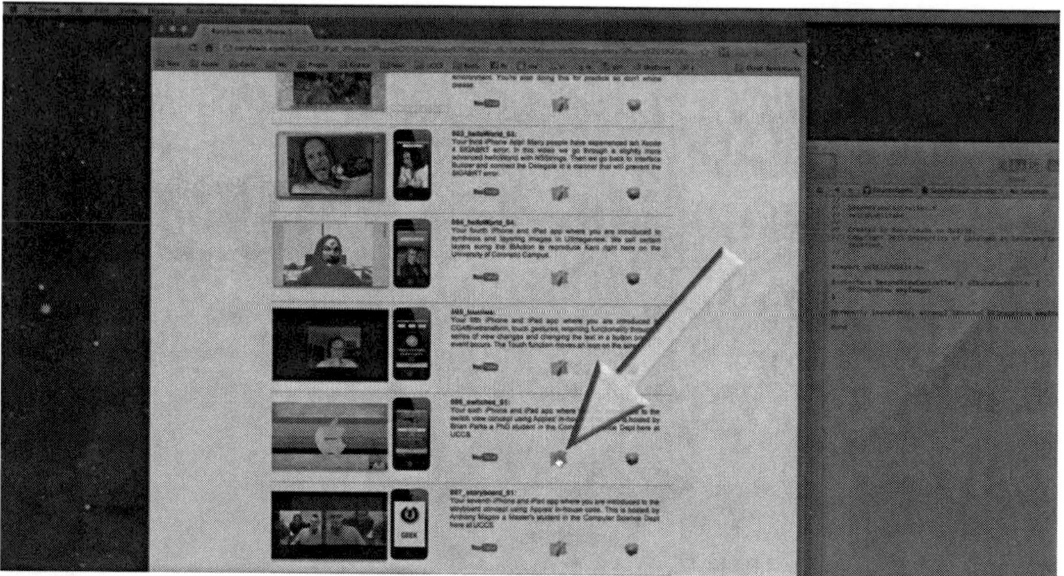

Figure 8–23. *Download the source code here.*

23. As shown in Figure 8–23, after going to `bit.ly/oEQcu6`, click the Xcode icon to download the source code to your desktop. What you are thinking here is that if you compare your code to the source code, you can find and fix the bug. Simple enough with this file, but what if you were trying to find the problem in 30,000 lines of source code? You would not be able to just eyeball it to find the error. Let's see how to get around that problem.

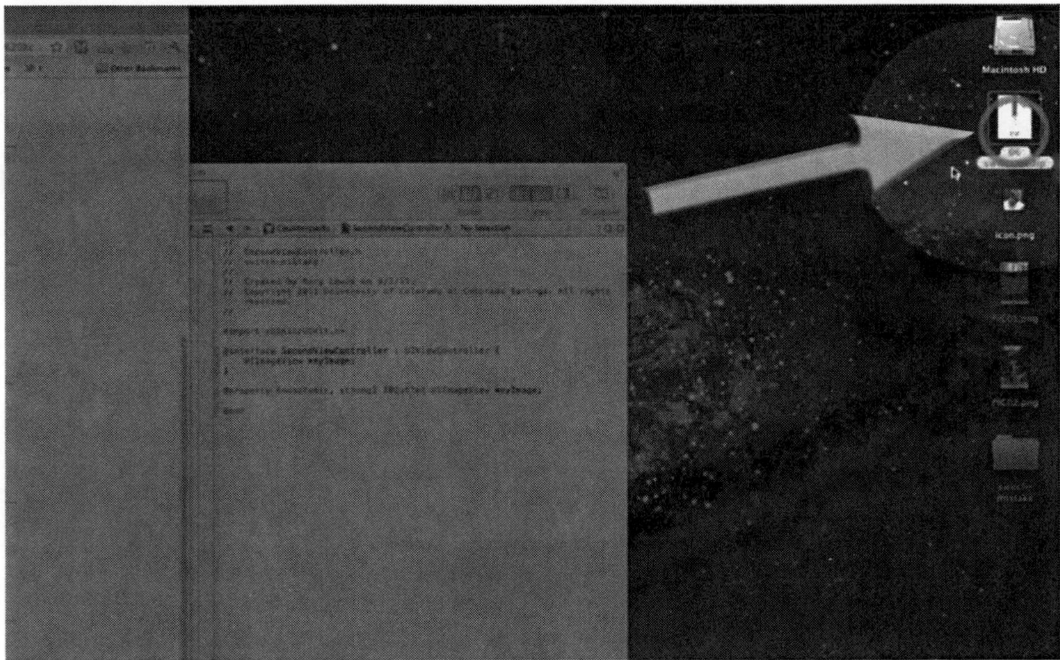

Figure 8–24. *Unzip the source code.*

24. As shown in Figure 8–24, when the source code arrives, preferably to your desktop, unzip it and open the folder.

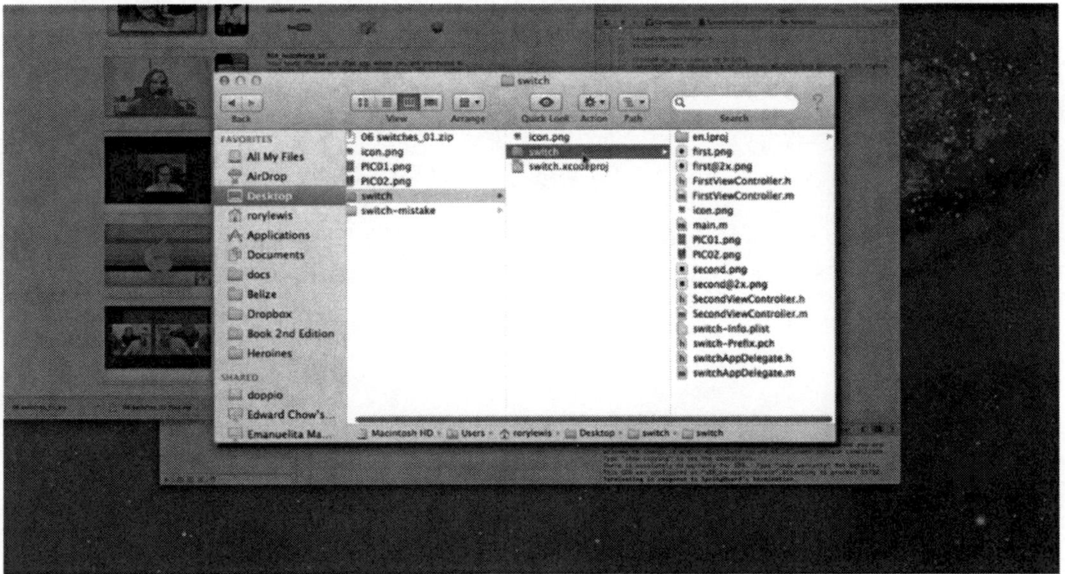

Figure 8–25. *Open the folder so you can see the* `SecondViewController.m` *file.*

25. After you have unzipped the folder containing the source code, you just want to keep it there for now. Make sure you have your eye on the target, which is the `SecondViewController.m` file, as illustrated in Figure 8–25.

Figure 8–26. *Open a new Finder window.*

26. As shown in Figure 8–26, you need to locate `FileMerge.app`. Press ⌘N to open a new window, because you need to keep the other folder containing the source code open. That way, you will be able to drag that `SecondViewController.m` file into `FileMerge.app` when you locate it inside this window.

Figure 8–27. *Go to the Developer tool.*

27. You need to go to the *Developer* tool to start navigating your way to `FileMerge.app`, so hit ⌘⇧G, enter "/Developer" in the pop up, and hit ↩, as shown in Figure 8–27.

Figure 8–28. *Navigate to* `FileMerge.app`*.*

28. Once in the Developer folder, navigate to *Applications* ➤ *Utilities* and open `FileMerge.app`, as shown in Figure 8–28.

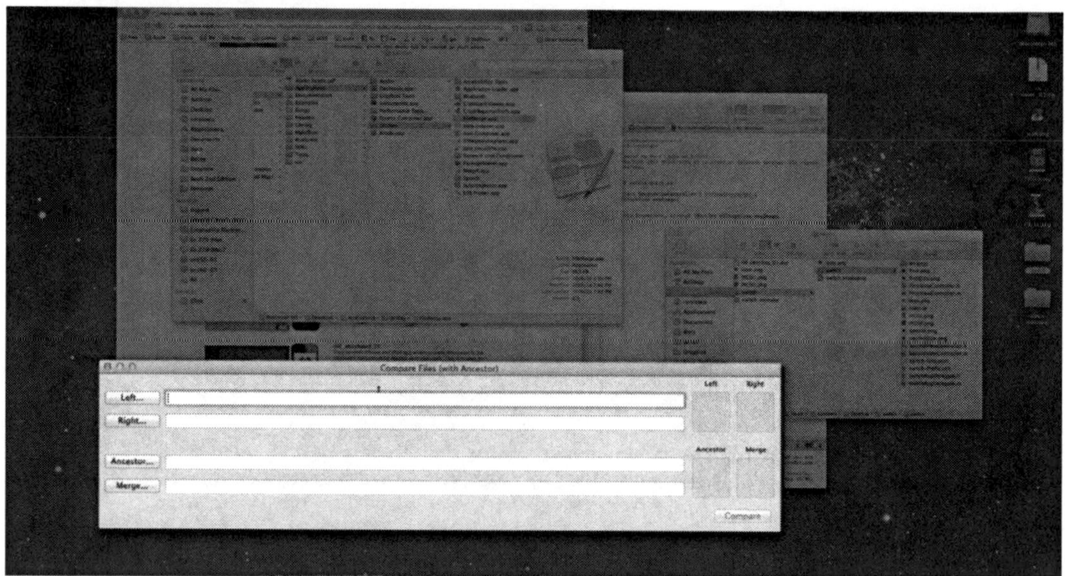

Figure 8–29. ***`FileMerge.app` opened***

29. `FileMerge.app` does not have the spark and flare that one might have imagined. It seems benign, but it does the job. Essentially, you want to drag your `SecondViewController.m` file location into the *Left* panel, and then the correct source code into the *Right* panel. The opened `FileMerge.app` is seen in Figure 8–29.

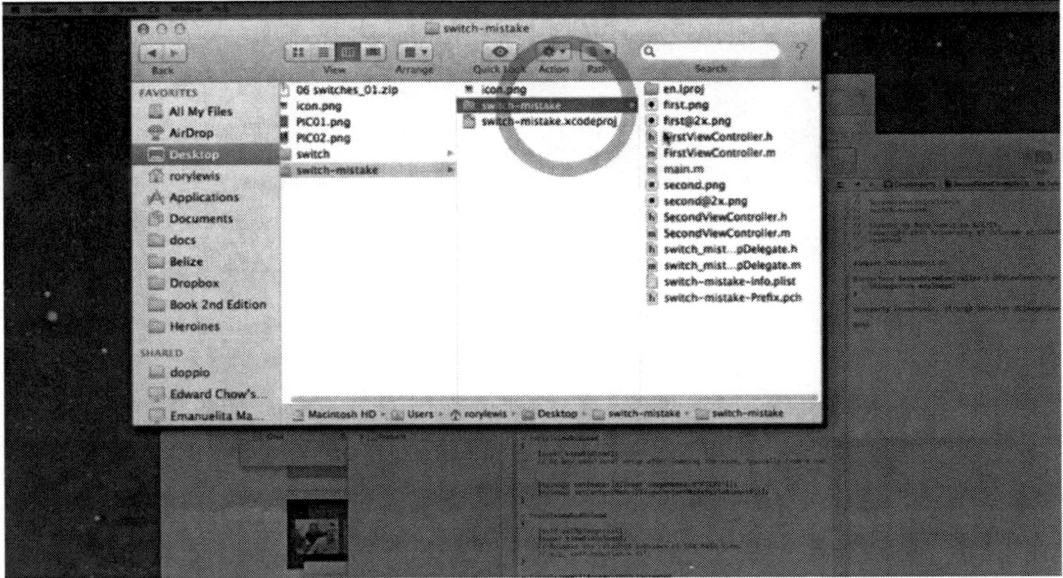

Figure 8–30. *Open your folder containing the Second View Controller.*

30. Figure 8–30 illustrates the opened folder containing your `SecondViewController` file. You need to drag your code into `FileMerge`, so open the folder containing your code. Select the `SecondViewController` file and drag it into `FileMerge.app`.

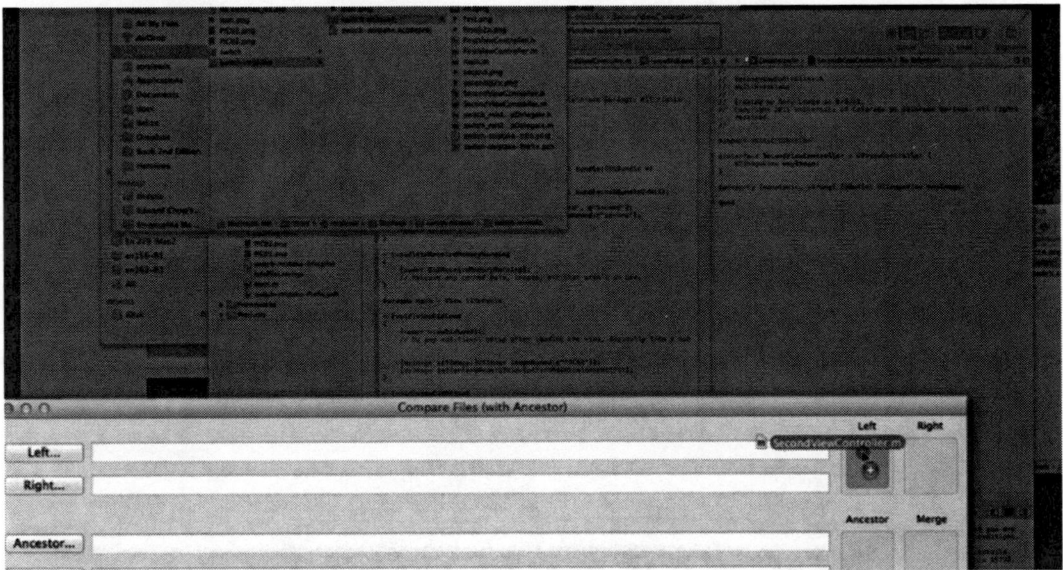

Figure 8–31. *Dragging your `SecondViewController.m` into the Left panel of `FileMerge.app`*

31. Figure 8–31 shows the `SecondViewController.m` being dragged into the Left panel of `FileMerge.app`. Do it.

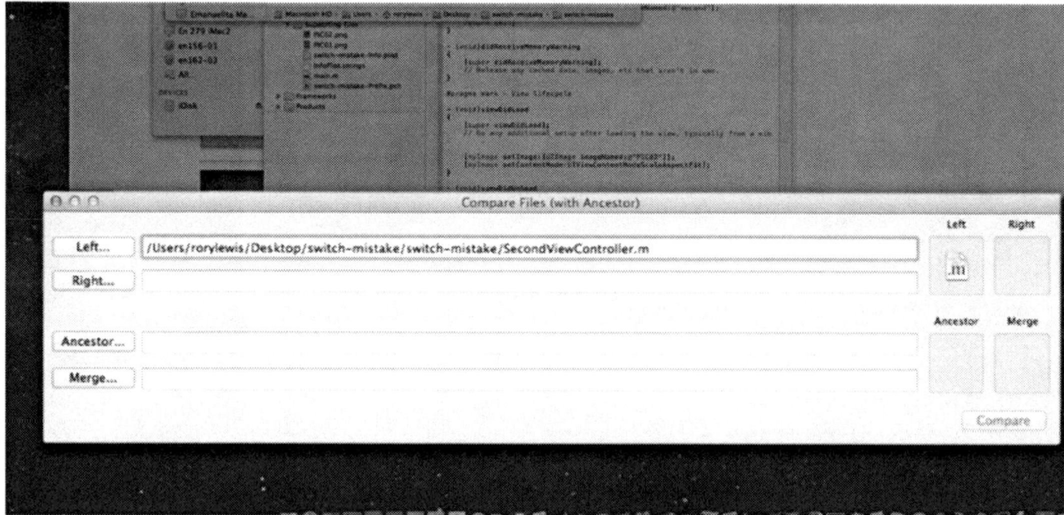

Figure 8–32. *`SecondViewController.m` properly located in the Left panel*

32. As shown in Figure 8–32, when you drag `SecondViewController.m` into the Left panel, it pulls out the address. Now, you need to pull the correct source code into the Right panel.

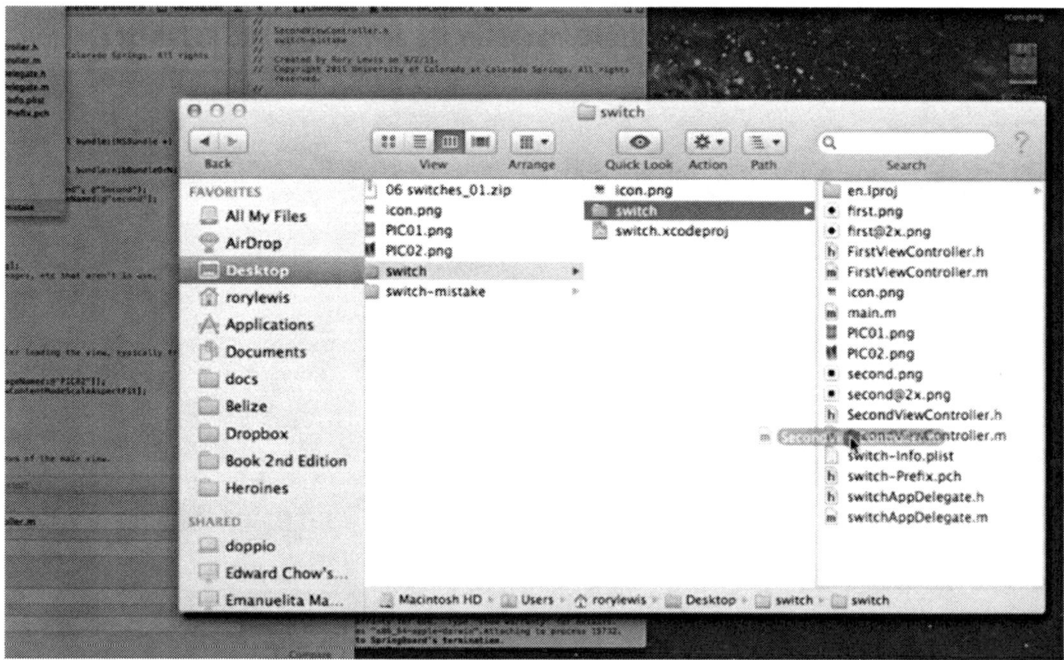

Figure 8–33. *Start dragging the correct source code into `FileMerge.app`.*

33. Now, drag the correct source code from the unzipped folder that I made you keep open into `FileMerge.app`. This is shown in Figure 8–33.

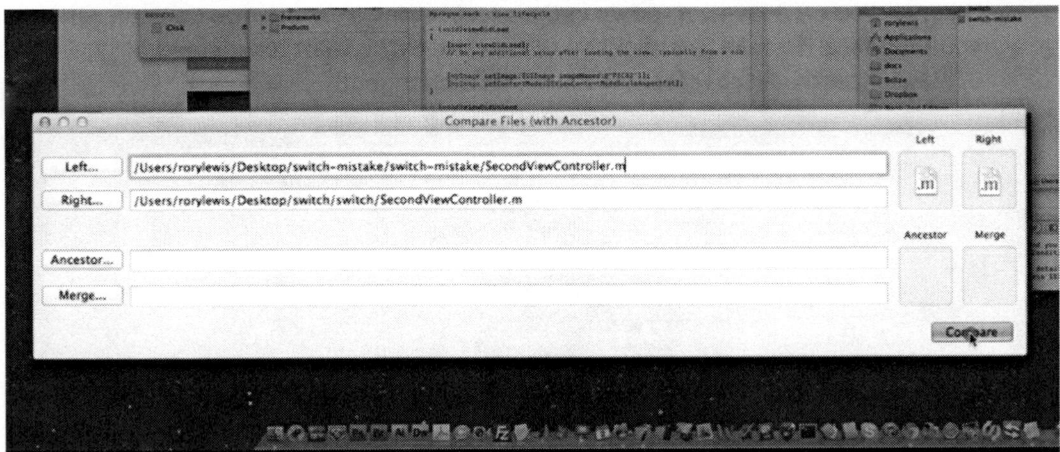

Figure 8–34. *Compare.*

34. Figure 8–34 shows both files correctly located in `FileMerge.app`. Click *Compare* or hit ↩ to get it working.

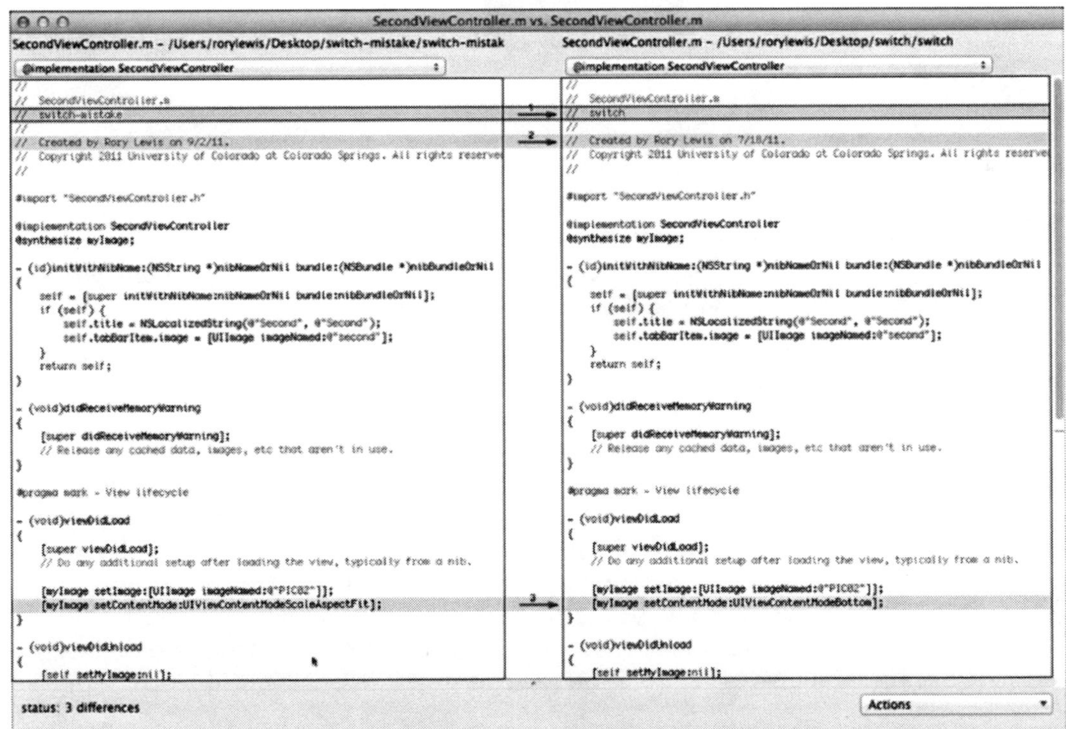

Figure 8–35. `FileMerge.app` *doing its thing.*

35. As you can see in Figure 8–35, once `FileMerge` opens there are some lines of text that clearly will be different, such as your name and my name, your date and my date, and so on. However, down in the `viewDidLoad` method, you can see where you made the mistake. It should be `UIViewContentModeBottom` instead of `UIViewContentModeScaleAspectFit`. So, let's change it!

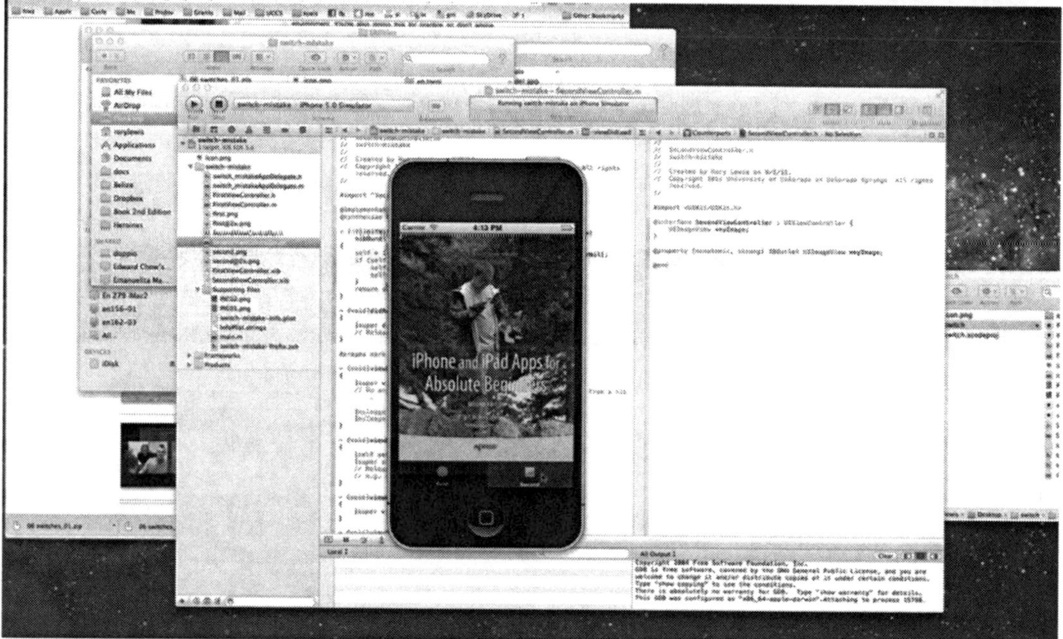

Figure 8–36. *All is well!*

36. Once you have gone back into Xcode and correctly changed `UIViewContentModeScaleAspectFit` to `UIViewContentModeBottom`, your app will run perfectly, as shown in Figure 8–36.

Digging the Code

The most-used tool in Xcode, by far, is setting breakpoints in the Xcode editor. Running your application and then seeing the state of your code at each breakpoint can illustrate if a variable is being recognized, what it's returning, and so forth. Breakpoints are very powerful. To add a breakpoint at a line, double-click in the gutter of your code (located to the left of that line), hold it, and click the "+" button. Check the *Continue* checkbox if you don't want the debugger to actually stop code execution at that breakpoint. Teaching breakpoints is described in many more advanced Apress Xcode books, such as *Pro iOS 5 Tools*, shown in Figure 8–37.

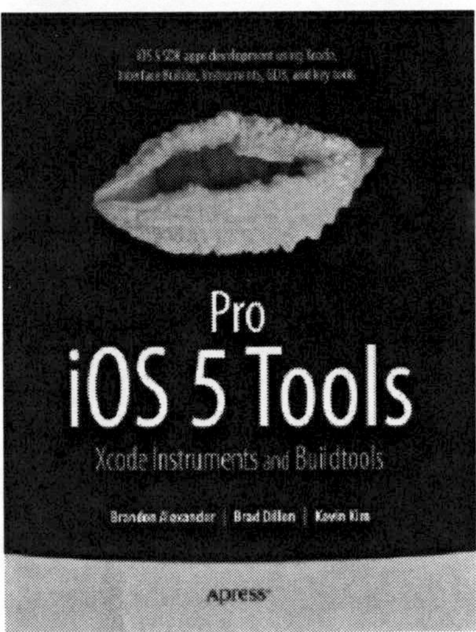

Figure 8–37. *Pro iOS 5 Tools*

Pro iOS 5 Tools goes in depth into the subjects of the following review, such as the Debugger Console, LLVM, and Organize. For now though, here is a brief overview that glosses over more advanced tools that are not in the domain of this Absolute Beginner book.

Debugger Console

The next most important and widely used coder's tool is the Debugger Console window. It is an efficient way for coders to communicate with the GDB. You can go to the console window in Xcode from the *Run* menu by pressing ⌘⇧R. You can also choose *Edit Active Scheme* from the Scheme pop-up to select either the LLVM compiler or the GDB under *Run item* in the left column. I prefer the LLVM compiler, because that's where all the new Fix-it red flags do their job (see the next section). For most of the code in this book, the LLVM will be adequate. Nonetheless, if you still would like to use GDB, then go to the Info panel and choose the debugger you want to use from the Debugger pop-up menu. To view output and type commands for GDB, first make sure that your output window is open, and then make sure the middle bottom of the View group is enabled.

Fix-it

Assuming that you will stay with the LLVM compiler, Fix-it scans your source text as you type and marks syntax errors with a red underscore and a red flag in your gutter. You can read the Fix-it message by clicking the symbol, and it will provide you with the reasons why it thinks you have a possible syntax error. Often, on smaller errors, Fix-it repairs your code automatically.

Documentation

The next tool that I see being widely used because of its easy access is Xcode's documentation. All you do is open the *Organizer* window (⌘⇧2), click the *Documentation* button located in the toolbar, and then click the jump bar to navigate up and down. See Figure 8–38.

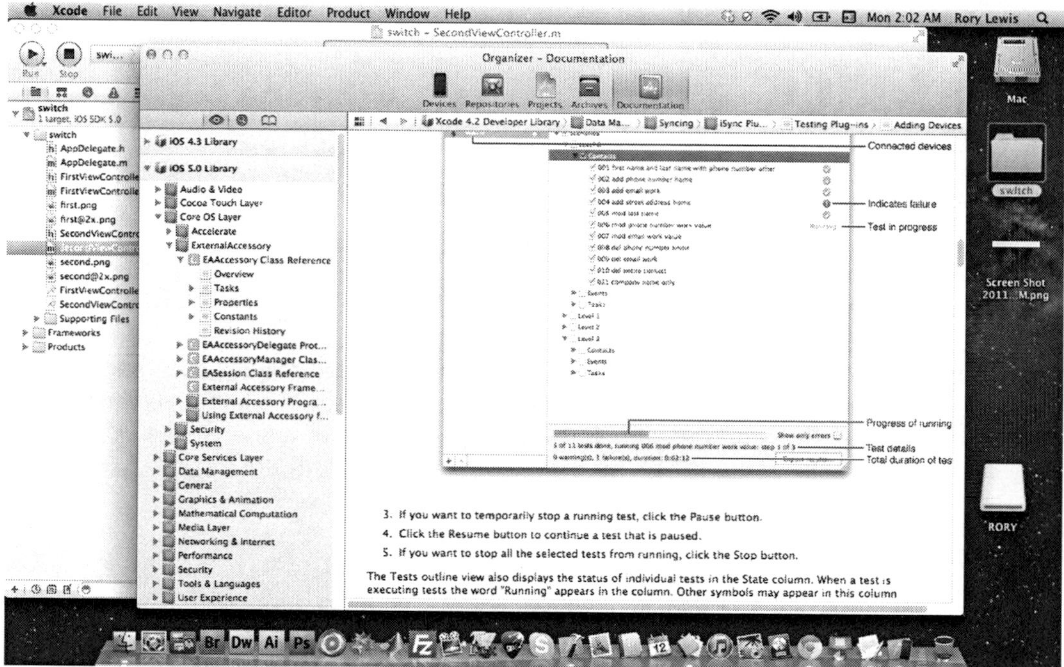

Figure 8–38. *Organizer*

Xcode 4.2 also provides online help for the Xcode IDE. This can be accessed by clicking on the disclosure triangle next to Xcode Help in the documentation navigator or by choosing **Help ➤ Xcode Help.** You will find that most of these online help documents come along with a video. You will also want to know that many of the Xcode's help articles are also available as contextual help, as explained at the Apple site here: `bit.ly/oY2jG9`. What this means is that the help tutorials can be reached from the shortcut menus by control-clicking any of the main UI areas in the workspace or Organizer window.

Quick Help in Xcode 4.2 and onward is more powerful than it ever was. At this stage, we just plough through our tutorials, but you will find it useful as you evolve as a programmer. Option-single-click to open Quick Help, as illustrated in Figure 8–39.

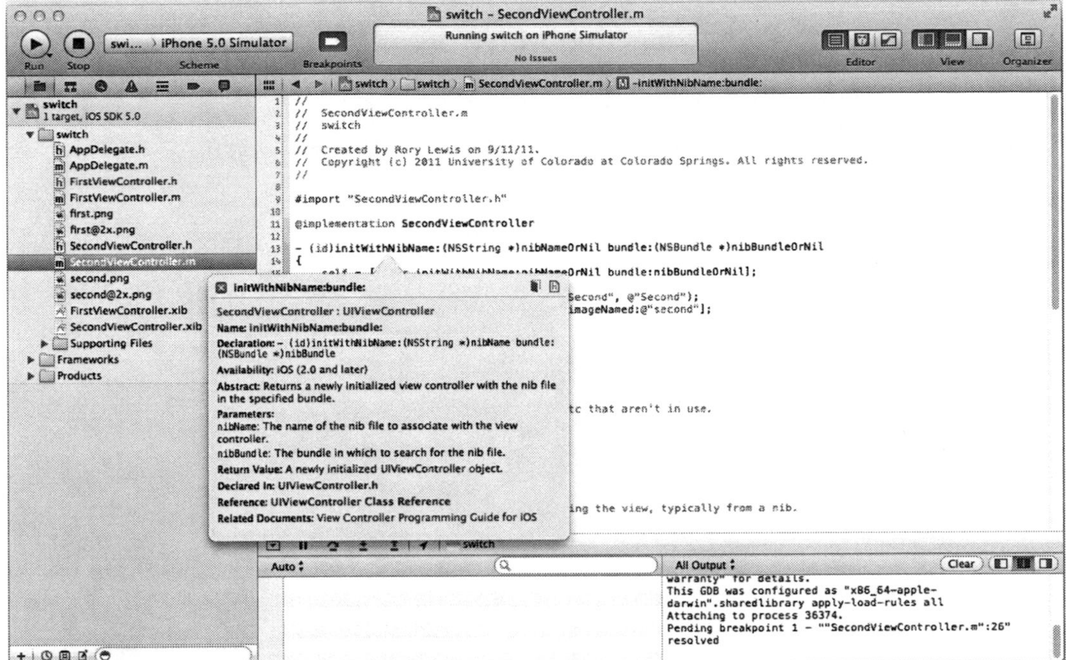

Figure 8–39. *Quick Help*

Static Analysis

Static analysis in Xcode 4.2 allows you to perform analysis on, debug, and edit your code within the workspace window. Simply click the project you want to debug in your project navigator and then choose **Product ➤ Analyze**. The analyzer grinds through your code, and then the navigator opens with a list of the issues it located. Blue rectangles with arrows will point you to your bugs.

In the Chapter Ahead

In Chapter 9, you will experience learning to code an app for iPhone and iPad that combines two potent iOS 5 tools: storyboarding and MapKits. It's a simple app that has massive teaching and learning curves behind it. The app you will build simply has a pin drop on a previously disclosed longitudinal and latitudinal location. The important aspect is linking up storyboarding and MapKits.

Chapter 9

MapKit & Storyboarding

I have been looking forward to writing this chapter on the MapKit framework and Storyboarding since I first conceived this book. This and the next two chapters will represent the culmination of our work together. Our journey is almost over and it is fitting that we finish with a bang. I am confident that integrating the MapKit framework, Storyboarding, TableViews, and iTunes will not disappoint you. This is not a trivial matter. Our journey over the last three chapters will be as follows: Chapter 9 will be Storyboarding and the MapKit framework. Chapter 10 will be Storyboarding, TableViews, and the MapKit framework. Finally, in Chapter 11, we will tackle Storyboarding and the iTunes stores (the place where you will place your apps). We will get more into Chapter 11 later, but suffice to say, I will show you how the most compelling apps incorporate Storyboarding, the MapKit framework, TableViews, and the Internet/iTunes store.

In this chapter, we will see that some of the coolest and most successful apps are based on the MapKit framework. We will place this framework on top of the Storyboarding platform and doing so will represent a tremendous accomplishment. The major reason I saved these concepts for last is that the topics require some experience to not overwhelm the student. Teaching this course to a lecture hall full of eager, and mostly novice, programmers, I learned the hard way that when I succumbed to the students' enthusiasm and tried to teach MapKit midway through the semester, I invariably led the entire class into a brick wall.

Even though MapKit provides us the means to write powerful and vivid apps, it also demands that we be quite aware of and fully understand methods, classes, and frameworks. Incorporating this application with Storyboarding further compounds this challenge. Originally, the scope of this book didn't include all of those concepts; but in the end, there was no way I could write the book and leave out MapKit!

So, before we begin, we need to sit back and look at a few things. MapKit, as a toolbox, is a challenging set of utilities and devices, but we will cover some of the basics and learn how we can use them with Storyboarding to successfully and creatively navigate the example in this chapter. We will first talk about *frameworks* and *classes*. Then, we will see what MapKit can already do without us having to program anything at all. After that, we will dig deeper to see what other programmers have done using MapKit and we will glean what we can from them. We've already looked at Storyboarding; but now we want to add some truly innovative code. After honing our understanding of methods, and once we have acquired a respectable grasp of frameworks, classes, and other Apple goodies contained in MapKit, we'll gently tackle the exercise.

In the latter half of the chapter, I will serve an extended dessert in the "Digging My Students' MapKit Code" section. Rather than finishing with an eclectic mix of technical references, I will present three of my students' efforts in MapKit–related projects. I am hopeful that when we look at what these representative students were able to accomplish very shortly after they passed my class, we will all feel even more inspired to set our course for the next challenge.

My objective is to get us all to a place where we can say: *I have programmed a basic iPad MapKit app with Storyboarding, and I understand how to move forward with confidence into the more advanced goal of coordinating Storyboarding, TableViews, and the MapKit framework in Chapter 10.*

A Little about Frameworks

When Steve Jobs was fired from Apple, he formed a business called NeXT. In the early '90s, his company produced beautiful, black, streamlined computers that made me drool with envy. A few of my professors owned a NeXT computer and I was aware of their capabilities. The most profound aspect of this outfit was not that they cranked out these black, streamlined boxes, but rather that they utilized a language called Objective–C. Jobs had found that, even though it was difficult to program in this complex language, the code it produced was able to "talk to" the microprocessor quite elegantly. So, what does this have to do with MapKit?

What NeXT did was create *frameworks* of complex Objective–C code, which we can regard much like the tools that a carpenter might have in his toolbox. When we use MapKit, we are bringing into our own code a framework of map–related tools—just as a carpenter may have one set of tools for cabinetry and another specially made set specifically for making intricate furniture. These specialized tools will differ significantly from the type of tools that a roofing carpenter might use.

To this end, we will bring two frameworks into Xcode that we have not used before. It will be almost as if we had been learning techniques as a flooring and cabinetry carpenter in Chapters 1–8; however, today we are going to the hardware store to get outfitted for our next gig, which will be audio–video installations in walls and ceilings. Therefore, before we continue on to the next program, we are going to have to go buy two brand–new tools. One of our new tools, the CoreLocation framework, shows us where we are geographically. The other tool, MapKit, enables us to interact with maps in a number of different of ways.

As we know, the way users interact with the iPad and iPhone is completely unlike anything ever seen before. Before the advent of these slick devices, 99% of all interactions with computers were based upon the mouse and a keyboard. As we have been learning from the examples we already programmed, we have used unique methods and classes to jump between screens and to sense when a user is pinching, tapping, or scrolling on the screen. To this already formidable set of tools, we are now going to add CoreLocation and MapKit frameworks.

Most of the programming we have explored up until now has been relatively transparent. However, in this chapter, it won't be quite so perceptible. We will have to really maintain our concentration in order to keep track of and understand how MapKit knows where we are on a map. We'll examine how it follows our finger interactions and how it knows where we are in terms of the various screens and views associated with maps.

One of the central areas of iPad/iPhone app development is *event handling*. Since this section confused many of my previous students, I will consciously do my best to keep us all focused on what we need to know from this area. If we get a firm grasp of the concepts of frameworks and classes, we will not be burdened by being overly concerned with event handling. We can get an idea of the scale of this topic by considering that while part of our app is keeping track of interacting both with a map and a GPS satellite, another portion of our code has to always be looking at when the user is going to direct the program to a new event.

Important Things to Know

There are three important things to know about the foundation of Storyboard and map–related applications in the iPad and iPhone arena. These two critical apps in Chapter 9 and 10 rely on four important tools: Storyboarding, MapKit, CoreLocation, and the `MKAnnotationView` class reference. As I have already indicated, we are not going to involve ourselves with how these sophisticated tools work so much as we are going to practice the art of deciding *when* to reach for *which* tool in our newly expanded toolbox.

Among other things, these tools allow us to effortlessly create a beautiful flow of technology with Storyboarding, display maps in our applications, use annotations, work with Geocoding (which works with longitude and latitude), and interact with our location (via CoreLocation).

When we want to interact effortlessly with Google Maps, we will use the Apple–provided MapKit framework. When we want to obtain our location or do cool things using GPS–satellite technology (with Google Maps)—we will use the CoreLocation framework. When we want to put it all together and seamlessly integrate with our user—we will take all the aforementioned technology and place it onto Storyboarding. Finally, when we want to place pins on a map, create references, draw chevron marks, or insert an image of our dog showing where he is on a map—we will call these *annotations* and, thus, use `MKAnnotationView`.

Preinstalled MapKit Apps

In order to take maximum advantage of the new ideas presented in this chapter, and be prepared to stretch and expand into a new level of creativity, we will first take a tour of the existing apps, preinstalled on the iPad and iPhone. It is important that we become familiar with these so that we can more easily add bells and whistles to our own creations—and that is on top of these ready–made "map apps," as described at `Apple.com`.

Find Yourself

Say we're in an unfamiliar neighborhood looking for a nearby restaurant. With iPhone, we can pinpoint our location on a map so we can figure out how to get there from where we are. iPhone 4 finds our location quickly and accurately using a combination of GPS, Wi–Fi, and cellular towers. As we move, iPhone automatically updates our location. When we arrive, we can drop a pin to mark our location and share it with others via email or MMS.

Figure 9–1. *Find yourself—a powerful zooming map function on the iPhone/iPad.*

Search for a location

We need a shot of espresso. Where's the nearest cafe? iPhone with the MapKit framework has the answer. Just type "coffee" in the search field within Maps and suddenly nearby coffee houses appear on the map; all represented by pins. Searching works with specific addresses and business names, too. When we find what we're looking for, we tap the pin to bring up more information, such as phone numbers, web addresses, and more. The "pin" extracts all the annotations we programmed in our MKAnnotationView.

Figure 9–2. *Search for a location—use this in conjunction with, or in lieu of, the visual map (with highlighted route).*

Change the view. See traffic

Maps on iPhone 4 look amazingly crisp and detailed on the high-resolution Retina display. We can switch between map view, satellite view, and hybrid view. We can even see a street view of a particular address. We can double-tap or pinch to zoom in and out on a map. Maps on iPhone also provide us with live traffic information, as well as indicating traffic speed along our route in easy-to-read green, yellow, and red highlights.

Figure 9–3. *Change the view and see traffic—shows the orientation with built–in compass (on Model 3GS) directions that indicate which way we are looking.*

We can forget printing out directions from our computer. With iPhone, we can view a list of turn–by–turn directions or follow a highlighted map route and track our progress with GPS. We can choose to see walking or driving directions, or even see what time the next train or bus leaves with public transit directions. The Compass app works with the built–in digital compass to tell us which direction our iPhone is facing. In addition, in the Maps app, the compass rotates the onscreen map to match the direction we're facing.

Figure 9–4. *Directions and seeing what direction we're facing—one of the many possibilities when running 'Maps' on iPhone/iPad.*

Figure 9–5. *FlightTrack uses the MapKit framework to track flights and then integrates with gate changes, schedules, and the rest of the personal data on any given ticket.*

Cool and Popular MapKit Apps Inspire Us

A funny thing happened along the way to teaching MapKits and Storyboarding to my students: Most thought they knew what MapKits were but actually, they had no idea how awesome the MapKit framework really was. So, before we dive into this chapter, we will take a few minutes to learn about the fantastic features of the MapKit framework.

> **CASE IN POINT:** One of my former students recently started working at Apple on iOS 5. She did exceptionally well in MapKits and, of all the departments within iOS 5 that she could have worked in, they placed her in the MapKit framework. One of the first things she told me was how huge this division was and how even though she loved MapKits—she had no idea that so many teams with so many incredibly intelligent people were all working on one thing: MapKits!

I found that it really helped my students when, after showing them the prebuilt apps, we spent some time reviewing some super-cool third-party MapKit apps—to inspire them and get their brains storming. So, imagine you are sitting with us and taking this brief tour as well. Here are 11 MapKit apps that caught my eye, some of which I use regularly.

- **FlightTrack:** This MapKit app lets us manage every aspect of our domestic and international flights with real-time updates and beautiful, zoomable maps. We can receive updates on gates, delays, and cancellations so we can book an alternate flight. The app covers more than 5000 airports and 1400 airlines. See Figure 9–5.
- **Metro Paris Subway:** Never get lost in the City of Light. Metro Paris Subway is a comprehensive guide to traveling through Paris, including official metro, RER, and bus maps and schedules. Complete with an interactive map and route planner, Metro Paris Subway will have us navigating like a real Parisian in no time. See Figure 9–6.
- **MapMyRide:** I use this MapKit app all the time. I simply turn it on and start riding around on my bike. It tracks my speed, time, and mileage, as well as the incline. It takes into account my age, gender, and body weight; then it tells me how many calories I burned. (On a good day, I can burn off two doughnuts!) The point is, this application calculates all these things while I'm just riding along huffing and puffing! When I get home, I can see the route on my computer. It does most of its work by using and manipulating preinstalled MapKit apps.
- **QuikMaps:** This do-it-yourself map app allows you to doodle on the map. It integrates with a number of places, including your website, Google Earth, or even your GPS.

- **360 Cities: The World In Virtual Reality:** This shows 360–degree panoramas of over 50 world cities and 6000 panoramas. It is the perfect technology for real estate agents, tour guides, and adventurers.
- **Cool Maps: 7 Wonders of the World:** This shows the seven wonders of the ancient world, and the seven wonders of the modern world, including natural wonders, underwater wonders, strange wonders, and local wonders. I am very impressed with how slick the programmers have made the touch and feel of the app.
- **Blipstar:** This app converts Internet business URL addresses to their corresponding brick–and–mortar stores and presents it all on a cool map.
- **Twitter Spy:** This app lets people see where the person who is tweeting them is currently located. Yep—wacky and crazy, but true.
- **Geo IP Tool:** This app displays the longitude and latitude information of businesses on the Web. Then it provides us with a choice of the best ways to get there.
- **Map Tunneling Tool:** This one is just clever fun. Imagine where we would come out if we began digging a hole straight down—from wherever. *Is the answer always China?*
- **Tall Eye:** This app shows you where you will go if you walk directly, in a straight line, around the earth, starting at one point and staying on a specific bearing all the way around.

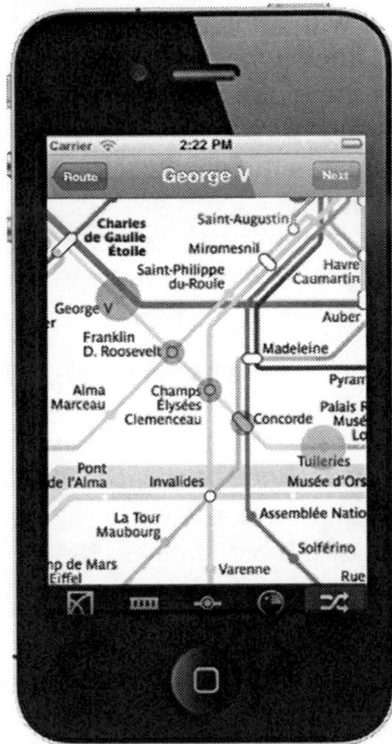

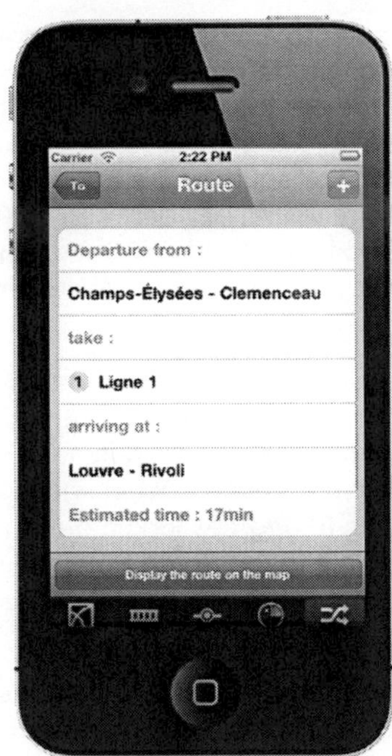

Figure 9–6. *Metro Paris Subway: Parsing GPS data from the trains in the subways helps us to know when a train going in our direction will appear at the nearest train station.*

myStory_01: A Single–View Application

In this exercise, we are going to begin with some boilerplate code and splash screens and icons that suit our basic requirements. Then, we will modify it from there. We will tour some of the same building blocks and files that we've seen throughout this book, and we will be challenged to see what areas of the code are pretty much the same as what we've already encountered and what areas are different—given the nature of this application.

The ability to recognize patterns and see structures just under the surface is a powerful aptitude that we all have, but we programmers cultivate ours to a heightened degree. We will play a little game to see if we can anticipate some of the moves we will have to take.

Possible Prepping for the App

We are going to consider a wide variety of components that we will use to build in to our app. Before that, though, I want to make sure we all have a firm grasp of some important terminology. For this project, we programmers need to recall some basic earth science and geography so that our code will be as effective as possible.

When we direct the computer to animate a pin dropping down, with annotations, onto a specific location, giving "longitude" and "latitude," we need to know what these terms really mean. *Lines of latitude* are the imaginary lines that circle the globe "horizontally," running east to west (or west to east). These invisible lines are measured in degrees, minutes, and seconds, north or south of the Equator. The Equator is the elliptical locus of points on the Earth's surface midway between the poles, which physically are *real* points—defined by the Earth's rotation on its axis. Lines of latitude are often referred to as parallels. The North Pole is 90 degrees north latitude; the South Pole is 90 degrees south latitude.

Lines of longitude, often called meridians, are imaginary "vertical" lines (ellipses) that cross through the North and South Poles. They are also measured in degrees, minutes, and seconds, east or west of the Prime Meridian, an arbitrary standard that runs through Greenwich, England. Unlike the Equator, which goes all the way around the world—360 degrees, the Prime Meridian (0 degrees longitude) is a semi-circle (semi-ellipse), extending from the North Pole to the South Pole; the other half of the arc is called the International Date Line, and it is defined as 180 degrees east and/or 180 degrees west longitude.

For our Chapter 9 app, the example I used to demonstrate the "pin drop" on location is my office at the University of Colorado at Colorado Springs. We, of course, can use any location we choose. We may want to use our own address, or a well-known landmark. To do this, we must get the latitude and longitude values of that location—most likely from Google Maps or a direct GPS reading. There are many sites on the Internet where we can find these coordinates; Figure 9–7 illustrates one of them, `http://bit.ly/vGszNu`.

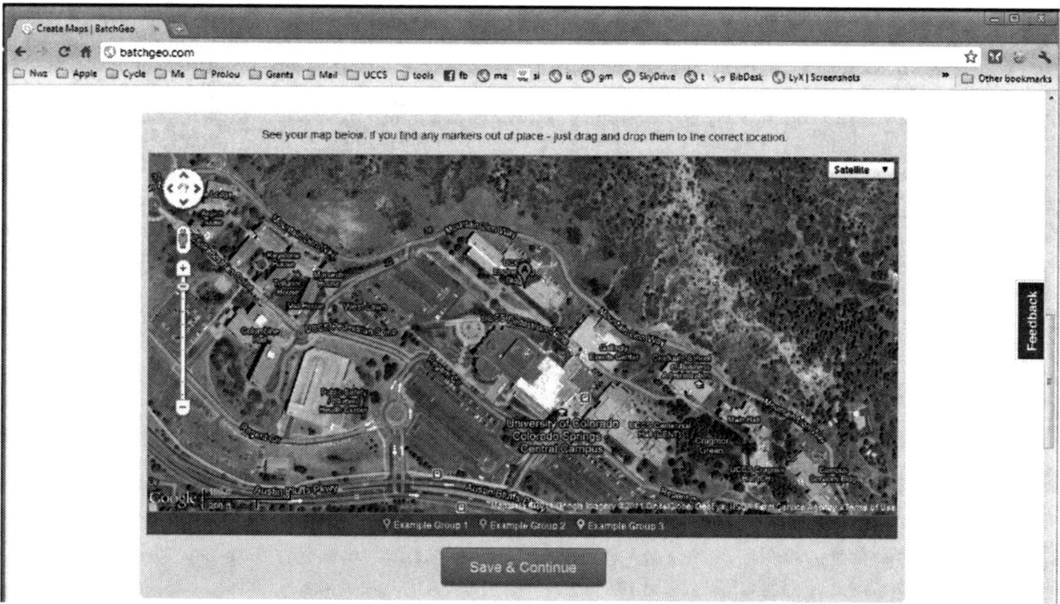

Figure 9–7. *Batchgeo (www.batchgeocode.com/lookup) is one of many Internet sites where one can enter an address and receive its longitudinal and latitudinal coordinates.*

Here's a thought—let's start to the end of our process and think backwards for a minute. Go ahead and jump forward in this chapter for a sneak peek at what the app will look like—what results it will return if all goes well. In Figure 9–34, we see a picture of a hybrid map showing a red pin that's sitting on top of a building. That's the Engineering Building at the University of Colorado at Colorado Springs; the pin is located right above my office. The next picture has what we call an *annotation*, which is the text. "Dr. Rory Lewis" is the title, and "University of Colorado at Colorado Springs" is the subtitle.

Later in the tutorial, we will see that we need to be careful about the title and the subtitle. We also control the color of the pin and we decide on the style of animation—how the pin drops onto the map image.

This is a good place for a reminder of the title of this book: *iPhone and iPad Apps for Absolute Beginners*. Take a deep breath! Even if we were all meeting our greatest expectations of learning the most we ever have and even if we were all meeting our greatest expectations of ourselves—learning so much complexity in such a short time, we would still *not* be an expert in this challenging area of MapKit code! At this point, my humble goal is not fluency, but reasonable familiarity and a sense of what lies ahead.

If that sounds right, let's get on with it.

Preliminaries

As in previous chapters, please download and extract images and boilerplate code for this chapter. Navigate to http://bit.ly/oDqzvY and download its contents. The images include three icon files, two splash screens, and two files of boilerplate code. Later, I will explain what these icons, splash screens, and boilerplates mean. Right now though, we will just download it to our desktop. Then, we will extract the files onto our beautifully clean desktop.

Sample code that I programmed on the video is available for download here: http://bit.ly/qd6iDT. After extracting all the files, remember to delete the `011_myStory_01.zip` and `myStory_01` folders. This is to avoid overwriting files and/or potential conflicts with the exercise code. To view the screencast of this chapter's exercise, go to http://bit.ly/owk24r.

A New Single View Template

Let's get started and choose the template.

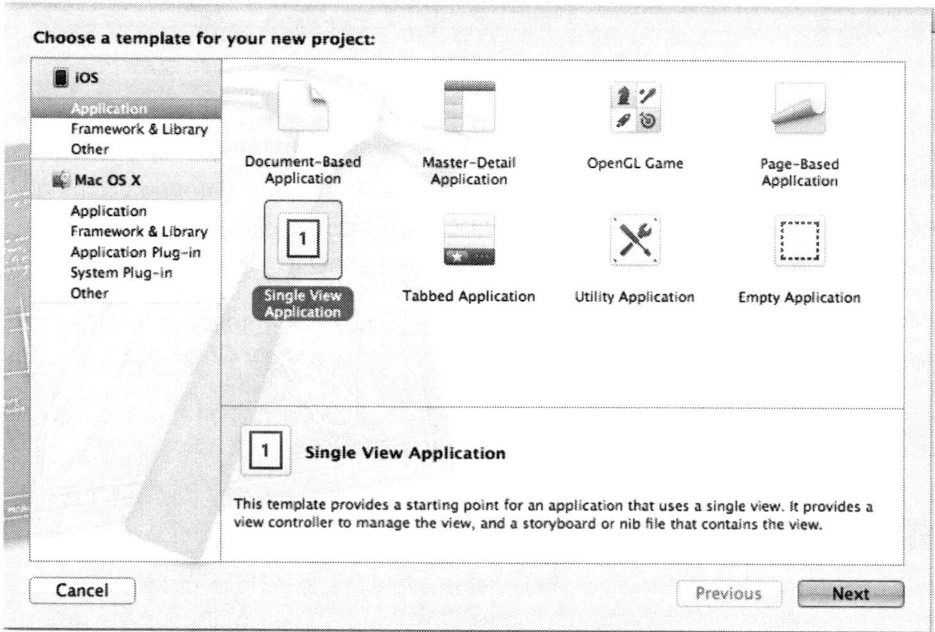

Figure 9–8. *Select the Single View Application icon, and then press Return or hit Next.*

1. Open Xcode and enter ⌘⇧N, as shown in Figure 9–8. Then click on the View-based Application template. We will call it `myStory_01` and then we will save it to our desktop. A folder bearing that name appears on the desktop.

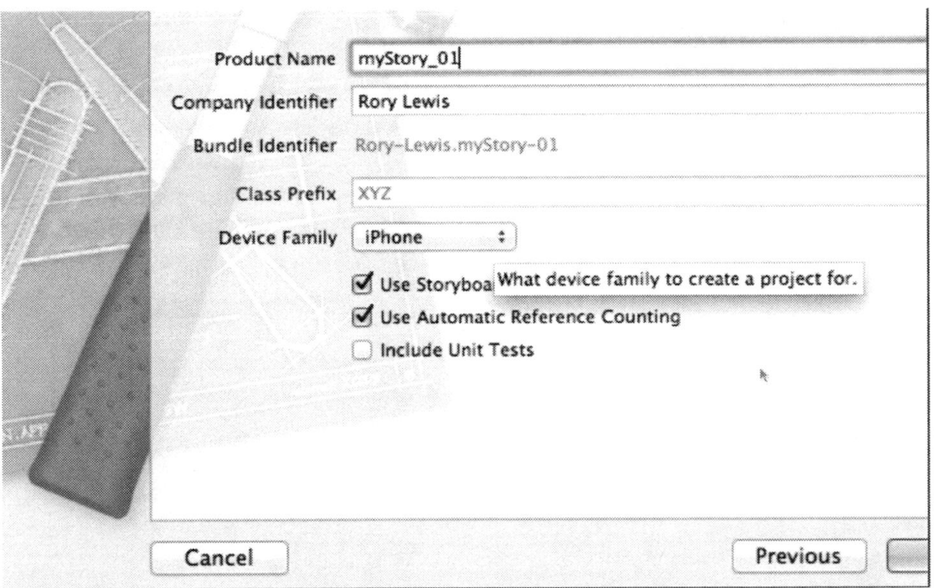

Figure 9–9. *Name your app myStory_01 making sure Storyboard and automatic referencing is on.*

2. In order to follow along as closely as possible, because it will get complex later, we will name our project "myStory_01." To do so, select iPhone, not iPad or Universal, leave the Class Prefix and Include Unit Tests options alone and as shown in Figure 9–9. Check that the Storyboard and Automatic Referencing option is on.

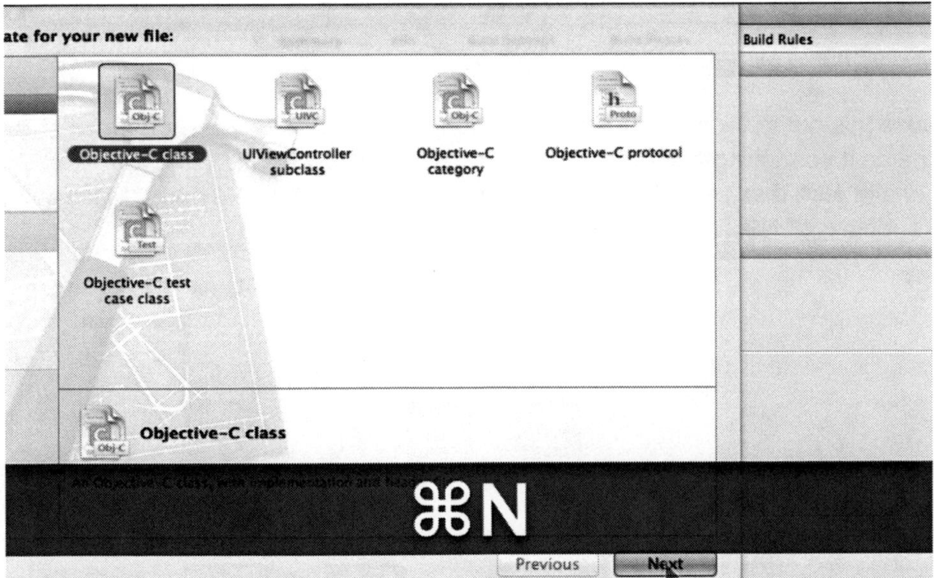

Figure 9–10. *Create an Objective–C class for your annotations.*

Preliminaries: Adding the Annotation File

3. While we're here setting up our project, we need to create an annotation file and import some frameworks. Let's start with the annotation file. As previously mentioned, we need a means to control our annotation. For that, we will create an Objective-C class that will control all the characteristics we want to display on this annotation. Click the Classes folder and enter ⌘N as shown in Figure 9–10. When finished, click Next.

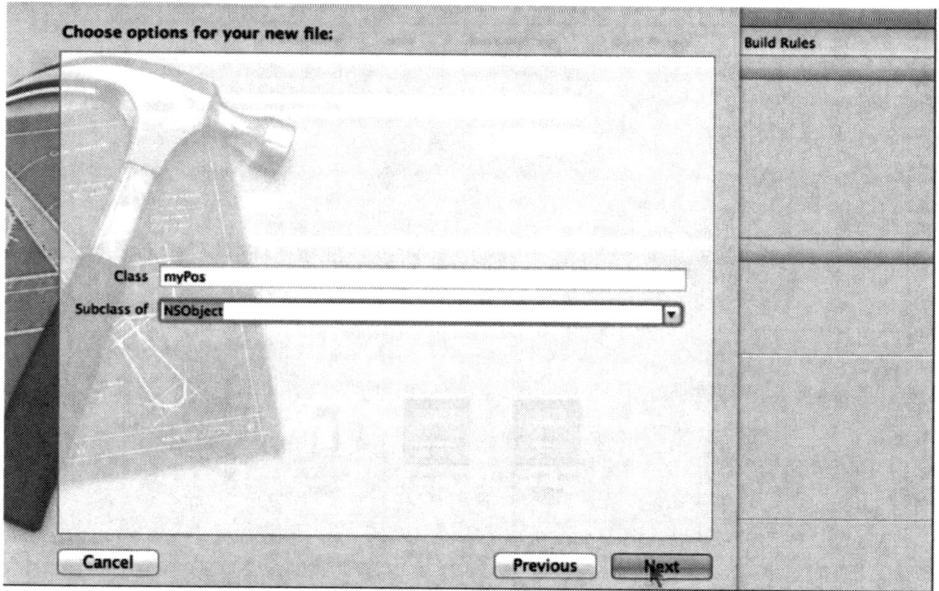

Figure 9–11. *Name it myPos and make sure it's an NSObject subclass.*

4. Because this controller will be in charge of controlling annotations for our position, let's name it something that correlates to *my position;* how about name it "myPos." Also, make sure that it is not a subclass of UIView or any other subclass. Make sure it's a subclass of NSobject. This is shown in Figure 9–11.

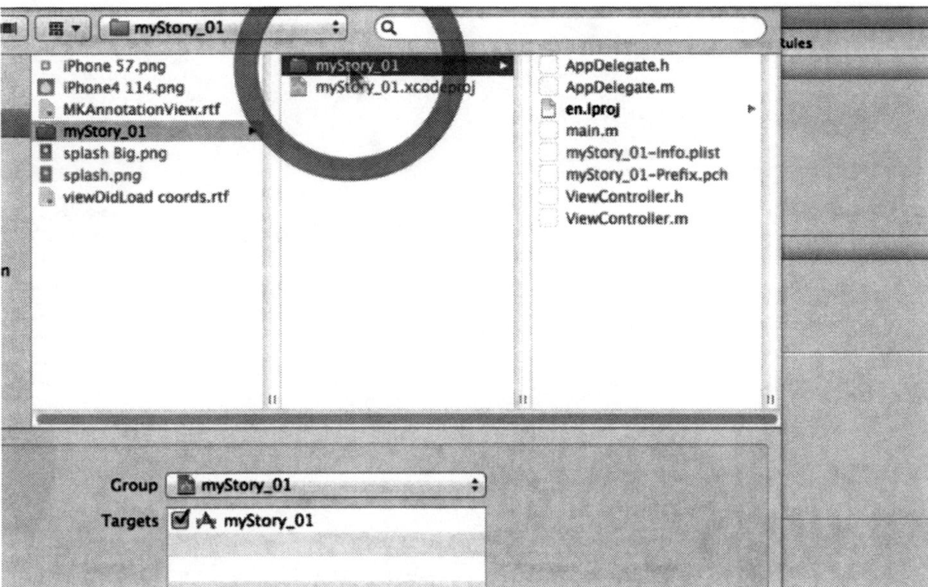

Figure 9–12. *Save it inside you myStory_01 folder.*

5. Make sure to save this *inside* the myStory_01 folder. This will make it much easier to export and is simply a good habit to have when we start sharing classes and objects with other programmers. See Figure 9–12.

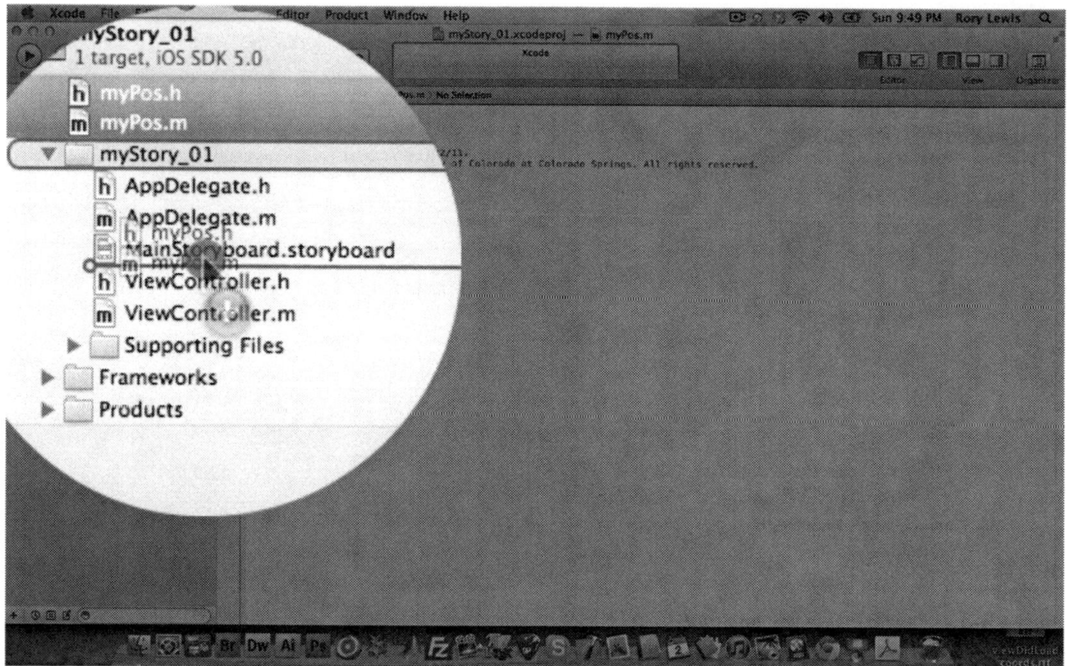

Figure 9–13. *Move the newly created NSObjects into the correct folder.*

6. As shown in Figure 9–13, our two newly created NSObjects named `myPos.h` and `myPos.m` are located in the root directory of our project. We need to move them to the correct place in the correct folder. I typically order the files I will be coding in the sequence I will code them under the nib or storyboard files. We usually do not work a lot with the AppDelegate files so I keep them on top and out of the way. Because I will start coding the NSObjects that keep track of my position, we will put them immediately under the Storyboard.

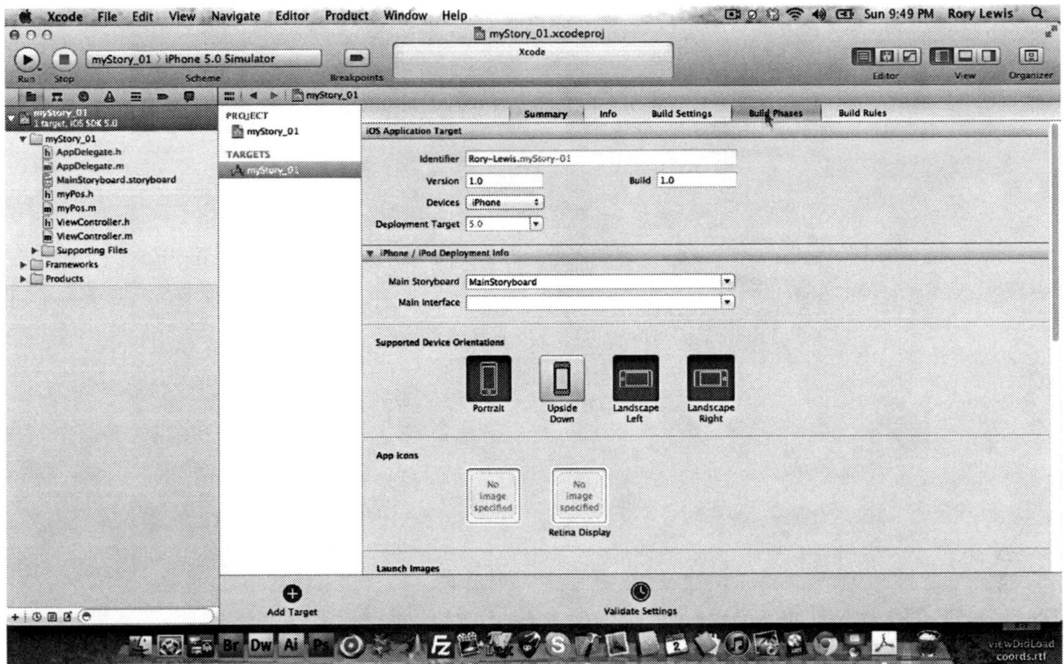

Figure 9–14. *Go to the myStory_01 root directory and select the Build Phases tab.*

Preliminaries: Adding Frameworks

7. The first thing we need to do is add two frameworks: For a newbie, we would say: "Frameworks are huge gobs of super code that is used for specialized stuff. It is too big to be carried around all the time but if we write an app that needs a framework—then we drag this framework into our code." Yeah, but we're not a newbie anymore—we're heading at a fast and furious pace to becoming a bona fide geek, respected by others left in the swamps of technology—so, let's look at this. Yes, it is specialized code. We will put it in a hierarchical directory that encapsulates s dynamic shared libraries such as, nib files, image files, localized strings, header files, and reference documentation in a single package. In our app, we will use Corelocation and MapKit frameworks and when we bring them into our app, the system loads them into memory as needed and shares the one copy of the resource among all applications whenever possible. So, we will go to our root directory and click on the Build Phases tab as shown in Figure 9–14.

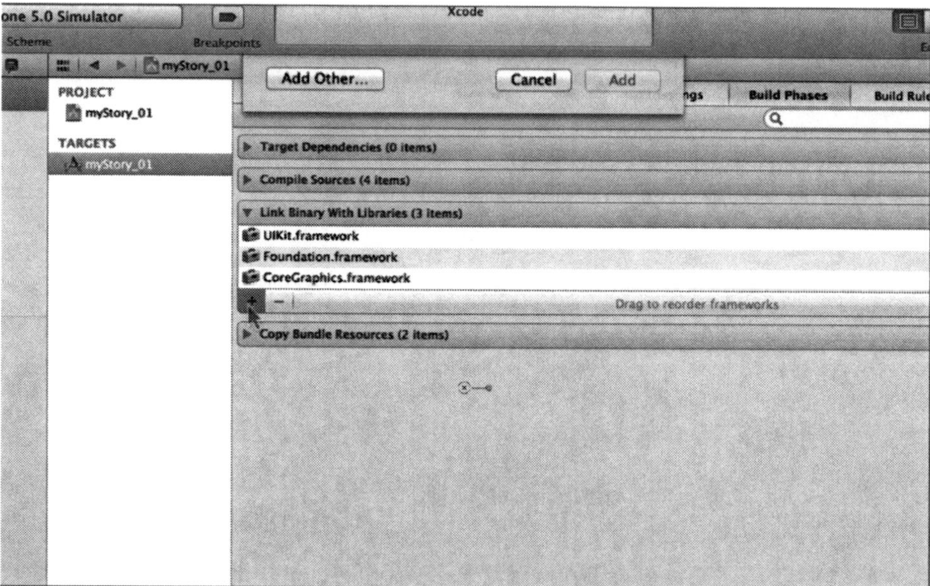

Figure 9–15. *Click on the Link Binaries with Libraries bar and click on the "+".*

8. As shown in Figure 9–15, click on the Link Binaries with Libraries bar and click on the "+".

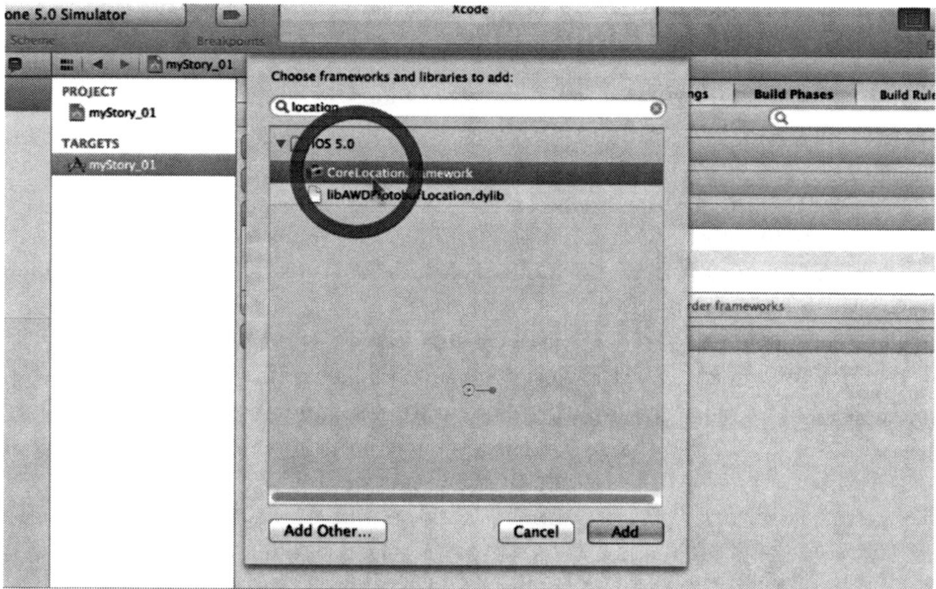

Figure 9–16. *Select the Corelocation Framework.*

9. We will either scroll through all our options or enter *location* in the search bar and select Corelocation Frameworks. Then we will press Add or Enter/Return as shown in Figure 9–16.

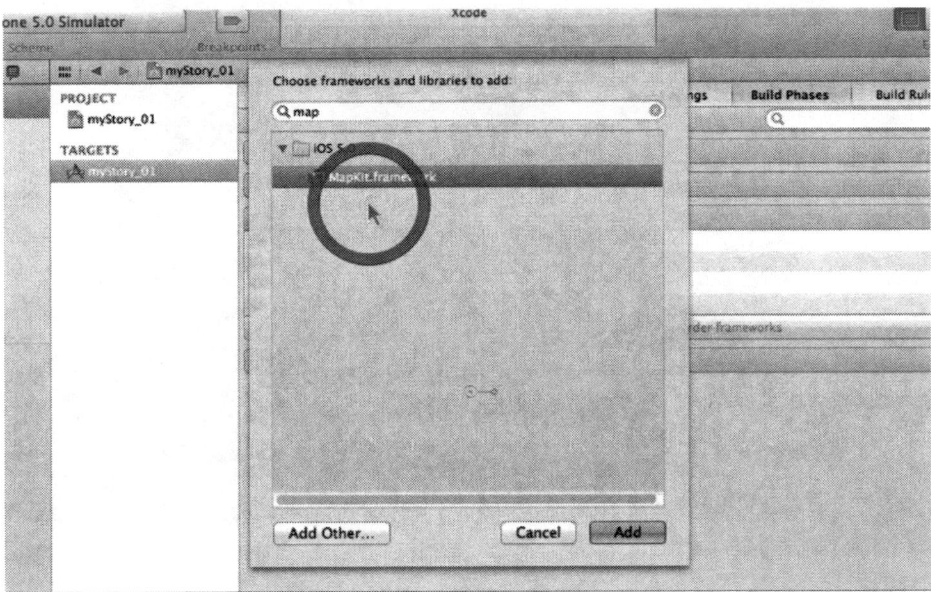

Figure 9–17. *Select the MapKit Framework.*

10. Repeating step 9, we will now do the same for MapKit. We will either scroll through all of our options or enter *location* in the search bar and select MapKit Framework. Then press Add or Enter/Return as shown in Figure 9–17.

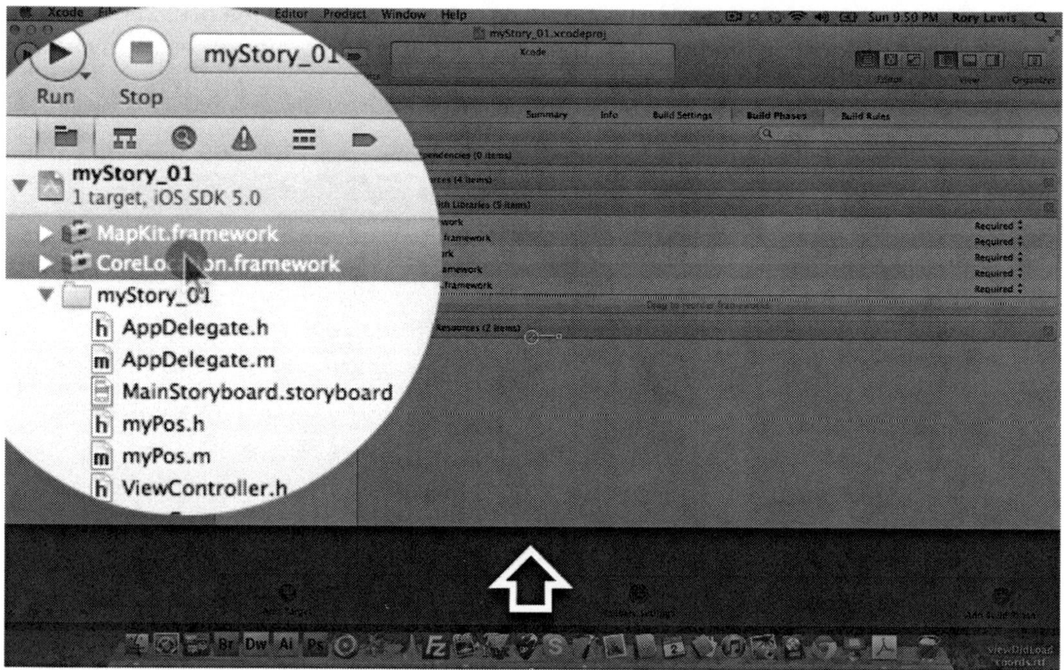

Figure 9–18. ***Move the imported Frameworks to the Frameworks folder.***

11. As shown in Figure 9–18, we will grab our two newly imported Frameworks that are by default stored in the root directory. We will then move those to our frameworks folder. It is important that we create good habits and store all of our Frameworks in the correct folder.

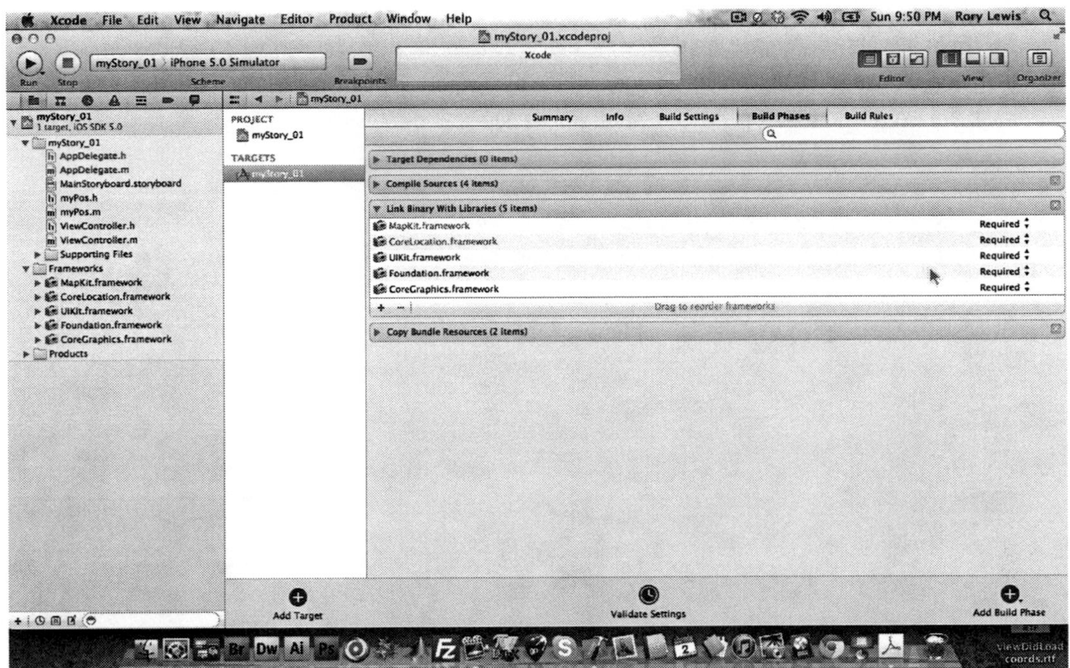

Figure 9–19. *Check your directories and files against mine.*

12. Before we move on, we need to make sure that we check our project against the example shown in Figure 9–19. We need to make sure that our NSObjects `myPos.h`, `myPos.m` and that our Corelocation and MapKit Frameworks are placed like those in the example. With this step completed, we will move on; place our images and then start coding.

Bring in the Images!

We want to have five essential images for every app we make. For convenience, these are included in the package available for download from my website at http://bit.ly/oDqzvY. They include the essential icons and two splash screens. These include the 57 by 57 px for the iPhone classic, the 72 x 72 px for the iPad, and the 114 x 114 px for the iPhone 4S Retina Display. I've also designed two splash screen images that are available for your use. Splash screen images appear on the screen of the app while the apps code loads. They usually only appear for less than a second, but they give the user something cool to look at—and they set the tone for the super cool app that is loading. You will need two splash screens because you have to accommodate the various iPad and iPhone configurations the user using your app might have. The 640 by 960 px splash screen for iPads and iPhone Retinas and a 320 by 480 px for the classic iPhone are included. After you have downloaded them, you can always use them as a template for your future apps.

NOTE: In this application, we are only using the iPhone. In the next chapter, when we design myStory_02, we will use both the IPhone and the iPad where we can use all the icons. So, just keep the extra iPad icon for later use when you design your own icons.

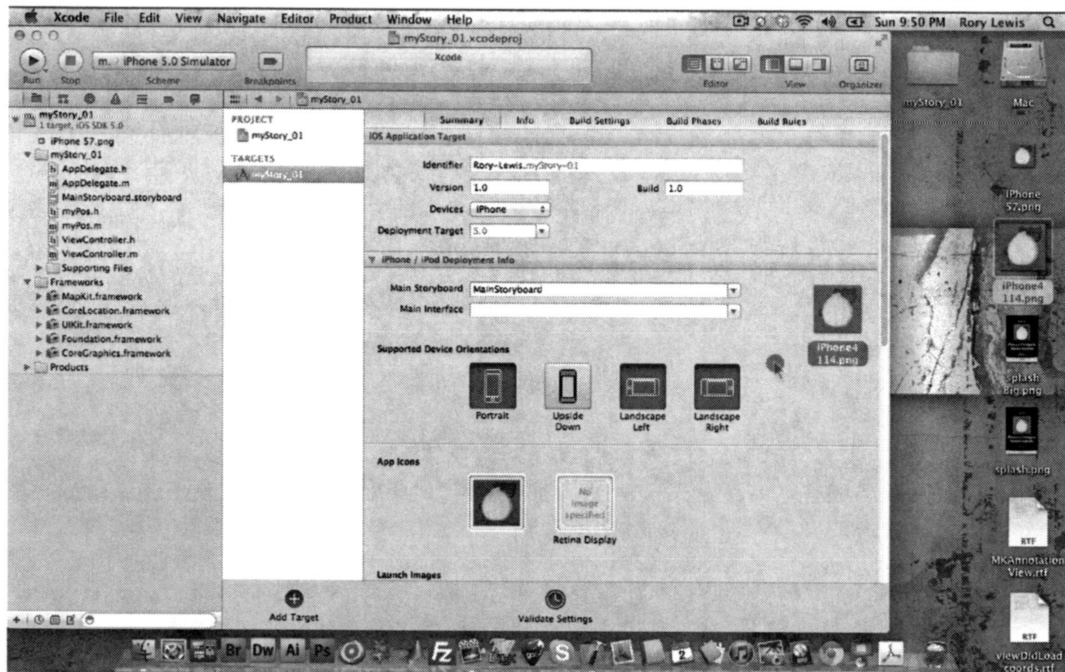

Figure 9–20. Drag in the icons.

13. Staying in the root directory after importing the frameworks, drag the icon images into the icon boxes. Figure 9–20 shows the 57 x 57 px classic iPhone icon in its box and the Retina icon being drug over to it.

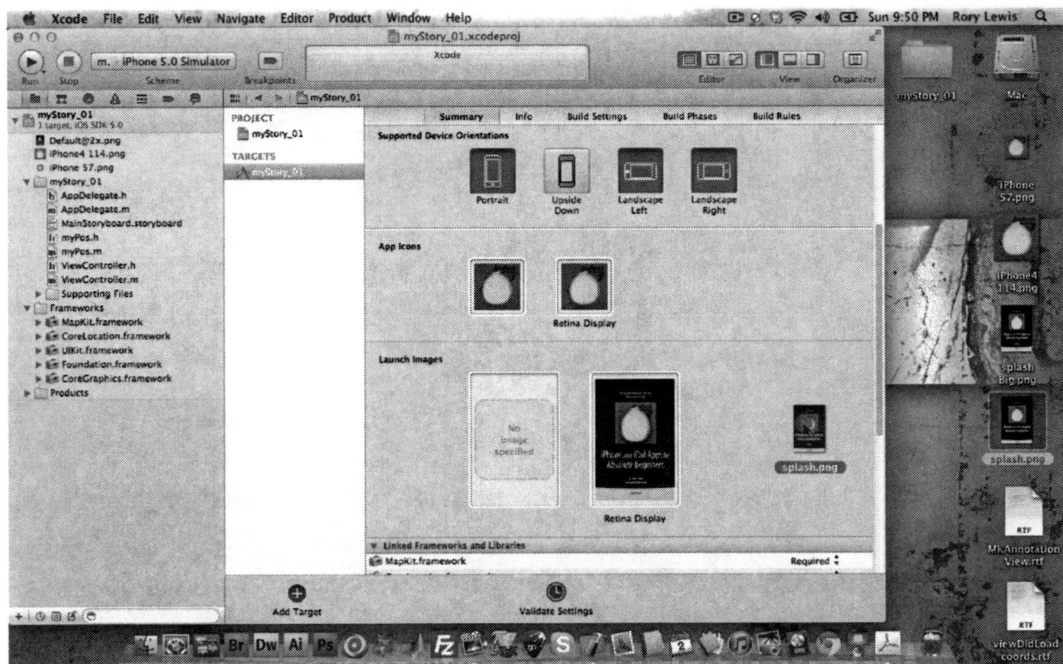

Figure 9–21. ***Drag in the icons.***

14. Similar to step 13, after importing the icons, we now need to import our splash screen images into their boxes. Figure 9–21 shows the iPhone Retina 320 by 480 px classic splash screen already in place with the classic iPhone 640 x 960 px splash screen being dragged in. Once we are finished dragging these images in, we are ready to start with the code.

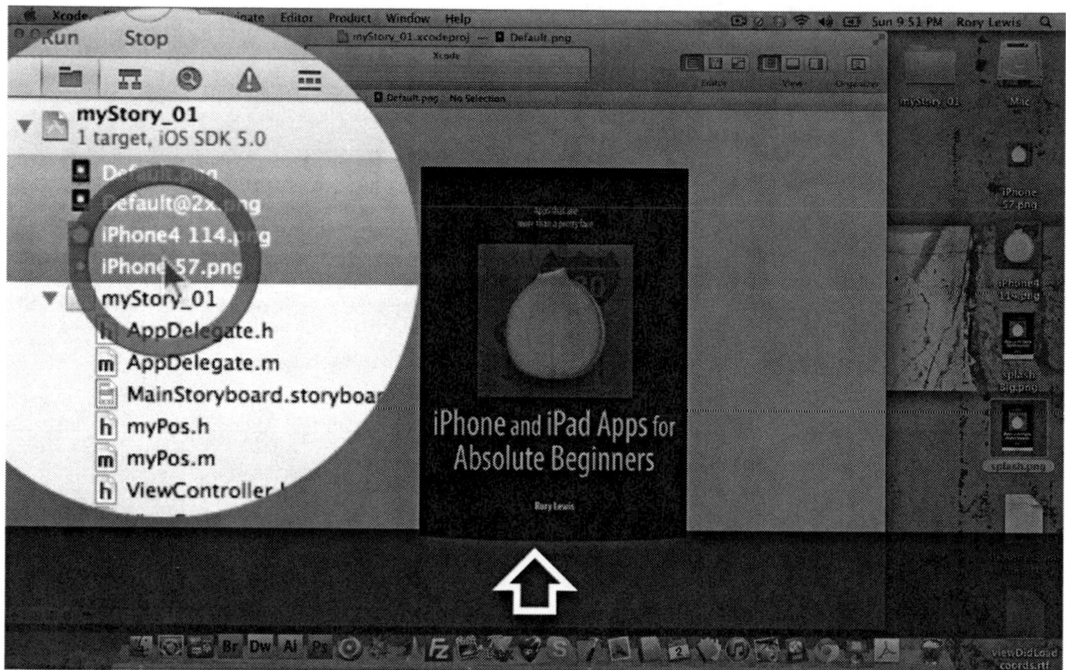

Figure 9–22. *Drag in your icons so you can take them to the correct folder.*

15. Before we start to code, we need to make sure that all our files are in the correct folders. At this point, we know that Xcode will recognize the correct icons and splash screens—but look where they are! They're in the root directory again. Grab them, as shown in Figure 9–22, and move them into the supporting files folder.

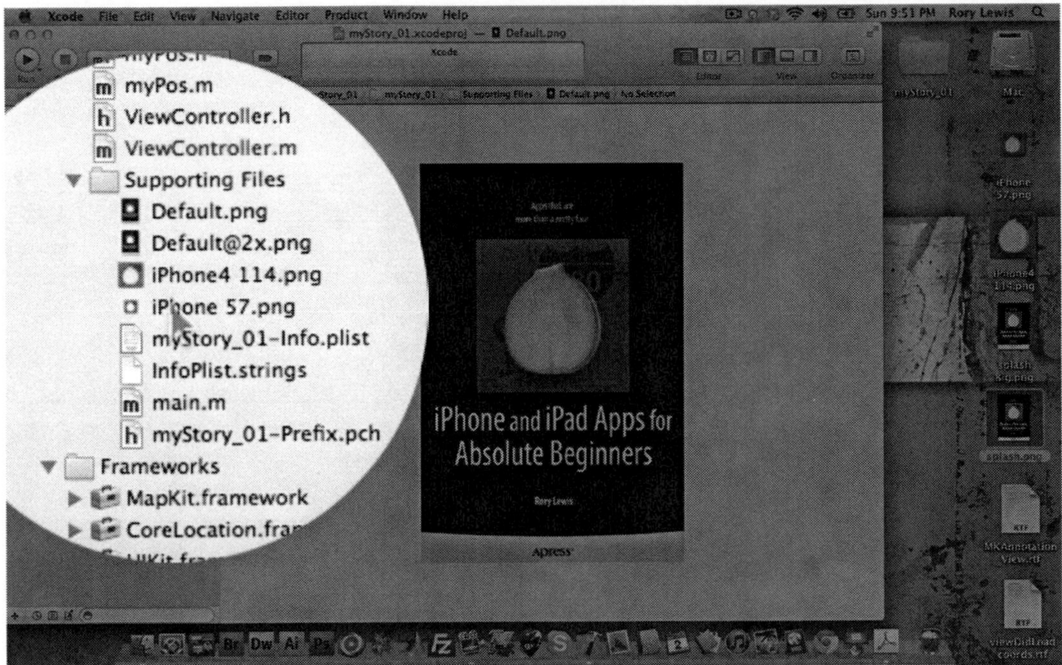

Figure 9–23. *Drop the project icons into the supporting files' folder.*

16. The supporting Files folder is probably not open. That's OK. As we drag the icons with our mouse, we will need to slow down as we hover over the supporting Files folder so it will open up. Once it opens up, drop the files into the folder as shown in Figure 9–23.

Figure 9–24. *Ready to paint .... erh .... code.*

17. Take a good look at Figure 9–24. We are now ready to code. We need to get used to wanting to see our coding canvas laid out before we ever start writing our code. This is very much like a painter who will first buy a canvas, get paint, turpentine, brushes, rags and a model of what will be painted before the first dab is ever painted. This is what we've just done. We need to get used to first setting everything up before we write our code.

> **NOTE:** I cannot understand why some students invariably dive into the code immediately upon receiving an in class assignment. I also always stop them immediately and make them prep as we have done here and throughout this book. It is during this time while I bring in all my files and create whatever new frameworks and NSObjects that I need that my mind goes into a semi meditative state and I quietly plan out how I will write the code. During this time, my mind tries out all kinds of different options and by the time I am finished prepping, I am completely ready to code.

Coding the myPos NSObject

Remember that myStory_01 is a lead-in or segue into myStory_02, which is where the real action is. In fact, many MapKit apps will need a separate NSObject to keep track of many positions. In this small app, we do not necessarily have to program the myPos.h and myPos.m files at all. But you need to get used to always creating an NSObject myPos to keep track of your position or an array of positions to feed into the annotations and MapKit framework. So, follow along with me as I explain in detail what we will be doing here. In myStory_02, I skip over some of these steps because I assume we all did our homework and programmed myStory_01 many times until we could do it without this book or any accompanying notes.

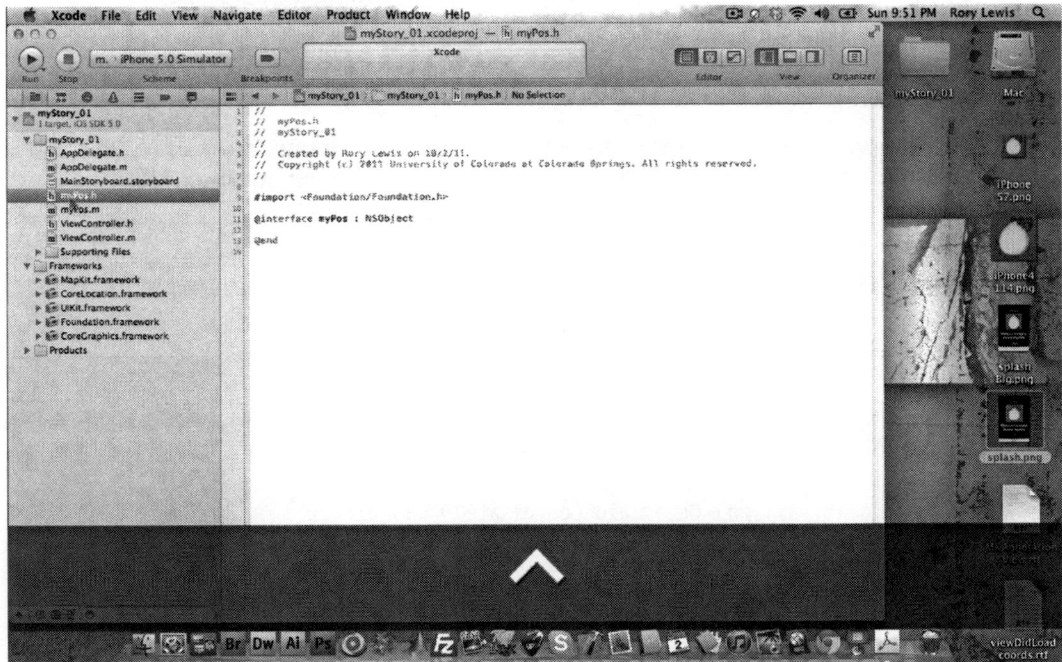

Figure 9–25. *myPos.h as it looks upon opening it.*

18. Click on the myPos.h file located in your myStory_01 folder inside the root folder. Upon opening it, as shown in Figure 9–25, we see the following:

```
#import <Foundation/Foundation.h>
@interface myPos : NSObject
@end
```

- The first thing we do is add a MapKit framework for our annotations by entering #import <MapKit/MkAnnotation.h> to the @interface myPos : NSObject directive.

- We also need to add `<MKAnnotation>`, which is a *protocol*. I explain protocols in Digging the Code, but for now, it means we'll have to write our own annotation object that implements this protocol. Just remember that an object that adopts this protocol must implement a property we call the coordinate property. Which, of course, we will do.
- We also set our `CLLocation` Class Reference to incorporate the geographical coordinates and altitude of our device with a variable that we'll name `coordinate`, as seen in Figure 9–26. We do that with this line:

```
CLLocationCoordinate2D coordinate;
```

- Now, we need two `NSString` variables to hold our titles and subtitles, which we will name `*title` and `*subtitle` as follows:

```
NSString *title;
NSString *subtitle;
```

- Finally, we create `@property` statements for the coordinate, title, and subtitle, as shown in the code that follows. Once we have made these additions, we will save our work as shown in Figure 9–26.

```
#import <Foundation/Foundation.h>
#import <MapKit/MkAnnotation.h>

@interface myPos : NSObject <MKAnnotation>
{
    CLLocationCoordinate2D coordinate;
    NSString *title;
    NSString *subtitle;
}

@property (nonatomic, assign) CLLocationCoordinate2D coordinate;
@property (nonatomic, copy)  NSString *title;
@property (nonatomic, copy) NSString *subtitle;

@end
```

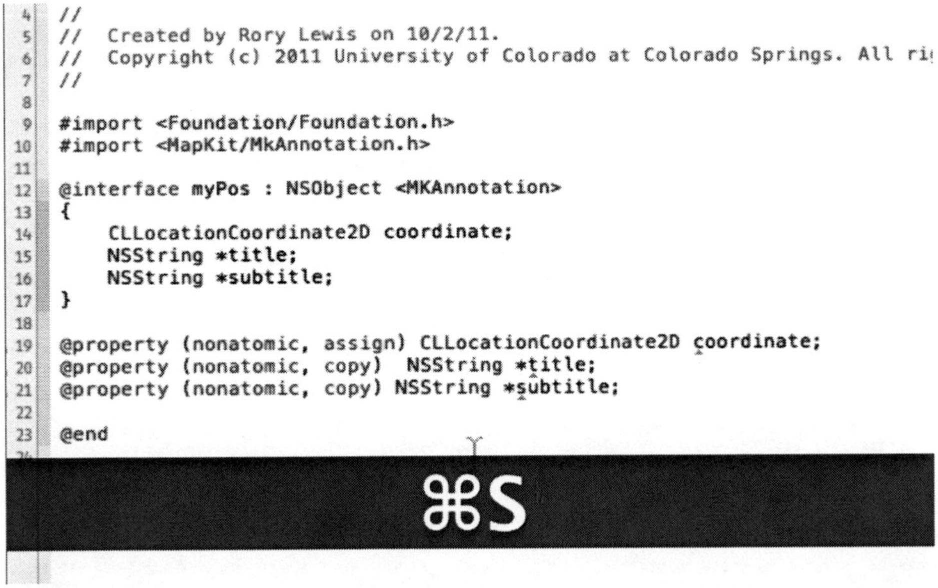

```
//
//  Created by Rory Lewis on 10/2/11.
//  Copyright (c) 2011 University of Colorado at Colorado Springs. All ri

#import <Foundation/Foundation.h>
#import <MapKit/MkAnnotation.h>

@interface myPos : NSObject <MKAnnotation>
{
    CLLocationCoordinate2D coordinate;
    NSString *title;
    NSString *subtitle;
}

@property (nonatomic, assign) CLLocationCoordinate2D coordinate;
@property (nonatomic, copy)  NSString *title;
@property (nonatomic, copy) NSString *subtitle;

@end
```

⌘S

Figure 9–26. *The MyPos.h incorporates the geographical coordinates and altitude of our device.*

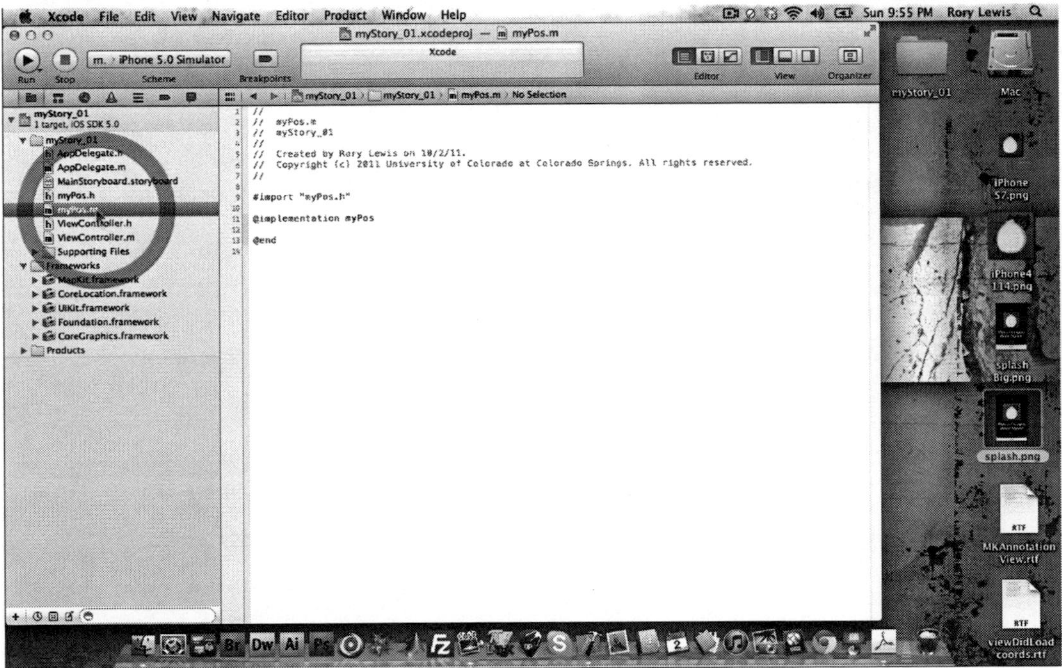

Figure 9–27. *This is how our myPos implementation file looks when we open it.*

19. We are now ready to code the myPos implementation file. We will click on the myPos.m file located in our myStory_01 folder inside the root folder. Figure 9–27 shows how the myPos.m file looks when we open it. Here we simply synthesize our coordinate, title, and subtitle with a @synthesize statement, which includes `coordinate`, `title`, and `subtitle`. Once done, our file should look similar to Figure 9–28. We will save our work on this file.

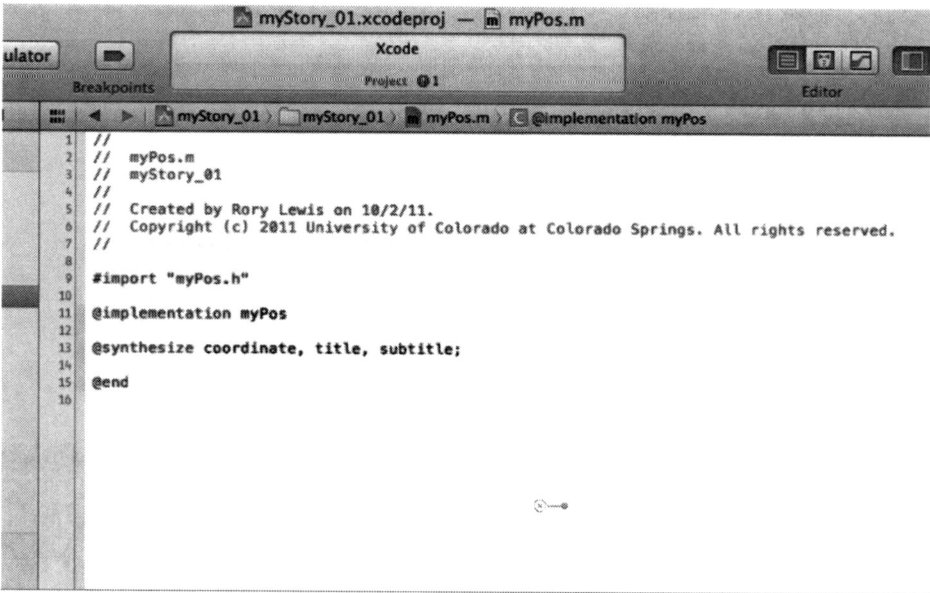

Figure 9–28. *This is how the myPos implementation file looks after the synthesis.*

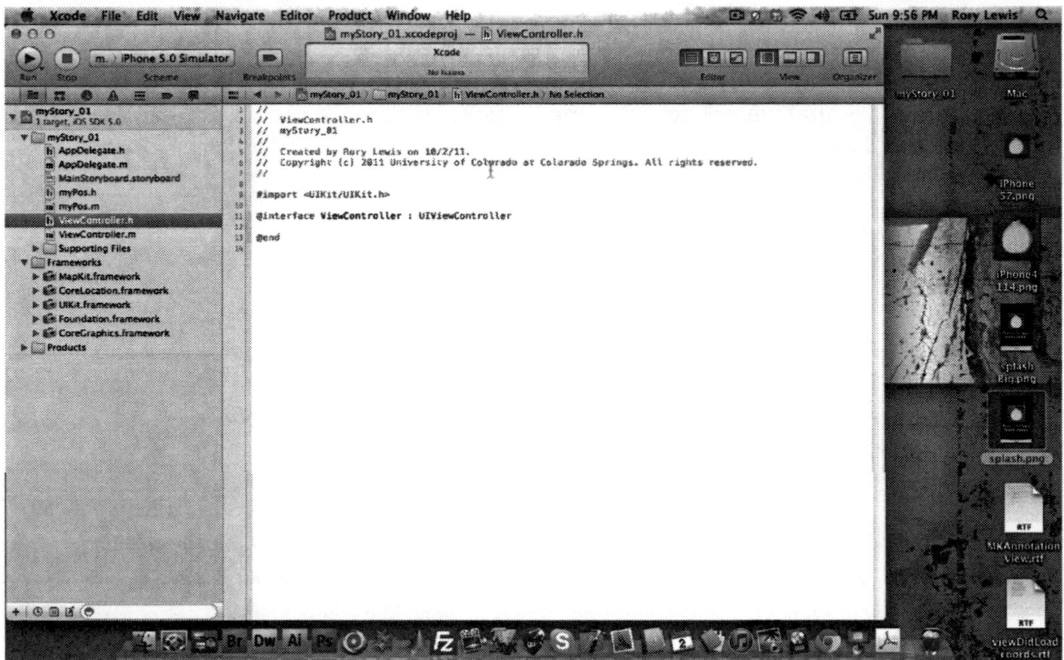

Figure 9–29. *Open the view controller.*

Coding the View Controller

We will start by declaring our classes, methods, and outlets in our `ViewController.h` file and then implementing them in our `ViewController.m` file. I have included some boilerplate code that we can drop into the implementation file. However, I am going go over each line separately, so it will be better if you follow along without dropping in the boilerplate code.

20. We will start, as always, with the header file. We will open up our header file by clicking on `ViewController.h` inside the root folder below the myPos.m file or thereabout. When we first open it up, it will look similar to Figure 9–29 and as shown below.

```
#import <UIKit/UIKit.h>
@interface ViewController : UIViewController
@end
```

- The first thing we need to do is tell our app that we have imported the MapKit framework; we do this by `#import <MapKit/MapKit.h>` under the line `#import <UIKit/UIKit.h>`. The next thing we will do is tell the header file that we will be using the `MKMapViewDelegate` protocol. This protocol defines a set of optional methods that our app will use to receive map update records.
- Next, we will add the `<MKMapViewDelegate>` protocol for the controller class.
- We are now able to add an outlet with a pointer to the `MKMapView` class. We do this by typing in `MKMapView *mapView`, which declares an object of type `MKMapView`.
- The last thing we need to do is define the `@property`, by entering.

```
@property (nonatomic, retain) IBOutlet MKMapView *mapView
```

> **NOTE** Some people may say: "Whoah! You only declared the IBOutllet outside the interface!" Well, actually, whether we stated IBOutlet MKMapView *mapView inside the interface or "outside," they really are both still inside and there is no need to declare it twice. I prefer to use outlets on @properties because it makes memory management of the objects loaded from the storyboard clearer. I go deeper into this in Memory Management of Storyboard Objects in Digging the Code.

- Once done, save it. Our code should appear as follows and as shown In Figure 9–30:

```
#import <UIKit/UIKit.h>
#import <MapKit/MapKit.h>

@interface ViewController : UIViewController <MKMapViewDelegate>
{
    MKMapView *mapView;
}

@property (nonatomic, retain) IBOutlet MKMapView *mapView;

@end
```

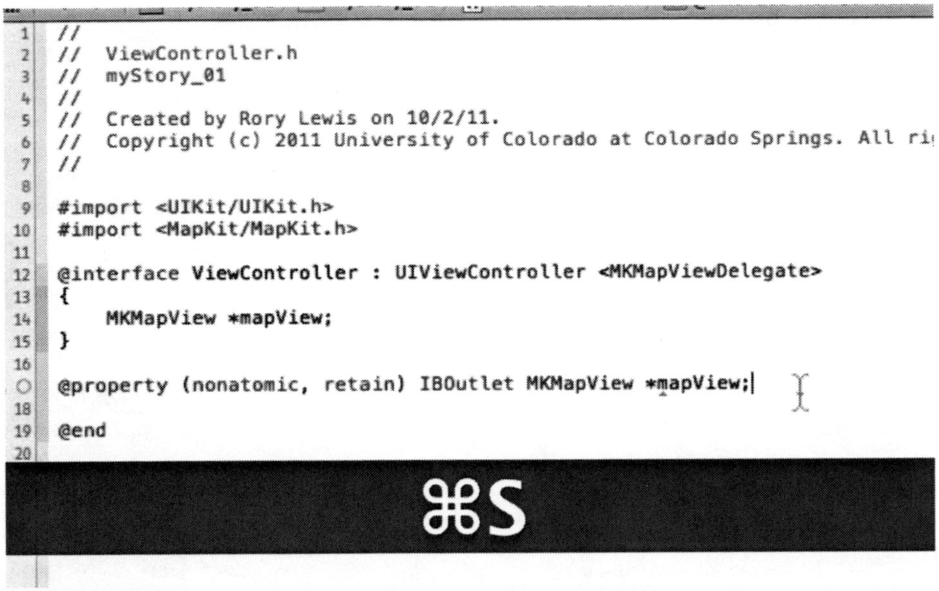

```
//
//  ViewController.h
//  myStory_01
//
//  Created by Rory Lewis on 10/2/11.
//  Copyright (c) 2011 University of Colorado at Colorado Springs. All ri
//

#import <UIKit/UIKit.h>
#import <MapKit/MapKit.h>

@interface ViewController : UIViewController <MKMapViewDelegate>
{
    MKMapView *mapView;
}

@property (nonatomic, retain) IBOutlet MKMapView *mapView;

@end
```

⌘S

Figure 9–30. *A completed ViewController header file.*

Dealing with the View Controller's Implementation

As mentioned in the introduction to this chapter, controlling and working with the MapKit and CoreLocation frameworks is not a trivial matter. Daunting as these areas can be, I could not leave them out of this book. We proceed on the basis that we have learned by now to look for familiar patterns, integrate what we can, and just follow directions when things get a bit complicated or beyond our immediate understanding!

Let's think about this—after doing the necessary importing of our myPos header file and the synthesis of the ViewController that we just set up in the header file—we need to do two things:

- Set up the coordinates of my office into the viewDidLoad method; and then,
- Make a pin drop down onto this exact latitude and longitude set forth in the viewDidLoad and put an annotation on it that states this is the office of Dr. Lewis.

In our case, we will set the map type to a Hybrid map. If we prefer, though, we may choose to use a Satellite map or a Street map. Remember, at this point, we will bring in the location of my office at the University of Colorado at Colorado Springs, we can go ahead and use mine, or you can choose your own point.

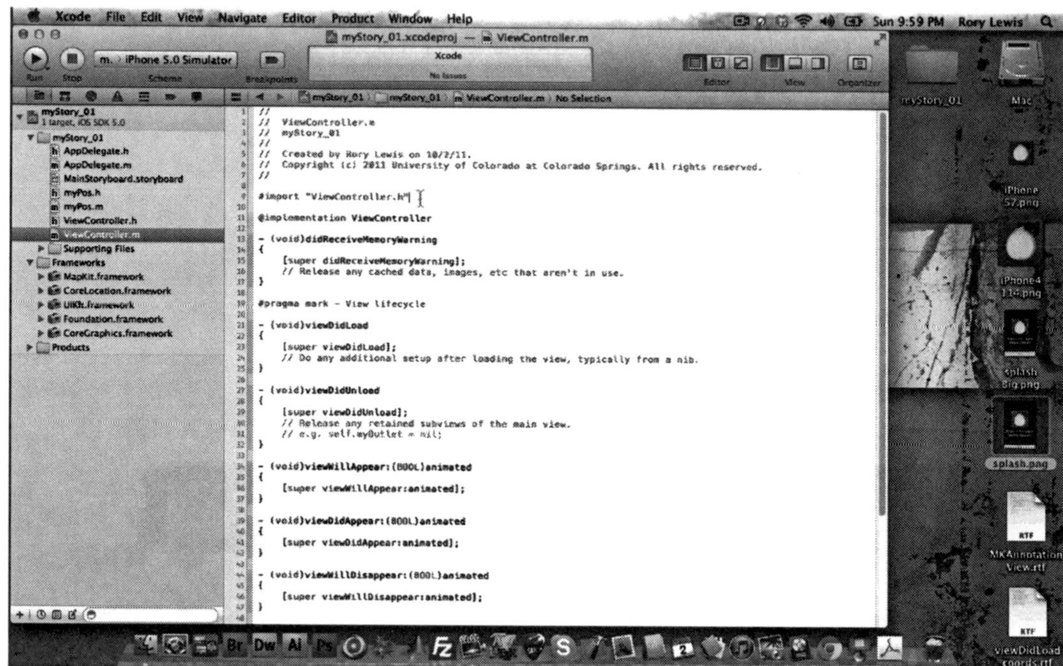

Figure 9–31. *The ViewController's implementation file before coding.*

21. When you first open up the viewController.m file, you will see the default code as shown in Figure 9–31. Let's first bring in the header file and synthesis:

- Right under the `#import "ViewController.h"` We want to import our mypos header file by coding

```
#import "myPos.h"
```

- Now, under the `@implementation,` we will add our synthesis of the mapView:

```
@synthesize mapView;
```

- Now, we can either drop in the boiler plate code from the file called viewDidLoad coord.rtf right over and in place of the comment `// Do any additional` … in the `viewDidLoad` method under the `[super viewDidLoad];` as shown:

```
[super viewDidLoad];
// Do any additional setup after loading the view, typically from a nib.
```

- The boilerplate code is as follows, but we will go step-by-step through it.

```
[mapView setMapType:MKMapTypeStandard];
[mapView setZoomEnabled:YES];
[mapView setScrollEnabled:YES];
mapView.mapType=MKMapTypeHybrid;
```

```
MKCoordinateRegion region = { {0.0, 0.0 }, { 0.0, 0.0 } };
region.center.latitude = 38.893432;
region.center.longitude = -104.800161;
region.span.longitudeDelta = 0.01f;
region.span.latitudeDelta = 0.01f;
[mapView setRegion:region animated:YES];
[mapView setDelegate:self];

myPos *ann = [[myPos alloc] init];
ann.title = @"Dr. Rory Lewis";
ann.subtitle = @"University of Colorado at Colorado Springs";
ann.coordinate = region.center;
[mapView addAnnotation:ann];
```

22. Now, going through this line by line;

- First, we make it standard and enable zoom and scroll:

```
[mapView setMapType:MKMapTypeStandard];
[mapView setZoomEnabled:YES];
[mapView setScrollEnabled:YES];
```

- Then, we do a reset on the previous coordinates by setting all the coordinate regions to zeros.

```
MKCoordinateRegion region = { {0.0, 0.0 }, { 0.0, 0.0 } };
```

- Then, we enter coordinates of our place of interest—which, for me, is my office at the University of Colorado at Colorado Springs. I enter `Region.center.latitude = 38.893432;` (the positive value denotes north of the Equator) and `region.center.longitude = -104.800161;` (the negative sign denotes west of the Prime Meridian).

```
region.center.latitude = 38.893432;
region.center.longitude = -104.800161;
```

- Related to these parameters, we need to set the latitude and longitude Delta `= 0.01f`. If your math or physics is rusty, recall that "delta" refers to the change, or difference, between two values.

```
region.span.longitudeDelta = 0.01f;
region.span.latitudeDelta = 0.01f;
```

- I have chosen to animate the pin when it drops.

```
[mapView setRegion:region animated:YES];
```

- The next action is to set the view controller class as the *delegate*, which is the role that will handle the interaction between the frameworks of our mapView. We do this with:

```
[mapView setDelegate:self];
```

> **NOTE:** Regarding the dropped pin and the attached label: We need to make the annotation object the holder of the information of our coordinates. Our annotation view is the type of view associated with the annotation object. Our annotation object needs to comply with all the rules we will set forth in our `MKAnnotation` protocol. In order to create this annotation object, we must define a new class, *which we did* when we created the `myPos` classes.

- We now need to instantiate this `myPos` object and add it to our map. To do this, we add the delegate function that will display the annotations onto our map. We start by having `myPos` name a pointer we'll call ann.

```
myPos *ann = [[myPos alloc] init];
```

- Next, we set the title, and in my case, I chose to use my name.

```
ann.title = @"Dr. Rory Lewis";
```

- We handle the subtitle similarly: `ann.subtitle = @"University of Colorado at Colorado Springs"`.

```
ann.subtitle = @"University of Colorado at Colorado Springs";
```

- We also want the pin to drop in the center of the map: `ann.coordinate = region.center`.

```
ann.coordinate = region.center;
```

- Reference all of the above with `[mapView addAnnotation:ann]`.

```
[mapView addAnnotation:ann];
```

At this point, we will take advantage of the next boilerplate method of code that most MapKit maps use. Unlike the viewDidLoad coord.rtf, the MKAnnotationView.rtf is a chunk of code we all use. Read the note below:

> **NOTE:** We seldom change chunks of code like viewDidLoad coord.rtf and by the time this book is printed, it may be part of a new function or a new class. The reason is that when people start using the same piece of code over and over, referring to it as "boilerplate code," that's about the time Apple decides to make a new class or function out of it, and sets it to a specific name. So, keep on using it and get the message through to Apple!

For now, there are a few things we all need to know about this code:

- It creates a *delegate method* that manages our annotation during zooming and scrolling. In other words, it keeps track of where we are—even when the user scrolls, zooms in, or zooms out of our map.

- It creates a *static identifier*, which controls our "queue meaning." If it can't *dequeue* our annotation, it will allocate one that we choose. I have also included code that changes the pin color to red. In addition, I have allowed *callout views*.

Paste the MKAnnotationView.rtf right after the `- (void)viewDidLoad` method and right before the `- (void)viewDidUnload` method. After you have pasted it there, your implementation file should look like the following.

```
#import "ViewController.h"
#import "myPos.h"

@implementation ViewController
@synthesize mapView;

- (void)didReceiveMemoryWarning
{
    [super didReceiveMemoryWarning];
    // Release any cached data, images, etc., that aren't in use.
}

#pragma mark - View lifecycle

- (void)viewDidLoad
{
    [super viewDidLoad];
        [mapView setMapType:MKMapTypeStandard];
        [mapView setZoomEnabled:YES];
        [mapView setScrollEnabled:YES];
        mapView.mapType=MKMapTypeHybrid;

        MKCoordinateRegion region = { {0.0, 0.0 }, { 0.0, 0.0 } };
        region.center.latitude = 38.893432;
        region.center.longitude = -104.800161;
        region.span.longitudeDelta = 0.01f;
        region.span.latitudeDelta = 0.01f;
        [mapView setRegion:region animated:YES];
        [mapView setDelegate:self];

        myPos *ann = [[myPos alloc] init];
        ann.title = @"Dr. Rory Lewis";
        ann.subtitle = @"University of Colorado at Colorado Springs";
        ann.coordinate = region.center;
        [mapView addAnnotation:ann];
}

- (MKAnnotationView *)mapView:(MKMapView *)mV viewForAnnotation:(id
<MKAnnotation>)annotation
{
        MKPinAnnotationView *pinView = nil;
        if(annotation != mapView.userLocation)
        {
                static NSString *defaultPinID = @"com.rorylewis";
                pinView = (MKPinAnnotationView *)[mapView
dequeueReusableAnnotationViewWithIdentifier:defaultPinID];
                if ( pinView == nil )
```

```
                            pinView = [[MKPinAnnotationView alloc]
initWithAnnotation:annotation reuseIdentifier:defaultPinID];

                pinView.pinColor = MKPinAnnotationColorRed;
                pinView.canShowCallout = YES;
                pinView.animatesDrop = YES;
        }
        else
        {
                [mapView.userLocation setTitle:@"I am here"];
        }

    return pinView;
}

- (void)viewDidUnload
{
    [super viewDidUnload];
    // Release any retained subviews of the main view.
    // e.g. self.myOutlet = nil;
}

- (void)viewWillAppear:(BOOL)animated
{
    [super viewWillAppear:animated];
}
- (void)viewDidAppear:(BOOL)animated
{
    [super viewDidAppear:animated];
}

- (void)viewWillDisappear:(BOOL)animated
{
        [super viewWillDisappear:animated];
}
- (void)viewDidDisappear:(BOOL)animated
{
        [super viewDidDisappear:animated];
}
-
(BOOL)shouldAutorotateToInterfaceOrientation:(UIInterfaceOrientation)interfaceOrientatio
n
{
    // Return YES for supported orientations
    return (interfaceOrientation != UIInterfaceOrientationPortraitUpsideDown);
}

@end
```

The Storyboard

Go ahead and open the Storyboard file. It will look similar to what you see in Figure 9–32.

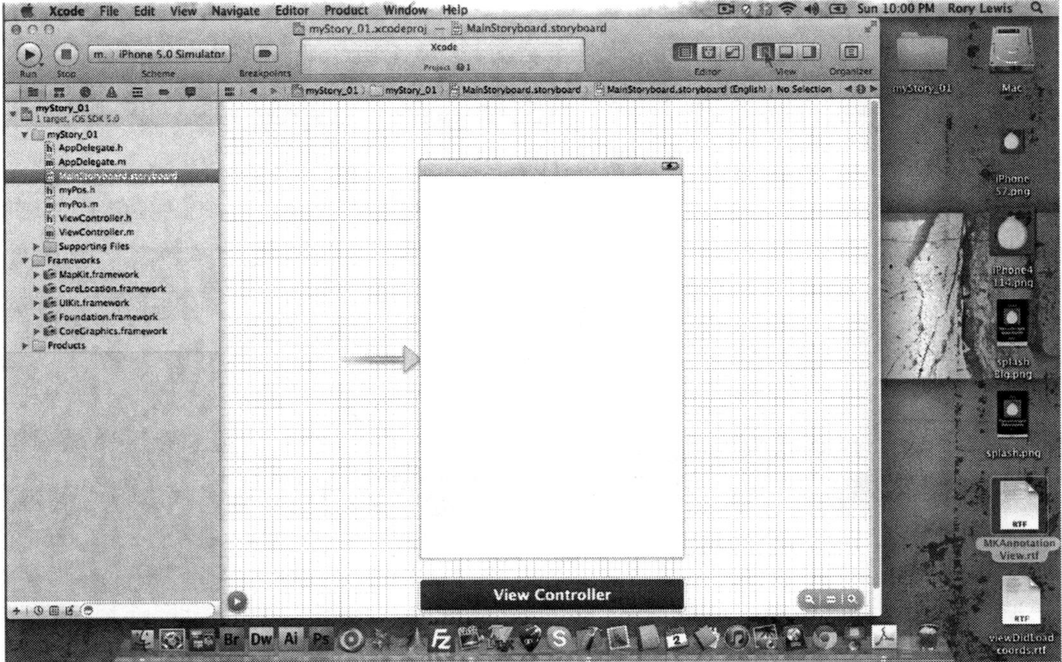

Figure 9–32. *Open Storyboarding*

As I have already mentioned quite a few times, I specifically chose myStory_01 as a segue to myStory_02, which will have a very complex Storyboard. In this app, I just want you to deal with setting up the MapKit framework. In myStory_02, we will set up the MapKit framework as we did here; then, we will set up a pretty tableView onto a Storyboard. Doing it all at one time would not be practical and I do know this. So, for how—this segment of the Storyboarding will be relatively easy—just a couple of steps. In myStory_02, this will not be the case. So, give your brain a break and follow along as we set up this very simple, one–piece Storyboard.

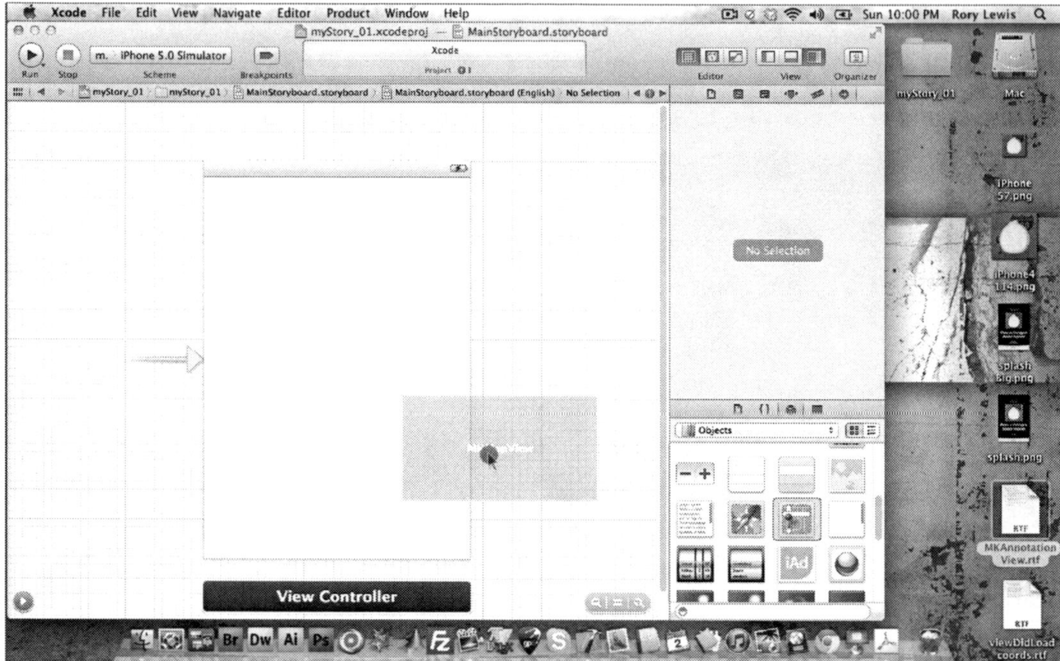

Figure 9–33. *Drag a MKMapView onto the view.*

23. With the Storyboard open—close the Inspector and open up the Utilities folder. Then drag a Map View (MKMapView) onto your view as shown in Figure 9–33.

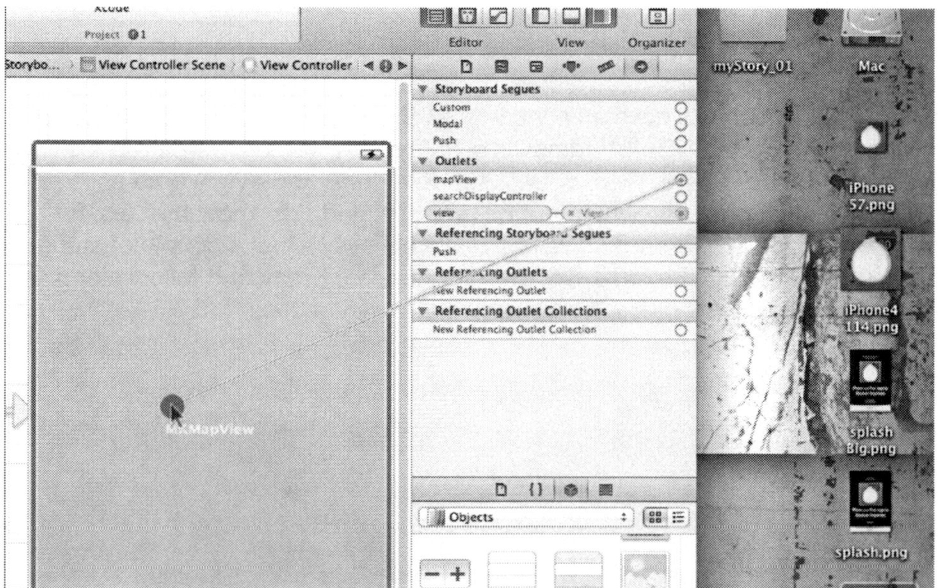

Figure 9–34. *Open the Connection Inspector and control drag to the MKMapView.*

24. We need to connect the `mapView` to the `MKMapView`. In the Document Outline Bar, select the View Controller and then click on the Connection Inspector and control–drag from the `mapView` to the `MKMapView`.

```
(MKAnnotationView *)mapView:(MKMapView *):
```

25. That's it! Run it. When we see a splash screen appear, we drop a pin right onto my office or the location we chose. See Figure 9–35.

Figure 9–35. *MapKIts and Storyboarding! Splash screen appears and then a pin drops onto a specified location!*

Congratulations! Once again, we have successfully implemented an app of fair complexity and we started with a body of code that we merely modified. As we compare our own Simulator to the images ahead, bask in the glow of accomplishment.

Then, perhaps after a brief rest, I hope that we might venture forward to see if some student examples in the "Digging My Students' MapKit Code" section whet our appetite for further development and challenge.

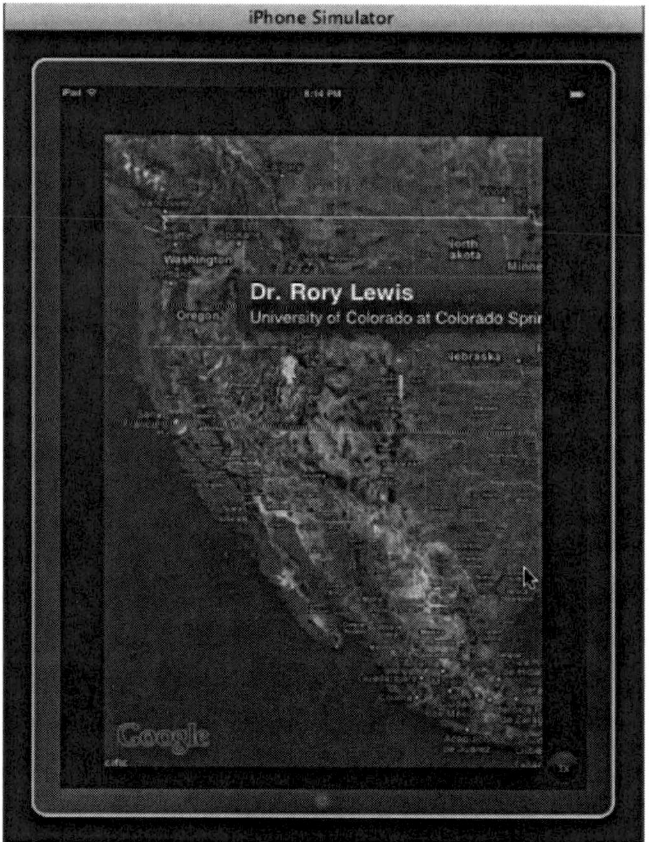

Figure 9–36. *At this point, I have my students implement it in class on the iPad. Try it out. The zoom is really far out as is shown here.*

Digging the Code

Here, in Digging the Code, we will go over protocols, memory management of Storyboard objects, parsing servers for MapKits, and reviewing some of my student's cool MapKit apps. Since it will open up new doors, I suggest that, if anything, we all read the parsing section well enough to be able to discuss and talk about it. When it comes to parsing, many coders fall short during interviews and discussions.

Protocols

Protocols are a list of methods that are not officially part of a language, but that a class can implement. We typically use protocols when we need to define methods for implementation by other classes. The aforementioned is my view. Apple, on the other hand, defines protocols a little differently. Apple officially states that protocols declare methods available for implementation by any class. Protocols are useful in at least three situations:

- To declare methods that others are expected to implement,
- To declare the interface to an object while concealing its class,
- To capture similarities among classes not hierarchically related.

Memory Management of Storyboard Objects

In Objective-C, `ivar` stands for Instance Variable. Now, `IBOutlets` are part of the public interface of a class and this is why I personally believe that it's better to declare our methods inside the `@property` implementation detail. Remember that `IBOutlet` ivars call setters, if they exist; however, if no setter is found, the object loaded from the nib is directly retained. This means that advertising the property as the `IBOutlet` at least makes it clear that the property's setter will always be used and follow whatever memory management rule has been set for that property. Apple puts it this way:

> *"Objects in the nib file are created with a retain count of 1 and then autoreleased. As it rebuilds the object hierarchy, UIKit reestablishes connections between the objects using setValue:forKey:, which uses the available setter method or retains the object by default if no setter method is available. This means that (assuming you follow the pattern shown in "Outlets") any object for which you have an outlet remains valid. If there are any top-level objects you do not store in outlets, however, you must retain either the array returned by the loadNibNamed:owner:options: method or the objects inside the array to prevent those objects from being released prematurely."*

Simply put, if given the choice, as in step 20, to either do it the way we did it:

```
#import <UIKit/UIKit.h>
#import <MapKit/MapKit.h>

@interface ViewController : UIViewController <MKMapViewDelegate>
{
    MKMapView *mapView;
}

@property (nonatomic, retain) IBOutlet MKMapView *mapView;

@end
```

Or this way:

```
#import <UIKit/UIKit.h>
#import <MapKit/MapKit.h>

@interface ViewController : UIViewController <MKMapViewDelegate>
{
    IBOutlet MKMapView *mapView;
```

```
}

@property (nonatomic, retain) MKMapView *mapView;

@end
```

The most interesting aspect of this is that if you simply drag your IBOutlet from the Storyboard Interface Builder into your header file—Xcode will make these decisions for you. It is "better" to use the first example and declare the IBOutlet in your @property, but that's only 'style' and you may work in an environment that uses the second method or the 'new' method we used in the first few chapters of this book.

Do yourself a favor and just do it the way I showed you—the first way.

Digging My Students' MapKit Code

When people come up to me and say, "Hey, Dr. Lewis, I have this really *great idea* for a new app...," it is amazing how often it involves using the MapKit framework. We have seen how fun and sexy this stuff is, and by now, you have likely also gathered that delving into the code can turn into quite a complexity.

As a final buffet of tasty, high-calorie, high-tech fun, and flash, I am going to share some final project scenarios with you. I certainly hope you actively follow along here, but I also want to honor the fact that you're done. You already succeeded in making it to the end of Chapter 9. So, remember, this section is like one of those "bonus feature" DVDs that Hollywood loves to include—at no extra cost. *Relax and enjoy!*

Parsing to MapKit from the Internet

A little background: I presented my class the MapKit session very much as I laid out the first example of this chapter. Then, we moved into one of the coolest things there is with MapKit—the ability to parse, or read live info, from the ether. This feature allows users to "see" the info on their map. I'll explain this to a degree before I present three student final projects.

One of the most intriguing things we can do with MapKit is get real live information from the Internet and configure it in a way that makes the Google Map on the user's iPhone come alive with live information (weather, traffic, geographical phenomena, taxis, planes, and so on). For example, one of the most popular apps for the San Francisco Bay Area is a program demonstrated in *iPhone Cool Projects* (Wolfgang Ante, et al., Apress, 2009) (see Figure 9–28) called "Routesy Bay Area San Francisco Muni and BART," written by Steven Peterson.

Peterson parses all the data from the BART (Bay Area Rapid Transit, `http://www.bart.gov/`) web server that keeps track of how close to schedule its trains are, the location of the trains, and their speeds. The app parses all this data and makes it useful and relevant to users *at their specific locations* in the San Francisco Bay Area. In Figure 9–29, you will see their app's red icon, and then several iPhone images. The left one shows all the places a user can catch buses and trains. The middle picture uses the same code we used in our example with a *core location* to show a user's current location with a blue icon, and where a requested station is. The right image reports to the user the relevant information on the best train given the context, the timing, etc. The app provides data for the next three trains that will be arriving at the train station nearest the user.

In essence, the MapKit code on the iPhone is, among other things, a *parsing* utility. It retrieves live information from a server that most people don't even know exists, and it puts a stream of data to a novel and useful purpose.

Because of the immediate and practical results that users of Peterson's app, and others like it, can reap, I figured this would be a perfect theme to round out this book. I'll first go over some of my "Parsing with the MapKit framework" lecture notes. Then I will show you several solid final projects created by my students on that basis.

With my students' blessing, the code for their projects (as shown below) is available for download from my website. This gives you the opportunity to have the code on your Mac while I simultaneously point out how you can modify it, learn the key features from it, or just put it on your iPad and show the folks at the bar these cool apps.

Figure 9–37. *Apress's* iPhone Cool Projects.

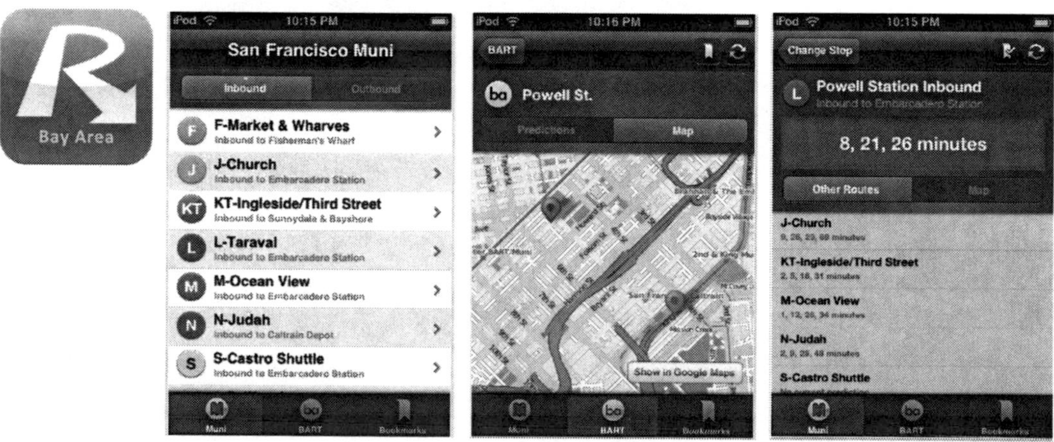

Figure 9–38. *App icon and examples of three action screens—parsing app: "Routesy Bay Area San Francisco Muni and BART." It combines data from the web and MapKit.*

The code for these three student Final Projects is located as follows:

- Stephen A. Moraco (Son): `http://www.rorylewis.com/xCode/011b_TrafficCam.zip`
- Stephen M. Moraco (Father): `http://www.rorylewis.com/xCode/011a_APRSkit.zip`
- Satish Rege: `http://www.rorylewis.com/xCode/011c_MyTraffic.zip`

MapKit Parsing

Remember, this is digging deep into the code at a level that is outside the scope of the book. However, all of the following instructions are seen in my students' code, which you are welcome to download. For now, just read along and see if you can follow their pattern of parsing, creating delegate objects, and so forth.

Before we look at their actual apps, consider a hypothetical scenario: Imagine there is a Grateful Dead Server that broadcasts an update on every Deadhead's geographical location—at least those who allow themselves to be visible on the grid. This hypothetical app allows a (serious) fan of the Grateful Dead to locate all the other Deadheads nearby at any given time. These fans can meet and share bootlegs, hang out, and generally relate on a plane that only other Grateful Dead disciples can appreciate.

Starting Point

If we were to create such an app, just as in the "Routesy" example, we would allow users to see where they are by bringing up the Attributes Inspector and turning on a Shows User Location switch. We would create a controller called *DeadHeadsView* that creates an instance of a parser we'll call `Gratefuldead`. Then, we would make it set itself as the delegate so it receives the feedback and calls a `getGratefuldead` data method.

Getting Data from the Web

As our parser sifts through the XML on the Grateful Dead Server, we would want it to grab `Gratefuldead` element data and create an instance of each *Gratefuldead* object. So, for each instance it creates, it calls back to us with an `addGratefuldead` method. We would need to implement our `Gratefuldead` and *Parser* methods on our `deadHeadsViewcontroller`. We might find that it's easier to think of our `GratefuldeadParser.h` this way:

```
+ (id)GratefuldeadParser; // this creates it
- (void)getGratefuldeadData; // this activates it
```

Add Methods to View Controller

Before adding implementation methods on our `DeadHeadsView` controller, we would need to implement the protocol with `GratefuldeadParser` Delegate and import its header file `#import <GratefuldeadParser.h>`. At this point, we'd be finished with the header, and we'd move to the implementation file.

First, we'd copy the two implementation methods from `GratefuldeadParser.h` and paste these two methods after the `@synthesize` statement:

```
@implementation DeadHeadsViewCOntroller

@synthesize deadView

- (void)getGratefuldeadData:(Gratefuldead *)Gratefuldead;
-(void)parserFinished
```

Test the Parser Feed

To test the Grateful Dead Server, we would see if we could log some messages. Let's separate the two methods, delete the semicolons, add brackets, and then enter "log" as shown:

```
- (void)getGratefuldeadData☹Gratefuldead *)Gratefuldead {
NSLog(@"Hippie Message");
}

-(void)parserFinished{
NSLog(@"located a Dead Head at %@", Gratefuldead.place");
}
```

Start the Parser Method

Having implemented our delegate methods, we would need to do three things:

1. Code the parser method. Put it into a method we could call `(void)viewWillAppear`. This would be called on by a view controller when its view is about to be displayed. If we were to do it this way, note that we would always want to call in our `- (void)viewWillAppear` method.

2. Create an instance of our parser that we would call *`GratefuldeadParser`*. With this, we'd get `GratefuldeadParser *parser = [GratefuldeadParser gratefuldeadParser]`. We want to make ourselves the delegate, which means that, now, *`GratefuldeadParser parser.delegate = self`*.

3. Two actions in this step: first, tell the parser to get the Gratefuldead data:

```
[parser getGratefuldeadData];
```

Second, handle its import:

```
#import "GratefuldeadParser.h"
```

Then, when the - (void)viewWillAppear is invoked, it would create an instance of *GratefuldeadParser*. As it receives the locations of all the Deadheads, it shows us where they are!

Do you recall how we made sure that the user of the app would appear on the map as a blue dot? I want you to think of the blue dot as just an annotation view. When added to the deadView, it essentially asks its delegate for its location.

> **NOTE:** If we return anything other than *nil*, then our annotation view, instead of the blue one, will be used and then return that view.

So, looking at this, we return nil when the annotation does not equal the user's current location.

```
- (MKAnnotationView *)deadView:(MKDeadView *)deadView
                 viewForAnnotation:(id <MKAnnotation>)annotation {
MKAnnotationView *view = nil;
return view;
```

But here's the thing; we do *not* want to return nil for our Gratefuldead locations. Conversely, we want to do cool things when our annotation is not equal to the deadView userLocation property, which itself is an annotation:

```
if(annotation != deadView.userLocation) {

                // THIS IS WHERE WE DO OUR COOL STUFF
               // BECAUSE IT'S A DEADHEAD, NOT THE USER
 }
```

At this point, we use the *dequeueReusableAnnotationViewWithIdentifier*, delegate method, which is available for reuse the instant they are off screen. It has a handy way of storing annotations in a separate data structure and then automatically adding and removing them from your map as the user's events require it. Note that dequeueReusableAnnotationViewWithIdentifier is about getting the reusable annotation view from the map, and it has nothing to do with adding or removing annotations:

```
GratefuldeadAnnotation *eqAnn = (GratefuldeadAnnotation*)annotation;
view = [self.deadView  dequeueReusableAnnotationViewWithIdentifier:@"GratefuldeadLoc"];
       if(nil == view) {
        view = [[[MKPinAnnotationView alloc] initWithAnnotation:eqAnn
                                             reuseIdentifier:@"GratefuldeadLoc"]
autorelease];
}
```

The annotation view goes and looks in its reuse queue to see if there are any views that can be reused if (nil == view) { … If there are none, it returns nil, which means we need to create a new one *view = [[[MKPinAnnotationView alloc] initWithAnnotation:eqAnn*.

There are many creative ways to make your annotations appear with animated chevrons, bells and whistles, Grateful Dead beads, and so on. You can see what's out there and available to make the iCandy portion of your annotations however you might wish.

In this regard, at this point of writing your code, the most important step is to review your code for errors using your NSLog debugger; this will determine whether it connects to a server of your choice. Once complete, it becomes an issue of parsing the XML. Then, the final step is to shop for iCandy for the annotations.

Three MapKit Final Projects: *CS–201 iPhone Apps, Objective–C*

The following are three apps that draw heavily on parsing information from the Internet. The first two come from a father and son, both named Stephen Moraco, and the third is from Satish Rege. They were all kind enough to write unedited bios as to why they took the class. They also included detailed lecture notes, the apps shown in this book, and what they got out of the course.

BIOGRAPHICAL INFO FOR EXAMPLES 1 AND 2

Stephen A. Moraco (Son)
Stephen M. Moraco (Father)

Steve A. (Figure 9–39) is in his senior year in high school. He has been concurrently enrolled at UCCS and has taken courses for dual credit (both high school and college). I, Stephen M. (Figure 9–40), am a professional software engineer working for Agilent Technologies, Inc. Both of us have iPhones and have an interest in learning to write applications for the iPhone. The UCCS course caught our attention as a way we could learn this together. In fact, we really enjoyed Dr. Lewis' CS201 classes, in which we toured the iPhone SDK and practiced writing a number of applications. The discussions in class and then between the two of us as we were driving home always had us excited about things we could do with the iPhone. Our final projects came from these discussions. Dr. Lewis, thank you for offering this course. It provided, in our case, a wonderful time of shared learning. We couldn't have had a more enjoyable time.

Figure 9–39. *Stephen A. Moraco (Son)*

Figure 9–40. *Stephen M. Moraco (Father)*

Final Project—Example 1

Stephen M. Moraco's app is one that is close to his heart. Being an amateur radio hobbyist, he decided to parse Bob Bruning's WB4APR site, where Bob had developed an Automatic Position Reporting System (APRS). Very much like the example that I gave in class, locating Deadheads, Stephen, the father, made an app that can locate all the Amateur Radio Operators that are within a user-specified distance from where they are at the time. I will not go over all of Stephen's code because you can download it and go over it carefully. The portions I think you should take note of are as follows: His `APRSmapViewController` header file sets out the road map with 3 IBOutlets, 1 IBAction, and a ViewController:

```
@property (nonatomic, retain) IBOutlet MKMapView *mapView;
@property (nonatomic, retain) APRSwebViewController *webBrowserController;
@property (nonatomic, retain) IBOutlet UISegmentedControl *ctlMapTypeChooser;
@property (nonatomic, retain) IBOutlet UIActivityIndicatorView *aiActivityInd;

-(IBAction)selectMapMode:(id)sender;
```

In the `APRSkit_MoracoDadAppDelegate` implementation file, he uses the following code to give the user a chance to log in. See Figure 9–41 for the results. The particulars of this step, seen in the - *(void)applicationDidFinishLaunching* method, also houses the distance (radius) from the user that the system will search for matches:

```
- (void)applicationDidFinishLaunching:(UIApplication *)application {

     NSLog(@"MapAPRS_MoracoDadAppDelegate:applicationDidFinishLaunching - ENTRY");
    // Override point for customization after app launch

     [window addSubview:[navigationController view]];
           [window makeKeyAndVisible];

     // preload our applcation defaults
     NSUserDefaults *upSettings = [NSUserDefaults standardUserDefaults];
     NSString *strDefaultCallsign = [upSettings stringForKey:kCallSignKey];
     if(strDefaultCallsign == nil)
     {
          strDefaultCallsign = strEmptyString;
     }
     self.callSign = strDefaultCallsign;
     //[strDefaultCallsign release];

     NSString *strDefaultSitePassword = [upSettings stringForKey:kSitePasswordKey];
     if(strDefaultSitePassword == nil)
     {
          strDefaultSitePassword = strEmptyString;
     }
     self.sitePassword = strDefaultSitePassword;

     NSString *strDefaultDistanceInMiles = [upSettings
stringForKey:kDistanceInMilesKey];
     if(strDefaultDistanceInMiles == nil)
     {
          strDefaultDistanceInMiles = @"30";
```

```
        }
        self.distanceInMiles = strDefaultDistanceInMiles;
        //[strDefaultSitePassword release];
        // INCORRECT DECR [upSettings release];
}
```

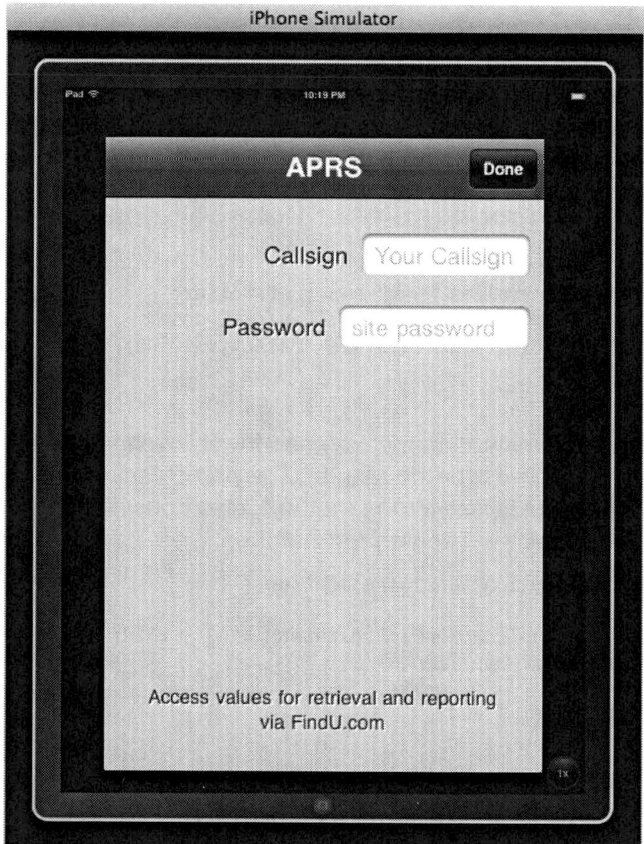

Figure 9–41. *CS–201 Final Project—Stephen M. Moraco's APRS set–up screen where users enter their Amateur Radio call signs and passwords.*

One of the first things Stephen did when he went to the website was make a list of all the attributes in the *XML* feed. The following list shows what he saw.

- Column–1 was the call sign, CALLSIGN
- Column–2 was the URL to Message traffic if available
- Column–3 was the URL to Weather page if available
- Column–4 was the Latitude
- Column–5 was the Longitude
- Column–6 was the distance from me (in miles)
- Column–7 was the DD:HH:MM:SS of the last report

To account for this data, he made eight pointers in his APRSstationParser.m file. Note that he has an extra one for possible unknown columns.

```
NSString *kCallSignCol          = @"Callsign";
NSString *kMsgURLCol            = @"MsgURL";
NSString *kWxURLCol             = @"WxURL";
NSString *kLatitudeCol          = @"Lat";
NSString *kLongitudeCol         = @"Long";
NSString *kDistanceCol          = @"Distance";
NSString *kLastReportCol        = @"LastReport";
NSString *kUnknownCol           = @"???";// re didn't recognize column #
```

Then, in the same file, he made case statements:

```
    case 1:
                m_strColumnName = kCallSignCol;
                break;
           case 2:
                m_strColumnName = kMsgURLCol;
                break;
           case 3:
                m_strColumnName = kWxURLCol;
                break;
           case 4:
                m_strColumnName = kLatitudeCol;
                break;
           case 5:
                m_strColumnName = kLongitudeCol;
                break;
           case 6:
                m_strColumnName = kDistanceCol;
                break;
           case 7:
                m_strColumnName = kLastReportCol;
                break;
           default:
                m_strColumnName = kUnknownCol;
                break;
```

Also, in the APRSkit_MoracoDadAppDelegate implementation file, the -*(void)recenterMap* method scans all annotations to determine geographical center and, just as we did in this chapter's exercise, to calculate the region of the map to display. Stephen does likewise after his three if statements. Figure 9–42 shows an image of the pins dropping.

```
- (void)recenterMap {
     NSLog(@" - APRSpinViewController:recenterMap - ENTRY");
          NSArray *coordinates = [self.mapView
valueForKeyPath:@"annotations.coordinate"];
     CLLocationCoordinate2D maxCoord = {-90.0f, -180.0f};
     CLLocationCoordinate2D minCoord = {90.0f, 180.0f};
     for(NSValue *value in coordinates) {
          CLLocationCoordinate2D coord = {0.0f, 0.0f};
          [value getValue:&coord];
               if(coord.longitude > maxCoord.longitude) {
                    maxCoord.longitude = coord.longitude;
               }
```

```
                if(coord.latitude > maxCoord.latitude) {
                    maxCoord.latitude = coord.latitude;
                }
                if(coord.longitude < minCoord.longitude) {
                    minCoord.longitude = coord.longitude;
                }
                if(coord.latitude < minCoord.latitude) {
                    minCoord.latitude = coord.latitude;
                }
    }
```

Note that in the `APRSstation` class, Stephen represents the details parsed from the APRS, which sets the location of the pins.

```
#import <CoreLocation/CoreLocation.h>

@interface APRSstation : NSObject {
    NSString   *m_strCallsign;
    NSDate     *m_dtLastReport;
    NSNumber   *m_nDistanceInMiles;
    NSString   *m_strMsgURL;
    NSString   *m_strWxURL;
    NSString   *m_strTimeSinceLastReport;
    CLLocation *m_locPosition;
    int         m_nInstanceNbr;
}

@property(nonatomic, copy) NSString *callSign;
@property(nonatomic, copy) NSNumber *distanceInMiles;
@property(nonatomic, retain) NSDate *lastReport;
@property(nonatomic, copy) NSString *timeSinceLastReport;
@property(nonatomic, copy) NSString *msgURL;
@property(nonatomic, copy) NSString *wxURL;
@property(nonatomic, retain) CLLocation *position;

@end
```

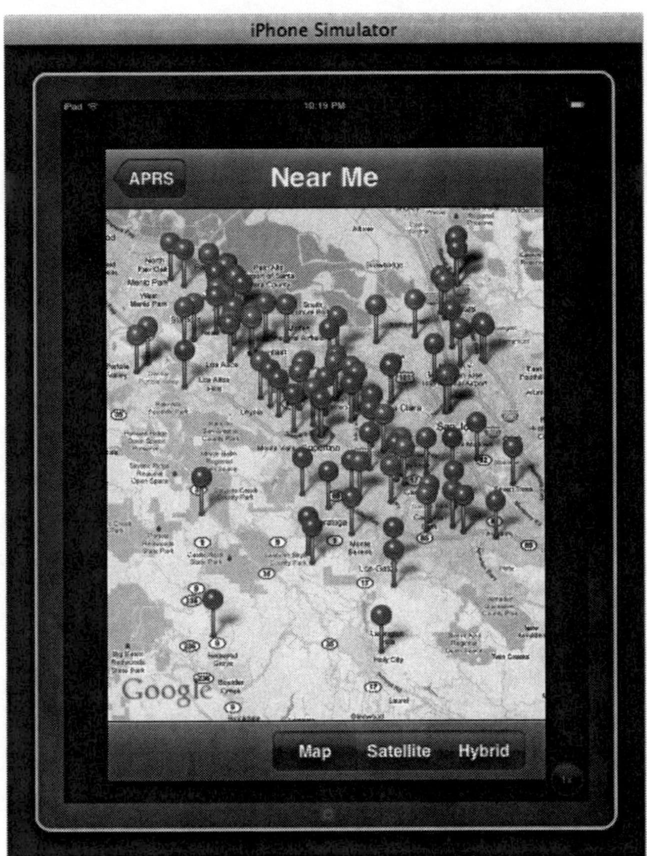

Figure 9–42. *CS-201 Final Project—Stephen M. Moraco's Animated pins drop down within the specified radius of the user's location. Here on the iPad simulator, the pins drop in the surrounding areas of Apple Headquarters.*

Another cool thing Stephen did was to distinguish between the amateur radio stations that have their own websites and those that do not. For the ones that have web sites, on the annotation view, he includes a chevron which, when clicked, yields the web page. See Figures 9–42 and 9–43. This code is directly under the switch cases in the `APRSstationParser.m` file.

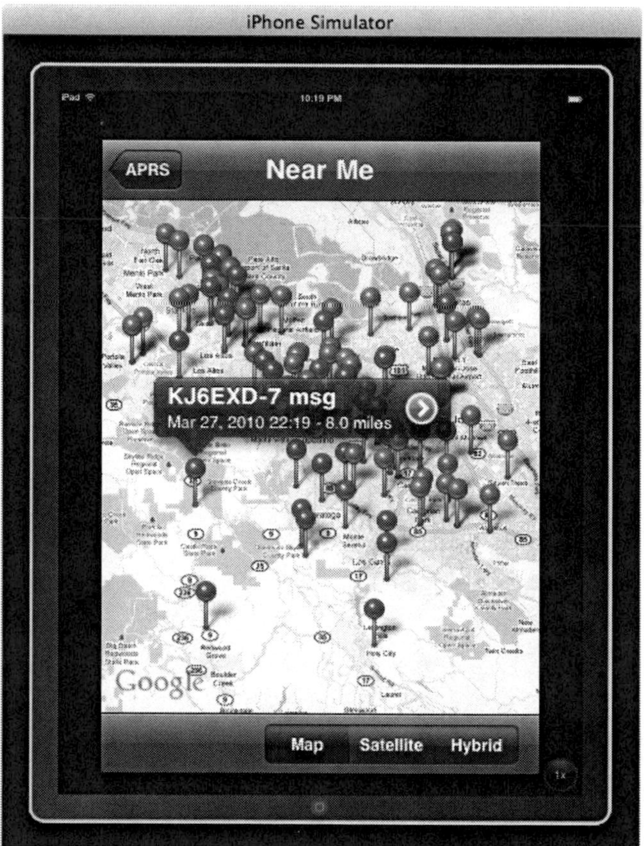

Figure 9–43. *CS–201 Final Project—Stephen M. Moraco's app provides Annotations to appear when one clicks on a pin and where a linked website is on the APRS server, a blue chevron appears where one may click to go to the amateur radio station's website. In this case, amateur radio station KJ6EXD–7 does have a website.*

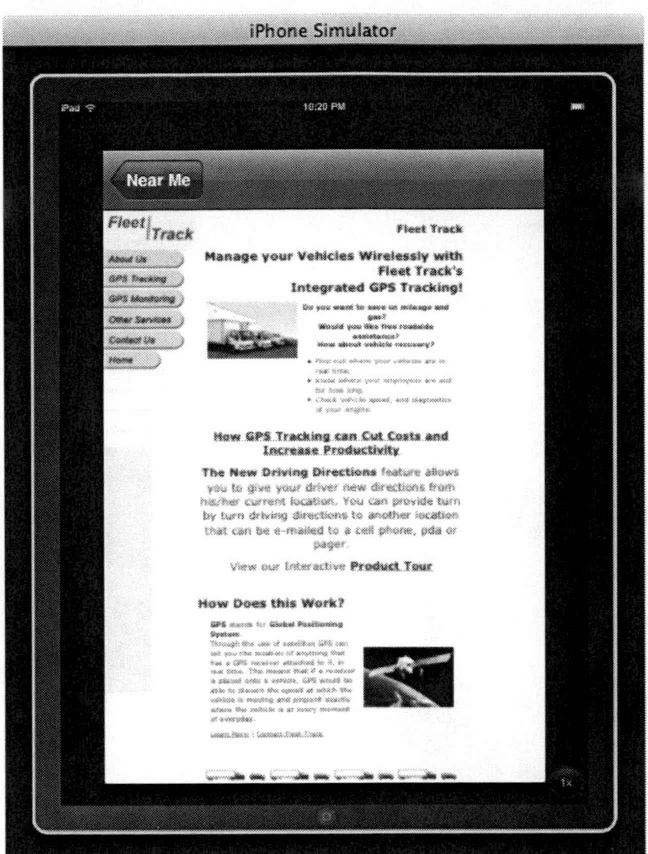

Figure 9–44. *CS–201 Final Project—Stephen M. Moraco's App showing the KJ6EXD–7 website embedded in the iPad.*

In the APRSmapViewController implementation file, Stephen includes, among other things, a bare–bones methodology to switch between map, satellite, and hybrid views. An example of this is seen when we show the closest radio station to the user, which, in simulator mode is Apple Headquarters. See Figure 9–44, where the view is in Hybrid mode.

```
-(IBAction)selectMapMode:(id)sender
{
    UISegmentedControl *scChooser = (UISegmentedControl *)sender;
    int nMapStyleIdx = [scChooser selectedSegmentIndex];
    NSLog(@"APRSmapViewController:selectMapMode - New Style=%d",nMapStyleIdx);

    switch (nMapStyleIdx) {
        case 0:
            self.mapView.mapType = MKMapTypeStandard;
            break;
        case 1:
            self.mapView.mapType = MKMapTypeSatellite;
            break;
        case 2:
            self.mapView.mapType = MKMapTypeHybrid;
```

```
                break;
            default:
                NSLog(@"APRSmapViewController:selectMapMode - Unknown Selection?!");
                break;
        }
}
```

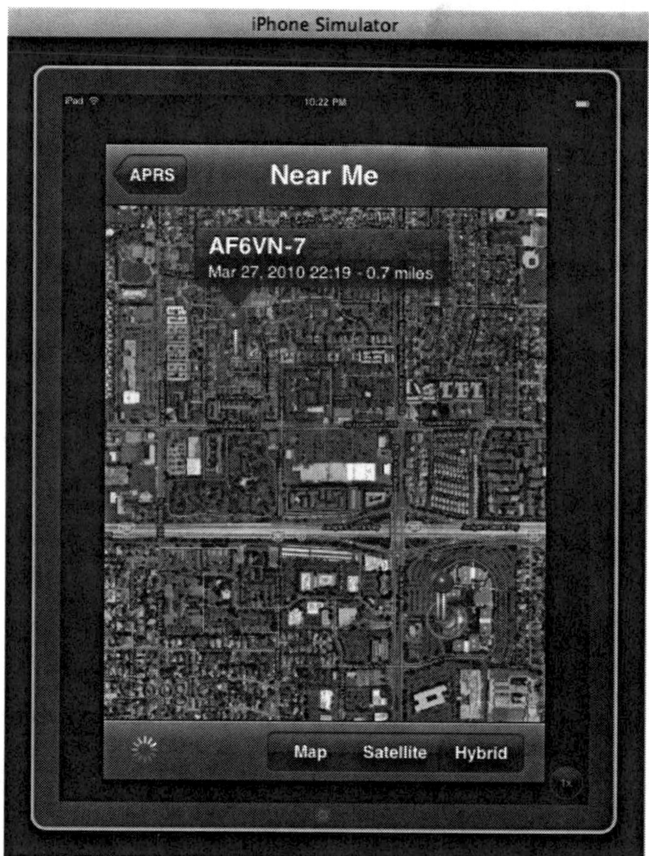

Figure 9–45. *CS–201 Final Project—Stephen M. Moraco's App showing the closest amateur radio station to Apple Headquarters in the Hybrid map view.*

Finally, as a finishing touch, which I always encourage students to complete; Stephen included a nice About page in the `AboutView` nib. See Figure 9–45.

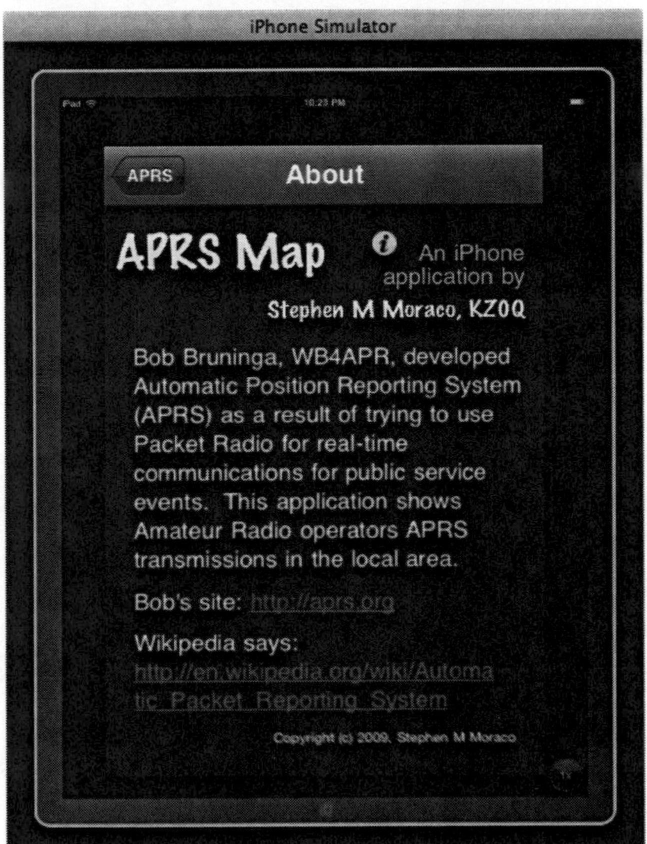

Figure 9–46. *CS–201 Final Project—Stephen M. Moraco's App showing his "About Page" —totally cool!*

> **NOTE:** In order to run the code, you will need to have a password and username. You have two options: 1) Acquire your own, or 2) Download any of these three apps, which are essentially the same.

```
http://itunes.apple.com/us/app/pocketpacket/id336500866?mt=8
http://itunes.apple.com/us/app/ibcnu/id314134969?mt=8
http://itunes.apple.com/us/app/aprs/id341511796?mt=8
```

Final Project—Example 2

Stephen A. Moraco is a gifted high school student who attended my class. His app parses the National Weather Cam network at `http://www.mhartman-wx.com/wcn/`. This can be seen in the `TrafficCamParser` implementation file *`static NSString *strURL =http://www.mhartman-wx.com/wcn/wcn_db.txt`*.

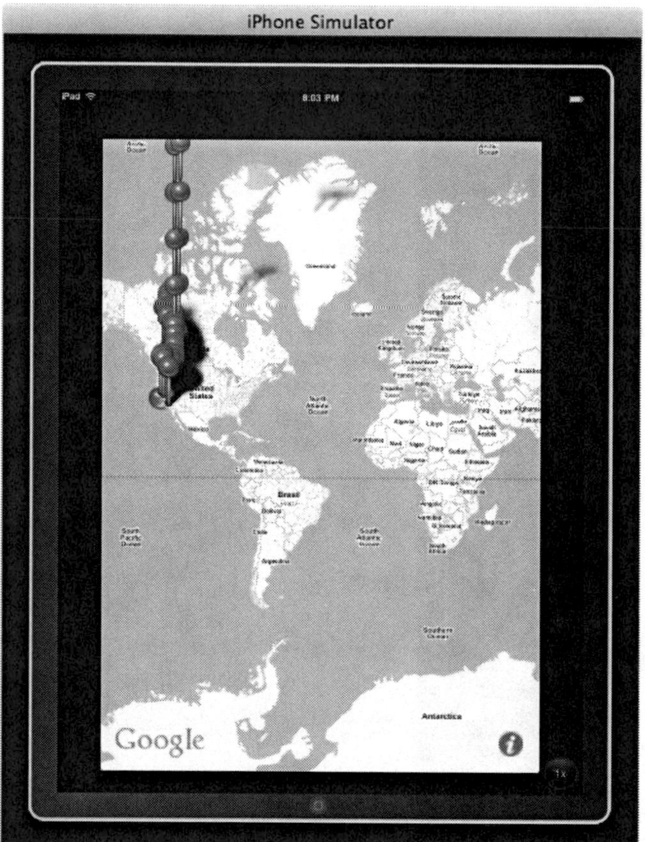

Figure 9–47. *CS-201 Final Project—Stephen A. Moraco's App launches with hundreds of pins plummeting from the sky as they fill up a specified area around the user's "current" location at Apple Headquarters.*

He found that he needed to use an adapter to filter out bad meta tags in the <head></head> sections. There was so much extraneous matter on the server it was crashing the code. To take care of this, he had to make rules to replace "^" with </field><field>, replace
's with blank space, replace "<font size=\"-1\">(" and ")
" with </field><field>, start and end with <CAM><field> and </field></CAM> and remove </font> tags, remove nonbreaking spaces. I've added numbering to help you see the start of each line, as the word wrap confuses me, too!

```
1.  NSString *strNoParaQueryResults = [strQueryResults
    stringByReplacingOccurrencesOfString:@"<font size=\"-1\">("
    withString:@"</field><field>"];
2.  strNoParaQueryResults = [strNoParaQueryResults
    stringByReplacingOccurrencesOfString:@")<br>" withString:@"</field><field>"];
3.  strNoParaQueryResults = [strNoParaQueryResults
    stringByReplacingOccurrencesOfString:@"</font>" withString:@""];
4.  strNoParaQueryResults = [strNoParaQueryResults
    stringByReplacingOccurrencesOfString:@" " withString:@""];
5.  strNoParaQueryResults = [strNoParaQueryResults
    stringByReplacingOccurrencesOfString:@"></a>" withString:@"></img></a>"];
```

```
6.  strNoParaQueryResults = [strNoParaQueryResults
    stringByReplacingOccurrencesOfString:@"width=150" withString:@"width=\"150\""];
7.  strNoParaQueryResults = [strNoParaQueryResults
    stringByReplacingOccurrencesOfString:@"height=100" withString:@"height=\"100\""];
8.  strNoParaQueryResults = [strNoParaQueryResults
    stringByReplacingOccurrencesOfString:@"width=100" withString:@"width=\"100\""];
9.  strNoParaQueryResults = [strNoParaQueryResults
    stringByReplacingOccurrencesOfString:@"height=150" withString:@"height=\"150\""];
10. strNoParaQueryResults = [strNoParaQueryResults
    stringByReplacingOccurrencesOfString:@"border=0" withString:@"border=\"0\""];
11. strNoParaQueryResults = [strNoParaQueryResults
    stringByReplacingOccurrencesOfString:@"\"\"" withString:@"\""];
12. strNoParaQueryResults = [strNoParaQueryResults
    stringByReplacingOccurrencesOfString:@".jpg " withString:@".jpg\" "];
13. strNoParaQueryResults = [strNoParaQueryResults
    stringByReplacingOccurrencesOfString:@"&" withString:@"and"];
14. strNoParaQueryResults = [strNoParaQueryResults
    stringByReplacingOccurrencesOfString:@"<font size=\"-1\">" withString:@""];
15. strNoParaQueryResults = [strNoParaQueryResults
    stringByReplacingOccurrencesOfString:@"</b<" withString:@"</b><"];
```

The `TrafficCamAnnotation.h` header files used is straightforward and simple, using the *+ (id)annotationWithCam:(TrafficCam *)Cam*; and - `(id)initWithCam:(TrafficCam *)Cam`; pointers as described earlier for my hypothetical `GratefuldeadParser.h`. In this case, *+ (id)annotationWithCam:(TrafficCam *)Cam*; creates parsed file and - `(id)initWithCam:(TrafficCam *)Cam`; initializes it. The result of all this hard work, taking care of the non-useful code, is seen in the clean annotation. See Figure 9–47.

```
#import <MapKit/MapKit.h>
#import <CoreLocation/CoreLocation.h>

@class TrafficCam;

@interface TrafficCamAnnotation : NSObject <MKAnnotation> {
     CLLocationCoordinate2D Coordinate;
     NSString *Title;
     NSString *Subtitle;
     TrafficCam *Cam;
}

@property(nonatomic, assign) CLLocationCoordinate2D coordinate;
@property(nonatomic, retain) NSString *title;
@property(nonatomic, retain) NSString *subtitle;
@property(nonatomic, retain) TrafficCam *cam;

+ (id)annotationWithCam:(TrafficCam *)Cam;
- (id)initWithCam:(TrafficCam *)Cam;

@end
```

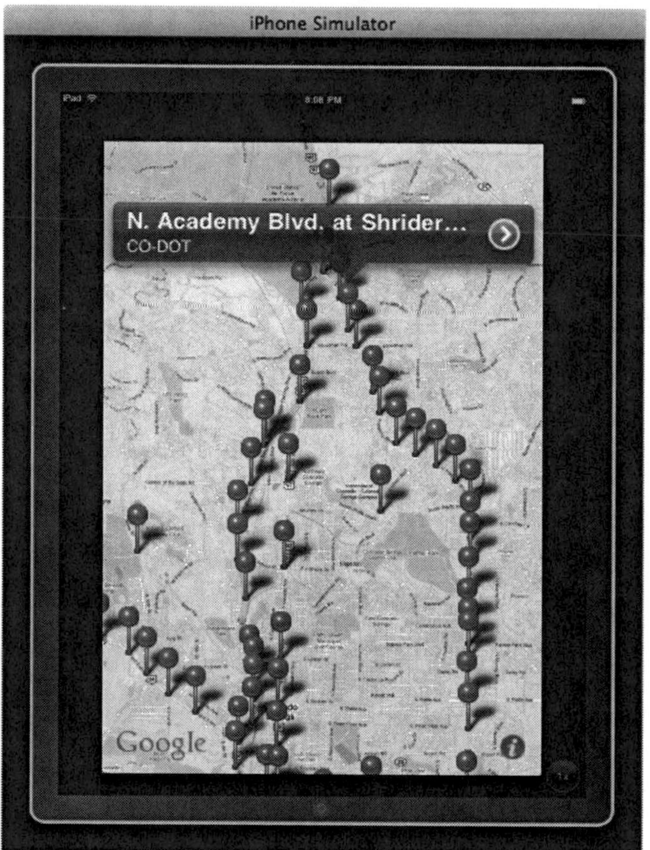

Figure 9–48. *CS–201 Final Project—Stephen A. Moraco's App zoomed into the Colorado Springs area. The annotation of North Academy at Shrider appears because the author clicked on that intersection.*

Stephen also found he could not automatically use the camera video views. Working around this challenge was not a trivial task in `TrafficCamSettingsViewController.m`. One example was to allow orientations other than the default portrait orientation:

```
BOOL)shouldAutorotateToInterfaceOrientation:(UIInterfaceOrientation)interfaceOrientation
{
    // Return YES for supported orientations
    return (interfaceOrientation == UIInterfaceOrientationPortrait);
}
```

He had to arrange this code in order to have beautifully spaced video cam images fitting nicely in the screen, as illustrated in Figure 9–48.

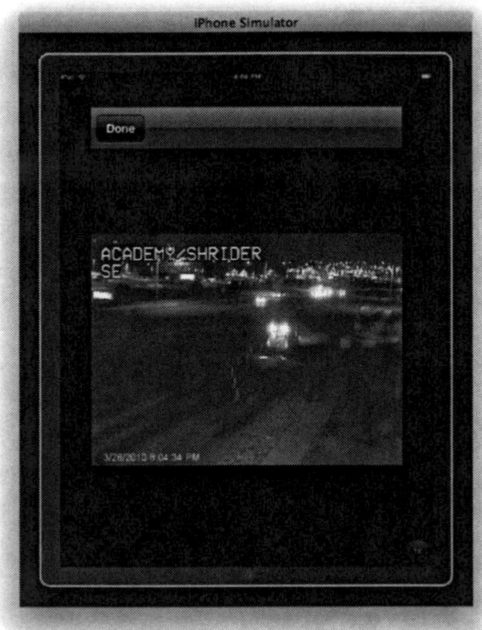

Figure 9–49. *CS–201 Final Project—Stephen A. Moraco's App zoomed into the Colorado Springs area. The annotation of North Academy at Shrider appears because the author clicked on that intersection.*

BIOGRAPHICAL INFO FOR EXAMPLE 3

Satish Rege

Why do I want to be an iPhone developer? Simple—the iPhone imparts the computing, the communicating, and the multimedia experience of a large computing system in the palm of your hand. It provides rich resources and user interface primitives to express creative capabilities in a synergistic way. These iPhone properties attracted me to want to learn iPhone development tools to express my own ideas. Rory's course was an excellent introduction that covered a multitude of iPhone capabilities and made them easy to master.

Figure 9–50. *Satish Rege*

Final Project—Example 3

Satish (Figure 9–42) always came up with simple eloquent code for all his homework assignments. When I graded the weekly assignments, I realized that Satish had the knack of being able to put into 20 lines of code what others would often take three times as much to do the same thing. For his final project, Satish's app allows one to look up ahead at the traffic at intersections to come, and, if there is a traffic jam at one intersection, to recommend another.

At least in theory, that is how it works. Satish saved a lot of heartache by starting at one location he knew would be a tough intersection: I–25 Northbound. He focused on controller implementation files and then he rotates back and forth from there depending on location in Colorado Springs. He has 27 cases for the 27 cameras in Colorado Springs. Simple, elegant, beautiful.

Figure 9–51 shows the list. Figures 9–52 and 9–53 show two examples of the traffic views.

```
//Choose the camera depending on your co-ordinate

     switch (cameraCordinate) {
          case 1:
               url = [NSURL
URLWithString:@"http://www.springsgov.com/trafficeng/bImage.ASP?camID=17"];     //Camera
- S Academy/ I-25 North
               break;
          case 2:
               url = [NSURL
URLWithString:@"http://www.springsgov.com/trafficeng/bImage.ASP?camID=18"];     //Camera
- HWY 85/87/I-25 N
               break;

>>>>>>
>>>>>>
>>>>>>
          case 26:
               url = [NSURL
URLWithString:@"http://www.springsgov.com/trafficeng/bImage.ASP?camID=33"];     //
Camera - Monument/ I-25 N
               break;
          case 27:
               url = [NSURL
URLWithString:@"http://www.springsgov.com/trafficeng/bImage.ASP?camID=49"];     //Camera
- CountyLine/ I-25 SE
               break;
```

Figure 9–51. *CS–201 Final Project—Rege's app selects the traffic lights closest to the user as he or she is driving down the street.*

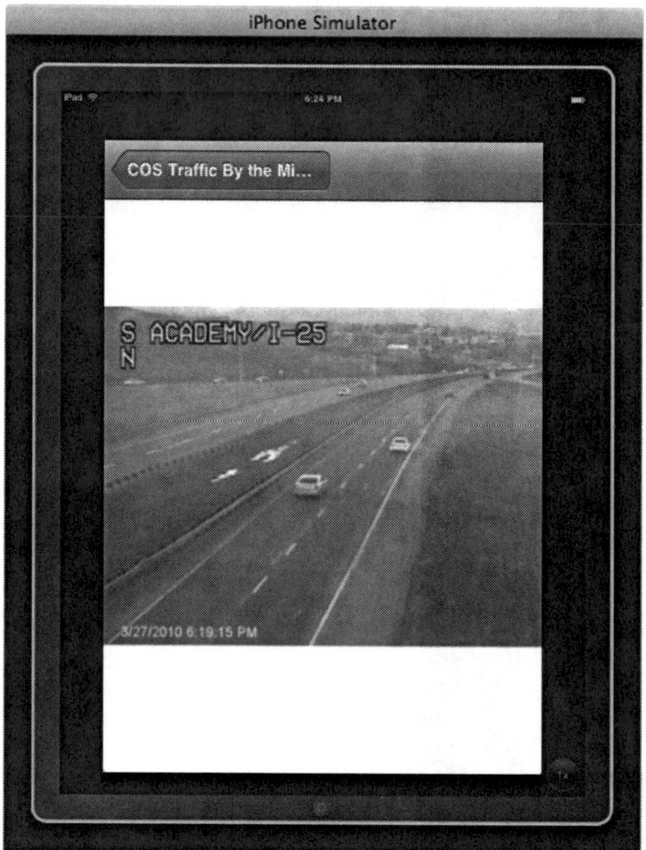

Figure 9–52. *CS–201 Final Project—Rege's traffic monitoring app showing the embedded camera view.*

Figure 9–53. *CS–201 Final Project—Satish Rege's app showing another embedded camera view.*

Zoom Out… Seeing the Big Picture

It's important to know where we came from, where we are now, and where we are going next. Not to get too metaphysical, but this chapter is a bit of a metaphor for our lives. Where were you five years ago? Last year? One day before you bought this book? Where do you intend to be six months from now?

That's why this subject is so popular. People love to know where they are! People love to know, and love to be shown how to get from "here" to "there."

You know how men stereotypically refuse to stop and ask for directions? I know I do—it is because I should just *know* where I'm going. When GPS came on the scene, I was impressed. But when Apple included one, by way of 'Maps,' in my first iPhone, I was totally blown away. All of a sudden, I had the ability to consult the oracle *and* maintain my male ego at the same time!

That's power, that's authority… and that's the same revolution we all joined. Now that you have completed this book, and successfully navigated through these exercises—some easier, some tougher—you are well on your way in the world of programming.

As I stated earlier, my goals for you in this chapter were humble. However, as in any really challenging and worthwhile pursuit, practice makes perfect. If you are exhausted, but still excited about these ideas and possibilities, then I count that as full success—both for you and for myself.

Some of you are perhaps thinking about topics that we did not cover in this book: the accelerometer, cameras/videos, peer–to–peer protocol, RSS feeds, mail clients/POP servers, etc. If these areas interest you, my hope is that your mind is already racing off in these new directions. That means you *do* know where you are, and that you know where you *want to go*. Life is good!

Chapter 10

MapKit & Tables with Storyboarding

There are five things I want you to bear in mind regarding this chapter:

- **Continuation of Chapter 9:** Chapter 10 takes what you learned in Chapter 9 and injects it with steroids. You will need to go over what you learned in Chapter 9 and go right into Chapter 10. In the lecture hall, I make my students in class run Chapter 9 in twenty minutes, that's if they want a grade and then, immediately after emailing me a screenshot of their completed project, we go right into Chapter 10. May I suggest that, if you have taken a couple of days off after ending Chapter 9, that you too make yourself repeat Chapter 9 a couple of times until you can do it under twenty minutes. Even if you have to do it 15 times, do it over and over again before trying this chapter.
- **Non-trivial:** When you're done with Chapter 10, you will have really accomplished something you can be proud of. Yes, on one hand students shriek with laughter when we debate what level of geekdom a student will be at a certain point, but the truth is that after you've completed this app, you will be able to get work as an Objective-C programmer, or at least be able to hold a decent conversation with an interviewer who will not believe you classified yourself as an absolute beginner. Neither did Apple when they hired a student of mine to work in their iOS 5 development in Cupertino. Eight months earlier, she'd never owned a Mac and was studying the first edition of this book, so take this seriously; this chapter will be a defining chapter in your life.

- **Big Picture:** As true as you are reading these words, there WILL be a time when this code will bog you down and, if you were in my lecture hall and I saw you overwhelmed and freaking out, I would walk up to you and remind you of the Big Picture. Throughout this chapter, I will bring you back to the Big Picture, which, in a nutshell, is a storyboard containing a table that is populated with many city names. We go to Google's server and fetch the geospatial addresses of each of these cities and, when the user taps on one of the cities listed in your table, we travel along another segue that instantiates a MapKit that drops a pin in the center of that city.
- **Chapter Outline:** Chapter 10 has very little preliminaries because I want you to seamlessly keep your momentum from Chapter 9 right into 10. I will explain where the help files and videos are, how to use them if you choose to, and how these are different from previous help files.
- **DO NOT GIVE UP:** Chapter 10 tests you and I want you to break through. Listen to me when I say that nobody is going to do Chapter 10 in one try! You will have to start from scratch repeatedly. This issue of starting over is, in fact, the ***key***: After spending a little time debugging, just start again from scratch. Please do not say to yourself: "*Oh I can't get this, look I've tried this 5 times and I can't get through it!*" It's OK to fail and start again and I really want you to get through this. I want to see you go to the forum and tell everybody you got through Chapter 10! OK? Yeah!

NOTE: It has come to my attention that a few of my students do not pronounce the word segue correctly. Here are some of the amazing renditions of this word I've heard from my students: "Seeg", "Seg-you", "Zeeyoo", "Suh-goo-wee", and, of course, "Sega", as in the game system! Really! If you did not know it already *Segue* is pronounced as follows: "Seg-way". That's my way of defining it. The proper and correct way, as defined by The Merriam-Webster Dictionary, is as follows:

se·gue\ se-( )gwā, sā-\

1 : proceed to what follows without pause—used as a direction in music

2 : perform the music that follows like that which has preceded—used as a direction in music

Origin of SEGUE: Italian, there follows, from seguire to follow, from Latin sequi — First Known Use: circa 1740.

myStory_02: A Single-View Application

In myStory_02, we divide the project into Parts 1 and 2. In Part 1, we use storyboarding to create a simple table that is populated by an array of cities. The length of the list will be whatever the "count" of the number of cities on the list is that you have or make up. When a user selects one of the cities on the list, nothing really happens. However, it's important to know that your application works at this point before moving forward. You can take a sneak peek at this by going to Figure 10–26. Then, in Part 2, we send the list of cities that populate our table to the Google server where we parse the server for the longitudinal and latitudinal addresses for each city. We store these address and, when the user selects a city, we "go" from the table, through the segue, and onto a View with a UIMapKit that instantiates a map of the city with a pin dropping into the city-center.

Possible Prepping for the App

Let's prep ourselves with two sets of terminology: "Parsing" and "going up onto the internet". We will be using the word "parse" quite a lot and, even though I was reticent to include parsing when I designed my course and this book, I decided on erring on teaching you something that is so fundamental to be able to code in this day and age: parsing is writing code that allows you to enter a server and extract only the terms you want from your database. For example, the Google server may have 6,000 associated pointers, links, and terms associated with the city of Durban, South Africa. We will parse the Google server, ignoring everything except for the longitudinal and latitudinal address of Durban. Think of the millions of application that need to go to a server somewhere and extract only the information that the user wants? This is critical coding, and I'm going to show you exactly how to do this (and make it look really cool on your iPad).

Of course you know that the Internet is not "up" in the air or a cloud. Yes, a certain amount of data is sent up to satellites but then comes back down to earth and travels through lines until it gets to a server. Having iPad and iPhone apps that can grab important data from a particular server is critical. I once had a student who wrote a final class project app that parsed the server of Colorado Springs' traffic cameras located here in Colorado. After parsing the correct images from the city server, he sent a couple of snap shots per second of each intersection back to the iPhone app so the user could "see ahead" at intersections and make decisions based on the amount of traffic at the intersection. Beautiful! However, as bright as this student was, when standing in the front of the lecture hall, he pointed to the sky when he described how he wrote the code to parse the server. I asked him if he knew that the server was located only 4 miles from campus. He looked at me and said: "So, it does not go up into the cloud?"

Even I point up at the clouds when I say go onto the internet but I want you to remember that, when we parse the Google server, we don't care where it is or how we got there. We are only concerned with whether our code correctly parses the server for only the information that is important to us.

Preliminaries

This chapter's download files are a little different from previous tutorials. Of course one does not have to download anything. You can follow along with the book and run the app perfectly sans the video, the source code, or the download files. I suggest you first try to do it without the video, download files, or source code. However, if you feel inclined to utilize the download files, you will want to pay attention to the following. The download files contain 6 images and 9 boilerplate codes. They are set forth as shown in Table 10–1:

Table 10–1. *Download files.*

Name of File	When Used	Description
01 Part 1myMasterTableViewController m	Coding Part 1	Private interface for our NSArray of cities. This is not in the header: so it's not public.
02 Part 1myMasterTableViewController m	Coding Part 1	Our NSArray of cities we insert into our viewDidLoad method.
03 Part 1myMasterTableViewController m	Coding Part 1	Code to enable viewing of the city names in each cell we insert into our tableView method.
04 Part 2myPos h	Coding Part 2	All of myPos.h
05 Part 2myPos m	Coding Part 2	All of myPos.m
06 Part 2myDetailViewController h	Coding Part 2	All of myDetailViewController.h
07 Part 2myDetailViewController m	Coding Part 2	Top Matter: #imports, our configureView private method, @implementation, and @ synthesize.
08 Part 2myDetailViewController m	Coding Part 2	Our setDetailItem method to update the view, our configureViewmethod to parse the Google server and update the user interface for the detail item and three connection methods.
09 Part 2myMasterTableViewController m	Coding Part 2	The prepareForSegue method that we insert into MasterTableViewController only for Part 2.
iPad 72	Not Used	The 72 × 72 pixel iPad Icon: This is for your convenience if you choose to do the Universal approach and have it compile for both the iPad and the iPhone.

Name of File	When Used	Description
iPhone 57	Preliminaries	The 57 × 57 pixel iPhone icon.
iPhone4 114	Preliminaries	The 114 ×114 pixel Retina iPhone icon.
splash Big	Preliminaries	The iPhone splash screen.
splash	Preliminaries	The 114 ×114 pixel Retina iPhone splash screen

These download files can be located at `http://bit.ly/nvc3Xk`. One can download the sample code that I programmed on the video here: `http://bit.ly/raKxPe`. To view the screencast of this chapter's exercise, go to `http://bit.ly/pEsztt`.

THE BIG PICTURE

We will have **many** versions of the big picture in this chapter. First, we will view the code form "30,000" feet, taking a very broad overall view of our landscape. Then, as we drill downward, we will always keep track of the big picture. Here's the first big picture:

1. Populate a table with a list of cities
2. Code a pin to drop to the center of a selected cities' map

A New Single View Template

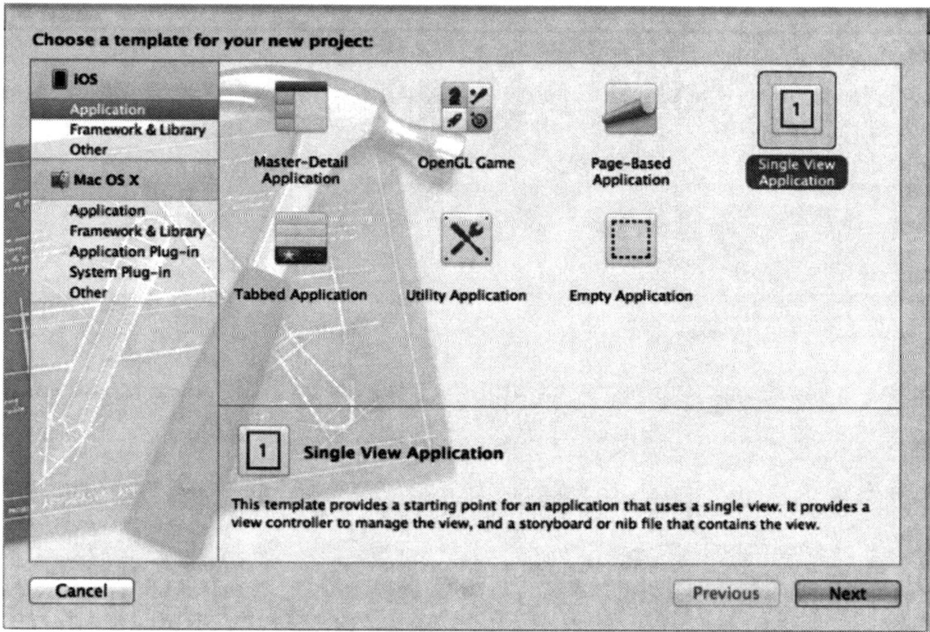

Figure 10–1. *Select the Single View Application icon, and press return or next.*

1. As in myStory_01, we will use a Single View Application. So open Xcode and enter `⌘⇧N`, as shown in Figure 10–1. After selecting the Single View Application, press enter/return.

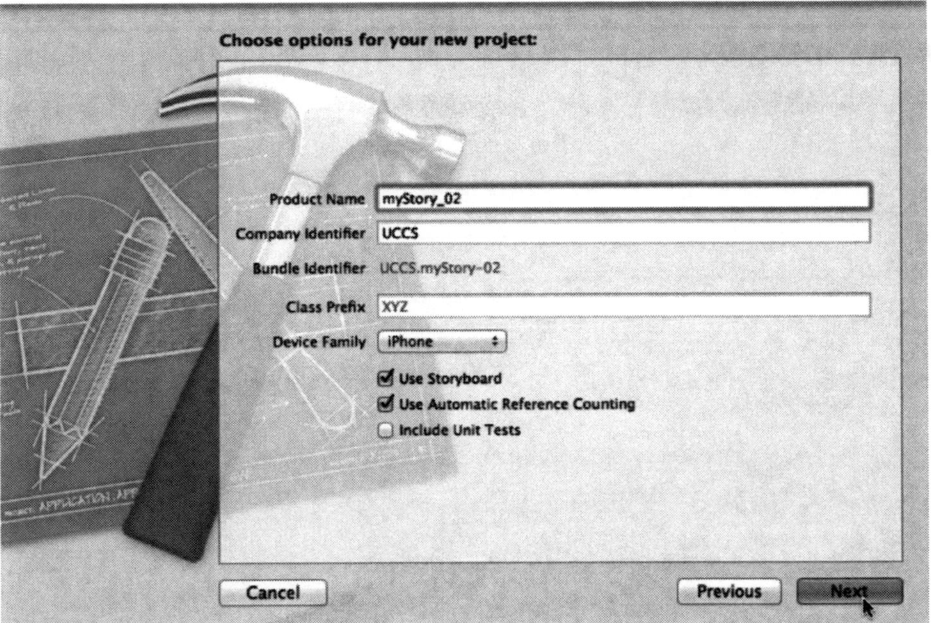

Figure 10–2. *Name your app myStory_02 making sure Storyboard and automatic referencing is on.*

2. In order to follow along with me as closely as you can, name it "myStory_02", select "iPhone", check the "Use Storyboard" and "Use Automatic Reference Counting" but leave the "Class Prefix" and "Include Unit Tests" unchecked, as shown in Figure 10–2. Automatic Referencing is really out of the scope of this book but, in very basic terms, Automatic Reference Counting (ARC) is code that invokes your Mac's automatic memory management for Objective-C objects and blocks. This frees the experienced programmer from the need to explicitly insert retains and releases.

Bring in the Images!

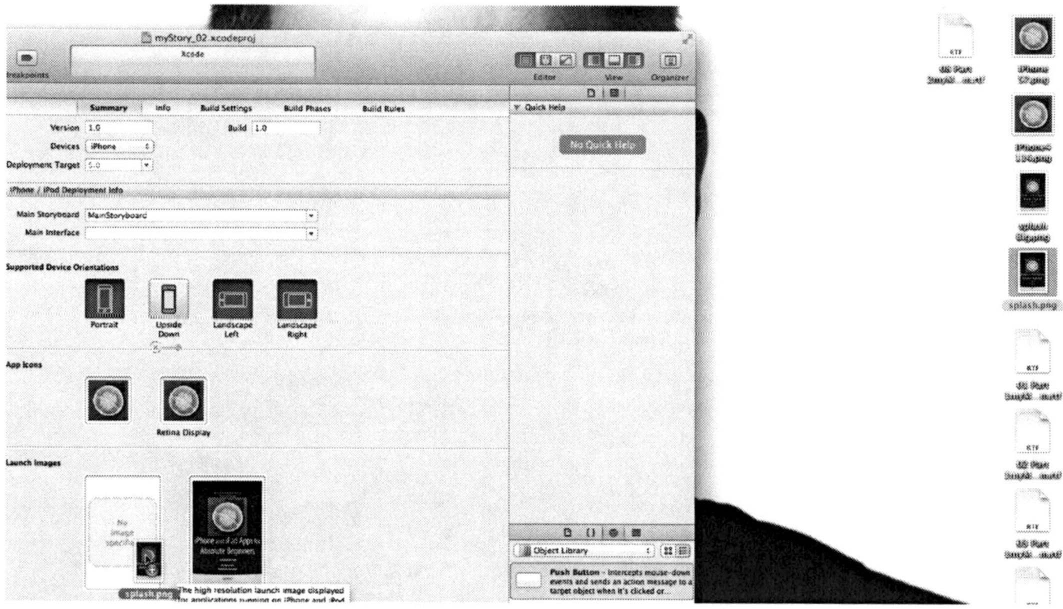

Figure 10–3. ***Drag in your graphics.***

3. Just as we did in myStory_01 after going to my website at `http://bit.ly/oqnNM7` and downloading the images and boilerplate code onto your desktop, drag in the 57 by 57 px for the iPhone classic, the 114 × 114 px for the iPhone 4S Retina Display. Also bring in the 640 × 960px splash screen for iPad and iPhone Retina displays and, as shown in Figure 10–3, drag in the 320 by 480px for the classic iPhone.

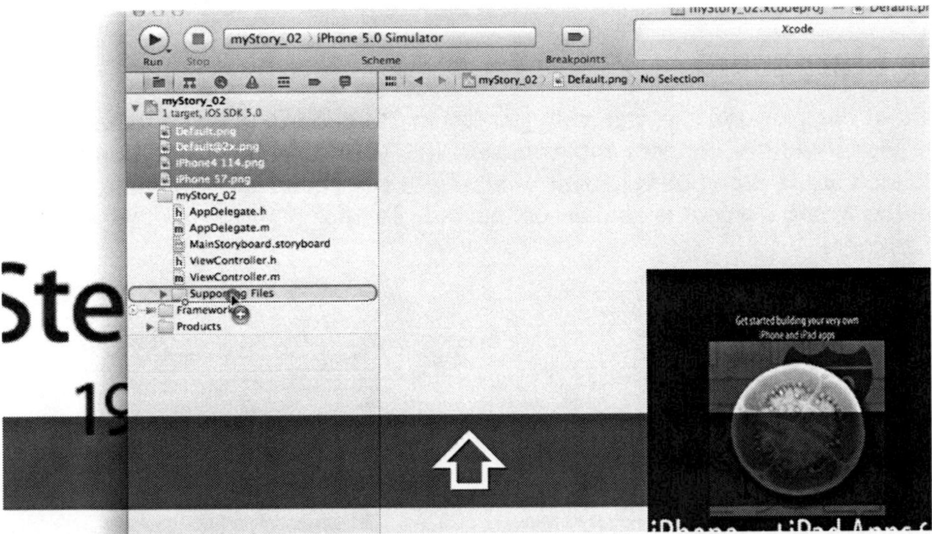

Figure 10–4. *Drag the images into the Supporting Files Folder.*

4. Because we always want to keep thing nice and orderly and in their proper place, you will see that the files holding the images you just dragged into Xcode are in the root directory. We want to drag them into their proper location – the Supporting Files folder. This is illustrated in Figure 10–4.

Organize Storyboard

One of the most benign ways one can really get lost in Storyboarding is not focusing on exactly how your structures connect and associate with your objects in Storyboarding. It is so easy to look at the Storyboard canvas and believe everything is great while not noticing that the wrong element is actually connected. So, make sure you follow along exactly as I am here.

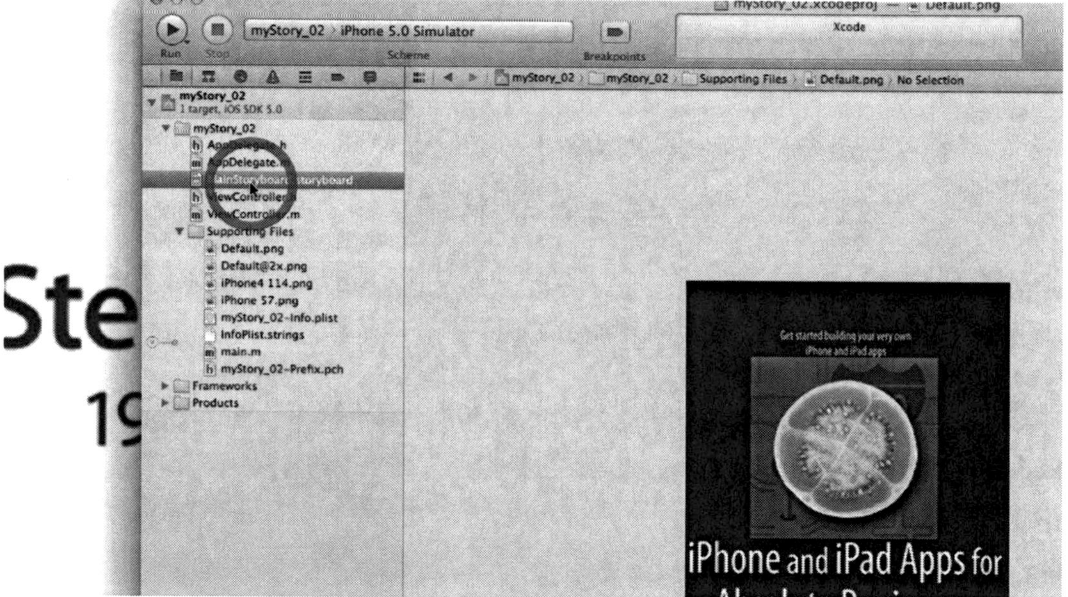

Figure 10–5. *Select the Storyboard.*

5. Select the storyboard, as shown in Figure 10–5.

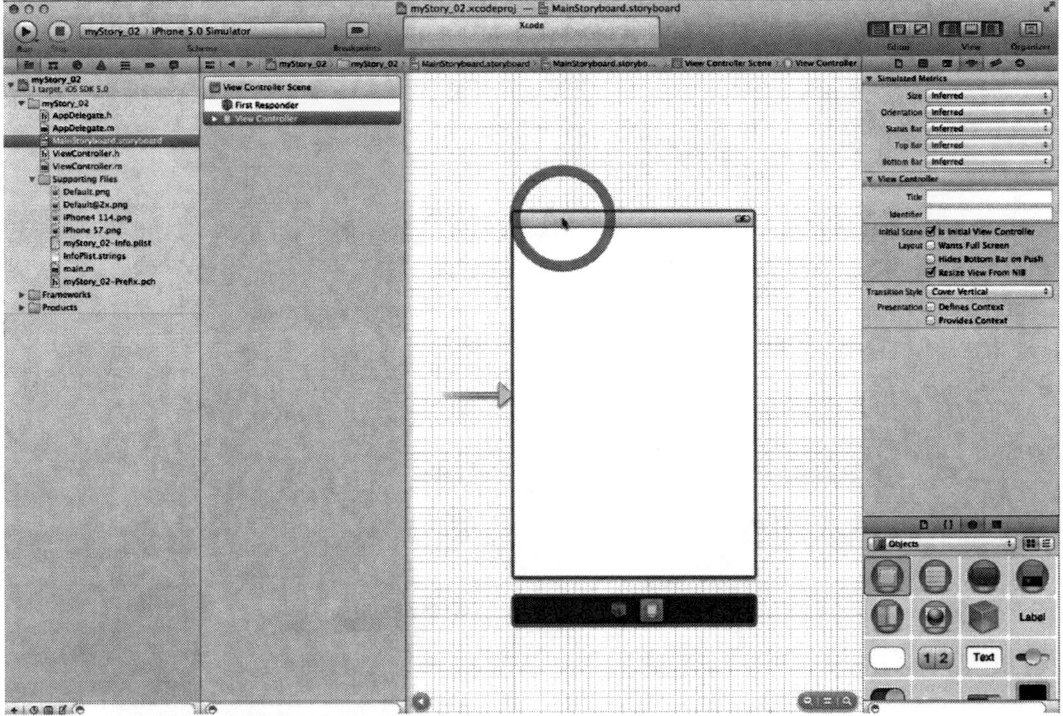

Figure 10–6. *We do not want a View Controller here.*

6. When Storyboard first opens up, you'll see a View Controller, as shown in Figure 10–6. We are selecting the default view Controller because we need to delete it. This is quite easy to grasp: we want a TableView with all its bells and whistles, the ones that are not there if you merely add a table onto a View Controller. We will make our own view Controller later. Right now, we need to delete the default View Controller, so go ahead and do it, as shown in Figure 10–6.

THE BIG PICTURE

1. Populate a table with a list of cities
   a. Create a Table View
2. Code a pin to drop to the center of a selected cities' map

Adding the Table View Controller

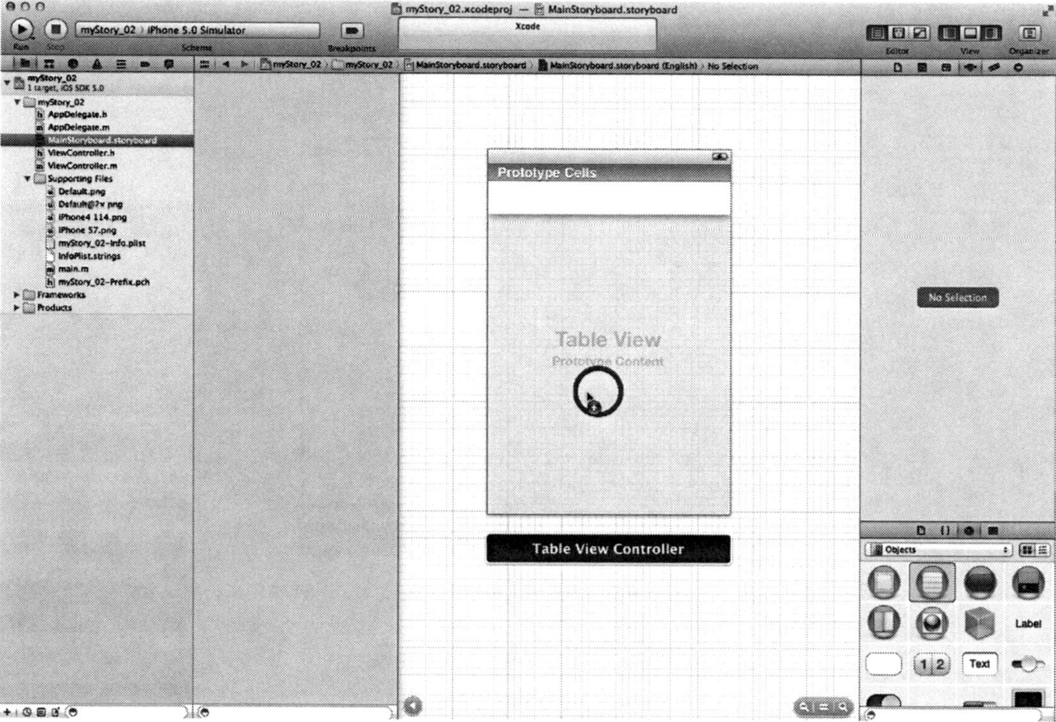

Figure 10–7. *Drag a Table View Controller onto the canvas.*

7. As mentioned, we need to have a fully loaded Table View to hold our array of cities and interact with Storyboarding and MapKit. So drag a Table View Controller onto the canvas, as shown in Figure 10–7.

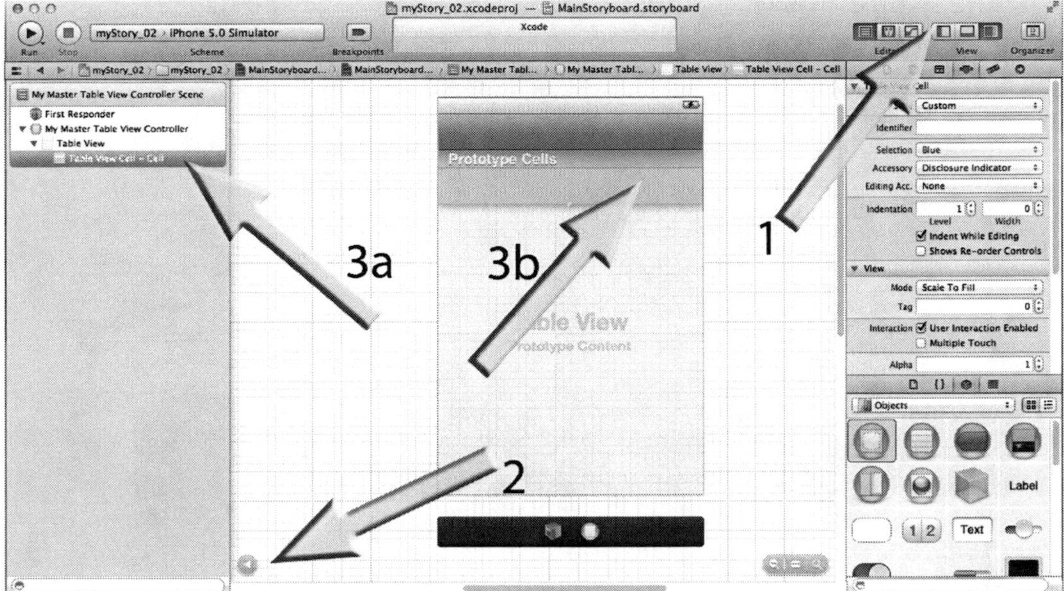

Figure 10–8. *Selecting the Table View Cell - Cell*

8. Something that is really cool and innovative about Storyboarding is that, we can edit the Table View right here in Storyboarding. The tricky thing is that navigating yourself around the canvas can be challenging.

   a. In order to select the Table View Cell - Cell if you need to unclutter your screen. First Close Navigator (Figure 10–8, arrow 1)

   b. Then make sure that your Document Outline is open (Figure 10–8, arrow 2)

   c. Then, in your My Master Table View Controller Scene, select the Table View Cell - Cell open (Figure 10–8, arrow 3a).

   d. Now, it is true that you could select it by clicking the prototype cell on the Storyboard (Figure 10–8, arrow 3b). However, I do NOT want you to get into the habit of selecting objects on the canvas because many experienced Objective-C coders have learned the very hard way that sometimes the object we think we've selected is actually under the object we actually selected. Many painful hours later, or redoing the code and bugging endlessly, we found our error. The other reason for not getting into the habit of selecting on the Storyboard is that by making you open the Document Outline and selecting the correct object in its pane, it helps one visualize where we are.

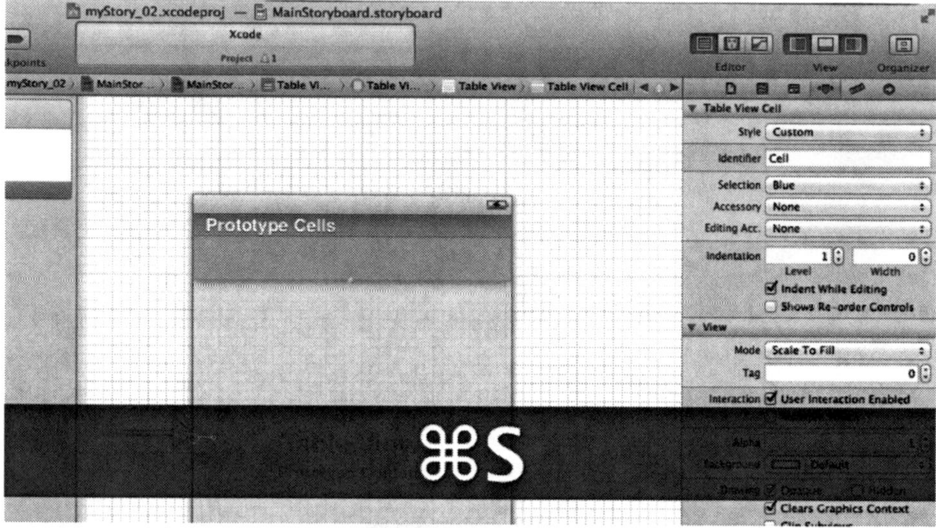

Figure 10–9. ***Name the Identifier "Cell" and save your work.***

9. We are going to want to reuse the nib cells. In other words, rather than create a massive list of cells, we'll just use one and reuses it for whatever the number of cities we have in our array. This means we need to give its Identifier a name that we can reuse, so let's just call it "Cell", as shown in Figure 10–9.

THE BIG PICTURE

1. Populate a table with a list of cities
    a. Create a Table View
    b. Make the Table views Identifier be a cell
2. Code a pin to drop to the center of a selected cities' map

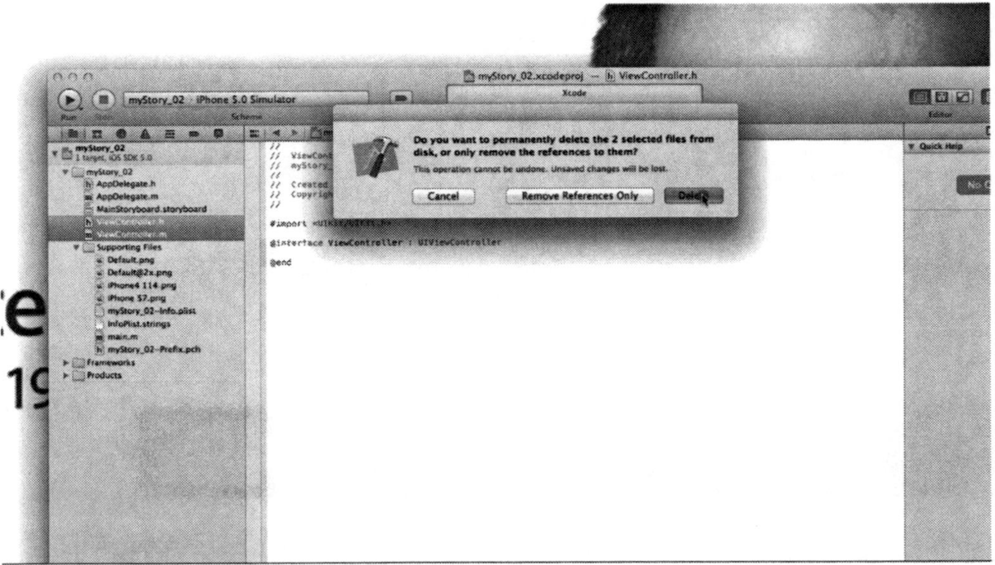

Figure 10–10. *Delete the original view Controller.*

10. We see that what we just built in the Storyboard was built with the original View Controller. We need to build our own View Controller so delete both its header and implementation files, as shown in Figure 10–10.

> **NOTE:** Make sure that you delete the entire class, not just its references.

THE BIG PICTURE: EXPANDED STEPS 10 - 17

1. Populate a table with a list of cities
    - 1.1. Create a Table View
    - 1.2. Organize our classes
        - 1.2.1. Delete the default ViewController
        - 1.2.2. Create 3 Classes
            - 1.2.2.1. Two UIViewController Subclasses
                - 1.2.2.1.1. myMasterTableViewController
                - 1.2.2.1.2 myDetailViewController
            - 1.2.2.2. One Objective C class
                - 1.2.2.2.1. myPos
2. Code a pin to drop to the center of a selected cities' map

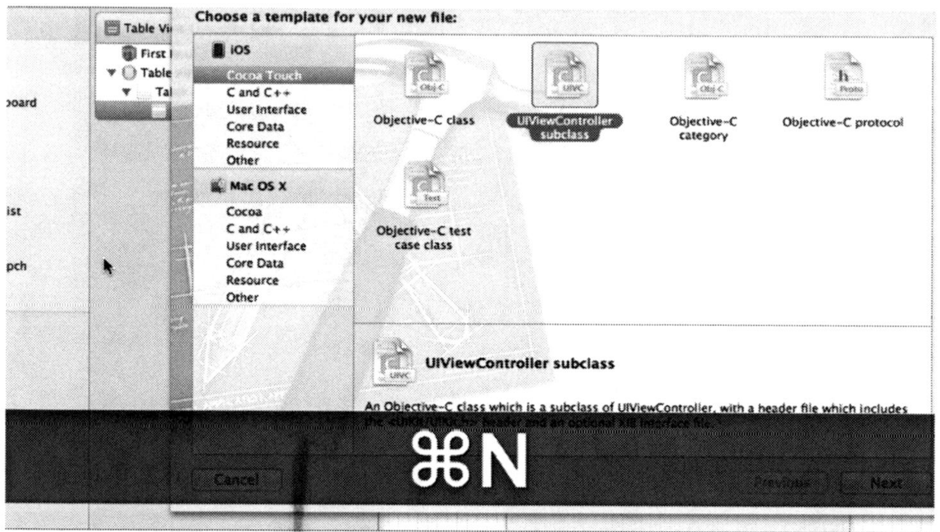

Figure 10–11. *Create the first of our two UIViewController subclasses.*

11. Now that we've deleted the table's default `ViewController`, we need a new backing class file to hold our cities and code structures that will enable a table to be populated with a list of cities. We will need two `UIViewController` subclasses, one to do exactly this and another to grab all the data we need from the Google server. We will also need a "*My Position* " (`myPos`) Objective-C class just like we did in myStory_01 to hold the current location. So let's start building these 3 classes: Enter⌘N and select a `UIViewController` subclass, as shown in Figure 10–11.

THE BIG PICTURE

1. Populate a table with a list of cities
    - 1.1. Create a Table View
    - 1.2. Organize our classes
        - 1.2.1. Delete the default ViewController
        - 1.2.2. Create 3 Classes
            - 1.2.2.1. Two UIViewController Subclasses
                - **1.2.2.1.1. myMasterTableViewController**
                - **1.2.2.1.2. myDetailViewController**
            - 1.2.2.2. One Objective C class
2. Code a pin to drop to the center of a selected cities' map

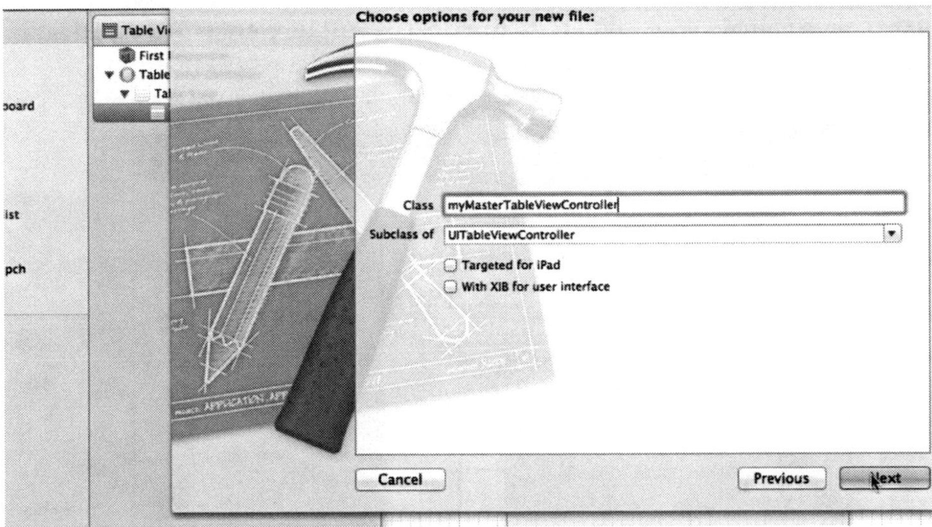

Figure 10–12. *Name it myMasterTableViewController.*

12. We need to make sure that this new class we are creating is a subclass of `UITableViewController` because we need it to know how to do table actions, such as hold our cities in the table. So, after you name it `myMasterTableViewController`, please make sure you make sure it's a subclass of `UITableViewController` because, if you don't, you'll be crying later. See Figure 10–12.

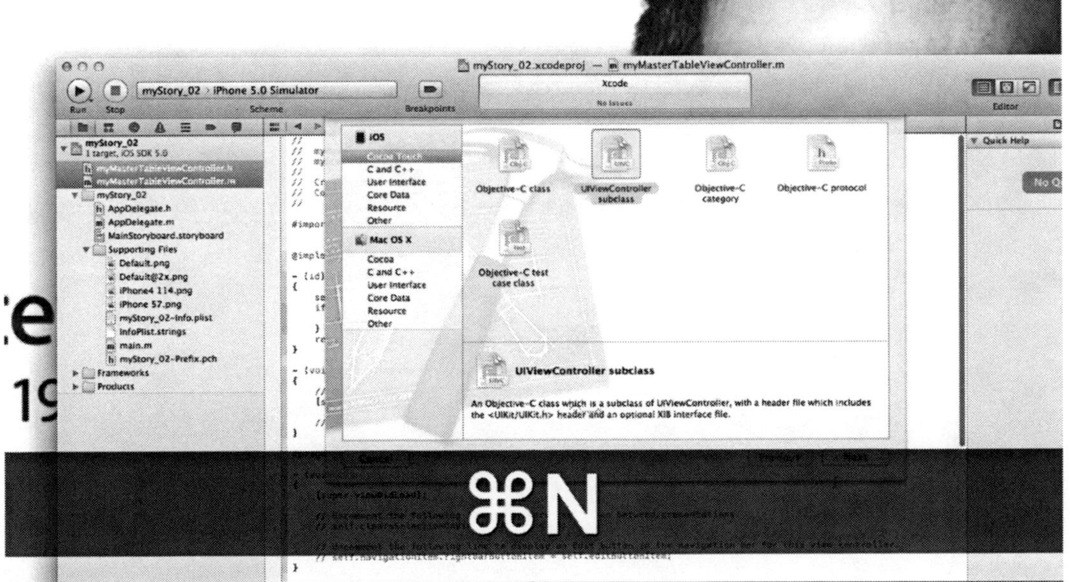

Figure 10–13. *Create the first of our two UIViewController subclasses.*

13. Once you have created your `myMasterTableViewController`, enter ⌘N again and select another UIViewController subclass, as shown in Figure 10–13.

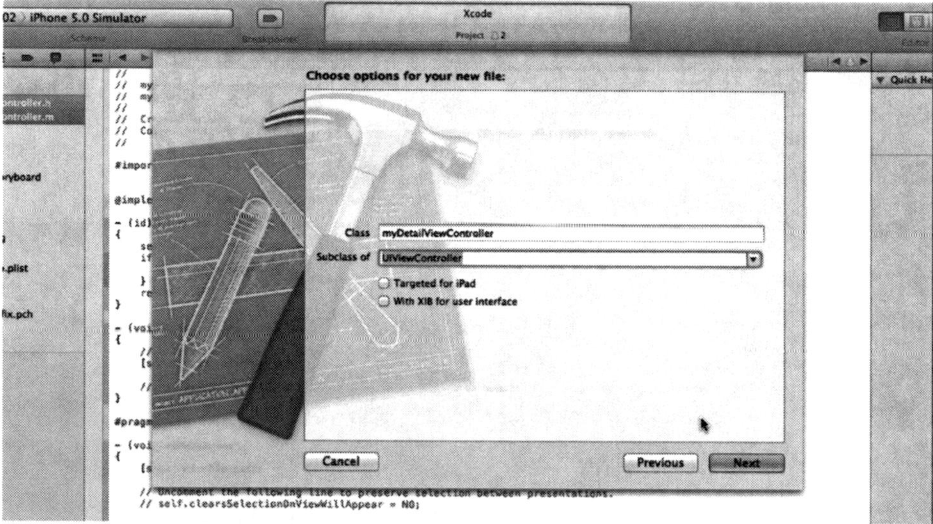

Figure 10–14. *Name thisUIViewController subclass myDetailViewController.*

14. ThisUIViewController subclass is going to be more involved with parsing the Google server and interacting between `myPos` and the View the user sees. So, after naming it `myDetailViewController`, make sure it's *not* a subclass of a `UITableViewController` but rather a subclass of a UIViewController, as shown in Figure 10–14.

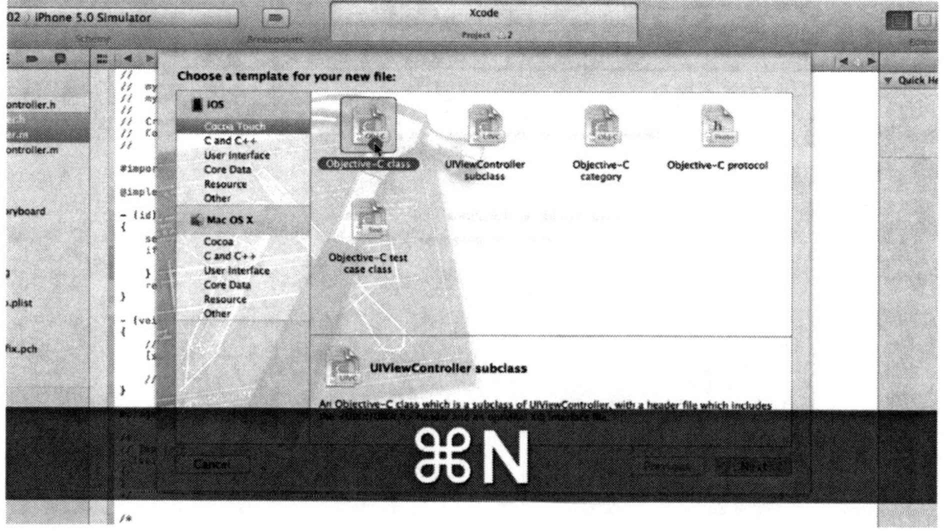

Figure 10–15. *Select an Objective-C class*

15. We've created our two UIViewController subclasses and now we need to create our 3rd class, an Objective-C class. So let's do it: enter ⌘N again and select an Objective -C class, as shown in Figure 10–22

THE BIG PICTURE

1. Populate a table with a list of cities
   1.1. Create a Table View
   1.2. Organize our classes
      1.2.1. Delete the default ViewController
      1.2.2. Create 3 Classes
         1.2.2.1. Two UIViewController Subclasses
         1.2.2.2. One Objective C class
            1.2.2.2.1. myPos
2. Code a pin to drop to the center of a selected cities' map

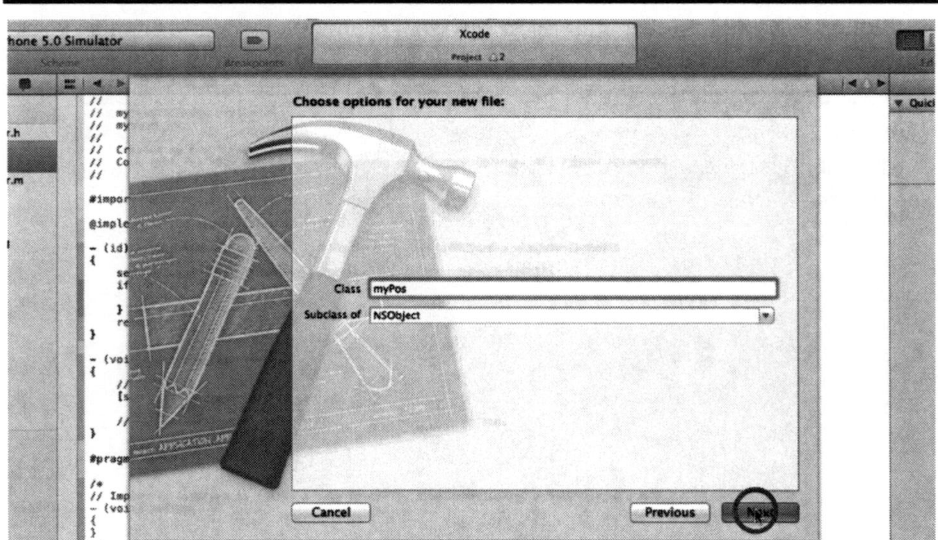

Figure 10–16. *Name it myPos*

16. Just as we did in myStory_01, this needs to be an `NSObject` subclass. Once you've made sure of this and named it `myPos`, click next or press enter, as shown in Figure 10–16. Let's move on.

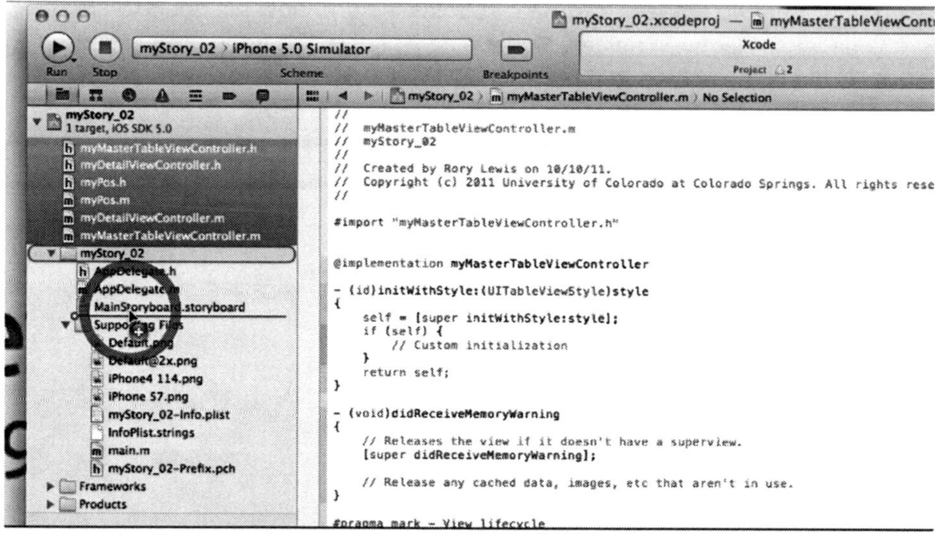

Figure 10–17. *Housekeeping part1: Drag the files into your myStory_02 folder.*

17. These classes need to be placed into our myStory_02 file because, if you don't and you're my student, you lose a letter grade for your project. If you're not one of my students and working for somebody, they will not look kindly upon you at all. If you're working for yourself and you do not organize your files, then God help you because not only will your life become very miserable with huge amounts of negative karma pouring all over you, but the folks in the iTunes store who ratify your code will have zero respect for you if they see messy organization and then your life will really be bad. Get the picture? This is shown in Figure 10–17.

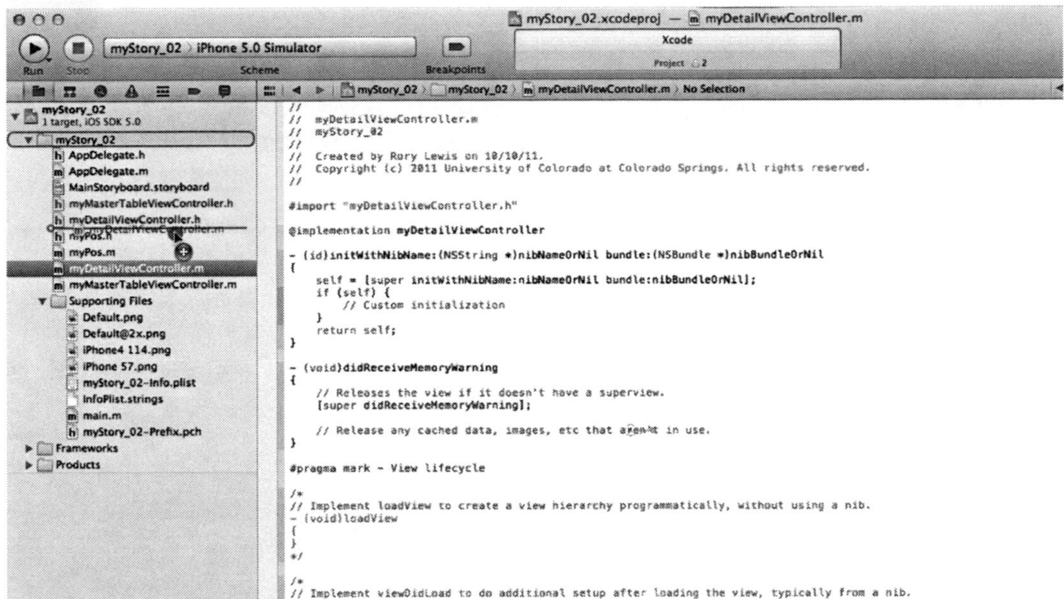

Figure 10–18. *Housekeeping part 2: organize your header and implementation files.*

18. After you have brought your files into your mySTory_02 folder, you will notice that your .h and .m files are together. This is not good. You need to put each class' header and implementation files together as shown in Figure 10–18

Coding myMasterTableViewController

In the video, I simply drop in the boilerplate code to save time. Here we will go through each line so that you can learn. So if you have any problem with writing all this code, please get over it. It's the only way you can learn how to code. Rather than throwing a bucket of paint onto the surface of a canvas, we are going talk about how each little stroke of code makes a beautiful Mona Lisa. A beautiful app that makes you feel great about yourself, teaches you how to write apps, and make money! OK, let's get to it. We need to do five things: create a private interface for our `NSArray` of cities, insert the actual `NSArray` of cities, have the table return 1 section, have the number of rows equal the number of cities, and enable viewing of the city names in each cell.

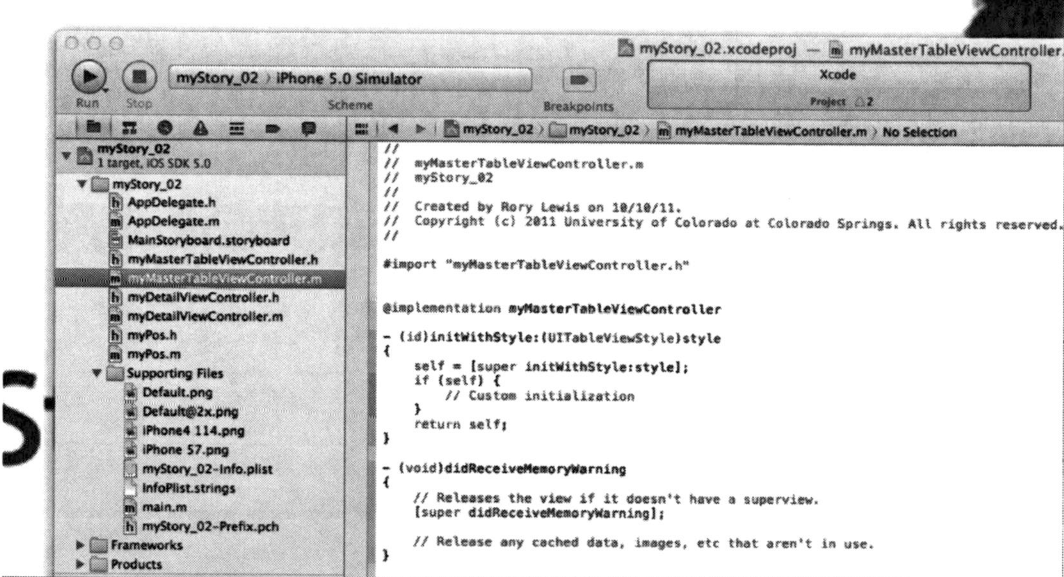

Figure 10–19. *This is how your myMasterTableViewController implementation file looks when you open it.*

19. We are now ready to code the myMasterTableViewController implementation file. Click on the myMasterTableViewController.m file located in your myStory_02 folder inside the root folder. Figure 10–19 shows how the myMasterTableViewController.m file looks when we open it.

THE BIG PICTURE: CODING MYMASTERTABLEVIEWCONTROLLER: STEPS 20 TO 22

1. Populate a table with a list of cities
   - 1.1. Create a Table View
   - 1.2. Organize our classes
   - **1.3. Code myMasterTableViewController.m**
     - **1.3.1. Create a Private interface for our NSArray of cities**
     - **1.3.2. Insert our NSArray of cities into viewDidLoad**
     - **1.3.3. Have the table return 1 section**
     - **1.3.4. Have the number of rows equal the number of cities**
     - **1.3.5. Enable viewing of the city names in each cell**
   - 1.4. Enable Storyboard to bring up the Table
     - 1.4.1. Associate the Table View with myMasterTableViewController
2. Code a pin to drop to the center of a selected cities' map

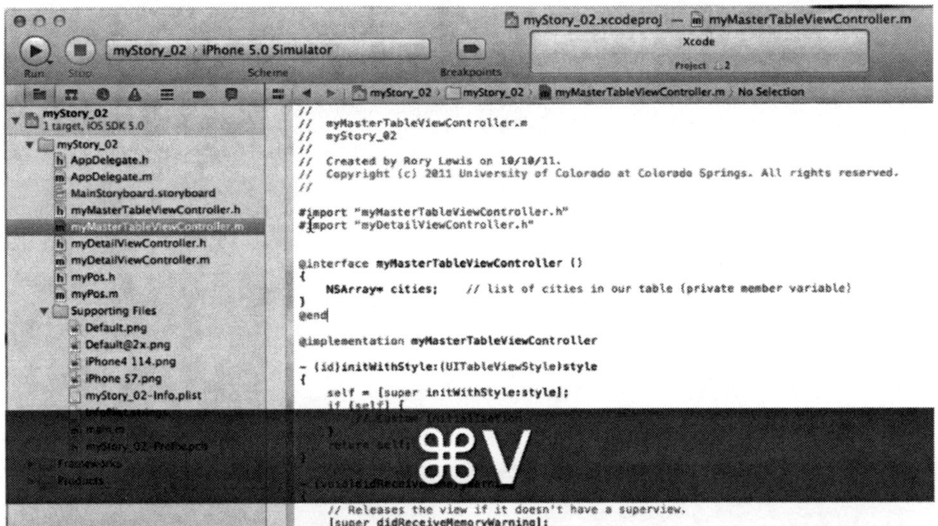

Figure 10–20. *Select and open myMasterTableViewController.m.*

20. Figure 10–20 shows the boilerplate paste of the private interface for our NSArray located in your download file *"01 Part 1myMasterTableViewController.m"*. We are going to type it in though and talk about it. We need to do two things. First, we are going to import the myDetailViewController header file and then create our private interface that contains a list of cities. We'll make it an `NSArray` with a pointer that will contain our cities, as you will see further below in the code. For now though, just remember that to make it a private member variable (we're doing it mainly as an exercise we could put this in the header file but then its public and I want to show you how to make it private because often lists of things need to be private). To make it private, we need to start with our `@interface` with name of the class followed by closed brackets `()` and then end it with an `@end`, as shown below

```
#import "myDetailViewController.h"

@interfacemyMasterTableViewController ()
{
NSArray* cities;
}
@end
```

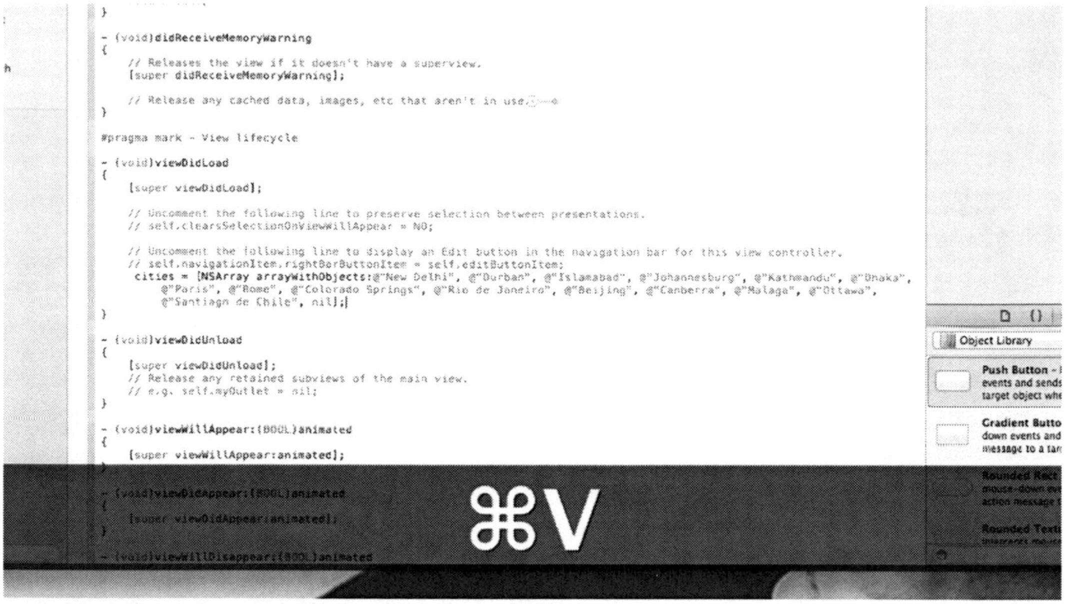

Figure 10–21. *Create an array with a list of cities.*

21. We need to allocate the array we are pointing to in our private array. In other words, we need to create an array, which we have already called "cities" in our private Interface. We are initializing the "cities" variable with a new array we will construct. So let's make cities be an `NSArray` that has objects in it. It goes on until it sees the `nil` at the end of it. Feel free to enter your own cities if you like. See the code below and the code in "*02 Part myMasterTableViewController m*" being pasted In Figure 10–21.

```
cities = [NSArrayarrayWithObjects:@"New Delhi", @"Durban", @"Islamabad",
@"Johannesburg", @"Kathmandu", @"Dhaka", @"Paris", @"Rome", @"Colorado Springs", @"Rio
de Janeiro", @"Beijing", @"Canberra", @"Malaga", @"Ottawa", @"Santiago de Chile", nil];
```

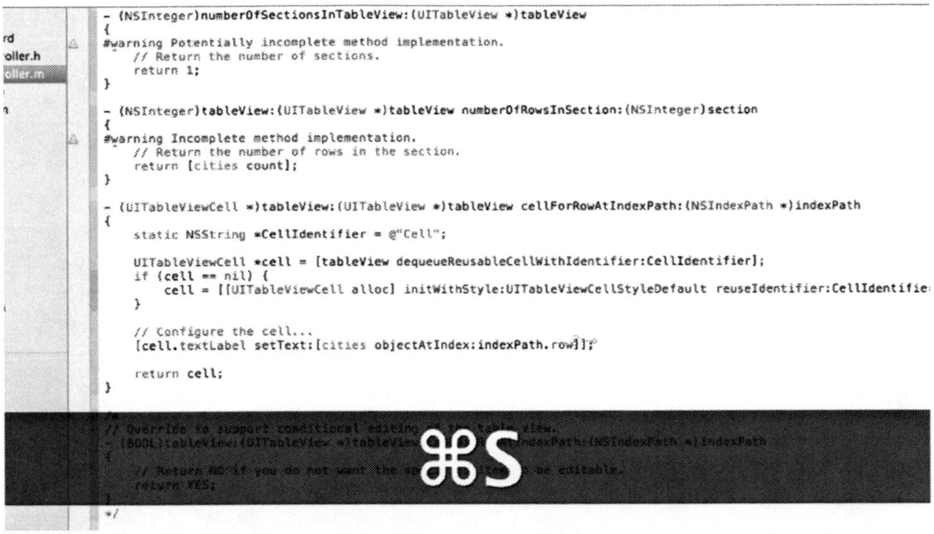

Figure 10–22. *Finish coding myMasterTableViewController.m*

22. We need to do three small tweaks to make sure our table can handle the list of cities we gave it and pop it onto the TableView. We need to have the table return 1 section, have the number of rows equal the number of cities, and, finally, enable viewing of the city names in each cell:

    a. Have the table return 1 section: Go to `numberOfSectionsInTableView` and add the `return1` after the comment. By default, it contains return 0 already. Be advised to remove or change this. Otherwise, you may wind up with two return statements and be very upset.

NOTE: The normal weight code is the default code that the clever people at Apple have already coded for us. The bold text is what you will need to enter.

```
- (NSInteger)numberOfSectionsInTableView:(UITableView *)tableView
{
    // Return the number of sections.
    return 1;
}
```

    b. We now need to modify the table view methods for our purposes. We need to first have the number of rows equal the number of cities. Go to `numberOfRowsInSection` and we'll make the number of rows be dynamic, which means that no matter the amount of cities we put into the table, we'll make the return be the `count` of the total cities:

```
- (NSInteger)tableView:(UITableView *)tableView numberOfRowsInSection:(NSInteger)section
{
```

```
    // Return the number of rows in the section.
    return [cities count];
}
```

c. Lastly we need to make sure that the city names show up in the cell. We need to grab the appropriate city names that we will show in each cell from the index and insert it into the `textLabel`. Go to the bottom of `tableViewcellForRowAtIndexPath` and enter the following.

> **NOTE:** Right now I do not want you to be concerned about the meaning of each line of grey code that Apple has coded on our behalf. At this point, I just want you to accept that it works and we will continue.

```
- (UITableViewCell *)tableView:(UITableView *)tableView
cellForRowAtIndexPath:(NSIndexPath *)indexPath
{
   static NSString *CellIdentifier = @"Cell";
    UITableViewCell *cell = [tableView
dequeueReusableCellWithIdentifier:CellIdentifier];
    if (cell == nil) {
        cell = [[UITableViewCell alloc] initWithStyle:UITableViewCellStyleDefault
reuseIdentifier:CellIdentifier];
    }
    // Configure the cell...
    [cell.textLabel setText:[cities objectAtIndex:indexPath.row]];
    return cell;
}
```

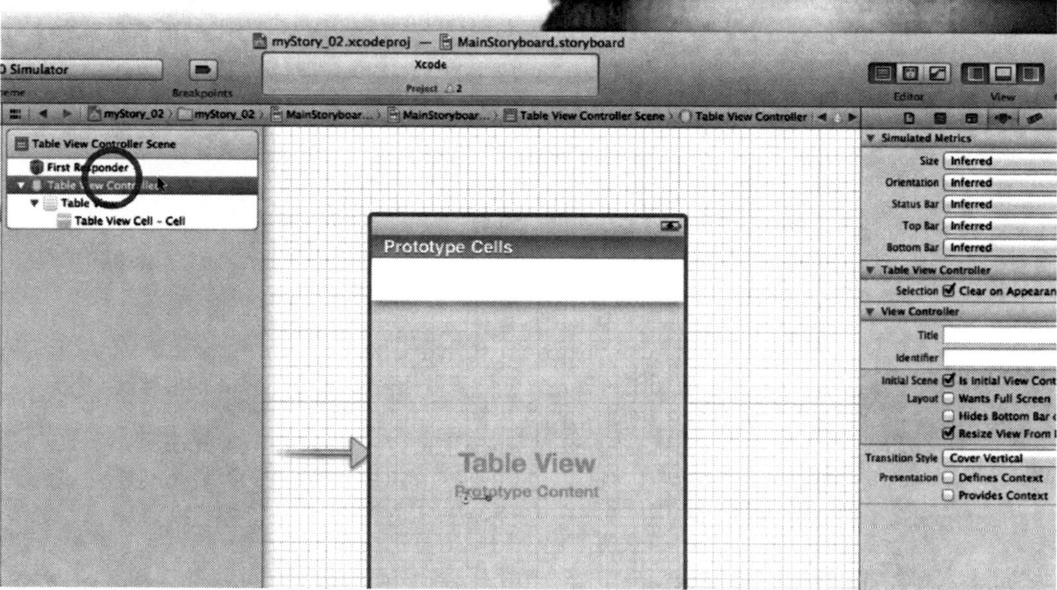

Figure 10–23. *Go back to Storyboard and select the Table View Controller.*

23. We need to associate the Table View with `myMasterTableViewController`. Go back into Storyboard and select the Table View Controller in the Document Outline, as shown in Figure 10–23.

THE BIG PICTURE: CODING MYMASTERTABLEVIEWCONTROLLER: STEPS 24 TO 26.

1. Populate a table with a list of cities
   1.1. Create a Table View
   1.2. Organize our classes
   1.3. Code myMasterTableViewController.m
   1.4. Enable Storyboard to bring up the Table
      1.4.1. Associate the Table View with myMasterTableViewController
2. Code a pin to drop to the center of a selected cities' map

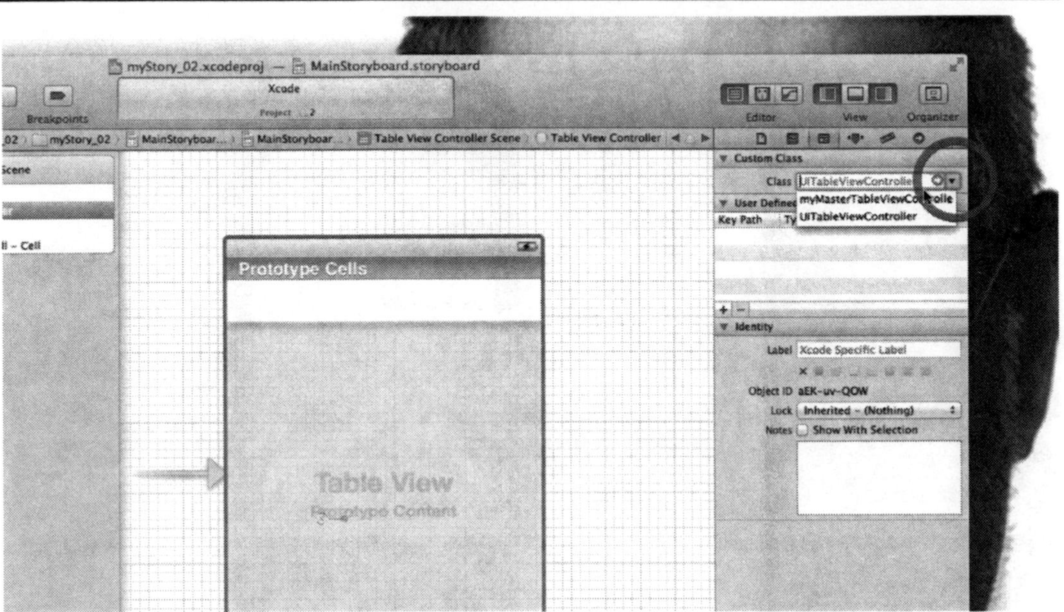

Figure 10–24. *Select myMasterTableViewController.*

24. Select the Identity inspector in the Utilities. Then, in Custom Class, open the drop down menu in Class and select `myMasterTableViewController`, as shown in Figure 10–24. This ensures that all the code we wrote in Steps 20-22 is now going grind away underneath our Table View and make magic!

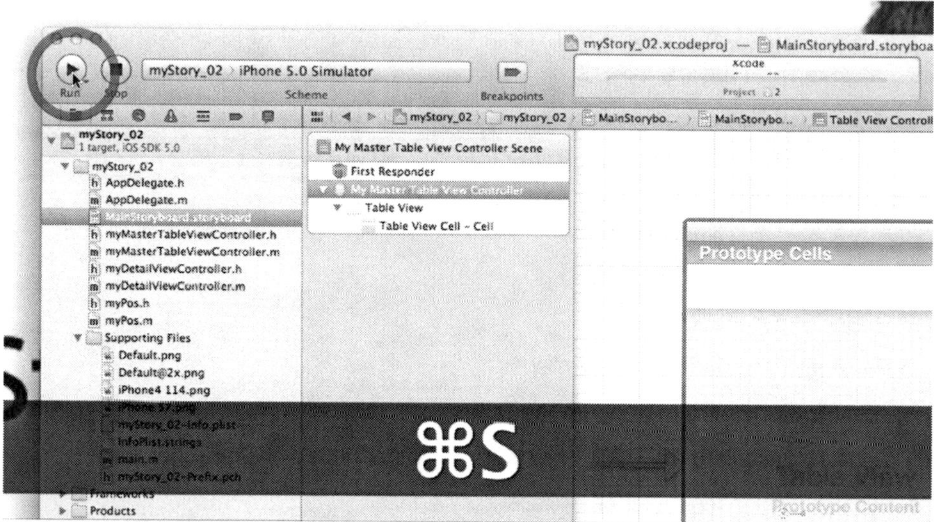

Figure 10–25. *Run It.*

25. We need to run it. See Figure 10–25.

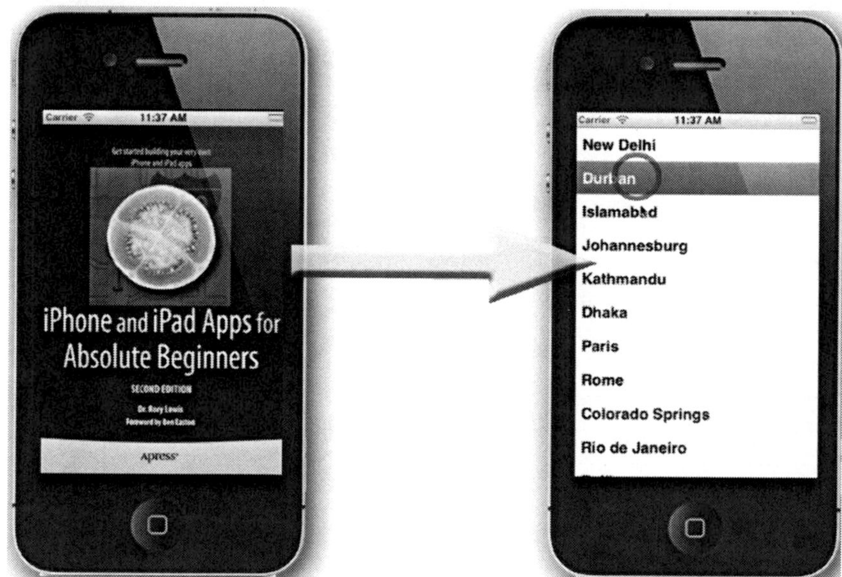

Figure 10–26. *A beautiful Splash screen takes us to a populated table.*

26. Make sure we see a splash screen appear and then a table populated with our list of cities, as shown in Figure 10–26. Sure enough, we see a splash screen, Lulu fruit and all. Then we see a table that is populated with our cities. It's not doing much at all when you click on it, but it's there. We're done with the first part of myStory_02.

THE BIG PICTURE

1. **Populate a table with a list of cities (COMPLETED – see Figure 10–26)**
2. Code a pin to drop to the center of a selected cities' map (NEXT SECTION)

Part 2

Let's take a deep breath and look around. If it was the lecture hall, I'd have you look at the latest greatest "Fail" videos on YouTube or play a Grateful Dead song like Ripple. Yes, the students know I'm completely whacko but, having had an acute brain injury and epilepsy, I know a little bit about the brain and, as a human, I know we need to rest.

We've successfully populated our table with a list of cities. Now, in Part Two, we will send that list of cities to Google, parse out the geospatial addresses of each city, store them, and then shoot them out to the MapKit when a user selects a city on our list.

Looking at the big picture below, one can see that we need to add the MapKit framework, do the code to make this work, and then tweak Storyboard to accept out new code.

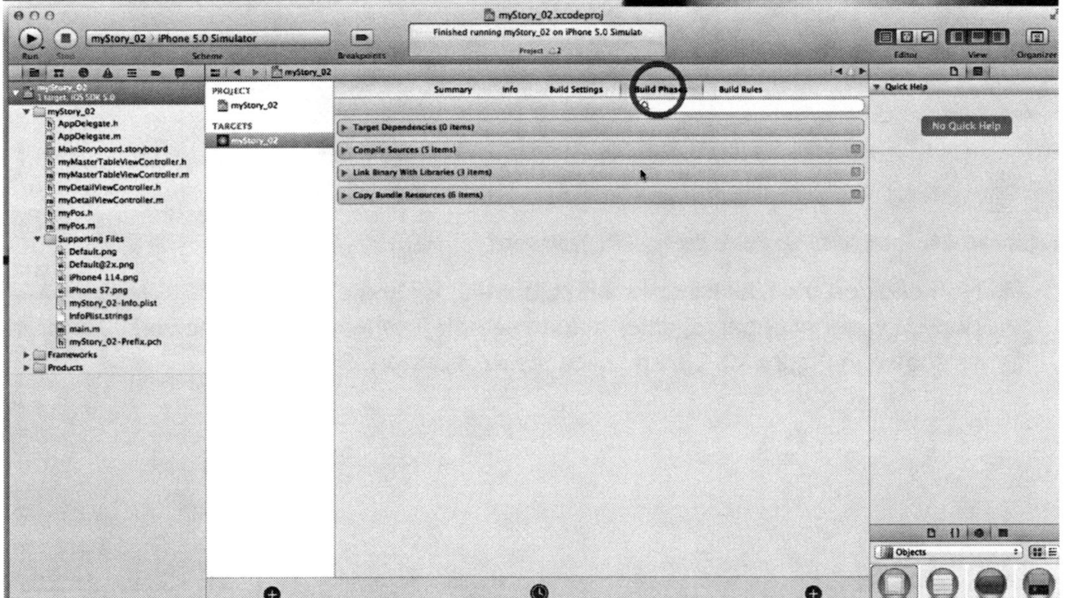

Figure 10–27. ***Click on Build Phases to so you can add the MapKit framework.***

27. We need to add the MapKit framework just as we did on myStory_01. So go to your root directory and click on the Build Phases tab, as shown in Figure 10–27.

THE BIG PICTURE: OVERVIEW OF PART 2

1. Populate a table with a list of cities (COMPLETED)
2. **Code a pin to drop to the center of a selected cities' map**
   2.1. **Add MapKit framework**
   2.2. **Write code**
   2.3. **Tweak Storyboard to accept our new code.**

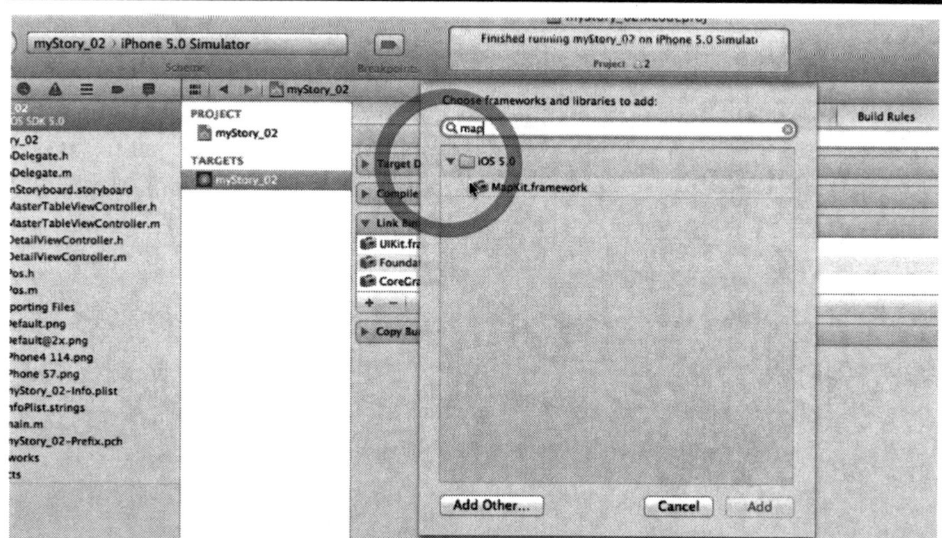

Figure 10–28. *Enter "map" to locate the MapKits framework!*

28. Now click on the Link Binaries with Libraries bar and click on the "+". When the pop-up window appears, enter map to search for the MapKit framework. Select it, as shown in Figure 10–28, and click the Add button.

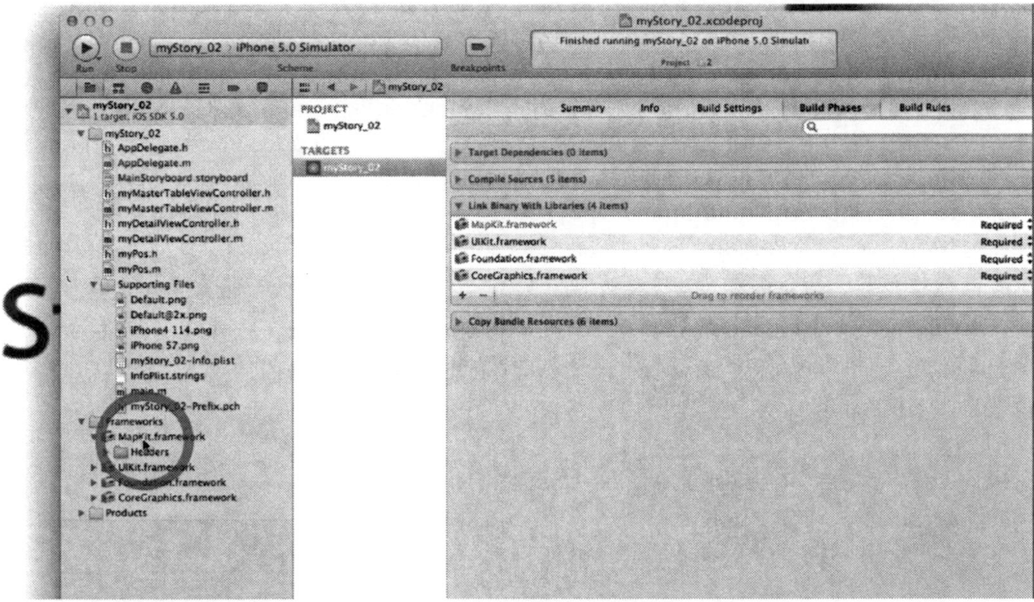

Figure 10–29. *Move the MapKit framework from the root folder to the Frameworks folder.*

29. The MapKit framework appears in the root directory just as it did in Figure 9-18 in myStory_01. Except there we also had Corelocation. Here we do not because we'll use Google's. Again, you will need to drag it to where the framework belongs, the Frameworks folder, as shown in Figure 10–29.

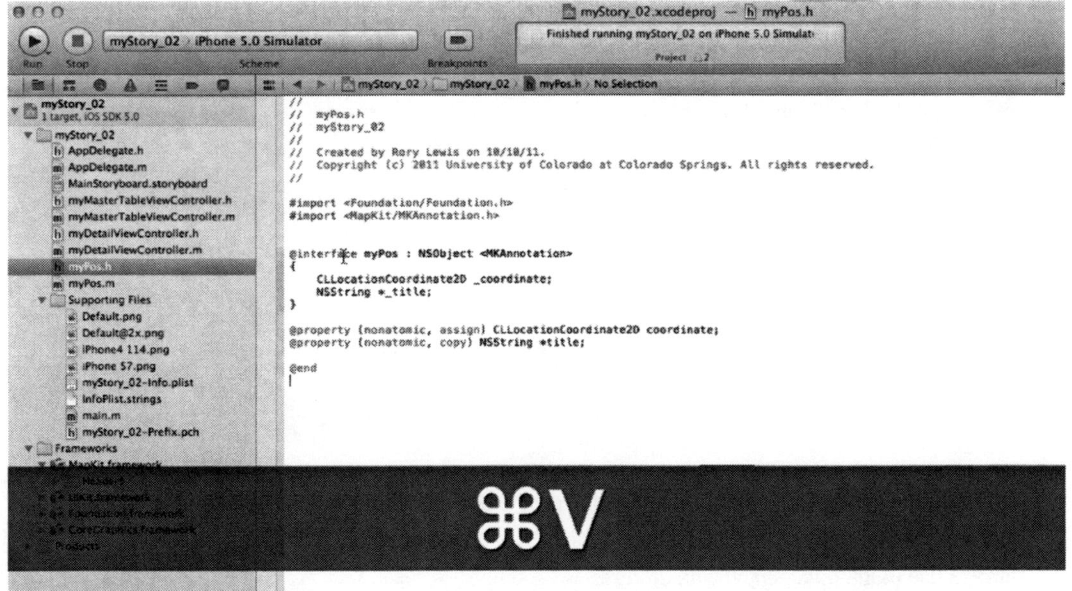

Figure 10–30. *Open myPos header file and either code or paste in the proper code.*

30. We will now code the myPos header file. I highly encourage you to not simply paste it into your header file as I did on the video. You will learn NOTHING by doing that. Follow along with me and you will learn how to code. Remember that myPos is handling the public interface and, in its header file, we need to set the two main fields, which are the name and the geospatial address of our cities. The names of the cities will be stored at the address pointed to by title. The geospatial longitudinal and latitudinal addresses of each city will be handled by 2-Dimensional location method and stored in a variable we'll name coordinate.

> **NOTE:** The CLLocationCoordinate2D is a structure that contains our geospatial coordinate using the World Geodetic System (WGS 84) reference frame, which is takes it locations from the core of the earth and know that it's off by 2 centimeters!

When we first open the myPos.h file, we see the following:

```
#import <Foundation/Foundation.h>
@interface myPos : NSObject
@end
```

The first thing we do is add MapKit by entering #import <MapKit/MKAnnotation.h>. Next we insert <MKAnnotation> after the given @interface myPos : NSObject. We use the MKAnnotation protocol every time we need to use annotation-related information in a map view. Next, we set our CLLocation class reference to incorporate the geospatial coordinates and altitude of our device by entering CLLocationCoordinate2Dcoordinate, which will use a variable I've called coordinate. We also need to store the name of the city, which we will do in the title using NSString. Finally, we create @property statements for both the location and title of each city. Your code for the myPos header file will now look as shown in Figure 10–30 or as follows:

```
#import <Foundation/Foundation.h>
#import <MapKit/MKAnnotation.h>

@interface myPos : NSObject <MKAnnotation>
{
    CLLocationCoordinate2D _coordinate;
    NSString *_title;
}

@property (nonatomic, assign) CLLocationCoordinate2D coordinate;
@property (nonatomic, copy) NSString *title;

@end
```

> **NOTE:** In the @property for our name of the city, which is a string we use (nonatomic, copy), I just want you to remember that, without getting all screwed up in the details, as a general rule, always use (nonatomic, copy) with strings.

THE BIG PICTURE: CODING OVERVIEW

1. Populate a table with a list of cities (COMPLETED)
2. Code a pin to drop to the center of a selected cities' map
   2.1. Add MapKit framework
   2.2. Write code
      2.2.1. myPos for keeping track of selected cities and their coordinates
      2.2.2. myDetailViewController to parse Google amongst other things
      2.2.3. myMasterTableViewController to control the segue to MapKits.
   2.3. Tweak Storyboard to accept our new code.

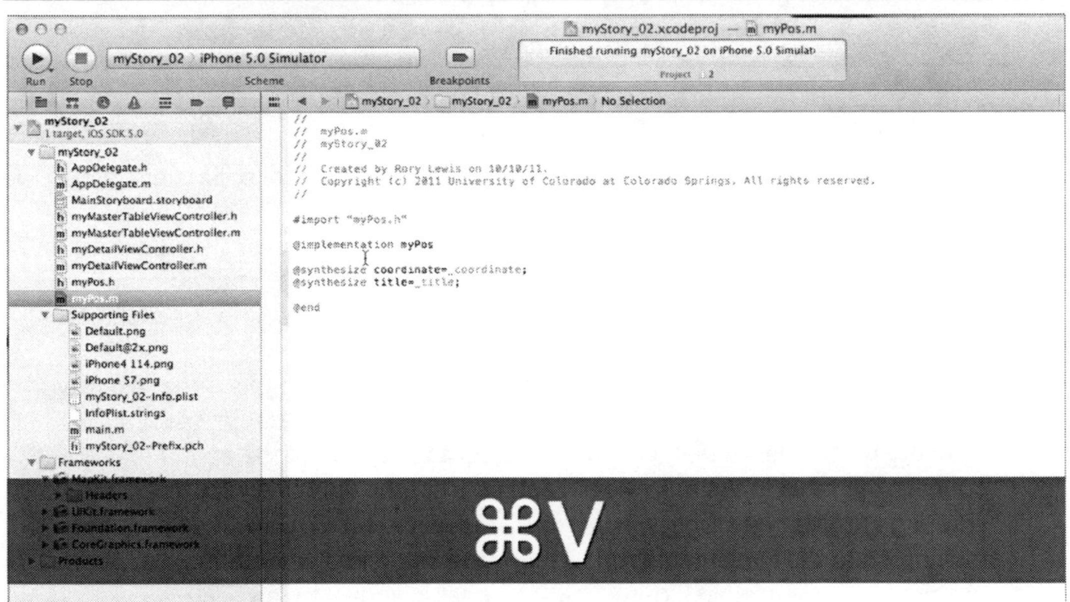

Figure 10–31. *Now we open up the myPos Implementation file.*

31. All we need to do in the implementation of the `myPos` header file is synthesize your coordinate and titles. The final code is shown in Figure 10–31.

```
#import "myPos.h"
@implementation myPos

@synthesize coordinate=_coordinate;
@synthesize title=_title;

@end
```

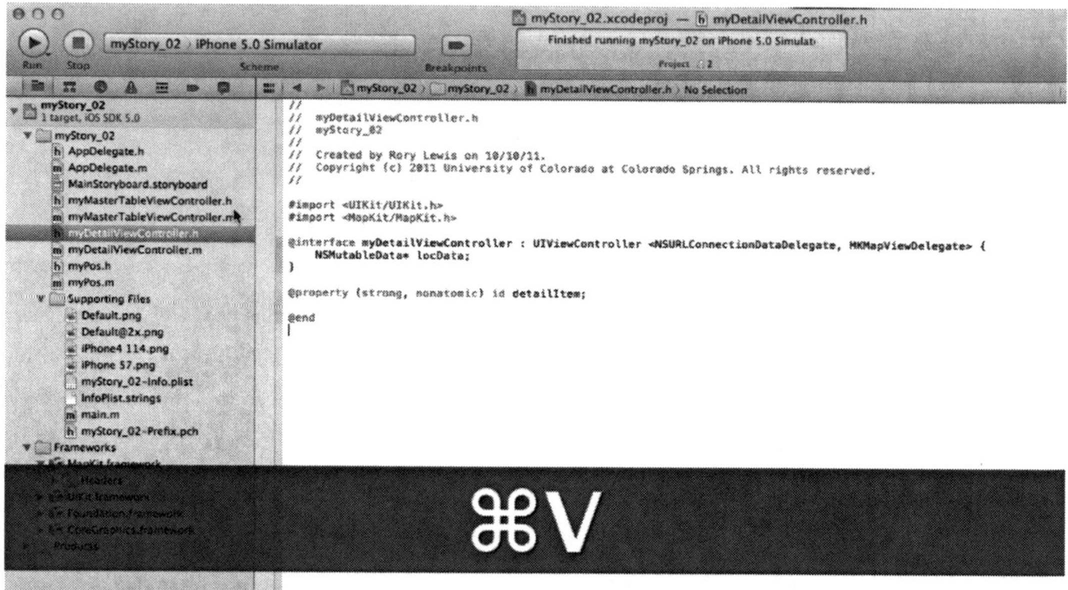

Figure 10–32. *Open the myDetailViewController header file to paste or code it.*

32. We now need to build the `myDetailViewController` class. Let's first import our MapKit and MapKit header file by entering `#import <MapKit/MapKit.h>` after the `#import <UIKit/UIKit.h>`. Now, looking at `@interface myDetailViewController`, we need to base it on the `UIViewController` and we are going support the `myDetailViewController` class with protocols first for connecting datadelegates and secondly for supporting map viewdelegates by coding `<NSURLConnectionDataDelegate, MKMapViewDelegate>`. With this done, we assign our local data to the `NSMutableData` as shown. Next we need to make a public property for the detail item, which we will set to prepare for the segue that will connect the table to the map view. Last, let's set the `@property` for this by entering `@property (strong, nonatomic) id detailItem`. Save it all and, before moving on to the implementation of this code in the implementation file, please check your code against Figure 10–32 or what is shown below.

```
#import <UIKit/UIKit.h>
#import <MapKit/MapKit.h>

@interface myDetailViewController : UIViewController <NSURLConnectionDataDelegate,
MKMapViewDelegate> {
    NSMutableData* locData;
}

@property (strong, nonatomic) id detailItem;

@end
```

Coding the myDetailViewController.m file

You are about to embark on the most advanced section of code I have used in the book. This is the section that will most probably let you down and crash. Because of this, I am open to you pasting a couple of the larger sections of code from my code. I want you to keep your cool and just follow along. I will show you how to code this and where to paste each specific set of boilerplate code. But first, let's take another look at the big picture.

THE BIG PICTURE: MYDETAILVIEWCONTROLLER.M EXPANDED.

1. Populate a table with a list of cities (COMPLETED)

2. Code a pin to drop to the center of a selected cities' map

- 2.1. Add MapKit framework
- 2.2. Write code
  - 2.2.1. myPos for keeping track of selected cities and their coordinates
  - 2.2.2. myDetailViewController to parse Google amongst other things
    - 2.2.2.1. Program the header file (completed)
    - **2.2.2.2. Program the implementation file**
      - **2.2.2.2.1. Import the myPos header file**
      - **2.2.2.2.2. Create a private interface**
      - **2.2.2.2.3. Synthesize the detailItem**
      - **2.2.2.2.4. Code the detailItem method and update its view**
      - **2.2.2.2.5. Code the configureView method**
        - **2.2.2.2.5.1. Go to googleapis.com**
        - **2.2.2.2.5.2. Parse the longitudinal and latitudinal cords.**
        - **2.2.2.2.5.3. Update the user interface for the detail item**
        - **2.2.2.2.5.4. Setup zoom and pin drop.**
  - 2.2.3. myMasterTableViewController to control the segue to MapKits.
- 2.3. Tweak Storyboard to accept our new code.

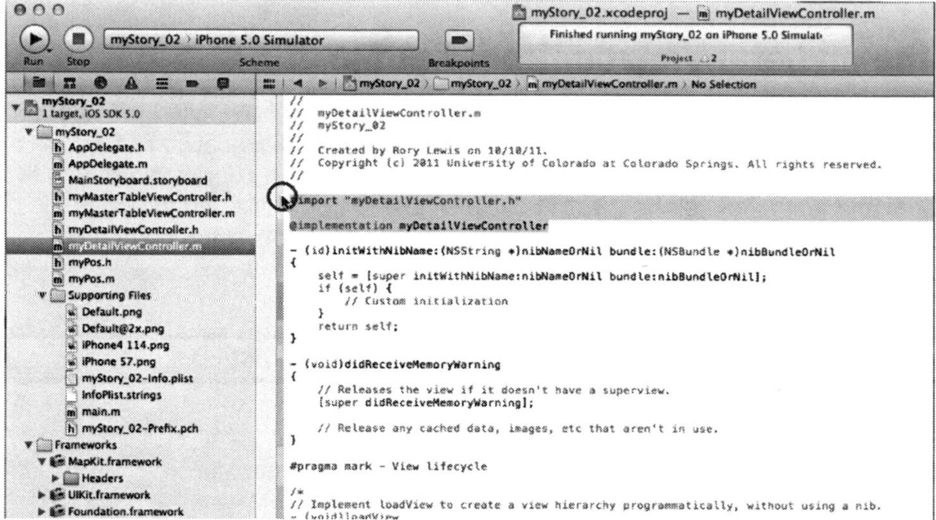

Figure 10–33. *Open up the myDetailViewController implementation file.*

33. As one can see from looking at the Big Picture, the `myDetailViewController` is going to contain a significant amount of code so let's start by coding the code found in the "07 Part 2myDetailViewController m" boiler plate code. Open the file, as shown in Figure 10–33.

    a. We first need to import the myPos.h file because, when we setup the zoom and pin drop code, we use title and coordinate for the myPos annotation.

```
#import "MyPos.h"
```

    b. Next we need configure our view as a private method by using a forward declaration of our method that you will code later. You can see what I mean here by looking at the code before my comment below `// private method`. We are declaring `configureView`. Do you see it anywhere yet? Nope? That's because we have yet to code it. But we will. It's private because it starts with the `@interface [name of this class]` followed by a () and then ends with an @end

```
@interface myDetailViewController ()
- (void)configureView;  // private method
@end
```

    c. Lastly, for this top section, we need to synthesize the property.

```
@synthesize detailItem=_detailItem;
```

This is all the code in the "06 Part 2myDetailViewController h" file and it should look as follows:

```
#import "myDetailViewController.h"
#import "myPos.h"
```

```
@interface myDetailViewController ()
- (void)configureView;  // private method
@end

@implementation myDetailViewController

@synthesize detailItem=_detailItem;
```

Don't be concerned if at this point you receive a warning about an incomplete interface, we will be taking care of it right now. But before moving on, let's look at the Big Picture again. As one can see, we have just completed 2.2.2.2.1 thru to 2.2.2.2.3.in step 33. In the next two steps (34 and 35), we will complete 2.2.2.2.4 thru to 2.2.2.2.5. (Everything between "Code the configureView method" and "Setup zoom and pin drop".)

THE BIG PICTURE

1. Populate a table with a list of cities (COMPLETED)
2. Code a pin to drop to the center of a selected cities' map
   - 2.1. Add MapKit framework
   - 2.2. Write code
     - 2.2.1. myPos for keeping track of selected cities and their coordinates
     - 2.2.2. myDetailViewController to parse Google amongst other things
       - 2.2.2.1. Program the header file (completed)
       - 2.2.2.2. Program the implementation file
         - 2.2.2.2.1. Import the myPos header file (Completed)
         - 2.2.2.2.2. Create a private interface (Completed)
         - 2.2.2.2.3. Synthesize the detailItem (Completed)
         - **2.2.2.2.4. Code the detailItem method and update its view**
         - **2.2.2.2.5. Code the configureView method**
           - **2.2.2.2.5.1. Go to googleapis.com**
           - **2.2.2.2.5.2. Parse the longitudinal and latitudinal cords.**
           - **2.2.2.2.5.3. Update the user interface for the detail item**
           - **2.2.2.2.5.4. Setup zoom and pin drop**
     - 2.2.3. myMasterTableViewController to control the segue to MapKits
   - 2.3. Tweak Storyboard to accept our new code

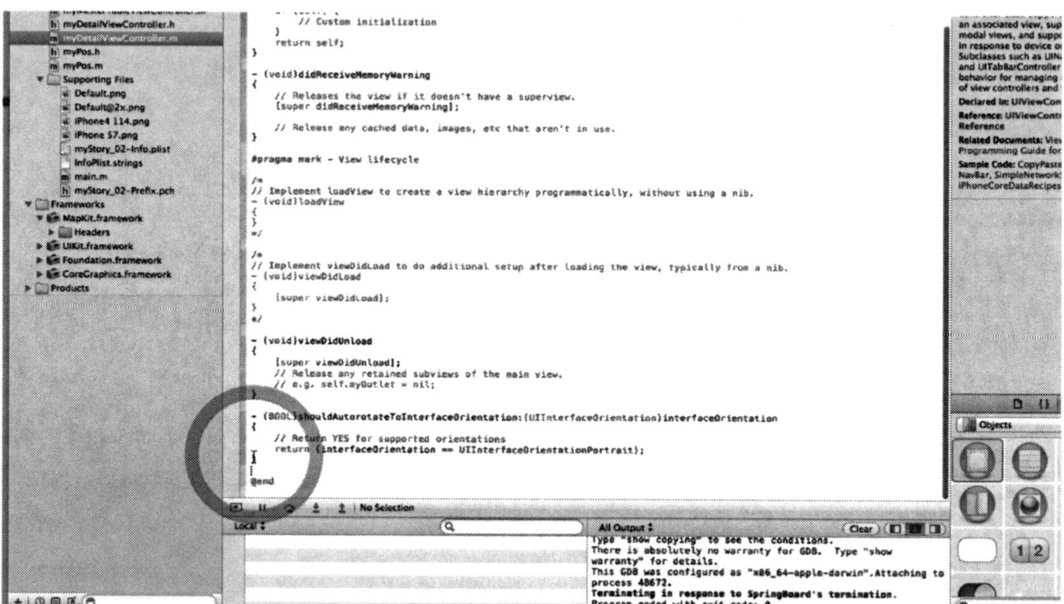

Figure 10–34. *Place your cursor in-between @end and the end of shouldAutorotate.*

34. We are now going to code a means to access the Google server, fetch data, and bring it back to the iPhone or iPad. For parsing and other heavy-duty code, I like to insert such code soon after the `shouldAutorotateToInterfaceOrientation` method but of course before the @end of the class I am coding. In our case, we have no choice but you will see that, in the `myMasterDetailViewController` when we insert the segue method, this can be far from the bottom of the code. So place your cursor as indicated and illustrated in Figure 10–34.

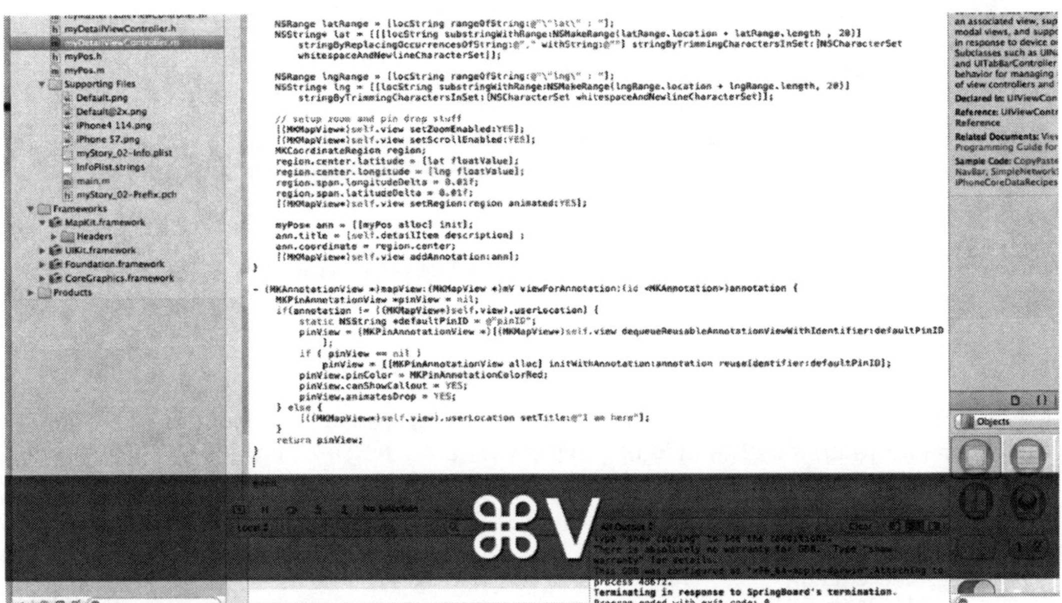

Figure 10–35. *Let's parse the Google server.*

35. I do not have a problem with you pasting the "08 Part 2myDetailViewController m" boilerplate code that parses the Google server because we all use it over and over. We all use and tweak it here and there. If you skipped my instruction in step 34, make you sure you know where to paste it. I will also go through the critical sections that you need to know and tweak. The odds are that Apple will soon make a class or framework to do this because we all use this code to parse servers. After pasting the code where it need to be, let's go through it.

a. Go back to where we began this last section of code. We first need to import the myPos.h file because, when we setup the zoom and pin drop code, we use title and coordinate for the `myPos` annotation. The first method we see is the `setDetailItem`, as shown below. We set the `detailItem` so it can be used and then, once it's stored locally, we'll configure the view which, in other words, means making a new map that will redraw itself when a change is needed. The `configureView` is the huge method that is next in the myDetailViewController.m

```
- (void)setDetailItem:(id)newDetailItem
{
if (_detailItem != newDetailItem) {
_detailItem = newDetailItem;

// Update the view.
        [selfconfigureView];
    }
}
```

b. The next item we look at is the configureView method that is a utility method and called internally. This is where the real action happens. First, let's look at how we get onto the server. We go to the server associated with mapURI, which in our case is the API geocode at Google, maps.googleapis.com. We're going to ask it for a city and make the code take care of the spaces, whether denoted by a space or a "%20"

```
NSString* mapURI =
@"http://maps.googleapis.com/maps/api/geocode/json?address=city&sensor=false";
        mapURI = [mapURI stringByReplacingOccurrencesOfString:@"city"
withString:[self.detailItem description]];
        NSURL* mapURL = [NSURL URLWithString:[mapURI
stringByReplacingOccurrencesOfString:@" " withString:@"%20"]];
```

Well, you can see above that we've told the server that we want data but the issue is how the server returns that data to us. This is where the NSURL protocols we'll use do the work but we have to call them by calling connection

```
NSURLConnection* connection = [NSURLConnection connectionWithRequest:[NSURLRequest
requestWithURL:mapURL] delegate:self];
        if (connection)
            locData = [NSMutableData data];
```

Here you can see how "connection" consists of three parts:

- connection:(NSURLConnection *)connection didReceiveResponse
- connection:(NSURLConnection *)connection didReceiveData
- connectionDidFinishLoading:(NSURLConnection *)connection

The connectionDidFinishLoading:(NSURLConnection *)connection is the method that actually collects the longitudinal and latitudinal data from the Google server and stores it.

```
- (void)connectionDidFinishLoading:(NSURLConnection *)connection {

NSRegularExpression* regex =
[NSRegularExpressionregularExpressionWithPattern:@"location.*?\\}"
options:NSRegularExpressionDotMatchesLineSeparators
error:nil];
NSString* dataString = [[NSStringalloc]
initWithData:locDataencoding:NSASCIIStringEncoding];
NSTextCheckingResult* locResult = [regex firstMatchInString:dataString
options:0range:NSMakeRange(0, [dataString length])];
NSString* locString = [dataString substringWithRange:[locResult range]];

NSRange latRange = [locString rangeOfString:@"\"lat\" : "];
NSString* lat = [[[locString substringWithRange:NSMakeRange(latRange.location +
latRange.length , 20)] stringByReplacingOccurrencesOfString:@","withString:@""]
stringByTrimmingCharactersInSet:[NSCharacterSetwhitespaceAndNewlineCharacterSet]];

NSRange lngRange = [locString rangeOfString:@"\"lng\" : "];
NSString* lng = [[locString substringWithRange:NSMakeRange(lngRange.location +
lngRange.length, 20)]
stringByTrimmingCharactersInSet:[NSCharacterSetwhitespaceAndNewlineCharacterSet]];
```

```
// setup zoom and pin drop stuff
    [(MKMapView*)self.viewsetZoomEnabled:YES];
    [(MKMapView*)self.viewsetScrollEnabled:YES];
MKCoordinateRegion region;
    region.center.latitude = [lat floatValue];
    region.center.longitude = [lng floatValue];
    region.span.longitudeDelta = 0.01f;
    region.span.latitudeDelta = 0.01f;
    [(MKMapView*)self.viewsetRegion:region animated:YES];

MyPos* ann = [[MyPosalloc] init];
    ann.title = [self.detailItemdescription] ;
    ann.coordinate = region.center;
    [(MKMapView*)self.viewaddAnnotation:ann];
}
```

c. Since we also need to handle the map delegation as a protocol, we have one more piece of code to handle here. Most of this, we do not use, but it does drop the pin for us. In the lecture hall, I make my students play around with changing the animation, the pin color, and the `setTitle`. Suffice to say we just drop it in as you too will find yourself doing. I encourage you to also play with at least the `pinView.pinColor = MKPinAnnotationColorRed`, the `pinView.canShowCallout = YES`, and the `pinView.animatesDrop = YES`.

```
(MKAnnotationView *)mapView:(MKMapView *)mV
viewForAnnotation:(id<MKAnnotation>)annotation {
    MKPinAnnotationView *pinView = nil;
    if(annotation != ((MKMapView*)self.view).userLocation) {
        static NSString *defaultPinID = @"pinID";
        pinView = (MKPinAnnotationView *)[(MKMapView*)self.view
dequeueReusableAnnotationViewWithIdentifier:defaultPinID];
        if ( pinView == nil )
            pinView = [[MKPinAnnotationView alloc] initWithAnnotation:annotation
reuseIdentifier:defaultPinID];
        pinView.pinColor = MKPinAnnotationColorRed;
        pinView.canShowCallout = YES;
        pinView.animatesDrop = YES;
    } else {
        [((MKMapView*)self.view).userLocation setTitle:@"I am here"];
    }
    return pinView;
}

@end
```

But the most important thing that I stress here is that you CANNOT be freaked out if you do not know what every piece of the code does. You do not know what every single part of your car's engine does to drive it. Similarly, you have enough right here above to know how to connect to a server, parse out what you want, and animate it as you like. Enough said. Get over it and move on. If as you move on you find you need to parse a server, go ahead, use this code, tinker around with it, and make it work.

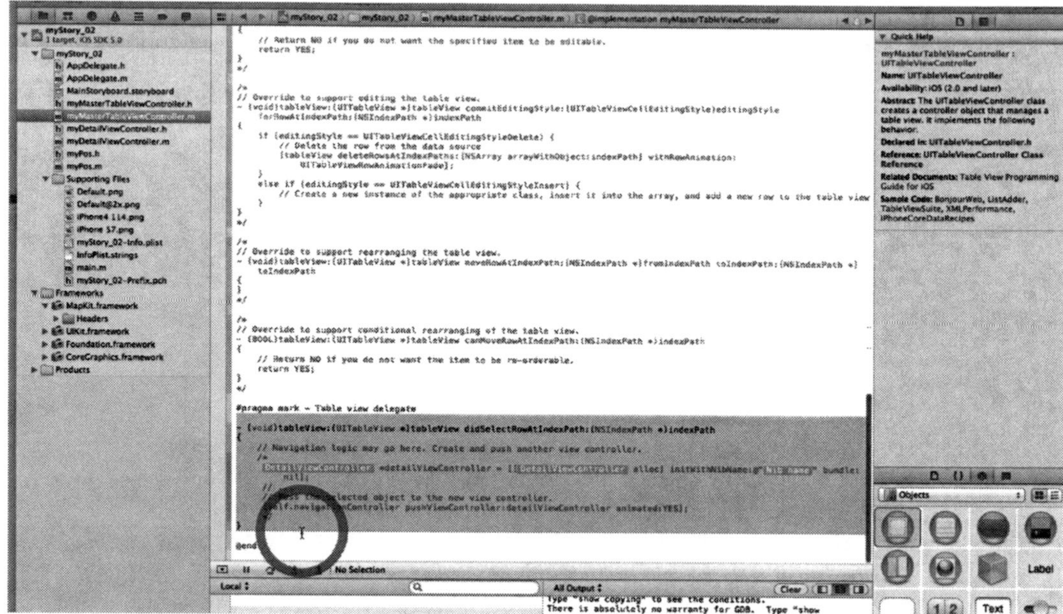

Figure 10–36. *Select and delete the tableView method.*

36. OK, we are through with the `myDetailViewController` and it's now time to do some housekeeping in the `myMasterTableViewController`. So, open it up and scroll down to the bottom of the myMasterTableViewController.m until you get to the `tableView` method. What I want you to see here is that this is the method we used when we used the table View delegate before storyboarding. The thing is that we now use storyboarding, so we no longer need it. Select it all, as shown in Figure 10–36, and either comment it out or delete it. In the video, I delete it out.

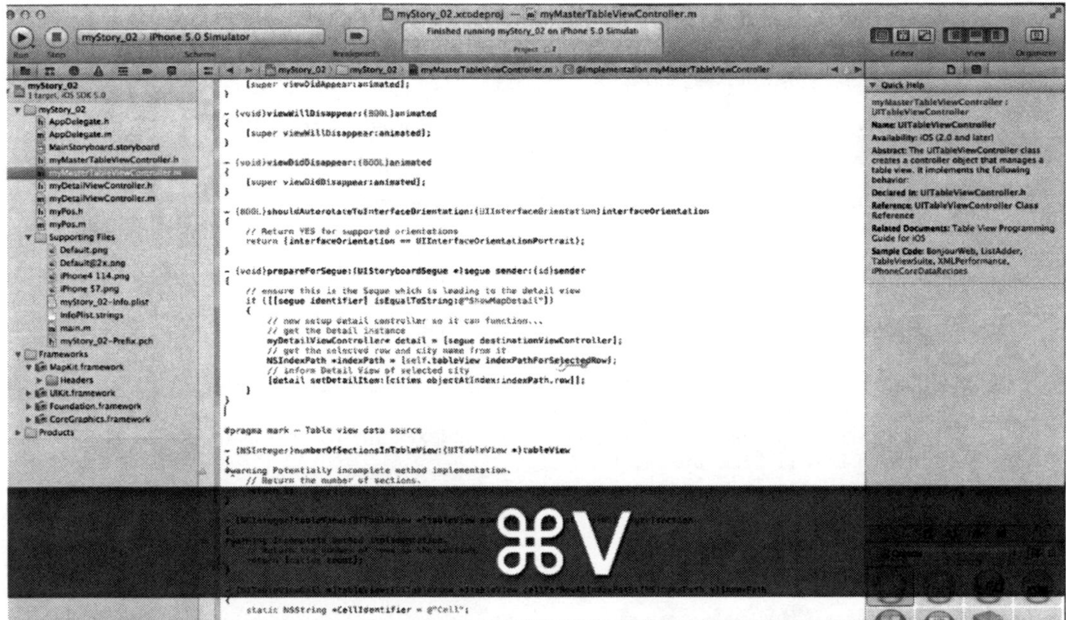

Figure 10–37. *Create the prepareForSegue method.*

37. Staying in the myMasterTableViewController implementation file, we need to look ahead and imagine that we are just about to create a segue that leads from our table to the MapKit, which in essence takes the place of the tableView method we just deleted. We will need a method to handle this. Again, you can either download the "09 Part 2myMasterTableViewController.m" boilerplate file or you can code along with me. Go to the end of the shouldAutorotateToInterfaceOrientation method, create a couple of blank line, and let's start coding or pasting the code in and following along.

   a. The first thing to note here is that we have already imported the myDetailViewController.h file in step 20.

   b. Now we need to tell the myDetailViewController what city to show and we do this with:

```
NSIndexPath *indexPath = [self.tableView indexPathForSelectedRow];
```

   c. We need to also make it only tell myDetailViewController if we're going to navigate through the segue. But the problem is that we need to tell the compiler the name of the segue it needs to keep a look out for us but we've yet to give this segue a name. So let's give it a name now!

   d. Let's call it ShowMapDetail. We also need the code that we will need to check if this segue is being used and then, if the segue called ShowMapDetail is, in fact, being used.

e. We know we are going to be going to a `detailViewController` so we grab the city name from the current and selected row because the user just clicked one.

f. We also set and create a detail item, the details of the city, as follows:

```
- (void)prepareForSegue:(UIStoryboardSegue *)segue sender:(id)sender
{
    // ensure this is the Seque which is leading to the detail view
    if ([[segue identifier] isEqualToString:@"ShowMapDetail"])
    {
        // now setup detail controller so it can function...
        // get the Detail instance
        MyDetailViewController* detail = [segue destinationViewController];
        // get the selected row and city name from it
        NSIndexPath *indexPath = [self.tableView indexPathForSelectedRow];
        // inform Detail View of selected city
        [detail setDetailItem:[cities objectAtIndex:indexPath.row]];
    }
}
```

Tweaking the Storyboard

We now have written or pasted all the code we need to parse the Google server for the geospatial specifics of each city we populated in our list on Part 1, and we also have the code to route these coordinates through a segue, which does not exist yet, through to a MapKit that will have a pin drop down into the middle of the selected city. In short, we need something that will contain our MapKit Framework and, to do this, we will add a navigation controller and a detail view. We will have to create a new View Controller and bring it onto the canvas. Then we need to connect the Master View to the Detail View and add a MapView to its Navigation. Looking at the big picture expanded, we see the following below.

THE BIG PICTURE: STORYBOARD TWEAKING EXPANDED

1. Populate a table with a list of cities (COMPLETED)
2. Code a pin to drop to the center of a selected cities' map
    - 2.1. Add MapKit framework
    - 2.2. Write code
    - 2.3. Tweak Storyboard to accept our new code.
        - **2.3.1. Add Navigation Controller**
        - **2.3.2. Add Detail View that will contain our MapKit Framework**
        - **2.3.3. Drag a View Controller onto the canvas**

2.3.4. Add a Push transition from the Master View to the Detail View - Name it "Detail View"

2.3.5. Add a MapView to its Navigation: - Drag the Map view above the View

2.3.6. Associate the Map View with the backing class of myDetailViewController

2.3.6.1. Select the View Controller Detail View in the view Controller Scene in the Document Outline

2.3.6.2. Select the Identity inspector in the Utilities

2.3.6.3. In Custom Class go to the drop down menu in Class

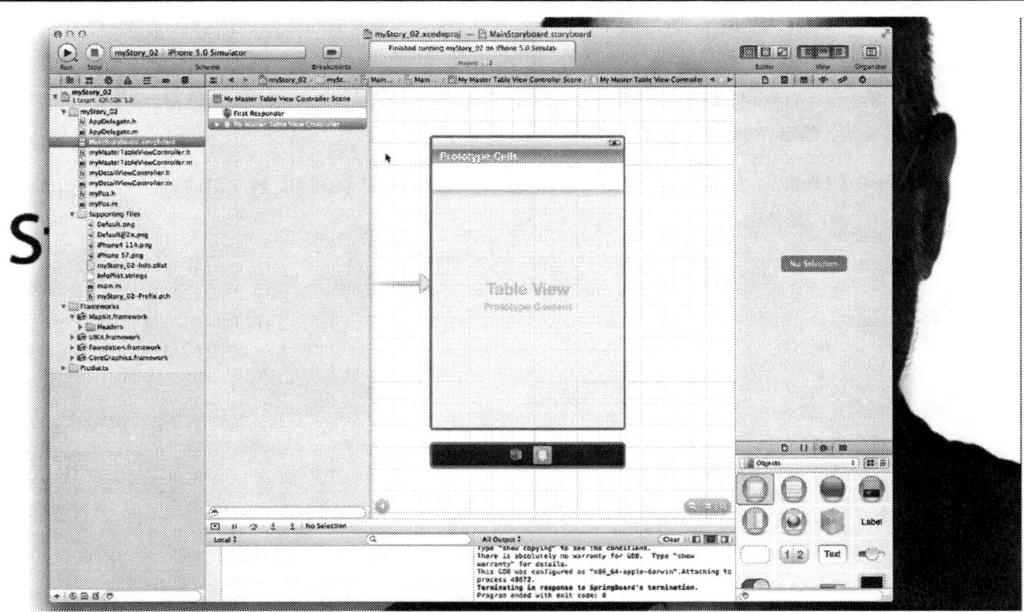

Figure 10–38. *Open up the Storyboard for some final tweaking.*

38. With this said, let's open up the Storyboard, as shown in Figure 10–38

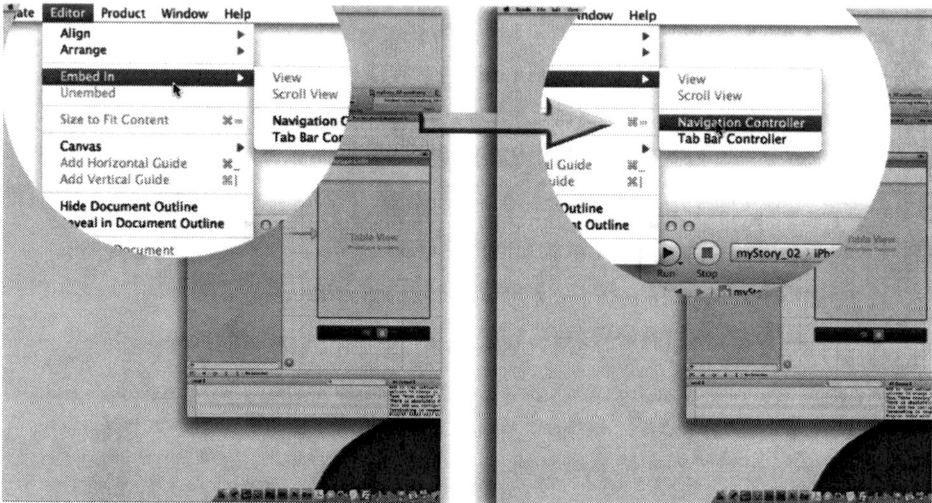

Figure 10–39. *Add a Navigation Controller.*

39. We need to add a Navigation controller, so select Editor ➤ Embed ➤ Navigation Controller, as shown in Figure 10–39.

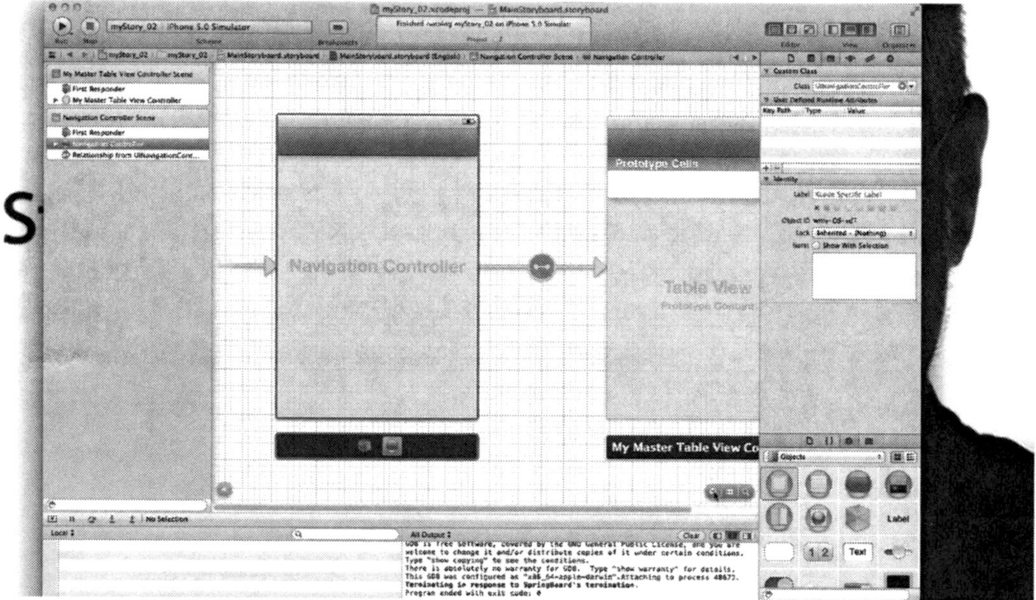

Figure 10–40. *The new Navigation Controller automatically connects to the Table View.*

40. As we can see in Figure 10–40, the new navigation controller automatically connects to our Table View. Make some space on your Storyboard by closing the Navigator.

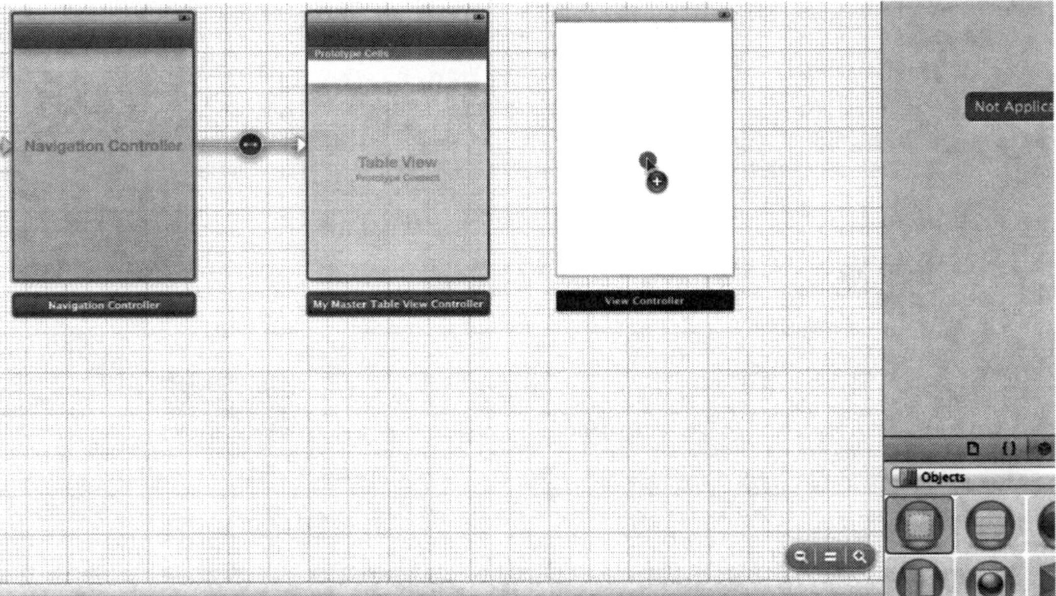

Figure 10–41. *Add Detail View that will contain our MapKit Framework.*

41. Zoom out so you can see more of the canvas. Now scroll to the left so you have a large area of blank canvas to the right of your Table View. Now grab a View Controller and drag it onto the canvas to the right of the Table View, as shown in Figure 10–41.

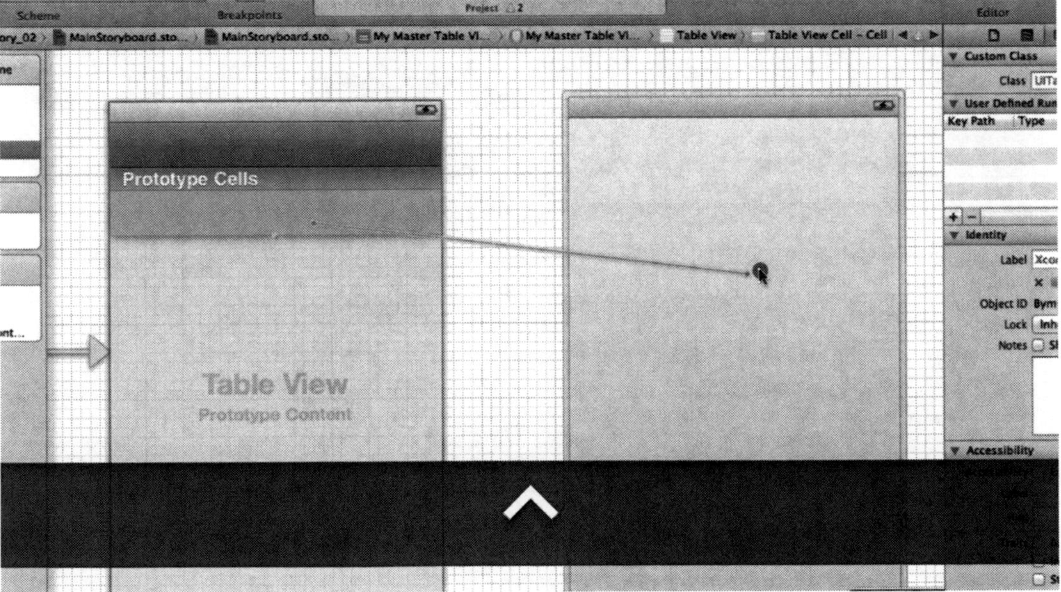

Figure 10–42. *Create a segue.*

42. We now need to connect the Master View and the Detail View with a segue - specifically with a push. To do this, I want you to select the cell in the Master View and then control drag from the cell to the View, as shown in Figure 10–42.

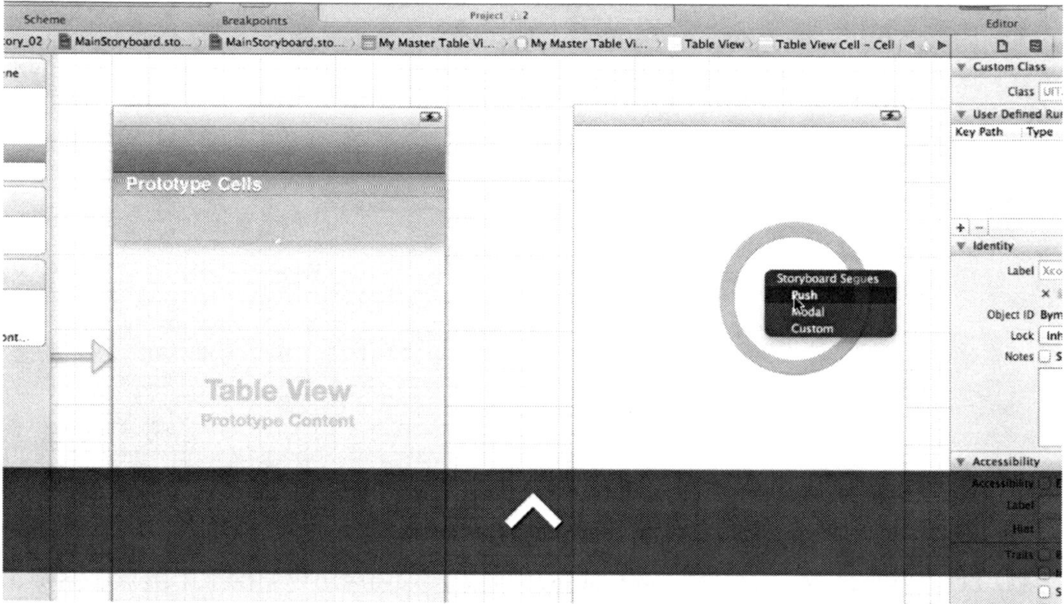

Figure 10–43. *Select Push.*

43. After you have controlled dragged from the cell to the View, you will see a drop down menu occur with three options of segue connectivity: Push, Modal, and Custom. We want to select Push. This is shown in Figure 10–43.

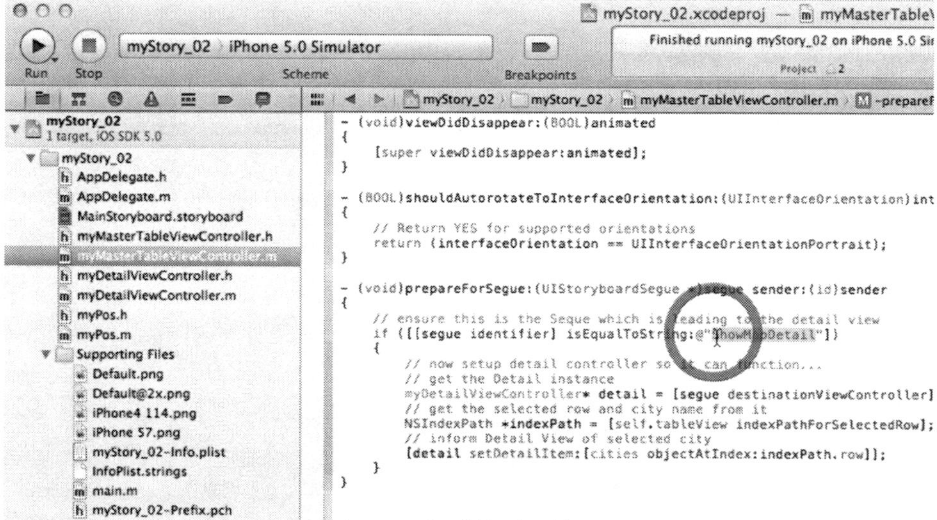

Figure 10–44. *Remember the name we gave the segue?*

44. We now need to give the segue that we just created the name we gave it in the prepare for segue method in the myMasterTableViewController.m class. In case you forgot the name you gave it, or even if you remember it, go back and copy the name of the segue so that your brain can make the connections. This is illustrated in Figure 10–44

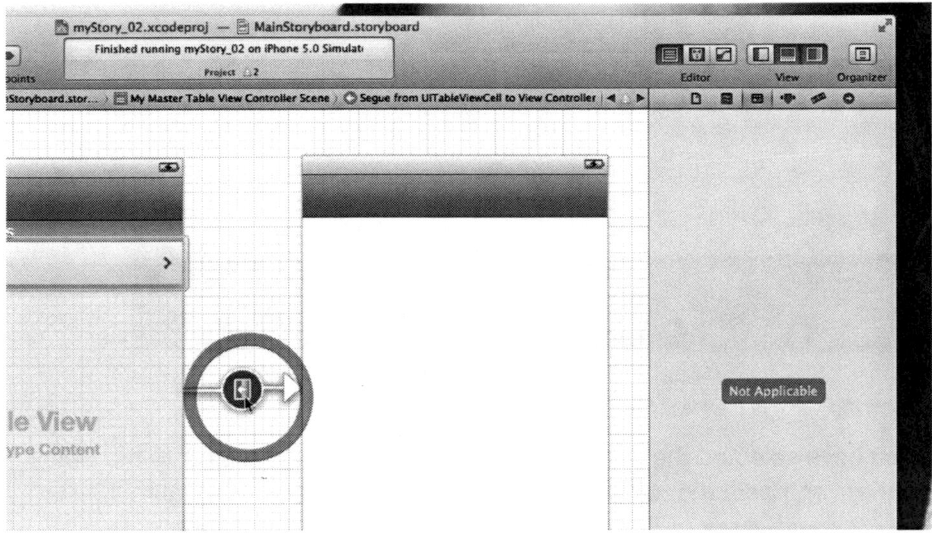

Figure 10–45. *Select the segue.*

45. This may sound really unnecessary but students have the most difficult time naming segues because they forget to first select it. I know it's new but it's amazing how many forget to do this. For this reason, I've taken the time to specifically include this image in the book. Select the segue, as shown in 10–45, and then we will give it its name.

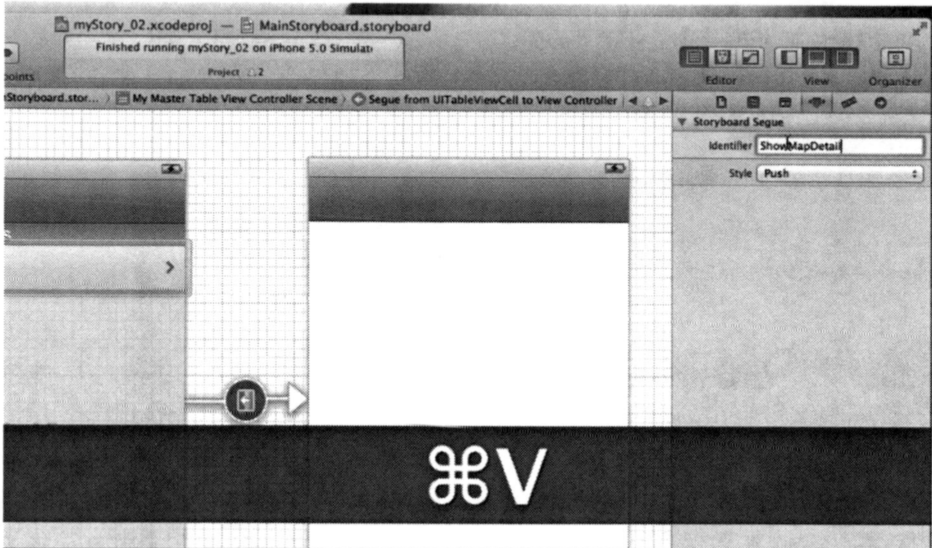

Figure 10–46. *Paste the name in the Identifier.*

46. Once you have selected the segue connecting the `UITableViewCell` to the Detail View Controller, paste the name in the Identifier box, as shown in Figure 10–46.

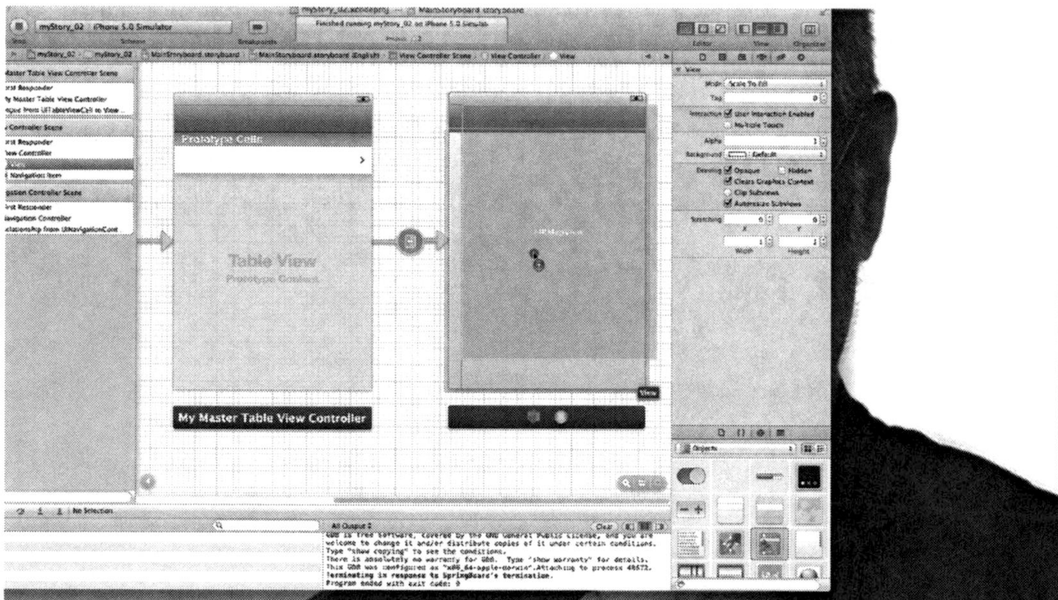

Figure 10–47. *Drag a Map View onto the View.*

47. We now have everything connected for the map to appear on the view except ... ahh - the Map View! Grab a Map View from the Library and drag it onto the View, as shown in Figure 10–47.

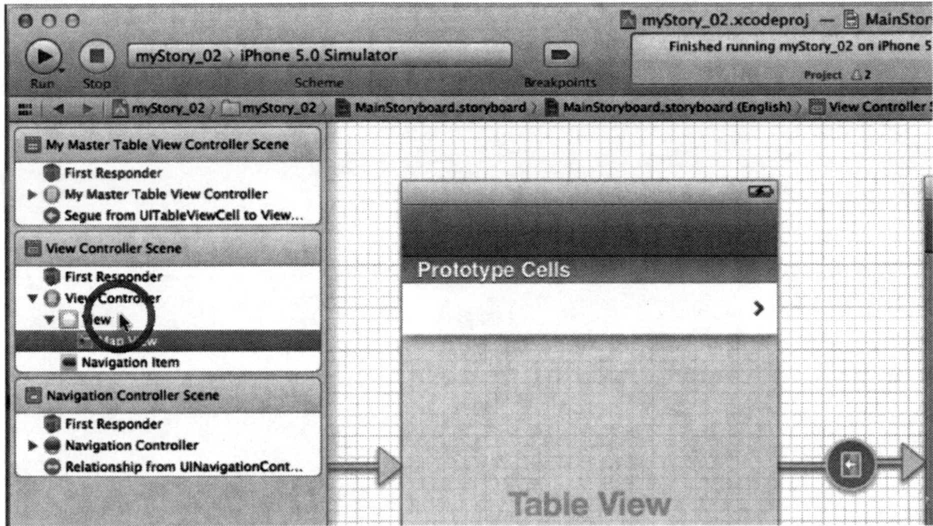

Figure 10–48. *Select the Map View.*

48. We now need to make the Map View become the Primary View. As you can see in Figure 10–48, the View is above the Map View. In geek terms, we say that the Map View is subordinate to the View and the View is currently the primary view. Remember how I said that Views lying on top of one another can be very confusing. Well, there's a reason I'm investing three images into this point.

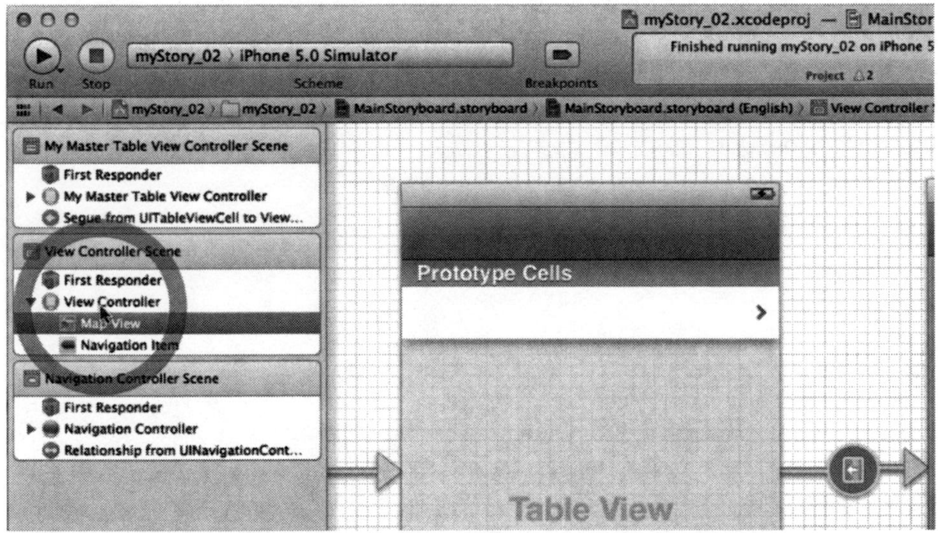

Figure 10–49. *Drag Map View on top of the View.*

49. Right now, the Map View that we just dragged onto the View is subordinate to the view. To make the view go away and have the Map View be the primary view, select the View Controller in the view Controller Scene in the Document Outline and then drag the Map View above the View, as shown in Figure 10–49.

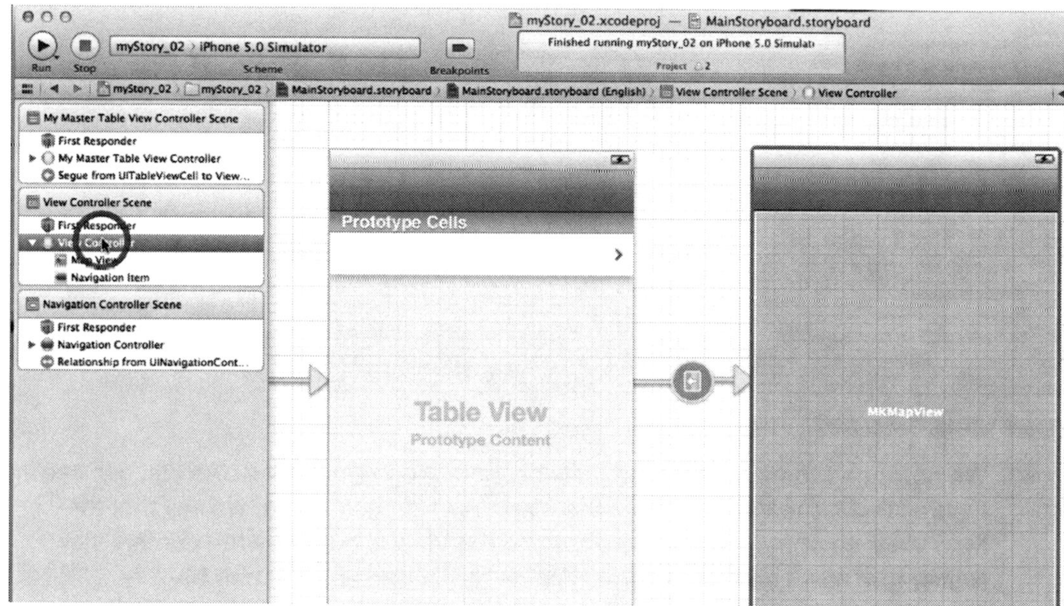

Figure 10–50. *Now Map View is the Primary View.*

50. Once the Map View is above the View, the View disappears and the MapView will be the Primary view. This is critical because nothing else will work if this doesn't happen! Make sure you can master this. Don't move on unless your screen looks like the screen in Figure 10–50.

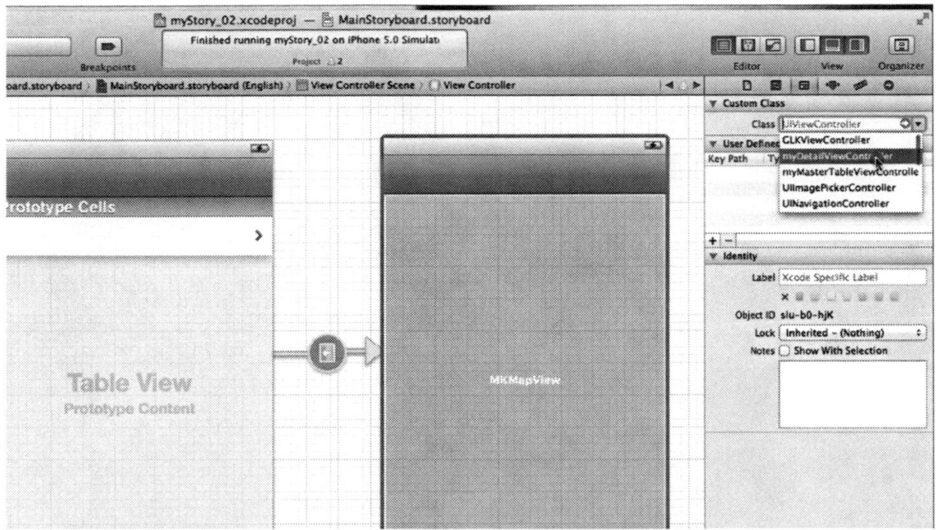

Figure 10–51. *Associate the Map View with your myDetailViewController.*

51. Remember the tons of work you did for the myDetailViewController.m? Well, that's all got to work underneath the Map View we have just created. Select the View Controller Detail in the View Controller Scene in the Document Outline. Select the Identity inspector in the Utilities. Then in the Custom Class, go to the drop down menu in Class and select `myDetailViewController`, as shown in Figure 10–51.

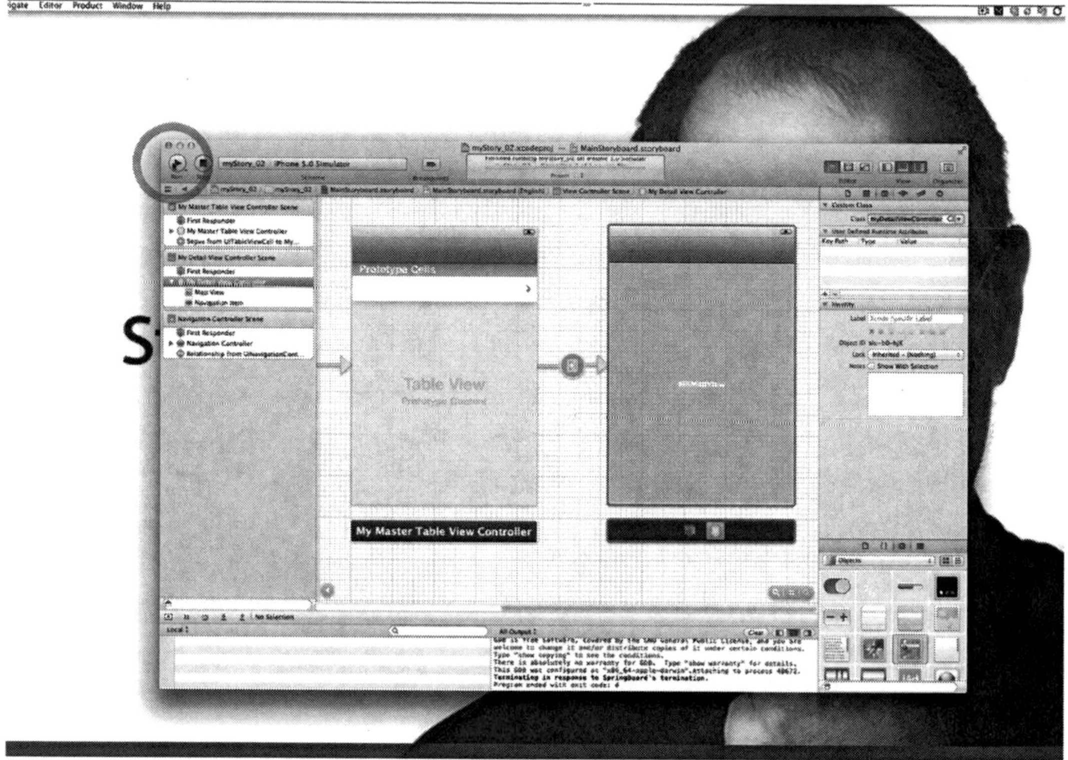

Figure 10–52. *Run it.*

52. Run it.

Figure 10–53. *Splash goes to Table View, then selecting a city, Durban.*

53. Yes, it is beautiful, isn't it? All that hard work, huh? The Splash appears, then we see the table we populated with cities but now we see the beautiful disclosures on the right side of each cell that are telling us that if we click on the cell then something very cool will happen. We then click on the cell and it segues in a Map view, as shown in the right image in Figure 10–54.

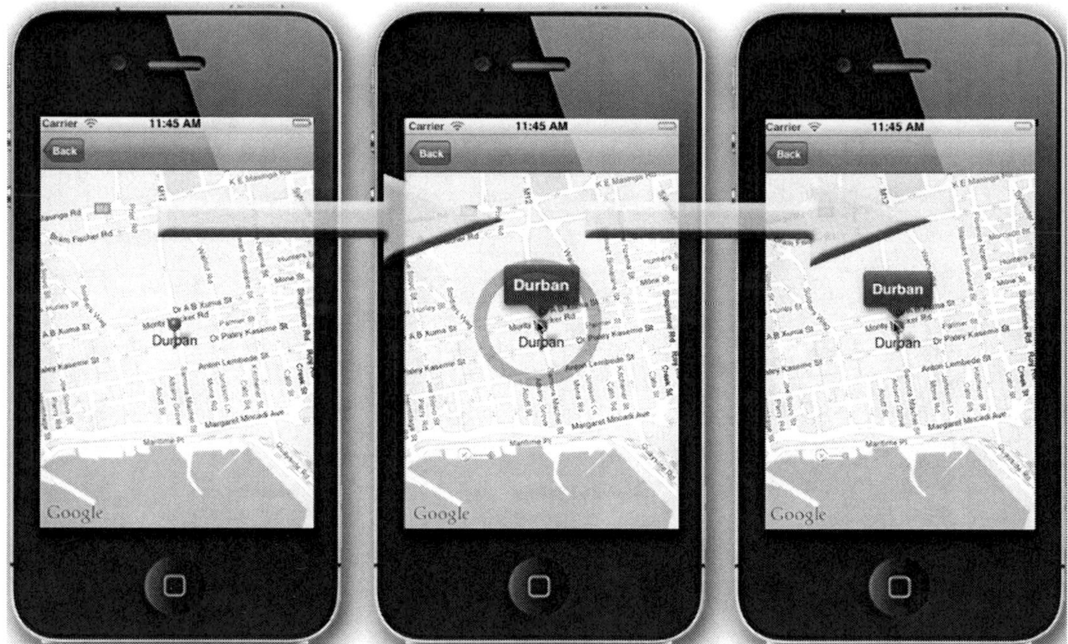

Figure 10–54. *The pin drops and the annotation works.*

54. Congratulations. The one thing I am going to have you do as an exercise is name the Navigation Bar the "Detail View" and also call the Table View the "Master" in the navigation bar. Go back to where you were in Figure 10–47 and simply double click near the center of the navigation bar and name it whatever you like actually. The reason I leave this out is because students often think that the name we give the navigation bar actually has some effect on the code. I've seen quite a few students changing the name on the navigation bars trying to debug their code. Leaving the names out shows you that these names have zero affect at all.

These two series have been very long. There is nothing beyond the code that I want to show you. In fact, there have been quite a few times that we have gone beyond the scope of "Beginner", let alone absolute beginner. So we will not dig down any more into the code than what we have already done. Now take a break, relax, and glow in the satisfaction!

Chapter 11

Storyboarding to Multimedia Platforms

This is the last chapter of the book and I have been looking forward to writing this chapter for a long time. This is the capstone app if you will. The app that teaches you how to market your restaurant, business, or whatever you like to various multimedia platforms. I chose to promote a band for this app because it includes iTunes and many of my students struggle with iTunes. We will take care of that right here. In the lecture hall, I first walk through the app with the students as they imagine they are in a distant place and time and they've discovered a band called The Beatles. They then market that band on the Web, YouTube, and iTunes. In the second half of this project, the students create their own business that they market in a similar but much more creative manner.

Unfortunately, due to copyright issues, it is not permissible to show pictures of the Beatles in a book that is not authorized by the Beatles. For the purposes of this book, I've created some dummy sites on the web with pictures of myself playing guitar and iTunes sites where I have songs from many years ago (1997). I will show you where to get the Beatles URLs (public domain) and how to make the site (first for the Beatles as I do in class) and then how to find other bands or other types of media to pretend to promote. Hopefully, you will have your own business, such as a restaurant, bead shop, consulting service, or whatever, that you can then make a promotional app of and shoot it up to the iTunes store so that people can download it for free.

How does this work? Remember back in Figure 1-21, I explained the exact process of how one can make money from an app on the Internet? Well, here I teach you how to market your business and set your app up, possibly for free to begin with. Let's say you have a babysitting business. After you learn how to manage the Beatles website, you can make an app for the babysitting business and shoot it up to the app store for free downloads. In the old days, we used to hand out cards – now we hand out apps. You let parents and potential parents of your babysitting store know that they can download your babysitting business' app for free and, with a password that only works for a limited time (and only if they are a potential parent), view their baby on a live webcam any time of day. They can see other children being taken care of by your staff. They can get updates on snow days, on birthdays, and pay their bills online all through your app. By word of mouth, those parents will tell other parents how great your business is based solely on how convenient and cool your app was.

The same applies to other businesses; you just need to be creative. Innovativeness is your department but hey! You had to have a huge streak of innovation to buy this book and, if you're still reading this, you're well into the realm of Geekdom so I have full faith that you have everything you need to make a wonderful app for your business, another person's business, or yourself. All you need is the technical know-how and I will teach you that right here, right now, so let's go!

myiTunes: A Master-Detail Application

myiTunes is based upon one of the more daunting methods of creating a storyboarding app: the Master-Detail Application. However, Master-Detail Applications empower the iPad iOS 5's split view and popover together with incredible storyboarding technology. More so, as if this were not enough, we also throw into the mix the ability to access iTunes, Facebook, Google+, pages that have videos, and, of course, the two iPad splash screens with cool icons that all add up to a beautiful, marketable app just waiting to boost you, your business, or another person's business up into the stratosphere—loudly!

iTunes has some controversial, quirky, and not so user-friendly means of accessing its iTunes music store. I will go through this step by step, including the ability to look up bands, videos, and podcasts. There are some other multimedia platforms I do not cover in the example because that would be overload, but I will show you exactly how to convert your media from images to video and so forth. I also include the code to access these other forms of multimedia and the boilerplate code that you download. So, even though we do not use all these types of media in the boilerplate, they are there for you to use as you so choose.

One thing about terminology before we proceed: we will be talking about split views and popovers in this app. These are the supercool tables and drop-down menus that, depending how you hold your iPad, invoke a table for the user to use. The split view shows 2 panels, side-by-side. In landscape mode, the master view is 320px wide. However, when you go to portrait orientation, the split view appears as a popover that looks like it's lying on top of the existing view. It looks like a drop-down menu sitting on top of what was underneath it (see Figure 11–25). It cannot be that it works like a dialog box or drop-down menu. One student recently asked me: "Dr. Lewis, can we pimp out the popover!?" Hmmm… nope! You cannot tweak, pimp out, and change much. But the issue is whether you want to or not, and the answer is 'probably not'. Popovers are sophisticated, elegant, and show the user that you, the developer who programmed them, are awesome!

So let's get on with the preliminaries so we can make a start on our app.

Preliminaries

This chapter's download files are similar in nature to Chapter 10's boilerplates and images. Except that, as mentioned before, I include code that we do not use in this app but that you may want to use when you create your own app using alternative or additional media. It's all there for you to use. On the video and in the code, there is a substantial amount of code prewritten by me. However, I explain it all in intense detail in this chapter so I suggest that you try and code it all by yourself. If you find you need to use the boilerplate code after a while, then go ahead and use it, but please first try doing it on your own. If you do have to use the boilerplate code, then go ahead and try typing in the code line by line after you had success running the boilerplate code. If you cannot make it work, even using the boilerplate code, then download my exact Xcode file and, after making my code run, see exactly where you missed something.

These download files can be found at `http://bit.ly/sL26vN`. One can download the sample code that I programmed on the video here: `http://bit.ly/uN1uV1`. To view the screencast of this chapter's exercise, go to `http://bit.ly/tPatpA`. If you need more help, go to the forum at `http://bit.ly/oLVwpY`.

THE BIG PICTURE

Just as we did in Chapter 10 when we began to write larger sets of code, we will use "The Big Picture" with its many views. First, we will view the code from "30,000" feet, taking a very broad overall view of our landscape. Then, as we drill downward, we will always keep track of the big picture.

1. Set up the popover in the storyboard
2. Code the interaction to the multimedia platforms
3. Tweak the popover to grab the platforms correctly

A New Master-Detail Template

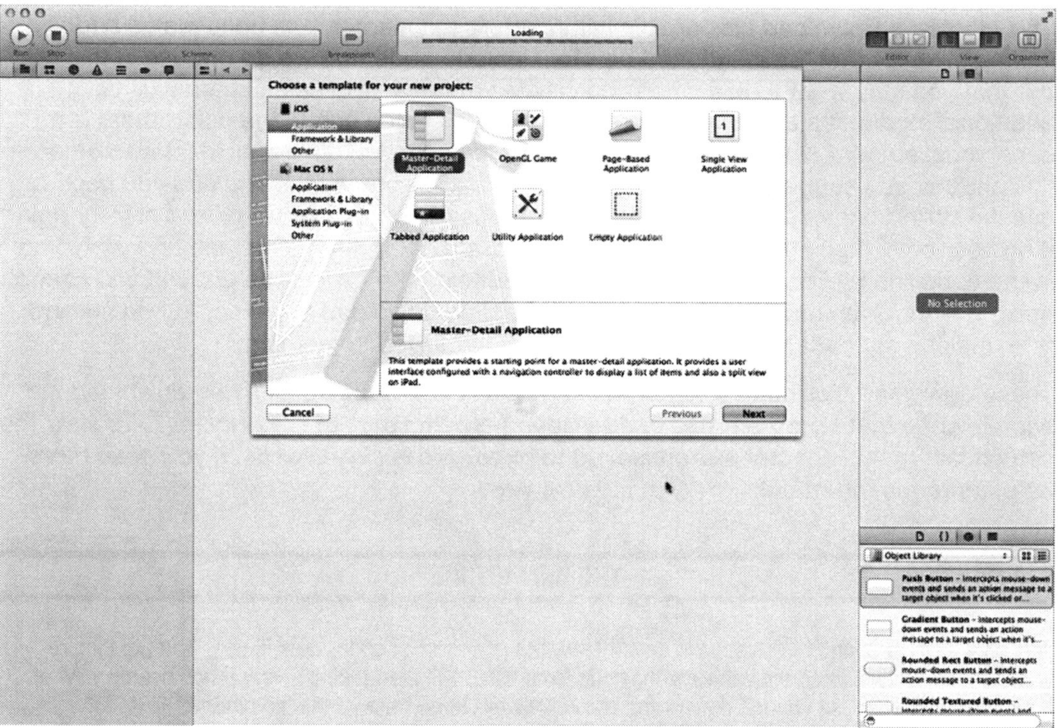

Figure 11–1. *Select the Master-Detail Application icon, and press return or next.*

1. We will use a Master-Detail Application. So open Xcode and enter ⌘⇧N, as shown in Figure 11–1. After selecting the Master-Detail Application, press enter/return.

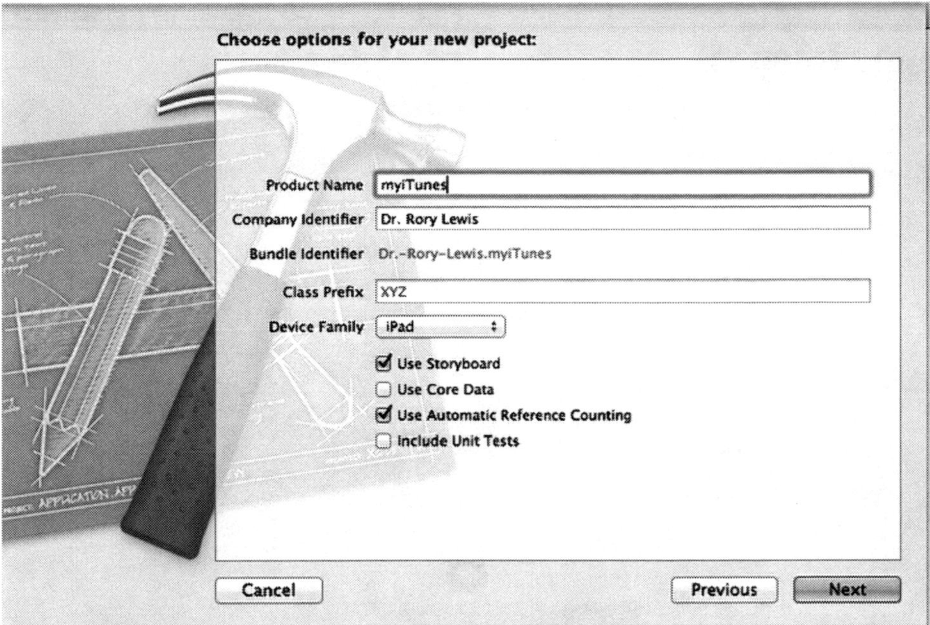

Figure 11–2. *Name your app myiTunes making sure Storyboard and automatic referencing is on.*

2. In order to follow along with me as closely as you can, name it “myiTunes,” select “iPad,” check the “Use Storyboard,” and “Use Automatic Reference Counting,” but leave the “Class Prefix” and “Include Unit Tests” unchecked as shown in Figure 11–2.

Bring in the Images!

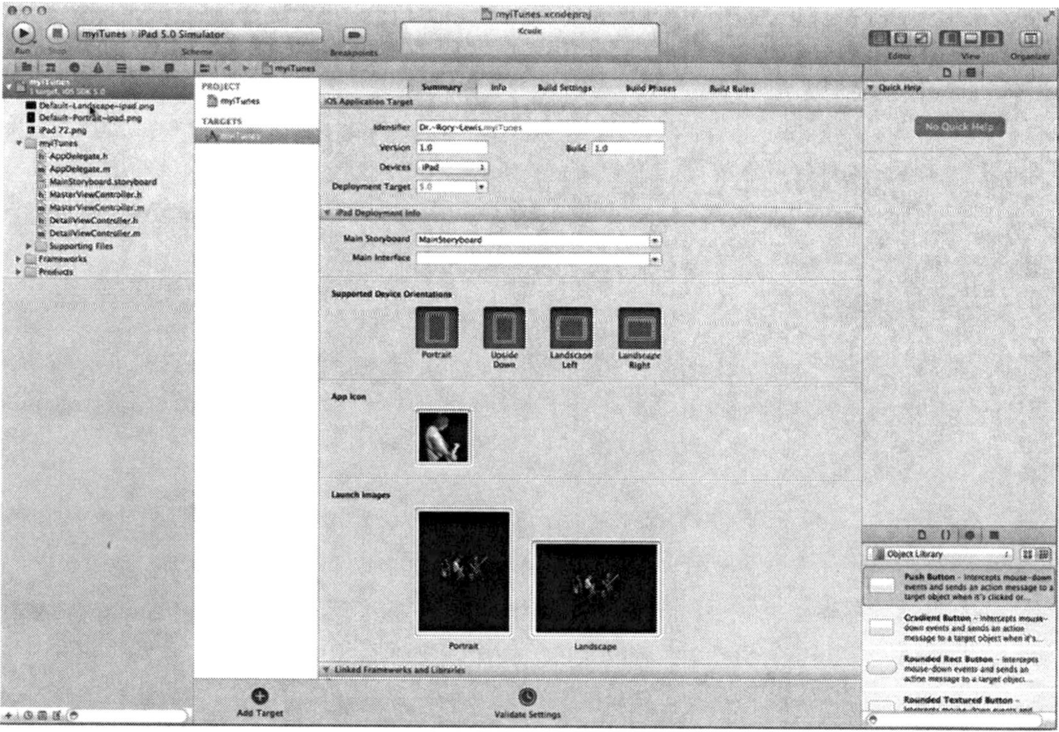

Figure 11–3. *Drag in your graphics.*

3. Just as we did in myStory_01 after going to my website at `http://bit.ly/uN1uV1` and downloading the images and boilerplate code onto your desktop, drag in the 72 × 72 px iPad icon, iPad 72, into the App Icon box, drag the 769 × 1004 px Default-Portrait iPad splash screen into the Launch 'Images Landscape box, and drag the 1024 × 748 px Default-Landscape iPad splash screen into the Launch Images' Portrait box as shown in Figure 11–3.

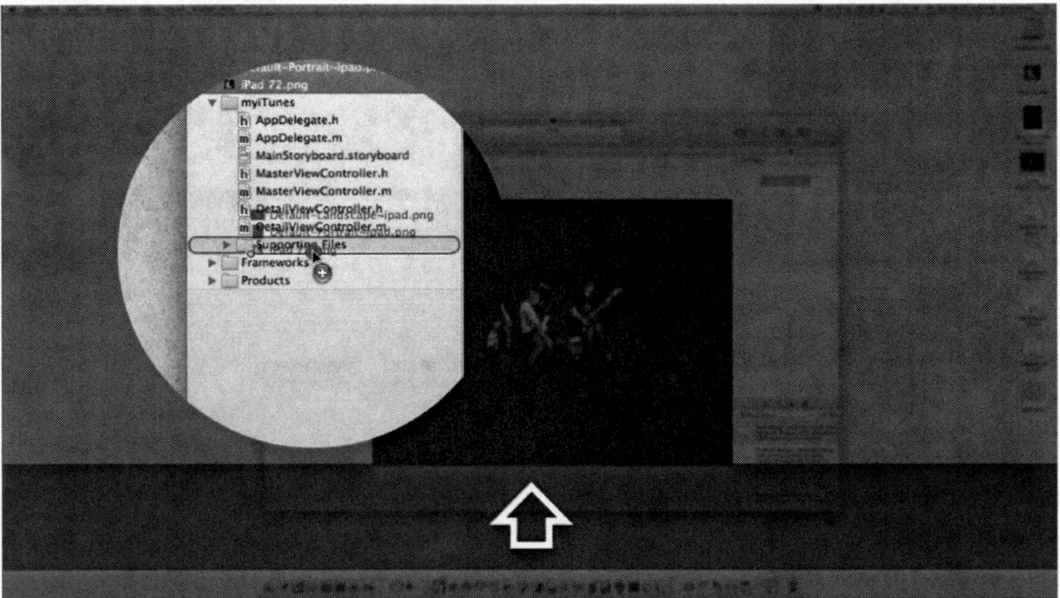

Figure 11–4. *Drag the images into the Supporting Files Folder.*

4. Because we always want to keep things nice, orderly, and in their proper place, you will see that the files holding the images you just dragged into Xcode are in the root directory. We want to drag them into their proper location: the Supporting Files folder. This is illustrated in Figure 11–4.

Organize the Popover in Storyboard

The first thing we will do is set up the popover in the storyboard. I am going to be fairly inventive and artful but not go overboard with beautiful popover bells and whistles because I do not want to take away from my two goals: teaching you to set up the storyboard and teaching you to write the code behind the storyboard. However, once you complete this project, you will have opened the door to all the rooms where you can later tinker around. But, for right now, let's keep it simple.

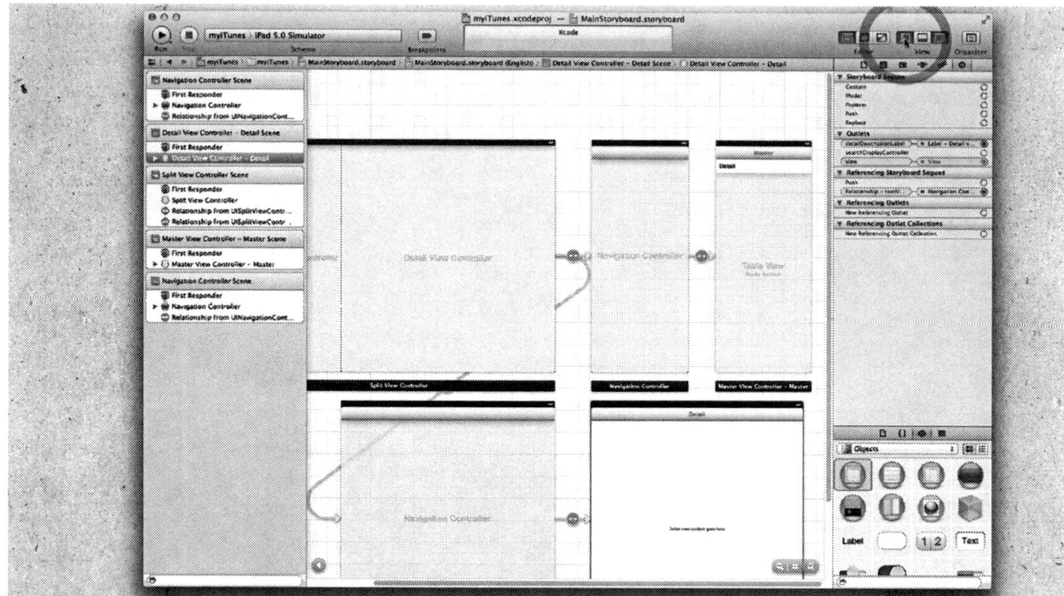

Figure 11–5. *Select Storyboard and close the Navigator.*

5. Select MainStoryboard.storyboard and close the Navigator as shown in Figure 11–5.

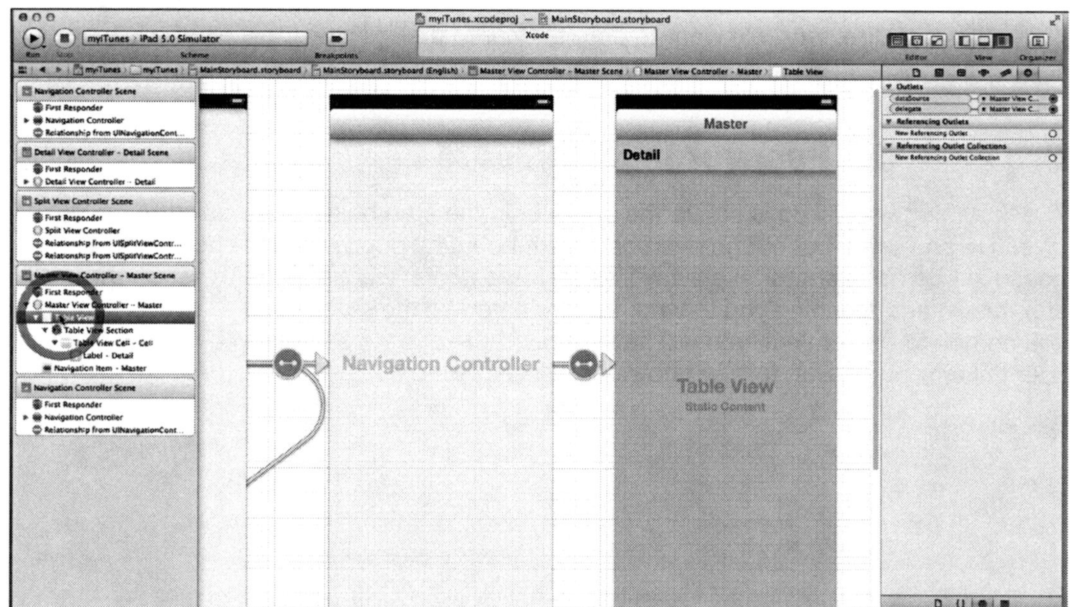

Figure 11–6. *We do not want a View Controller here.*

6. Before we get too far, I want you to take a look at Figure 11–14 and take a look at all the Table views and their levels located in the left hand side bar called the Document Outline inside the box called Master View Controller - Master Scene. Compare how populated it is compared to our lone Table view in our Master View Controller - Master Scene. That's quite a lot of work there.

   There are two ways to populate these Table Views with what you want. They are the "long boring" way and the "organized and very efficient" way. We plan ahead and we do this by sticking to a simple rule:

   Create one Table view with all its sub-attributes. Then, once you have one done exactly the way you want it, duplicate the entire set.

   We are selecting the default view Controller because we need to delete it. As far as the big picture is concerned, we will create one group exactly as we want it to be, as indicated by 1.1 in "The Big Picture".

   So go ahead and open the Documents Outline and select Table View in my Master View Controller–Master scene as shown in Figure 11–6.

THE BIG PICTURE

1. Set up the popover in the storyboard
   - **1.1. Create a Group**
     - 1.1.1. Set up the attributes of each Table View Cell – Cell in the group
   - 1.2. Duplicate the Group as required
   - 1.3. Label all the cells
2. Code the interaction to the multimedia platforms
3. Tweak the popover to grab the platforms correctly

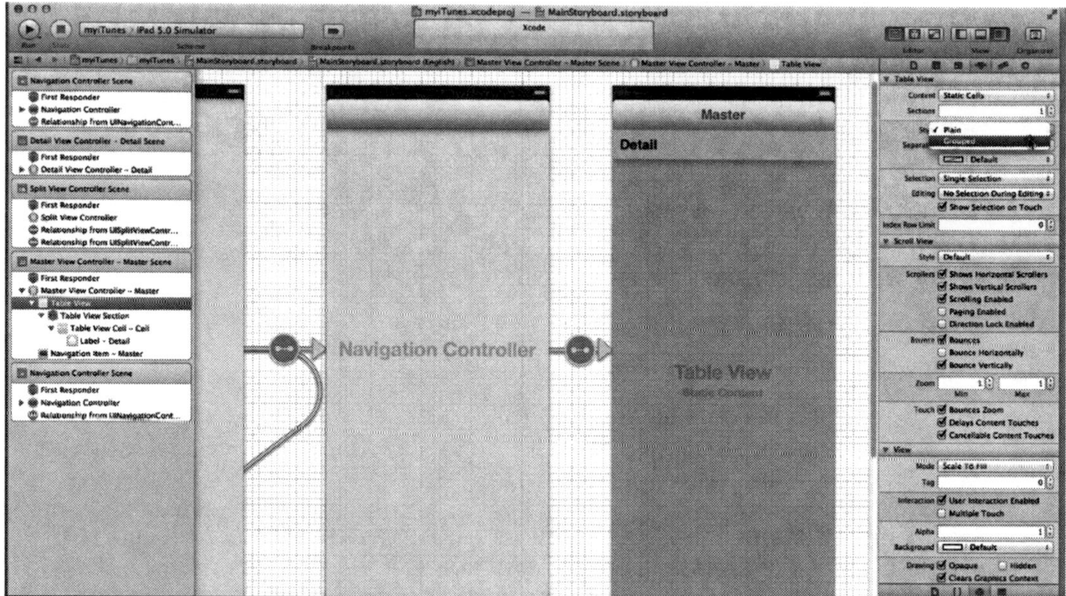

Figure 11–7. *Create a grouped-style set of static cells.*

7. Open the Attributes Inspector in the Utilities pane and then go down and ensure Static Cells from the Content drop-down menu. Next select "Grouped" Style to give us space for headers for separation as shown in Figure 11–7.

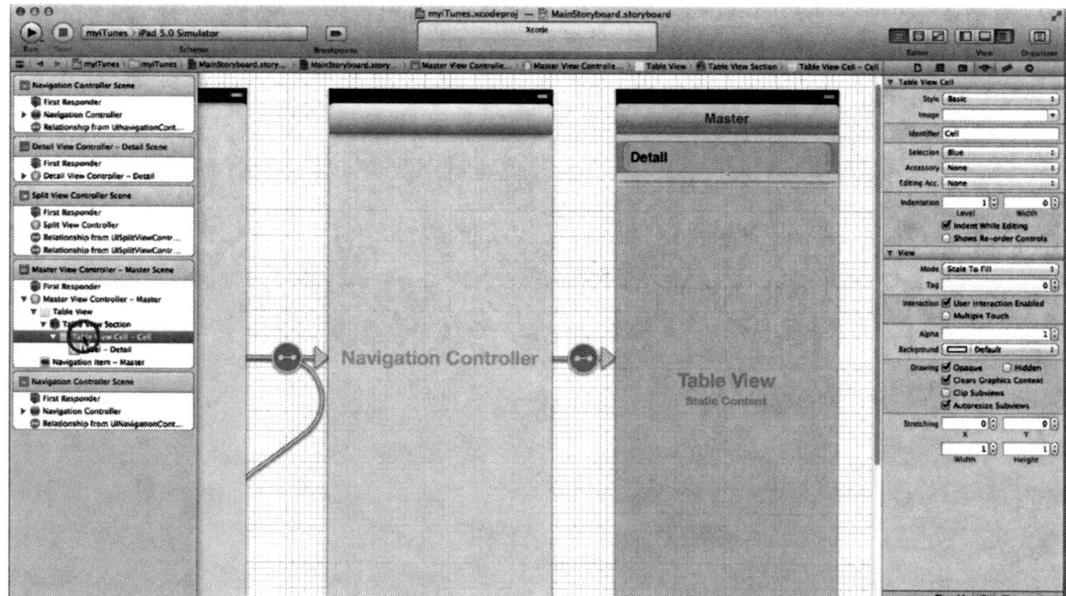

Figure 11–8. *Selecting the Table View Cell - Cell*

8. This can be benign but tricky so pay attention to this very simple step: go back to the Documents Outline and, inside your Master View Controller – Master scene, go down two levels from the Table View you have just been working on. As shown in Figure 11–8, you should now be at the Table View Cell—Cell. If you select the wrong level, you will only realize you're lost when you're very lost.

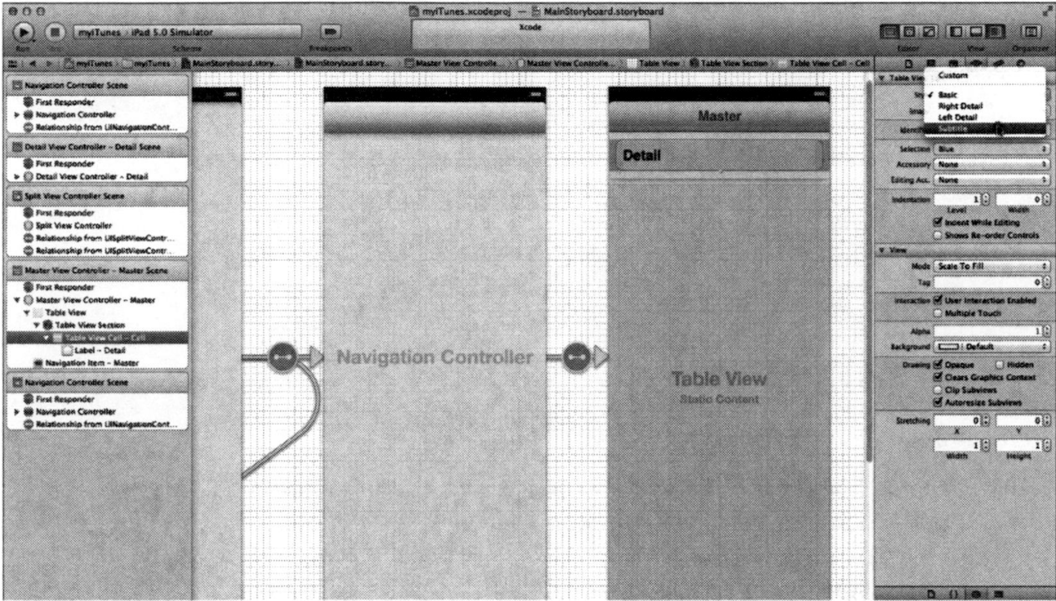

Figure 11–9. *Create subtitles for each Table View Cell – Cell.*

9. We want to create subtitles in each Table View Cell—Cell because they tell us, and most importantly the user, what we will see or where we will be going if we select this option. So, go back to the Attributes Inspector in the utilities pane and then go down and select Subtitle from the Style as shown in Figure 11–9.

> **NOTE:** As we travel here for the first time while we set up the cells, note that there are many fun and awesome tricks you can use when you travel back here again. I mentioned that we will be opening "doors" that lead into rooms with lots of bells and whistles. This is one of them! Keep looking around as we travel to these different rooms.

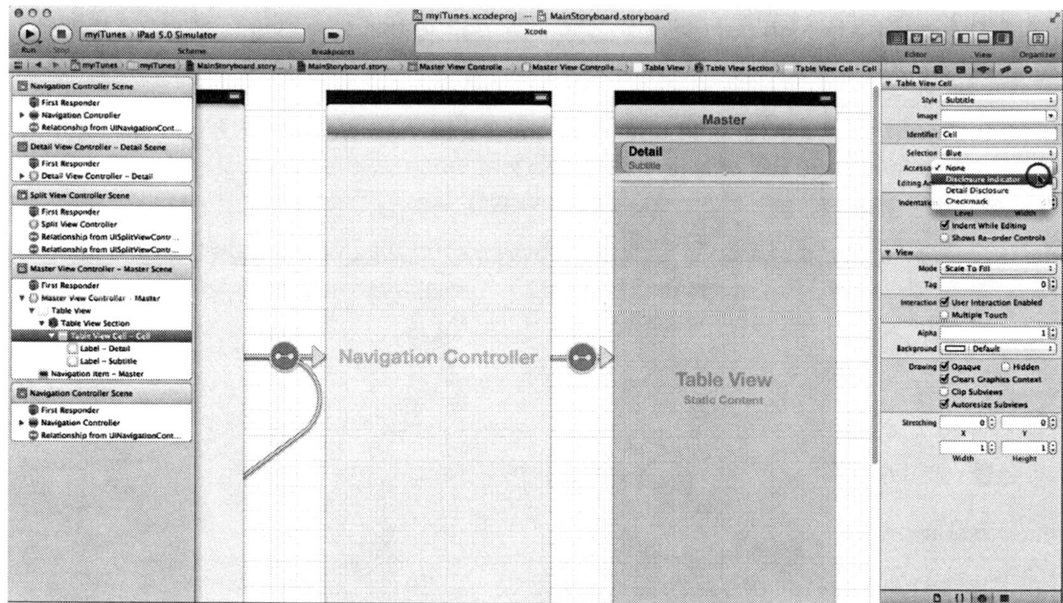

Figure 11–10. *Create disclosure indicators for each Table View Cell – Cell.*

10. Looking at Figure 11–10, we can now see that, under Detail in our cell, there is a Subtitle. This is exactly what we want. Now, while we're here, why don't we also add disclosure indicators ">" that give the user a sense of the direction that they will be travelling in when they select a particular cell? Yup, that's a great idea! Go to the Accessory section just under the Style section you were in and select Disclosure Indicator as shown in Figure 11–10

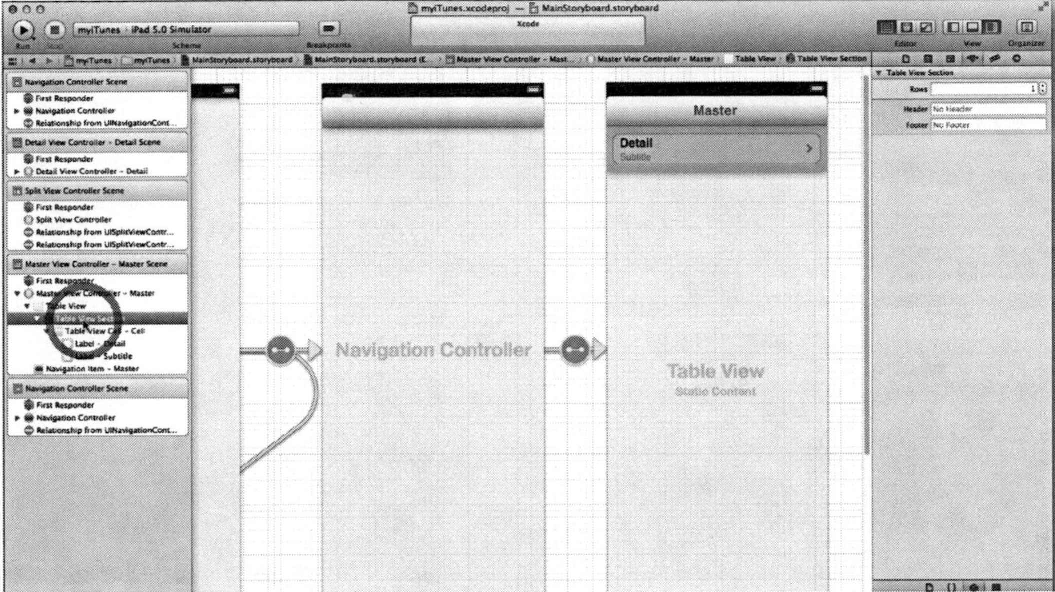

Figure 11–11. *Go back up one level to the Table View Section.*

11. Ahh… look at that beautiful Disclosure and subtitle we've just created in Figure 11–11. Beautiful! Before we get too lost, look at The Big Picture and see that we are about to embark on setting up the Table View Section (1.1.2.). Go back to the Documents Outline and select the Table View Section as shown in Figure 11–11.

THE BIG PICTURE

1. Set up the popover in the storyboard
   1.1. Create a Group
      1.1.1. Set up the attributes of each Table View Cell – Cell in the group
         1.1.1.1. Static Cells, Grouped Style, subtitles, and disclosure indicators
      1.1.2. Set up the Table View Section
         1.1.2.1. Create a header and create 2 rows
   1.2. Duplicate the Group as required
      1.2.1. Go to the Master scene and make 4 sections
   1.3. Label all the cells
2. Code the interaction to the multimedia platforms
3. Tweak the popover to grab the platforms correctly

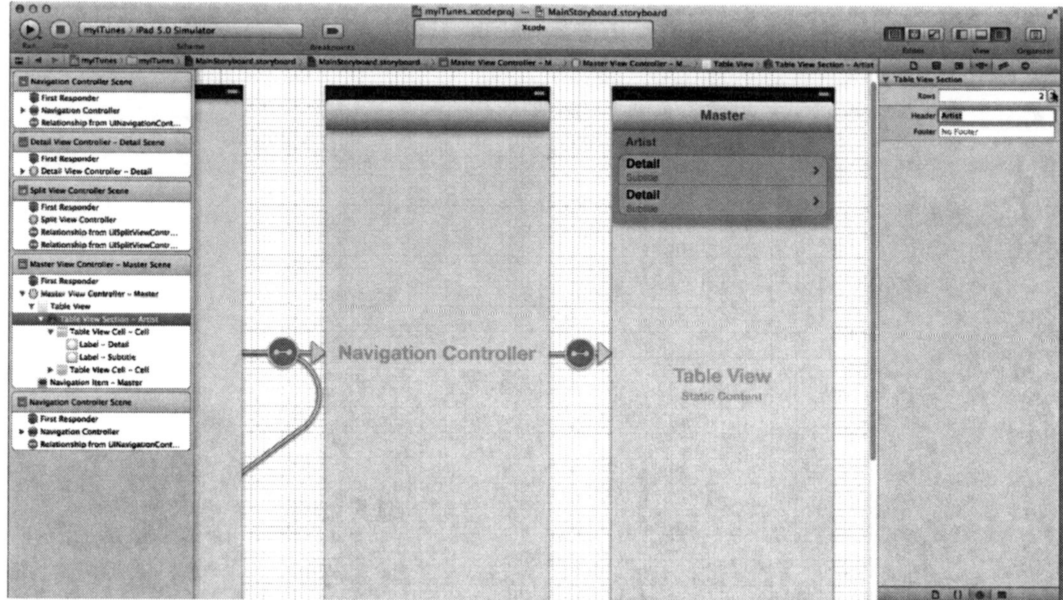

Figure 11–12. *Name the first group "Artist" and create two rows.*

12. Keep in mind that we have yet to label any of our Table View Cell—Cells yet. I only do this in step 1.3 in The Big Picture, which is the last step for two reasons. First, it takes time and, second, we will change them. However, in this instance, we need to go to the Header in the Attributes inspector and simply give it a "dummy" label that will give us something, anything, to edit when we duplicate these cells. So, go ahead and label this group with the name of our first group, which will be Artists. Then, create 2 rows as shown in Figure 11–12 because we will only have two rows of cells in each group. You may want more. You will always want to err on the side of creating more cells because then you can delete them very easily, but if you have to recreate cells, you often will have to spend time formatting them.

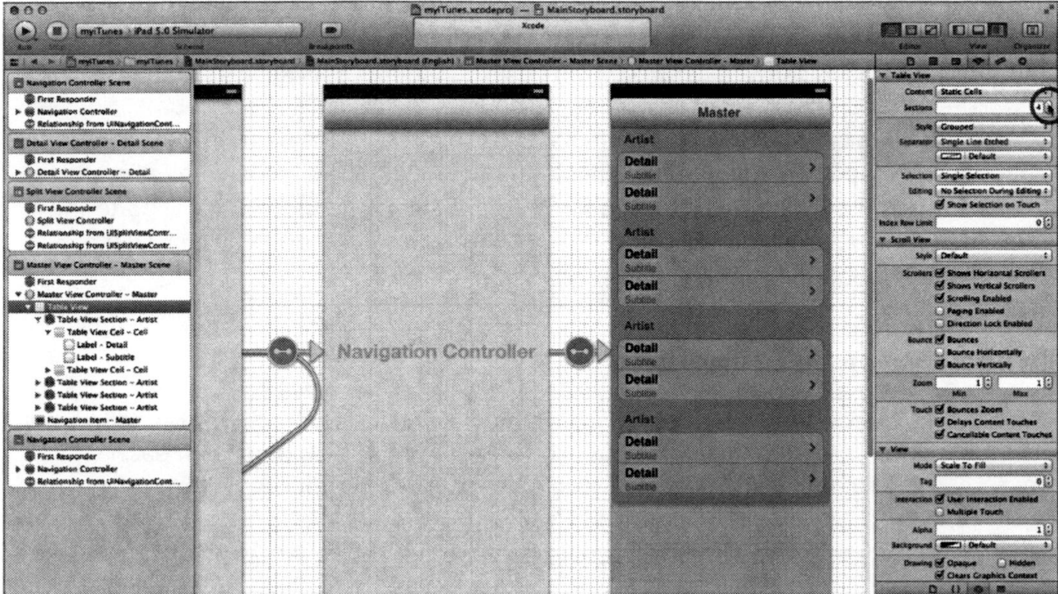

Figure 11–13. *Only now do we create all of our sections.*

13. We have now created one group exactly as we want it. So now go back to the original Table View where we began and make 4 sections as shown in Figure 11–13.

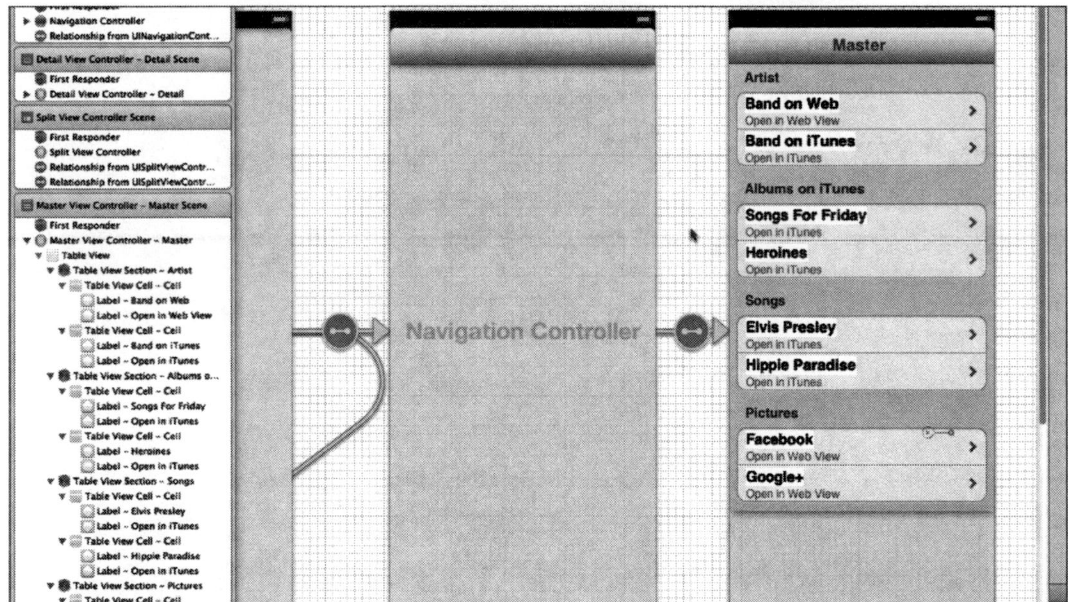

Figure 11–14. *Name the cells and headers.*

14. Of course you will do things differently when you create your own but for now let's name our four groups: Artists, Albums on iTunes, Songs, and Pictures. These 4 groups will facilitate our "Band's" (I will give you the Beatles links when we get to the code) presence on the Web, and iTunes, under Artists, then Albums. For the Beatles, there will be many albums. For our example, we're only using 2, and likewise for Songs and Pictures. Note that in the subtitles, some are telling the user that they will go to iTunes and some are telling the user they will go to the Internet. Name all the cells as shown in Figure 11–14. Remember that you can simply double-click on the cell to create a name.

Coding the myiTunes App

I really want to keep this really, really, really simple! Two broad things will be done when we code: first create code that hooks up to what we want to happen when each cell is pressed and then make sure our views connect correctly with the WebViews.

THE BIG PICTURE

1. Set up the popover in the storyboard
2. **Code the interaction to the multimedia platforms**
    2.1. MasterView Controller
        2.1.1. Code for each cell that is selected
    2.2. DetailView Controller
        2.2.1. Connecting the views to the WebViews
3. Tweak the popover to grab the platforms correctly

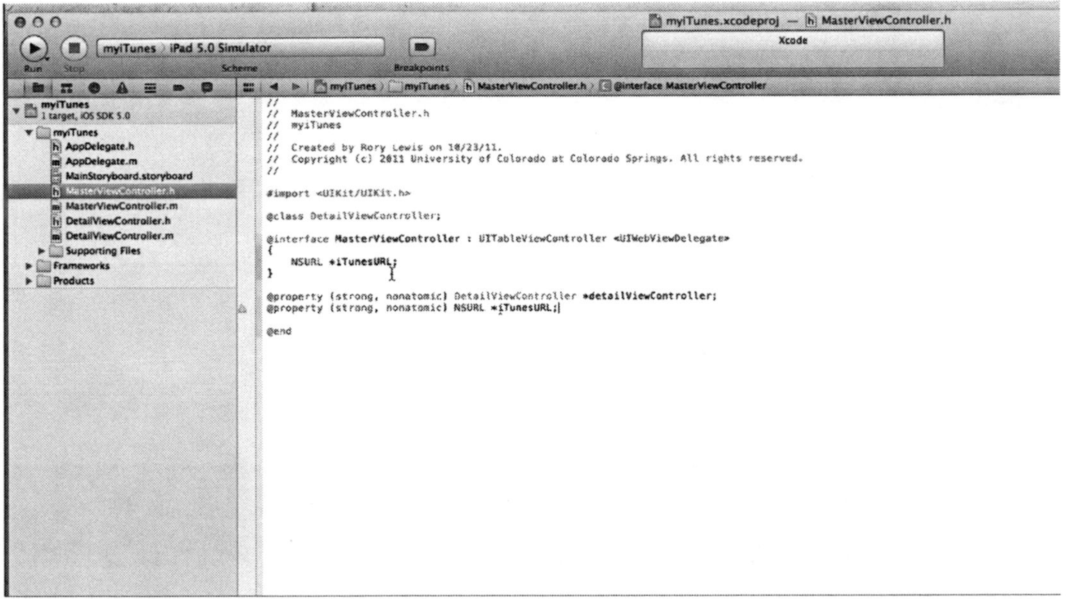

Figure 11–15. *Create a NSURL to hook up to iTunes.*

15. We start by looking at the MasterViewController so let's first make sure that our header allows us to do all the things we need to do in our implementation file. Save everything, close the utilities, open the navigator, and open up the MasterViewController.h. We start by creating an NSURL to connect to iTunes. I've named this pointer iTunesURL as shown in Figure 11–22. Before we simply blurt out that we want an NSURL *iTunesURL, we need to bring in a protocol that will define this method. In our case, we specifically need to define a method that delegates or gives to us all the good stuff necessary for a UIWebView object that will handle the iTunes web content we want loaded. As we did before in myStory_02, we will use the UIWebViewDelegate Protocol Reference <UIWebViewDelegate>. Please make sure that you also create the @property as shown below.

```
#import <UIKit/UIKit.h>
@class myDetailViewController;
@interface myMasterViewController : UITableViewController <UIWebViewDelegate>
{
    NSURL *iTunesURL;
}


@property (strong, nonatomic) myDetailViewController *detailViewController;
@property (strong, nonatomic) NSURL *iTunesURL;
@end
```

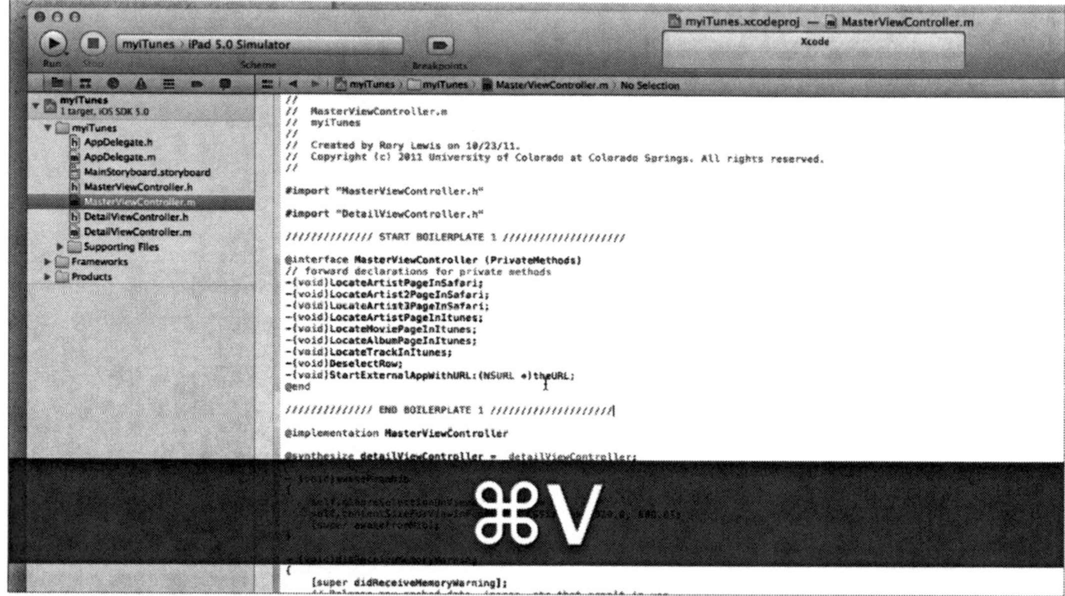

Figure 11–16. *Paste the first Boilerplate.*

16. Open up the MasterViewController implementation file and then select all the contents of the first Boilerplate file (Boilerplate 01). After that, paste the contents in-between the #import "myDetailViewController.h" line and the @implementation MasterViewController line as shown in Figure 11–16. This code is nothing else but forward declarations of private methods I've written to accommodate the various types of media we link to in this app and media that you may use in later apps. Specifically we have 3:

    a. LocateArtistPageInSafari

    b. LocateArtistPageInItunes, a LocateMoviePageInItunes (we do not use this one but I thought you may like to have it at your disposal) and

    c. StartExternalAppWithURL:(NSURL *)theURL).

    Once you paste the first boilerplate in, it should look as follows:

```
#import "MasterViewController.h"
#import "myDetailViewController.h"
////////////// START BOILERPLATE 1 ////////////////////
@interface MasterViewController (PrivateMethods)
// forward declarations for private methods
-(void)LocateArtistPageInSafari;
-(void)LocateArtist2PageInSafari;
-(void)LocateArtist3PageInSafari;
-(void)LocateArtistPageInItunes;
-(void)LocateMoviePageInItunes;
-(void)LocateAlbumPageInItunes;
-(void)LocateTrackInItunes;
```

```
-(void)DeselectRow;
-(void)StartExternalAppWithURL:(NSURL *)theURL;
@end

////////////// END BOILERPLATE 1 ////////////////////
@implementation myMasterViewController
@synthesize detailViewController = _detailViewController;
```

Figure 11–17. *Synthesize the iTunesURL.*

17. We cannot get too wrapped up in the header protocol and forget that we need to synthesize the iTunesURL we set up in our header file. This is shown in Figure 11–23 and also below.

```
////////////// END BOILERPLATE 1 ////////////////////
@implementation MasterViewController
@synthesize detailViewController = _detailViewController;
@synthesize iTunesURL;
- (void)awakeFromNib
{
    self.clearsSelectionOnViewWillAppear = NO;
    self.contentSizeForViewInPopover = CGSizeMake(320.0, 600.0);
    [super awakeFromNib];
}
```

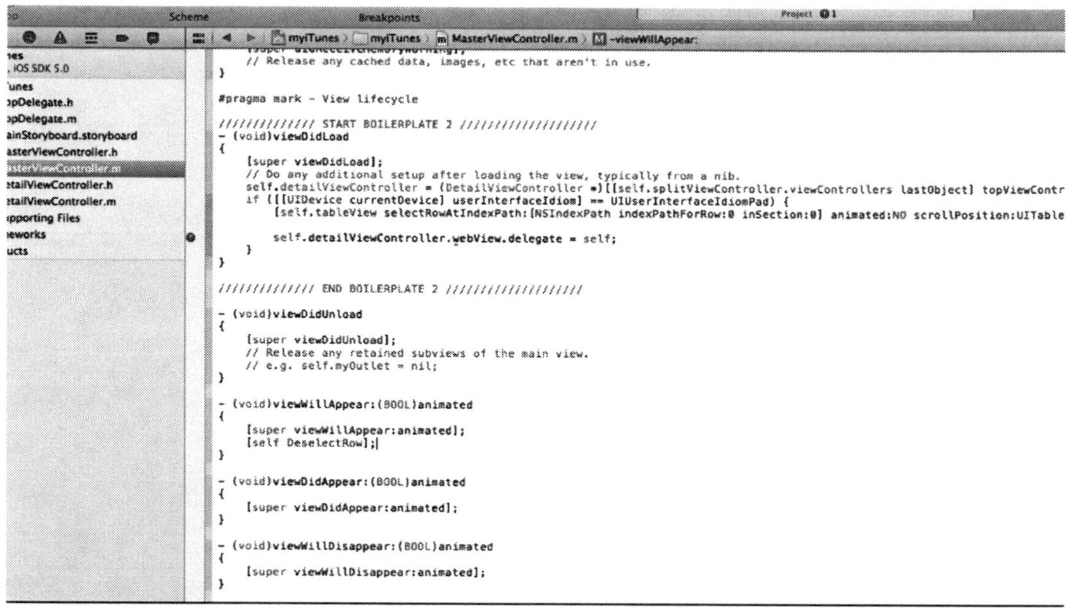

Figure 11–18. *Insert boilerplate 2.*

18. The viewDidLoad that comes along with the Master-Detail default Instantiation is not exactly what we need. There are two ways to do this and I prefer the first way, which is to code it yourself. Here you will see why we need to add onto it. For those of you who may feel you're being overwhelmed, that's cool too. Hang in there and let me go over how to tweak the viewDidLoad. After that, we'll show you how to use the boilerplate. As you know, the grey lettering is the code that is automatically instantiated. Essentially I've added an "If" statement. Mmm.... what is this if statement doing? All we're doing here is saying that we have code here that is specific to the iPad, and we want to make sure that the interface that's being used on the current device is the correct one.

```
- (void)viewDidLoad
{
    [super viewDidLoad];
        // Do any additional setup after loading the view, typically from a nib.
    self.detailViewController = (DetailViewController
*)[[self.splitViewController.viewControllers lastObject] topViewController];
    if ([[UIDevice currentDevice] userInterfaceIdiom] == UIUserInterfaceIdiomPad) {
        [self.tableView selectRowAtIndexPath:[NSIndexPath indexPathForRow:0 inSection:0]
animated:NO scrollPosition:UITableViewScrollPositionMiddle];
        self.detailViewController.webView.delegate = self;
    }
}
```

Now, for those of you who feel a little more comfortable pasting in the boilerplate code , open boilerplate 02 and select everything. Then select all of viewDidLoad and paste it over it so that it looks similar to what is shown in Figure 11–18 and as shown here:

```
- (void)didReceiveMemoryWarning
```

```
{
    [super didReceiveMemoryWarning];
    // Release any cached data, images, etc that aren't in use.
}

#pragma mark - View lifecycle
/////////////// START BOILERPLATE 2 /////////////////////
- (void)viewDidLoad
{
    [super viewDidLoad];
        // Do any additional setup after loading the view, typically from a nib.
    self.detailViewController = (DetailViewController
*)[[self.splitViewController.viewControllers lastObject] topViewController];
    if ([[UIDevice currentDevice] userInterfaceIdiom] == UIUserInterfaceIdiomPad) {
        [self.tableView selectRowAtIndexPath:[NSIndexPath indexPathForRow:0 inSection:0]
animated:NO scrollPosition:UITableViewScrollPositionMiddle];
        self.detailViewController.webView.delegate = self;
    }
}

/////////////// END BOILERPLATE 2 /////////////////////
- (void)viewDidUnload
{
    [super viewDidUnload];
    // Release any retained subviews of the main view.
    // e.g. self.myOutlet = nil;
```

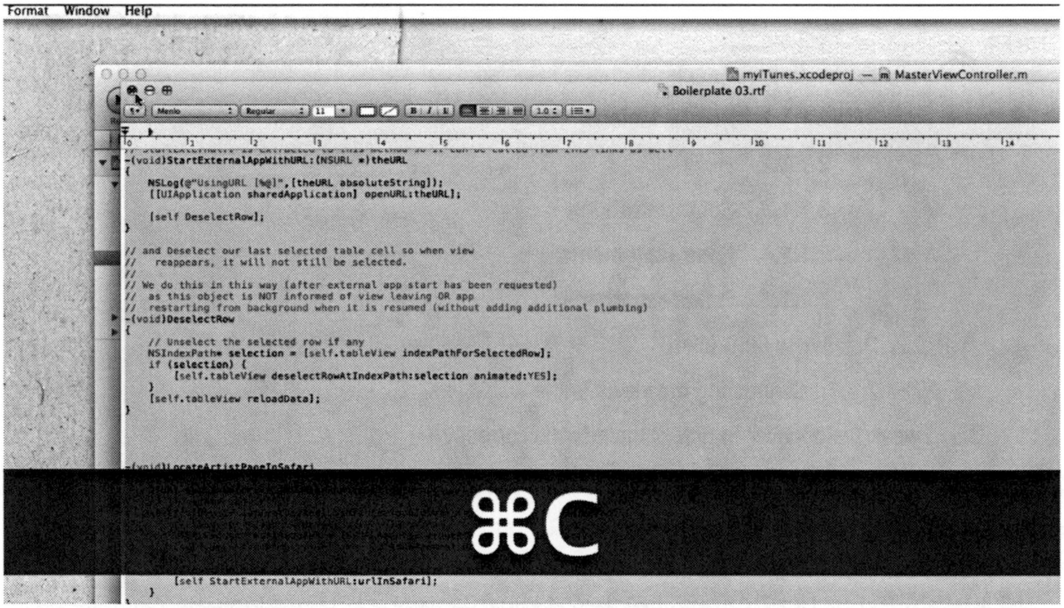

Figure 11–19. *Boilerplate 3*

19. We now need to delete everything from `shouldAutorotateToInterfaceOrientation` down to the @end. Once it is deleted, select all the contents of boilerplate 3, as shown in Figure 11–19, and paste it in its place. This code is the crux of it all so let's go through it now. Let's start by looking at The Big Picture to see that we have completed 2.1.1.1 through to 2.1.1.2. We need to make sure our app still runs regardless of the orientation of the iPad (split view, in landscape, and popover in portrait) and have a set of cases of events that we will trigger if a cell is selected. We have eight cells so we will have eight cases ranging from 0 through to 7. We will then program our private methods to deal with special circumstances.

> **NOTE:** Since we are first coding the `MasterViewController`, Xcode will give you some warnings and error signs at this point. Ignore them for now.

THE BIG PICTURE

1. Set up the popover in the storyboard
2. Code the interaction to the multimedia platforms
   - 2.1. MasterView Controller
     - 2.1.1. Code for each cell that is selected
       - 2.1.1.1. Header Material
       - 2.1.1.2. viewDidLoad
       - **2.1.1.3. Set orientations**
       - **2.1.1.4. Case statements**
       - **2.1.1.5. Private methods**
   - 2.2. DetailView Controller
     - 2.2.1. Connecting the views to the WebViews
3. Tweak the popover to grab the platforms correctly

The original `shouldAutorotateToInterfaceOrientation` is shown in grey below and we'll only use it if it's an iPad.

```
- (BOOL)shouldAutorotateToInterfaceOrientation:(UIInterfaceOrientation)↩
interfaceOrientation
{
    // Return YES for supported orientations
    if ([[UIDevice currentDevice] userInterfaceIdiom] == UIUserInterfaceIdiomPhone) {
        return (interfaceOrientation != UIInterfaceOrientationPortraitUpsideDown);
    } else {
```

```
        return YES;
    }
}
```

We need to do a couple of things now. We need to convert our section and row numbers from a linear index to rows when counting from top to bottom. For those of you who are looking carefully at each line of code, I need to point out that the next two lines assume that the 1st section is 2 rows and all others are 1.

```
NSInteger nSelectedRowIdx = (indexPath.section > 0) ? indexPath.section+1 : 0;
//now 0,2,3,4
nSelectedRowIdx += indexPath.row;
//now 0,1,2,3,4
```

If you're happy that this all relates each case to a specific line (the top line in each cell), then that's OK too. Just use this every time you do it. In fact, just paste it in and change the case statements below and you will be fine.

```
- (void)tableView:(UITableView *)tableView didSelectRowAtIndexPath:(NSIndexPath
*)indexPath
{
    NSInteger nSelectedRowIdx = indexPath.section *2 + indexPath.row;
    switch (nSelectedRowIdx) {
```

Now we need to make the case statements that will tag along the rows we have ordered sequentially. We have four sections: ARTIST, ALBUMS IN ITUNES, SONGS, and PICTURES. We need to have two selections called cases within each of them, so let's lay it out in The Big Picture for a minute.

THE BIG PICTURE

1. Set up the popover in the storyboard
2. Code the interaction to the multimedia platforms
    - 2.1. MasterView Controller
        - 2.1.1. Code for each cell that is selected
            - 2.1.1.1. Header Material
            - 2.1.1.2. viewDidLoad
            - 2.1.1.3. Set orientations
            - **2.1.1.4. Case statements**
                - **2.1.1.4.1. ARTISTS**
                    - **2.1.1.4.1.1. Case 0**
                    - **2.1.1.4.1.2. Case 1**
                - **2.1.1.4.2. ALBUMS**
                    - **2.1.1.4.2.1. Case 2**
                    - **2.1.1.4.2.2. Case 3**

2.1.1.4.3. SONGS

2.1.1.4.3.1. Case 4

2.1.1.4.3.2. Case 5

2.1.1.4.4. PICTURES

2.1.1.4.4.1. Case 6

2.1.1.4.4.2. Case 7

2.1.1.5. Private methods (Helper routines to process redirects prior to handing off to application open)

2.1.1.5.1.

2.2. DetailView Controller

2.2.1. Connecting the views to the WebViews

3. Tweak the popover to grab the platforms correctly

Accordingly, the code is as follows:

```
        case 0: // in Safari (Artist)
            [self LocateArtistPageInSafari];
            break;

        case 1: // in iTunes (Artist)
            //[self LocateArtistPageInItunes];
        {
            NSURL *urlInItunes = [NSURL URLWithString:@"http://itunes.apple.com/➥
us/artist/rory-lewis/id65902515?uo=4"];
            [self StartExternalAppWithURL:urlInItunes];
        }
            break;
        case 2: // in iTunes (Songs)
                      //[self LocateArtistPageInItunes];
        {
            NSURL *urlInItunes = [NSURL URLWithString:@"http://itunes.apple.com/➥
us/album/songs-for-friday/id408548641?uo=4"];
            [self StartExternalAppWithURL:urlInItunes];
        }
            break;
        case 3: // in iTunes (Songs)
            //[self LocateArtistPageInItunes];
        {
            NSURL *urlInItunes = [NSURL URLWithString:@"http://itunes.apple.com/us/➥
album/heroines/id461113548?uo=4"];
            [self StartExternalAppWithURL:urlInItunes];
        }
            break;
        case 4: // in iTunes (Songs)
            //[self LocateArtistPageInItunes];
        {
            NSURL *urlInItunes = [NSURL URLWithString:@"http://itunes.apple.com/us/➥
album/elvis-presley/id461113548?i=461113566&uo=4"];
```

```
            [self StartExternalAppWithURL:urlInItunes];
        }
            break;
        case 5: // in iTunes (Songs)
            //[self LocateArtistPageInItunes];
        {
            NSURL *urlInItunes = [NSURL URLWithString:@"http://itunes.apple.com/➥
us/album/hippie-paradise/id408548641?i=408549591&uo=4"];
            [self StartExternalAppWithURL:urlInItunes];
        }
            break;
        case 6: // in Safari (Artist)
            [self LocateArtist2PageInSafari];
            break;

        case 7: // in Safari (Artist)
            [self LocateArtist3PageInSafari];
            break;

    }

    //[self DeselectRow];
}
```

We now need to create our helper routines to process redirects prior to handing off to the open application. Specifically, we need to process a `LinkShare/TradeDoubler/DGM` URL to something iPhone can handle, if you choose to use a universal app on your own that does include the iPhone. For more information you can go to `http://developer.apple.com/library/ios/#qa/qa1629/_index.htm`.

```
- (void)openReferralURL:(NSURL *)referralURL {
    //NSURLConnection *connection =
    (void)[[NSURLConnection alloc] initWithRequest:[NSURLRequest
requestWithURL:referralURL] delegate:self startImmediately:YES];
}
```

Now we save the most recent URL for a safety measure (just in case multiple redirects occur). Note that `iTunesURL` is an `NSURL` property in this class declaration:

```
- (NSURLRequest *)connection:(NSURLConnection *)connection willSendRequest:(NSURLRequest
*)request redirectResponse:(NSURLResponse *)response {
    self.iTunesURL = [response URL];
    NSLog(@"RxURL [%@]",[self.iTunesURL absoluteString]);
    return request;
}
```

OK, no more redirects. So we use the last URL that we saved:

```
- (void)connectionDidFinishLoading:(NSURLConnection *)connection {
    [self StartExternalAppWithURL:self.iTunesURL];
}
```

This is a little technical, but we need to have an iTMS link (a special kind of url/link protocol used for iTunes' links and URLs) to get out there into the ether. We have this little method called `StartExternalAppWithURL` in order to allow our iTMS links:

```
-(void)StartExternalAppWithURL:(NSURL *)theURL
{
```

```
    NSLog(@"UsingURL [%@]",[theURL absoluteString]);
    [[UIApplication sharedApplication] openURL:theURL];
    [self DeselectRow];
}
```

Almost done. We just need to deselect our last selected table cell so, when our view reappears, it will not still be selected. We do this after our external app start has been requested because this object is NOT informed of view leaving OR the app restarting from the background when it is resumed without adding additional plumbing.

```
-(void)DeselectRow
{
    // Unselect the selected row if any
    NSIndexPath* selection = [self.tableView indexPathForSelectedRow];
    if (selection) {
        [self.tableView deselectRowAtIndexPath:selection animated:YES];
    }
    [self.tableView reloadData];
}
```

Last bit—three Artist pages in Safari (`case 0`) and the cases for 6 and 7.

```
-(void)LocateArtistPageInSafari
{
    NSURL *urlInSafari = [NSURL URLWithString:@"http://bit.ly/poi91o"];
    // if we have an iPAD...
    if ([[UIDevice currentDevice] userInterfaceIdiom] == UIUserInterfaceIdiomPad) {
        // then open page in detail view (UIWebView)
        NSURLRequest *urlRequest = [NSURLRequest requestWithURL:urlInSafari];
        [self.detailViewController.webView loadRequest:urlRequest];
    } else {
        // else we have an iPhone/iPod Touch so open in external safari
        [self StartExternalAppWithURL:urlInSafari];
    }
}

-(void)LocateArtist2PageInSafari
{
    NSURL *urlInSafari = [NSURL URLWithString:@"http://on.fb.me/nFwQj6"];
    // if we have an iPAD...
    if ([[UIDevice currentDevice] userInterfaceIdiom] == UIUserInterfaceIdiomPad) {
        // then open page in detail view (UIWebView)
        NSURLRequest *urlRequest = [NSURLRequest requestWithURL:urlInSafari];
        [self.detailViewController.webView loadRequest:urlRequest];
    } else {
        // else we have an iPhone/iPod Touch so open in external safari
        [self StartExternalAppWithURL:urlInSafari];
    }
}

-(void)LocateArtist3PageInSafari
{
    NSURL *urlInSafari = [NSURL URLWithString:@"http://bit.ly/nxY8AZ"];
    // if we have an iPAD...
    if ([[UIDevice currentDevice] userInterfaceIdiom] == UIUserInterfaceIdiomPad) {
        // then open page in detail view (UIWebView)
        NSURLRequest *urlRequest = [NSURLRequest requestWithURL:urlInSafari];
        [self.detailViewController.webView loadRequest:urlRequest];
```

```
    } else {
        // else we have an iPhone/iPod Touch so open in external safari
        [self StartExternalAppWithURL:urlInSafari];
    }
}

@end
```

Coding DetailViewController

That was something else, wasn't it!? Just as an aside, something that will make you laugh. When I first began to get my head wrapped around storyboarding for my class, we were working on the beta version and it kept changing every week. Not only had I never seen a storyboard before, but the code was changing constantly and I had to teach it in front of the lecture hall. I had many sleepless nights. But here is the deal. If you master this app and storyboarding, you are well on your way to huge success in programming. You do not have to know all of the above, you can simply learn when to use it. In our `DetailViewController`, we need to set up our `UIWebview` but first let's have a look at The Big Picture.

THE BIG PICTURE

1. Set up the popover in the storyboard
2. Code the interaction to the multimedia platforms
    - 2.1. MasterView Controller
    - **2.2. DetailView Controller**
        - **2.2.1. Connecting the views to the WebViews**
3. Tweak the popover to grab the platforms correctly

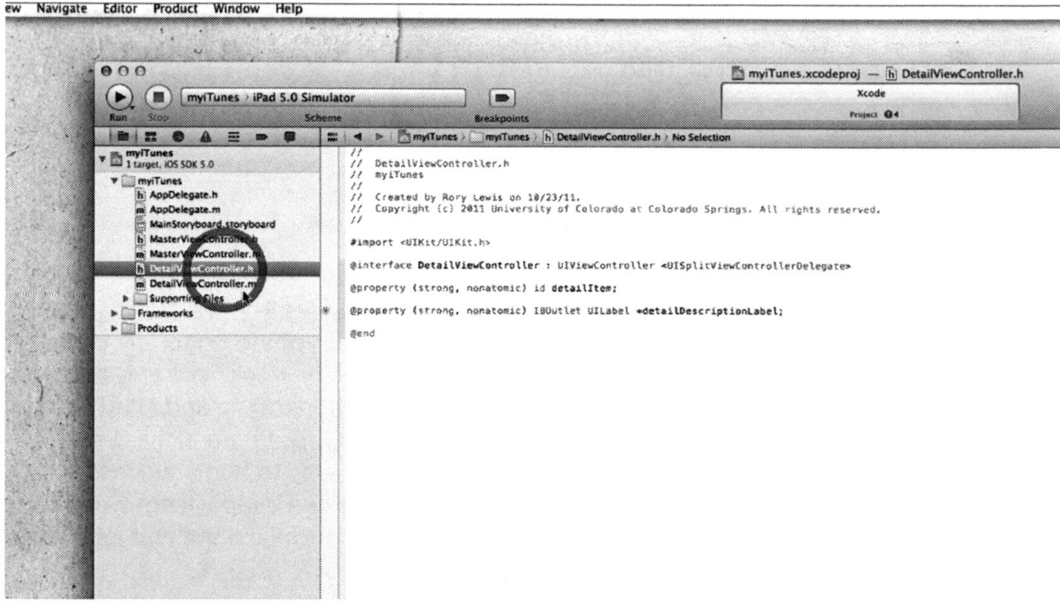

Figure 11–20. *Select and open the DetailViewController header file.*

20. Save your `MasterViewController` and open the `DetailViewController.h` file as shown in Figure 11–20. Then add the code shown below. Note that when we go back to tweak the storyboard, we will connect this to our `UIWebView`.

```
#import <UIKit/UIKit.h>
@interface DetailViewController : UIViewController <UISplitViewControllerDelegate>
@property (strong, nonatomic) id detailItem;
@property (strong, nonatomic) IBOutlet UILabel *detailDescriptionLabel;
@property (strong, nonatomic) IBOutlet UIWebView *webView;
@end
```

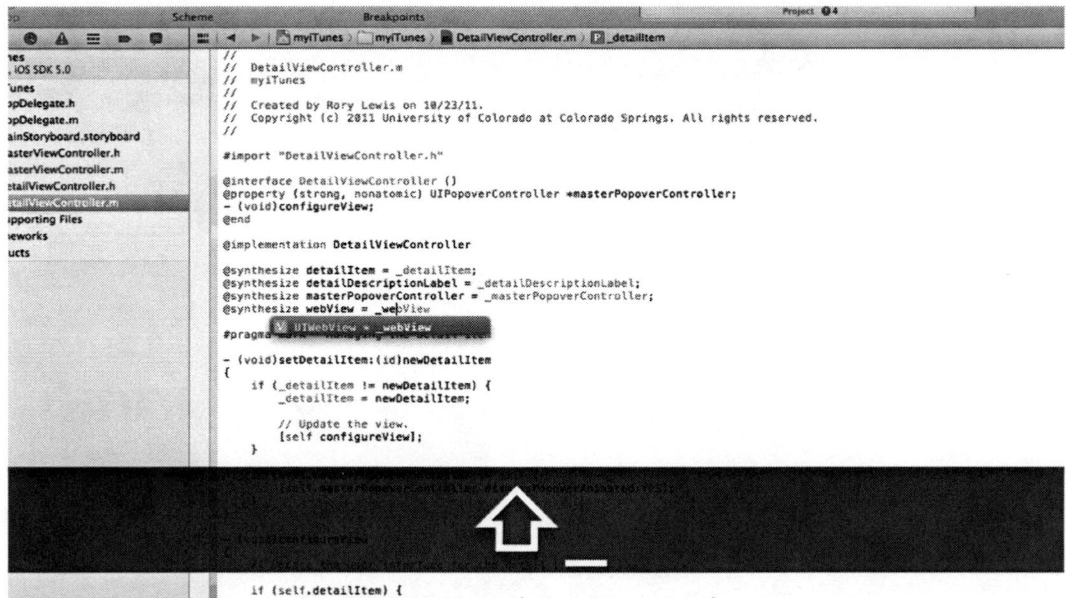

Figure 11–21. *Synthesize the webView in the implementation file.*

21. Now open your `DetailViewController.m` file and synthesize the `webView` as shown in Figure 11–21 and here:

```
#import "DetailViewController.h"
@interface DetailViewController ()
@property (strong, nonatomic) UIPopoverController *masterPopoverController;
- (void)configureView;
@end

@implementation DetailViewController
@synthesize detailItem = _detailItem;
@synthesize detailDescriptionLabel = _detailDescriptionLabel;
@synthesize masterPopoverController = _masterPopoverController;
@synthesize webView = _webView;
#pragma mark - Managing the detail item
```

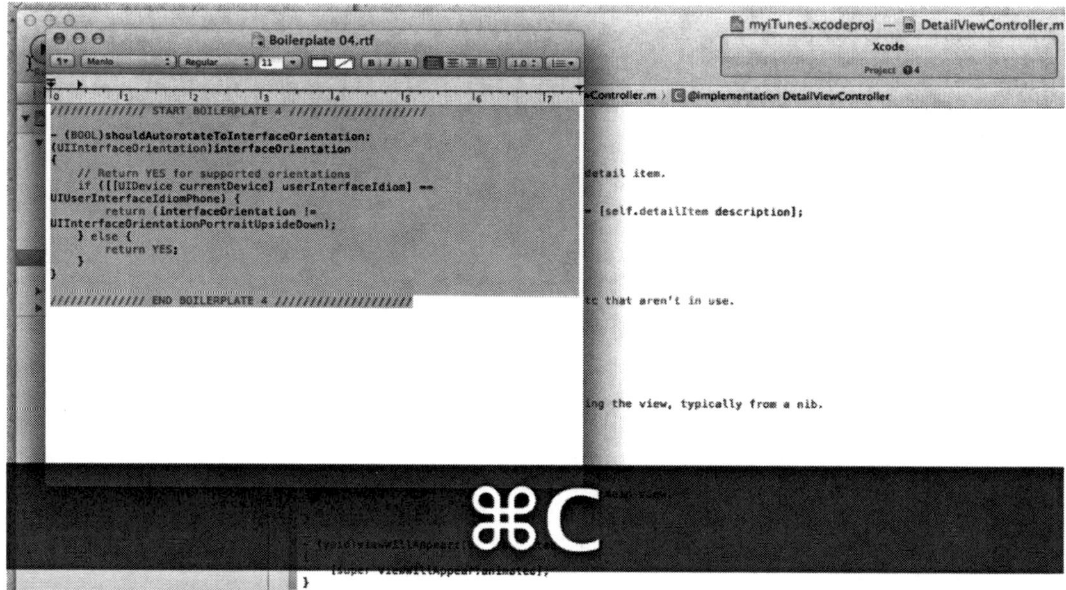

Figure 11–22. *Select Boilerplate 4.*

22. We now need to redo our shouldAutorotateToInterfaceOrientation method to take care of the Portrait and Landscape issues as mentioned before. Go ahead and delete the shouldAutorotateToInterface Orientation and either write these few lines of code or paste in its place the contents of Boilerplate 4.

```
////////////// START BOILERPLATE 4 ////////////////////
- (BOOL)shouldAutorotateToInterfaceOrientation:(UIInterfaceOrientation)↵
interfaceOrientation
{
    // Return YES for supported orientations
    if ([[UIDevice currentDevice] userInterfaceIdiom] == UIUserInterfaceIdiomPhone) {
        return (interfaceOrientation != UIInterfaceOrientationPortraitUpsideDown);
    } else {
        return YES;
    }
}
////////////// END BOILERPLATE 4 ////////////////////
```

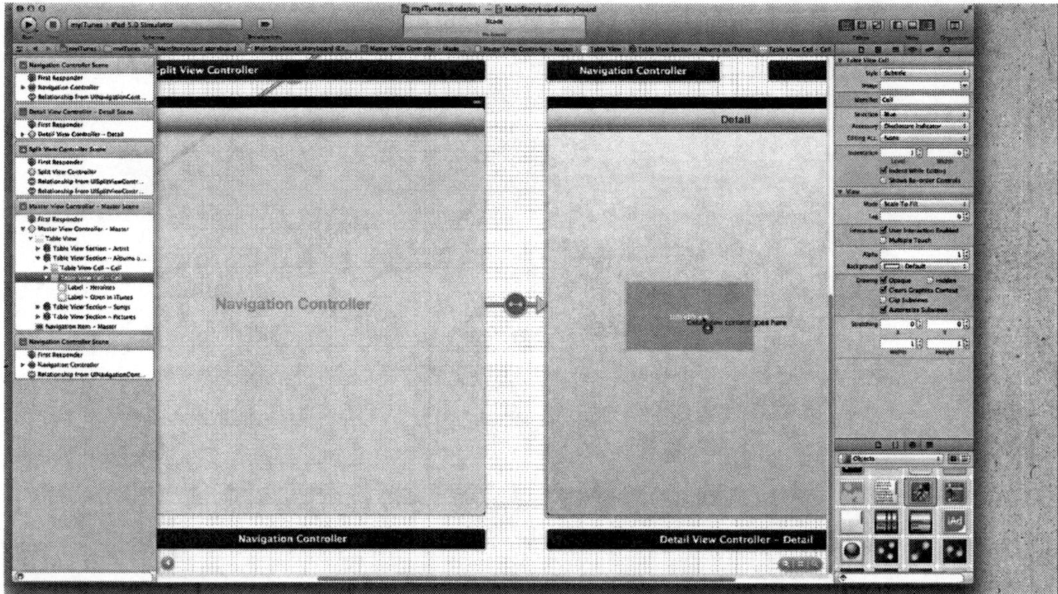

Figure 11–23. *Go back to Storyboard and select the Table View Cell – Cell and drag a Web View onto the Detail View.*

23. Save everything and go back into storyboard, close the Navigator, open up the Utilities and, in the Utilities, open up the Library. Our Table View Cell is where our web views will be shown so we need a web view located there. Go back to Storyboard and select the Table View Cell – Cell and drag a Web View onto the Detail View as shown in Figure 11–23.

Finalizing the Storyboard

We are almost done. The only thing we need to still do is connect something that was not there when we began – the `webView` – `UIWebView` connection in the code. Now that it's there, we need to go back into storyboard and connect them.

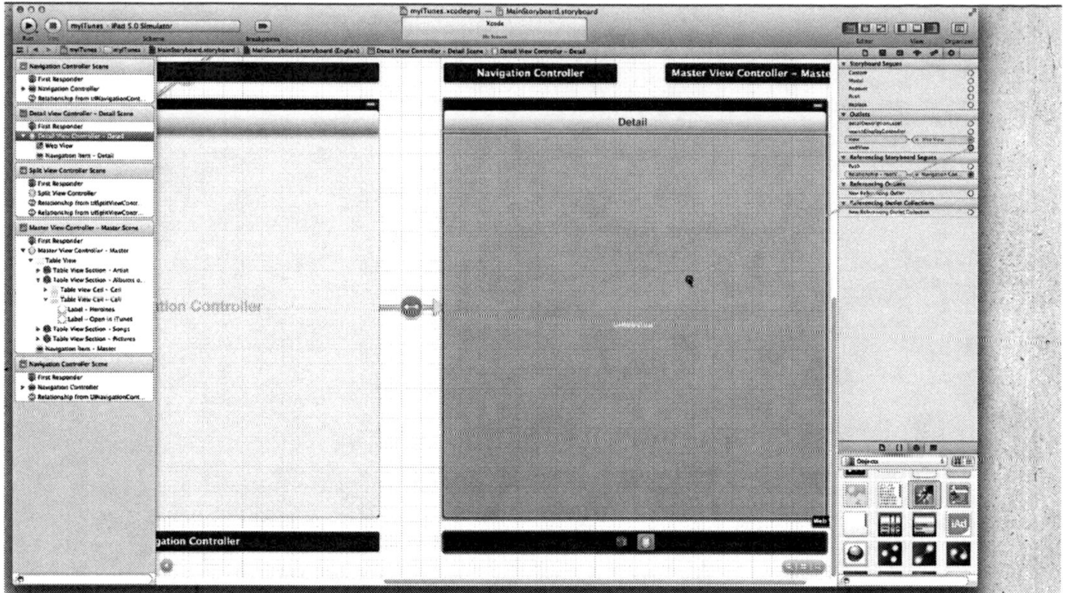

Figure 11–24. *Select myMasterTableViewController.*

24. Now go back to the Documents Outline and, inside the **Detail View Controller - Detail Scene,** grab the Web View and drag it up over the **Navigation Item - Detail** above the View into your **Detail View Controller - Detail**. Now your View disappears just as we did in `myStory_02`. Keeping the **Detail View Controller - Detail** selected as shown in the upper left-hand side in Figure 11–24, go back over to your Connection Inspector and control-drag from the `webView` to the `UIWebView` as shown in Figure 11–24. Save it.

> **NOTE**: Now connect your iPad to your Mac and, rather than selecting iPad simulator, select iOS Device. You can run it on the simulator if you like but **iTunes cannot run inside the simulator** so all the iTunes links will not work. Once you have connected your iPad to your Mac, press run.

Figure 11–25. *From the icon through to the Popover*

25. Once your app has completed building, which may take up to 17 seconds, you will see the icon appear as shown in Figure 11–25. Once you press the icon, you will immediately see the popover screen. The first time you select it, it will not show anything underneath. However, once you select a page and then select the popover again, it keeps the underlying image below the popover as shown in Figure 11–26.

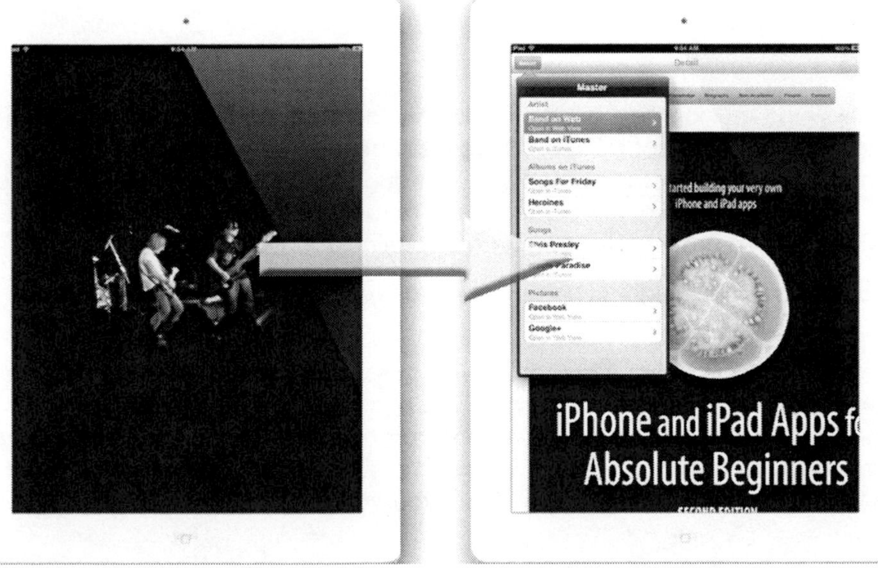

Figure 11–26. *A beautiful Splash screen presents itself while the screen loads.*

26. Once we select a cell, the splash screen appears while the page loads from the Internet or from iTunes. Here, in the right hand image, we see the popover placed on top of the first image.

Figure 11–27. *Orientation working with iTunes*

27. We need to have a little patience with orientation correcting itself with iTunes. This is something Apple needs to work on. Just be patient. Figure 11–27 shows the 2nd selection on the left hand side and the first iTunes selection on the right hand side.

In Ending

This has been a wonderful journey, but it's really only the start. As I've gone through this second edition, I cannot help but think of all the fresh minds that will read these exercises and struggle through them, then break through to create awesome apps and make money! How many more of my students and readers of this book will work at Apple!? Wow! It's been a great motivation for me to think about this.

On a sad note, as I was finishing this book, Steve Jobs passed away. God bless you, Steve.

I hope to see you all on the forum. I do not answer questions submitted to me by email but I will answer those exact same questions if you post them on the forum (`http://bit.ly/oLVwpY`) because then everybody can share my answers. I would also like to encourage you to help. No matter how much of a beginner you are, get into the forum and help others. Helping others speeds up your journey.

Peace.

Dr. Lewis

Index

Special Characters and Numerics

A

B

C

D

E

F

J

K

L

M

N

R

S

T

U

V

W

X

Y

Z

CPSIA information can be obtained at www.ICGtesting.com
Printed in the USA
LVOW050524200112
264765LV00002B/1/P